Exclusive Offer
40%
Discount

You have successfully read and understood *Paul Wilmott introduces Quantitative Finance, Second Edition*, now its time to upgrade to *Paul Wilmott on Quantitative Finance, Second Edition, 3 volume set.*

As a valued reader, we are pleased to offer you an exclusive 40% discount off the price of the book. Simply complete and return the form overleaf.

Paul Wilmott on Quantitative Finance, Second Edition, serves as a comprehensive reference on both traditional and new derivatives and financial engineering techniques. Explaining finance in an accessible manner, Wilmott covers all the current financial theories in quantitative finance and makes them easy to understand and implement.

0-470-01870-4
978-0-470-01870-5
1472 pages
Hardback
3 volume set

How to Order

Please send me_____cop(y)ies of

Paul Wilmott on Quantitative Finance, second edition,
0-470-01870-4
978-0-470-01870-5
1472 pages
Hardback
3 volume set

Postage rates

UK   ☐ £3.70   Amounts shown are for the total order

Europe Surface mail ☐ £5.35/€8.00   Air mail ☐ £12.75/€19.00

Outside Europe

        Surface mail ☐ £7.75   Air mail ☐ £14.95

Subtotal: _____

Add postage: _____

Total: _____

Payment methods

☐ Cheque enclosed, payable to John Wiley & Sons Ltd

☐ Credit/charge card

    ☐ Maestro   ☐ Mastercard   ☐ Visa   ☐ American Express

Card Number   _ _ _ _   _ _ _ _   _ _ _ _   _ _ _ _   _ _ _

Start Date _ _   _ _   Expiry Date _ _   _ _   Maestro issue number _ _

Card Security Code   _ _ _ _   Required for Maestro, Mastercard, Visa, American Express

CARDHOLDER'S SIGNATURE _____

CARDHOLDER'S NAME _____

CARDHOLDER'S REGISTERED ADDRESS _____

_____

POSTCODE _____ COUNTRY _____

TELEPHONE _____ E-MAIL _____

☐ Invoice for prepayment   Purchase order number_____enclosed

EU customers please include your VAT number _____

We will refund your payment if books are returned in resaleable condition within 30 days

Delivery address

PLEASE USE CAPITALS

NAME _____

JOB TITLE _____

COMPANY/UNIVERSITY _____

ADDRESS _____

_____

POSTCODE _____ COUNTRY _____

Promotion Code FXK

How to order

■ Phone our Customer Services Dept
   UK   Dial free   0800 243407
   Overseas   +44 1243 843294

■ Fax this form to: +44 1243 843296

■ Post this form to:
     Customer Services Dept
     John Wiley & Sons Ltd
     1 Oldlands Way, Bognor Regis
     West Sussex, PO22 9SA
     England

■ E-mail to cs-books@wiley.co.uk
   Please include your postal address

■ Online at www.wiley.com

Please quote the promotion code shown at the bottom of this page

Delivery will be arranged by John Wiley & Sons Ltd, on your behalf via Wiley Distribution Services Ltd. Alternatively you may collect your order by prior arrangement. We can also quote for delivery by courier. Please e-mail cs-books@wiley.co.uk for details.

Please allow 21 days for delivery. Whilst every effort is made to ensure that the contents of this leaflet are accurate, all information is subject to change without notice.

STAY INFORMED BY POST OR E-MAIL

Check out our new alerting service at:
www.wiley.com/email

Alternatively please indicate your areas of interest:

_____

_____

_____

YOUR PERSONAL DATA

We, John Wiley & Sons Ltd, will use the information you have provided to fulfil your request. In addition, we would like to:

1. Use your information to keep you informed by post of titles and offers of interest to you and available from us or other Wiley Group companies worldwide, and may supply your details to members of the Wiley Group for this purpose.

☐ Please tick the box if you do not wish to receive this information

2. Share your information with other carefully selected companies so that they may contact you by post with details of titles and offers that may be of interest to you.

☐ Please tick the box if you do not wish to receive this information.

If, at any time, you wish to stop receiving information, please contact The Database Marketing Dept (databasegroup@wiley.co.uk) at John Wiley & Sons Ltd, The Atrium, Southern Gate, Chichester, West Sussex. PO19 8SQ, UK.

10419 04/08

Paul Wilmott Introduces Quantitative Finance

Second Edition

Paul Wilmott Introduces Quantitative Finance

Second Edition

www.wilmott.com

John Wiley & Sons, Ltd

Copyright © 2007   John Wiley & Sons Ltd, The Atrium, Southern Gate, Chichester,
                        West Sussex PO19 8SQ, England

                        Telephone (+44) 1243 779777

Email (for orders and customer service enquiries): cs-books@wiley.co.uk
Visit our Home Page on www.wiley.com

Reprinted October 2007, June, 2008, December 2009, October 2010, June 2011, February 2012, March
2013, January 2014, May 2015, August 2015, January 2017, September 2017, April 2018

Copyright © 2007 Paul Wilmott

Other Wiley Editorial Offices

John Wiley & Sons Inc., 111 River Street, Hoboken, NJ 07030, USA

Jossey-Bass, 989 Market Street, San Francisco, CA 94103-1741, USA

Wiley-VCH Verlag GmbH, Boschstr. 12, D-69469 Weinheim, Germany

John Wiley & Sons Australia Ltd, 42 McDougall Street, Milton, Queensland 4064, Australia

John Wiley & Sons (Asia) Pte Ltd, 2 Clementi Loop #02-01, Jin Xing Distripark, Singapore 129809

John Wiley & Sons Canada Ltd, 6045 Freemont Blvd, Mississauga, ONT, L5R 4J3, Canada

Wiley also publishes its books in a variety of electronic formats. Some content that appears
in print may not be available in electronic books.

Anniversary Logo Design: Richard J. Pacifico

Library of Congress Cataloging-in-Publication Data

Wilmott, Paul.
  Paul Wilmott introduces quantitative finance. — 2nd ed.
    p. cm.
  ISBN 978-0-470-31958-1
  1. Finance — Mathematical models. 2. Options (Finance) — Mathematical models. 3. Options (Finance) — Prices —
Mathematical models. I. Title. II Title: Quantitative finance.
  HG173.W493 2007
  332 — dc22   2007015893

British Library Cataloguing in Publication Data

A catalogue record for this book is available from the British Library

ISBN 978-0-470-31958-1 (P/B)

Typeset in 10/12pt Helvetica by Laserwords Private Limited, Chennai, India
Printed and bound by CPI Group (UK) Ltd, Croydon, CR0 4YY

To a rising Star

contents

Preface

In this book I present classical quantitative finance. The book is suitable for students on advanced undergraduate finance and derivatives courses, MBA courses, and graduate courses that are mainly taught, as opposed to ones that are based on research. The text is quite self-contained, with, I hope, helpful sidebars ('Time Out') covering the more mathematical aspects of the subject for those who feel a little bit uncomfortable. Little prior knowledge is assumed, other than basic calculus, even *stochastic* calculus is explained here in a simple, accessible way.

By the end of the book you should know enough quantitative finance to understand most derivative contracts, to converse knowledgeably about the subject at dinner parties, to land a job on Wall Street, and to pass your exams.

The structure of the book is quite logical. Markets are introduced, followed by the necessary math and then the two are melded together. The technical complexity is never that great, nor need it be. The last three chapters are on the numerical methods you will need for pricing. In the more advanced subjects, such as credit risk, the mathematics is kept to a minimum. Also, plenty of the chapters can be read without reference to the mathematics at all. The structure, mathematical content, intuition, etc., are based on many years' teaching at universities and on the Certificate in Quantitative Finance, and training bank personnel at all levels.

The accompanying CD contains spreadsheets and Visual Basic programs implementing many of the techniques described in the text. The CD icon will be seen throughout the book, indicating material to be found on the CD, naturally. There is also a full list of its contents at the end of the book.

You can also find an Instructors Manual at www.wiley.com/go/pwiqf2 containing answers to the end-of-chapter questions in this book. The questions are, in general, of a mathematical nature but suited to a wide range of financial courses.

This book is a shortened version of *Paul Wilmott on Quantitative Finance, second edition*. It's also more affordable than the 'full' version. However, I hope that you'll eventually upgrade, perhaps when you go on to more advanced, research-based studies, or take that job on The Street.

PWOQF is, I am told, a standard text within the banking industry, but in *Paul Wilmott Introduces Quantitative Finance* I have specifically the university student in mind.

The differences between the university and the full versions are outlined at the end of the book. And to help you make the leap, we've included a form for you to upgrade, giving you a nice discount. Roughly speaking, the full version includes a great deal of non-classical, more modern approaches to quantitative finance, including several non-probabilistic models. There are more mathematical techniques for valuing exotic options and more markets are covered. The numerical methods are described in more detail.

If you have any problems understanding anything in the book, find errors, or just want a chat, email me at `paul@wilmott.com`. I'll do my very best to respond as quickly as possible. Or visit `www.wilmott.com` to discuss quantitative finance, and other subjects, with other people in this business.

I would like to thank the following people. My partners in various projects: Paul and Jonathan Shaw and Gil Christie at 7city, unequaled in their dedication to training and their imagination for new ideas. Also Riaz Ahmad, Seb Lleo and Siyi Zhou who have helped make the Certificate in Quantitative Finance so successful, and for taking some of the pressure off me. Everyone involved in the magazine, especially Aaron Brown, Alan Lewis, Bill Ziemba, Caitlin Cornish, Dan Tudball, Ed Lound, Ed Thorp, Elie Ayache, Espen Gaarder Haug, Graham Russel, Henriette Präst, Jenny McCall, Kent Osband, Liam Larkin, Mike Staunton, Paula Soutinho and Rudi Bogni. I am particularly fortunate and grateful that John Wiley & Sons have been so supportive in what must sometimes seem to them rather wacky schemes. I am grateful to James Fahy for his work on my websites, and apologies for always failing to provide a coherent brief. Thanks also to David Epstein for help with the exercises, again; and, of course, to Nassim Nicholas Taleb for entertaining chats.

Thanks to John, Grace, Sel and Stephen, for instilling in me their values. Values which have invariably served me well. And to Oscar and Zachary who kept me sane throughout many a series of unfortunate events!

Finally, thanks to my number one fan, Andrea Estrella, from her number one fan, me.

ABOUT THE AUTHOR

Paul Wilmott's professional career spans almost every aspect of mathematics and finance, in both academia and in the real world. He has lectured at all levels, and founded a magazine, the leading website for the quant community, and a quant certificate program. He has managed money as a partner in a very successful hedge fund. He lives in London, is married, and has two sons. Although he enjoys quantitative finance his ideal job would be designing Kinder Egg toys.

You will see this icon whenever a method is implemented on the CD.

More info about the particular meaning of an icon is contained in its 'speech box'.

products and markets: equities, commodities, exchange rates, forwards and futures

The aim of this Chapter...

...is to describe some of the basic financial market products and conventions, to slowly introduce some mathematics, to hint at how stocks might be modeled using mathematics, and to explain the important financial concept of 'no free lunch.' By the end of the chapter you will be eager to get to grips with more complex products and to start doing some proper modeling.

In this Chapter...

- an introduction to equities, commodities, currencies and indices
- the time value of money
- fixed and floating interest rates
- futures and forwards
- no-arbitrage, one of the main building blocks of finance theory

1.1 **INTRODUCTION**

This first chapter is a very gentle introduction to the subject of finance, and is mainly just a collection of definitions and specifications concerning the financial markets in general. There is little technical material here, and the one technical issue, the 'time value of money,' is extremely simple. I will give the first example of 'no arbitrage.' This is important, being one part of the foundation of derivatives theory. Whether you read this chapter thoroughly or just skim it will depend on your background.

1.2 **EQUITIES**

The most basic of financial instruments is the **equity, stock** or **share**. This is the ownership of a small piece of a company. If you have a bright idea for a new product or service then you could raise capital to realize this idea by selling off future profits in the form of a stake in your new company. The investors may be friends, your Aunt Joan, a bank, or a venture capitalist. The investor in the company gives you some cash, and in return you give him a contract stating how much of the company he owns. The **shareholders** who own the company between them then have some say in the running of the business, and technically the directors of the company are meant to act in the best interests of the shareholders. Once your business is up and running, you could raise further capital for expansion by issuing new shares.

This is how small businesses begin. Once the small business has become a large business, your Aunt Joan may not have enough money hidden under the mattress to invest in the next expansion. At this point shares in the company may be sold to a wider audience or even the general public. The investors in the business may have no link with the founders. The final point in the growth of the company is with the quotation of shares on a regulated stock exchange so that shares can be bought and sold freely, and capital can be raised efficiently and at the lowest cost.

Figures 1.1 and 1.2 show screens from Bloomberg giving details of Microsoft stock, including price, high and low, names of key personnel, weighting in various indices, etc. There is much, much more info available on Bloomberg for this and all other stocks. We'll be seeing many Bloomberg screens throughout this book.

In Figure 1.3 I show an excerpt from *The Wall Street Journal Europe* of 14th April 2005. This shows a small selection of the many stocks traded on the New York Stock Exchange. The listed information includes highs and lows for the day as well as the change since the previous day's close.

The behavior of the quoted prices of stocks is far from being predictable. In Figure 1.4 I show the Dow Jones Industrial Average over the period January 1950 to March 2004. In Figure 1.5 is a time series of the Glaxo–Wellcome share price, as produced by Bloomberg.

If we could predict the behavior of stock prices in the future then we could become very rich. Although many people have claimed to be able to predict prices with varying degrees of accuracy, no one has yet made a completely convincing case. In this book I am going to take the point of view that prices have a large element of randomness. This does *not* mean that we cannot model stock prices, but it does mean that the modeling must be done in a probabilistic sense. No doubt the reality of the situation lies somewhere between

```
MSFT US $ C 95+¹⁵/₁₆ Q Q194¹⁵/₁₆/95Q                    DL18 Equity DES
As of Sep10 DELAYED Vol 17,227,500 Op 95¹/₁₆ Q  Hi 95⅝ Q  Lo 94 Q
                    DESCRIPTION                          Page  1 /10
MSFT US              MICROSOFT CORP            12) CN All News/Research
Computer Software                             13) CWP Company Web Page
CUSIP 594918104                               14) HH Hoover's Handbook
Microsoft Corporation develops, manufactures, licenses, sells, and supports
software products.  The Company offers operating system software, server
application software, business and consumer applications software, software
development tools, and Internet and intranet software.  Microsoft also develops
the MSN network of Internet products and services.

      STOCK DATA    Round Lot    100 | 8)DVD    DIVIDENDS  - None
1)GPO Current Price      USD      95 |      Indicated Gross Yld
      52Wk High 7/19/1999 USD 100³/₄ |      Dividend Growth
      52Wk Low  10/ 8/1998 USD  43⁷/₈ |      Ex-Date      Type       Amt
      YTD Chng ( 37.00%)  USD  25³²/₃₂|
2)TRA 1 Yr Total Return       82.25% |      3/29/99    Split    2 for 1
3)CH1 Shares Out as of 4/30 5103.859M| EARNINGS - Ann Date 10/20/99 (Est)
      Market Cap    USD 484866.63M | 9)ERN Trailing 12mo EPS   USD   1.395
Float   3576.78M  Short Int 24.823M | 10)EE Est EPS    6/2000 USD   1.566
5)BETA Beta   vs. SPX         1.25 | 11)GE P/E   68.10  Est P/E    60.66
6)OCM Options avail & Stk Marginable| LT Growth   25.21 Est PEG     2.41
Par Value = .0000125

Copyright 1999 BLOOMBERG L.P.  Frankfurt:69-920410  Hong Kong:2-977-6000  London:171-330-7500  New York:212-318-2000
Princeton:609-279-3000  Singapore:226-3000  Sydney:2-9777-8686  Tokyo:3-3201-8900  Sao Paulo:11-3048-4500
                                                                    I741-53-0 11-Sep-99 15:35:34
Bloomberg
PROFESSIONAL
```

Figure 1.1 Details of Microsoft stock. Source: Bloomberg L.P.

```
Page                                            DL18 Equity DES
Hit 1 <GO> for a more detailed company management profile (MGMT).
MSFT US              MICROSOFT CORP                    Page  2 /10
One Microsoft Way          T:425-882-8080       F:425-936-8000
Bldg 8 Southwest           2) http://www.microsoft.com/msft/
Redmond,WA   98052-6399    TR AG ChaseMellon Shareholder Services
United States              # OF EMPLOYEES      27,055
WILLIAM H GATES III        CHAIRMAN/CEO
STEVEN A BALLMER           PRESIDENT
ROBERT J HERBOLD           EXEC VP/COO
GREGORY B MAFFEI           SENIOR VP/CFO
TIM HALLADAY               INVESTOR RELATIONS CONTACT
STEVE SCHIRO               VP:CONSUMER CUSTOMER UNIT
Type   Common Stock   PAR $ .00001 | 3)WGT MEMBER         TICKER  WEIGHT
PRIMARY EXCHANGE   NASDAQ N-Mkt |  S&P 500 INDEX        SPX    4.368%
COUNTRY          United States |  NASDAQ 100 STOCK     NDX   14.287%
FISCAL YEAR END      JUNE      |  S&P 100 INDEX        OEX    8.752%
SIC Code  7372  PREPAKG SOFTW  |  TRIB WORLD INDEX     TRIB   5.245%
VALOREN    000951692           |  AMEX INSTITUTION     XII    6.540%
WPK Number 870747              |  AMEX COMPUTER TE     XCI   23.453%
SEDOL      2588173             |  PHILA NATIONAL O     XOC   21.223%
Sicovam    903099              |  CBOE TECHNOLOGY      TXX    4.157%
ISIN       US5949181045        |  S&P INDUSTRIALS      SPXI   5.316%
                               |  S&P CAPITAL GOOD     SPCAPC 15.140%

Copyright 1999 BLOOMBERG L.P.  Frankfurt:69-920410  Hong Kong:2-977-6000  London:171-330-7500  New York:212-318-2000
Princeton:609-279-3000  Singapore:226-3000  Sydney:2-9777-8686  Tokyo:3-3201-8900  Sao Paulo:11-3048-4500
                                                                    I741-53-0 11-Sep-99 15:35:41
Bloomberg
PROFESSIONAL
```

Figure 1.2 Details of Microsoft stock continued. Source: Bloomberg L.P.

THE WALL STREET JOURNAL EUROPE.

NEW YORK STOCK EXCHANGE TRANSACTIONS

Figure 1.3 *The Wall Street Journal Europe* of 14th April 2005.

complete predictability and perfect randomness, not least because there have been many cases of market manipulation where large trades have moved stock prices in a direction that was favorable to the person doing the moving. Having said that, I will digress slightly in Appendix B where I describe some of the popular methods for supposedly predicting future stock prices.

See the simulation on the CD

To whet your appetite for the mathematical modeling later, I want to show you a simple way to simulate a random walk that looks something like a stock price. One of the simplest random processes is the tossing of a coin. I am going to use ideas related to coin tossing as a model for the behavior of a stock price. As a simple experiment start with the number 100 which you should think of as the price of your stock, and toss a coin. If you throw a head multiply the number by 1.01, if you throw a tail multiply by 0.99. After one toss your number will be either 99 or 101. Toss again. If you get a head multiply your *new* number by 1.01 or by 0.99 if you throw a tail. You will now have either $1.01^2 \times 100$, $1.01 \times 0.99 \times 100 = 0.99 \times 1.01 \times 100$ or $0.99^2 \times 100$. Continue this process and plot your value on a graph each time you throw the coin. Results of one particular experiment are shown in Figure 1.6. Instead of physically tossing a coin, the series used in this plot was generated on a spreadsheet like that in Figure 1.7. This uses the Excel spreadsheet function RAND() to generate a uniformly distributed random number between 0 and 1. If this number is greater than one half it counts as a 'head' otherwise a 'tail.'

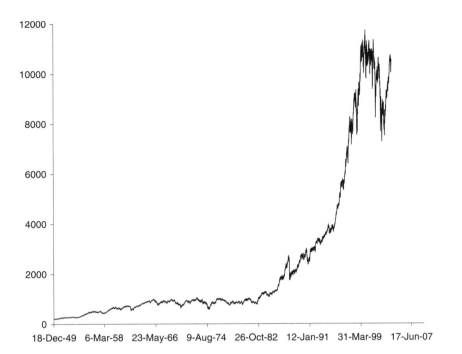

Figure 1.4   A time series of the Dow Jones Industrial Average from January 1950 to March 2004.

Figure 1.5   Glaxo–Wellcome share price (volume below). Source: Bloomberg L.P.

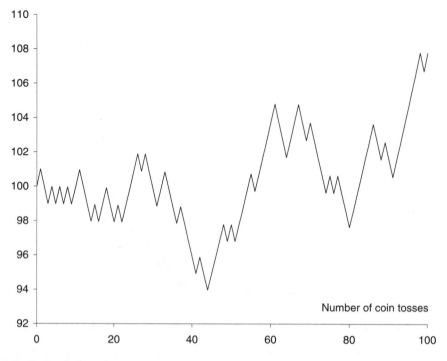

Figure 1.6   A simulation of an asset price path?

Time Out...

More about coin tossing

Notice how in the above experiment I've chosen to *multiply* each 'asset price' by a factor, either 1.01 or 0.99. Why didn't I simply *add* a fixed amount, 1 or −1, say? This is a very important point in the modeling of asset prices; as the asset price gets larger so do the changes from one day to the next. It seems reasonable to model the asset price changes as being proportional to the current level of the asset, they are still random but the magnitude of the randomness depends on the level of the asset. This will be made more precise in later chapters, where we'll see how it is important to model the return on the asset, its percentage change, rather than its absolute value. And, of course, in this simple model the 'asset price' cannot go negative.

If we use the multiplicative rule we get an approximation to what is called a **lognormal random walk**, also **geometric random walk**. If we use the additive rule we get an approximation to a **Normal** or **arithmetic random walk**.

As an experiment, using Excel try to simulate both the arithmetic and geometric random walks, and also play around with the probability of a rise in asset price; it doesn't have to be one half. What happens if you have an arithmetic random walk with a probability of rising being less than one half?

1.2.1 Dividends

The owner of the stock theoretically owns a piece of the company. This ownership can only be turned into cash if he owns so many of the stock that he can take over the company and keep all the profits for himself. This is unrealistic for most of us. To the average investor the value in holding the stock comes from the **dividends** and any growth in the stock's value. Dividends are lump sum payments, paid out every quarter or every six months, to the holder of the stock.

The amount of the dividend varies from time to time depending on the profitability of the company. As a general rule companies like to try to keep the level of dividends about the same each time. The amount of the dividend is decided by the board of directors of the company and is usually set a month or so before the dividend is actually paid.

When the stock is bought it either comes with its entitlement to the next dividend (**cum**) or not (**ex**). There is a date at around the time of the dividend payment when the stock goes from cum to ex. The original holder of the stock gets the dividend but the person who buys it obviously does not. All things being equal a stock that is cum dividend is better than one that is ex dividend. Thus at the time that the dividend is paid and the stock goes ex dividend there will be a drop in the value of the stock. The size of this drop in stock value offsets the disadvantage of not getting the dividend.

This jump in stock price is in practice more complex than I have just made out. Often capital gains due to the rise in a stock price are taxed differently from a dividend, which is often treated as income. Some people can make a lot of risk-free money by exploiting tax 'inconsistencies.'

	A	B	C	D	E
1	Initial stock price	100		Stock	
2	Up move	1.01		100	
3	Down move	0.99		101	
4	Probability of up	0.5		99.99	
5				98.9901	
6		= B1		99.98	
7				98.9802	
8				99.97	
9		=D6*IF(RAND()>1-$B$4,$B$2,$B$3)		03	
10				99.96001	
11				98.96041	
12				99.95001	
13				100.9495	
14				99.94001	
15				98.94061	
16				97.95121	
17				98.93072	
18				97.94141	
19				98.92083	
20				99.91004	
21				98.91094	
22				97.92183	
23				98.90104	
24				97.91203	
25				98.89115	
26				99.88007	
27				100.8789	
28				101.8877	
29				100.8688	
30				101.8775	
31				100.8587	

Figure 1.7   Simple spreadsheet to simulate the coin-tossing experiment.

1.2.2   Stock splits

Stock prices in the US are usually of the order of magnitude of $100. In the UK they are typically around £1. There is no real reason for the popularity of the number of digits, after all, if I buy a stock I want to know what percentage growth I will get, the absolute level of the stock is irrelevant to me, it just determines whether I have to buy tens or thousands of the stock to invest a given amount. Nevertheless there is some psychological element to the stock size. Every now and then a company will announce a **stock split**. For example, the company with a stock price of $90 announces a three-for-one stock split. This simply means that instead of holding one stock valued at $90, I hold three valued at $30 each.[1]

---

[1] In the UK this would be called a two-for-one split.

```
<HELP> for explanation, <MENU> for similar functions.        DL18 Equity DVD
Hit # <GO> to view details.
              DIVIDEND/SPLIT  SUMMARY                        Page  1/ 1
MSFT US        MICROSOFT CORP                        Currency ■■
 12 Month Yield      n.a.
 Indicated Yield     n.a.


   Graph Selections                      GRAPH NOT AVAILABLE
   B-Both
   G-Gross Yield
   Y-Adjust for Splits

   Range  1990  to  1999   Type 1-All          Frequency Irregular
    Declared Ex-Date  Record   Payable        Amount     Type
 1)  1/25/99  3/29/99  3/12/99  3/26/99        2 for 1    Stock Split
 2)  1/26/98  2/23/98  2/ 6/98  2/20/98        2 for 1    Stock Split
 3) 11/12/96 12/ 9/96 11/22/96 12/ 6/96        2 for 1    Stock Split
 4)  4/25/94  5/23/94  5/ 6/94  5/20/94        2 for 1    Stock Split
 5)  6/ 3/92  6/15/92  6/ 3/92  6/12/92        3 for 2    Stock Split
 6)  5/ 8/91  6/27/91  6/18/91  6/26/91        3 for 2    Stock Split
 7)  3/13/90  4/16/90  3/26/90  4/13/90        2 for 1    Stock Split



Copyright 1999 BLOOMBERG L.P.   Frankfurt:69-920410  Hong Kong:2-977-6000  London:171-330-7500  New York:212-318-2000
Princeton:609-279-3000    Singapore:226-3000    Sydney:2-9777-8686     Tokyo:3-3201-8900    Sao Paulo:11-3048-4500
                                                                    I741-53-0 11-Sep-99 15:36:49
■Bloomberg
PROFESSIONAL
```

Figure 1.8   Stock split info for Microsoft. Source: Bloomberg L.P.

1.3   **COMMODITIES**

Commodities are usually raw products such as precious metals, oil, food products, etc. The prices of these products are unpredictable but often show seasonal effects. Scarcity of the product results in higher prices. Commodities are usually traded by people who have no need of the raw material. For example they may just be speculating on the direction of gold without wanting to stockpile it or make jewelry. Most trading is done on the futures market, making deals to buy or sell the commodity at some time in the future. The deal is then closed out before the commodity is due to be delivered. Futures contracts are discussed below.

Figure 1.9 shows a time series of the price of pulp, used in paper manufacture.

1.4   **CURRENCIES**

Another financial quantity we shall discuss is the **exchange rate**, the rate at which one currency can be exchanged for another. This is the world of **foreign exchange**, or **Forex** or **FX** for short. Some currencies are pegged to one another, and others are allowed to float freely. Whatever the exchange rates from one currency to another, there must be consistency throughout. If it is possible to exchange dollars for pounds and then the pounds for yen, this implies a relationship between the dollar/pound, pound/yen and dollar/yen exchange rates. If this relationship moves out of line it is possible to make **arbitrage profits** by exploiting the mispricing.

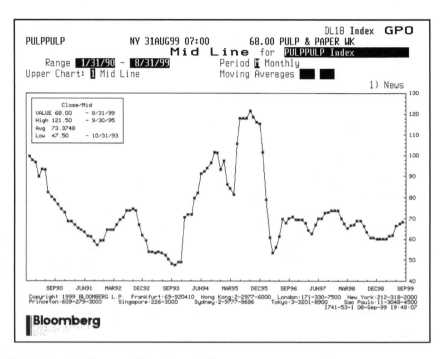

Figure 1.9 Pulp price. Source: Bloomberg L.P.

Dow Jones and Dow Jones Stoxx Indexes

Dividend yield*	Price-to-earnings ratio*	Dows Jones Index	PERFORMANCE (euros) Last	Daily	52-wk.	PERFORMANCE (U.S. dollars) Last	Daily	52-wk.
2.03%	16	**World** -a				252.11	**-0.12%**	13.9%
2.02	16	**Stoxx Global 1800**	258.90	**-0.80%**	7.7%	249.78	**-0.04**	13.7
2.80	13	**Stoxx 600**	330.70	**-0.09**	14.6	319.08	**0.69**	21.0
2.93	12	**Stoxx Large 200**	357.10	**-0.09**	13.4	342.72	**0.68**	19.8
2.23	17	**Stoxx Mid 200**	296.40	**-0.10**	19.6	284.38	**0.67**	26.3
2.21	18	**Stoxx Small 200**	181.90	**0.04**	19.4	174.48	**0.81**	26.1
2.14	15	**Stoxx Growth**	1468.50	**-0.11**	12.7	1668.87	**0.66**	19.0
3.41	12	**Stoxx Value**	1544.90	**-0.03**	14.6	1756.49	**0.74**	21.1
2.77	14	**Euro Stoxx**	353.60	**-0.37**	15.9	341.21	**0.40**	22.4
2.94	13	**Euro Stoxx Large 200**	380.80	**-0.39**	15.0	365.14	**0.38**	21.4
2.06	18	**Euro Stoxx Mid 200**	314.50	**-0.26**	19.2	301.50	**0.51**	25.9
2.14	20	**Euro Stoxx Small 200**	195.90	**-0.36**	19.2	187.66	**0.41**	25.9
4.81%	12	**Stoxx Select Dividend 30**	2791.80	**0.00%**	15.7%	3086.74	**0.77%**	22.2%
4.07	11	**Euro Stoxx Select Div 30**	2804.30	**-0.23**	23.3	3112.55	**0.54**	30.2
3.53	15	**U.S. Select Dividend** -b				818.86	**-0.17**	8.7
5.50	18	**Australia LPT** -b, c	2068.60	**0.37**	20.9			
2.45	15	**Sustainability**	1058.80	**-0.57**	9.3	1154.88	**0.19**	15.5
1.67	16	**Islamic Market** -a				1921.94	**-0.03**	10.0
1.94	15	**Islamic Market 100**	1926.90	**-0.69**	1.5	2130.43	**0.08**	7.2
5.64	15	**Islamic Turkey** -c	2372.80	**-0.27**	17.9			
4.25	1	**Bahrain** -c	181.40	**-0.44**	8.3			
1.72	17	**Wilshire 5000**				12971.03	**-0.39**	6.4
		DJ-AIG Commodity	182.80	**0.22**	-1.2	171.55	**1.00**	4.3
		Euro Currency	108.10	**0.38**	4.6			

*Fundamentals are based on data in U.S. dollar. Footnotes: a-in US dollar. b-dividends reinvested. c-in local currency. Note: All data as of 2 p.m. ET.

Source: Dow Jones Indexes

Cross rates U.S.-dollar and euro foreign-exchange rates in global trading

	USD	GBP	CHF	SEK	RUB	NOK	JPY	ILS	EUR	DKK	CDN	AUD
Australia	1.3092	2.4838	1.0716	0.1839	0.0491	0.2104	0.0113	0.3009	1.6916	0.2267	1.1720	...
Canada	1.1171	2.1193	0.9144	0.1569	0.0419	0.1795	0.0096	0.2567	1.4433	0.1934	...	0.8533
Denmark	5.7745	10.9557	4.7268	0.8110	0.2166	0.9281	0.0499	1.3270	7.4612	...	5.1694	4.4109
Euro	0.7739	1.4683	0.6335	0.1087	0.0290	0.1244	0.0067	0.1779	...	0.1340	0.6928	0.5912
Israel	4.3515	8.2559	3.5620	0.6111	0.1632	0.6994	0.0376	...	5.6226	0.7536	3.8955	3.3239
Japan	115.8300	219.7585	94.8144	16.2671	4.3447	18.6162	...	26.6184	149.6639	20.0589	103.6928	88.4767
Norway	6.2220	11.8047	5.0931	0.8738	0.2334	...	0.0537	1.4299	8.0394	1.0775	5.5700	4.7527
Russia	26.6600	50.5807	21.8229	3.7441	...	4.2848	0.2302	6.1266	34.4474	4.6168	23.8664	20.3642
Sweden	7.1205	13.5094	5.8286	...	0.2671	1.1444	0.0615	1.6363	9.2004	1.2331	6.3744	5.4390
Switzerland	1.2217	2.3178	...	0.1716	0.0458	0.1963	0.0105	0.2807	1.5785	0.2116	1.0936	0.9332
U.K.	0.5271	...	0.4314	0.0740	0.0198	0.0847	0.0046	0.1211	0.6810	0.0913	0.4718	0.4026
U.S.	...	1.8972	0.8186	0.1404	0.0375	0.1607	0.0086	0.2298	1.2921	0.1732	0.8952	0.7638

Source: Reuters via WSJ Market Data Group

MSCI indexes

Developed and emerging-market
from MSCI Barra as of Aug. 21, 2

Dividend yield	Price-to-earnings ratio	Morgan Stanley Index
2.20%	16	**ALL COUNTRY (AC) WO**
2.20	16	World (Developed Mark
2.10	17	World ex-EMU
2.10	16	World ex-UK
2.60	15	EAFE
2.50	13	Emerging Markets (EM
3.00	14	**EUROPE**
3.00	13	EMU
2.80	14	Europe ex-UK
3.70	12	Europe Value
2.20	17	Europe Growth
2.00	23	Europe Small Cap
2.10	14	EM Europe
3.30	13	UK
2.80	15	Nordic Countries
1.30	16	Russia
2.50	15	South Africa
3.00	15	**AC ASIA PACIFIC EX-JA**
1.10	20	Japan
2.30	15	China
1.30	20	India
1.80	10	Korea
4.00	15	Taiwan
...	...	**US BROAD MARKET**
1.30	27	US Small Cap
2.70	12	**EM LATIN AMERICA**

*Twenty-three developed and 26 emergin

Figure 1.10 *The Wall Street Journal Europe* of 22nd August 2006, currency exchange rates.

Figure 1.10 is an excerpt from *The Wall Street Journal Europe* of 22nd August 2006. At the bottom of this excerpt is a matrix of exchange rates. A similar matrix is shown in Figure 1.11 from Bloomberg.

Although the fluctuation in exchange rates is unpredictable, there is a link between exchange rates and the interest rates in the two countries. If the interest rate on dollars is raised while the interest rate on pounds sterling stays fixed we would expect to see sterling depreciating against the dollar for a while. Central banks can use interest rates as a tool for manipulating exchange rates, but only to a degree.

```
<HELP> for explanation, <MENU> for similar functions.          DL18 Curncy FXC

15:40
Sat  9/11        KEY  CROSS  CURRENCY  RATES

        USD    EUR    JPY    GBP    CHF    CAD    AUD    NZD    HKD    DKK    SEK
SEK  8.2937 8.6039 7.6285 13.423 5.3473 5.6248 5.4038 4.4168 1.0680 1.1564  ....
DKK  7.1720 7.4402 6.5968 11.608 4.6241 4.8640 4.6729 3.8194  .92352  .... .86475
HKD  7.7659 8.0563 7.1430 12.569 5.0070 5.2668 5.0599 4.1357  .... 1.0828 .93636
NZD  1.8778 1.9480 1.7272 3.0392 1.2107 1.2735 1.2235  .... .24180 .26182 .22641
AUD  1.5348 1.5922 1.4117 2.4841 .98956 1.0409  .... .81736 .19763 .21400 .18506
CAD  1.4745 1.5296 1.3562 2.3865 .95068  .... .96071 .78524 .18987 .20559 .17779
CHF  1.5510 1.6090 1.4266 2.5103  .... 1.0519 1.0106 .82599 .19972 .21626 .18701
GBP  .61786 .64096 .56830  .... .39836 .41903 .40256 .32904 .07956 .08615 .07450
JPY  108.72 112.79  .... 175.96 70.097 73.733 70.837 57.899 14.000 15.159 13.109
EUR  .96395  .... .88663 1.5602 .62150 .65375 .62806 .51335 .12413 .13440 .11623
USD   .... 1.0374 .91979 1.6185 .64475 .67820 .65155 .53255 .12877 .13943 .12057
                (x100)
 Spot  Enter 1M,2M etc. for forward rates       E EURO/     █ Use XDF Currencies
        Hit -1,-2...<Page> for previous days        LEGACY   █ Show change only

  monitoring enabled:    decrease   increase   no change   BLOOMBERG Composite
  Copyright 1999 BLOOMBERG L.P.  Frankfurt:69-920410 Hong Kong:2-977-6000  London:171-330-7500  New York:212-318-2000
  Princeton:609-279-3000     Singapore:226-3000    Sydney:2-9777-8686    Tokyo:3-3201-8900    Sao Paulo:11-3048-4500
                                                                       I741-53-0 11-Sep-99 15:40:06
 ▌Bloomberg
  PROFESSIONAL
```

Figure 1.11   Key cross currency rates. Source: Bloomberg L.P.

At the start of 1999 Euroland currencies were fixed at the rates shown in Figure 1.12.

1.5   INDICES

For measuring how the stock market/economy is doing as a whole, there have been developed the stock market **indices**. A typical index is made up from the weighted sum of a selection or **basket** of representative stocks. The selection may be designed to represent the whole market, such as the Standard & Poor's 500 (S&P500) in the US or the Financial Times Stock Exchange index (FTSE100) in the UK, or a very special part of a market. In Figure 1.4 we saw the DJIA, representing major US stocks. In Figure 1.13 is shown JP Morgan's Emerging Market Bond Index.

The EMBI+ is an index of emerging market debt instruments, including external-currency-denominated Brady bonds, Eurobonds and US dollar local markets instruments. The main components of the index are the three major Latin American countries, Argentina, Brazil and Mexico. Bulgaria, Morocco, Nigeria, the Philippines, Poland, Russia and South Africa are also represented.

Figure 1.14 shows a time series of the MAE All Bond Index which includes Peso and US dollar denominated bonds sold by the Argentine Government.

1.6   THE TIME VALUE OF MONEY

The simplest concept in finance is that of the **time value of money**; $1 today is worth more than $1 in a year's time. This is because of all the things we can do with $1 over the

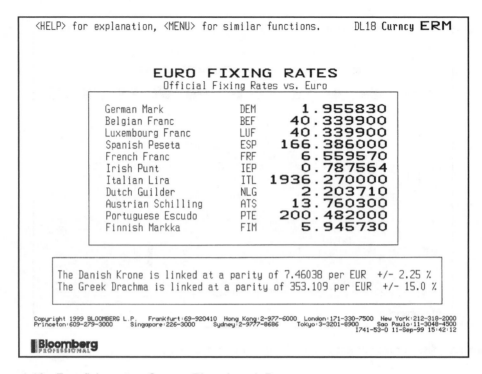

Figure 1.12 Euro fixing rates. Source: Bloomberg L.P.

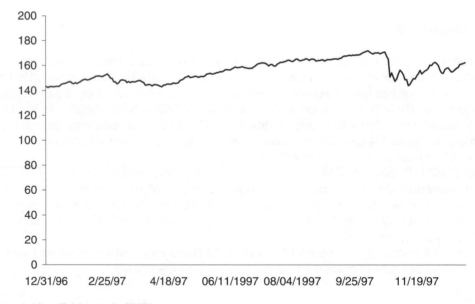

Figure 1.13 JP Morgan's EMBI +.

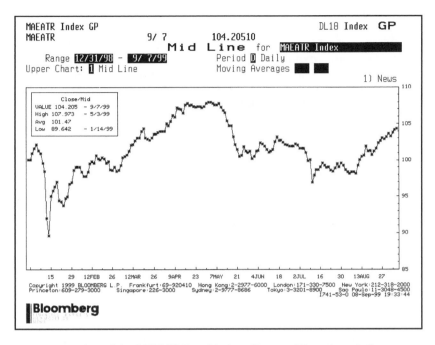

```
MAEATR Index GP                                    DL18 Index  GP
MAEATR              9/ 7        104.20510
                              Mid Line  for  MAEATR Index
        Range 12/31/98 - 9/ 7/99       Period 0 Daily
Upper Chart: 1 Mid Line                Moving Averages
                                                       1) News      110
```

Figure caption content in chart:
```
          Close/Mid
VALUE 104.205 - 9/7/99
High  107.973 - 5/3/99
Avg   101.47
Low    89.642 - 1/14/99
```

```
   15   29  12FEB 26  12MAR 26  9APR 23  7MAY 21  4JUN 18  2JUL 16  30  13AUG 27
Copyright 1999 BLOOMBERG L.P.  Frankfurt:69-920410  Hong Kong:2-2977-6000  New York:212-318-2000
Princeton:609-279-3000  Singapore:226-3000  Sydney:2-9777-8686  Tokyo:3-3201-8900  Sao Paulo:11-3048-4500
                                              I741-53-0 08-Sep-99 19:33:44
```

Figure 1.14 A time series of the MAE All Bond Index. Source: Bloomberg L.P.

next year. At the very least, we can put it under the mattress and take it out in one year. But instead of putting it under the mattress we could invest it in a gold mine, or a new company. If those are too risky, then lend the money to someone who is willing to take the risks and will give you back the dollar with a little bit extra, the **interest**. That is what banks do, they borrow your money and invest it in various risky ways, but by spreading their risk over many investments

they reduce their overall risk. And by borrowing money from many people they can invest in ways that the average individual cannot. The banks compete for your money by offering high interest rates. Free markets and the ability to quickly and cheaply change banks ensure that interest rates are fairly consistent from one bank to another.

$Time\ Out...$

Symbols

It had to happen sooner or later, and the first chapter is as good as anywhere. Our first mathematical symbol is nigh.

Please don't be put off by the use of symbols if you feel more comfortable with numbers and concrete examples. I know that math is the one academic subject that can terrify adults, just because of poor teaching in schools. If you fall into this category, just go with the flow, concentrate on the words, the examples and the Time Outs, and before you know it...

I am going to denote interest rates by r. Although rates vary with time I am going to assume for the moment that they are constant. We can talk about several types of interest. First of all there is **simple** and **compound interest**. Simple interest is when the interest you receive is based only on the amount you initially invest, whereas compound interest is when you also get interest on your interest. Compound interest is the only case of relevance. And compound interest comes in two forms, **discretely compounded** and **continuously compounded**. Let me illustrate how they each work.

Suppose I invest $1 in a bank at a discrete interest rate of r paid once *per annum*. At the end of one year my bank account will contain

$$1 \times (1+r).$$

If the interest rate is 10% I will have one dollar and ten cents. After two years I will have

$$1 \times (1+r) \times (1+r) = (1+r)^2,$$

or one dollar and twenty-one cents. After n years I will have $(1+r)^n$. That is an example of discrete compounding.

Now suppose I receive m interest payments at a rate of r/m *per annum*. After one year I will have

$$\left(1 + \frac{r}{m}\right)^m. \tag{1.1}$$

Now I am going to imagine that these interest payments come at increasingly frequent intervals, but at an increasingly smaller interest rate: I am going to take the limit $m \to \infty$. This will lead to a rate of interest that is paid continuously. Expression (1.1) becomes[2]

I BELIEVE THAT 99% OF FINANCE REQUIRES ONLY BASIC MATH

$$\left(1 + \frac{r}{m}\right)^m = e^{m \log\left(1 + \frac{r}{m}\right)} \sim e^r.$$

That is how much money I will have in the bank after one year if the interest is continuously compounded. And similarly, after a time t I will have an amount

$$\left(1 + \frac{r}{m}\right)^{mt} \sim e^{rt} \tag{1.2}$$

in the bank. Almost everything in this book assumes that interest is compounded continuously.

---

[2] The symbol $\sim$, called 'tilde,' is like 'approximately equal to,' but with a slightly more technical, in a math sense, meaning. The symbol $\to$ means 'tends to.'

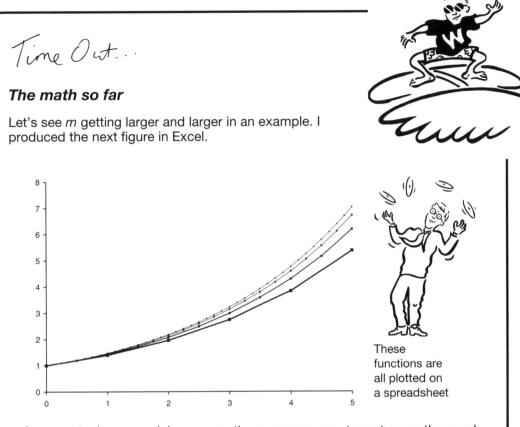

Time Out...

The math so far

Let's see m getting larger and larger in an example. I produced the next figure in Excel.

These functions are all plotted on a spreadsheet

As m gets larger and larger, so the curve seems to get smoother and smoother, eventually becoming the exponential function. We'll be seeing this function a lot. In Excel the exponential function e^x (also written $\exp(x)$) is EXP( ).

What mathematics have we seen so far? To get to (1.2) all we needed to know about are the two functions, the **exponential function** e (or exp) and the **logarithm** log, and Taylor series. Believe it or not, you can appreciate almost all finance theory by knowing these three things together with 'expectations.' I'm going to build up to the basic Black–Scholes and derivatives theory assuming that you know all four of these. Don't worry if you don't know about these things, in Appendix A I review these requisites.

En passant, what would the above figures look like if interest were simple rather than compound? Which would you prefer to receive?

Another way of deriving the result (1.2) is via a differential equation. Suppose I have an amount $M(t)$ in the bank at time t, how much does this increase in value from one day to the next? If I look at my bank account at time t and then again a short while later, time $t + dt$, the amount will have increased by

$$M(t + dt) - M(t) \approx \frac{dM}{dt} dt + \cdots,$$

where the right-hand side comes from a Taylor series expansion. But I also know that the interest I receive must be proportional to the amount I have, M, the interest rate, r, and the time step, dt. Thus

$$\frac{dM}{dt}dt = rM(t)\,dt.$$

Dividing by dt gives the ordinary differential equation

$$\frac{dM}{dt} = rM(t)$$

the solution of which is

$$M(t) = M(0)\,e^{rt}.$$

If the initial amount at $t = 0$ was \$1 then I get (1.2) again.

OUR FIRST (AND SIMPLEST) DIFFERENTIAL EQUATION

Time Out...

Differential equations

This is our first **differential equation**; hang on in there, it'll become second nature soon.

Whenever you see d something over d something else you know you're looking at a slope, or gradient, also known as rate of change or sensitivity. So here we've got the rate of change of money with time, i.e. rate of growth of money in the bank. You don't need to know how I solved this differential equation really. In Appendix A I explain all about slope, sensitivities and differential equations.

This first differential equation is an example of an **ordinary differential equation**, there is only one **independent variable** t. M is the **dependent variable**, its value depends on t. We'll also be seeing **partial differential equations** where there is more than one independent variable. And we'll also see quite a few **stochastic differential equations**. These are equations with a random term in them, used for modeling the randomness in the financial world. For the next few chapters there will be no more mention of differential equations. Whew.

This equation relates the value of the money I have now to the value in the future. Conversely, if I know I will get one dollar at time T in the future, its value at an earlier time t is simply

$$\frac{1}{e^{r(T-t)}} = e^{-r(T-t)}.$$

I can relate cashflows in the future to their **present value** by multiplying by this factor. As an example, suppose that r is 5%, i.e. $r = 0.05$, then the present value of $1,000,000 to be received in two years is

$$\$1,000,000 \times e^{-0.05 \times 2} = \$904,837.$$

The present value is clearly less than the future value.

Interest rates are a very important factor determining the present value of future cashflows. For the moment I will only talk about one interest rate, and that will be constant. In later chapters I will generalize.

1.7 FIXED-INCOME SECURITIES

In lending money to a bank you may get to choose for how long you tie your money up and what kind of interest rate you receive. If you decide on a fixed-term deposit the bank will offer to lock in a fixed rate of interest for the period of the deposit, a month, six months, a year, say. The rate of interest will not necessarily be the same for each period, and generally the longer the time that the money is tied up the higher the rate of interest, although this is not always the case. Often, if you want to have immediate access to your money then you will be exposed to interest rates that will change from time to time, since interest rates are not constant.

These two types of interest payments, **fixed** and **floating**, are seen in many financial instruments. **Coupon-bearing bonds** pay out a known amount every six months or year, etc. This is the **coupon** and would often be a fixed rate of interest. At the end of your fixed term you get a final coupon and the return of the **principal**, the amount on which the interest was calculated. **Interest rate swaps** are an exchange of a fixed rate of interest for a floating rate of interest. Governments and companies issue bonds as a form of borrowing. The less creditworthy the issuer, the higher the interest that they will have to pay out. Bonds are actively traded, with prices that continually fluctuate.

1.8 INFLATION-PROOF BONDS

A very recent addition to the list of bonds issued by the US Government is the **index-linked bond**. These have been around in the UK since 1981, and have provided a very successful way of ensuring that income is not eroded by inflation.

In the UK inflation is measured by the **Retail Price Index** or **RPI**. This index is a measure of year-on-year inflation, using a 'basket' of goods and services including mortgage interest payments. The index is published monthly. The coupons and principal of the index-linked bonds are related to the level of the RPI. Roughly speaking, the amounts of the coupon and principal are scaled with the increase in the RPI over the period from the issue of the bond to the time of the payment. There is one slight complication in that the actual RPI level used in these calculations is set back *eight months*. Thus the base measurement is eight months before issue and the scaling of any coupon is with respect to the increase in the RPI from this base measurement to the level of the RPI eight months before the coupon is paid. One of the reasons for this complexity is that the initial estimate of the RPI is usually corrected at a later date.

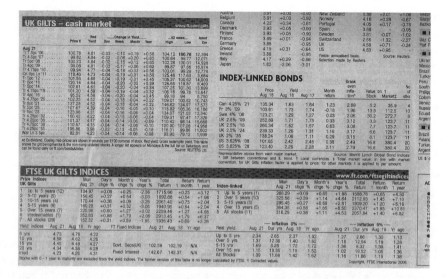

Figure 1.15   UK gilts prices from *The Financial Times* of 22nd August 2006.

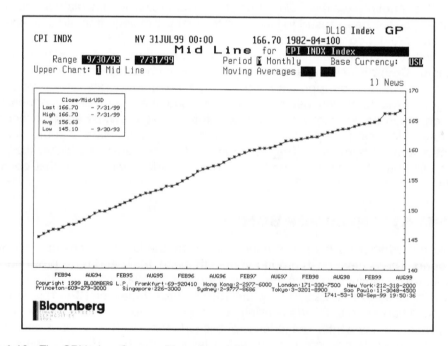

Figure 1.16   The CPI index. Source: Bloomberg L.P.

Figure 1.15 shows the UK gilts prices published in *The Financial Times* of 22nd August 2006. The index-linked bonds are on the right.

In the US the inflation index is the **Consumer Price Index** (**CPI**). A time series of this index is shown in Figure 1.16.

I will not pursue the modeling of inflation or index-linked bonds in this book. I would just like to say that the dynamics of the relationship between inflation and short-term interest rates is particularly interesting. Clearly the level of interest rates will affect the rate of inflation directly through mortgage repayments, but also interest rates are often used by central banks as a tool for keeping inflation down.

1.9 FORWARDS AND FUTURES

FORWARDS AND FUTURES ARE VERY IMPORTANT CONTRACTS

A **forward contract** is an agreement where one party promises to buy an asset from another party at some specified time in the future and at some specified price. No money changes hands until the **delivery date** or **maturity** of the contract. The terms of the contract make it an obligation to buy the asset at the delivery date, there is no choice in the matter. The asset could be a stock, a commodity or a currency.

The amount that is paid for the asset at the delivery date is called the **delivery price**. This price is set at the time that the forward contract is entered into, at an amount that gives the forward contract a value of zero initially. As we approach maturity the value of *this particular forward contract* that we hold will change in value, from initially zero to, at maturity, the difference between the underlying asset and the delivery price.

In the newspapers we will also see quoted the **forward price** for different maturities. These prices are the delivery prices for forward contracts of the quoted maturities, should we enter into such a contract *now*.

Try to distinguish between the value of a particular contract during its life and the specification of the delivery price at initiation of the contract. It's all very subtle. You might think that the forward price is the market's view on the asset value at maturity; this is not quite true as we'll see shortly. In theory, the market's expectation about the value of the asset at maturity of the contract is irrelevant.

A **futures contract** is very similar to a forward contract. Futures contracts are usually traded through an exchange, which standardizes the terms of the contracts. The profit or loss from the futures position is calculated every day and the change in this value is paid from one party to the other. Thus with futures contracts there is a gradual payment of funds from initiation until maturity.

Because you settle the change in value on a daily basis, the value of a futures contract at any time during its life is zero. The futures price varies from day to day, but must at maturity be the same as the asset that you are buying.

I'll show later that provided interest rates are known in advance, forward prices and futures prices of the same maturity must be identical.

Forwards and futures have two main uses, in speculation and in hedging. If you believe that the market will rise you can benefit from this by entering into a forward or futures contract. If your market view is right then a lot of money will change hands (at maturity or every day) in your favor. That is speculation and is very risky. Hedging is the opposite, it is avoidance of risk. For example, if you are expecting to get paid in yen in six months' time, but you live in America and your expenses are all in dollars, then you could enter into a futures contract to lock in a guaranteed exchange rate for the amount of your yen income. Once this exchange rate is locked in you are no longer exposed to fluctuations in the dollar/yen exchange rate. But then you won't benefit if the yen appreciates.

1.9.1   A first example of no arbitrage

Although I won't be discussing futures and forwards very much they do provide us with our first example of the **no-arbitrage** principle. I am going to introduce some more mathematical notation now, it will be fairly consistent throughout the book. Consider a forward contract that obliges us to hand over an amount $F at time T to receive the underlying asset. Today's date is t and the price of the asset is currently $S(t)$, this is the **spot price**, the amount for which we could get immediate delivery of the asset. When we get to maturity we will hand over the amount $F and receive the asset, then worth $S(T)$. How much profit we make cannot be known until we know the value $S(T)$, and we cannot know this until time T. From now on I am going to drop the '$' sign from in front of monetary amounts.

We know all of F, $S(t)$, t and T, but is there any relationship between them? You might think not, since the forward contract entitles us to receive an amount $S(T) - F$ at expiry and this is unknown. However, by entering into a special portfolio of trades *now* we can eliminate all randomness in the future. This is done as follows.

Enter into the forward contract. This costs us nothing up front but exposes us to the uncertainty in the value of the asset at maturity. Simultaneously sell the asset. It is called **going short** when you sell something you don't own. This is possible in many markets, but with some timing restrictions. We now have an amount $S(t)$ in cash due to the sale of the asset, a forward contract, and a short asset position. But our net position is zero. Put the cash in the bank, to receive interest.

When we get to maturity we hand over the amount F and receive the asset, this cancels our short asset position regardless of the value of $S(T)$. At maturity we are left with a guaranteed $-F$ in cash as well as the bank account. The word 'guaranteed' is important because it emphasizes that it is independent of the value of the asset. The bank account contains the initial investment of an amount $S(t)$ with added interest, this has a value at maturity of

$$S(t)e^{r(T-t)}.$$

Our net position at maturity is therefore

$$S(t)e^{r(T-t)} - F.$$

OUR FIRST EXAMPLE OF NO ARBITRAGE

Since we began with a portfolio worth zero and we end up with a predictable amount, that predictable amount should also be zero. We can conclude that

$$F = S(t)e^{r(T-t)}. \tag{1.3}$$

This is the relationship between the spot price and the forward price. It is a linear relationship, the forward price is proportional to the spot price.

Table 1.1 Cashflows in a hedged portfolio of asset and forward.

Holding	Worth today (t)	Worth at maturity (T)
Forward	0	$S(T) - F$
−Stock	$-S(t)$	$-S(T)$
Cash	$S(t)$	$S(t)e^{r(T-t)}$
Total	0	$S(t)e^{r(T-t)} - F$

TODAY'S CASHFLOW IS ZERO, THE FUTURE CASHFLOW IS KNOWN, SO . . . . .

The cashflows in this special hedged portfolio are shown in Table 1.1.

$Time\ Out...$

No arbitrage again

Example: The spot asset price S is 28.75, the one-year forward price F is 30.20 and the one-year interest rate is 4.92%. Are these numbers consistent with no arbitrage?

$$F - Se^{r(T-t)} = 30.20 - 28.75e^{0.0492\times 1} = 0.0001.$$

This is effectively zero to the number of decimal places quoted.

If we know any three out of S, F, r and $T - t$ we can find the fourth, assuming there are no arbitrage possibilities. Note that the forward price in no way depends on what the asset price is expected to do, whether it is expected to increase or decrease in value.

In Figure 1.17 is a path taken by the spot asset price and its forward price. As long as interest rates are constant, these two are related by (1.3).

If this relationship is violated then there will be an arbitrage opportunity. To see what is meant by this, imagine that F is less than $S(t)e^{r(T-t)}$. To exploit this and make a riskless arbitrage profit, enter into the deals as explained above. At maturity you will have $S(t)e^{r(T-t)}$ in the bank, a short asset and a long forward. The asset position cancels when you hand over the amount F, leaving you with a profit of $S(t)e^{r(T-t)} - F$. If F is greater than that given by (1.3) then you enter into the opposite positions, going short the forward. Again you make a riskless profit. The standard economic argument then says that investors will act quickly to exploit the opportunity, and in the process prices will adjust to eliminate it.

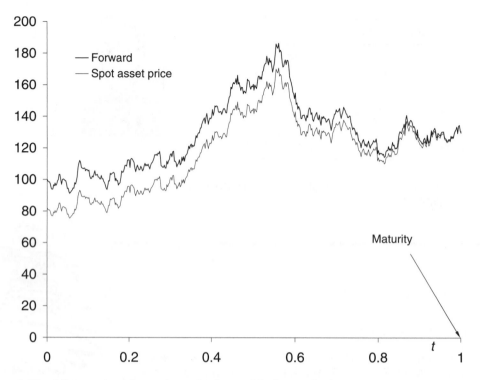

Figure 1.17 A time series of a spot asset price and its forward price.

1.10 MORE ABOUT FUTURES

Futures are usually traded through an exchange. This means that they are very liquid instruments and have lots of rules and regulations surrounding them. Here are a few observations on the nature of futures contracts.

Available assets A futures contract will specify the asset which is being invested in. This is particularly interesting when the asset is a natural commodity because of non-uniformity in the type and quality of the asset to be delivered. Most commodities come in a variety of grades. Oil, sugar, orange juice, wheat, etc. futures contracts lay down rules for precisely what grade of oil, sugar, etc. may be delivered. This idea even applies in some financial futures contracts. For example, bond futures may allow a range of bonds to be delivered. Since the holder of the short position gets to choose which bond to deliver he naturally chooses the cheapest.

The contract also specifies how many of each asset must be delivered. The quantity will depend on the market.

Delivery and settlement The futures contract will specify when the asset is to be delivered. There may be some leeway in the precise delivery date. Most futures contracts are closed out before delivery, with the trader taking the opposite position before maturity. But if the position is not closed then delivery of the asset is made. When the asset is another financial contract settlement is usually made in cash.

Margin   I said above that changes in the value of futures contracts are settled each day. This is called **marking to market**. To reduce the likelihood of one party defaulting, being unable or unwilling to pay up, the exchanges insist on traders depositing a sum of money to cover changes in the value of their positions. This money is deposited in a **margin account**. As the position is marked to market daily, money is deposited or withdrawn from this margin account.

Margin comes in two forms, the **initial margin** and the **maintenance margin**. The initial margin is the amount deposited at the initiation of the contract. The total amount held as margin must stay above a prescribed maintenance margin. If it ever falls below this level then more money (or equivalent in bonds, stocks, etc.) must be deposited. The levels of these margins vary from market to market.

Margin has been much neglected in the academic literature. But a poor understanding of the subject has led to a number of famous financial disasters, most notably Metallgesellschaft and Long Term Capital Management. We'll discuss the details of these cases in Chapter 26, and we'll also be seeing how to model margin and how to margin hedge.

1.10.1   Commodity futures

Futures on commodities don't necessarily obey the no-arbitrage law that led to the asset/future price relationship explained above. This is because of the messy topic of storage. Sometimes we can only reliably find an upper bound for the futures price. Will the futures price be higher or lower than the theoretical no-storage-cost amount? Higher. The holder of the futures contract must compensate the holder of the commodity for his storage costs. This can be expressed in percentage terms by an adjustment s to the risk-free rate of interest.

But things are not quite so simple. Most people actually holding the commodity are benefiting from it in some way. If it is something consumable, such as oil, then the holder can benefit from it immediately in whatever production process they are engaged in. They are naturally reluctant to part with it on the basis of some dodgy theoretical financial calculation. This brings the futures price back down. The benefit from holding the commodity is commonly measured in terms of the **convenience yield** c:

$$F = S(t)e^{(r+s-c)(T-t)}.$$

Observe how the storage cost and the convenience yield act in opposite directions on the price. Whenever

$$F < S(t)e^{r(T-t)}$$

the market is said to be in **backwardation**. Whenever

$$F > S(t)e^{r(T-t)}$$

the market is in **contango**.

1.10.2   FX futures

There are no problems associated with storage when the asset is a currency. We need to modify the no-arbitrage result to allow for interest received on the foreign currency r_f. The result is

$$F = S(t)e^{(r-r_f)(T-t)}.$$

The confirmation of this is an easy exercise.

1.10.3 Index futures

Futures contracts on stock indices are settled in cash. Again, there are no storage problems, but now we have dividends to contend with. Dividends play a role similar to that of a foreign interest rate on FX futures. So

$$F = S(t)e^{(r-q)(T-t)}.$$

Here q is the dividend yield. This is clearly an approximation. Each stock in an index receives a dividend at discrete intervals, but can these all be approximated by one continuous dividend yield?

1.11 SUMMARY

The above descriptions of financial markets are enough for this introductory chapter. Perhaps the most important point to take away with you is the idea of no arbitrage. In the example here, relating spot prices to futures prices, we saw how we could set up a very simple portfolio which completely eliminated any dependence on the future value of the stock. When we come to value derivatives, in the way we just valued a forward, we will see that the same principle can be applied albeit in a far more sophisticated way.

FURTHER READING

- For general financial news visit `www.bloomberg.com` and `www.reuters.com`. CNN has online financial news at `www.cnnfn.com`. There are also online editions of *The Wall Street Journal*, `www.wsj.com`, *The Financial Times*, `www.ft.com` and *Futures and Options World*, `www.fow.com`.

- For more information about futures see the Chicago Board of Trade website `www.cbot.com`.

- Many, many financial links can be found at Wahoo!, `www.io.com/~gibbonsb/wahoo.html`.

- See Bloch (1995) for an empirical analysis of inflation data and a theoretical discussion of pricing index-linked bonds.

- In the main, we'll be assuming that markets are random. For insight about alternative hypotheses see Schwager (1990, 1992).

- See Brooks (1967) for how the raising of capital for a business might work in practice.

- Cox, *et al.* (1981) discuss the relationship between forward and future prices.

EXERCISES

1. A company makes a three-for-one stock split. What effect does this have on the share price?

2. A company whose stock price is currently S pays out a dividend DS, where $0 \leq D \leq 1$. What is the price of the stock just after the dividend date?

3. The dollar sterling exchange rate (colloquially known as 'cable') is 1.83, £1 = $1.83. The sterling euro exchange rate is 1.41, £1 = €1.41. The dollar euro exchange rate is 0.77, $1 = €0.77. Is there an arbitrage, and if so, how does it work?

4. You put $1000 in the bank at a continuously compounded rate of 5% for one year. At the end of this first year rates rise to 6%. You keep your money in the bank for another eighteen months. How much money do you now have in the bank including the accumulated, continuously compounded, interest?

5. A spot exchange rate is currently 2.350. The one-month forward is 2.362. What is the one-month interest rate assuming there is no arbitrage?

6. A particular forward contract costs nothing to enter into at time t and obliges the holder to buy the asset for an amount F at expiry T. The asset pays a dividend DS at time t_d, where $0 \leq D \leq 1$ and $t \leq t_d \leq T$. Use an arbitrage argument to find the forward price $F(t)$.

   Hint: Consider the point of view of the writer of the contract when the dividend is reinvested immediately in the asset.

CHAPTER 2
derivatives

The aim of this Chapter...

...is to describe the basic forms of option contracts, make the reader comfortable with the jargon, explain the relevant pages of financial newspapers, give a basic understanding of the purpose of options, and to expand on the 'no free lunch,' or no-arbitrage, idea. By the end of the chapter you will be familiar with the most common forms of derivatives.

In this Chapter...

- the definitions of basic derivative instruments
- option jargon
- no arbitrage and put-call parity
- how to draw payoff diagrams
- simple option strategies

2.1 **INTRODUCTION**

The previous chapter dealt with some of the basics of financial markets. I didn't go into any detail, just giving the barest outline and setting the scene for this chapter. Here I introduce the theme that is central to the book, the subject of options, a.k.a. derivatives or contingent claims. This chapter is non-technical, being a description of some of the most common option contracts, and explanation of the market-standard jargon. It is in later chapters that I start to get technical.

Options have been around for many years, but it was only on 26th April 1973 that they were first traded on an exchange. It was then that The Chicago Board Options Exchange (CBOE) first created standardized, listed options. Initially there were just calls on 16 stocks. Puts weren't even introduced until 1977. In the US options are traded on CBOE, the American Stock Exchange, the Pacific Stock Exchange and the Philadelphia Stock Exchange. Worldwide, there are over 50 exchanges on which options are traded.

2.2 **OPTIONS**

If you are reading the book in a linear fashion, from start to finish, then the last topics you read about will have been futures and forwards. The holder of future or forward contracts is *obliged* to trade at the maturity of the contract. Unless the position is closed before maturity the holder must take possession of the commodity, currency or whatever is the subject of the contract, regardless of whether the asset has risen or fallen. Wouldn't it be nice if we only had to take possession of the asset if it had risen?

The simplest **option** gives the holder the *right* to trade in the future at a previously agreed price but takes away the obligation. So if the stock falls, we don't have to buy it after all.

> A **call option** is the right to buy a particular asset for an agreed amount at a specified time in the future

As an example, consider the following call option on Microsoft stock. It gives the holder the right to buy one of Microsoft stock for an amount $25 in one month's time. Today's stock price is $24.5. The amount '25' which we can pay for the stock is called the **exercise price** or **strike price**. The date on which we must **exercise** our option, if we decide to, is called the **expiry** or **expiration date**. The stock on which the option is based is known as the **underlying asset**.

Let's consider what may happen over the next month, up until expiry. Suppose that nothing happens, that the stock price remains at $24.5. What do we do at expiry? We could exercise the option, handing over $25 to receive the stock. Would that be sensible? No, because the stock is only worth $24.5, either we wouldn't exercise the option or if we really wanted the stock we would buy it in the stock market for the $24.5. But what if the stock price rises to $29? Then we'd be laughing, we would exercise the option, paying $25 for a stock that's worth $29, a profit of $4.

We would exercise the option at expiry if the stock is above the strike and not if it is below. If we use S to mean the stock price and E the strike then at expiry the option is worth

$$\max(S - E, 0).$$

This function of the underlying asset is called the **payoff function**. The 'max' function represents the optionality.

Why would we buy such an option? Clearly, if you own a call option you want the stock to rise as much as possible. The higher the stock price the greater will be your profit. I will discuss this below, but our decision whether to buy it will depend on how much it costs; the option is valuable, there is no downside to it unlike a future. In our example the option was valued at $1.875. Where did this number come from? The valuation of options is one of the subjects of this book, and I'll be showing you how to find this value later on.

What if you believe that the stock is going to fall, is there a contract that you can buy to benefit from the fall in a stock price? Yes, there is.

> A **put option** is the right to *sell* a particular asset for an agreed amount at a specified time in the future

The holder of a put option wants the stock price to fall so that he can sell the asset for more than it is worth. The payoff function for a put option is

$$\max(E - S, 0).$$

Now the option is only exercised if the stock falls below the strike price.

Figure 2.1 is an excerpt from *The Wall Street Journal Europe* of 14th April 2005 showing options on various stocks. The table lists closing prices of the underlying stocks and the last traded prices of the options on the stocks. To understand how to read this let us examine the prices of options on Apple. Go to 'AppleC' in the list, there are several instances. The closing price on 13th April 2005 was $41.35 (the LAST column, second from the right). Calls and puts are quoted here with strikes of $37.50, $40, ..., $47.50, $50, others may exist but are not included in the newspaper. The expiries mentioned are April, May and July. Part of the information included here is the volume of the transactions in each series; we won't worry about that but some people use option volume as a trading indicator. From the data, we can see that the April calls with a strike of $40 were worth $2.40. The puts with same strike and expiry were worth $1.20. The April calls with a strike of $42.50 were worth $1.20 and the puts with same strike and expiry were worth $2.45. Note that the higher the strike, the lower the value of the calls but the higher the value of the puts. This makes sense when you remember that the call allows you to buy the underlying for the strike, so that the lower the strike price the more this right is worth to you. The opposite is true for a put since it allows you to sell the underlying for the strike price.

There are more strikes and expiries available for options on indices, so let's now look at the Index Options section of *The Wall Street Journal Europe* 5th January 2000, this is shown in Figure 2.2.

In Figure 2.3 are the quoted prices of the March and June DJIA calls against the strike price. Also plotted is the payoff function *if the underlying were to finish at its current value at expiry*, the current closing price of the DJIA was 10,997.93.

This plot reinforces the fact that the higher the strike the lower the value of a call option. It also appears that the longer time to maturity the higher the value of the call. Is it obvious that this should be so? As the time to expiry decreases what would we see happen? As

June 113.10 113.20 113.06 113.16 0.14 113.20 111.28 1,001,156
Sept 113.07 113.07 113.03 113.11 0.14 113.07 111.83 14,652
vol Wed 631,483; open int 1,015,808, +6,768.

10 Yr. Euro-BUND (EUREX)-€100,000; pts of 100%
June 119.56 119.69 119.45 119.65 0.27 120.02 113.45 1,202,848

U.S. LISTED OPTIONS

Wednesday, April 13, 2005

Volume and close for actively traded equity options, with results for the corresponding put or call contract as of 3 pm New York trading. Open interest is total outstanding for all exchanges and reflects previous trading day. Close when possible is shown for the underlying stock or primary market.
XC-Composite. p-Put. o-Strike price adjusted for split.

Most Active Contracts

OPTION/STRIKE			VOL	EXCH	LAST	NET CHG	LAST	OPEN INT
Nasd100Tr	Apr 05	36		68,323	XC	0.25	-0.45	36.27	133,909
AppleC	Apr 05	45		62,651	XC	0.50	-0.20	41.35	75,417
Pfizer	Apr 05	27.50		60,465	XC	0.30	0.25	27.31	72,714
A M D	Apr 05	18		48,681	XC	0.30	0.10	17.24	37,705
AppleC	Apr 05	42.50		40,352	XC	1.20	-0.60	41.35	114,921
Nasd100Tr	Apr 05	36	p	32,808	XC	0.15	0.10	36.27	312,947
AppleC	Apr 05	40	p	26,640	XC	1.20	0.50	41.35	67,675
AppleC	Apr 05	37.50	p	26,487	XC	0.45	0.15	41.35	46,494
AppleC	Apr 05	47.50		25,496	XC	0.25	-0.10	41.35	64,825
AppleC	Apr 05	50		23,850	XC	0.10	-0.05	41.35	35,877
Nasd100Tr	Apr 05	37		20,604	XC	0.05	-0.05	36.27	194,602
Pfizer	May 05	27.50		20,012	XC	0.70	0.30	27.31	45,569
Lilly	Apr 05	55		19,661	XC	3.90	3.60	56.48	25,672
AppleC	Apr 05	40		18,353	XC	2.40	-0.90	41.35	63,299
PhmHldTr	Apr 05	75		17,941	XC	0.70	0.55	74.70	12,064
Nasd100Tr	Apr 05	37	p	17,479	XC	0.80	0.35	36.27	169,293
MorgStan	Apr 05	55		17,335	XC	0.15	-0.25	53.62	18,546
Lilly	Apr 05	60		16,631	XC	0.95	0.90	56.48	30,432
A M D	Apr 05	17		15,267	XC	0.60	...	17.24	27,839
Lilly	Apr 05	50	p	15,218	XC	1.10	1.00	56.48	25,899
Nasd100Tr	Jan 07	44		14,500	XC	1.75	-0.15	36.27	14,509
Yahoo	Jul 05	30		14,142	XC	0.80	0.15	33.65	21,953
SPDR	Apr 05	118		13,028	XC	0.30	-0.70	117.98	23,661
Merck	Apr 05	35		12,132	XC	0.25	0.20	34.80	28,018
AppleC	May 05	45		11,842	XC	1.45	-0.55	41.35	17,188
PhmHldTr	May 05	75		11,475	XC	1.60	1.00	74.70	17,959
Nasd100Tr	May 05	36	p	11,081	XC	0.65	0.20	36.27	136,071
AppleC	Jul 05	35	p	10,945	XC	1.45	0.30	41.35	38,103
BrMySq	Apr 05	25	p	10,218	XC	0.40	0.30	25.89	5,605
SemiHTr	Aug 05	32.50	p	9,734	XC	2.45	0.35	31.57	27,948
MCI Inc	Sep 05	27.50		9,608	XC	0.65	0.15	26.25	22,081
Nasd100Tr	Apr 05	35		9,383	XC	1.20	-0.45	36.27	30,988
eBay	May 05	35		9,103	XC	1.60	-0.35	33.12	23,721
Gen El	Apr 05	35	p	9,053	XC	0.10	0.05	35.83	34,528
Citigrp	Apr 05	45	p	9,018	XC	0.15	0.10	45.95	31,483
BrMySq	Apr 05	25		8,904	XC	1.10	0.73	25.89	25,573
Google	Apr 05	195		8,716	XC	0.40	-1.05	192	19,841
AppleC	Apr 05	42.50	p	8,551	XC	2.45	0.85	41.35	43,082
PhmHldTr	May 05	70		8,535	XC	5.20	2.10	74.70	18,406
IvaxCp	Apr 05	20		8,508	XC	0.60	0.50	18.70	5,123

DJ INDEXES

Figure 2.1 *The Wall Street Journal Europe* of 14th April 2005, Stock Options. Reproduced by permission of Dow Jones & Company, Inc.

INDEX OPTIONS TRADING

Tuesday, January 4, 2000

Volume, close, net change and open interest for all contracts. Volume figures are unofficial. Open interest reflects previous trading day. p-Put. c-Call. The totals for call and put volume and open interest are midday figures.

CHICAGO

CB MEXICO INDEX(MEX)

Strike			Vol.	3 pm Close	Net. Chg.	Open Int.
Jun	90	c	5	19 3/8	−1 3/8	13
Mar	110	c	10	4 1/4	−1 1/8	46
Call Vol.			**15**	**Open Int.**		**116**
Put Vol.			**0**	**Open Int.**		**338**

CB TECHNOLOGY(TXX)

Strike			Vol.	3 pm Close	Net. Chg.	Open Int.
Jan	650	p	10	1/8	−6 1/8	26
Feb	820	p	10	8 1/8	+1 3/8	10
Feb	900	p	60	17 1/4	+3 1/2	30
Call Vol.			**0**	**Open Int.**		**319**
Put Vol.			**80**	**Open Int.**		**381**

DJ INDUS AVG(DJX)

Strike			Vol.	3 pm Close	Net. Chg.	Open Int.
Jan	90	p	540	1/16	...	9,881
Jan	92	p	180	1/16	...	1,546
Feb	92	p	150	3/16	...	150
Mar	92	c	1	21 1/2	−1	1
Jun	92	p	5	1 1/2	+5/16	9,117
Jan	96	p	13	1/8	+1/16	23,136
Feb	96	p	23	9/16	+1/4	1,340
Mar	96	p	50	1	+3/16	10,585
Jun	96	p	795	1 7/8	+1/4	6,974
Jan	100	p	35	5/16	+3/16	9,841
Feb	100	p	112	1 1/16	+1/4	2,983
Mar	100	c	82	13 1/4	−3 3/4	258
Mar	100	p	15	1 3/8	+7/16	9,170
Jun	100	p	5	2 3/4	+3/4	5,023
Jan	102	p	1,088	5/16	+1/8	4,358
Feb	102	p	365	1 1/16	+1/4	1,750
Mar	102	p	30	1 13/16	+3/8	3,147
Jan	104	c	111	9 1/8	−7/8	2,654
Jan	104	p	449	1/2	+1/4	3,671
Feb	104	p	4	1 3/16	...	227
Mar	104	c	2	10 1/4	−1 5/8	1,051
Mar	104	p	8	1 5/8	+3/8	2,367
Jun	104	p	5	3 1/2	+3/4	1,632
Jan	105	p	1,281	3/4	+3/8	959
Jan	106	c	10	7 1/8	−1	377
Jan	106	p	28	3/4	+3/8	1,999
Mar	106	c	8	9 3/8	−2 1/4	783
Mar	106	p	1	2 5/16	+5/16	757
Jun	106	c	2	12 1/2	+1/8	3
Jan	108	c	23	4 1/2	−3 5/8	618
Jan	108	p	159	1 3/8	+9/16	2,157
Feb	108	p	25	2 1/2	+5/8	272
Mar	108	c	8	7 3/8	−3	3,594
Mar	108	p	8	3 1/8	+9/16	4,769
Jun	108	c	12	10 1/4	−2 3/4	311
Jan	109	c	6	3 7/8	−3 3/8	30
Jan	109	p	43	1 1/2	+11/16	689
Jan	110	c	143	2 3/4	−3 1/8	1,519
Jan	110	p	213	1 13/16	+13/16	5,035
Feb	110	c	13	4 5/8	−2	63
Feb	110	p	58	3	+15/16	514
Mar	110	c	34	5 7/8	−2 5/8	7,029

Strike			Vol.	3 pm Close	Net. Chg.	Open Int.
Feb	470	c	2	27 1/8	−4	8
Feb	470	p	1	8	+3/8	615
Jan	480	c	15	11	−14 3/4	19
Mar	480	p	1	15 1/2	−1/8	2,364
Jan	485	c	2	10	−6 7/8	9
Jan	490	c	4	9 3/8	−1 3/4	75
Feb	490	c	86	12 3/8	−6 3/8	219
Mar	490	c	3	23	−2	100
Mar	490	p	3	18 1/2	+1/2	100
Feb	500	c	400	8 1/4	−5	186
Feb	500	p	100	20 3/4	+1 1/4	195
Jan	510	c	5	2	−2 1/4	5
Feb	510	c	10	5 3/4	−3 1/4	21
Mar	520	c	3	6 1/2	−3 3/4	5
Call Vol.			**533**	**Open Int.**		**8,978**
Put Vol.			**266**	**Open Int.**		**14,765**

S & P 100 INDEX(OEX)

Strike			Vol.	3 pm Close	Net. Chg.	Open Int.
Mar	540	p	33	1 1/8	+1/4	486
Jan	550	p	796	1/16	−1/16	6,551
Jan	560	p	60	3/16	+1/16	1,498
Feb	560	p	10	5/8	...	272
Jan	580	p	226	1/4	+1/8	1,195
Feb	580	p	32	3/4	+1/8	231
Jan	600	p	400	3/16	...	3,531
Feb	600	c	1	187	−17	1
Feb	600	p	14	1	+1/8	1,088
Jan	610	c	1	172	−18	25
Jan	610	p	251	5/16	+1/16	1,200
Jan	620	p	95	3/8	+1/8	2,490
Feb	620	c	1	165	−19	10
Feb	620	p	43	2	...	496
Mar	620	p	81	4 3/8	+1 1/8	712
Jan	630	p	29	3/8	+1/16	1,623
Jan	640	c	3	144	−12 1/2	199
Jan	640	p	50	7/16	−1/16	2,022
Feb	640	c	1	146	−19	31
Feb	640	p	60	3 1/8	+3/4	838
Mar	640	p	41	5 1/8	+1 3/4	315
Apr	640	p	6	6 1/4	+1/8	32
Jan	650	p	36	9/16	−3/16	4,315
Jan	660	p	90	1	+1/2	3,318
Feb	660	c	1	125	−7 1/4	5
Feb	660	p	42	4 1/8	+1	1,083
Mar	660	c	4	132	−18	59
Mar	660	p	90	7	+1	789
Apr	660	p	2	8 7/8	+2 1/8	4
Jan	670	c	18	99 1/2	−31 1/2	137
Jan	670	p	413	1 1/4	+1/4	2,349
Feb	670	p	44	4 7/8	+7/8	125
Jan	680	c	706	102	−7 3/8	1,309
Jan	680	p	244	1 9/16	+7/16	3,464
Feb	680	p	92	6	+2 1/8	223
Mar	680	p	76	10 1/4	+3 1/2	1,657
Jan	690	p	291	1 3/4	+3/8	4,583
Feb	690	c	4	91	−14 1/4	11
Feb	690	p	171	6 1/2	+2 1/4	1,977
Jan	695	p	283	2 3/8	+7/8	1,415
Jan	700	c	124	73	−18 7/8	6,023
Jan	700	p	968	2 1/4	+5/8	12,174
Feb	700	p	278	7 1/2	+2	1,305
Mar	700	p	7	10	+1/2	2,731
Apr	700	p	3	18 1/2	+5 1/2	98
Jan	705	p	245	2 5/8	+5/8	1,569
Jan	710	c	74	61 1/2	−19 1/2	2,386
Jan	710	p	726	3 1/4	+1 3/8	7,712
Feb	710	p	6	9 3/8	+2 3/4	580
Jan	715	p	237	3 1/4	+1 1/4	3,720

Strike			Vol.	3 pm Close	Net. Chg.	Open Int.
Feb	1500	c	669	12	−12 1/4	5,484
Feb	1500	p	55	78 1/2	+9	116
Mar	1500	c	1,001	32 1/2	−4 1/2	13,524
Mar	1500	p	17	83	+8	740
Jan	1525	c	541	3/4	−3 1/4	5,628
Jan	1525	p	203	97	+16	278
Feb	1525	c	181	7 3/4	−8 1/4	1,861
Mar	1525	c	1,606	15	−25 1/2	7,549
Mar	1525	p	500	114	+28	218
Jan	1550	c	789	3/8	−5/8	13,957
Feb	1550	c	221	3 5/8	−4 7/8	3,059
Feb	1550	p	2	111	+25	77
Mar	1550	c	1,397	11	−5 1/2	9,956
Jan	1575	c	10	3/8	+1/8	2,102
Feb	1575	c	6	2	−3 5/8	1,779
Mar	1575	c	209	6 3/4	−6	619
Mar	1575	p	10	152 1/2	+38 1/2	11
Feb	1600	c	155	1	−1 7/16	1,925
Mar	1600	c	502	3 3/4	−3 1/4	9,199
Mar	1650	c	55	1 1/4	−1 3/4	2,052
Jan	1700	p	1	267	+15	373
Mar	1700	c	100	1	−1/8	1,416
Mar	1700	p	3	264	+22	32
Call Vol.			**36,803**	**Open Int.**		**820,987**
Put Vol.			**45,134**	**Open Int.**		**975,013**

AMERICAN

COMP TECH(XCI)

Strike			Vol.	3 pm Close	Net. Chg.	Open Int.
Jan	860	p	3	16 1/4	...	...
Jan	1120	c	22	259 3/4	+160 1/8	22
Jan	1170	p	3	7	+2 7/8	3
Call Vol.			**22**	**Open Int.**		**71**
Put Vol.			**6**	**Open Int.**		**60**

JAPAN INDEX(JPN)

Strike			Vol.	3 pm Close	Net. Chg.	Open Int.
Mar	170	c	2	25 1/4	+3 3/4	651
Mar	175	c	9	21	−1	39
Jan	180	p	30	11/16	−1/8	125
Mar	180	c	8	17 1/2	+3 1/2	3,390
Jan	185	c	10	9 5/8	+1/8	10
Jan	185	p	10	11/16	+1/4	91
Feb	185	p	10	3	−3/4	10
Mar	185	c	1	14 3/8	−1 1/4	99
Jan	190	p	35	2 1/8	+1/16	145
Mar	190	c	156	10 3/4	−1 1/2	252
Jan	195	c	1	3 5/8	−7/8	42
Feb	195	p	35	5 3/4	−4 1/8	39
Mar	195	c	4	8 1/4	−1/8	101
Call Vol.			**556**	**Open Int.**		**23,806**
Put Vol.			**120**	**Open Int.**		**7,561**

MS CYCLICAL(CYC)

Strike			Vol.	3 pm Close	Net. Chg.	Open Int.
Jan	520	p	125	3 1/8	...	125
Feb	520	p	2,000	7 1/2	−1/2	5,000
Feb	560	c	2,000	22	−4	5,000
Jan	590	c	20	4 1/2	−7 1/2	400
Call Vol.			**2,020**	**Open Int.**		**12,676**
Put Vol.			**2,125**	**Open Int.**		**11,224**

MS HITECH 35(MSH)

Strike			Vol.	3 pm Close	Net. Chg.	Open Int.
Jan	1560	c	50	310 1/4	+10 1/4	39
Jan	1570	c	850	303 3/4	−36 1/4	865
Jan	1580	c	50	291 1/4	+23 1/2	14
Feb	1600	p	275	45	+10	260
Jan	1610	p	60	14 3/4	−8 1/8	21
Jan	1630	c	4	218 3/8	−11 7/8	3

Figure 2.2 *The Wall Street Journal Europe* of 5th January 2000, Index Options. Reproduced by permission of Dow Jones & Company, Inc.

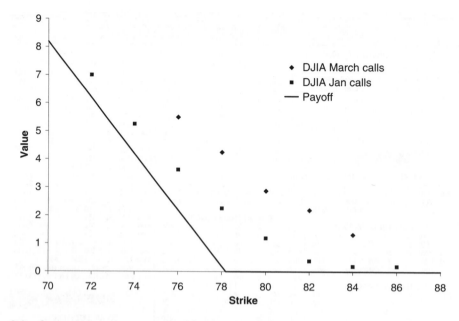

Figure 2.3   Option prices versus strike, March and June series of DJIA.

there is less and less time for the underlying to move, so the option value must converge to the payoff function.

Time Out...

Plotting

When plotting using Excel you'll find it best to use the 'XY Scatter' option. This allows you to get the correct scale on the horizontal axis without any hassle. Also, don't use the smoothing option as it can give spurious wiggles in the plots.

One of the most interesting features of calls and puts is that they have a non-linear dependence on the underlying asset. This contrasts with futures which have a linear dependence on the underlying. This non-linearity is very important in the pricing of options, as the randomness in the underlying asset and the curvature of the option value with respect to the asset are intimately related.

Calls and puts are the two simplest forms of option. For this reason they are often referred to as **vanilla** because of the ubiquity of that flavor. There are many, many more kinds of options, some of which will be described and examined later on. Other terms

GLXO LN GBp ↑	1688	-13	L 5s L 1686/1689	L	Trd	Equity **OCM**

At 12:50 Vol 854,194 Op 1694 L Hi 1703 L Lo 1686 L Prev 1701

OPTION MONITOR 3   COMP   Center: 1687   1 ⟨GO⟩ to Edit Spreadsheet

	BID m	ASK m	LAST m	1CHG m	IVBD	IVAS	BEST	DEBS	GABS	VEBS	THEO	7DEC
GLXO LN CALLS				1 Day	Imp	Imp		Delta	Gamma	Vega		
	Bid Price	Ask Price	Last Trade	Net Change	Volat Bid	Volat Ask	Best Price	Best Price	Best Price	Best Price	Theo. Value	7 Day Decay
GLXOCT99	1686.0	1689.0	1688.0	-13.0			1687					
1) 1200	489.50	504.50	509.50	unch	N.A.	69.97	504.50	.942	.0003	.674	494.09	4.6870
2) 1250	440.00	455.00	460.00	unch	N.A.	63.58	455.00	.936	.0003	.689	444.92	4.6853
3) 1300	390.50	405.50	410.50	unch	N.A.	57.36	405.50	.928	.0004	.837	396.33	4.6828
4) 1350	342.00	357.00	362.00	unch	N.A.	52.29	357.00	.915	.0005	.853	348.72	4.8888
5) 1400	294.50	309.50	314.50	unch	N.A.	48.07	309.50	.895	.0007	1.018	302.62	5.2385
6) 1450	249.00	264.00	268.50	unch	29.45	45.11	264.00	.864	.0008	1.194	258.66	5.8316
7) 1500	203.00	218.00	224.00	unch	30.67	42.27	220.00	.823	.0011	1.538	217.53	6.3538
8) 1600	125.00	137.50	136.00	-6.00	29.86	37.59	136.00	.706	.0017	2.013	146.02	7.0423
9) 1700	69.00	76.00	80.00	unch	30.95	34.02	76.00	.516	.0020	2.280	90.956	7.4785
10) 1800	32.00	38.00	40.00	unch	30.62	33.12	37.00	.319	.0019	2.005	52.713	6.2390
11) 1900	16.00	20.00	21.50	unch	32.84	35.47	20.00	.190	.0013	1.552	28.386	4.8611
12) 2000	6.00	9.00	9.00	unch	32.53	35.83	9.00	.099	.0008	1.041	14.273	2.9660
13) 2100	2.00	4.00	3.50	unch	32.32	36.52	3.50	.044	.0005	.581	6.728	1.4568
14) 2200		2.00	1.00	unch	N.A.	38.08	1.00	.015	.0002	.232	2.968	.5272
15) 2300		1.50	.50	unch	N.A.	41.58	.50	.008	.0001	.132	1.262	.2929
16) 2400		1.00	.50	unch	N.A.	43.98	.50	.007	.0001	.126	.502	.2977
17) 2500		1.00	.50	unch	N.A.	48.40	.50	.007	.0001	.101	.195	.3010

Copyright 1999 BLOOMBERG L.P.   Frankfurt:69-920410 Hong Kong:2-977-6000 London:171-330-7500 New York:212-318-2000
Princeton:609-279-3000   Singapore:226-3000   Sydney:2-9777-8686   Tokyo:3-3201-8900   Sao Paulo:11-3048-4500
                                                                    I574-414-0 08-Sep-99 11:50:14

Bloomberg PROFESSIONAL

Figure 2.4   Prices for Glaxo–Wellcome calls expiring in October. Source: Bloomberg L.P.

used to describe contracts with some dependence on a more fundamental asset are **derivatives** or **contingent claims**.

Figure 2.4 shows the prices of call options on Glaxo–Wellcome for a variety of strikes. All these options are expiring in October. The table shows many other quantities that we will be seeing later on.

2.3 DEFINITION OF COMMON TERMS

The subjects of mathematical finance and derivatives theory are filled with jargon. The jargon comes from both the mathematical world and the financial world. Generally speaking the jargon from finance is aimed at simplifying communication, and to put everyone on the same footing.[1] Here are a few loose definitions to

be going on with, some you have already seen and there will be many more throughout the book.

- **Premium:** The amount paid for the contract initially. How to find this value is the subject of much of this book.

- **Underlying (asset):** The financial instrument on which the option value depends. Stocks, commodities, currencies and indices are going to be denoted by S. The option payoff is defined as some function of the underlying asset at expiry.

---

[1] I have serious doubts about the purpose of most of the math jargon.

- **Strike (price)** or **exercise price:** The amount for which the underlying can be bought (call) or sold (put). This will be denoted by E. This definition only really applies to the simple calls and puts. We will see more complicated contracts in later chapters and the definition of strike or exercise price will be extended.

- **Expiration (date)** or **expiry (date):** Date on which the option can be exercised or date on which the option ceases to exist or give the holder any rights. This will be denoted by T.

- **Intrinsic value:** The payoff that would be received if the underlying is at its current level when the option expires.

- **Time value:** Any value that the option has above its intrinsic value. The uncertainty surrounding the future value of the underlying asset means that the option value is generally different from the intrinsic value.

- **In the money:** An option with positive intrinsic value. A call option when the asset price is above the strike, a put option when the asset price is below the strike.

- **Out of the money:** An option with no intrinsic value, only time value. A call option when the asset price is below the strike, a put option when the asset price is above the strike.

- **At the money:** A call or put with a strike that is close to the current asset level.

- **Long position:** A positive amount of a quantity, or a positive exposure to a quantity.

- **Short position:** A negative amount of a quantity, or a negative exposure to a quantity. Many assets can be sold short, with some constraints on the length of time before they must be bought back.

2.4   **PAYOFF DIAGRAMS**

The understanding of options is helped by the visual interpretation of an option's value at expiry. We can plot the value of an option at expiry as a function of the underlying in what is known as a **payoff diagram**. At expiry the option is worth a known amount. In the case of a call option the contract is worth $\max(S - E, 0)$. This function is the bold line in Figure 2.5.

Figure 2.6 shows Bloomberg's standard option valuation screen and Figure 2.7 shows the value against the underlying and the payoff.

The payoff for a put option is $\max(E - S, 0)$; this is the bold line plotted in Figure 2.8.

Figure 2.9 shows Bloomberg's option valuation screen and Figure 2.10 shows the value against the underlying and the payoff.

These payoff diagrams are useful since they simplify the analysis of complex strategies involving more than one option.

Make a mental note of the thin lines in all of these figures. The meaning of these will be explained very shortly.

2.4.1   Other representations of value

The payoff diagrams shown above only tell you about what happens at expiry, how much money your option contract is worth at that time. It makes no allowance for how much

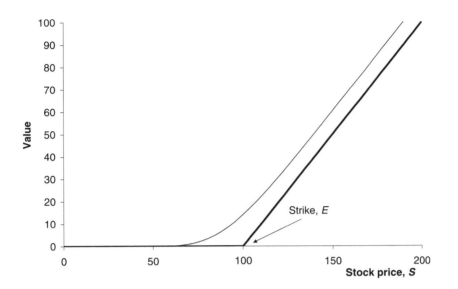

Figure 2.5 Payoff diagram for a call option.

```
<HELP> for explanation, <MENU> for similar functions.    DL18 Equity OV
              Standard  Option  Valuation          Page 1/2
      MSFT        US      MICROSOFT CORP       Currency: USD
                                                   Hit 1 GO for save/send screen
                                                   Hit 2 GO for notes
  Price of MSFT US Equity95                         Hit 3 GO for dividends
                                                   Hit MENU for exotic option types
                                                   Hit PAGE for scenario graph
  Strike:         95      100.000% (USD)Rate: 4.742%Semiannual
  Exercise Type:       E European
  Put or Call:         C Call

  Time to Expiration:      90 05:09 Model Type: 1 Default
  Trade:           9/11/99 15:52
  Expiration:     12/10/99 21:02
  Settle Date:     9/11/99
  Exercise Delay:        0


    Option Valuation and Risk Parameters           Dividends
          Value   Percent  Time Value:      7.26294  Dividend Yield     0.00%
  Price:  7.262938   7.645% Theta:          0.04277  Ex-Date        Amount
  Volatility:  35.821%     Premium:         7.64520     No dividends proj.
  Delta:        0.56123 Parity:             0.00000
  Gamma:        0.02330 Gearing:           13.08011
  Vega:         0.18619 Rho                 0.11433
  Copyright 1999 BLOOMBERG L.P.   Frankfurt:69-920410  Hong Kong:2-977-6000  London:171-330-7500  New York:212-318-2000
  Princeton:609-279-3000    Singapore:226-3000    Sydney:2-9777-8686    Tokyo:3-3201-8900    Sao Paulo:11-3048-4500
                                                                I741-53-0 11-Sep-99 15:52:51
  Bloomberg
  PROFESSIONAL
```

Figure 2.6 Bloomberg option valuation screen, call. Source: Bloomberg L.P.

premium you had to pay for the option. To adjust for the original cost of the option, sometimes one plots a diagram such as that shown in Figure 2.11. In this **profit diagram** for a call option I have subtracted from the payoff the premium originally paid for the call option. This figure is helpful because it shows how far into the money the asset must be at expiry before the option becomes profitable. The asset value marked S^* is the point

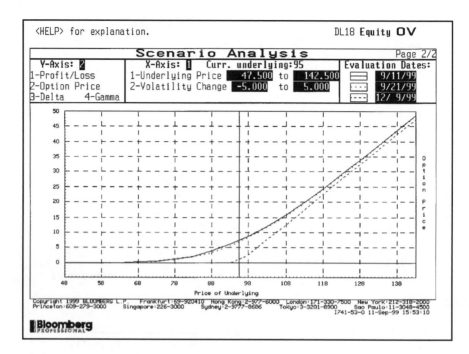

Figure 2.7 Bloomberg scenario analysis, call. Source: Bloomberg L.P.

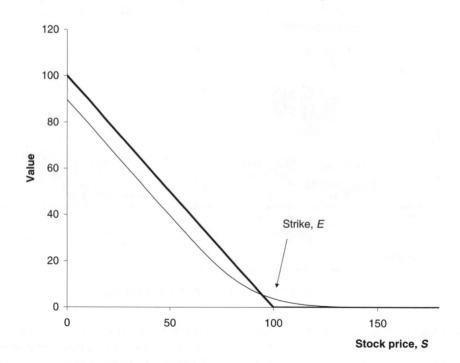

Figure 2.8 Payoff diagram for a put option.

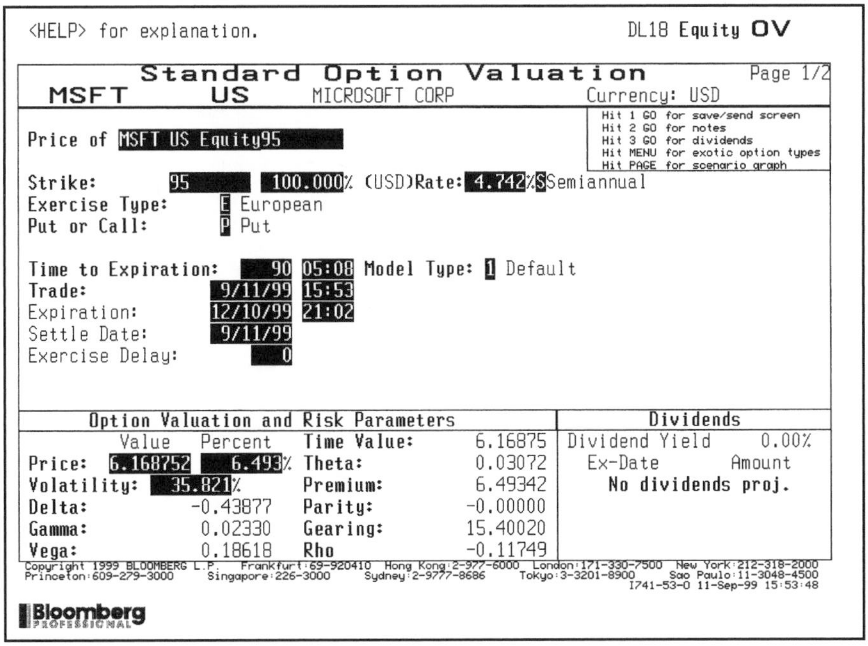

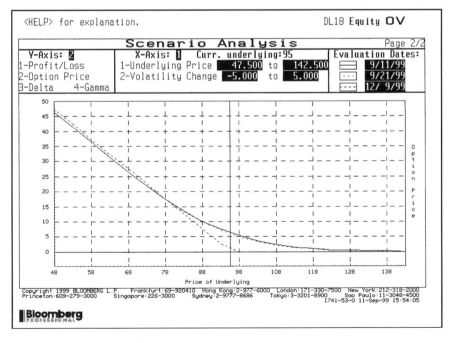

Figure 2.9 Bloomberg option valuation screen, put. Source: Bloomberg L.P.

Figure 2.10 Bloomberg scenario analysis, put. Source: Bloomberg L.P.

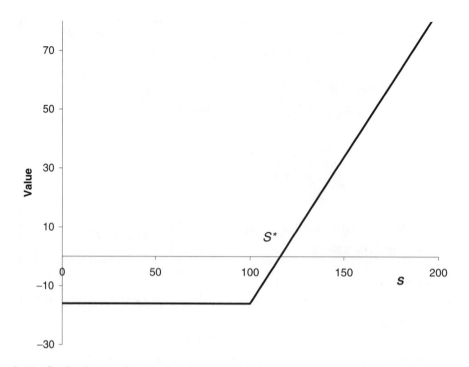

Figure 2.11 Profit diagram for a call option.

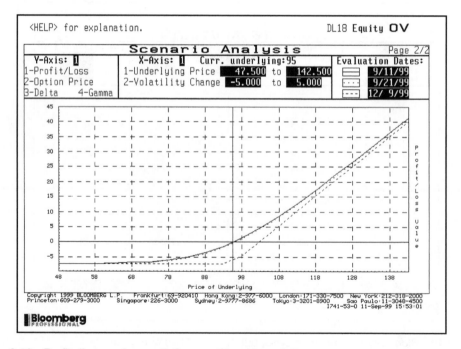

Figure 2.12 Profit diagram for a call. Source: Bloomberg L.P.

which divides profit from loss; if the asset at expiry is above this value then the contract has made a profit, if below the contract has made a loss.

As it stands, this profit diagram takes no account of the time value of money. The premium is paid up front but the payoff, if any, is only received at expiry. To be consistent one should either discount the payoff by multiplying by $e^{-r(T-t)}$ to value everything at the present, or multiply the premium by $e^{r(T-t)}$ to value all cashflows at expiry.

Figure 2.12 shows Bloomberg's call option profit diagram. Note that the profit today is zero; if we buy the option and immediately sell it we make neither a profit nor a loss (this is subject to issues of transaction costs).

2.5 WRITING OPTIONS

I have talked above about the rights of the purchaser of the option. But for every option that is sold, someone somewhere must be liable if the option is exercised. If I hold a call option entitling me to buy a stock some time in the future, who do I buy this stock from? Ultimately, the stock must be delivered by the person who **wrote** the option. The **writer** of an option is the

person who promises to deliver the underlying asset, if the option is a call, or buy it, if the option is a put. The writer is the person who receives the premium.

In practice, most simple option contracts are handled through an exchange so that the purchaser of an option does not know who the writer is. The holder of the option can even sell the option on to someone else via the exchange to close his position. However, regardless of who holds the option, or who has handled it, the writer is the person who has the obligation to deliver or buy the underlying.

The asymmetry between owning and writing options is now clear. The purchaser of the option hands over a premium in return for special rights, and an uncertain outcome. The writer receives a guaranteed payment up front, but then has obligations in the future.

2.6 MARGIN

Writing options is very risky. The downside of buying an option is just the initial premium, the upside may be unlimited. The upside of writing an option is limited, but the downside could be huge. For this reason, to cover the risk of default in the event of an unfavorable outcome, the **clearing houses** that register and settle options insist on the deposit of a margin by the writers

of options. Clearing houses act as counterparty to each transaction. Margin was described in Chapter 1.

2.7 MARKET CONVENTIONS

Most of the simpler options contracts are bought and sold through exchanges. These exchanges make it simpler and more efficient to match buyers with sellers. Part of this simplification involves the conventions about such features of the contracts as the available strikes and expiries. For example, simple calls and puts come in **series**. This refers to the strike and expiry dates. Typically a stock has three choices of expiries trading at any time. Having standardized contracts traded through an exchange promotes liquidity of the instruments.

Some options are an agreement between two parties, often brought together by an intermediary. These agreements can be very flexible and the contract details do not need to satisfy any conventions. Such contracts are known as **over the counter** or **OTC** contracts. I give an example at the end of this chapter.

2.8 THE VALUE OF THE OPTION BEFORE EXPIRY

We have seen how much calls and puts are worth at expiry, and drawn these values in payoff diagrams. The question that we can ask, and the question that is central to this book, is 'How much is the contract worth *now*, before expiry?' How much would you pay for a contract, a piece of paper, giving you rights in the future? You may have no idea what the stock price will do between now and expiry in six months, say, but clearly the contract has value. At the very least you know that there is no downside to owning the option, the contract gives you specific rights but no *obligations*. Two things are clear about the contract value before expiry: the value will depend on how high the asset price is today and how long there is before expiry.

The higher the underlying asset today, the higher we might expect the asset to be at expiry of the option and therefore the more valuable we might expect a call option to be. On the other hand a put option might be cheaper by the same reasoning.

The dependence on time to expiry is more subtle. The longer the time to expiry, the more time there is for the asset to rise or fall. Is that good or bad if we own a call option? Furthermore, the longer we have to wait until we get any payoff, the less valuable will that payoff be simply because of the time value of money.

I will ask you to suspend disbelief for the moment (it won't be the first time in the book) and trust me that we will be finding a 'fair value' for these options contracts. The aspect of finding the 'fair value' that I want to focus on now is the dependence on the asset price and time. I am going to use V to mean the value of the option, and it will be a function of the value of the underlying asset S at time t. Thus we can write $V(S, t)$ for the value of the contract.

We know the value of the contract *at expiry*. If I use T to denote the expiry date then at $t = T$ the function V is known, it is just the payoff function. For example if we have a call option then

$$V(S, T) = \max(S - E, 0).$$

This is the function of S that I plotted in the earlier payoff diagrams. Now I can tell you what the fine lines are in Figures 2.5 and 2.8, they are the values of the contracts $V(S, t)$ *at some time before expiry*, plotted against S. I have not specified how long before expiry, since the plot is for explanatory purposes only.

Time Out...

Functions of two variables

The option value is a function of two variables, asset price S and time t. If it helps, think of V as being the height of a mountain with the two variables being distances in the northerly and westerly directions. Later we're going to be looking at the slope of this mountain in each of the two directions . . . these will be sensitivities of the option price to changes in the asset and in time. These slopes or gradients are what you experience in your car when you see a sign such as '1-in-10 gradient.' That is precisely the same as a slope of 0.1.

2.9   **FACTORS AFFECTING DERIVATIVE PRICES**

The two most important factors affecting the prices of options are the value of the underlying asset S and the time to expiry t. These quantities are **variables** meaning that they inevitably change during the life of the contract; if the underlying did not change then the pricing would be trivial. This contrasts with the **parameters** that affect the price of options.

Examples of parameters are the interest rate and strike price. The interest rate will have an effect on the option value via the time value of money since the payoff is received in the future. The interest rate also plays another role which we will see later. Clearly the strike price is important, the higher the strike in a call, the lower the value of the call.

If we have an equity option then its value will depend on any dividends that are paid on the asset during the option's life. If we have an FX option then its value will depend on the interest rate received by the foreign currency.

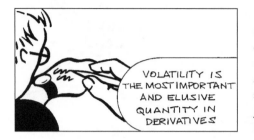

There is one important parameter that I have not mentioned, and which has a major impact on the option value. That parameter is the **volatility**. Volatility is a measure of the amount of fluctuation in the asset price, a measure of the randomness. Figure 2.13 shows two simulated asset price paths, the more jagged of the two has the higher volatility. The technical definition of volatility is the 'annualized standard deviation of the asset returns.' I will show how to measure this parameter in Chapter 4.

Volatility is a particularly interesting parameter because it is so hard to estimate. And having estimated it, one finds that it never stays constant and is unpredictable.

The distinction between parameters and variables is very important. I shall be deriving equations for the value of options, partial differential equations. These equations will involve differentiation with respect to the variables, but the parameters, as their name suggests, remain as parameters in the equations.

Volatility and timescales

Time Out...

Volatility

Remember our first coin-tossing experiment back in Chapter 1? Try this again, but instead of multiplying by a factor of 1.01 or 0.99, use factors of 1.02 and 0.98. Now plot the time series. This is an example of a more volatile path. If you're feeling strong, try the following experiment.

Play around with different scale factors, 1.01 and 0.99, 1.02 and 0.98, 1.05 and 0.95, keeping them symmetric about 1 to start with. Now try different 'timescales,' i.e. toss the coin only once every two units of time, then once every four units. Would you call a path with large but infrequent moves as volatile as one with smaller but more frequent moves?

2.10 **SPECULATION AND GEARING**

If you buy a far out-of-the-money option it may not cost very much, especially if there is not very long until expiry. If the option expires worthless, then you also haven't lost very

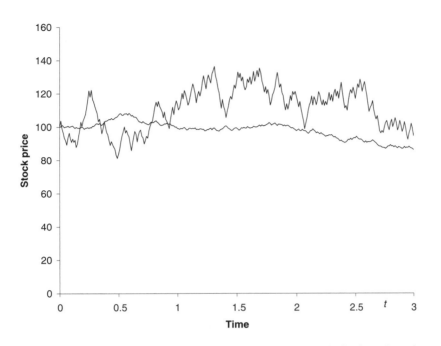

Figure 2.13 Two (simulated) asset price paths, one is much more volatile than the other.

much. However, if there is a dramatic move in the underlying, so that the option expires in the money, you may make a large profit relative to the amount of the investment. Let me give an example.

Example Today's date is 14th April and the price of Wilmott Inc. stock is $666. The cost of a 680 call option with expiry 22nd August is $39. I expect the stock to rise significantly between now and August, how can I profit if I am right?

Buy the stock Suppose I buy the stock for $666. And suppose that by the middle of August the stock has risen to $730. I will have made a profit of $64 per stock. More importantly my investment will have risen by

$$\frac{730 - 666}{666} \times 100 = 9.6\%.$$

Buy the call If I buy the call option for $39, then at expiry I can exercise the call, paying $680 to receive something worth $730. I have paid $39 and I get back $50. This is a profit of $11 per option, but in percentage terms I have made

$$\frac{\text{value of asset at expiry} - \text{strike} - \text{cost of call}}{\text{cost of call}} \times 100 = \frac{730 - 680 - 39}{39} \times 100 = 28\%.$$

This is an example of **gearing** or **leverage**. The out-of-the-money option has a high gearing, a possible high payoff for a small investment. The downside of this leverage is that the call option is more likely than not to expire completely worthless and you will lose all of your investment. If Wilmott Inc. remains at $666 then the stock investment has the same value but the call option experiences a 100% loss.

Highly leveraged contracts are very risky for the writer of the option. The buyer is only risking a small amount; although he is very likely to lose, his downside is limited to his initial premium. But the writer is risking a large loss in order to make a probable small profit. The writer is likely to think twice about such a deal unless he can offset his risk by buying other contracts. This offsetting of risk by buying other related contracts is called **hedging**.

Gearing explains one of the reasons for buying options. If you have a strong view about the direction of the market then you can exploit derivatives to make a better return, if you are right, than buying or selling the underlying.

2.11 **EARLY EXERCISE**

The simple options described above are examples of **European options** because exercise is only permitted *at expiry*. Some contracts allow the holder to exercise *at any time* before expiry, and these are called **American options**. American options give the holder more rights than their European equivalent and can therefore be more valuable, and they can never be less valuable. The main point of interest with American-style contracts is deciding *when* to exercise. In Chapter 3 I will discuss American options, and show how to determine when it is *optimal* to exercise, so as to give the contract the highest value.

Note that the terms 'European' and 'American' do not in any way refer to the continents on which the contracts are traded.

Finally, there are **Bermudan options**. These allow exercise on specified dates, or in specified periods. In a sense they are half way between European and American since exercise is allowed on some days and not on others.

ANOTHER EXAMPLE OF NO ARBITRAGE. FROM NOW ON THEY WON'T BE SO EASY

2.12 **PUT-CALL PARITY**

Imagine that you buy one European call option with a strike of E and an expiry of T and that you write a European put option with the same strike and expiry. Today's date is t. The payoff you receive at T for the call will look like the line in the first plot of Figure 2.14. The payoff for the put is the line in the second plot in the figure. Note that the sign of the payoff is negative, you *wrote* the option and are liable for the payoff. The payoff for the portfolio of the two options is the sum of the individual payoffs, shown in the third plot. The payoff for this portfolio of options is

$$\max(S(T) - E, 0) - \max(E - S(T), 0) = S(T) - E,$$

where $S(T)$ is the value of the underlying asset at time T.

The right-hand side of this expression consists of two parts, the asset and a fixed sum E. Is there another way to get exactly this payoff? If I buy the asset today it will cost me $S(t)$ and be worth $S(T)$ at expiry. I don't know what the value $S(T)$ will be but I do know how to guarantee to get that amount, and that is to buy the asset.

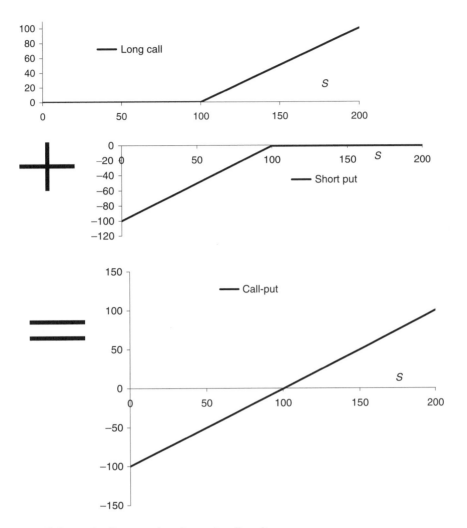

Figure 2.14 Schematic diagram showing put-call parity.

What about the E term? To lock in a payment of E at time T involves a cash flow of $Ee^{-r(T-t)}$ at time t. The conclusion is that the portfolio of a long call and a short put gives me exactly the same payoff as a long asset, short cash position. The equality of these cashflows is independent of the future behavior of the stock and is model independent:

$$C - P = S - Ee^{-r(T-t)},$$

where C and P are today's values of the call and the put respectively. This relationship holds at any time up to expiry and is known as **put-call parity**. If this relationship did not hold then there would be riskless arbitrage opportunities.

In Table 2.1 I show the cashflows in the perfectly hedged portfolio. In this table I have set up the cashflows to have a guaranteed value of zero at expiry.

FUTURE CASHFLOW
IS ZERO, SO TODAY'S
MUST BE AS WELL

Table 2.1 Cashflows in a hedged portfolio of options and asset.

Holding	Worth today (t)	Worth at expiry (T)
Call	C	$\max(S(T) - E, 0)$
−Put	$-P$	$-\max(E - S(T), 0)$
−Stock	$-S(t)$	$-S(T)$
Cash	$Ee^{-r(T-t)}$	E
Total	$C - P - S(t) + Ee^{-r(T-t)}$	0

Time Out...

A simulation of put-call parity

Below are four plots, all with time along the horizontal axis. The first is of some asset price. The second is the value of a call option on that asset. You don't need to know details of the contract, such as strike and expiry. Nor do you need to know how I calculated the value.

The third plot is of a put option (same strike and expiry as the call, whatever they were). The fourth plot is stock value minus call value plus put value. Observe how it grows exponentially, just like cash in the bank. This is a graphical illustration of put-call parity.

See how this might work in practice on the CD

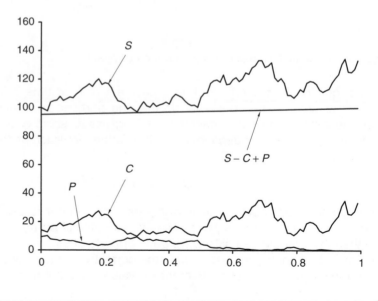

2.13 **BINARIES OR DIGITALS**

The original and still most common contracts are the vanilla calls and puts. Increasingly important are the **binary** or **digital options**. These contracts have a payoff at expiry that is discontinuous in the underlying asset price. An example of the payoff diagram for one of these options, a **binary call**, is shown in Figure 2.15. This contract pays $1 at expiry, time T, if the asset price is then greater than the exercise price E. Again, and as with the rest of the figures in this chapter, the bold line is the payoff and the fine line is the contract value some time before expiry.

Why would you invest in a binary call? If you think that the asset price will rise by expiry, to finish above the strike price then you might choose to buy either a vanilla call or a binary call. The vanilla call has the best upside potential, growing linearly with S beyond the strike. The binary call, however, can never pay off more than the $1. If you expect the underlying to rise dramatically then it may be best to buy the vanilla call. If you believe that the asset rise will be less dramatic then buy the binary call. The gearing of the vanilla call is greater than that for a binary call if the move in the underlying is large.

Figure 2.16 shows the payoff diagram for a **binary put**, the holder of which receives $1 if the asset is *below* E at expiry. The binary put would be bought by someone expecting a modest fall in the asset price.

There is a particularly simple binary put-call parity relationship. What do you get at expiry if you hold both a binary call and a binary put with the same strikes and expiries? The answer is that you will always get $1 regardless of the level of the underlying at expiry. Thus

$$\text{Binary call} + \text{Binary put} = e^{-r(T-t)}.$$

What would the table of cashflows look like for the perfectly hedged digital portfolio?

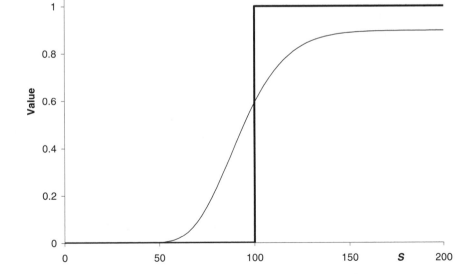

Figure 2.15 Payoff diagram for a binary call option.

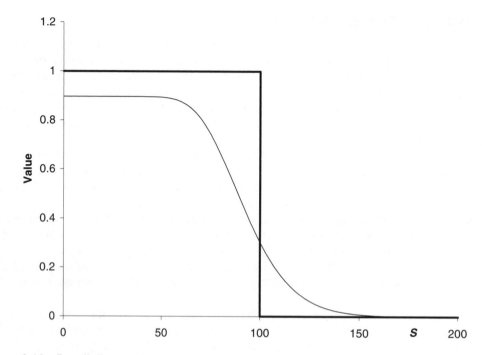

Figure 2.16 Payoff diagram for a binary put option.

2.14 **BULL AND BEAR SPREADS**

A payoff that is similar to a binary option can be made up with vanilla calls. This is our first example of a **portfolio of options** or an **option strategy**.

Suppose I buy one call option with a strike of 100 and write another with a strike of 120 and with the same expiration as the first then my resulting portfolio has a payoff that is shown in Figure 2.17. This payoff is zero below 100, 20 above 120 and linear in between. The payoff is continuous, unlike the binary call, but has a payoff that is superficially similar. This strategy is called a **bull spread** (or a **call spread**) because it benefits from a bull, i.e. rising, market.

The payoff for a general bull spread, made up of calls with strikes E_1 and E_2, is given by

$$\frac{1}{E_2 - E_1}(\max(S - E_1, 0) - \max(S - E_2, 0)),$$

where $E_2 > E_1$. Here I have bought/sold $(E_2 - E_1)^{-1}$ of each of the options so that the maximum payoff is scaled to 1.

If I write a put option with strike 100 and buy a put with strike 120 I get the payoff shown in Figure 2.18. This is called a **bear spread** (or a **put spread**), benefiting from a bear, i.e. falling, market. Again, it is very similar to a binary put except that the payoff is continuous.

Because of put-call parity it is possible to build up these payoffs using other contracts.

A strategy involving options of the same type (i.e. calls or puts) is called a **spread**.

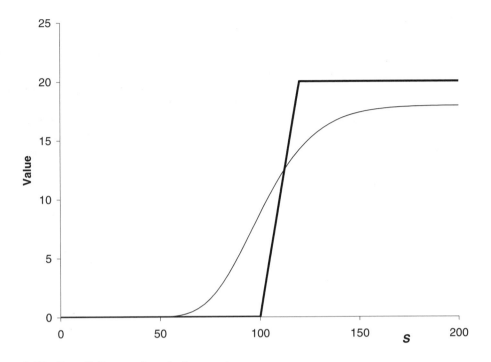

Figure 2.17 Payoff diagram for a bull spread.

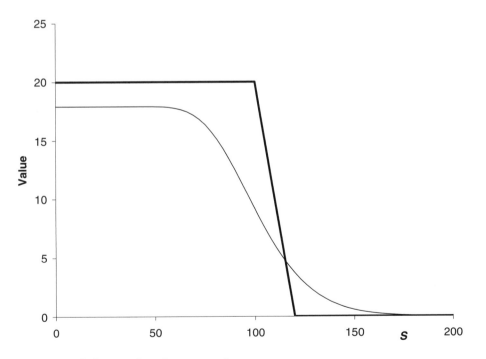

Figure 2.18 Payoff diagram for a bear spread.

2.15 **STRADDLES AND STRANGLES**

If you have a precise view on the behavior of the underlying asset you may want to be precise in your choice of option; simple calls, puts, and binaries may be too crude.

The **straddle** consists of a call and a put with the same strike. The payoff diagram is shown in Figure 2.19. Such a position is usually bought at the money by someone who expects the underlying to either rise or fall, but not to remain at the same level. For example, just before an anticipated major news item stocks often show a 'calm before the storm.' On the announcement the stock suddenly moves either up or down depending on whether or not the news was favorable to the company. They may also be bought by technical traders who see the stock at a key support or resistance level and expect the stock to either break through dramatically or bounce back.

The straddle would be sold by someone with the opposite view, someone who expects the underlying price to remain stable.

Figure 2.20 shows the Bloomberg screen for setting up a straddle. Figure 2.21 shows the profit and loss for this position at various times before expiry. The profit/loss is the option value less the upfront premium.

The **strangle** is similar to the straddle except that the strikes of the put and the call are different. The contract can be either an **out-of-the-money strangle** or **an in-the-money strangle**. The payoff for an out-of-the money strangle is shown in Figure 2.22. The motivation behind the purchase of this position is similar to that for the purchase of a straddle. The difference is that the buyer expects an even larger move in the underlying one way or the other. The contract is usually bought when the asset is around the middle of the two strikes and is cheaper than a straddle. This cheapness means that the gearing

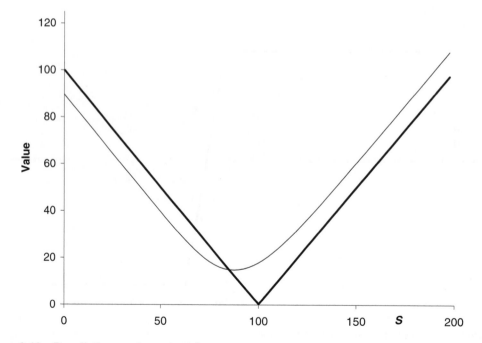

Figure 2.19 Payoff diagram for a straddle.

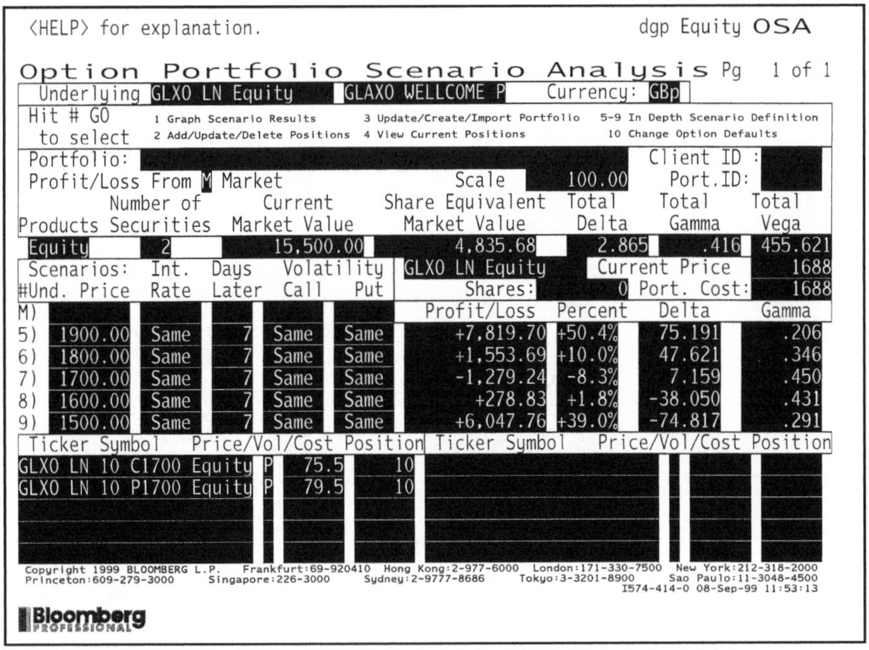

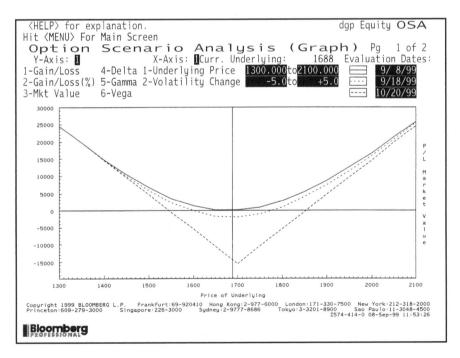

Figure 2.20 A portfolio of two options making up a straddle. Source: Bloomberg L.P.

Figure 2.21 Profit/loss for the straddle at several times before expiry. Source: Bloomberg L.P.

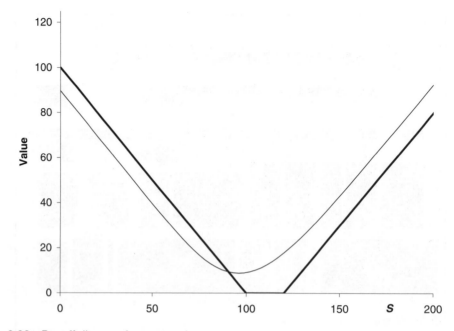

Figure 2.22 Payoff diagram for a strangle.

for the out-of-the-money strangle is higher than that for the straddle. The downside is that there is a much greater range over which the strangle has no payoff at expiry, for the straddle there is only the one point at which there is no payoff.

There is another reason for a straddle or strangle trade that does not involve a view on the direction of the underlying. These contracts are bought or sold by those with a view on the direction of volatility, they are one of the simplest **volatility trades**. Because of the relationship between the price of an option and the volatility of the asset one can speculate on the direction of volatility. Do you expect the volatility to rise? If so, how can you benefit from this? Until we know more about this relationship, we cannot go into this in more detail.

Straddles and strangles are rarely held until expiry.

A strategy involving options of different types (i.e. both calls and puts) is called a **combination**.

2.16 RISK REVERSAL

The **risk reversal** is a combination of a long call, with a strike above the current spot, and a short put, with a strike below the current spot. Both have the same expiry. The payoff is shown in Figure 2.23.

The risk reversal is a very special contract, popular with practitioners. Its value is usually quite small between the strikes and related to the market's expectations of the behavior of volatility.

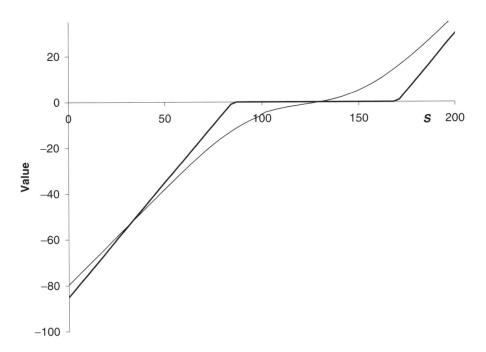

Figure 2.23 Payoff diagram for a risk reversal.

2.17 **BUTTERFLIES AND CONDORS**

A more complicated strategy involving the purchase and sale of options with *three* different strikes is a **butterfly spread**. Buying a call with a strike of 90, writing two calls struck at 100 and buying a 110 call gives the payoff in Figure 2.24. This is the kind of position you might enter into if you believe that the asset is not going anywhere, either up or down. Because it has no large upside potential (in this case the maximum payoff is 10) the position will be relatively cheap. With options, cheap is good.

The **condor** is like a butterfly except that four strikes, and four call options, are used. The payoff is shown in Figure 2.25.

2.18 **CALENDAR SPREADS**

All of the strategies I have described above have involved buying or writing calls and puts with different strikes *but all with the same expiration*. A strategy involving options with different expiry dates is called a **calendar spread**. You may enter into such a position if you have a precise view on the timing of a market move as well as the direction of the move. As always the motive behind such a strategy is to reduce the payoff at asset values and times which you believe are irrelevant, while increasing the payoff where you think it will matter. Any reduction in payoff will reduce the overall value of the option position.

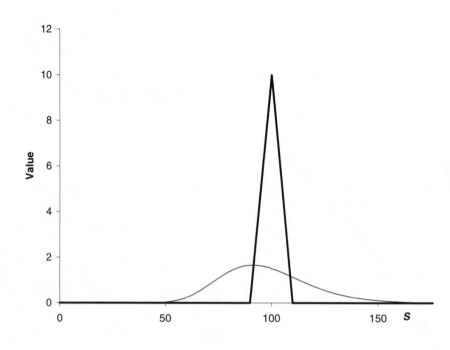

Figure 2.24 Payoff diagram for a butterfly spread.

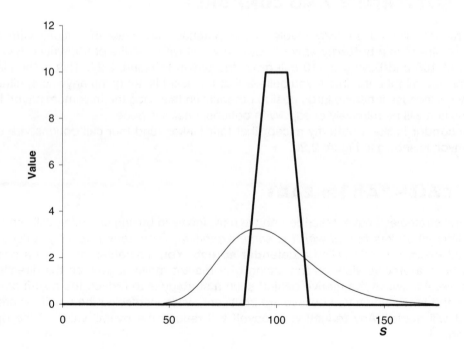

Figure 2.25 Payoff diagram for a condor.

2.19 LEAPS AND FLEX

LEAPS or **long-term equity anticipation securities** are longer-dated exchange-traded calls and puts. They began trading on the CBOE in the late 1980s. They are standardized so that they expire in January each year and are available with expiries up to three years. They come with three strikes, corresponding to at the money and 20% in and out of the money with respect to the underlying asset price when issued.

Figure 2.26 shows LEAPS quoted in *The Wall Street Journal Europe*.

In 1993 the CBOE created **FLEX** or **FLexible EXchange-traded options** on several indices. These allow a degree of customization, in the expiry date (up to five years), the strike price and the exercise style.

2.20 WARRANTS

A contract that is very similar to an option is a **warrant**. Warrants are call options issued by a company on its own equity. The main differences between traded options and warrants are the timescales involved, warrants usually have a longer lifespan, and on exercise the company issues new stock to the warrant holder. On exercise, the holder of a *traded* option receives stock that has already been issued. Exercise is usually allowed any time before expiry, but after an initial waiting period.

The typical lifespan of a warrant is five or more years. Occasionally **perpetual warrants** are issued, these have no maturity.

2.21 CONVERTIBLE BONDS

Convertible bonds or **CBs** have features of both bonds and warrants. They pay a stream of coupons with a final repayment of principal at maturity, but they can be converted into the underlying stock before expiry. On conversion rights to future coupons are lost. If the

LEAPS-LONG TERM

DJ INDUS AVG – CB						
Dec 01	104	p	42	7¾	+ ¾	475
Dec 01	140	p	44	22¼	+ 2½	106
S & P 100 INDEX – CB						
Dec 01	140	c	5	38	+ 6	105
S & P 500 INDEX – CB						
Dec 00	70	p	60	7/16	+ 1/8	8993
Dec 00	90	p	5	1 3/16	+ ¼	15789
Dec 00	100	p	4	1 15/16	+ ½	18242
Dec 00	110	p	85	2¾	+ ¼	15068
Dec 00	112½	p	1	3	+ 3/8	7496
Dec 00	115	p	22	3 5/8	+ 5/8	19282
Dec 00	117½	p	10	7 5/8	+ 1 3/8	839
Dec 00	120	p	52	4 3/8	+ 5/8	17787
Dec 00	125	p	6	5 1/8	+ 5/8	5809
Dec 00	130	p	18	6¼	+ 7/8	7322
Dec 00	140	p	90	9	+ 1¼	10159
Dec 00	145	p	2	9½	+ ¾	935
Call Volume			**39**	**Open Int 6,469,087**		
Put Volume			**20**	**Open Int 4,671,720**		

Figure 2.26 *The Wall Street Journal Europe* of 5th January 2000, LEAPS. Reproduced by permission of Dow Jones & Company, Inc.

stock price is low then there is little incentive to convert to the stock, the coupon stream is more valuable. In this case the CB behaves like a bond. If the stock price is high then conversion is likely and the CB responds to the movement in the asset. Because the CB can be converted into the asset, its value has to be at least the value of the asset. This makes CBs similar to American options; early exercise and conversion are mathematically the same.

2.22 OVER THE COUNTER OPTIONS

Not all options are traded on an exchange. Some, known as over the counter or OTC options, are sold privately from one counterparty to another. In Figure 2.27 is the term

Preliminary and Indicative
For Discussion Purposes Only

Over-the-counter Option linked to the S&P500 Index

Option Type	European put option, with contingent premium feature
Option Seller	XXXX
Option Buyer	[dealing name to be advised]
Notional Amount	USD 20MM
Trade Date	[]
Expiration Date	[]
Underlying Index	S&P500
Settlement	Cash settlement
Cash Settlement Date	5 business days after the Expiration Date
Cash Settlement Amount	Calculated as per the following formula:
	$\quad$ #Contracts * max[0, S&Pstrike − S&Pfinal]
	$\quad$ where #Contracts = Notional Amount /
	$\quad$ S&Pinitial
	This is the same as a conventional put option:
	S&Pstrike will be equal **to 95% of the closing price on the Trade Date**
	S&Pfinal will be the level of the Underlying Index at the valuation time on the Expiration Date
	S&Pinitial is the level of the Underlying Index at the time of execution
Initial Premium Amount	[2%] of Notional Amount
Initial Premium Payment Date	5 business days after Trade Date
Additional Premium Amounts	[1.43%] of Notional Amount per Trigger Level
Additional Premium Payment Dates	The Additional Premium Amounts shall be due only if the Underlying Index at any time from and including the Trade Date and to and including the Expiration Date is equal to or greater than any of the Trigger Levels.
Trigger Levels	103%, 106% and 109% of **S&P500initial**
Documentation	ISDA
Governing law	New York

This indicative term sheet is neither an offer to buy or sell securities or an OTC derivative product which includes options, swaps, forwards and structured notes having similar features to OTC derivative transactions, nor a solicitation to buy or sell securities or an OTC derivative product. The proposal contained in the foregoing is not a complete description of the terms of a particular transaction and is subject to change without limitation.

Figure 2.27 Term sheet for an OTC 'put.'

sheet for an OTC put option, having some special features. A **term sheet** specifies the precise details of an OTC contract. In this OTC put the holder gets a put option on S&P500, but more cheaply than a vanilla put option. This contract is cheap because part of the premium does not have to be paid until and unless the underlying index trades above a specified level. Each time that a new level is reached an extra payment is triggered. This feature means that the contract is not vanilla, and makes the pricing more complicated. We will be discussing special features like the ones in this contract in later chapters. Quantities in square brackets will be set at the time that the deal is struck.

2.23 **SUMMARY**

We now know the basics of options and markets, and a few of the simplest trading strategies. We know some of the jargon and the reasons why people might want to buy an option. We've also seen another example of no arbitrage in put-call parity. This is just the beginning. We don't know how much these instruments are worth, how they are affected by the price of the underlying, how much risk is involved in the buying or writing of options. And we have only seen the very simplest of contracts; there are many, many more complex products to examine. All of these issues are going to be addressed in later chapters.

FURTHER READING

- McMillan (1996) and Options Institute (1995) describe many option strategies used in practice.

- Most exchanges have websites. The London International Financial Futures Exchange website contains information about the money markets, bonds, equities, indices and commodities. See `www.liffe.com`. For information about options and derivatives generally, see `www.cboe.com`, the Chicago Board Options Exchange website. The American Stock Exchange is on `www.amex.com` and the New York Stock Exchange on `www.nyse.com`.

- Derivatives have often had bad press (and there's probably more to come). See Miller (1997) for a discussion of the pros and cons of derivatives.

- The best books on options are Hull (2005) and Cox & Rubinstein (1985), modesty forbids me mentioning others. (Oh, all right then, *PWOQF2*.)

EXERCISES

1. Find the value of the following portfolios of options at expiry, as a function of the share price:
    (a) Long one share, long one put with exercise price E,
    (b) Long one call and one put, both with exercise price E,
    (c) Long one call, exercise price E_1, short one call, exercise price E_2, where $E_1 < E_2$,

(d)   Long one call, exercise price E_1, long one put, exercise price E_2. There are three cases to consider,

(e)   Long two calls, one with exercise price E_1 and one with exercise price E_2, short two calls, both with exercise price E, where $E_1 < E < E_2$.

2.   What is the difference between a payoff diagram and a profit diagram? Illustrate with a portfolio of short one share, long two calls with exercise price E.

3.   A share currently trades at $60. A European call with exercise price $58 and expiry in three months trades at $3. The three month default-free discount rate is 5%. A put is offered on the market, with exercise price $58 and expiry in three months, for $1.50. Do any arbitrage opportunities now exist? If there is a possible arbitrage, then construct a portfolio that will take advantage of it. (This is an application of put-call parity.)

4.   A three-month, 80 strike, European call option is worth $11.91. The 90 call is $4.52 and the 100 call is $1.03. How much is the butterfly spread?

5.   Using the notation $V(E)$ to mean the value of a European call option with strike E, what can you say about $\frac{\partial V}{\partial E}$ and $\frac{\partial^2 V}{\partial E^2}$ for options having the same expiration?

Hint: Consider call and butterfly spreads and the absence of arbitrage.

CHAPTER 3
the binomial model

The aim of this Chapter...

...is to describe the simplest model for asset prices that can be, and is, used for pricing derivatives, to introduce the two fundamental building blocks of quantitative finance and to explain a very important (but very counter-intuitive) financial concept. By the end of this chapter you will be able to write a program for pricing basic derivatives. I hope you won't be too confused by the important-but-counter-intuitive financial concept... even if you are, we'll come back to it many more times.

In this Chapter...

- a simple model for an asset price random walk

- delta hedging

- no arbitrage

- the basics of the binomial method for valuing options

- risk neutrality

3.1   **INTRODUCTION**

In this chapter I'm going to present a very simple and popular model for the random behavior of an asset, for the moment think 'equity.' This simple model will allow us to start valuing options. Undoubtedly, one of the reasons for the popularity of this model is that it can be implemented without any higher mathematics (such as differential calculus). This is a positive point, however the downside is that it is harder to attain greater levels of sophistication or numerical analysis in this setting.

Later we'll be seeing a more sophisticated model, but the ideas we first encounter in this chapter will be seen over and over again. These are the fundamental concepts of hedging and no arbitrage.

The binomial model is very important because it shows that you don't need a simple formula for everything. Indeed, it is extremely important to have a way of valuing options that only relies on a simple model and fast, accurate numerical methods. Often in real life a contract may contain features that make analytic solution very hard or impossible. Some of these features may be just a minor modification to some other, easily-priced, contract but even minor changes to a contract can have important effects on the value and especially on the method of solution. The classic example is of the American put. Early exercise may seem to be a small change to a contract but the difference between the values of a European and an American put can be large and certainly there is no simple closed-form solution for the American option and its value must be found numerically.

Time Out...

Simplicity itself

The math in this chapter is all very straightforward, addition, subtraction, multiplication and, occasionally, division.

Before I describe this model I want to stress that the binomial model may be thought of as being either a genuine *model* for the behavior of equities, or, alternatively, as a *numerical method* for the solution of the Black–Scholes equation.[1] Or it can be thought of as a *teaching aid* to explain delta hedging, risk elimination and risk-neutral valuation.

Having said what is good about the binomial I would like to say what, to my mind, is bad about it.

First, as a model of stock price behavior it is poor. The binomial model says that the stock can either go up by a known amount or down by a known amount, there are but two possible stock prices 'tomorrow.' This is clearly unrealistic. This is important because

---

[1] In this case, it is very similar to an explicit finite-difference method. We'll see the famous Black–Scholes equation and finite-difference methods later.

from this model follow certain results that hinge entirely on there only being two prices for the stock tomorrow. Introduce a third state and the results collapse.

Second, as a numerical scheme it is prehistoric compared with modern numerical methods. We go into these numerical methods in some detail in this book but several volumes could be written on sophisticated numerical methods alone. I would advise the reader to study the binomial model for the intuition it gives, but do not rely on it for numerical calculations.

But as a teaching aid for explaining difficult concepts, the binomial model is fantastic. Indeed, it is said that the binomial model even helps MBA students understand options. However, I don't believe in such dumbing down. I don't think that quantitative finance should be dumbed down, just like I don't believe that brain surgery should be dumbed down.

My advice is that once you have become comfortable with the ideas that come out of this chapter you should relegate the binomial method to the back of your mind.

3.2 EQUITIES CAN GO DOWN AS WELL AS UP

The most 'accessible' approach to option pricing is the **binomial model**. This requires only basic arithmetic and no complicated stochastic calculus. In this model we will see the ideas of hedging and no arbitrage used. The end result is a simple algorithm for determining the correct value for an option.

We are going to examine a very simple model for the behavior of a stock, and based on this model see how to value options.

- We will have a stock, and a call option on that stock expiring tomorrow.

- The stock can either rise or fall by a known amount between today and tomorrow.

- Interest rates are zero.

Figure 3.1 gives an example. The stock is currently worth $100 and can rise to $101 or fall to $99 between today and tomorrow.

Which of the two prices is realized tomorrow is completely random. There is a certain probability of the stock rising and one minus that probability of the stock falling. In this example the probability of a rise to 101 is 0.6, so that the probability of falling to 99 is 0.4. See Figure 3.2.

Now let's introduce the call option on the stock. This call option has a strike of $100 and expires tomorrow.

If the stock price rises to 101, what will then be the option's payoff? See Figure 3.3. It is just $101 - 100 = 1$.

And if the stock falls to 99 tomorrow, what is then the payoff? See Figure 3.4. The answer is zero, the option has expired out of the money.

If the stock rises the option is worth 1, and if it falls it is worth 0. There is a 0.6 probability of getting 1 and a 0.4 probability of getting zero. Interest rates are zero. . .

What is the option worth today?

No, the answer is *not* 0.6. If that is what you thought, based on calculating simple expectations, then I successfully 'led you up the garden path' to the wrong answer.

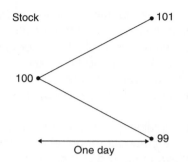

Figure 3.1 The stock can rise or fall over the next day, only two future prices are possible.

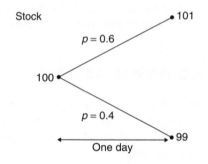

Figure 3.2 Probabilities associated with the future stock prices.

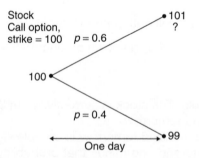

Figure 3.3 What is the option payoff if the stock rises?

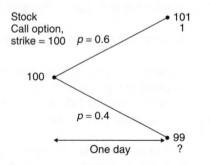

Figure 3.4 What is the option payoff if the stock falls?

3.3 **THE OPTION VALUE**

The correct answer is. . .

$$\frac{1}{2}.$$

Why?

To see how this can be the only correct answer we must first construct a *portfolio* consisting of one option and short $\frac{1}{2}$ of the underlying stock. This portfolio is shown in Figure 3.7.

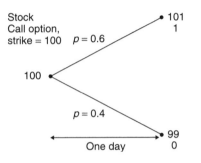

Figure 3.5   Now we know the option values in both 'states of the world.'

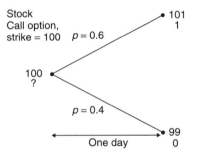

Figure 3.6   What is the option worth today?

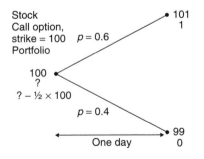

Figure 3.7   Long one option, short half of the stock.

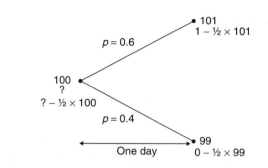

Figure 3.8 The portfolio values at expiration.

If the stock rises to 101 then this portfolio is worth

$$1 - \tfrac{1}{2} \times 101;$$

the one being from the option payoff and the $-\tfrac{1}{2} \times 101$ being from a short $(-)$ position $\left(\tfrac{1}{2}\right)$ in the stock (now worth 101).

If the stock falls to 99 then this portfolio is worth

$$0 - \tfrac{1}{2} \times 99;$$

the zero being from the option payoff and the $-\tfrac{1}{2} \times 99$ being from a short $(-)$ position $\left(\tfrac{1}{2}\right)$ in the stock (now worth 99). See Figure 3.8.

In either case, tomorrow, at expiration, the portfolio takes the value

$$-\frac{99}{2}$$

and that is regardless of whether the stock rises or falls.

We have constructed a perfectly risk-free portfolio.

If the portfolio is worth $-99/2$ tomorrow, and interest rates are zero, how much is this portfolio worth today?

It must also be worth $-99/2$ today.

This is an example of **no arbitrage**: There are two ways to ensure that we have $-99/2$ tomorrow.

1. Buy one option and sell one half of the stock.

2. Put the money under the mattress.

Both of these 'portfolios' must be worth the same today. Therefore, using '?' as in the figure to represent the unknown option value

$$? - \tfrac{1}{2} \times 100 = \text{the option value} - \tfrac{1}{2} \times 100 = -\tfrac{1}{2} \times 99$$

and so

$$? = \text{the option value} = \frac{1}{2}.$$

3.4 **WHICH PART OF OUR 'MODEL' DIDN'T WE NEED?**

The value of an option does not depend on the probability of the stock rising or falling. This is equivalent to saying that the stock growth rate is irrelevant for option pricing. This is because we have **hedged** the option with the stock. See Figure 3.9. We do not care whether the stock rises or falls. See Figure 3.10.

We *do* care about the stock price range, however. The stock volatility is very important in the valuation of options.

Three questions follow from the above simple argument:

- Why should this 'theoretical price' be the 'market price'?
- How did I know to sell $\frac{1}{2}$ of the stock for hedging?
- How does this change if interest rates are non-zero?

3.5 **WHY SHOULD THIS 'THEORETICAL PRICE' BE THE 'MARKET PRICE'?**

This one is simple. Because if the theoretical price and the market price are not the same, then there is risk-free money to be made. If the option costs less than 0.5 simply buy it and hedge to make a profit. If it is worth more than 0.5 in the market then sell it and hedge, and make a guaranteed profit.

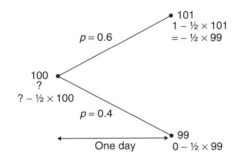

Figure 3.9 The portfolio is 'hedged.'

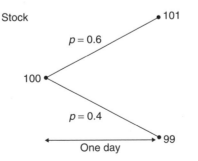

Figure 3.10 Which parameter(s) didn't we need?

It's not quite this simple because it is possible for arbitrage opportunities to exist, and to exist for a long time. We also really need there to be some practical mechanism for arbitrage to be 'removed.' In practice this means we really need there to be a couple of agents perhaps undercutting each other in such a way that the arb opportunity disappears: A sells the option for 0.55, gets all the business and makes a guaranteed 0.05 profit. Along comes B who sells the option for just 0.53, now he takes away all the business from A, who responds by dropping his price to 0.52, etc. So really, supply and demand should act to make the option price converge to the 0.5.

3.5.1   The role of expectations

The expected payoff is definitely 0.6 for this option. It's just that this has nothing to do with the option's value. Let's take a quick look at the role of this expectation.

Would anyone pay 0.6 or more for the option? No, unless they were **risk seeking**.

Would anyone pay 0.55? Perhaps, if they liked the idea of an expected return of

$$\frac{0.6 - 0.55}{0.55} \approx 9\%.$$

The person writing the option would be very pleased with the guaranteed profit of 0.05.

3.6   HOW DID I KNOW TO SELL $\frac{1}{2}$ OF THE STOCK FOR HEDGING?

Introduce a symbol. Use Δ to denote the quantity of stock that must be sold for hedging. We start off with one option, $-\Delta$ of the stock, giving a portfolio value of

$$? - \Delta \times 100.$$

Tomorrow the portfolio is worth

$$1 - \Delta \times 101$$

if the stock rises, or

$$0 - \Delta \times 99$$

if it falls.

The key step is the next one; make these two equal to each other:

$$1 - \Delta \times 101 = 0 - \Delta \times 99.$$

Therefore

$$\Delta(101 - 99) = 1$$

$$\Delta = 0.5.$$

Another example: Stock price is 100, can rise to 103 or fall to 98. Value a call option with a strike price of 100. Interest rates are zero.

Again use Δ to denote the quantity of stock that must be sold for hedging.

The portfolio value is

$$? - \Delta \times 100.$$

Tomorrow the portfolio is worth either

$$3 - \Delta 103$$

or

$$0 - \Delta 98.$$

So we must make

$$3 - \Delta 103 = 0 - \Delta 98.$$

That is,

$$\Delta = \frac{3 - 0}{103 - 98} = \frac{3}{5} = 0.6.$$

The portfolio value tomorrow is then

$$-0.6 \times 98.$$

With zero interest rate, the portfolio value today must equal the risk-free portfolio value tomorrow:

$$? - 0.6 \times 100 = -0.6 \times 98.$$

Therefore the option value is 1.2.

3.6.1   The general formula for Δ

Delta hedging means choosing Δ such that the portfolio value does not depend on the direction of the stock.

When we generalize this (using symbols instead of numbers later on) we will find that

$$\Delta = \frac{\text{Range of option payoffs}}{\text{Range of stock prices}}.$$

We can think of Δ as the sensitivity of the option to changes in the stock.

3.7   HOW DOES THIS CHANGE IF INTEREST RATES ARE NON-ZERO?

Simple. We delta hedge as before to construct a risk-free portfolio. (And we use exactly the same delta.) Then we present value that back in time, by multiplying by a discount factor.

Example: Same as first example, but now $r = 0.1$.

The discount factor for going back one day is

$$\frac{1}{1 + 0.1/252} = 0.9996.$$

The portfolio value today must be the *present value* of the portfolio value tomorrow

$$? - 0.5 \times 100 = -0.5 \times 99 \times 0.9996.$$

So that

$$? = 0.51963.$$

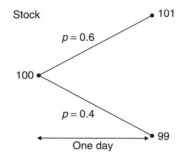

Figure 3.11 What is the expected stock price?

3.8 IS THE STOCK ITSELF CORRECTLY PRICED?

Earlier, I tried to trick you into pricing the option by looking at the expected payoff. Suppose, for the sake of argument, that I had been successful in this. I would then have asked you what was the expected stock price tomorrow; forget the option.

The expected stock value tomorrow is

$$0.6 \times 101 + 0.4 \times 99 = 100.2.$$

In an expectation's sense, the stock itself seems incorrectly priced. Shouldn't it be valued at 100.2 today? Well, we already kind of know that expectations aren't the way to price options, so this is also not the way to price stock. But we can go further than that, and make some positive statements.

We ought to pay less than the future expected value because the stock is risky. We want a positive expected return to compensate for the risk. This is an idea we will be seeing in detail later on, in Chapter 21 on portfolio management.

We can plot the stock (and all investments) on a risk/return diagram, see Figure 3.12. Risk is measured by standard deviation and return is the expected return. The figure shows two investments, the stock and, at the origin, the bank investment. The bank investment has zero risk, and in our first example above, has zero expected return.

We will see in Chapter 21 that we can get to other places in the risk/return space by dividing our money between several investments. In the present case, if we put half our

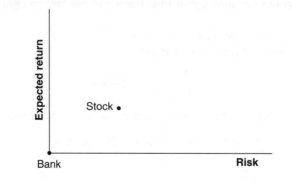

Figure 3.12 Risk and return for the stock and the risk-free investment.

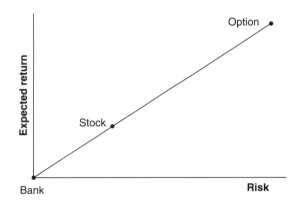

Figure 3.13 Now we have three investments, including the option.

money in the bank and half in the stock we will find ourselves with an investment that is exactly half way between the two dots in the figure. We can get to any point on the straight line between the risk-free dot and the stock dot by splitting our money between these two, we can even get to any place on the extrapolated straight line in Figure 3.13 by borrowing money at the risk-free rate to invest in the stock.

3.9 COMPLETE MARKETS

The option also has an expected return and a risk. In our example the expected return and the risk for the option are both much, much greater than for the stock. We can plot the option on the same risk/return diagram. Where do you think it might be? Above the extrapolated line, on it, or below it?

It turns out that the option lies *on* the straight line, see Figure 3.13. This means that we can 'replicate' an option's risk and return characteristic with stock and the risk-free investment. Option payoffs can be **replicated** by stocks and cash. Any two points on the straight lines can be used to get us to any other point. So, we can get a risk-free investment using the option and the stock, and this is hedging. And, the stock can be replicated by cash and the option.

A conclusion of this analysis is that options are redundant in this 'world,' i.e. in this model. We say that **markets are complete**. The practical implication of complete markets is that options are hedgeable and can therefore be priced without any need to know probabilities. We can hedge an option with stock to 'replicate' a risk-free investment, Figure 3.14, and we can replicate an option using stock and a risk-free investment, Figures 3.15 and 3.16. We could also, of course, replicate stock with an option and risk-free investment.

3.10 THE REAL AND RISK-NEUTRAL WORLDS

In our world, the **real world**, we have used our statistical skills to estimate the future possible stock prices (99 and 101) and the probabilities of reaching them (0.4 and 0.6).

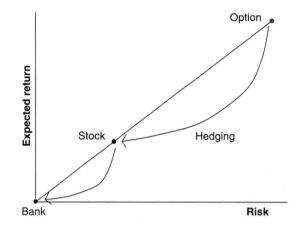

Figure 3.14 Hedging.

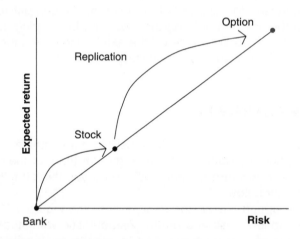

Figure 3.15 Replication.

Some properties of the real world:

- We know all about delta hedging and risk elimination.
- We are very sensitive to risk, and expect greater return for taking risk.
- It turns out that only the two stock prices matter for option pricing, not the probabilities.

People often refer to the **risk-neutral world** in which people don't care about risk. The risk-neutral world has the following characteristics:

- We don't care about risk, and don't expect any extra return for taking unnecessary risk.
- We don't ever need statistics for estimating probabilities of events happening.
- We believe that everything is priced using simple expectations.

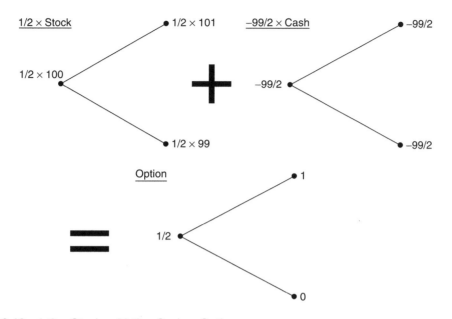

Figure 3.16 $1/2 \times$ Stock $- 99/2 \times$ Cash $=$ Option.

Imagine yourself in the risk-neutral world, looking at the stock price model. Suppose all you know is that the stock is currently worth $100 and could rise to $101 or fall to $99.

If the stock is correctly priced today, using simple expectations, what would you deduce to be the probabilities of the stock price rising or falling?

The symmetry makes the answer to this rather obvious. If the stock is correctly priced using expectations then the probabilities ought to be 50% chance of a rise and 50% chance of a fall. The calculation we have just performed goes as follows...

On the risk-neutral planet they calculate **risk-neutral probabilities** p' from the equation

$$p' \times 101 + (1 - p') \times 99 = 100.$$

From which $p' = 0.5$.

Do not think that this p' is in any sense real. No, the real probabilities are still 60% and 40%. This calculation assumes something that is fundamentally wrong, that simple expectations are used for pricing. No allowance has been made for risk.

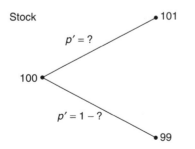

Figure 3.17 What is the probability of the stock rising?

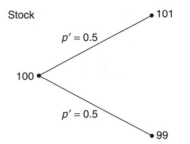

Figure 3.18 Risk-neutral probabilities.

Never mind, let's stay with this risk-neutral world and see what they think the option value is. We won't tell them yet that the calculation they have just done is 'wrong.'

How would they then value the call option? Since they reckon the probabilities to be 50–50 and they use simple expectations to calculate values with no regard to risk then they would price the option using the expected payoff with their probabilities, i.e.

$$0.5 \times 1 + 0.5 \times 0 = 0.5.$$

See Figure 3.19. This is called the **risk-neutral expectation**.

Damn and blast! They have found the correct answer for the wrong reasons! To put it in a nutshell, they have twice used their basic assumption of pricing via simple expectations to get to the correct answer. Two wrongs in this case do make a right. First of all they calculate a probability from a price, and then a price from a probability. The two 'errors' were in opposite directions and canceled each other out.

And this technique will always work.

In the risk-neutral world they have exactly the same price for the option (but for different reasons).

3.10.1 Non-zero interest rates

When interest rates are non-zero we must perform exactly the same operations, but whenever we equate values at different times we must allow for present valuing.

With $r = 0.1$ we calculate the risk-neutral probabilities from

$$0.9996 \times (p' \times 101 + (1 - p') \times 99) = 100.$$

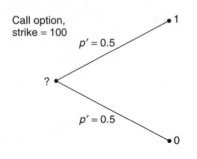

Figure 3.19 Pricing the option.

So

$$p' = 0.51984.$$

The expected option payoff is now

$$0.51984 \times 1 + (1 - 0.51984) \times 0 = 0.51984.$$

And the present value of this is

$$0.9996 \times 0.51984 = 0.51963.$$

And this must be the option value. (It is the same as we derived the 'other' way.)

Risk-neutral pricing is a very powerful technique, and we will be seeing a lot more of it. Just remember one thing for the moment, that the risk-neutral probability p' that we have just calculated (the 0.5 in the first example) is not real, it does not exist, it is a mathematical construct. The real probability of the stock price was always in our example 0.6, it's just that this never was used in our calculations.

3.11 AND NOW USING SYMBOLS

Let's generalize, so that instead of 100, 101, 99, 0.6, etc., we use symbols for everything. In the binomial model we assume that the asset, which initially has the value S, can, during a time step δt, either

- rise to a value $u \times S$ or
- fall to a value $v \times S$,

with $0 < v < 1 < u$.

- The probability of a rise is p and so the probability of a fall is $1 - p$.

Note: By *multiplying* the asset price by constants rather than *adding* constants, we will later be able to build up a whole tree of prices. (This will be a discrete-time version of what you will soon come to know as a lognormal random walk.)

- The three constants u, v and p are chosen to give the binomial walk the same characteristics as the asset we are modeling.

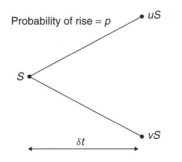

Figure 3.20 The model, using symbols.

Now remember that I said that I don't want you using the binomial model, other than to gain intuition? Well, to help you in that I want to wean you off the model starting now. To that end I am going to use notation that will be important from Chapter 4 onwards, and is notation we all use in proper quant finance. Instead of using, u, v and p we are going to write everything in terms of the mean and the standard deviation of the random walk. That involves writing u, v and p in terms of what are known as the drift and the volatility. The drift is the average rate at which the asset rises and the volatility is a measure of its randomness.

In order to do this I have to introduce new symbols to represent the drift and volatility of the asset: μ the drift of the asset and σ the volatility. And we still have a time step δt over which the asset move takes place.

I'm going to give some expressions now for u, v and p and then explain where they come from:

$$u = 1 + \sigma\sqrt{\delta t},$$

$$v = 1 - \sigma\sqrt{\delta t}$$

and

$$p = \frac{1}{2} + \frac{\mu\sqrt{\delta t}}{2\sigma}. \tag{3.1}$$

To see what these mean let's look at the average change in asset price during the time step and the standard deviation.

3.11.1   Average asset change

The expected asset price after one time step is

$$puS + (1 - p)vS = \left(\frac{1}{2} + \frac{\mu\sqrt{\delta t}}{2\sigma}\right)\left(1 + \sigma\sqrt{\delta t}\right)S$$

$$+ \left(\frac{1}{2} - \frac{\mu\sqrt{\delta t}}{2\sigma}\right)\left(1 - \sigma\sqrt{\delta t}\right)S = (1 + \mu\,\delta t)S.$$

So the expected change in the asset is $\mu S\,\delta t$.

- The expected **return** is $\mu\,\delta t$.

3.11.2   Standard deviation of asset price change

The variance of change in asset price is

$$S^2\left(p(u - 1 - \mu\,\delta t)^2 + (1 - p)(v - 1 - \mu\,\delta t)^2\right)$$

$$= S^2\left(\left(\frac{1}{2} + \frac{\mu\sqrt{\delta t}}{2\sigma}\right)\left(\sigma\sqrt{\delta t} - \mu\,\delta t\right)^2 + \left(\frac{1}{2} - \frac{\mu\sqrt{\delta t}}{2\sigma}\right)\left(\sigma\sqrt{\delta t} + \mu\,\delta t\right)^2\right)$$

$$= S^2(\sigma^2\delta t - \mu^2\delta t^2).$$

The standard deviation of asset changes is (approximately) $S\sigma\sqrt{\delta t}$.

- The standard deviation of returns is (approximately) $\sigma\sqrt{\delta t}$.

3.12 **AN EQUATION FOR THE VALUE OF AN OPTION**

Suppose that we know the value of the option at the time $t + \delta t$. For example, this time may be the expiration of the option, say.

Now construct a portfolio at time t consisting of one option and a short position in a quantity Δ of the underlying. At time t this portfolio has value

$$\Pi = V - \Delta S,$$

where the option value V is for the moment unknown. You'll recognize this as exactly what we did before, but now we're using symbols instead of numbers.

At time $t + \delta t$ the option takes one of two values, depending on whether the asset rises or falls

$$V^+ \quad \text{or} \quad V^-.$$

At the same time the portfolio becomes either

$$V^+ - \Delta uS \quad \text{or} \quad V^- - \Delta vS.$$

Since we know V^+, V^-, u, v and S the values of both of these expressions are just linear functions of Δ.

3.12.1 Hedging

Having the freedom to choose Δ, we can make the value of this portfolio the same whether the asset rises or falls. This is ensured if we make

$$V^+ - \Delta uS = V^- - \Delta vS.$$

This means that we should choose

$$\Delta = \frac{V^+ - V^-}{(u - v)S} \tag{3.2}$$

for hedging. This is just the range of option prices divided by the range of asset prices.

The portfolio value is then

$$V^+ - \Delta uS = V^+ - \frac{u(V^+ - V^-)}{(u - v)}$$

if the stock rises or

$$V^- - \Delta vS = V^- - \frac{v(V^+ - V^-)}{(u - v)}$$

if it falls.

And, of course, these two expressions are the same.

Let's denote this portfolio value by

$$\Pi + \delta\Pi.$$

This just means the original portfolio value plus the change in value.

3.12.2 No arbitrage

Since the value of the portfolio has been guaranteed, we can say that its value must coincide with the value of the original portfolio plus any interest earned at the risk-free rate; this is the no-arbitrage argument.

Thus

$$\delta\Pi = r\Pi\,\delta t.$$

Putting everything together we get

$$\Pi + \delta\Pi = \Pi + r\Pi\,\delta t = \Pi(1 + r\,\delta t) = V^+ - \frac{u(V^+ - V^-)}{(u-v)}$$

with

$$\Pi = V - \Delta S = V - \frac{V^+ - V^-}{(u-v)S}S = V - \frac{V^+ - V^-}{(u-v)}$$

And the end result is

$$(1 + r\,\delta t)\left(V - \frac{V^+ - V^-}{(u-v)}\right) = V^- - \frac{v(V^+ - V^-)}{(u-v)}.$$

On a spreadsheet

Rearranging as an equation for V we get

$$(1 + r\,\delta t)V = (1 + r\,\delta t)\frac{V^+ - V^-}{u-v} + \frac{uV^- - vV^+}{(u-v)}.$$

This is an equation for V given V^+, and V^-, the option values at the next time step, and the parameters u and v describing the random walk of the asset.

But it can be written more elegantly than this.

This equation can also be written as

$$V = \frac{1}{1 + r\,\delta t}\left(p'V^+ + (1 - p')V^-\right), \qquad (3.3)$$

where

$$p' = \frac{1}{2} + \frac{r\sqrt{\delta t}}{2\sigma}. \qquad (3.4)$$

The right-hand side of Equation (3.3) is just like a discounted expectation; the terms inside the parentheses are the sum of probabilities multiplied by events.

If only the expression contained p, the real probability of a stock rise, then this expression would be the expected value at the next time step.

We see that the probability of a rise or fall is irrelevant as far as option pricing is concerned since p did not appear in Equation (3.3). But what if we interpret p' as a probability? Then we could 'say' that the option price is the present value of an expectation. But not the real expectation.

We are back with risk-neutral expectations again.

Let's compare the expression for p' with the expression for the actual probability p:

$$p' = \frac{1}{2} + \frac{r\sqrt{\delta t}}{2\sigma}$$

but

$$p = \frac{1}{2} + \frac{\mu\sqrt{\delta t}}{2\sigma}.$$

The two expressions differ in that where one has the interest rate r the other has the drift μ, but are otherwise the same. Strange.

- We call p' the **risk-neutral probability**. It's like the real probability, but the real probability if the drift rate were r instead of μ.

Observe that the risk-free interest rate plays two roles in option valuation. It's used once for discounting to give present value, and it's used as the drift rate in the risk-neutral asset price random walk.

3.13 **WHERE DID THE PROBABILITY p GO?**

What happened to the probability p and the drift rate μ?

Interpreting p' as a probability, (3.3) is the statement that

- the option value at any time is the present value of the risk-neutral expected value at any later time.

In reading books or research papers on mathematical finance you will often encounter the expression 'risk-neutral' this or that, including the expression risk-neutral probability. You can think of an option value as being the present value of an expectation, only it's not the real expectation.

Don't worry we'll come back to this several more times until you get the hang of it.

3.14 **COUNTER-INTUITIVE?**

- Two stocks A and B.

- Both have the same value, same volatility and are denominated in the same currency.

- Both have call options with the same strike and expiration.

- Stock A is doubling in value every year, stock B is halving.

Therefore both call options have the same value. But which would you buy? That one stock is doubling and the other halving is irrelevant. That option prices don't depend on the direction that the stock is going can be difficult to accept initially.

3.15 **THE BINOMIAL TREE**

The binomial model, just introduced, allows the stock to move up or down a prescribed amount over the next time step. If the stock starts out with value S then it will take either the value uS or vS after the next time step. We can extend the random walk to the next time step. After two time steps the asset will be at either u^2S, if there were two up moves, uvS, if an up was followed by a down or vice versa, or v^2S, if there were two consecutive down moves. After three time steps the asset can be at u^3S, u^2vS, etc. One can imagine extending this random walk out all the way until expiry. The resulting structure looks like Figure 3.21 where the nodes represent the values taken by the asset. This structure is called the **binomial tree**. Observe how the tree bends due to the geometric nature of the asset growth. Often this tree is drawn as in Figure 3.22 because it is easier to draw, but this doesn't quite capture the correct structure.

The top and bottom branches of the tree at expiry can only be reached by one path each, either all up or all down moves. Whereas there will be several paths possible for each of the intermediate values at expiry. Therefore the intermediate values are more likely to be reached than the end values if one were doing a simulation. The binomial tree therefore contains within it an approximation to the probability density function for the lognormal random walk.

3.16 **THE ASSET PRICE DISTRIBUTION**

The probability of reaching a particular node in the binomial tree depends on the number of distinct paths to that node and the probabilities of the up and down moves. Since up and down moves are approximately equally likely and since there are more paths to the interior prices than to the two extremes we will find that the probability distribution of future prices is roughly bell shaped. In Figure 3.23 is shown the number of paths to each node after four time steps and the probability of getting to each. In Figure 3.24 this is interpreted as probability density functions at a sequence of times.

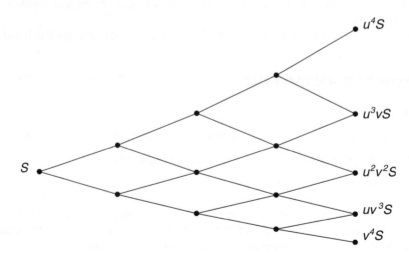

Figure 3.21   The binomial tree.

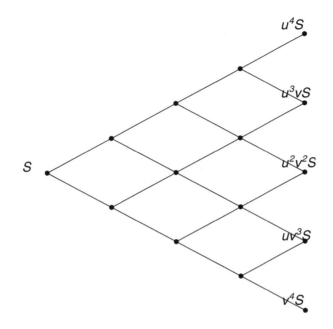

Figure 3.22 The binomial tree: a schematic version.

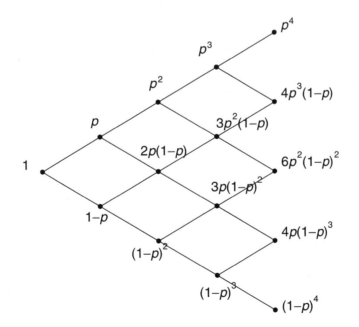

Figure 3.23 Counting paths.

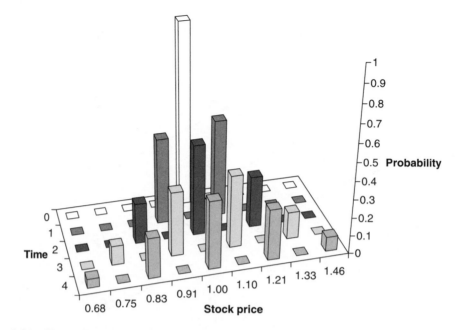

Figure 3.24 The probability distribution of future asset prices.

A few steps in a tree

3.17 **VALUING BACK DOWN THE TREE**

We certainly know V^+ and V^- at expiry, time T, because we know the option value as a function of the asset; this is the payoff function.

If we know the value of the option at expiry we can find the option value at the time $T - \delta t$ for all values of S on the tree. But knowing these values means that we can find the option values one step further back in time.

• Thus we work our way back down the tree until we get to the root.

This root is the current time and asset value, and thus we find the option value today.

This algorithm is shown schematically over the next few pages. In this example I have used the choices of u, v and p' described in the appendix to this chapter with $S = 100$, $\delta t = 1/12$, $r = 0.1$, and $\sigma = 0.2$. The option is a European call with a strike of 100 and four months to expiration.

Using these numbers we have $u = 1.0604$, $v = 0.9431$ and $p' = 0.5567$. As an example, after one time step the asset takes either the value $100 \times 1.0604 = 106.04$ or $100 \times .9431 = 94.31$. Working back from expiry, the option value at the time step before expiry when $S = 119.22$ is given by

$$e^{-0.1 \times 0.0833}(0.5567 \times 26.42 + (1 - 0.5567) \times 12.44) = 20.05.$$

Working right back down the tree to the present time, the option value when the asset is 100 is 6.13.

Tree of asset prices

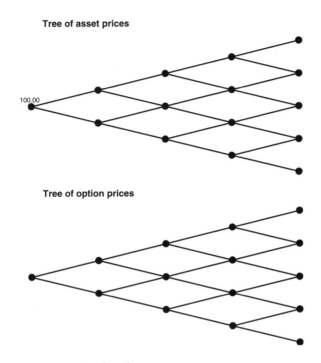

Tree of option prices

Figure 3.25 The two trees, asset and option.

Tree of asset prices

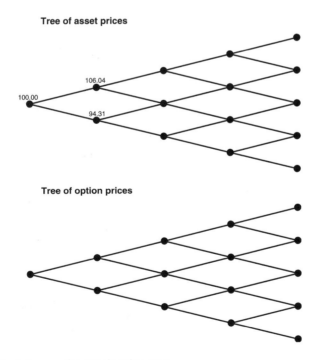

Tree of option prices

Figure 3.26 Start building up the stock-price tree.

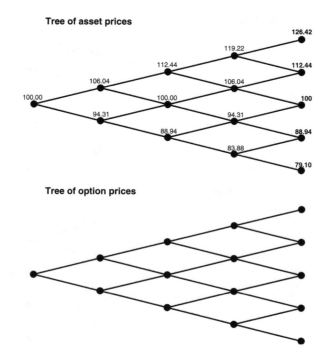

Figure 3.27   The finished stock tree.

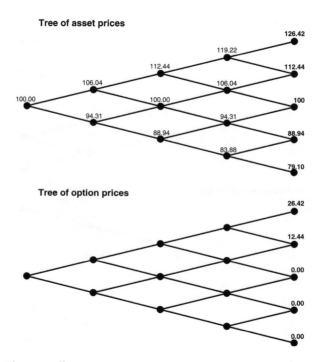

Figure 3.28   The option payoff.

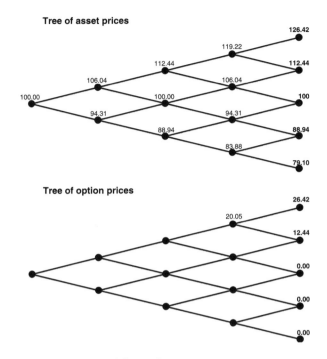

Figure 3.29 Work backwards one 'node' at a time.

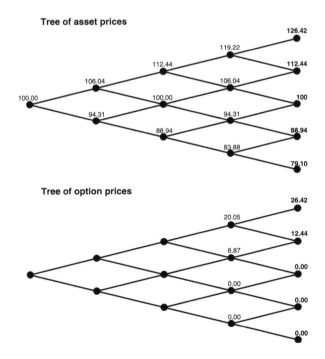

Figure 3.30 First time step completed.

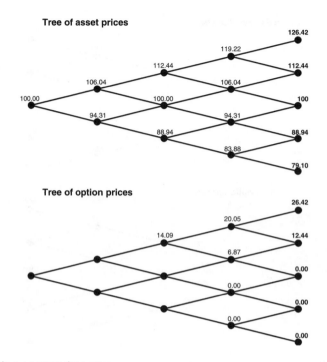

Figure 3.31 Starting on next time step.

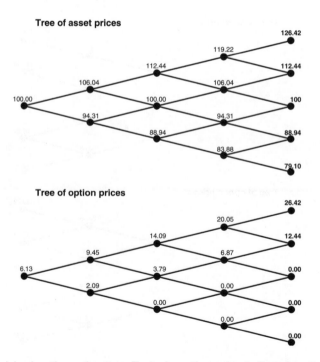

Figure 3.32 The finished option-price tree. Today's option price is therefore 6.13.

3.18 PROGRAMMING THE BINOMIAL METHOD

In practice, the binomial method is programmed rather than done on a spreadsheet. Here is a function that takes inputs for the underlying and the option, using an externally defined payoff function.[2] Key points to note about this program concern the building up of the arrays for the asset $S()$ and the option $V()$. First of all, the asset array is built up only in order to find the final values of the asset at each node at the final time step, expiry. The asset values on other nodes are never used. Second, the argument j refers to how far up the asset is from the lowest node *at that time step*.

```
Function Price(Asset As Double, Volatility _
                As Double, IntRate _
                As Double, Strike _
                As Double, Expiry _
                As Double, NoSteps _
                As Integer)
ReDim S(0 To NoSteps)
ReDim V(0 To NoSteps)
time step = Expiry / NoSteps
DiscountFactor = Exp(-IntRate * time step)
temp1 = Exp((IntRate + Volatility * Volatility) _
                            * time step)
temp2 = 0.5 * (DiscountFactor + temp1)
u = temp2 + Sqr(temp2 * temp2 - 1)
d = 1 / u
p = (Exp(IntRate * time step) - d) / (u - d)

S(0) = Asset
For n = 1 To NoSteps
    For j = n To 1 Step -1
        S(j) = u * S(j - 1)
    Next j
        S(0) = d * S(0)
Next n

For j = 0 To NoSteps
    V(j) = Payoff(S(j), Strike)
Next j

For n = NoSteps To 1 Step -1
    For j = 0 To n - 1
        V(j) = (p * V(j + 1) + (1 - p) * V(j)) _
            * DiscountFactor
    Next j
Next n
Price = V(0)
End Function
```

CODE IMPLEMENTING THE BINOMIAL METHOD FOR A EUROPEAN OPTION

Working code

---

[2] This parameterization of the binomial method is the one explained in the appendix to this chapter.

Here is the externally defined payoff function `Payoff(S, Strike)` for a call.

```
Function Payoff(S, K)
Payoff = 0
If S > K Then Payoff = S - K
End Function
```

Because I never use the asset nodes other than at expiry I could have used only the one array in the above, with the same array being used for both *S* and *V*. I have kept them separate to make the program more transparent. Also, I could have saved the values of *V* at all of the nodes; in the above I have only saved the node at the present time. Saving all the values will be important if you want to see how the option value changes with the asset price and time, if you want to calculate greeks for example.

In Figure 3.33 I show a plot of the calculated option price against the number of time steps using this algorithm. The inset figure is a close-up. Observe the oscillation. In this example, an odd number of time steps gives an answer that is too high and an even an answer that is too low.

3.19 THE GREEKS

The greeks are defined as derivatives of the option value with respect to various variables and parameters. These greeks will later be very important when we talk about risk management. It is important to distinguish whether the differentiation is with respect to a variable or a parameter (it could, of course, be with respect to both). If the differentiation is only with respect to the asset price and/or time then there is sufficient information in our binomial tree to estimate the derivative. It may not be an accurate estimate, but it will be *an* estimate. The option's delta, gamma and theta, defined below can all be estimated from the tree.

On the other hand, if you want to examine the sensitivity of the option with respect to one of the parameters, then you must perform another binomial calculation.

Let me take these two cases in turn.

From the binomial model the option's delta is defined by

$$\frac{V^+ - V^-}{(u - v)S}.$$

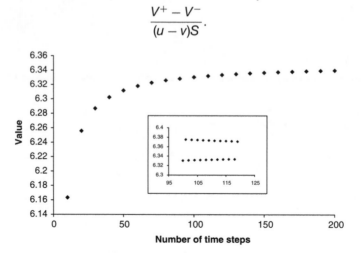

Figure 3.33 Option price as a function of number of time steps.

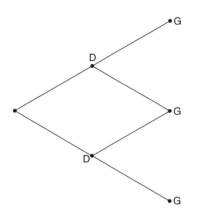

Figure 3.34 Calculating the delta and gamma.

We can calculate this quantity directly from the tree. Referring to Figure 3.34, the delta uses the option value at the two points marked 'D,' together with today's asset price and the parameters u and v. This is a simple calculation.

In the limit as the time step approaches zero, the delta becomes

$$\frac{\partial V}{\partial S}.$$

The gamma of the option is also defined as a derivative of the option with respect to the underlying, the sensitivity of the delta to the asset.

$$\frac{\partial^2 V}{\partial S^2}.$$

To estimate this quantity using our tree is not so clear. (It will be much easier when we use a finite-difference grid.) However, gamma, being the sensitivity of the delta to the underlying, is a measure of how much we must rehedge at the next time step. But we can calculate the delta at points marked with a D in Figure 3.34 from the option value one time step further in the future. The gamma is then just the change in the delta from one of these to the other divided by the distance between them. This calculation uses the points marked 'G' in Figure 3.34.

The theta of the option is the sensitivity of the option price to time, assuming that the asset price does not change. (Again, this is easier to calculate from a finite-difference grid.) An obvious choice for the discrete-time definition of theta is to interpolate between V^+ and V^- to find a theoretical option value *had the asset not changed* and use this to estimate

$$\frac{\partial V}{\partial t}.$$

This results in

$$\frac{\frac{1}{2}(V^+ + V^-) - V}{\delta t}.$$

As the time step gets smaller and smaller these greeks approach the Black–Scholes continuous-time values, which we'll be seeing shortly.

Estimating the other type of greeks, the ones involving differentiation with respect to parameters, is slightly harder. They are harder to calculate in the sense that you must perform a second binomial calculation. I will illustrate this with the calculation of the option's vega.

The vega is the sensitivity of the option value to the volatility

$$\frac{\partial V}{\partial \sigma}.$$

Suppose we want to find the option value and vega when the volatility is 20%. The most efficient way to do this is to calculate the option price twice, using a binomial tree, with two different values of σ. Calculate the option value using a volatility of $\sigma \pm \epsilon$, for a small number ϵ; call the values you find $V_{\pm}$. The option value is approximated by the average value

$$V = \tfrac{1}{2}(V_+ + V_-)$$

and the vega is approximated by

$$\frac{V_+ - V_-}{2\epsilon}.$$

The importance of these greeks in risk management will become increasingly apparent as you read this book.

3.20 EARLY EXERCISE

American-style exercise is easy to implement in a binomial setting. The algorithm is identical to that for European exercise with one exception. We use the same binomial tree, with the same u, v and p, but there is a slight difference in the formula for V. We must ensure that there are no arbitrage opportunities at any of the nodes.

For reasons which will become apparent, I'm going to change my notation now, making it more complex but more informative. Introduce the notation S_j^n to mean the asset price at the nth time step, at the node j from the bottom, $0 \leq j \leq n$. This notation is consistent with the code above. In our lognormal world we have

$$S_j^n = Su^j v^{n-j},$$

where S is the current asset price. Also introduce V_j^n as the option value at the same node. Our ultimate goal is to find V_0^0 knowing the payoff, i.e. knowing V_j^M for all $0 \leq j \leq M$ where M is the number of time steps.

Returning to the American option problem, arbitrage is possible if the option value goes below the payoff at any time. If our theoretical value falls below the payoff then it is time to exercise. If we do then exercise the option its value and the payoff must be the same. If we find that

$$\frac{V_{j+1}^{n+1} - V_j^{n+1}}{u - v} + \frac{1}{1 + r\,\delta t}\frac{uV_j^{n+1} - vV_{j+1}^{n+1}}{u - v} \geq \text{Payoff}(S_j^n)$$

then we use this as our new value. But if

$$\frac{V_{j+1}^{n+1} - V_j^{n+1}}{u - v} + \frac{1}{1 + r\,\delta t}\frac{uV_j^{n+1} - vV_{j+1}^{n+1}}{u - v} < \text{Payoff}(S_j^n)$$

we should exercise, giving us a better value of

$$V_j^n = \text{Payoff}(S_j^n).$$

We can put these two together to get

$$V_j^n = \max\left(\frac{V_{j+1}^{n+1} - V_j^{n+1}}{u - v} + \frac{1}{1 + r\,\delta t}\frac{uV_j^{n+1} - vV_{j+1}^{n+1}}{u - v}, \text{Payoff}(S_j^n)\right)$$

instead of (3.3). This ensures that there are no arbitrage opportunities. This modification is easy to code, but note that the payoff is a function of the asset price at the node in question. This is new and not seen in the European problem for which we did not have to keep track of the asset values on each of the nodes.

Below is a function for calculating the value of an American-style option. Note the differences between this program and the one for the European-style exercise. The code is the same except that we keep track of more information and the line that updates the option value incorporates the no-arbitrage condition.

```
Function USPrice(Asset As Double, Volatility _
                 As Double, IntRate As _
                 Double, Strike As _
                 Double, Expiry As _
                 Double, NoSteps _
                 As Integer)
ReDim S(0 To NoSteps, 0 To NoSteps)
ReDim V(0 To NoSteps, 0 To NoSteps)
time step = Expiry / NoSteps
DiscountFactor = Exp(-IntRate * time step)
temp1 = Exp((IntRate + Volatility * Volatility) * time step)
temp2 = 0.5 * (DiscountFactor + temp1)
u = temp2 + Sqr(temp2 * temp2 - 1)
d = 1 / u
p = (Exp(IntRate * time step) - d) / (u - d)

S(0, 0) = Asset
For n = 1 To NoSteps
    For j = n To 1 Step -1
        S(j, n) = u * S(j - 1, n - 1)
    Next j
        S(0, n) = d * S(0, n - 1)
Next n

For j = 0 To NoSteps
    V(j, NoSteps) = Payoff(S(j, NoSteps), Strike)
Next j
For n = NoSteps To 1 Step -1
    For j = 0 To NoSteps - 1
        V(j, n - 1) = max((p * V(j + 1, n) + (1 - p) * V(j, n)) _
            * DiscountFactor, Payoff(S(j, n - 1), Strike))
    Next j

Next n
USPrice = V(0, 0)
End Function
```

CODE FOR A US OPTION, IT'S NOT THAT MUCH DIFFERENT FROM THE EURO PROGRAM

Working code

3.21   **THE CONTINUOUS-TIME LIMIT**

As I mentioned, the binomial model is useful for explaining delta hedging and risk neutrality but not so great as a numerical method. But it can also lead us to the famous Black–Scholes equation. The binomial model is a discrete-time model whereas Black–Scholes is in continuous time. So let's examine (3.3) as $\delta t \to 0$.

First of all, we have chosen

$$u \sim 1 + \sigma \sqrt{\delta t}$$

and

$$v \sim 1 - \sigma \sqrt{\delta t}.$$

Next we write

$$V = V(S, t), \quad V^+ = V(uS, t + \delta t) \quad \text{and} \quad V^- = V(vS, t + \delta t).$$

Expanding these expressions in Taylor series[3] for small δt and substituting into (3.2) we find that

$$\Delta \sim \frac{\partial V}{\partial S} \quad \text{as} \quad \delta t \to 0.$$

Thus the binomial delta becomes, in the limit, the Black–Scholes delta.

Similarly, we can substitute the expressions for V, V^+ and V^- into (3.3) to find

$$\frac{\partial V}{\partial t} + \tfrac{1}{2}\sigma^2 S^2 \frac{\partial^2 V}{\partial S^2} + rS \frac{\partial V}{\partial S} - rV = 0.$$

This is the Black–Scholes equation. Again, the drift rate μ has disappeared from the equation. We'll be seeing a better derivation of this equation soon.

This famous equation will be derived later using stochastic calculus rather than via the binomial model. The stochastic calculus derivation is far more useful than the binomial, being far easier to generalize. And from the next chapter on there will be no more mention of u, v and p and the binomial model, everything will be in terms of drift rate and volatility (and even the drift rate disappears from most basic models, so it's really only volatility we'll be talking about).

3.22   **SUMMARY**

In this chapter I described the basics of the binomial model, deriving pricing equations and algorithms for both European- and American-style exercises. The method can be extended in many ways, to incorporate dividends, to allow Bermudan exercise, to value path-dependent contracts and to price contracts depending on other stochastic variables such as interest rates. I have not gone into the method in any detail for the simple reason that the binomial method is just a simple version of an explicit finite-difference scheme. As such it will be discussed in depth in Chapter 28. Finite-difference methods have an obvious advantage over the binomial method; they are far more flexible. I've said it a million times already, it seems, but let me say one more time: The binomial model is great for getting intuition about delta hedging and risk-neutral pricing but not for real-life pricing. So we won't be seeing any more of the binomial model from Chapter 4 on.

---

[3] If you are rusty on Taylor series then Appendix A contains a useful recap.

FURTHER READING

- The original binomial concept is due to Cox. *et al*. (1979).

- Almost every book on options describes the binomial method in more depth than I do. One of the best is Hull (2005) who also describes its use in the fixed-income world.

WELCOME TO MY WORLD

I'd like to introduce you to the inhabitants of planet Risk Neutral, in a distant, imaginary part of the universe. The people of Risk Neutral are strange, ethereal creatures, with little care for the pleasures of the flesh. Satisfaction to them comes from the world of the mind, the world of ideas, concepts, symbols, and especially abstract probability theory. Yes, they're very much like UK academics.

Risk Neutrals do not care for money. Their culture has no concept of 'risk.' Since they have no concept of risk, they also do not have any need to be compensated for taking risk. To them value and expectation are identical.

If we were to send a delegation of Earthlings to planet Risk Neutral with our binomial model and option pricing question they might behave as follows.

'Gentlemen of Risk Neutral,' we say, 'please would you put your undoubted mathematical skills to use on our perplexing problem from the world of finance?'

'We can but try,' they reply.

'We have a stock that is currently valued at $100. Tomorrow it will be worth either $101 or $99. The probability of the stock being at $101 is...' We are just about to say '60%,' the result of many months of painstaking statistical analysis. But before we can finish our sentence we are interrupted.

'Do not tell us the probability. We are perfectly capable of working this out for ourselves.'

How is this possible? How can the Risk Neutrals calculate this probability without any more data than the $100, the $101 and the $99?

Recall that Risk Neutrals do not understand risk, that they ought to have a positive expectation for a risky investment. Therefore they reckon that the $100 must be the expected stock price tomorrow, suitably discounted. (They do have interest-bearing bank accounts on Risk Neutral. But at the time of our visit interest rates were conveniently zero.)

'What is the probability then?' we ask.

'Clearly it is 50%.'

If interest rates are zero then they have solved the simple problem

$$p'101 + (1 - p')99 = 100.$$

The p' is therefore 0.5.

Now this is wrong. The probability is not 0.5, it *is* 0.6. However, we Earthlings are far too polite to disabuse them. After all we have only just met. So we continue with our problem. We explain to them about the idea of options and payoffs.

'The option payoff is one dollar if the stock rises and zero otherwise, what is the value of the option today?'

'It must be zero point five multiplied by one, plus zero point five multiplied by zero. So zero point five.' Their answer is 0.5. They have calculated a simple expectation based on their incorrect probability.

Yet this is correct. They have found the correct answer despite making a fundamental mistake; they have valued in terms of expectations. But this mistake has been made twice. Once they have calculated probability from price, and the second time price from probability. The second mistake reverses the first.

This method pricing always works. If interest rates were not zero on Risk Neutral then they would need to present value twice in the above calculations, in both the stock expectations calculation that yielded the risk-neutral probability p' and in the option valuation calculation. On the Risk Neutral planet they believe, erroneously, that all traded investments grow on average at the risk-free interest rate.

As we are leaving the planet to return to Earth we overhear two Risk Neutrals talking about trying their hand[4] at investing in the options market. They are in for a shock. They are very rapidly going to learn about risk. They may have successfully priced the option, but they have yet to discover hedging.

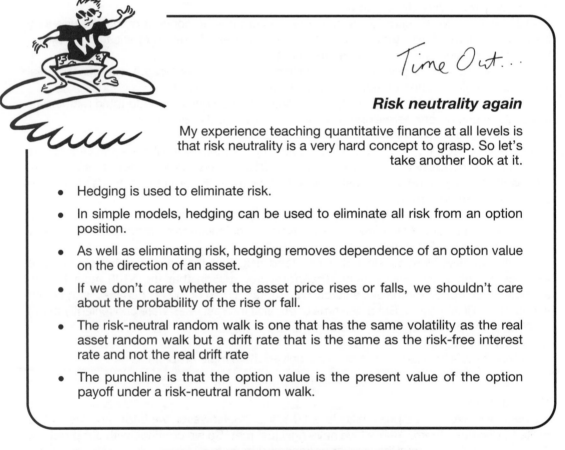

Time Out...

Risk neutrality again

My experience teaching quantitative finance at all levels is that risk neutrality is a very hard concept to grasp. So let's take another look at it.

- Hedging is used to eliminate risk.

- In simple models, hedging can be used to eliminate all risk from an option position.

- As well as eliminating risk, hedging removes dependence of an option value on the direction of an asset.

- If we don't care whether the asset price rises or falls, we shouldn't care about the probability of the rise or fall.

- The risk-neutral random walk is one that has the same volatility as the real asset random walk but a drift rate that is the same as the risk-free interest rate and not the real drift rate

- The punchline is that the option value is the present value of the option payoff under a risk-neutral random walk.

APPENDIX: ANOTHER PARAMETERIZATION

The three constants u, v and p are chosen to give the binomial walk the same drift and standard deviation as the stock we are trying to model. Having only these two equations for the three parameters gives us one degree of freedom in this choice. I've chosen the parametrization that results in the tidiest math. But this degree of freedom is often used

---

[4] Actually it's more like a paw.

to give the random walk the further property that after an up and a down movement (or a down followed by an up) the asset returns to its starting value, S.[5] This gives us the requirement that

$$v(uS) = u(vS) = S$$

i.e.

$$uv = 1. \tag{3.5}$$

For the binomial random walk to have the correct drift over a time period of δt we need

$$puS + (1 - p)vS = SE\left[e^{(\mu - \frac{1}{2}\sigma^2)\delta t + \sigma\phi\sqrt{\delta t}}\right] = Se^{\mu \, \delta t},$$

i.e.

$$pu + (1 - p)v = e^{\mu \, \delta t}.$$

Where all these exponentials and things come from will be clear after the next chapter, so you may want to read this appendix again later. Rearranging this equation we get

$$p = \frac{e^{\mu \, \delta t} - v}{u - v}. \tag{3.6}$$

Then for the binomial random walk to have the correct variance we need (details omitted)

$$pu^2 + (1 - p)v^2 = e^{(2\mu + \sigma^2)\delta t}. \tag{3.7}$$

Equations (3.5), (3.6) and (3.7) can be solved to give

$$u = \frac{1}{2}\left(e^{-\mu \, \delta t} + e^{(\mu + \sigma^2)\delta t}\right) + \frac{1}{2}\sqrt{\left(e^{-\mu \, \delta t} + e^{(\mu + \sigma^2)\delta t}\right)^2 - 4}.$$

Approximations that are good enough for most purposes are

$$u \approx 1 + \sigma \, \delta t^{1/2} + \frac{1}{2}\sigma^2 \delta t,$$

$$v \approx 1 - \sigma \, \delta t^{1/2} + \frac{1}{2}\sigma^2 \delta t$$

and

$$p \approx \frac{1}{2} + \frac{(\mu - \frac{1}{2}\sigma^2)\delta t^{1/2}}{2\sigma}.$$

Of course, if this is being used for pricing options you must replace the μ with r everywhere.

---

[5] Other choices are possible. For example, sometimes the probability of an up move is set equal to the probability of a down move, i.e. $p = 1/2$.

EXERCISES

1. Solve the three equations for u, v and p using the alternative condition $p = \frac{1}{2}$ instead of the condition that the tree returns to where it started, i.e. $uv = 1$.

2. Starting from the approximations for u and v, check that in the limit $\delta t \to 0$ we recover the Black–Scholes equation.

3. A share price is currently $80. At the end of three months, it will be either $84 or $76. Ignoring interest rates, calculate the value of a three-month European call option with exercise price $79. You must use both the methods of setting up the delta-hedged portfolio, and the risk-neutral probability method.

4. A share price is currently $92. At the end of one year, it will be either $86 or $98. Calculate the value of a one-year European call option with exercise price $90 using a single-step binomial tree. The risk-free interest rate is 2% p.a. with continuous compounding. You must use both the methods of setting up the delta-hedged portfolio, and the risk-neutral probability method.

5. A share price is currently $45. At the end of each of the next two months, it will change by going up $2 or going down $2. Calculate the value of a two month European call option with exercise price $44. The risk-free interest rate is 6% p.a. with continuous compounding. You must use both the methods of setting up the delta-hedged portfolio, and the risk-neutral probability method.

6. A share price is currently $63. At the end of each three month period, it will change by going up $3 or going down $3. Calculate the value of a six month American put option with exercise price $61. The risk-free interest rate is 4% p.a. with continuous compounding. You must use both the methods of setting up the delta-hedged portfolio, and the risk-neutral probability method.

7. A share price is currently $15. At the end of three months, it will be either $13 or $17. Ignoring interest rates, calculate the value of a three-month European option with payoff $\max(S^2 - 159, 0)$, where S is the share price at the end of three months. You must use both the methods of setting up the delta-hedged portfolio, and the risk-neutral probability method.

8. A share price is currently $180. At the end of one year, it will be either $203 or $152. The risk-free interest rate is 3% p.a. with continuous compounding. Consider an American put on this underlying. Find the exercise price for which holding the option for the year is equivalent to exercising immediately. This is the break-even exercise price. What effect would a decrease in the interest rate have on this break-even price?

9. A share price is currently $75. At the end of three months, it will be either $59 or $92. What is the risk-neutral probability that the share price increases? The risk-free interest rate is 4% p.a. with continuous compounding.

CHAPTER 4
the random behavior of assets

The aim of this Chapter...

...is to demonstrate mathematical modeling in practice, to take the reader from an analysis of stock price data towards a probabilistic model for the behavior of asset prices. The fundamental model we build up will later be used as the starting point for deriving the famous Black–Scholes model for option prices. By the end of this chapter the reader will feel comfortable performing a simple analysis of any financial data.

In this Chapter...

- more notation commonly used in mathematical finance

- how to examine time-series data to model returns

- the Wiener process, a mathematical model of randomness

- a simple model for equities, currencies, commodities and indices

4.1 **INTRODUCTION**

In the first few chapters you've seen some basic financial instruments, and you've seen some of the important financial concepts such as no arbitrage and hedging. Now we are going to go right back to first principles with data analysis and modeling. We'll also start to see some stochastic calculus. No more of that binomial nonsense, although it gave us some useful insight at the time. (Do you get the sense that I have a mission here?) In this chapter I describe a simple continuous-time model for equities and other financial instruments, inspired by our earlier coin-tossing experiment. This takes us into the world of stochastic calculus and Wiener processes. Although there is a great deal of theory behind the ideas I describe, I am going to explain everything in as simple and accessible manner as possible. We will be modeling the behavior of equities, currencies and commodities, but the ideas are applicable to the fixed-income world as well.

4.2 **THE POPULAR FORMS OF 'ANALYSIS'**

There are three forms of 'analysis' commonly used in the financial world:

- Fundamental

- Technical

- Quantitative

Fundamental analysis is all about trying to determine the 'correct' worth of a company by an in-depth study of balance sheets, management teams, patent applications, competitors, lawsuits, etc. In other words, getting to the heart of the firm, doing lots of accounting and projections and what-not. This sounds like a really sensible way to model a company and hence its stock price. There are unfortunately two difficulties with this approach. First it is very, very hard. You need a degree in accounting and plenty of patience. And even then all the most important stuff can be hidden 'off balance sheet.' Second, and more importantly, 'The market can stay irrational longer than you can stay solvent' (Keynes). In other words, even if you have the perfect model for the value of a firm it doesn't mean you can make money. You have to find some mispricing and then hope that the rest of the world starts to see your point of view. And this may never happen. If fundamental analysis is hard, then the next form of analysis is the exact opposite, because it is so easy.

Technical analysis is when you don't care anything about the company other than the information contained within its stock price history. You draw trendlines, look for specific patterns in the share price and make predictions accordingly. This is the subject of Appendix B. Most academic evidence suggests that most technical analysis is bunk.

The final form of analysis is the one we are really concerned with in this book, and is the form that has been most successful over the last 50 years, forming a solid foundation for portfolio theory, derivatives pricing and risk management. It is **quantitative analysis**. Quantitative analysis is all about treating financial quantities such as stock prices or interest rates as random, and then choosing the best models for that randomness. Let's see why randomness is important and then build up a simple, random, stock price model.

4.3 **WHY WE NEED A MODEL FOR RANDOMNESS: JENSEN'S INEQUALITY**

Why is 'randomness' so crucial to modeling the world of derivatives? Why can't we just try to forecast the future stock price as best we can and figure out the option's payoff? To best see the importance of randomness in option theory let's take a look at some very simple mathematics, called **Jensen's inequality**.

The stock price today is 100. Let's suppose that in one year's time it could be 50 or 150, with both equally likely. See Figure 4.1. How can we value an option on this stock, a call option with a strike of 100 expiring in one year, say?

Two ways spring to mind.

With those two possible scenarios we could say that we expect the stock price to be at 100 in one year, this being the average of the possible future values. The payoff for the call option would then be 0, since it is exactly at the money. And the present value of this is zero. Could this be the way to value an option?

Probably not. You expect the value to be greater than zero, since half the time there is some payoff.

Alternatively we could look at the two possible payoffs and then calculate that expectation. If the stock falls to 50 then the payoff is zero, if it rises to 150 then the payoff is 50.

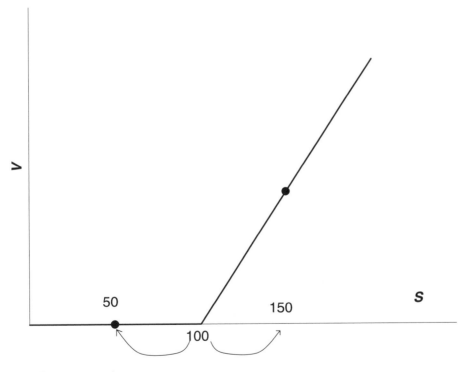

Figure 4.1   Future scenarios.

The average payoff is therefore 25, which we could present value to give us some idea of the option's value.

It turns out that the second calculation is closer to what we do in practice to value options (although we know that the *real* probabilities don't come into the calculation) and we'll see lots of this throughout the book. But that calculation also illustrates another point of great importance, that the order in which we do the payoff calculation and the expectation matters. In this example we had

$$\text{Payoff (Expected [Stock price])} = 0$$

whereas

$$\text{Expected [Payoff(Stock price)]} = 25.$$

This is an example of Jensen's inequality. Let's use some symbols. If we have a convex function $f(S)$ (in our example the payoff function for a call) of a random variable S (in our example the stock price) then

$$E[f(S)] \geq f(E[S]). \tag{4.1}$$

We can even get an idea of how much greater the left-hand side is than the right-hand side by using a Taylor series approximation around the mean of S. Write

$$S = \bar{S} + \epsilon,$$

where $\bar{S} = E[S]$, so the $E[\epsilon] = 0$. Then

$$E[f(S)] = E\left[f(\bar{S} + \epsilon)\right] = E\left[f(\bar{S}) + \epsilon f'(\bar{S}) + \tfrac{1}{2}\epsilon^2 f''(\bar{S}) + \cdots\right]$$

$$\approx f(\bar{S}) + \tfrac{1}{2}f''(\bar{S})E\left[\epsilon^2\right]$$

$$= f(E[S]) + \tfrac{1}{2}f''(E[S])E\left[\epsilon^2\right].$$

So the left-hand side of (4.1) is greater than the right by approximately

$$\tfrac{1}{2}f''(E[S])\, E\left[\epsilon^2\right].$$

This shows the importance of two concepts:

- $f''(E[S])$: The **convexity** of an option. As a rule this adds value to an option. It also means that any intuition we may get from linear contracts (forwards and futures) might not be helpful with non-linear instruments such as options.

- $E\left[\epsilon^2\right]$: Randomness in the underlying, and its **variance**. As stated above, modeling randomness is the key to modeling options.

Now we have seen a hint as to why randomness is so important, let's start modeling some assets! The new model we'll be seeing for assets is not unlike the binomial model just described, just a lot more realistic.

4.4 SIMILARITIES BETWEEN EQUITIES, CURRENCIES, COMMODITIES AND INDICES

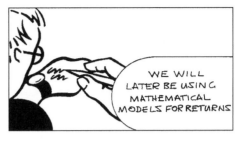

WE WILL LATER BE USING MATHEMATICAL MODELS FOR RETURNS

When you invest in something, whether it is a stock, commodity, work of art or a racehorse, your main concern is that you will make a comfortable return on your investment. By **return** we tend to mean the percentage growth in the value of an asset, together with accumulated dividends, over some period:

$$\text{Return} = \frac{\text{Change in value of the asset} + \text{accumulated cashflows}}{\text{Original value of the asset}}.$$

I want to distinguish here between the percentage or relative growth and the absolute growth. Suppose we could invest in either of two stocks, both of which grow on average by $10 *per annum*. Stock A has a value of $100 and stock B is currently worth $1000. Clearly the former is a better investment, at the end of the year stock A will probably be worth around $110 (if the past is anything to go by) and stock B $1010. Both have gone up by $10, but A has risen by 10% and B by only 1%. If we have $1000 to invest we would be better off investing in ten of asset A than one of asset B. This illustrates that when we come to model assets, it is the return that we should concentrate on. In this respect, all of equities, currencies, commodities and stock market indices can be treated similarly. What return do we expect to get from them?

Part of the business of estimating returns for each asset is to estimate how much unpredictability there is in the asset value. In the next section I am going to show that randomness plays a large part in financial markets, and start to build up a model for asset returns incorporating this randomness.

Time Out...

Returns

Here is another way of understanding why returns are more important than actual stock price. Suppose I told you that one stock had a value of 5 and another 500. You would think nothing of it. Now suppose I told you that one currency had an interest rate of 5% and another had an interest rate of 500%. Whoa...you'd be somewhat surprised by the currency with the 500% interest rate, wouldn't you? There's a big clue in such an observation. We don't care about the absolute value of a stock price, only its return. So let's analyze and model returns. When we come to modeling interest rates we won't have such a valuable clue to help us. This makes interest rate modeling harder than equity modeling.

4.5 **EXAMINING RETURNS**

In Figure 4.2 I show the quoted price of Perez Companc, an Argentinian conglomerate, over the period February 1995 to November 1996. This is a very typical plot of a financial asset. The asset shows a general upward trend over the period but this is far from guaranteed. If you bought and sold at the wrong times you would lose a lot of money. The unpredictability that is seen in this figure is the main feature of financial modeling. Because there is so much randomness, any mathematical model of a financial asset must acknowledge the randomness and have a probabilistic foundation.

On a spreadsheet, I include some data for you to play with

Remembering that the returns are more important to us than the absolute level of the asset price, I show in Figure 4.3 how to calculate returns on a spreadsheet. Denoting the asset value on the ith day by S_i, then the return from day i to day $i+1$ is given by

$$\frac{S_{i+1} - S_i}{S_i} = R_i.$$

(I've ignored dividends here, they are easily allowed for, especially since they only get paid two or four times a year typically.) Of course, I didn't need to use data spaced at intervals of a day, I will comment on this later.

In Figure 4.4 I show the daily returns for Perez Companc. This looks very much like 'noise,' and that is exactly how we are going to model it. The mean of the returns

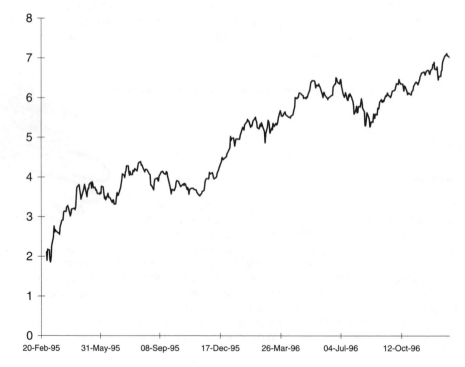

Figure 4.2   Perez Companc from February 1995 to November 1996.

Date	Perez	Return			
01-Mar-95	2.11		Average return	0.002916	
02-Mar-95	1.90	-0.1	Standard deviation	0.024521	
03-Mar-95	2.18	0.149906			
06-Mar-95	2.16	-0.01081			
07-Mar-95	1.91	-0.11258	=AVERAGE(C3:C463)		
08-Mar-95	1.86	-0.02985			
09-Mar-95	1.97	0.061538			
10-Mar-95	2.27	0.15	=STDEVP(C3:C463)		
13-Mar-95	2.49	0.099874			
14-Mar-95	2.76	0.108565			
15-Mar-95	2.61	-0.05426			
16-Mar-95	2.67	0.021858			
17-Mar-95	2.64	-0.0107			
20-Mar-95	2.60	-0.01622	=(B13-B12)/B12		
21-Mar-95	2.59	-0.00275			
22-Mar-95	2.59	-0.00275			
23-Mar-95	2.55	-0.01232			
24-Mar-95	2.73	0.069307			
27-Mar-95	2.91	0.064815			
28-Mar-95	2.92	0.002899			
29-Mar-95	2.92	0			
30-Mar-95	3.12	0.069364			
31-Mar-95	3.14	0.005405			
03-Apr-95	3.13	-0.00269			
04-Apr-95	3.24	0.037736			
05-Apr-95	3.25	0.002597			
06-Apr-95	3.28	0.007772			
07-Apr-95	3.21	-0.02057			
10-Apr-95	3.02	-0.06037			
11-Apr-95	3.08	0.019553			
12-Apr-95	3.19	0.035616			
17-Apr-95	3.21	0.007936			
18-Apr-95	3.17	-0.01312			
19-Apr-95	3.24	0.021277			

IT COULDN'T
BE EASIER

Figure 4.3 Spreadsheet for calculating asset returns.

distribution is

$$\overline{R} = \frac{1}{M} \sum_{i=1}^{M} R_i \tag{4.2}$$

and the sample standard deviation is

$$\sqrt{\frac{1}{M-1} \sum_{i=1}^{M} (R_i - \overline{R})^2}, \tag{4.3}$$

where M is the number of returns in the sample (one fewer than the number of asset prices). From the data in this example we find that the mean is 0.002916 and the standard deviation is 0.024521.

Notice how the mean daily return is much smaller than the standard deviation. This is very typical of financial quantities over short timescales. On a day-by-day basis you will tend to see the noise in the stock price, and will have to wait months perhaps before you can spot the trend.

The frequency distribution of this time series of daily returns is easily calculated, and very instructive to plot. In Excel use Tools | Data Analysis | Histogram. In Figure 4.5 is

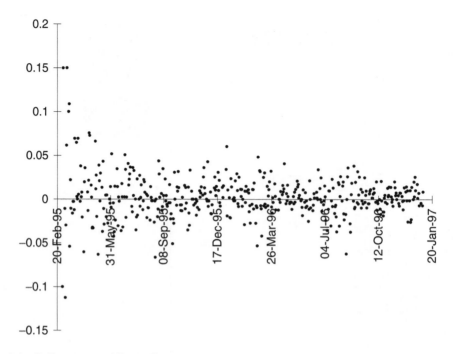

Figure 4.4   Daily returns of Perez Companc.

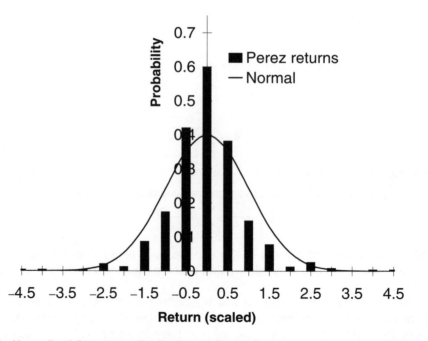

Figure 4.5   Normalized frequency distribution of Perez Companc and the standardized Normal distribution.

shown the frequency distribution of daily returns for Perez Companc. This distribution has been scaled and translated to give it a mean of zero, a standard deviation of one and an area under the curve of one. On the same plot is drawn the probability density function for the standardized Normal distribution function

$$\frac{1}{\sqrt{2\pi}}e^{-\frac{1}{2}\phi^2},$$

where ϕ is a standardized Normal variable.[1] The two curves are not identical but are fairly close.

Supposing that we believe that the empirical returns are close enough to Normal for this to be a good approximation, then we have come a long way towards a model. I am going to write the returns as a random variable, drawn from a Normal distribution with a known, constant, non-zero mean and a known, constant, non-zero standard deviation:

$$R_i = \frac{S_{i+1} - S_i}{S_i} = \text{mean} + \text{standard deviation} \times \phi.$$

Figure 4.6 shows the returns distribution of Glaxo–Wellcome as calculated by Bloomberg. This has not been normalized.

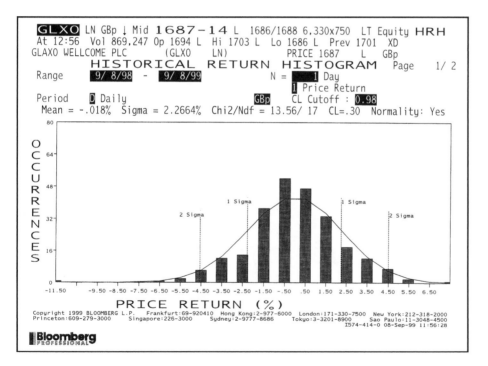

Figure 4.6 Glaxo–Wellcome returns histogram. Source: Bloomberg L.P.

---

[1] Think of a number, any number ... funny, that's the number I was thinking of.

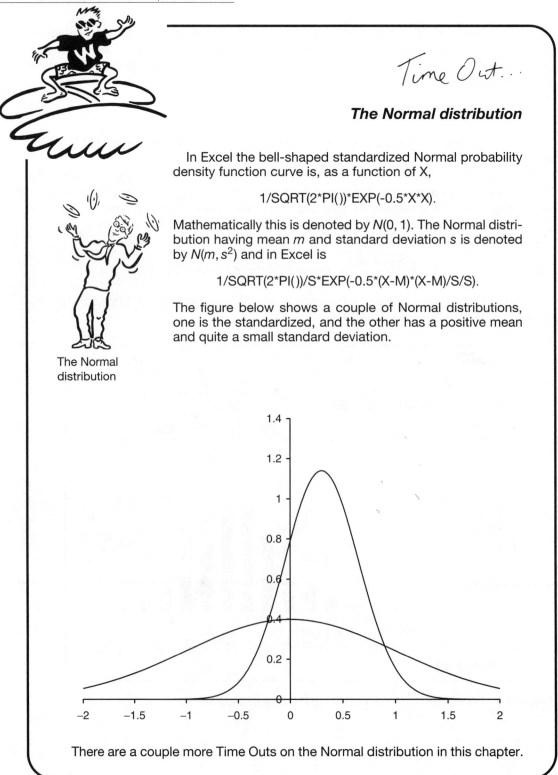

Time Out...

The Normal distribution

In Excel the bell-shaped standardized Normal probability density function curve is, as a function of X,

1/SQRT(2*PI())*EXP(-0.5*X*X).

Mathematically this is denoted by $N(0, 1)$. The Normal distribution having mean m and standard deviation s is denoted by $N(m, s^2)$ and in Excel is

1/SQRT(2*PI())/S*EXP(-0.5*(X-M)*(X-M)/S/S).

The figure below shows a couple of Normal distributions, one is the standardized, and the other has a positive mean and quite a small standard deviation.

The Normal distribution

There are a couple more Time Outs on the Normal distribution in this chapter.

4.6 **TIMESCALES**

How do the mean and standard deviation of the returns' time series, as estimated by (4.2) and (4.3), scale with the time step between asset price measurements? In the example the time step is one day, but suppose I sampled at hourly intervals or weekly, how would this affect the distribution?

Call the time step δt. The mean of the return scales with the size of the time step. That is, the larger the time between sampling the more the asset will have moved in the meantime, *on average*. I can write

$$\text{mean} = \mu\,\delta t,$$

for some μ which we will assume to be constant. This is the same μ as in Chapter 3, representing the annualized average return or the drift.

Ignoring randomness for the moment, our model is simply

$$\frac{S_{i+1} - S_i}{S_i} = \mu\,\delta t.$$

Rearranging, we get

$$S_{i+1} = S_i(1 + \mu\,\delta t).$$

If the asset begins at S_0 at time $t = 0$ then after one time step $t = \delta t$ and

$$S_1 = S_0(1 + \mu\,\delta t).$$

After two time steps $t = 2\,\delta t$ and

$$S_2 = S_1(1 + \mu\,\delta t) = S_0(1 + \mu\,\delta t)^2,$$

and after M time steps $t = M\,\delta t = T$ and

$$S_M = S_0(1 + \mu\,\delta t)^M.$$

This is just

$$S_M = S_0\,(1 + \mu\,\delta t)^M = S_0 e^{M\log(1+\mu\,\delta t)} \approx S_0 e^{\mu M\,\delta t} = S_0 e^{\mu T}.$$

In the limit as the time step tends to zero with the total time T fixed, this approximation becomes exact. This result is important for two reasons.

First, in the absence of any randomness the asset exhibits exponential growth, just like cash in the bank.

Second, the model is meaningful in the limit as the time step tends to zero. If I had chosen to scale the mean of the returns distribution with any other power of δt it would have resulted in either a trivial model ($S_T = S_0$) or infinite values for the asset.

The second point can guide us in the choice of scaling for the random component of the return. How does the standard deviation of the return scale with the time step δt? Again, consider what happens after $T/\delta t$ time steps each of size δt (i.e. after a total time of T). Inside the square root in expression (4.3) there are a large number of terms,

$T/\delta t$ of them. In order for the standard deviation to remain finite as we let δt tend to zero, the individual terms in the expression must each be of $O(\delta t)$. Since each term is a square of a return, the standard deviation of the asset return over a time step δt must be $O(\delta t^{1/2})$:

$$\text{standard deviation} = \sigma \, \delta t^{1/2},$$

where σ is some parameter measuring the amount of randomness, the larger this parameter the more uncertain is the return. This σ is the same σ we saw in Chapter 3. It is the annualized standard deviation of asset returns.

Putting these scalings explicitly into our asset return model

$$R_i = \frac{S_{i+1} - S_i}{S_i} = \mu \, \delta t + \sigma \phi \, \delta t^{1/2}. \tag{4.4}$$

I can rewrite Equation (4.4) as

$$S_{i+1} - S_i = \mu S_i \, \delta t + \sigma S_i \phi \, \delta t^{1/2}. \tag{4.5}$$

The left-hand side of this equation is the change in the asset price from time step i to time step $i + 1$. The right-hand side is the 'model.' We can think of this equation as a model for a **random walk** of the asset price. This is shown schematically in Figure 4.7. We know exactly where the asset price is today but tomorrow's value is unknown. It is distributed about today's value according to (4.5).

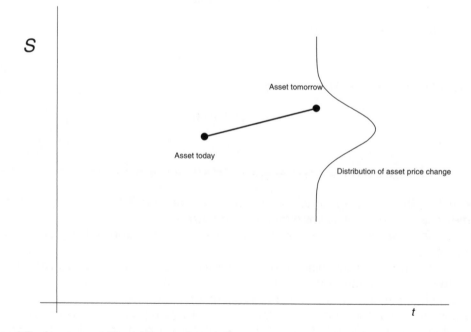

Figure 4.7   A representation of the random walk.

Time Out...

Binomial versus Normal

We've been considering two models for the asset return, the binomial and the Normal. The figure below shows what these two look like. Although completely different, they both should have the same mean return and standard deviation as the asset we are modeling.

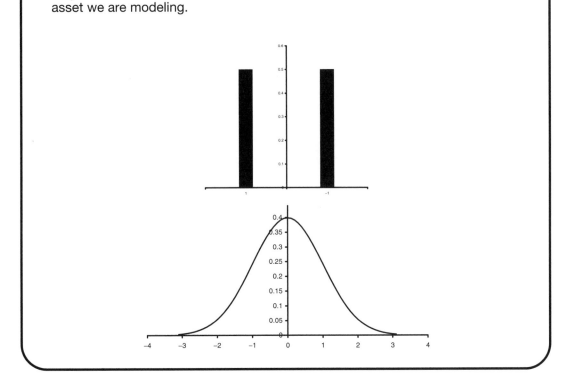

4.6.1 The drift

The parameter μ is called the **drift rate**, the **expected return** or the **growth rate** of the asset. Statistically it is very hard to measure since the mean scales with the usually small parameter δt. It can be estimated by

$$\mu = \frac{1}{M \, \delta t} \sum_{i=1}^{M} R_i.$$

The unit of time that is usually used is the year, in which case μ is quoted as an *annualized* growth rate.

In the classical option pricing theory the drift plays almost no role. So even though it is hard to measure, this doesn't matter too much.[2]

4.6.2   The volatility

The parameter σ is called the **volatility** of the asset. It can be estimated by

$$\sqrt{\frac{1}{(M-1)\,\delta t}\sum_{i=1}^{M}(R_i - \overline{R})^2}.$$

Again, this is almost always quoted in annualized terms.

The volatility is the most important and elusive quantity in the theory of derivatives. I will come back again and again to its estimation and modeling.

Because of their scaling with time, the drift and volatility have different effects on the asset path. The drift is not apparent over short timescales for which the volatility dominates. Over long timescales, for instance decades, the drift becomes important. Figure 4.8 is a realized path of the logarithm of an asset, together with its expected path and a 'confidence interval.' In this example the confidence interval represents one standard deviation. With the assumption of Normality this means that 68% of the time the asset should be within this range. The mean path is growing linearly in time and the confidence interval grows like the square root of time. Thus over short timescales the volatility dominates.

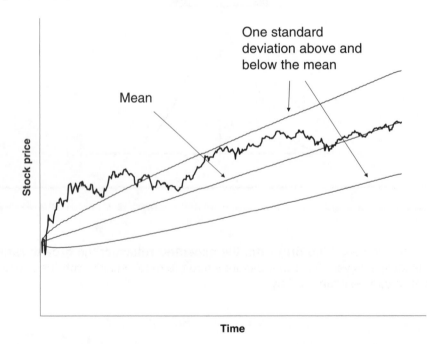

Figure 4.8   Path of the logarithm of an asset, its expected path and one standard deviation above and below.

---

[2] In non-classical theories and in portfolio management, it *does* often matter, very much.

4.7 **ESTIMATING VOLATILITY**

The most common estimate of volatility is simply

$$\sqrt{\frac{1}{(M-1)\,\delta t}\sum_{i=1}^{M}(R_i - \overline{R})^2}.$$

If δt is sufficiently small the mean return $\overline{R}$ term can be ignored. For small δt

$$\sqrt{\frac{1}{(M-1)\,\delta t}\sum_{i=1}^{M}\left(\log S(t_i) - \log S(t_{i-1})\right)^2}$$

can also be used, where $S(t_i)$ is the closing price on day t_i.

It is highly unlikely that volatility is constant for any given asset. Changing economic circumstances, seasonality, etc. will inevitably result in volatility changing with time. If you want to know the volatility today you must use some past data in the calculation. Unfortunately, this means that there is no guarantee that you are actually calculating *today's* volatility.

Typically you would use daily closing prices to work out daily returns and then use the past 10, 30, 100, ... daily returns in the formula above. Or you could use returns over longer or shorter periods. Since all returns are equally weighted, while they are in the estimate of volatility, any large return will stay in the estimate of vol until the 10 (or 30 or 100) days have past. This gives rise to a plateauing of volatility, and is totally spurious.

4.8 **THE RANDOM WALK ON A SPREADSHEET**

The random walk (4.5) can be written as a 'recipe' for generating S_{i+1} from S_i:

$$S_{i+1} = S_i\left(1 + \mu\,\delta t + \sigma\phi\,\delta t^{1/2}\right). \tag{4.6}$$

We can easily simulate the model using a spreadsheet. In this simulation we must input several parameters, a starting value for the asset, a time step δt, the drift rate μ, the volatility σ and the total number of time steps. Then, at each time step, we must choose a random number ϕ from a Normal distribution. I will talk about simulations in depth in Chapter 29, for the moment let me just say that an approximation to a Normal variable that is fast in a spreadsheet, and quite accurate, is simply to add up twelve random variables drawn from a uniform distribution over zero to one, and subtract six:

This is very simple to implement

$$\left(\sum_{i=1}^{12}\mathrm{RAND}()\right) - 6.$$

I USE THIS ALL THE TIME, IT'S QUICK AND EASY AND GOOD ENOUGH FOR MOST PURPOSES

The Excel spreadsheet function RAND() gives a uniformly distributed random variable.

	A	B	C	D	E	F	G	H
1	Asset	100		Time	Asset			
2	Drift	0.15		0	100			
3	Volatility	0.25		0.01	98.38844			
4	Timestep	0.01		0.02	94.28005			
5				0.03	95.40441			
6				0.04	92.79735			
7	=D4+$B$4			0.05	93.45168			
8				0.06	93.99664			
9				0.07	97.66597			
10				0.08	96.52319			
11	=E7*(1+$B$2*$B$4+$B$3*SQRT($B$4)*(RAND()+RAND()+RAND()+RAND()							
12	+RAND()+RAND()+RAND()+RAND()+RAND()+RAND()+RAND()+RAND()-6))							
13				0.11	99.60075			
14				0.12	99.01974			
15				0.13	100.8729			
16				0.14	101.2378			
17				0.15	102.4736			
18				0.16	102.7694			
19				0.17	100.7347			
20				0.18	102.7021			
21				0.19	107.3493			
22				0.2	109.887			
23				0.21	108.688			
24				0.22	110.7826			
25				0.23	112.8932			
26				0.24	111.0625			
27				0.25	111.6157			
28				0.26	112.5443			
29				0.27	111.9805			
30				0.28	115.6002			
31				0.29	117.9831			
32				0.3	115.2694			
33				0.31	117.4374			

Figure 4.9   Simulating the random walk on a spreadsheet.

In Figure 4.9 I show the details of a spreadsheet used for simulating the asset price random walk.

Time Out...

Excel and the approximation to the Normal

You can draw Normally distributed random numbers in Excel using NORMSINV(RAND()). But this is very slow. Below are the distributions for the real Normal and the approximate Normal using 10,000 random numbers. Not bad?

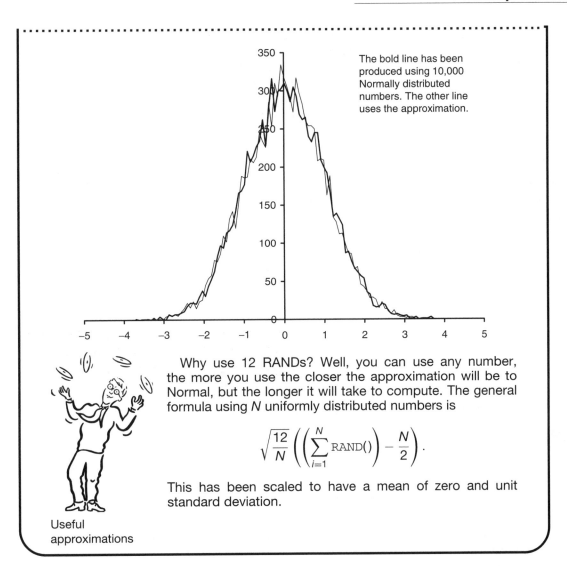

The bold line has been produced using 10,000 Normally distributed numbers. The other line uses the approximation.

Why use 12 RANDs? Well, you can use any number, the more you use the closer the approximation will be to Normal, but the longer it will take to compute. The general formula using N uniformly distributed numbers is

$$\sqrt{\frac{12}{N}}\left(\left(\sum_{i=1}^{N}\mathrm{RAND}()\right)-\frac{N}{2}\right).$$

This has been scaled to have a mean of zero and unit standard deviation.

Useful approximations

4.9 THE WIENER PROCESS

So far we have a model that allows the asset to take any value after a time step. This is a step forward but we have still not reached our goal of continuous time, we still have a discrete time step. This section is a brief introduction to the continuous-time limit of equations like (4.4). I will start to introduce ideas from the world of stochastic modeling and Wiener processes, delving more deeply in Chapter 5.

I am now going to use the notation $d\cdot$ to mean 'the change in' some quantity. Thus dS is the 'change in the asset price.' But this change will be in *continuous time*. Thus we will go to the limit $\delta t = 0$. The first δt on the right-hand side of (4.5) becomes dt but the second term is more complicated.

I cannot straightforwardly write $dt^{1/2}$ instead of $\delta t^{1/2}$. If I do go to the zero-time step limit then any random $dt^{1/2}$ term will dominate any deterministic dt term. Yet in our problem the factor in front of $dt^{1/2}$ has a mean of zero, so maybe it does not outweigh the drift after all. Clearly something subtle is happening in the limit.

It turns out, and we will see this in Chapter 5, that because the *variance* of the random term is $O(\delta t)$ we *can* make a sensible continuous-time limit of our discrete-time model. This brings us into the world of Wiener processes.

I am going to write the term $\phi \, \delta t^{1/2}$ as

$$dX.$$

You can think of dX as being a random variable, drawn from a Normal distribution with mean zero and variance dt:

$$E[dX] = 0 \quad \text{and} \quad E[dX^2] = dt.$$

This is not exactly what it is, but it is close enough to give the right idea. This is called a **Wiener process**. The important point is that we can build up a continuous-time theory using Wiener processes instead of Normal distributions and discrete time.

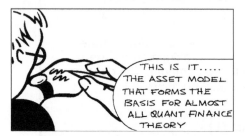

4.10 THE WIDELY ACCEPTED MODEL FOR EQUITIES, CURRENCIES, COMMODITIES AND INDICES

Our asset price model in the continuous-time limit, using the Wiener process notation, can be written as

$$dS = \mu S \, dt + \sigma S \, dX. \qquad (4.7)$$

This is our first **stochastic differential equation**. It is a continuous-time model of an asset price. It is the most widely accepted model for equities, currencies, commodities and indices, and the foundation of so much finance theory.

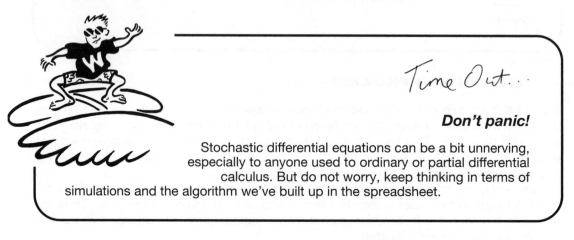

Time Out...

Don't panic!

Stochastic differential equations can be a bit unnerving, especially to anyone used to ordinary or partial differential calculus. But do not worry, keep thinking in terms of simulations and the algorithm we've built up in the spreadsheet.

We've now built up a simple model for equities that we are going to be using quite a lot. You could ask, if the stock market is so random how can fund managers justify their fee? Do

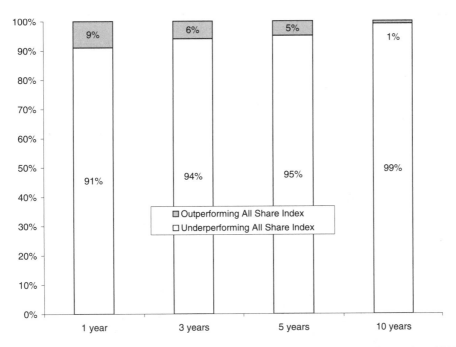

Figure 4.10   Fund performances compared with UK All Share Index. To end December 1998. Data supplied by Virgin Direct.

they manage to outsmart the market? Are they clairvoyant or aren't the markets random? Well, I won't swear that markets are random but I can say with confidence that fund managers don't outperform the market. In Figure 4.10 is shown the percentage of funds that outperform an index of all UK stocks. Whether we look at a one-, three-, five- or 10-year horizon we can see that the vast majority of funds can't even keep up with the market. And statistically speaking, there are bound to be a few that beat the market, but only by chance. Maybe one should invest in a fund that does the opposite of all other funds. Great idea except that the management fee and transaction costs probably mean that that would be a poor investment too. This doesn't prove that markets are random, but it's sufficiently suggestive that most of my personal share exposure is via an index-tracker fund.

Time Out...

Why do we like the Normal distribution?

The Normal distribution is a special and wonderful distribution. It occurs naturally in many walks of life, and has nice properties. Here's a little experiment that shows why it crops up naturally, and after this I'll give you a theorem.

Back to coin tossing. Toss one coin, heads you win one dollar, tails you lose one dollar. Figure 1 shows the probability distribution.

Now toss two coins, same rules, for each head you get one dollar, but lose one for each tail. The probability density function is shown in Figure 2.

The sequence of figures below shows the probability density function of winnings/losses after an increasing number of tosses. What do you notice? It's starting to look more and more like the bell-shaped Normal distribution.

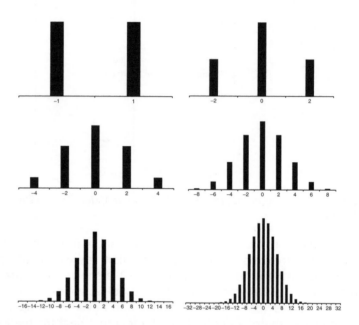

This is a simple demonstration of the **Central Limit Theorem**: Let $X_1, X_2, \ldots$ be a sequence of independent identically distributed (i.i.d.) random variables with finite means m and finite non-zero variances s^2 then the sum

$$S_n = X_1 + X_2 + \ldots + X_n$$

in the limit as $n \to \infty$ is distributed Normally with mean nm and variance ns^2. Or if we rescale,

$$S'_n = \frac{X_1 + X_2 + \ldots + X_n - nm}{\sqrt{n}s}$$

tends to the standardized Normal distribution.

The point is that if we add up enough i.i.d. random variables (with finite mean and standard deviation) we end up with something that's Normally distributed. And that's why the Normal distribution occurs all over the place.

4.11   **SUMMARY**

In this chapter I introduced a simple model for the random walk of asset. Initially I built the model up in discrete time, showing what the various terms mean, how they scale with the time step and showing how to implement the model on a spreadsheet.

Most of this book is about continuous-time models for assets. The continuous-time version of the random walk involves concepts such as stochastic calculus and Wiener processes. I introduced these briefly in this chapter and will now go on to explain the underlying theory of stochastic calculus to give the necessary background for the rest of the book.

FURTHER READING

- Mandelbrot (1963) and Fama (1965) did some of the early work on the analysis of financial data.

- Parkinson (1980) derived the high-low estimator and Garman & Klass (1980) derived the high-low-close estimator.

- For an introduction to random walks and Wiener processes see Øksendal (1992) and Schuss (1980).

- Some high frequency data can be ordered through Olsen Associates, `www.olsen.ch`. It's not free, but nor is it expensive.

- The famous book by Malkiel (1990) is well worth reading for its insights into the behavior of the stock market. Read what he has to say about chimpanzees, blindfolds and darts. In fact, if you haven't already got Malkiel's book make sure that it is the next book you read after finishing mine.

EXERCISES

1. A share has an expected return of 12% per annum (with continuous compounding) and a volatility of 20% per annum. Changes in the share price satisfy $dS = \mu S\, dt + \sigma S\, dX$. Simulate the movement of the share price, currently $100, over a year, using a time interval of one week.

2. What is the distribution of the price increase for the share movement described in Question 1?

3. Using daily share price data, find and plot returns for the asset. What are the mean and standard deviation for the sample you have chosen?

4. Compare interest rate data with your share price data. Are there any major differences? Is the asset price model

$$dS = \mu S\, dt + \sigma S\, dX$$

also suitable for modeling interest rates?

CHAPTER 5
elementary stochastic calculus

The aim of this Chapter...

...is to develop the theory behind the manipulation of random quantities, in particular stochastic differential equations like the one at the end of the previous chapter. This is very important for a thorough understanding of quantitative finance.

In this Chapter...

- all the stochastic calculus you need to know, and no more
- the meaning of Markov and martingale
- Brownian motion
- stochastic integration
- stochastic differential equations
- Itô's lemma in one and more dimensions

5.1 INTRODUCTION

Stochastic calculus is very important in the mathematical modeling of financial processes. This is because of the underlying random nature of financial markets. Because stochastic calculus is such an important tool I want to ensure that it can be used by everyone. To that end, I am going to try to make this chapter as accessible and intuitive as possible. By the end, I hope that the reader will know what various technical terms mean (and rarely are they very complicated), but, more importantly, will also know how to use the techniques with the minimum of fuss.

Most academic articles in finance have a 'pure' mathematical theme. The mathematical rigor in these works is occasionally justified, but more often than not it only succeeds in obscuring the content. When a subject is young, as is mathematical finance (young*ish*), there is a tendency for technical rigor to feature very prominently in research. This is due to lack of confidence in the methods and results. As the subject ages, researchers will become more cavalier in their attitudes and we will see much more rapid progress.

Time Out...

Aaaaarghhhhhh!

If you don't feel comfortable with messy algebra, just skip to the end of the chapter where I outline the intuition behind stochastic calculus and give you a few rules of thumb to help you use it in practice. Actually, most of this chapter is just groundwork for the important mathematical 'tool' of Itô's lemma.

5.2 A MOTIVATING EXAMPLE

Toss a coin. Every time you throw a head I give you $1, every time you throw a tail you give me $1. Figure 5.1 shows how much money you have after six tosses. In this experiment the sequence was THHTHT, and we finished even.

If I use R_i to mean the random amount, either $1 or −$1, you make on the ith toss then we have

$$E[R_i] = 0, \quad E[R_i^2] = 1 \quad \text{and} \quad E[R_i R_j] = 0.$$

In this example it doesn't matter whether or not these expectations are conditional on the past. In other words, if I threw five heads in a row it does not affect the outcome of the sixth toss. To the gamblers out there, this property is also shared by a fair die, a balanced roulette wheel, but not by the deck of cards in blackjack. In blackjack the same deck is used for game after game, the odds during one game depend on what cards were dealt out from the same deck in previous games. That is why you can in the long run beat the house at blackjack but not roulette.

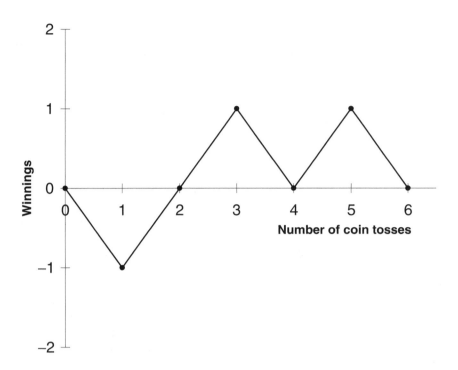

Figure 5.1   The outcome of a coin-tossing experiment.

Introduce S_i to mean the total amount of money you have won up to and including the ith toss so that

$$S_i = \sum_{j=1}^{i} R_j.$$

Later on it will be useful if we have $S_0 = 0$, i.e. you start with no money.

Time Out...

Just like coin tossing or the binomial tree

Very similar, but here we have something like an arithmetic random walk rather than geometric...we are adding or subtracting a quantity rather than multiplying.

If we now calculate expectations of S_i it *does* matter what information we have. If we calculate expectations of future events before the experiment has even begun then

$$E[S_i] = 0 \quad \text{and} \quad E[S_i^2] = E[R_1^2 + 2R_1R_2 + \cdots] = i.$$

On the other hand, suppose there have been five tosses already, can I use this information and what can we say about expectations for the sixth toss? This is the **conditional expectation**. The expectation of S_6 conditional upon the previous five tosses gives

$$E[S_6|R_1,\ldots,R_5] = S_5.$$

MARKOV MEANS NO MEMORY BEYOND THE PRESENT. A PROPERTY OF MOST FINANCE MODELS

5.3 THE MARKOV PROPERTY

This result is special, the expected value of the random variable S_i conditional upon all of the past events *only depends on the previous value* S_{i-1}. This is the **Markov property**. We say that the random walk has no memory beyond where it is now. Note that it doesn't have to be the case that the expected value of the random variable S_i is the same as the previous value.

This can be generalized to say that given information about S_j for some values of $1 \le j < i$ then the only information that is of use to us in estimating S_i is the value of S_j for the largest j for which we have information.

Almost all of the financial models that I will show you have the Markov property. This is of fundamental importance in modeling in finance. I will also show you examples where the system has a small amount of memory, meaning that one or two other pieces of information are important. And I will also give a couple of examples where *all* of the random walk path contains relevant information.

5.4 THE MARTINGALE PROPERTY

The toin-cossing experiment possesses another property that can be important in finance. You know how much money you have won after the fifth toss. Your expected winnings after the sixth toss, and indeed after any number of tosses if we keep playing, is just the amount you already hold. That is, the conditional expectation of your winnings at any time in the future is just the amount you already hold:

$$E[S_i|S_j, j < i] = S_j.$$

This is called the **martingale property**.

5.5 QUADRATIC VARIATION

I am now going to define the **quadratic variation** of the random walk. This is defined by

$$\sum_{j=1}^{i} (S_j - S_{j-1})^2 .$$

Because you either win or lose an amount $1 after each toss, $|S_j - S_{j-1}| = 1$. Thus the quadratic variation is always i:

$$\sum_{j=1}^{i} (S_j - S_{j-1})^2 = i.$$

I want to use the coin-tossing experiment for one more demonstration. And that will lead us to a continuous-time random walk.

5.6 BROWNIAN MOTION

I am going to change the rules of my coin-tossing experiment. First of all I am going to restrict the time allowed for the six tosses to a period t, so each toss will take a time $t/6$. Second, the size of the bet will not be $1 but $\sqrt{t/6}$.

This new experiment clearly still possesses both the Markov and martingale properties, and its quadratic variation measured over the whole experiment is

$$\sum_{j=1}^{6} (S_j - S_{j-1})^2 = 6 \times \left(\sqrt{\frac{t}{6}}\right)^2 = t.$$

I have set up my experiment so that the quadratic variation is just the time taken for the experiment.

I will change the rules again, to speed up the game. We will have n tosses in the allowed time t, with an amount $\sqrt{t/n}$ riding on each throw. Again, the Markov and martingale properties are retained and the quadratic variation is still

$$\sum_{j=1}^{n} (S_j - S_{j-1})^2 = n \times \left(\sqrt{\frac{t}{n}}\right)^2 = t.$$

I am now going to make n larger and larger. All I am doing with my rule changes is to speed up the game, decreasing the time between tosses, with a smaller amount for each bet. But I have chosen my new scalings very carefully, the time step is decreasing like n^{-1} but the bet size only decreases by $n^{-1/2}$.

In Figure 5.2 I show a series of experiments, each lasting for a time 1, with increasing number of tosses per experiment.

As I go to the limit $n = \infty$, the resulting random walk stays finite. It has an expectation, conditional on a starting value of zero, of

$$E[S(t)] = 0$$

and a variance

$$E[S(t)^2] = t.$$

I use $S(t)$ to denote the amount you have won or the value of the random variable after a time t. The limiting process for this random walk as the time steps go to zero is called **Brownian motion**, and I will denote it by $X(t)$.

The important properties of Brownian motion are as follows.

- **Finiteness:** Any other scaling of the bet size or 'increments' with time step would have resulted in either a random walk going to infinity in a finite time, or a limit in which there was no motion at all. It is important that the increment scales with the square root of the time step.

- **Continuity:** The paths are continuous, there are no discontinuities. Brownian motion is the continuous-time limit of our discrete time random walk.

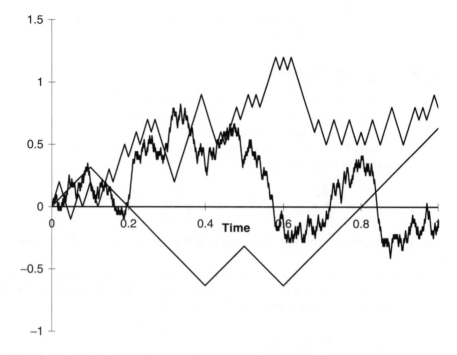

Figure 5.2   A series of coin-tossing experiments, the limit of which is Brownian motion.

- **Markov:** The conditional distribution of $X(t)$ given information up until $\tau < t$ depends only on $X(\tau)$.

- **Martingale:** Given information up until $\tau < t$ the conditional expectation of $X(t)$ is $X(\tau)$.

- **Quadratic variation:** If we divide up the time 0 to t in a partition with $n + 1$ partition points $t_i = i\,t/n$ then

$$\sum_{j=1}^{n} \left(X(t_j) - X(t_{j-1})\right)^2 \to t. \quad \text{(Technically 'almost surely.')}$$

- **Normality:** Over finite time increments t_{i-1} to t_i, $X(t_i) - X(t_{i-1})$ is Normally distributed with mean zero and variance $t_i - t_{i-1}$.

Having built up the idea and properties of Brownian motion from a series of experiments, we can discard the experiments, to leave the Brownian motion that is defined by its properties. These properties will be very important for our financial models.

5.7   **STOCHASTIC INTEGRATION**

I am going to define a **stochastic integral** by

$$W(t) = \int_0^t f(\tau)\, dX(\tau) = \lim_{n \to \infty} \sum_{j=1}^{n} f(t_{j-1}) \left(X(t_j) - X(t_{j-1})\right)$$

with

$$t_j = \frac{jt}{n}.$$

Before I manipulate this is any way or discuss its properties, I want to stress that the function $f(t)$ which I am integrating is evaluated in the summation at the *left-hand point* t_{j-1}. It will be crucially important that each function evaluation does not know about the random increment that multiplies it, i.e. the integration is **non anticipatory**. In financial terms, we will see that we take some action such as choosing a portfolio and only then does the stock price move. This choice of integration is natural in finance, ensuring that we use no information about the future in our current actions.

5.8 STOCHASTIC DIFFERENTIAL EQUATIONS

Stochastic integrals are important for any theory of stochastic calculus since they can be meaningfully defined. (And in the next section I show how the definition leads to some important properties.) However, it is very common to use a shorthand notation for expressions such as

WE'LL BE USING STOCHASTIC DIFFERENTIAL EQUATIONS ALL THE TIME

$$W(t) = \int_0^t f(\tau)\,dX(\tau). \tag{5.1}$$

That shorthand comes from 'differentiating' (5.1) and is

$$dW = f(t)\,dX. \tag{5.2}$$

Think of dX as being an increment in X, i.e. a Normal random variable with mean zero and standard deviation $dt^{1/2}$.

Equations (5.1) and (5.2) are meant to be equivalent. One of the reasons for this shorthand is that the equation (5.2) looks a lot like an ordinary differential equation. We *do not* go the further step of dividing by dt to make it look exactly like an ordinary differential equation because then we would have the difficult task of defining $\frac{dX}{dt}$.

Pursuing this idea further, imagine what might be meant by

$$dW = g(t)\,dt + f(t)\,dX. \tag{5.3}$$

This is simply shorthand for

$$W(t) = \int_0^t g(\tau)\,d\tau + \int_0^t f(\tau)\,dX(\tau).$$

Equations like (5.3) are called **stochastic differential equations**. Their precise meaning comes, however, from the technically more accurate equivalent stochastic integral. In this book I will use the shorthand versions almost everywhere, no confusion should arise.

5.9 THE MEAN SQUARE LIMIT

I am going to describe the technical term **mean square limit**. This is useful in the precise definition of stochastic integration. I will explain the idea by way of the simplest example.

Examine the quantity

$$E\left[\left(\sum_{j=1}^{n}(X(t_j) - X(t_{j-1}))^2 - t\right)^2\right] \tag{5.4}$$

where

$$t_j = \frac{jt}{n}.$$

This can be expanded as

$$E\left[\sum_{j=1}^{n}(X(t_j) - X(t_{j-1}))^4 + 2\sum_{i=1}^{n}\sum_{j<i}(X(t_i) - X(t_{i-1}))^2(X(t_j) - X(t_{j-1}))^2\right.$$

$$\left. -2t\sum_{j=1}^{n}(X(t_j) - X(t_{j-1}))^2 + t^2\right].$$

Since $X(t_j) - X(t_{j-1})$ is Normally distributed with mean zero and variance t/n we have

$$E\left[(X(t_j) - X(t_{j-1}))^2\right] = \frac{t}{n}$$

and

$$E\left[(X(t_j) - X(t_{j-1}))^4\right] = \frac{3t^2}{n^2}.$$

Thus (5.4) becomes

$$n\frac{3t^2}{n^2} + n(n-1)\frac{t^2}{n^2} - 2tn\frac{t}{n} + t^2 = O\left(\frac{1}{n}\right).$$

As $n \to \infty$ this tends to zero. We therefore say that

$$\sum_{j=1}^{n}(X(t_j) - X(t_{j-1}))^2 = t$$

in the 'mean square limit.' This is often written, for obvious reasons, as

$$\int_0^t (dX)^2 = t.$$

I am not going to use this result, nor will I use the mean square limit technique. However, when I talk about 'equality' in the following 'proof' I mean equality in the mean square sense.

5.10 FUNCTIONS OF STOCHASTIC VARIABLES AND ITÔ'S LEMMA

I am now going to introduce the idea of a function of a stochastic variable. In Figure 5.3 is shown a realization of a Brownian motion $X(t)$ and the function $F(X) = X^2$.

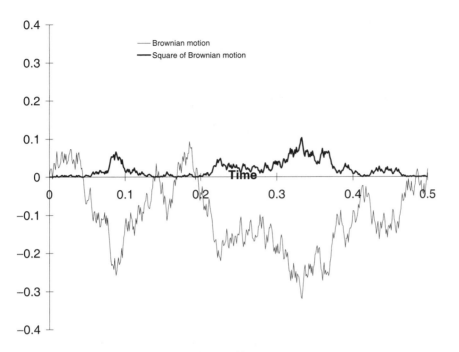

Figure 5.3 A realization of a Brownian motion and its square.

If $F = X^2$ is it true that $dF = 2X\,dX$? No. The ordinary rules of calculus do not generally hold in a stochastic environment. Then what are the rules of calculus?

I am going to 'derive' the most important rule of stochastic calculus, **Itô's lemma**. My derivation is more heuristic than rigorous, but at least it is transparent. I will do this for an arbitrary function $F(X)$.

In this derivation I will need to introduce various timescales. The first timescale is very, very small. I will denote it by

$$\frac{\delta t}{n} = h.$$

This timescale is so small that the function $F(X(t+h))$ can be approximated by a Taylor series:

$$F(X(t+h)) - F(X(t)) = (X(t+h) - X(t))\frac{dF}{dX}(X(t)) + \tfrac{1}{2}(X(t+h) - X(t))^2\frac{d^2F}{dX^2}(X(t)) + \dots$$

From this it follows that

$$(F(X(t+h)) - F(X(t))) + (F(X(t+2h)) - F(X(t+h))) + \dots + (F(X(t+nh))$$

$$-F(X(t+(n-1)h)))$$

$$= \sum_{j=1}^{n}(X(t+jh) - X(t+(j-1)h))\frac{dF}{dX}(X(t+(j-1)h))$$

$$+ \tfrac{1}{2}\frac{d^2F}{dX^2}(X(t))\sum_{j=1}^{n}(X(t+jh) - X(t+(j-1)h))^2 + \dots$$

In this I have used the approximation

$$\frac{d^2F}{dX^2}(X(t + (j - 1)h)) = \frac{d^2F}{dX^2}(X(t)).$$

This is consistent with the order of accuracy I require.

The first line in this becomes simply

$$F(X(t + nh)) - F(X(t)) = F(X(t + \delta t)) - F(X(t)).$$

The second is just the definition of

$$\int_t^{t+\delta t} \frac{dF}{dX} dX$$

and the last is

$$\frac{1}{2}\frac{d^2F}{dX^2}(X(t))\delta t,$$

in the *mean square sense*. Thus we have

$$F(X(t + \delta t)) - F(X(t)) = \int_t^{t+\delta t} \frac{dF}{dX}(X(\tau))dX(\tau) + \frac{1}{2}\int_t^{t+\delta t} \frac{d^2F}{dX^2}(X(\tau))d\tau.$$

I can now extend this result over longer timescales, from zero up to t, over which F *does* vary substantially to get

$$F(X(t)) = F(X(0)) + \int_0^t \frac{dF}{dX}(X(\tau))dX(\tau) + \frac{1}{2}\int_0^t \frac{d^2F}{dX^2}(X(\tau))d\tau.$$

This is the integral version of **Itô's lemma**, which is usually written as

$$dF = \frac{dF}{dX} dX + \frac{1}{2}\frac{d^2F}{dX^2} dt. \qquad (5.5)$$

We can now answer the question, if $F = X^2$ what stochastic differential equation does F satisfy? In this example

$$\frac{dF}{dX} = 2X \quad \text{and} \quad \frac{d^2F}{dX^2} = 2.$$

Therefore Itô's lemma tells us that

$$dF = 2X\,dX + dt.$$

This is *not* what we would get if X were a deterministic variable. In integrated form

$$X^2 = F(X) = F(0) + \int_0^t 2X \, dX + \int_0^t 1 \, d\tau = \int_0^t 2X \, dX + t.$$

Therefore

$$\int_0^t X \, dX = \tfrac{1}{2}X^2 - \tfrac{1}{2}t.$$

5.11 INTERPRETATION OF ITÔ'S LEMMA

Itô's lemma is going to be of great importance to us when we start to look at pricing options. If we can get comfortable with manipulating random quantities via simple rules of stochastic calculus then we will find most option theory quite straightforward.

To help in that regard, and to give you some insight into the role that Itô's lemma will be playing, take a look at the next figure, Figure 5.4.

In this figure you will see at the top a realization of a stock price, just a basic lognormal random walk. Below this is the value of an option on this stock.[1] What you will notice about these plots is that both have a direction to them (both are rising overall) and both have a random element (the bouncing around of the values).

Both look stochastic and we know that the stock price satisfies a stochastic differential equation

$$dS = \mu S \, dt + \sigma S \, dX,$$

so maybe the option value (call it $V(S, t)$) also satisfies a stochastic differential equation

$$dV = \underline{\hspace{1cm}} dt + \underline{\hspace{1cm}} dX.$$

The question is, then, what are the underlined bits? And that is precisely what Itô tells us.

This will be important later when we do the Black–Scholes theory, because knowing how much randomness there is in an option's value relative to a stock's value will give us a recipe for eliminating that randomness by buying an option and selling short a special quantity of the stock.

5.12 ITÔ AND TAYLOR

Having derived Itô's lemma, I am going to give some intuition behind the result and then slightly generalize it.

---

[1] It doesn't much matter whether it is a call, a put or something more exotic, the concept is relevant to all options.

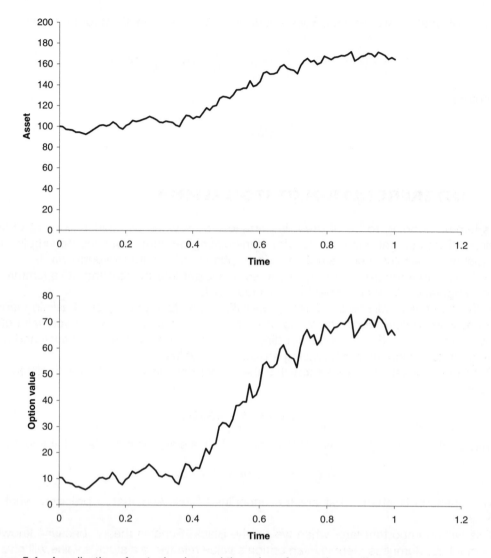

Figure 5.4 A realization of a stock price and the value of an option on that stock.

If we were to do a naive Taylor series expansion of F, completely disregarding the nature of X, and treating dX as a small increment in X, we would get

$$F(X + dX) = F(X) + \frac{dF}{dX}dX + \tfrac{1}{2}\frac{d^2F}{dX^2}dX^2,$$

ignoring higher-order terms. We could argue that $F(X + dX) - F(X)$ was just the 'change in' F and so

$$dF = \frac{dF}{dX}dX + \tfrac{1}{2}\frac{d^2F}{dX^2}dX^2.$$

This is very similar to (5.5) (and Taylor series *is* very similar to Itô), with the only difference being that there is a dX^2 instead of a dt. However, since in a sense

$$\int_0^t (dX)^2 = t$$

I could perhaps write

$$dX^2 = dt. \tag{5.6}$$

Although this lacks any rigor it does give the correct result. However, on a positive note you can, with little risk of error, use Taylor series with the 'rule of thumb' (5.6) and in practice you will get the right result. Although this is technically incorrect, you almost certainly won't get the wrong result. I will use this rule of thumb almost every time I want to differentiate a function of a random variable.

Time Out...

Intuition behind dX²' = 'dt

This is subtle. Pay close attention.

We shouldn't really think of dX^2 as being the square of a single Normally distributed random variable, mean zero, variance dt. No, we should think of it as the sum of squares of lots and lots (an infinite number) of independent and identically distributed Normal variables, each one having mean zero and a very, very small (infinitesimal) variance. What happens when you add together lots of i.i.d. variables? In this case we get a quantity with a mean of dt and a variance which goes rapidly to zero as the 'lots' approach 'infinity.'

To end this section I will generalize slightly. Suppose my stochastic differential equation is

$$dS = a(S)\,dt + b(S)\,dX, \tag{5.7}$$

say, for some functions $a(S)$ and $b(S)$. Here dX is the usual Brownian increment. Now if I have a function of S, $V(S)$, what stochastic differential equation does it satisfy? The answer is

$$dV = \frac{dV}{dS}\,dS + \tfrac{1}{2}b^2 \frac{d^2V}{dS^2}\,dt.$$

We could derive this properly or just cheat by using Taylor series with $dX^2 = dt$. I could, if I wanted, substitute for dS from (5.7) to get an equation for dV in terms of the pure Brownian motion X:

$$dV = \left(a(S)\frac{dV}{dS} + \tfrac{1}{2}b(S)^2\frac{d^2V}{dS^2}\right)dt + b(S)\frac{dV}{dS}\,dX.$$

5.13 ITÔ IN HIGHER DIMENSIONS

In financial problems we often have functions of one stochastic variable S and a deterministic variable t, time: $V(S, t)$. If

$$dS = a(S, t)\, dt + b(S, t)\, dX,$$

then the increment dV is given by

$$dV = \frac{\partial V}{\partial t}\, dt + \frac{\partial V}{\partial S}\, dS + \tfrac{1}{2}b^2 \frac{\partial^2 V}{\partial S^2}\, dt. \tag{5.8}$$

Again, this is shorthand notation for the correct integrated form. This result is obvious, as is the use of partial instead of ordinary derivatives.

Occasionally, we have a function of two, or more, random variables, and time as well: $V(S_1, S_2, t)$. An example would be the value of an option to buy the more valuable out of Nike and Reebok. I will write the behavior of S_1 and S_2 in the general form

$$dS_1 = a_1(S_1, S_2, t)dt + b_1(S_1, S_2, t)dX_1$$

and

$$dS_2 = a_2(S_1, S_2, t)\, dt + b_2(S_1, S_2, t)dX_2.$$

Note that I have *two* Brownian increments dX_1 and dX_2. We can think of these as being Normally distributed with variance dt, but *they are correlated*. The correlation between these two random variables I will call ρ. This can also be a function of S_1, S_2 and t but must satisfy

$$-1 \leq \rho \leq 1.$$

The 'rules of thumb' can readily be imagined:

$$dX_1^2 = dt, \quad dX_2^2 = dt \quad \text{and} \quad dX_1 dX_2 = \rho\, dt.$$

Itô's lemma becomes

$$dV = \frac{\partial V}{\partial t}\, dt + \frac{\partial V}{\partial S_1}dS_1 + \frac{\partial V}{\partial S_2}dS_2 + \tfrac{1}{2}b_1^2 \frac{\partial^2 V}{\partial S_1^2}\, dt + \rho b_1 b_2 \frac{\partial^2 V}{\partial S_1 \partial S_2}\, dt + \tfrac{1}{2}b_2^2 \frac{\partial^2 V}{\partial S_2^2}\, dt. \tag{5.9}$$

5.14 SOME PERTINENT EXAMPLES

In this section I am going to introduce a few common random walks and talk about their properties.

Remember that a stochastic differential equation model for variable S is something of the form

$$dS = \underline{\quad\quad}\, dt + \underline{\quad\quad}\, dX.$$

The bit in front of the dt is deterministic and the bit in front of the dX tells us how much randomness there is. Modeling is very much about choosing functions to go where the underlining is, it is about choosing the functional form for the deterministic part and the functional form for the amount of randomness. We will now look at some examples.

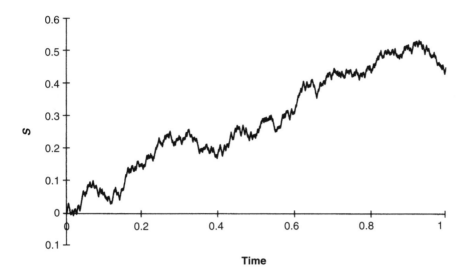

Figure 5.5 A realization of $dS = \mu\, dt + \sigma\, dX$.

5.14.1 Brownian motion with drift

The first example is like the simple Brownian motion but with a drift:

$$dS = \mu\, dt + \sigma\, dX.$$

A realization of this is shown in Figure 5.5. The point to note about this realization is that S has gone negative. This random walk would therefore not be a good model for many financial quantities, such as interest rates or equity prices. This stochastic differential equation can be integrated exactly to get

$$S(t) = S(0) + \mu t + \sigma(X(t) - X(0)).$$

Time Out...

Spreadsheet simulation

This random walk is simulated on the following spreadsheet.

	A	B	C	D	E	F
1	Start	100		Time	S	
2	μ	0.1		0	100	
3	σ	0.2		0.01	100.0171	
4				=B1 0.02	99.99066	
5	Timestep	0.01		0.03	99.96521	
6				0.04	99.97567	
7				0.05	99.93592	
8				0.06	99.95225	
9		=D8+$B$5		0.07	99.96202	
10				0.08	99.95202	
11				0.09	99.95474	
12		=E11+$B$2*$B$5+$B$3*SQRT($B$5)*		0.1	99.96519	
13		(RAND()+RAND()+RAND()+RAND()+R		11	99.94123	
14		AND()+RAND()+RAND()+RAND()+RA		12	99.94159	
15		ND()+RAND()+RAND()+RAND()-6)		13	99.94805	
16				14	99.95993	
17				0.15	99.95776	
18				0.16	99.95448	
19				0.17	99.93744	
20				0.18	99.90828	
21				0.19	99.9203	
22				0.2	99.94772	

The spreadsheet is easily changed to model other random walks

5.14.2 The lognormal random walk

My second example is similar to the above but the drift and randomness scale with S:

$$dS = \mu S\,dt + \sigma S\,dX. \tag{5.10}$$

A realization of this is shown in Figure 5.6.

How does the time series in Figure 5.6 which was generated on a spreadsheet using random returns compare qualitatively with the time series in Figure 5.7 which is the real series for Glaxo–Wellcome?

If S starts out positive it can never go negative; the closer that S gets to zero the smaller the increments dS. For this reason I have had to start the simulation with a non-zero value for S. This property of this random walk is clearly seen if we examine the function $F(S) = \log S$ using Itô's lemma. From Itô we have

$$dF = \frac{dF}{dS}\,dS + \tfrac{1}{2}\sigma^2 S^2 \frac{d^2F}{dS^2}\,dt = \frac{1}{S}\left(\mu S\,dt + \sigma S\,dX\right) - \tfrac{1}{2}\sigma^2\,dt$$

$$= \left(\mu - \tfrac{1}{2}\sigma^2\right)\,dt + \sigma\,dX.$$

This shows us that $\log S$ can range between minus and plus infinity but cannot reach these limits in a finite time, therefore S cannot reach zero or infinity in a finite time.

The integral form of this stochastic differential equation follows simply from the stochastic differential equation for $\log S$:

$$S(t) = S(0)e^{\left(\mu - \frac{1}{2}\sigma^2\right)t + \sigma(X(t) - X(0))}.$$

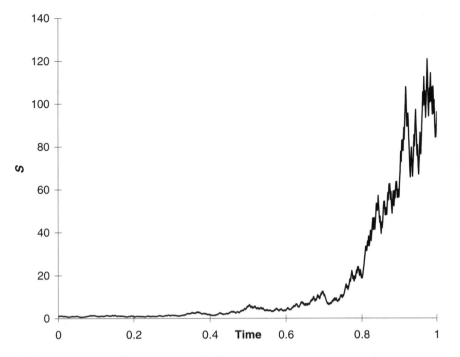

Figure 5.6 A realization of $dS = \mu S\, dt + \sigma S\, dX$.

Figure 5.7 Glaxo–Wellcome share price (volume below). Source: Bloomberg L.P.

The stochastic differential equation (5.10) will be particularly important in the modeling of many asset classes. And if we have some function $V(S, t)$ then from Itô it follows that

$$dV = \frac{\partial V}{\partial t} dt + \frac{\partial V}{\partial S} dS + \frac{1}{2}\sigma^2 S^2 \frac{\partial^2 V}{\partial S^2} dt.$$

(5.11)

5.14.3 A mean-reverting random walk

The third example is

$$dS = (v - \mu S) dt + \sigma\, dX.$$

A realization of this is shown in Figure 5.8.

This random walk is an example of a **mean-reverting** random walk. If S is large, the negative coefficient in front of dt means that S will move down on average, if S is small it rises on average. There is still no incentive for S to stay positive in this random walk. With r instead of S this random walk is the Vasicek model for the short-term interest rate.

Mean-reverting models are used for modeling a random variable that 'isn't going anywhere.' That's why they are often used for interest rates; Figure 5.9 shows the yield on a Japanese Government Bond.

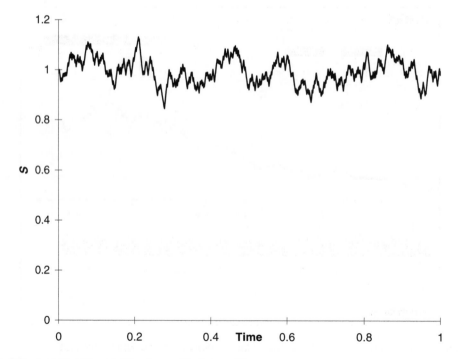

Figure 5.8 A realization of $dS = (v - \mu S) dt + \sigma\, dX$.

Figure 5.9 Time series of the yield on a JGB. Source: Bloomberg L.P.

5.14.4 And another mean-reverting random walk

The final example is similar to the third but I am going to adjust the random term slightly:

$$dS = (v - \mu S)\,dt + \sigma S^{1/2}\,dX.$$

Now if S ever gets close to zero the randomness decreases, perhaps this will stop S from going negative? Let's play around with this example for a while. And we'll see Itô in practice.

Write $F = S^{1/2}$. What stochastic differential equation does F satisfy? Since

$$\frac{dF}{dS} = \tfrac{1}{2}S^{-1/2} \quad \text{and} \quad \frac{d^2F}{dS^2} = -\tfrac{1}{4}S^{-3/2}$$

we have

$$dF = \left(\frac{4v - \sigma^2}{8F} - \tfrac{1}{2}\mu F\right)dt + \tfrac{1}{2}\sigma\,dX.$$

I have just turned the original stochastic differential equation with a variable coefficient in front of the random term into a stochastic differential equation with a constant random term. In so doing I have made the drift term nastier. In particular, the drift is now singular at $F = S = 0$. Something special is happening at $S = 0$.

Instead of examining $F(S) = S^{1/2}$, can I find a function $F(S)$ such that its stochastic differential equation has a zero drift term? For this I will need

$$(v - \mu S)\frac{dF}{dS} + \tfrac{1}{2}\sigma^2 S\frac{d^2F}{dS^2} = 0.$$

This is easily integrated once to give

$$\frac{dF}{dS} = A S^{-\frac{2\nu}{\sigma^2}} e^{\frac{2\mu S}{\sigma^2}} \qquad (5.12)$$

for any constant A. I won't take this any further but just make one observation. If

$$\frac{2\nu}{\sigma^2} \geq 1$$

we cannot integrate (5.12) at $S = 0$. This makes the origin **non attainable**. In other words, if the parameter ν is sufficiently large it forces the random walk to stay away from zero.

This particular stochastic differential equation for S will be important later on, it is the Cox, Ingersoll & Ross model for the short-term interest rate.

These are just four of the many random walks we will be seeing.

5.15 **SUMMARY**

This chapter introduced the most important tool of the trade, Itô's lemma. Itô's lemma allows us to manipulate functions of a random variable. If we think of S as the value of an asset for which we have a stochastic differential equation, a 'model,' then we can handle functions of the asset, and ultimately value contracts such as options.

If we use Itô as a tool we do not need to know why or how it works, only how to use it. Essentially all we require to successfully use the lemma is a rule of thumb, as explained in the text. Unless we are using Itô in highly unusual situations, then we are unlikely to make any errors.

FURTHER READING

- Neftci (1996) is the only readable book on stochastic calculus for beginners. It does not assume any knowledge about anything. It takes the reader very slowly through the basics as applied to finance.

- Once you have got beyond the basics, move on to Øksendal (1992) and Schuss (1980).

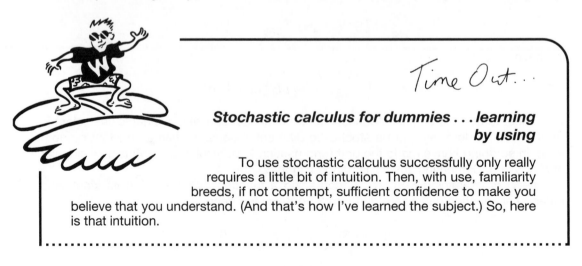

Time Out...

Stochastic calculus for dummies . . . learning by using

To use stochastic calculus successfully only really requires a little bit of intuition. Then, with use, familiarity breeds, if not contempt, sufficient confidence to make you believe that you understand. (And that's how I've learned the subject.) So, here is that intuition.

- Stochastic differential equations are like recipes for generating random walks, just as we saw in the previous chapter using Excel.

- If you have some quantity, let's call it S, that follows such a random walk, then any function of S is also going to follow a random walk. For example, if S is moving about randomly, then so is S^2.

- The question then becomes 'What is the random walk for this function of S?' That is, what is its recipe, or what is its stochastic differential equation?

- The answer to that comes from applying something very like Taylor series but with two tricks.

- The first trick is that when you do your Taylor series expansion, only keep terms of size dt or bigger ($dt^{1/2}$).

- The second trick is that every time you see a dX^2 term replace it with dt. Why? Because dX is really made up of lots of Normally distributed random variables, and so dX^2 becomes its expected value dt.

EXERCISES

In all of these $X(t)$ is Brownian motion.

1. By considering $X^2(t)$, show that

$$\int_0^t X(\tau)dX(\tau) = \tfrac{1}{2}X^2(t) - \tfrac{1}{2}t.$$

2. Show that

$$\int_0^t \tau\, dX(\tau) = tX(t) - \int_0^t X(\tau)\, d\tau.$$

3. Show that

$$\int_0^t X^2(\tau)dX(\tau) = \tfrac{1}{3}X^3(t) - \int_0^t X(\tau)\, d\tau.$$

4. Consider a function $f(t)$ which is continuous and bounded on $[0, t]$. Prove integration by parts, i.e.

$$\int_0^t f(\tau)dX(\tau) = f(t)X(t) - \int_0^t X(\tau)df(\tau).$$

5. Find $u(W, t)$ and $v(W, t)$ where

$$dW(t) = u\, dt + v\, dX(t)$$

and

(a) $W(t) = X^2(t),$

(b) $W(t) = 1 + t + e^{X(t)}$,

(c) $W(t) = f(t)X(t)$,

where f is a bounded, continuous function.

6.   If S follows a lognormal random walk, use Itô's lemma to find the differential equations satisfied by

(a) $f(S) = AS + B$,

(b) $g(S) = S^n$,

(c) $h(S, t) = S^n e^{mt}$,

where A, B, m and n are constants.

7.   If $dS = \mu S \, dt + \sigma S \, dX$, use Itô's lemma to find the stochastic differential equation satisfied by $f(S) = \log(S)$.

8.   The change in a share price satisfies

$$dS = A(S, t) \, dX + B(S, t) \, dt,$$

for some functions A, B, what is the stochastic differential equation satisfied by $f(S, t)$? Can A, B be chosen so that a function $g(S)$ has a zero drift, but non-zero variance?

9.   Two shares follow geometric Brownian motions, i.e.

$$dS_1 = \mu_1 S_1 \, dt + \sigma_1 S_1 \, dX_1,$$

$$dS_2 = \mu_2 S_2 \, dt + \sigma_2 S_2 \, dX_2.$$

The share price changes are correlated with correlation coefficient ρ. Find the stochastic differential equation satisfied by a function $f(S_1, S_2)$.

CHAPTER 6
the Black–Scholes model

The aim of this Chapter...

...is to explain in as simple and non-technical a manner as possible the original breakthrough in quantitative finance that led to such a growth in the industry and the development of the subject. By now you will know all the mathematical tools to follow this chapter, and by the end of the chapter will be ready to apply the ideas to new situations.

In this Chapter...

- the foundations of derivatives theory: delta hedging and no arbitrage

- the derivation of the Black–Scholes partial differential equation

- the assumptions that go into the Black–Scholes equation

- how to modify the equation for commodity and currency options

6.1 **INTRODUCTION**

This is, without doubt, the most important chapter in the book. In it I describe and explain the basic building blocks of derivatives theory. These building blocks are delta hedging and no arbitrage. They form a moderately sturdy foundation to the subject and have performed well since 1973 when the ideas became public.

In this chapter I begin with the stochastic differential equation model for equities and exploit the correlation between this asset and an option on this asset to make a perfectly risk-free portfolio. I then appeal to no arbitrage to equate returns on all risk-free portfolios to the risk-free interest rate, the so-called 'no free lunch' argument.

These ideas are identical to those we saw in Chapter 3, it's just that the math is different.

The arguments are trivially modified to incorporate dividends on the underlying and also to price commodity and currency options and options on futures.

This chapter is quite theoretical, yet all of the ideas contained here are regularly used in practice. Even though all of the assumptions can be shown to be wrong to a greater or lesser extent, the Black–Scholes model is profoundly important both in theory and in practice.

6.2 **A VERY SPECIAL PORTFOLIO**

In Chapter 2 I described some of the characteristics of options and options markets. I introduced the idea of call and put options, amongst others. The value of a call option is clearly going to be a function of various parameters in the contract, such as the strike price E and the time to expiry $T - t$, T is the date of expiry, and t is the current time. The value will also depend on properties of the asset itself, such as its price, its drift and its volatility, as well as the risk-free rate of interest.[1] We can write the option value as

$$V(S, t; \sigma, \mu; E, T; r).$$

Notice that the semi-colons separate different types of variables and parameters:

- S and t are variables;

- σ and μ are parameters associated with the asset price;

- E and T are parameters associated with the details of the particular contract;

- r is a parameter associated with the currency in which the asset is quoted.

I'm not going to carry all the parameters around, except when it is important. For the moment I'll just use $V(S, t)$ to denote the option value.

One simple observation is that a call option will rise in value if the underlying asset rises, and will fall if the asset falls. This is clear since a call has a larger payoff the greater the value of the underlying at expiry. This is an example of **correlation** between two financial instruments, in this case the correlation is positive. A put and the underlying have a negative correlation. We can exploit these correlations to construct a very special portfolio.

---

[1] Actually, I'm lying. One of these parameters does not affect the option value.

Use Π to denote the value of a portfolio of one long option position and a short position in some quantity Δ, **delta**, of the underlying:

$$\Pi = V(S, t) - \Delta S. \tag{6.1}$$

The first term on the right is the option and the second term is the short asset position. Notice the minus sign in front of the second term. The quantity Δ will for the moment be some constant quantity of our choosing. We will assume that the underlying follows a lognormal random walk

$$dS = \mu S\, dt + \sigma S\, dX.$$

It is natural to ask how the value of the portfolio changes from time t to $t + dt$. The change in the portfolio value is due partly to the change in the option value and partly to the change in the underlying:

$$d\Pi = dV - \Delta\, dS.$$

Notice that Δ has not changed during the time step; we have not anticipated the change in S. From Itô we have

$$dV = \frac{\partial V}{\partial t}\, dt + \frac{\partial V}{\partial S}\, dS + \tfrac{1}{2}\sigma^2 S^2 \frac{\partial^2 V}{\partial S^2}\, dt.$$

Thus the portfolio changes by

$$d\Pi = \frac{\partial V}{\partial t}\, dt + \frac{\partial V}{\partial S}\, dS + \tfrac{1}{2}\sigma^2 S^2 \frac{\partial^2 V}{\partial S^2}\, dt - \Delta\, dS. \tag{6.2}$$

Time Out...

Just like the binomial

Many people feel more at home with the binomial analysis than with the stochastic analysis of the Black–Scholes model. Well, in principle they are nearly identical, it's just that the math is a little bit more abstract with the Black–Scholes model.

For example, all that Equation (6.2) says is that our special portfolio takes different values depending on what the asset does over the next time step. In the binomial model there were two different values that the portfolio could take, represented by the up and down movements of the asset. In the Black–Scholes model there's a whole spectrum of possible values represented by the dS terms... so the dS terms represent the risk in the portfolio. And just as in the binomial model we're going to make these terms disappear.

From a technical point of view, in the binomial model we did lots of modeling, hedging, etc. first before arriving at the Black–Scholes partial differential equation by performing a Taylor series expansion. In the Black–Scholes analysis the Taylor series expansion, in its stochastic form, comes first and the hedging, etc. comes later.

6.3 **ELIMINATION OF RISK: DELTA HEDGING**

The right-hand side of (6.2) contains two types of terms, the deterministic and the random. The deterministic terms are those with the *dt*, and the random terms are those with the *dS*. Pretending for the moment that we know *V* and its derivatives then we know everything about the right-hand side of (6.2) *except for the value of dS*. And this quantity we can never know in advance.

THIS IS NOT JUST A THEORETICAL CONCEPT, IT IS USED IN REAL LIFE AS WELL

These random terms are the risk in our portfolio. Is there any way to reduce or even eliminate this risk? This can be done in theory (and *almost* in practice) by carefully choosing Δ. The random terms in (6.2) are

$$\left(\frac{\partial V}{\partial S} - \Delta\right) dS.$$

If we choose

$$\Delta = \frac{\partial V}{\partial S} \tag{6.3}$$

then the randomness is reduced to zero.

Any reduction in randomness is generally termed **hedging**, whether that randomness is due to fluctuations in the stock market or the outcome of a horse race. The perfect elimination of risk, by exploiting correlation between two instruments (in this case an option and its underlying), is generally called **delta hedging**.

Delta hedging is an example of a **dynamic hedging** strategy. From one time step to the next the quantity $\frac{\partial V}{\partial S}$ changes, since it is, like *V*, a function of the ever-changing variables *S* and *t*. This means that the perfect hedge must be continually rebalanced.

Delta hedging was effectively first described by Thorp & Kassouf (1967) but they missed the crucial (Nobel prize winning) next step. (We will see more of Thorp when we look at casino blackjack as an investment in Chapter 20.)

6.4 **NO ARBITRAGE**

After choosing the quantity Δ as suggested above, we hold a portfolio whose value changes by the amount

$$d\Pi = \left(\frac{\partial V}{\partial t} + \tfrac{1}{2}\sigma^2 S^2 \frac{\partial^2 V}{\partial S^2}\right) dt. \tag{6.4}$$

This change is completely *riskless*. If we have a completely risk-free change $d\Pi$ in the portfolio value Π then it must be the same as the growth we would get if we put the equivalent amount of cash in a risk-free interest-bearing account:

$$d\Pi = r\Pi \, dt. \tag{6.5}$$

This is an example of the **no-arbitrage** principle.

To see why this should be so, consider in turn what might happen if the return on the portfolio were, first, greater and, second, less than the risk-free rate. If we were guaranteed to get a return of greater than r from the delta-hedged portfolio then what we could do is borrow from the bank, paying interest at the rate r, invest in the risk-free option/stock portfolio and make a profit. If, on the other hand, the return were less than the risk-free rate we should go short the option, delta hedge it, and invest the cash in the bank. Either way, we make a riskless profit in excess of the risk-free rate of interest. At this point we say that, all things being equal, the action of investors buying and selling to exploit the arbitrage opportunity will cause the market price of the option to move in the direction that eliminates the arbitrage.

Time Out...

The money-in-the-bank equation

Equation (6.5) is the same as 'our first differential equation' for money in the bank. The notation has changed from M to Π.

6.5 THE BLACK–SCHOLES EQUATION

Substituting (6.1), (6.3) and (6.4) into (6.5) we find that

$$\left(\frac{\partial V}{\partial t} + \tfrac{1}{2}\sigma^2 S^2 \frac{\partial^2 V}{\partial S^2} \right) dt = r \left(V - S \frac{\partial V}{\partial S} \right) dt.$$

On dividing by dt and rearranging we get

$$\frac{\partial V}{\partial t} + \tfrac{1}{2}\sigma^2 S^2 \frac{\partial^2 V}{\partial S^2} + rS \frac{\partial V}{\partial S} - rV = 0. \qquad (6.6)$$

A simulation of delta hedging

This is the **Black–Scholes equation**. The equation was first written down in 1969, but a few years passed, with Fischer Black and Myron Scholes justifying the model, before it was published. The derivation of the equation was finally published in 1973, although the call and put formulæ had been published a year earlier.[2]

THE FAMOUS, NOBEL PRIZE - WINNING EQUATION THAT GOT DERIVATIVES THEORY STARTED

The Black–Scholes equation is a **linear parabolic partial differential equation**. In fact, almost all partial differential equations in finance are of a similar form. They are almost always linear,

---

[2] The pricing formulæ were being used even earlier by Ed Thorp to make money.

meaning that if you have two solutions of the equation then the sum of these is itself also a solution. Financial equations are also usually parabolic, meaning that they are related to the heat or diffusion equation of mechanics. One of the good things about this is that such equations are relatively easy to solve numerically.

The Black–Scholes equation contains all the obvious variables and parameters such as the underlying, time, and volatility, but there is no mention of the drift rate μ. Why is this? Any dependence on the drift dropped out at the same time as we eliminated the dS component of the portfolio. The economic argument for this is that since we can perfectly hedge the option with the underlying we should not be rewarded for taking unnecessary risk; only the risk-free rate of return is in the equation. This means that if you and I agree on the volatility of an asset we will agree on the value of its derivatives *even if we have differing estimates of the drift*.

Another way of looking at the hedging argument is to ask what happens if we hold a portfolio consisting of just the stock, in a quantity Δ, and cash. If Δ is the partial derivative of some option value then such a portfolio will yield an amount at expiry that is simply that option's payoff. In other words, we can use the same Black–Scholes argument to **replicate** an option just by buying and selling the underlying asset. This leads to the idea of a **complete market**. In a complete market an option can be replicated with the underlying, thus making options redundant. Why buy an option when you can get the same payoff by trading in the asset? Many things conspire to make markets incomplete such as transaction costs.

Time Out...

Slopes, gradients, etc.

The Black–Scholes partial differential equation is a relationship between the option value, the gradient in the S and t directions and the gradient of the gradient in the S direction. This sounds complicated. I can understand why. But it is really very simple when you actually come to solve the equation numerically. Here's a foretaste of what's in Chapter 28.

Imagine you're at expiry of a call option. At that time do you know the option value as a function of the underlying asset S? Yes, of course, it's just the payoff function

$$\max(S - E, 0).$$

So you know one term in Equation (6.6), the last one.

Do you know the slope of the option value in the S direction at expiry? You certainly do. It's zero for $S < E$ and one for $S > E$. (Let's not worry about what the value is *at* $S = E$, we'll leave that to others to lose sleep over.) So you know the second-to-last term in the equation. Mathematically, this is represented by the Heaviside function, $\mathcal{H}(\cdot)$, zero when its argument is negative and one when it is positive.

So

$$\frac{\partial V}{\partial S} = \mathcal{H}(S - E).$$

What about the slope of the slope in the S direction? Well, if the slope is zero or one, the slope of the slope is zero. So you know the second term in the equation.

$$\frac{\partial^2 V}{\partial S^2} = 0.$$

To recap, we've got

$$\frac{\partial V}{\partial t} + \tfrac{1}{2}\sigma^2 S^2 \times 0 + rS\mathcal{H}(S - E) - r\max(S - E, 0) = 0.$$

This is an equation for $\frac{\partial V}{\partial t}$. For example, if $S < E$ we have

$$\frac{\partial V}{\partial t} = 0.$$

If $S > E$ we have

$$\frac{\partial V}{\partial t} = -rS + rS - RE = -rE.$$

And the significance of this?

If we know $\frac{\partial V}{\partial t}$ then we know the slope of the option value in the t direction. If we know this slope then we can find the option value at the time *just before* expiry. If we are at time $T - \delta t$, where δt is small, then the option value will be approximately

$$V = 0 \quad \text{for} \quad S < E$$

and

$$V = S - E + rE\,\delta t \quad \text{for} \quad S > E.$$

See how we have found the option value one time step before expiry? We can keep repeating this procedure over and over, working backwards in time until we get to the present. And as the time step gets smaller, so this approximation to the option value gets more accurate.

One, not-so-minor point. How does the option value ever become non-zero for $S < E$? I guess we should worry about what happens at $S = E$ after all. This'll sort itself out later on, don't worry. What I've described here is the basis for the important numerical method known as the explicit finite-difference method, which we'll be seeing lots of later on.

6.6 THE BLACK–SCHOLES ASSUMPTIONS

What are the 'assumptions' in the Black–Scholes model? Here is a partial list, together with some discussion.

- **The underlying follows a lognormal random walk:** This is not entirely necessary. To find explicit solutions we will need the random term in the stochastic differential equation for S to be proportional to S. The 'factor' σ does not need to be constant to find solutions, but it must only be time dependent. As far as the validity of the equation is concerned it doesn't matter if the volatility is also asset-price dependent, but then the equation will either have very messy explicit solutions, if it has any at all, or have to be solved numerically. Then there is the question of the drift term μS. Do we need this term to take this form, after all it doesn't even appear in the equation? There is a technicality here that whatever the stochastic differential equation for the asset S, the domain over which the asset can range must be zero to infinity. This is a technicality I am not going into, but it amounts to another elimination of arbitrage. It is possible to choose the drift so that the asset is restricted to lie within a range; such a drift would not be allowed.

- **The risk-free interest rate is a known function of time:** This restriction is just to help us find explicit solutions again. If r were constant this job would be even easier. In practice, the interest rate is often taken to be time dependent but known in advance. Explicit formulæ still exist for the prices of simple contracts. In reality the rate r is not known in advance and is itself stochastic, or so it seems from data. I will discuss stochastic interest rates later. We've also assumed that lending and borrowing rates are the same.

- **There are no dividends on the underlying:** I will drop this restriction in a moment.

- **Delta hedging is done continuously:** This is definitely impossible. Hedging must be done in discrete time. Often the time between rehedges will depend on the level of transaction costs in the market for the underlying; the lower the costs, the more frequent the rehedging.

- **There are no transaction costs on the underlying:** The dynamic business of delta hedging is in reality expensive since there is a bid-offer spread on most underlyings. In some markets this matters and in some it doesn't.

- **There are no arbitrage opportunities:** This is a beauty. Of course there are arbitrage opportunities, a lot of people make a lot of money finding them.[3] It is extremely important to stress that we are ruling out model-dependent arbitrage. This is highly dubious since it depends on us having the correct model in the first place, and that is unlikely. I am happier ruling out model-independent arbitrage, i.e. arbitrage arising when two identical cashflows have different values. But even that can be criticized.

There are many more assumptions but the above are the most important.

6.7 **FINAL CONDITIONS**

The Black–Scholes equation (6.6) knows nothing about what kind of option we are valuing, whether it is a call or a put, nor what is the strike and the expiry. These points are dealt

---

[3] Life, and everything in it, is based on arbitrage opportunities and their exploitation. Evolution is statistical arbitrage.

with by the **final condition**. We must specify the option value V as a function of the underlying at the expiry date T. That is, we must prescribe $V(S, T)$, the payoff.

For example, if we have a call option then we know that

$$V(S, T) = \max(S - E, 0).$$

For a put we have

$$V(S, T) = \max(E - S, 0),$$

for a binary call

$$V(S, T) = \mathcal{H}(S - E)$$

and for a binary put

$$V(S, T) = \mathcal{H}(E - S),$$

where $\mathcal{H}(\cdot)$ is the **Heaviside function**, which is zero when its argument is negative and one when it is positive.

The imposition of the final condition will be explained in Chapters 7 and 8, and implemented numerically in later chapters.

As an aside, observe that both the asset, S, and 'money in the bank,' e^{rt}, satisfy the Black–Scholes equation.

6.8 OPTIONS ON DIVIDEND-PAYING EQUITIES

The first generalization we discuss is how to value options on stocks paying dividends. This is just about the simplest generalization of the Black–Scholes model. To keep things simple let's assume that the asset receives a continuous and constant dividend yield, D. Thus in a time dt each asset receives an amount $DS\,dt$. This must be factored into the derivation of the Black–Scholes equation. I take up the Black–Scholes argument at the point where we are looking at the change in the value of the portfolio:

$$d\Pi = \frac{\partial V}{\partial t}\,dt + \frac{\partial V}{\partial S}\,dS + \tfrac{1}{2}\sigma^2 S^2 \frac{\partial^2 V}{\partial S^2}\,dt - \Delta\,dS - D\Delta S\,dt.$$

The last term on the right-hand side is simply the amount of the dividend per asset, $DS\,dt$, multiplied by the number of the asset held, $-\Delta$. The Δ is still given by the rate of change of the option value with respect to the underlying, but after some simple substitutions we now get

$$\frac{\partial V}{\partial t} + \tfrac{1}{2}\sigma^2 S^2 \frac{\partial^2 V}{\partial S^2} + (r - D)S\frac{\partial V}{\partial S} - rV = 0. \tag{6.7}$$

6.9 CURRENCY OPTIONS

Options on currencies are handled in exactly the same way. In holding the foreign currency we receive interest at the foreign rate of interest r_f. This is just like receiving a continuous dividend. I will skip the derivation but we readily find that

$$\frac{\partial V}{\partial t} + \tfrac{1}{2}\sigma^2 S^2 \frac{\partial^2 V}{\partial S^2} + (r - r_f)S\frac{\partial V}{\partial S} - rV = 0. \tag{6.8}$$

6.10 **COMMODITY OPTIONS**

The relevant feature of commodities requiring that we adjust the Black–Scholes equation is that they have a **cost of carry**. That is, the storage of commodities is not without cost. Let us introduce q as the fraction of the value of a commodity that goes towards paying the cost of carry. This means that just holding the commodity will result in a gradual loss of wealth even if the commodity price remains fixed. To be precise, for each unit of the commodity held an amount $qS\,dt$ will be required during short time dt to finance the holding. This is just like having a negative dividend and so we get

$$\frac{\partial V}{\partial t} + \tfrac{1}{2}\sigma^2 S^2 \frac{\partial^2 V}{\partial S^2} + (r+q)S\frac{\partial V}{\partial S} - rV = 0. \tag{6.9}$$

6.11 **EXPECTATIONS AND BLACK–SCHOLES**

In the Black–Scholes equation there is no mention of the drift rate of the underlying asset μ. It seems that whether the asset is rising or falling in the long run, it doesn't affect the value of an option. This is highly counter-intuitive. But we saw exactly the same thing happening in the binomial model of Chapter 3. *At the same time as hedging away exposure to randomness, we hedge away exposure to direction.*

We also saw in Chapter 3 that an option value can be thought of as being an expectation. But a very special expectation. In words:

> The fair value of an option is the
> present value of the expected payoff at expiry
> under a risk-neutral random walk for the underlying

We can write

$$\text{option value} = e^{-r(T-t)}E\,[\text{payoff}(S)]$$

provided that the expectation is with respect to the risk-neutral random walk, not the *real* one.

But what do 'real' and 'risk neutral' mean exactly?

Real   refers to the actual random walk as seen, as realized. It has a certain volatility σ and a certain drift rate μ. We can simulate this random walk on a spreadsheet very easily, and calculate expected future option payoffs, for example.

Risk neutral   refers to an artificial random walk that has little to do with the path an asset is actually following. That is not strictly true, both the real and the risk-neutral random asset paths have the same volatility. The difference is in the drift rates. The risk-neutral random walk has a drift that is the same as the risk-free interest rate, r. So simulate risk-free random walks to calculate expectations if you want to work out theoretical option values. In Chapter 29 we will see how this is done in practice.

Time Out...

Real and risk neutral

This idea is probably more confusing than anything else in quantitative finance, but is extremely important. I will use the phrase 'risk-neutral (random walk)' several times in this book. Watch out for it, and remember that all it means is that you must pretend that the random walk of the underlying has a drift rate that is the same as the risk-free interest rate.

But remember also that such risk-neutral valuation is only valid *when hedging can be used to eliminate all risk.* If hedging is impossible, risk-neutral valuation is meaningless.

6.12 SOME OTHER WAYS OF DERIVING THE BLACK–SCHOLES EQUATION

The derivation of the Black–Scholes equation above is the classical one, and similar to the original Black and Scholes derivation. There are other ways of getting to the same result. Here are a few, without any of the details. The details, and more examples, are contained in the final reference in the Further reading.

6.12.1 The martingale approach

The value of an option can be shown to be an expectation, not a real expectation but a special, risk-neutral one. This is a useful result, since it forms the basis for pricing by simulation, see Chapter 29. The concepts of hedging and no arbitrage are obviously still used in this derivation. The major drawback with this approach is that it requires a probabilistic description of the financial world.

6.12.2 The binomial model

The binomial model is a discrete time, discrete asset price model for underlyings and again uses hedging and no arbitrage to derive a pricing algorithm for options. We have seen this in detail in Chapter 3. In taking the limit as the time step shrinks to zero we get the continuous-time Black–Scholes equation.

6.12.3 CAPM/utility

We'll be seeing the Capital Asset Pricing Model later, for the moment you just need to know that it is a model for the behavior of risky assets and a principle and algorithm for defining and finding optimal ways to allocate wealth among the assets. Portfolios are described in terms of their risk (standard deviation of returns) and reward (expected growth). If you include options in this framework then the possible combinations of risk and reward are not increased. This is because options are, in a sense, just functions of their underlyings. This is market completeness. The risk and reward on an option and on its underlying are related and the Black–Scholes equation follows.

6.13 NO ARBITRAGE IN THE BINOMIAL, BLACK–SCHOLES AND 'OTHER' WORLDS

With the Black–Scholes continuous-time model, as with the binomial discrete-time model, we have been able to eliminate uncertainty in the value of a portfolio by a judicious choice of a hedge. In both cases we find that it does not matter how the underlying asset moves, the resulting value of the portfolio is the same. This is especially clear in the binomial model. This hedging is only possible in these two simple, popular models. For consider a trivial generalization: the trinomial random walk.

In Figure 6.1 we see a representation of a trinomial random walk. After a time step δt the asset could have risen to uS, fallen to vS or not moved from S.

What happens if we try to hedge an option under this scenario? As before, we can 'hedge' with $-\Delta$ of the underlying but this time we would like to choose Δ so that the value of the portfolio (of one option and $-\Delta$ of the asset) is the same at time $t + \delta t$ no matter to which value the asset moves. In other words, we want the portfolio to have the same value for all *three* possible outcomes (see Figure 6.2). Unfortunately, we cannot choose a value for Δ that ensures this to be the case: this amounts to solving two equations (first portfolio value = second portfolio value = third portfolio value) with just one unknown (the delta). Hedging is not possible in the trinomial world. Indeed, perfect hedging, and thus the application of the 'no-arbitrage principle' is only possible in the two special cases: the Black–Scholes continuous time/continuous asset world, and the binomial world. And in the far more complex 'real' world, delta hedging is *not* possible.[4]

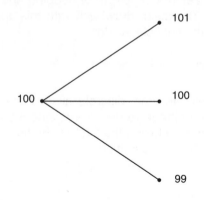

Figure 6.1 The trinomial tree.

---

[4] Is it good for the popular models to have such an unrealistic property? These models are at least a good *starting* point.

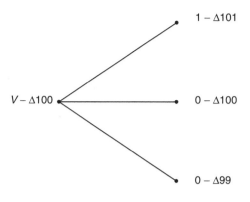

Figure 6.2 Is hedging possible?

6.14 **FORWARDS AND FUTURES**

Can we find values for forward and future contracts? How do they fit into the Black–Scholes framework? With ease. Let's look at the simpler forward contract first.

6.14.1 Forward contracts

Notation first. $V(S, t)$ will be the value of the forward contract at any time during its life on the underlying asset S, and maturing at time T. I'll assume that the delivery price is known and then find the forward contract's value. At the end of this section I'll turn this on its head to find the forward price. If you can't remember the differences between all these terms, take a look at Chapter 1 again.

Set up the portfolio of one long forward contract and short Δ of the underlying asset:

$$\Pi = V(S, t) - \Delta S.$$

This changes by an amount

$$d\Pi = \frac{\partial V}{\partial t}\, dt + \frac{\partial V}{\partial S}\, dS + \tfrac{1}{2}\sigma^2 S^2 \frac{\partial^2 V}{\partial S^2}\, dt - \Delta\, dS$$

from t to $t + dt$. Choose

$$\Delta = \frac{\partial V}{\partial S}$$

to eliminate risk. By applying the no-arbitrage argument we end up with exactly the Black–Scholes partial differential equation again.

The final condition for the equation is simply the difference between the asset price S and the fixed delivery price $\bar{S}$, say. So

$$V(S, T) = S - \bar{S}.$$

The solution of the equation with this final condition is

$$V(S, t) = S - \bar{S}e^{-r(T-t)}.$$

This is the forward contract's value during its life.

How does this relate to the setting of the delivery price in the first place, and the newspaper-quoted forward price?

The delivery price is set initially $t = t_0$ as the price that gives the forward contract zero value. If the underlying asset is S_0 at t_0 then

$$0 = S_0 - \bar{S}e^{-r(T-t_0)}$$

or

$$\bar{S} = S_0 e^{r(T-t_0)}.$$

And the forward price, as quoted? This (see Chapter 1 for a reminder) is the delivery price, as varying from day to day. So the forward price for the contract maturing at T is

$$\text{Forward price} = Se^{r(T-t)}.$$

6.15 FUTURES CONTRACTS

Emboldened by the above, let's try to calculate the futures price. This is more subtle, that's why I calculate it second. Use $F(S, t)$ to denote the futures price.

Remember that the value of the futures contract during its life is always zero because the change in value is settled daily. This cashflow must be taken into account in our analysis.

Set up a portfolio of one long futures contract and short Δ of the underlying:

$$\Pi = -\Delta S.$$

Where is the value of the futures contract? Is this a mistake? No, because it has no value it doesn't appear in the portfolio valuation equation. How does the portfolio change in value?

$$d\Pi = dF - \Delta \, dS.$$

The dF represents the cashflow due to the continual settlement. Applying Itô's lemma,

$$d\Pi = \frac{\partial F}{\partial t} dt + \frac{\partial F}{\partial S} dS + \tfrac{1}{2}\sigma^2 S^2 \frac{\partial^2 F}{\partial S^2} dt - \Delta \, dS.$$

Choose

$$\Delta = \frac{\partial F}{\partial S}$$

to eliminate risk. Set

$$d\Pi = r\Pi \, dt$$

to get

$$\frac{\partial F}{\partial t} + \tfrac{1}{2}\sigma^2 S^2 \frac{\partial^2 F}{\partial S^2} + rS\frac{\partial F}{\partial S} = 0.$$

Observe that there are only three terms in this, it is not the same as the Black–Scholes equation.

The final condition is

$$F(S, T) = S,$$

the futures price and the underlying must have the same value at maturity.

The solution is just

$$F(S, t) = Se^{r(T-t)}.$$

6.15.1   When interest rates are known, forward prices and futures prices are the same

We've just seen that the forward price and the futures price are the same when interest rates are constant. They are still the same when rates are known functions of time. Matters are more subtle when interest rates are stochastic. But we'll have to wait a few chapters to investigate this problem.

6.16   OPTIONS ON FUTURES

The final modification to the Black–Scholes model in this chapter is to value options on futures. Recalling that the future price of a non-dividend paying equity F is related to the spot price by

$$F = e^{r(T_F - t)}S$$

where T_F is the maturity date of the futures contract. We can easily change variables, and look for a solution $V(S, t) = \mathcal{V}(F, t)$. We find that

$$\frac{\partial \mathcal{V}}{\partial t} + \tfrac{1}{2}\sigma^2 F^2 \frac{\partial^2 \mathcal{V}}{\partial F^2} - r\mathcal{V} = 0. \tag{6.10}$$

The equation for an option on a future is actually simpler than the Black–Scholes equation.

6.17   SUMMARY

This was an important but not too difficult chapter. In it I introduced some very powerful and beautiful concepts such as delta hedging and no arbitrage. These two fundamental principles led to the Black–Scholes option pricing equation. Everything from this point on is based on, or is inspired by, these ideas.

FURTHER READING

- The history of option theory, leading up to Black–Scholes is described in Briys *et al.* (1998).

- The story of the derivation of the Black–Scholes equation, written by Bob Whaley, can be found in the 10th anniversary issue of *Risk* Magazine, published in December 1997.

- Of course, you must read the original work, Black & Scholes (1973) and Merton (1973).

- See Black (1976) for the details of the pricing of options on futures, and Garman & Kohlhagen (1983) for the pricing of FX options.

- For details of other ways to derive the Black–Scholes equation see Andreasen *et al.* (1998).

EXERCISES

1. Check that the following are solutions of the Black–Scholes equation:
   (a) $V(S,t) = S$,
   (b) $V(S,t) = e^{rt}$.

   Why are these solutions of particular note?

2. What is the most general solution of the Black–Scholes equation with each of the following forms?
   (a) $V(S,t) = A(S)$,
   (b) $V(S,t) = B(S)C(t)$.

3. Prove the following bounds on European call options $C(S,t)$, with expiry at time T, on an underlying share price S, with no dividends:
   (a)
   $$C \leq S,$$

   (b)
   $$C \geq \max(S - Ee^{-r(T-t)}, 0),$$

   (c)
   $$0 \leq C_1 - C_2 \leq (E_2 - E_1)e^{-r(T-t)},$$

   where C_1 and C_2 are calls with exercise prices E_1 and E_2 respectively, and $E_1 < E_2$.

4. Prove the following bounds on European put options $P(S,t)$, with expiry at time T, on an underlying share price S, with no dividends:
   (a)
   $$P \leq Ee^{-r(T-t)},$$

   (b)
   $$P \geq Ee^{-r(T-t)} - S,$$

   (c)
   $$0 \leq P_2 - P_1 \leq (E_2 - E_1)e^{-r(T-t)},$$

   where P_1 and P_2 are calls with exercise prices E_1 and E_2 respectively, and $E_1 < E_2$.

5. Prove the following bounds on European call options $C(S, t)$, on an underlying share price S, with no dividends:

    (a)

    $$C_A \geq C_B,$$

    where C_A and C_B are calls with the same exercise price E and expiry dates T_A and T_B respectively, and $T_A > T_B$.

    (b)

    $$C_2 \leq \frac{E_3 - E_2}{E_3 - E_1} C_1 + \frac{E_2 - E_1}{E_3 - E_1} C_3,$$

    where C_1, C_2 and C_3 are calls with the same expiry T, and have exercise prices E_1, E_2 and E_3 respectively, where $E_1 < E_2 < E_3$.

    Hint: Consider $E_2 = \lambda E_1 + (1 - \lambda) E_3$.

6. $C(S, t)$ and $P(S, t)$ are the values of European call and put options, with exercise price E and expiry at time T. Show that a portfolio of long the call and short the put satisfies the Black-Scholes equation. What boundary and final conditions hold for this portfolio?

7. Consider an option which expires at time T. The current value of the option is $V(S, t)$. It is possible to synthesize the option using vanilla European calls, all with expiry at time T. We assume that calls with all exercise prices are available and buy $f(E)$ of the call with exercise price E, which has value $C(S, t; E)$. The value of the synthesized option is then

    $$V(S, t) = \int_0^\infty f(E') C(S, t; E') dE'.$$

    Find the density of call options, $f(E)$, that we must use to synthesize the option.

    Hint: Synthesize the option payoff to find $f(E)$.

8. Find the random walk followed by a European option, $V(S, t)$. Use Black–Scholes to simplify the equation for dV.

9. Compare the equation for futures to Black–Scholes with a constant, continuous dividend yield. How might we price options on futures if we know the value of an option with the same payoff with the asset as underlying?

    Hint: Consider Black–Scholes with a constant, continous dividend yield $D = r$.

CHAPTER 7
partial differential equations

The aim of this Chapter...

...is to compare the Black–Scholes equation with mathematical models in other walks of life and so instill in the reader confidence in the relevance of partial differential equations, and to demonstrate some of the more useful solution methods...although we won't really be needing any of them.

In this Chapter...

- properties of the parabolic partial differential equation
- the meaning of terms in the Black–Scholes equation
- some solution techniques

7.1 **INTRODUCTION**

The analysis and solution of partial differential equations is a BIG subject. We can only skim the surface in this book. If you don't feel comfortable with the subject, then the list of books at the end should be of help. However, to understand finance, and even to solve partial differential equations numerically, does not require any great depth of understanding. The aim of this chapter is to give just enough background to the subject to permit any reasonably numerate person to follow the rest of the book; I want to keep the entry requirements to the subject as low as possible.

7.2 **PUTTING THE BLACK–SCHOLES EQUATION INTO HISTORICAL PERSPECTIVE**

The Black–Scholes partial differential equation is in two dimensions, S and t. It is a parabolic equation, meaning that it has a second derivative with respect to one variable, S, and a first derivative with respect to the other, t. Equations of this form are more colloquially known as **heat** or **diffusion equations**.

The equation, in its simplest form, goes back to almost the beginning of the 19th century. Diffusion equations have been successfully used to model

- diffusion of one material within another, smoke particles in air;

- flow of heat from one part of an object to another;

- chemical reactions, such as the Belousov–Zhabotinsky reaction which exhibits fascinating wave structure;

- electrical activity in the membranes of living organisms, the Hodgkin–Huxley model;

- dispersion of populations, individuals move both randomly and to avoid overcrowding;

- pursuit and evasion in predator–prey systems;

- pattern formation in animal coats, the formation of zebra stripes;

- dispersion of pollutants in a running stream.

In most of these cases the resulting equations are more complicated than the Black–Scholes equation.

The simplest heat equation for the temperature in a bar is usually written in the form

$$\frac{\partial u}{\partial t} = \frac{\partial^2 u}{\partial x^2}$$

where u is the temperature, x is a spatial coordinate and t is time. This equation comes from a heat balance. Consider the flow into and out of a small section of the bar. The flow of heat along the bar is proportional to the spatial gradient of the temperature

$$\frac{\partial u}{\partial x}$$

and thus the derivative of this, the *second* derivative of the temperature, is the heat retained by the small section. This retained heat is seen as a rise in the temperature, represented mathematically by

$$\frac{\partial u}{\partial t}.$$

The balance of the second x-derivative and the first t-derivative results in the heat equation. (There would be a coefficient in the equation, depending on the properties of the bar, but I have set this to one.)

7.3 THE MEANING OF THE TERMS IN THE BLACK–SCHOLES EQUATION

The Black–Scholes equation can be accurately interpreted as a reaction-convection-diffusion equation. The basic diffusion equation is a balance of a first-order t derivative and a second-order S derivative:

$$\frac{\partial V}{\partial t} + \tfrac{1}{2}\sigma^2 S^2 \frac{\partial^2 V}{\partial S^2}.$$

If these were the only terms in the Black–Scholes equation it would still exhibit the smoothing-out effect, that any discontinuities in the payoff would be instantly diffused away. The only difference between these terms and the terms as they appear in the basic heat or diffusion equation is that the diffusion coefficient is a function of one of the variables S. Thus we really have diffusion in a non-homogeneous medium.

The first-order S-derivative term

$$rS\frac{\partial V}{\partial S}$$

can be thought of as a convection term. If this equation represented some physical system, such as the diffusion of smoke particles in the atmosphere, then the convective term would be due to a breeze, blowing the smoke in a preferred direction.

The final term

$$-rV$$

is a reaction term. Balancing this term and the time derivative would give a model for decay of a radioactive body, with the half-life being related to r. (A better description, for which I am indebted to a delegate on a training course but whose name I've forgotten, is that this term is a 'passive smoking' effect.)

Putting these terms together and we get a reaction-convection-diffusion equation. An almost identical equation would be arrived at for the dispersion of pollutant along a flowing river with absorption by the sand. In this, the dispersion is the diffusion, the flow is the convection, and the absorption is the reaction.

7.4 BOUNDARY AND INITIAL/FINAL CONDITIONS

To uniquely specify a problem we must prescribe **boundary conditions** and an **initial** or **final condition**. Boundary conditions tell us how the solution must behave for all time at certain values of the asset. In financial problems we usually specify the behavior of the solution at $S = 0$ and as $S \to \infty$. We must also tell the problem how the solution begins. The Black–Scholes equation is a backward equation, meaning that the signs of the t derivative and the second S derivative in the equation are the same when written on the same side of the equals sign. We therefore have to impose a final condition. This is usually the payoff function at expiry.

The Black–Scholes equation in its basic form is linear and satisfies the superposition principle; add together two solutions of the equation and you will get a third. This is not true of non-linear equations. Linear diffusion equations have some very nice properties. Even if we start out with a discontinuity in the final data, due to a discontinuity in the payoff, this *immediately* gets smoothed out; this is due to the diffusive nature of the equation. Another nice property is the uniqueness of the solution. Provided that the solution is not allowed to grow too fast as S tends to infinity the solution will be unique. This precise definition of 'too fast' need not worry us, we will not have to worry about uniqueness for any problems we encounter.

7.5 SOME SOLUTION METHODS

We are not going to spend much time on the exact solution of the Black–Scholes equation. Such solution is important, but current market practice is such that models have features which preclude the exact solution. The few explicit, closed-form solutions that are used by practitioners will be covered in the next chapter.

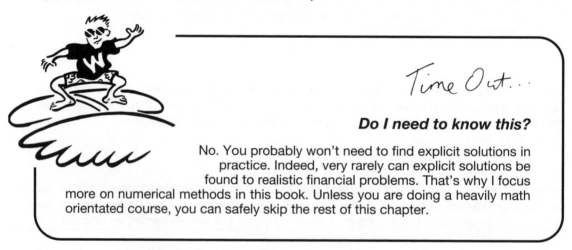

Time Out...

Do I need to know this?

No. You probably won't need to find explicit solutions in practice. Indeed, very rarely can explicit solutions be found to realistic financial problems. That's why I focus more on numerical methods in this book. Unless you are doing a heavily math orientated course, you can safely skip the rest of this chapter.

7.5.1 Transformation to constant coefficient diffusion equation

It can sometimes be useful to transform the basic Black–Scholes equation into something a little bit simpler by a change of variables. If we write

$$V(S, t) = e^{\alpha x + \beta \tau} U(x, \tau),$$

where

$$\alpha = -\tfrac{1}{2}\left(\frac{2r}{\sigma^2} - 1\right), \quad \beta = -\tfrac{1}{4}\left(\frac{2r}{\sigma^2} + 1\right)^2, \quad S = e^x \quad \text{and} \quad t = T - \frac{2\tau}{\sigma^2},$$

then $U(x, \tau)$ satisfies the basic diffusion equation

$$\frac{\partial U}{\partial \tau} = \frac{\partial^2 U}{\partial x^2}.$$ (7.1)

This simpler equation is easier to handle than the Black–Scholes equation. Sometimes that can be important, for example when seeking closed-form solutions, or in some simple numerical schemes. We shall not pursue this any further.

7.5.2 Green's functions

One solution of the Black–Scholes equation is

$$V'(S, t) = \frac{e^{-r(T-t)}}{\sigma S'\sqrt{2\pi(T-t)}} e^{-\left(\log(S/S') + \left(r - \frac{1}{2}\sigma^2\right)(T-t)\right)^2 / 2\sigma^2(T-t)}$$ (7.2)

for any S'. (You can verify this by substituting back into the equation, but we'll also be seeing it derived in the next chapter.) This solution is special because as $t \to T$ it becomes zero everywhere, except at $S = S'$. In this limit the function becomes what is known as a **Dirac delta function**. Think of this as a function that is zero everywhere except at one point where it is infinite, in such a way that its integral is one. How is this of help to us?

Expression (7.2) is a solution of the Black–Scholes equation for any S'. Because of the linearity of the equation we can multiply (7.2) by any constant, and we get another solution. But then we can also get another solution by adding together expressions of the form (7.2) but with different values for S'. Putting this together, and thinking of an integral as just a way of adding together many solutions, we find that

$$\frac{e^{-r(T-t)}}{\sigma\sqrt{2\pi(T-t)}} \int_0^\infty e^{-\left(\log(S/S') + \left(r - \frac{1}{2}\sigma^2\right)(T-t)\right)^2 / 2\sigma^2(T-t)} f(S')\frac{dS'}{S'}$$

is also a solution of the Black–Scholes equation for any function $f(S')$. (If you don't believe me, substitute it into the Black–Scholes equation.)

Because of the nature of the integrand as $t \to T$ (i.e. that it is zero everywhere except at S' and has integral one), if we choose the arbitrary function $f(S')$ to be the payoff function then this expression becomes the solution of the problem:

$$V(S, t) = \frac{e^{-r(T-t)}}{\sigma\sqrt{2\pi(T-t)}} \int_0^\infty e^{-\left(\log(S/S') + \left(r - \frac{1}{2}\sigma^2\right)(T-t)\right)^2 / 2\sigma^2(T-t)} \text{Payoff}(S')\frac{dS'}{S'}.$$

The function $V'(S, t)$ given by (7.2) is called the **Green's function**.

7.5.3 Series solution

Sometimes we have boundary conditions at two finite (and non-zero) values of S, S_u and S_d, say (we see examples in Chapter 13). For this type of problem, we postulate that the required solution of the Black–Scholes equation can be written as an infinite sum of special functions. First of all, transform to the nicer basic diffusion equation in x and τ. Now write the solution as

$$e^{\alpha x + \beta \tau} \sum_{i=0}^{\infty} a_i(\tau) \sin(i\omega x) + b_i(\tau) \cos(i\omega x),$$

for some ω and some functions a and b to be found. The linearity of the equation suggests that a sum of solutions might be appropriate. If this is to satisfy the Black–Scholes equation then we must have

$$\frac{da_i}{d\tau} = -i^2 \omega^2 a_i(\tau) \quad \text{and} \quad \frac{db_i}{d\tau} = -i^2 \omega^2 b_i(\tau).$$

You can easily show this by substitution. The solutions are thus

$$a_i(\tau) = A_i e^{-i^2 \omega^2 \tau} \quad \text{and} \quad b_i(\tau) = B_i e^{-i^2 \omega^2 \tau}.$$

The solution of the Black–Scholes equation is therefore

$$e^{\alpha x + \beta \tau} \sum_{i=0}^{\infty} e^{-i^2 \omega^2 \tau} (A_i \sin(i\omega x) + B_i \cos(i\omega x)). \tag{7.3}$$

We have solved the equation, all that we need to do now is to satisfy boundary and initial conditions.

Consider the example where the payoff at time $\tau = 0$ is $f(x)$ (although it would be expressed in the original variables, of course) but the contract becomes worthless if ever $x = x_d$ or $x = x_u$.[1]

Rewrite the term in brackets in (7.3) as

$$C_i \sin\left(i\omega' \frac{x - x_d}{x_u - x_d}\right) + D_i \cos\left(i\omega' \frac{x - x_d}{x_u - x_d}\right).$$

To ensure that the option is worthless on these two x values, choose $D_i = 0$ and $\omega' = \pi$. The boundary conditions are thereby satisfied. All that remains is to choose the C_i to satisfy the final condition:

$$e^{\alpha x} \sum_{i=0}^{\infty} C_i \sin\left(i\omega' \frac{x - x_d}{x_u - x_d}\right) = f(x).$$

This also is simple. Multiplying both sides by

$$\sin\left(j\omega' \frac{x - x_d}{x_u - x_d}\right),$$

and integrating between x_d and x_u we find that

$$C_j = \frac{2}{x_u - x_d} \int_{x_d}^{x_u} f(x) e^{-\alpha x} \sin\left(j\omega' \frac{x - x_d}{x_u - x_d}\right) dx.$$

This technique, which can be generalized, is the **Fourier series method**. There are some problems with the method if you are trying to represent a discontinuous function with a sum of trigonometrical functions. The oscillatory nature of an approximate solution with a finite number of terms is known as **Gibbs phenomenon**.

---

[1] This is an example of a double knock-out option, see Chapter 13.

7.6 **SIMILARITY REDUCTIONS**

Apart from the Green's function, we're not going to use any of the above techniques in this book; rarely will we even find explicit solutions. But one technique that we will find useful is the **similarity reduction**. I will demonstrate the idea using the simple diffusion equation, we will later use it in many other, more complicated problems.

The basic diffusion equation

$$\frac{\partial u}{\partial t} = \frac{\partial^2 u}{\partial x^2} \tag{7.4}$$

is an equation for the function u which depends on the two variables x and t. Sometimes, in very, very special cases, we can write the solution as a function of just one variable. Let me give an example. Verify that the function

$$u(x, t) = \int_0^{x/t^{1/2}} e^{-\frac{1}{4}\xi^2}\, d\xi$$

satisfies (7.4). But in this function x and t only appear in the combination

$$\frac{x}{t^{1/2}}.$$

Thus, in a sense, u is a function of only one variable.

A slight generalization, but also demonstrating the idea of similarity solutions, is to look for a solution of the form

$$u = t^{-1/2} f(\xi) \tag{7.5}$$

where

$$\xi = \frac{x}{t^{1/2}}.$$

Substitute (7.5) into (7.4) to find that a solution for f is

$$f = e^{-\frac{1}{4}\xi^2},$$

so that

$$t^{-1/2} e^{-\frac{1}{4}\frac{x^2}{t}}$$

is also a special solution of the diffusion equation.

Be warned, though. You can't always find similarity solutions; not only must the equation have a particularly nice structure but also the similarity form must be consistent with any initial condition or boundary conditions.

7.7 **OTHER ANALYTICAL TECHNIQUES**

The other two main solution techniques for linear partial differential equations are Fourier and Laplace transforms. These are such large and highly technical subjects that I really cannot begin to give an idea of how they work, space is far too short. But be reassured that it is probably not worth your while learning the techniques, since in finance they can be used to solve only a very small number of problems. If you want to learn something useful then move on to the next section.

7.8 NUMERICAL SOLUTION

Even though there are several techniques that we can use for finding solutions, in the vast majority of cases we must solve the Black–Scholes equation numerically. But we are lucky. Parabolic differential equations are just about the easiest equations to solve numerically. Obviously, there are any number of really sophisticated techniques, but if you stick with the simplest then you can't go far wrong. I want to stress that I am going to derive many partial differential equations from now on, and I am going to assume you trust me that we will at the end of the book see how to solve them.

7.9 SUMMARY

This short chapter is only intended as a primer on partial differential equations. If you want to study this subject in depth, see the books and articles mentioned below.

FURTHER READING

- Grindrod (1991) is all about reaction-diffusion equations, where they come from and their analysis. The book includes many of the physical models described above.

- Murray (1989) also contains a great deal on reaction-diffusion equations, but concentrating on models of biological systems.

- Wilmott & Wilmott (1990) describe the diffusion of pollutant along a river with convection and absorption by the river bed.

- The classical reference works for diffusion equations are Crank (1989) and Carslaw & Jaeger (1989). But also see the book on partial differential equations by Sneddon (1957) and the book on general applied mathematical methods by Strang (1986).

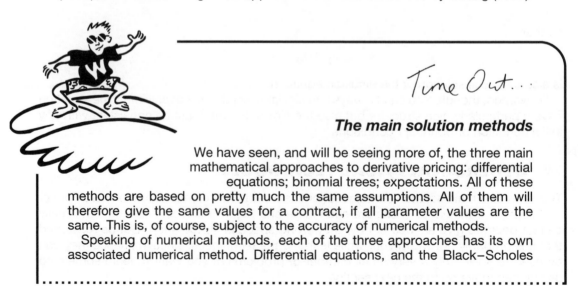

Time Out...

The main solution methods

We have seen, and will be seeing more of, the three main mathematical approaches to derivative pricing: differential equations; binomial trees; expectations. All of these methods are based on pretty much the same assumptions. All of them will therefore give the same values for a contract, if all parameter values are the same. This is, of course, subject to the accuracy of numerical methods.

Speaking of numerical methods, each of the three approaches has its own associated numerical method. Differential equations, and the Black–Scholes equation, in particular, can be solved by finite-difference methods. The whole of Chapter 28 is devoted to this subject. The binomial tree model is, interestingly, also its own numerical method, and we've seen that in some detail already in Chapter 3. Finally, pricing by calculating risk-neutral expectations is one of the subjects in Chapter 29 on Monte Carlo simulations.

EXERCISES

1. Consider an option with value $V(S, t)$, which has payoff at time T. Reduce the Black–Scholes equation, with final and boundary conditions, to the diffusion equation, using the following transformations:

   (a)

   $$S = Ee^x, \quad t = T - \frac{2\tau}{\sigma^2}, \quad V(S, t) = Ev(x, \tau),$$

   (b)

   $$v = e^{\alpha x + \beta \tau} u(x, \tau),$$

   for some α and β. What is the transformed payoff? What are the new initial and boundary conditions? Illustrate with a vanilla European call option.

2. The solution to the initial value problem for the diffusion equation is unique (given certain constraints on the behavior, it must be sufficiently smooth and decay sufficiently fast at infinity). This can be shown as follows:

   Suppose that there are two solutions $u_1(x, \tau)$ and $u_2(x, \tau)$ to the problem

   $$\frac{\partial u}{\partial \tau} = \frac{\partial^2 u}{\partial x^2}, \quad \text{on} \ -\infty < x < \infty,$$

   with

   $$u(x, 0) = u_0(x).$$

   Set $v(x, \tau) = u_1 - u_2$. This is a solution of the equation with $v(x, 0) = 0$. Consider

   $$E(\tau) = \int_{-\infty}^{\infty} v^2(x, \tau) \, dx.$$

   Show that

   $$E(\tau) \geq 0, \quad E(0) = 0,$$

   and integrate by parts to find that

   $$\frac{dE}{d\tau} \leq 0.$$

   Hence show that $E(\tau) \equiv 0$ and, consequently, $u_1(x, \tau) \equiv u_2(x, \tau)$.

3. Suppose that $u(x, \tau)$ satisfies the following initial value problem:

$$\frac{\partial u}{\partial \tau} = \frac{\partial^2 u}{\partial x^2}, \quad \text{on} \; -\pi < x < \pi, \; \tau > 0,$$

with

$$u(-\pi, \tau) = u(\pi, \tau) = 0, \quad u(x, 0) = u_0(x).$$

Solve for u using a Fourier sine series in x, with coefficients depending on τ.

4. Check that u_δ satisfies the diffusion equation, where

$$u_\delta = \frac{1}{2\sqrt{\pi\tau}} e^{-\frac{x^2}{4\tau}}.$$

5. Solve the following initial value problem for $u(x, \tau)$ on a semi-infinite interval, using a Green's function:

$$\frac{\partial u}{\partial \tau} = \frac{\partial^2 u}{\partial x^2}, \quad \text{on} \; x > 0, \; \tau > 0,$$

with

$$u(x, 0) = u_0(x) \text{ for } x > 0, \quad u(0, \tau) = 0 \text{ for } \tau > 0.$$

Hint: Define $v(x, \tau)$ as

$$v(x, \tau) = u(x, \tau) \text{ if } x > 0,$$
$$v(x, \tau) = -u(-x, \tau) \text{ if } x < 0.$$

Then we can show that $v(0, \tau) = 0$ and

$$u(x, \tau) = \frac{1}{2\sqrt{\pi\tau}} \int_0^\infty u_0(s)(e^{-(x-s)^2/4\tau} - e^{-(x+s)^2/4\tau}) \, ds.$$

6. Reduce the following parabolic equation to the diffusion equation.

$$\frac{\partial u}{\partial \tau} = \frac{\partial^2 u}{\partial x^2} + a\frac{\partial u}{\partial x} + b,$$

where a and b are constants.

7. Using a change of time variable, reduce

$$c(\tau)\frac{\partial u}{\partial \tau} = \frac{\partial^2 u}{\partial x^2},$$

to the diffusion equation when $c(\tau) > 0$.

Consider the Black–Scholes equation, when σ and r can be functions of time, but $k = 2r/\sigma^2$ is still a constant. Reduce the Black–Scholes equation to the diffusion equation in this case.

8. Show that if

$$\frac{\partial u}{\partial \tau} = \frac{\partial^2 u}{\partial x^2}, \quad \text{on } -\infty < x < \infty, \ \tau > 0,$$

with

$$u(x, 0) = u_0(x) > 0,$$

then $u(x, \tau) > 0$ for all τ.

Use this result to show that an option with positive payoff will always have a positive value.

9. If $f(x, \tau) \geq 0$ in the initial value problem

$$\frac{\partial u}{\partial \tau} = \frac{\partial^2 u}{\partial x^2} + f(x, \tau), \quad \text{on } -\infty < x < \infty, \ \tau > 0,$$

with

$$u(x, 0) = 0, \text{ and } u \to 0 \text{ as } |x| \to \infty,$$

then $u(x, \tau) \geq 0$. Hence show that if C_1 and C_2 are European calls with volatilities σ_1 and σ_2 respectively, but are otherwise identical, then $C_1 > C_2$ if $\sigma_1 > \sigma_2$.

Use put-call parity to show that the same is true for European puts.

CHAPTER 8
the Black–Scholes formulae and the 'greeks'

The aim of this Chapter...

...is to show how the basic Black–Scholes formulæ are derived from the Black–Scholes equation, and to introduce more sophisticated hedging strategies. The chapter contains lots of useful formulæ which are also summarized at the end.

In this Chapter...

- the derivation of the Black–Scholes formulæ for calls, puts and simple digitals

- the meaning and importance of the 'greeks,' delta, gamma, theta, vega and rho

- the difference between differentiation with respect to variables and to parameters

- formulæ for the greeks for calls, puts and simple digitals

8.1 INTRODUCTION

The Black–Scholes equation has simple solutions for calls, puts and some other contracts. In this chapter I'm going to walk you through the derivation of these formulæ step by step. This is one of the few places in the book where I do derive formulæ. The reason that I don't often derive formulæ is that the majority of contracts do not have explicit solutions for their theoretical value. Instead much of my emphasis will be placed on finding numerical solutions of the Black–Scholes equation.

We've seen how the quantity 'delta,' the first derivative of the option value with respect to the underlying, occurs as an important quantity in the derivation of the Black–Scholes equation. In this chapter I describe the importance of other derivatives of the option price, with respect to the variables (the underlying asset and time) and with respect to some of the parameters. These derivatives are important in the hedging of an option position, playing key roles in risk management. It can be argued that it is more important to get the hedging correct than to be precise in the pricing of a contract. The reason for this is that if you are accurate in your hedging you will have reduced or eliminated future uncertainty. This leaves you with a profit (or loss) that is set the moment that you buy or sell the contract. But if your hedging is inaccurate, then it doesn't matter, within reason, what you sold the contract for initially, future uncertainty could easily dominate any initial profit. Of course, life is not so simple, in reality we are exposed to model error, which can make a mockery of anything we do. However, this illustrates the importance of good hedging, and that's where the 'greeks' come in.

Time Out...

Close your eyes until I tell you to open them

Unless you are doing a highly mathsy course, you won't
need to know all the manipulations that follow.

8.2 DERIVATION OF THE FORMULÆ FOR CALLS, PUTS AND SIMPLE DIGITALS

The Black–Scholes equation is

$$\frac{\partial V}{\partial t} + \tfrac{1}{2}\sigma^2 S^2 \frac{\partial^2 V}{\partial S^2} + rS\frac{\partial V}{\partial S} - rV = 0. \tag{8.1}$$

This equation must be solved with final condition depending on the payoff: each contract will have a different functional form prescribed at expiry $t = T$, depending on whether it is a call, a put or something more fancy. This is the final condition that must be imposed to make the solution unique. We'll worry about final conditions later, for the moment concentrate on manipulating (8.1) into something we can easily solve.

The first step in the manipulation is to change from present value to future value terms. Recalling that the payoff is received at time T but that we are valuing the option at time t this suggests that we write

$$V(S, t) = e^{-r(T-t)}U(S, t).$$

This takes our differential equation to

$$\frac{\partial U}{\partial t} + \tfrac{1}{2}\sigma^2 S^2 \frac{\partial^2 U}{\partial S^2} + rS\frac{\partial U}{\partial S} = 0.$$

The second step is really trivial. Because we are solving a backward equation, discussed in Chapter 7, we'll write

$$\tau = T - t.$$

This now takes our equation to

$$\frac{\partial U}{\partial \tau} = \tfrac{1}{2}\sigma^2 S^2 \frac{\partial^2 U}{\partial S^2} + rS\frac{\partial U}{\partial S}.$$

When we first started modeling equity prices we used intuition about the asset price *return* to build up the stochastic differential equation model. Let's go back to examine the return and write

$$\xi = \log S.$$

With this as the new variable, we find that

$$\frac{\partial}{\partial S} = e^{-\xi}\frac{\partial}{\partial \xi} \quad \text{and} \quad \frac{\partial^2}{\partial S^2} = e^{-2\xi}\frac{\partial^2}{\partial \xi^2} - e^{-2\xi}\frac{\partial}{\partial \xi}.$$

Now the Black–Scholes equation becomes

$$\frac{\partial U}{\partial \tau} = \tfrac{1}{2}\sigma^2 \frac{\partial^2 U}{\partial \xi^2} + \left(r - \tfrac{1}{2}\sigma^2\right)\frac{\partial U}{\partial \xi}.$$

What has this done for us? It has taken the problem defined for $0 \leq S < \infty$ to one defined for $-\infty < \xi < \infty$. But more importantly, the coefficients in the equation are now all constant, independent of the underlying. This is a big step forward, made possible by the lognormality of the underlying asset. We are nearly there.

The last step is simple, but the motivation is not so obvious. Write

$$x = \xi + \left(r - \tfrac{1}{2}\sigma^2\right)\tau,$$

and $U = W(x, \tau)$. This is just a 'translation' of the coordinate system. It's a bit like using the forward price of the asset instead of the spot price as a variable. After this change of variables the Black–Scholes becomes the simpler

$$\frac{\partial W}{\partial \tau} = \tfrac{1}{2}\sigma^2 \frac{\partial^2 W}{\partial x^2}. \tag{8.2}$$

To summarize,

$$V(S, t) = e^{-r(T-t)}U(S, t) = e^{-r\tau}U(S, T - \tau) = e^{-r\tau}U(e^\xi, T - \tau)$$

$$= e^{-r\tau}U\left(e^{x - \left(r - \frac{1}{2}\sigma^2\right)\tau}, T - \tau\right) = e^{-r\tau}W(x, \tau).$$

To those of you who already know the Black–Scholes formulæ for calls and puts the variable x will ring a bell:

$$x = \xi + \left(r - \frac{1}{2}\sigma^2\right)\tau = \log S + \left(r - \frac{1}{2}\sigma^2\right)(T - t).$$

Having turned the original Black–Scholes equation into something much simpler, let's take a break for a moment while I explain where we are headed.

I'm going to derive an expression for the value of any option whose payoff is a known function of the asset price at expiry. This includes calls, puts and digitals. This expression will be in the form of an integral. For special cases, I'll show how to rewrite this integral in terms of the cumulative distribution function for the Normal distribution. This is particularly useful since the function can be found on spreadsheets, calculators and in the backs of books. But there are two steps before I can write down this integral.

The first step is to find a special solution of (8.2), called the fundamental solution. This solution has useful properties. The second step is to use the linearity of the equation and the useful properties of the special solution to find the *general solution* of the equation. Here we go.

I'm going to look for a special solution of (8.2) of the following form

$$W(x, \tau) = \tau^\alpha f\left(\frac{(x - x')}{\tau^\beta}\right), \tag{8.3}$$

where x' is an arbitrary constant. And I'll call this special solution $W_f(x, \tau; x')$. Note that the unknown function depends on only *one* variable $(x - x')/\tau^\beta$. As well as finding the function f we must find the constant parameters α and β. We can expect that if this approach works, the equation for f will be an ordinary differential equation since the function only has one variable. This reduction of dimension is an example of a similarity reduction, discussed in Chapter 7.

Substituting expression (8.3) into (8.2) we get

$$\tau^{\alpha-1}\left(\alpha f - \beta\eta\frac{df}{d\eta}\right) = \frac{1}{2}\sigma^2\tau^{\alpha-2\beta}\frac{d^2f}{d\eta^2}, \tag{8.4}$$

where

$$\eta = \frac{x - x'}{\tau^\beta}.$$

Examining the dependence of the two terms in (8.4) on both τ and η we see that we can only have a solution if

$$\alpha - 1 = \alpha - 2\beta \quad \text{i.e.} \quad \beta = \frac{1}{2}.$$

I want to ensure that my 'special solution' has the property that its integral over all ξ is independent of τ, for reasons that will become apparent. To ensure this, I require

$$\int_{-\infty}^{\infty} \tau^{\alpha} f((x - x')/\tau^{\beta}) \, dx$$

to be constant. I can write this as

$$\int_{-\infty}^{\infty} \tau^{\alpha+\beta} f(\eta) \, d\eta$$

and so I need

$$\alpha = -\beta = -\tfrac{1}{2}.$$

The function f now satisfies

$$-f - \eta \frac{df}{d\eta} = \sigma^2 \frac{d^2 f}{d\eta^2}.$$

This can be written

$$\sigma^2 \frac{d^2 f}{d\eta^2} + \frac{d(\eta f)}{d\eta} = 0,$$

which can be integrated once to give

$$\sigma^2 \frac{df}{d\eta} + \eta f = a,$$

where a is a constant. For my special solution I'm going to choose $a = 0$. This equation can be integrated again to give

$$f(\eta) = b e^{-\frac{\eta^2}{2\sigma^2}}.$$

I will choose the constant b such that the integral of f from minus infinity to plus infinity is one:

$$f(\eta) = \frac{1}{\sqrt{2\pi}\sigma} e^{-\frac{\eta^2}{2\sigma^2}}.$$

This is the special solution I have been seeking:[1]

$$W(x, \tau) = \frac{1}{\sqrt{2\pi\tau}\sigma} e^{-\frac{(x-x')^2}{2\sigma^2\tau}}.$$

Now I will explain why it is useful in our quest for the Black–Scholes formulæ.

In Figure 8.1 is plotted W as a function of x' for several values of τ. Observe how the function rises in the middle but decays at the sides. As $\tau \to 0$ this becomes more pronounced. The 'middle' is the point $x' = x$. At this point the function grows unboundedly

---

[1] It is just the probability density function for a Normal random variable with mean zero and standard deviation σ.

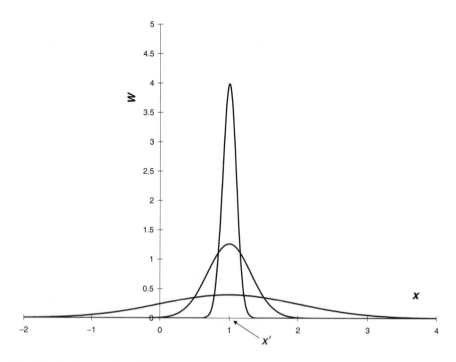

Figure 8.1 The fundamental solution.

and away from this point the function decays to zero as $\tau \to 0$. Although the function is increasingly confined to a narrower and narrower region its area remains fixed at one. These properties of decay away from one point, unbounded growth at that point and constant area, result in a **Dirac delta function** $\delta(x' - x)$ as $\tau \to 0$. The delta function has one important property, namely

$$\int \delta(x' - x)\, g\,(x')\, dx' = g(x)$$

where the integration is from any point below x to any point above x. Thus the delta function 'picks out' the value of g at the point where the delta function is singular, i.e. at $x' = x$. In the limit as $\tau \to 0$ the function W becomes a delta function at $x = x'$. This means that

$$\lim_{\tau \to 0} \frac{1}{\sigma\sqrt{2\pi\tau}} \int_{-\infty}^{\infty} e^{-\frac{(x'-x)^2}{2\sigma^2\tau}}\, g(x')\, dx' = g(x).$$

This property of the special solution, together with the linearity of the Black–Scholes equation, are all that are needed to find some explicit solutions.

Now is the time to consider the payoff. Let's call it

$$\text{Payoff}(S).$$

This is the value of the option at time $t = T$. It is the final condition for the function V, satisfying the Black–Scholes equation:

$$V(S, T) = \text{Payoff}(S).$$

In our new variables, this final condition is

$$W(x, 0) = \text{Payoff}(e^x).$$ (8.5)

I claim that the solution of this for $\tau > 0$ is

$$W(x, \tau) = \int_{-\infty}^{\infty} W_f(x, \tau; x') \text{Payoff}(e^{x'}) \, dx'.$$ (8.6)

To show this, I just have to demonstrate that the expression satisfies Equation (8.2) and the final condition (8.5). Both of these are straightforward. The integration with respect to x' is similar to a summation, and since each individual component satisfies the equation so does the sum/integral. Alternatively, differentiate (8.6) under the integral sign to see that it satisfies the partial differential equation. That it satisfies condition (8.5) follows from the special properties of the fundamental solution W_f.

Retracing our steps to write our solution in terms of the original variables, we get

$$V(S, t) = \frac{e^{-r(T-t)}}{\sigma \sqrt{2\pi(T-t)}} \int_0^\infty e^{-\left(\log(S/S') + \left(r - \frac{1}{2}\sigma^2\right)(T-t)\right)^2 / 2\sigma^2(T-t)} \text{Payoff}(S') \frac{dS'}{S'},$$ (8.7)

where I have written $x' = \log S'$.

This is the exact solution for the option value in terms of the arbitrary payoff function. In the next sections I will manipulate this expression for special payoff functions.

8.2.1   Formula for a call

The call option has the payoff function

$$\text{Payoff}(S) = \max(S - E, 0).$$

Expression (8.7) can then be written as

$$\frac{e^{-r(T-t)}}{\sigma \sqrt{2\pi(T-t)}} \int_E^\infty e^{-\left(\log(S/S') + \left(r - \frac{1}{2}\sigma^2\right)(T-t)\right)^2 / 2\sigma^2(T-t)} (S' - E) \frac{dS'}{S'}.$$

Return to the variable $x' = \log S'$, to write this as

$$\frac{e^{-r(T-t)}}{\sigma \sqrt{2\pi(T-t)}} \int_{\log E}^\infty e^{-\left(-x' + \log S + \left(r - \frac{1}{2}\sigma^2\right)(T-t)\right)^2 / 2\sigma^2(T-t)} (e^{x'} - E) \, dx'$$

$$= \frac{e^{-r(T-t)}}{\sigma \sqrt{2\pi(T-t)}} \int_{\log E}^\infty e^{-\left(-x' + \log S + \left(r - \frac{1}{2}\sigma^2\right)(T-t)\right)^2 / 2\sigma^2(T-t)} e^{x'} \, dx'$$

$$- E \frac{e^{-r(T-t)}}{\sigma \sqrt{2\pi(T-t)}} \int_{\log E}^\infty e^{-\left(-x' + \log S + \left(r - \frac{1}{2}\sigma^2\right)(T-t)\right)^2 / 2\sigma^2(T-t)} \, dx'.$$

Both integrals in this expression can be written in the form

$$\int_d^\infty e^{-\frac{1}{2}x'^2} \, dx'$$

for some *d* (the second is just about in this form already, and the first just needs a completion of the square).

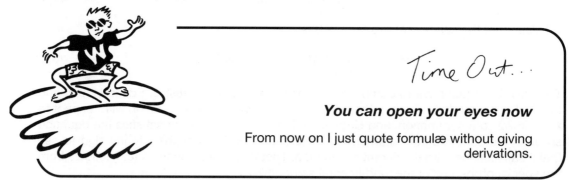

Apart from a couple of minor differences, this integral is just like the cumulative distribution function for the standardized Normal distribution[2] defined by

$$N(x) = \frac{1}{\sqrt{2\pi}} \int_{-\infty}^{x} e^{-\frac{1}{2}\phi^2} \, d\phi.$$

This function, plotted in Figure 8.2, is the probability that a Normally distributed variable is less than *x*.

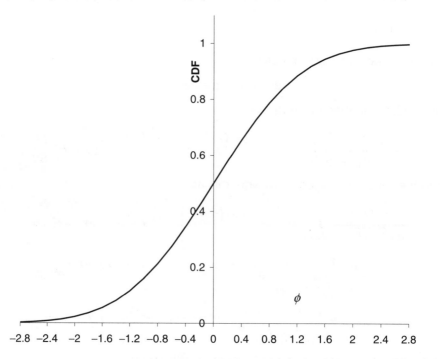

Figure 8.2 The cumulative distribution function for a standardized Normal random variable, $N(x)$.

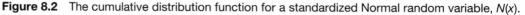

[2] I.e. having zero mean and unit standard deviation.

Thus the option price can be written as two separate terms involving the cumulative distribution function for a Normal distribution:

$$\text{Call option value} = SN(d_1) - Ee^{-r(T-t)}N(d_2)$$

where

$$d_1 = \frac{\log(S/E) + \left(r + \frac{1}{2}\sigma^2\right)(T-t)}{\sigma\sqrt{T-t}}$$

and

$$d_2 = \frac{\log(S/E) + \left(r - \frac{1}{2}\sigma^2\right)(T-t)}{\sigma\sqrt{T-t}}.$$

Excel representation of call value

When there is continuous dividend yield on the underlying, or it is a currency, then

Call option value

$$Se^{-D(T-t)}N(d_1) - Ee^{-r(T-t)}N(d_2)$$

$$d_1 = \frac{\log(S/E) + \left(r - D + \frac{1}{2}\sigma^2\right)(T-t)}{\sigma\sqrt{T-t}}$$

$$d_2 = \frac{\log(S/E) + \left(r - D - \frac{1}{2}\sigma^2\right)(T-t)}{\sigma\sqrt{T-t}}$$

$$= d_1 - \sigma\sqrt{T-t}$$

YOU'LL BE USING THIS SO MUCH THAT IT HELPS IF YOU'VE MEMORIZED IT

Time Out...

In Excel

In Excel the cumulative distribution function for the standardized Normal distribution is NORMSDIST(). The natural logarithm is LN().

The option value is shown in Figure 8.3 as a function of the underlying asset at a fixed time to expiry. In Figure 8.4 the value of the at-the-money option is shown as a function of time, expiry is $t = 1$. In Figure 8.5 is the call value as a function of both the underlying and time.

When the asset is 'at-the-money forward,' i.e. $S = Ee^{-(r-D)(T-t)}$, then there is a simple approximation for the call value (Brenner & Subrahmanyam, 1994):

$$\text{Call} \approx 0.4\, Se^{-D(T-t)}\sigma\sqrt{T-t}.$$

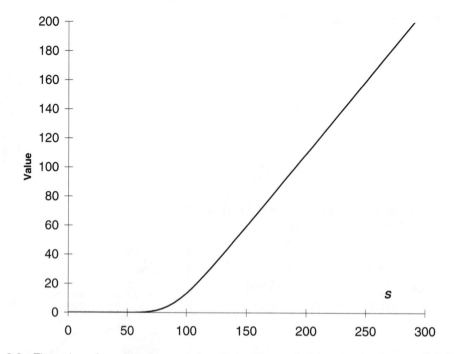

Figure 8.3 The value of a call option as a function of the underlying asset price at a fixed time to expiry.

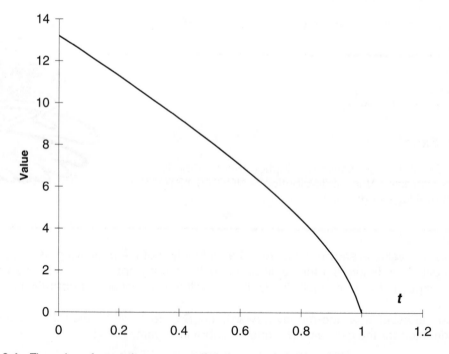

Figure 8.4 The value of an at-the-money call option as a function of time.

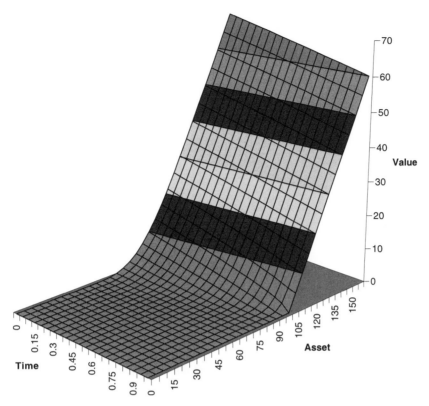

Figure 8.5 The value of a call option as a function of asset and time.

8.2.2 Formula for a put

The put option has payoff

$$\text{Payoff}(S) = \max(E - S, 0).$$

The value of a put option can be found in the same way as above, or using put-call parity

$$\text{Put option value} = -SN(-d_1) + Ee^{-r(T-t)}N(-d_2),$$

with the same d_1 and d_2.

When there is continuous dividend yield on the underlying, or it is a currency, then

> **Put option value**
> $$-Se^{-D(T-t)}N(-d_1) + Ee^{-r(T-t)}N(-d_2)$$

Excel
representation of
put value

YOU MEMORIZED THE CALL VALUE, I HOPE, NOW MEMORIZE THE PUT

The option value is shown in Figure 8.6 against the underlying asset and in Figure 8.7 against time. In Figure 8.8 is the option value as a function of both the underlying asset and time.

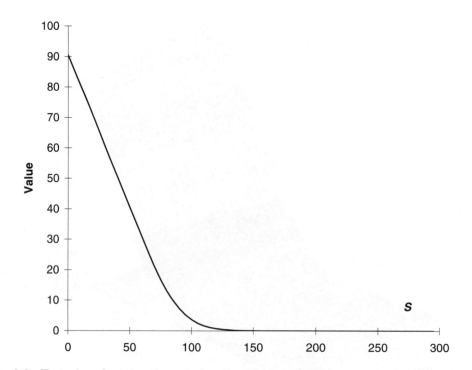

Figure 8.6   The value of a put option as a function of the underlying asset at a fixed time to expiry.

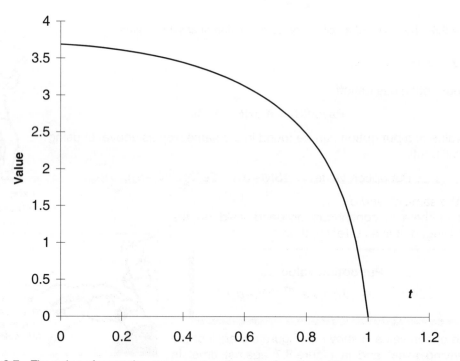

Figure 8.7   The value of an at-the-money put option as a function of time.

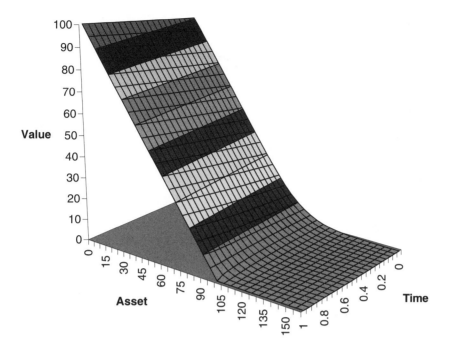

Figure 8.8 The value of a put option as a function of asset and time.

When the asset is at-the-money forward the simple approximation for the put value (Brenner & Subrahmanyam, 1994) is

$$\text{Put} \approx 0.4 \, Se^{-D(T-t)} \sigma \sqrt{T-t}.$$

8.2.3 Formula for a binary call

The binary call has payoff

$$\text{Payoff}(S) = \mathcal{H}(S - E),$$

where $\mathcal{H}$ is the Heaviside function taking the value one when its argument is positive and zero otherwise.

Incorporating a dividend yield, we can write the option value as

$$\frac{e^{-r(T-t)}}{\sigma\sqrt{2\pi(T-t)}} \int_{\log E}^{\infty} e^{-\left(x'-\log S-\left(r-D-\frac{1}{2}\sigma^2\right)(T-t)\right)^2 \Big/ 2\sigma^2(T-t)} \, dx'.$$

This term is just like the second term in the call option equation and so

Excel representation of binary values

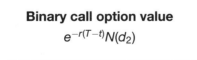

Binary call option value
$$e^{-r(T-t)}N(d_2)$$

The option value is shown in Figure 8.9.

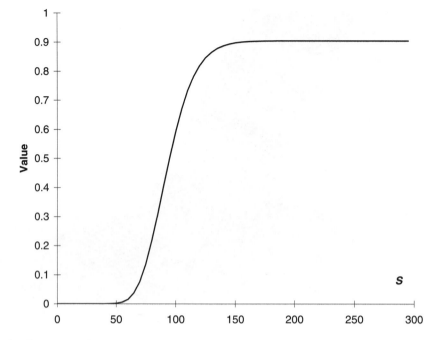

Figure 8.9 The value of a binary call option.

8.2.4 Formula for a binary put

The binary put has a payoff of one if $S < E$ at expiry. It has a value of

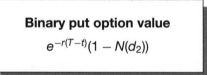

Binary put option value

$$e^{-r(T-t)}(1 - N(d_2))$$

since a binary call and a binary put must add up to the present value of $1 received at time T. The option value is shown in Figure 8.10.

THE DELTA IS OUR FIRST, AND MOST IMPORTANT, 'GREEK'

8.3 DELTA

The **delta** of an option or a portfolio of options is the sensitivity of the option or portfolio to the underlying. It is the rate of change of value with respect to the asset:

$$\Delta = \frac{\partial V}{\partial S}$$

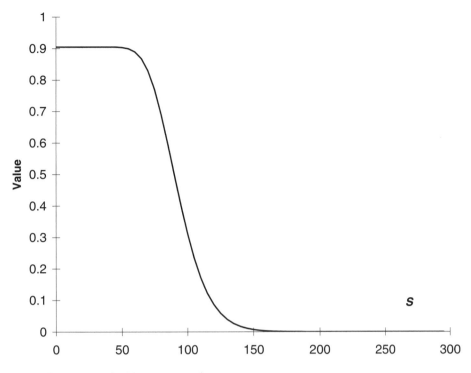

Figure 8.10   The value of a binary put option.

Here V can be the value of a single contract or of a whole portfolio of contracts. The delta of a portfolio of options is just the sum of the deltas of all the individual positions.

The theoretical device of delta hedging, introduced in Chapters 3 and 6, for eliminating risk is far more than that, it is a very important practical technique.

Roughly speaking, the financial world is divided up into speculators and hedgers. The speculators take a view on the direction of some quantity such as the asset price (or more abstract quantities such as volatility) and implement a strategy to take advantage of their view. Such people may not hedge at all.

Then there are the hedgers. There are two kinds of hedger: the ones who hold a position already and want to eliminate some very specific risk (usually using options) and the ones selling (or buying) the options because they believe they have a better price and can make money by hedging away *all* risk. It is the latter type of hedger that is delta hedging. They can only guarantee to make a profit by selling a contract for a high value if they can eliminate all of the risk due to the random fluctuation in the underlying.

Delta hedging means holding one of the option and short a quantity Δ of the underlying. Delta can be expressed as a function of S and t, I'll give some formulæ later in this section. This function varies as S and t vary. This means that the number of assets held must be continuously changed to maintain a **delta-neutral** position, this procedure is called **dynamic hedging**. Changing the number of assets held requires the continual purchase and/or sale of the stock. This is called **rehedging** or **rebalancing** the portfolio.

This delta hedging may take place very frequently in highly liquid markets where it is relatively costless to buy and sell. Thus the Black–Scholes assumption of continuous hedging may be quite accurate. In less liquid markets, you lose a lot on bid-offer spread and will therefore hedge less frequently. Moreover, you may not even be able to buy or sell in the quantities you want. Even in the absence of costs, you cannot be sure that your model for the underlying is accurate. There will certainly be some risk associated with the model. These issues make delta hedging less than perfect and in practice the risk in the underlying cannot be hedged away perfectly.

Some contracts have a delta that becomes very large at special times or asset values. The size of the delta makes delta hedging impossible; what can you do if you find yourself with a theoretical delta requiring you to buy more stock than exists? In such a situation the basic foundation of the Black–Scholes world has collapsed and you would be right to question the validity of any pricing formula. This happens at expiry close to the strike for binary options. Although I've given a formula for their price above and a formula for their delta below, I'd be careful using them if I were you.

Excel representation of delta values

Here are some formulæ for the deltas of common contracts (all formulæ assume that the underlying pays dividends or is a currency):

Deltas of common contracts

Call $\qquad e^{-D(T-t)}N(d_1)$

Put $\qquad e^{-D(T-t)}(N(d_1) - 1)$

Binary call $\dfrac{e^{-r(T-t)}N'(d_2)}{\sigma S\sqrt{T-t}}$

Binary put $-\dfrac{e^{-r(T-t)}N'(d_2)}{\sigma S\sqrt{T-t}}$

$$N'(x) = \frac{1}{\sqrt{2\pi}}e^{-\frac{1}{2}x^2}$$

Examples of these functions are plotted in Figure 8.11, with some scaling of the binaries.

8.4 GAMMA

THE GAMMA IS IMPORTANT WHEN EXAMINING THE HIGHER-ORDER BEHAVIOR OF A CONTRACT

The **gamma**, Γ, of an option or a portfolio of options is the second derivative of the position with respect to the underlying:

$$\Gamma = \frac{\partial^2 V}{\partial S^2}$$

Since gamma is the sensitivity of the delta to the underlying it is a measure of how much or how often a position must be rehedged in order to maintain a delta-neutral position.

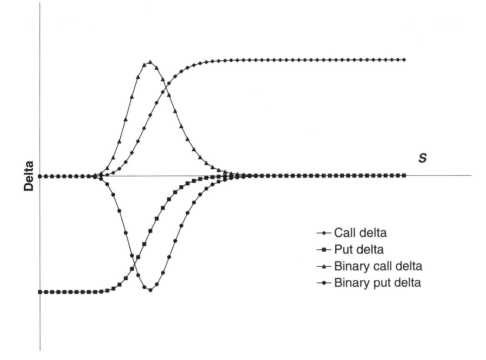

Figure 8.11 The deltas of a call, a put, a binary call and a binary put option. (Binary values scaled to a maximum value of one.)

Although the delta also varies with time this effect is dominated by the Brownian nature of the movement in the underlying.

In a delta-neutral position the gamma is partly responsible for making the return on the portfolio equal to the risk-free rate, the no-arbitrage condition of Chapter 6. The rest of this task falls to the time-derivative of the option value, discussed below. Actually, the situation is far more complicated than this because of the necessary discreteness in the hedging, there is a finite time between rehedges. In any delta-hedged position you make money on some hedges and lose some on others. In a long gamma position ($\Gamma > 0$) you make money on the large moves in the underlying and lose it on the small moves. The net effect is to get the risk-free rate of return on the portfolio.

Gamma also plays an important role when there is a mismatch between the market's view of volatility and the actual volatility of the underlying.

Because costs can be large and because one wants to reduce exposure to model error it is natural to try to minimize the need to rebalance the portfolio too frequently. Since gamma is a measure of sensitivity of the hedge ratio Δ to the movement in the underlying, the hedging requirement can be decreased by a gamma-neutral strategy. This means buying or selling more *options*, not just the underlying. Because the gamma of the underlying (its second derivative) is zero, we cannot add gamma to our position just with the underlying. We can have as many options in our position as we want, we choose the quantities of each such that both delta and gamma are zero. The minimal requirement is to hold two different types of option and the underlying. In practice, the option position is not readjusted too often because, if the cost of transacting in the underlying is large, then the cost of transacting in its derivatives is even larger.

Here are some formulæ for the gammas of common contracts:

Excel representation of gamma values

Gammas of common contracts

Call $\quad \dfrac{e^{-D(T-t)}N'(d_1)}{\sigma S\sqrt{T-t}}$

Put $\quad \dfrac{e^{-D(T-t)}N'(d_1)}{\sigma S\sqrt{T-t}}$

Binary call $\quad -\dfrac{e^{-r(T-t)}d_1 N'(d_2)}{\sigma^2 S^2 (T-t)}$

Binary put $\quad \dfrac{e^{-r(T-t)}d_1 N'(d_2)}{\sigma^2 S^2 (T-t)}$

Examples of these functions are plotted in Figure 8.12, with some scaling for the binaries.

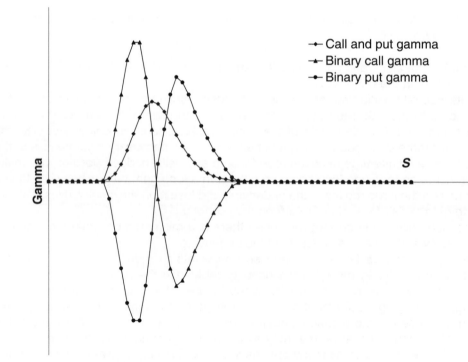

Figure 8.12 The gammas of a call, a put, a binary call and a binary put option.

8.5 **THETA**

Theta, Θ, is the rate of change of the option price with time.

$$\Theta = \frac{\partial V}{\partial t}$$

IF THE ASSET DOESN'T MOVE, THE OPTION WILL CHANGE BY THE THETA WITH TIME

The theta is related to the option value, the delta and the gamma by the Black–Scholes equation. In a delta-hedged portfolio the theta contributes to ensuring that the portfolio earns the risk-free rate. But it contributes in a completely certain way, unlike the gamma which contributes the right amount *on average*.

Here are some formulæ for the thetas of common contracts:

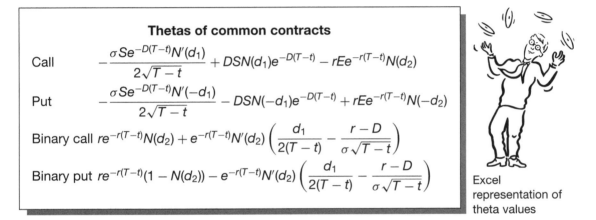

Thetas of common contracts

Call $\quad -\dfrac{\sigma S e^{-D(T-t)} N'(d_1)}{2\sqrt{T-t}} + DSN(d_1)e^{-D(T-t)} - rEe^{-r(T-t)}N(d_2)$

Put $\quad -\dfrac{\sigma S e^{-D(T-t)} N'(-d_1)}{2\sqrt{T-t}} - DSN(-d_1)e^{-D(T-t)} + rEe^{-r(T-t)}N(-d_2)$

Binary call $re^{-r(T-t)}N(d_2) + e^{-r(T-t)}N'(d_2)\left(\dfrac{d_1}{2(T-t)} - \dfrac{r-D}{\sigma\sqrt{T-t}}\right)$

Binary put $re^{-r(T-t)}(1 - N(d_2)) - e^{-r(T-t)}N'(d_2)\left(\dfrac{d_1}{2(T-t)} - \dfrac{r-D}{\sigma\sqrt{T-t}}\right)$

Excel representation of theta values

These functions are plotted in Figure 8.13.

8.6 **SPEED**

The **speed** of an option is the rate of change of the gamma with respect to the stock price.

$$\text{Speed} = \frac{\partial^3 V}{\partial S^3}$$

Traders use the gamma to estimate how much they will have to rehedge if the stock moves. The stock moves by $1 so the delta changes by whatever the gamma is. But that's only an approximation. The delta may change by more or less than this, especially if the stock moves by a larger amount, or the option is close to the strike and expiration. Hence the use of speed in a higher-order Taylor series expansion.

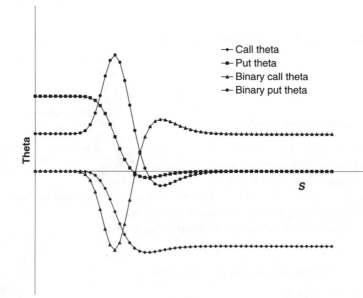

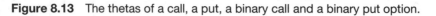

Figure 8.13 The thetas of a call, a put, a binary call and a binary put option.

Here are some formulæ for the speed of common contracts:

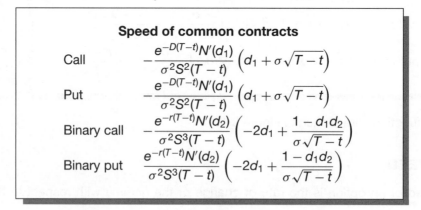

Speed of common contracts

Call $\quad -\dfrac{e^{-D(T-t)}N'(d_1)}{\sigma^2 S^2(T-t)}\left(d_1 + \sigma\sqrt{T-t}\right)$

Put $\quad -\dfrac{e^{-D(T-t)}N'(d_1)}{\sigma^2 S^2(T-t)}\left(d_1 + \sigma\sqrt{T-t}\right)$

Binary call $\quad -\dfrac{e^{-r(T-t)}N'(d_2)}{\sigma^2 S^3(T-t)}\left(-2d_1 + \dfrac{1 - d_1 d_2}{\sigma\sqrt{T-t}}\right)$

Binary put $\quad \dfrac{e^{-r(T-t)}N'(d_2)}{\sigma^2 S^3(T-t)}\left(-2d_1 + \dfrac{1 - d_1 d_2}{\sigma\sqrt{T-t}}\right)$

WE DON'T KNOW THE VOLATILITY PRECISELY. VEGA MEASURES SENSITIVITY OF VALUE TO VOL.

8.7 VEGA

Vega, a.k.a. zeta and kappa, is a very important but confusing quantity. It is the sensitivity of the option price to volatility.

$$\text{Vega} = \frac{\partial V}{\partial \sigma}$$

This is completely different from the other greeks[3] since it is a derivative with respect to a parameter and not a variable. This makes something of a difference when we come to find numerical solutions for such quantities.

In practice, the volatility of the underlying is not known with certainty. Not only is it very difficult to measure at any time, it is even harder to predict what it will do in the future. Suppose that we put a volatility of 20% into an option pricing formula, how sensitive is the price to that number? That's the vega.

As with gamma hedging, one can vega hedge to reduce sensitivity to the volatility. This is a major step towards eliminating some model risk, since it reduces dependence on a quantity that, to be honest, is not known very accurately.

There is a downside to the measurement of vega. It is only really meaningful for options having single-signed gamma everywhere. For example, it makes sense to measure vega for calls and puts but not binary calls and binary puts. I have included the formulæ for the vega of such contracts below, but they should be used with care, if at all. The reason for this is that call and put values (and options with single-signed gamma) have values that are monotonic in the

THE VEGA IS ONLY THEORETICALLY MEANINGFUL IN A SMALL NUMBER OF SITUATIONS. BEWARE

volatility: increase the volatility in a call and its value increases everywhere. However, contracts with a gamma that changes sign may have a vega measured at zero because as we increase the volatility the price may rise somewhere and fall somewhere else. Such a contract is very exposed to volatility risk but that risk is not measured by the vega.

Here are some formulæ for the vegas of common contracts:

Excel representation of vega values

Vegas of common contracts

Call	$S\sqrt{T-t}\,e^{-D(T-t)}N'(d_1)$
Put	$S\sqrt{T-t}\,e^{-D(T-t)}N'(d_1)$
Binary call	$-e^{-r(T-t)}N'(d_2)\dfrac{d_1}{\sigma}$
Binary put	$e^{-r(T-t)}N'(d_2)\dfrac{d_1}{\sigma}$

In Figure 8.14 is shown the value of an at-the-money call option as a function of the volatility. There is one year to expiry, the strike is 100, the interest rate is 10% and there are no dividends. No matter how far in or out

---

[3] It's not even Greek. Among other things it is an American car, a star (Alpha Lyræ), the real name of Zorro, there are a couple of 16th century Spanish authors called Vega, an op art painting by Vasarely and a character in the computer game 'Street Fighter.' And who could forget Vincent, and his brother, and his 'cousin'?

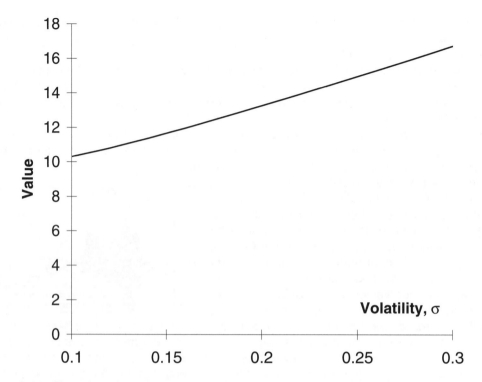

Figure 8.14 The value of an at-the-money call option as a function of volatility.

of the money this curve is always monotonically increasing for call options and put options, uncertainty adds value to the contract. The slope of this curve is the vega.

8.8 RHO

Rho, ρ, is the sensitivity of the option value to the interest rate used in the Black–Scholes formulæ:

$$\rho = \frac{\partial V}{\partial r}$$

In practice one often uses a whole term structure of interest rates, meaning a time-dependent rate $r(t)$. Rho would then be the sensitivity to the level of the rates assuming a parallel shift in rates at all times. Again, you must be careful for which contracts you measure rho.

Here are some formulæ for the rhos of common contracts:

Rhos of common contracts

Call $\quad E(T - t)e^{-r(T-t)}N(d_2)$

Put $\quad -E(T - t)e^{-r(T-t)}N(-d_2)$

Binary call $\quad -(T - t)e^{-r(T-t)}N(d_2) + \dfrac{\sqrt{T-t}}{\sigma}e^{-r(T-t)}N'(d_2)$

Binary put $\quad -(T - t)e^{-r(T-t)}(1 - N(d_2)) - \dfrac{\sqrt{T-t}}{\sigma}e^{-r(T-t)}N'(d_2)$

Excel representation of rho values

The sensitivities of common contract to the dividend yield or foreign interest rate are given by the following formulæ:

Sensitivity to dividend for common contracts

Call $\quad -(T - t)Se^{-D(T-t)}N(d_1)$

Put $\quad (T - t)Se^{-D(T-t)}N(-d_1)$

Binary call $\quad -\dfrac{\sqrt{T-t}}{\sigma}e^{-r(T-t)}N'(d_2)$

Binary put $\quad \dfrac{\sqrt{T-t}}{\sigma}e^{-r(T-t)}N'(d_2)$

8.9   **IMPLIED VOLATILITY**

The Black–Scholes formula for a call option takes as input the expiry, the strike, the underlying and the interest rate *together with the volatility* to output the price. All but the volatility are easily measured. How do we know what volatility to put into the formulæ? A trader can see on his screen that a certain call option with four months until expiry and a strike of 100 is trading at 6.51 with the underlying at 101.5 and a short-term interest rate of 8%. Can we use this information in some way?

Turn the relationship between volatility and an option price on its head, if we can see the price at which the option is trading, we can ask 'What volatility must I use to get the correct market price?' This is called the **implied volatility**. The implied volatility is the volatility of the underlying which when substituted into the Black–Scholes formula gives a theoretical price equal to the market price. In a sense it is the market's view of volatility over the life of the option. Assuming that we are using call prices to estimate the implied volatility then provided the option price is less than the asset and greater than zero then we can find a unique value for the implied volatility. (If the option price is outside these bounds then there's a very extreme arbitrage opportunity.) Because there is no simple formula for the implied volatility as a function of the option value we must solve the equation

$$V_{BS}(S_0, t_0; \sigma, r; E, T) = \text{known value}$$

for σ, where V_{BS} is the Black–Scholes formula. Today's asset price is S_0, the date is t_0 and everything is known in this equation except for σ. Below is an algorithm for finding the implied volatility from the market price of a call option to any required degree of accuracy. The method used is **Newton–Raphson** which uses the derivative of the option price with respect to the volatility (the vega) in the calculation. This method is particularly good for such a well-behaved function as a call value.

VB implementation

A SIMPLE VB FUNCTION FOR CALCULATING IMPLIED VOL FROM CALL PRICES

```
Function ImpVolCall(MktPrice As Double, _
            Strike As Double, Expiry As _
            Double, Asset As Double, _
            IntRate As Double, error _
            As Double)
Volatility = 0.2
dv = error + 1
While Abs(dv) > error
    d1 = Log(Asset / Strike) + (IntRate _
            + 0.5 * Volatility * Volatility) _
            * Expiry
    d1 = d1 / (Volatility * Sqr(Expiry))
    d2 = d1 - Volatility * Sqr(Expiry)
    PriceError = Asset * cdf(d1) - Strike _
            * Exp(-IntRate * Expiry) _
            * cdf(d2) - MktPrice
    Vega = Asset * Sqr(Expiry / 3.1415926 _
            / 2) * Exp(-0.5 * d1 * d1)
    dv = PriceError / Vega
    Volatility = Volatility - dv
Wend
ImpVolCall = Volatility
End Function
```

In this we need the cumulative distribution function for the Normal distribution. The following is a simple algorithm which gives an accurate, and fast, approximation to the cumulative distribution function of the standardized Normal:

$$\text{For } x \geq 0 \quad N(x) \approx 1 - \frac{1}{\sqrt{2\pi}} e^{-\frac{1}{2}x^2} \left(a_1 d + a_2 d^2 + a_3 d^3 + a_4 d^4 + a_5 d^5 \right)$$

where

$$d = \frac{1}{1 + 0.0.2316419x}$$

and

$$a1 = 0.31938153, \quad a2 = -0.356563782, \quad a3 = 1.781477937,$$

$$a4 = -1.821255978 \text{ and } a5 = 1.330274429.$$

For $x < 0$ use the fact that $N(x) + N(-x) = 1$.

```
Function cdf(x As Double) As Double
Dim d As Double
Dim temp as Double
Dim a1 As Double
Dim a2 As Double
Dim a3 As Double
Dim a4 As Double
Dim a5 As Double
d = 1 / (1 + 0.2316419 * Abs(x))
a1 = 0.31938153
a2 = -0.356563782
a3 = 1.781477937
a4 = -1.821255978
a5 = 1.330274429
temp = a5
temp = a4 + d * temp
temp = a3 + d * temp
temp = a2 + d * temp
temp = a1 + d * temp
temp = d * temp
cdf = 1 - 1 / Sqr(2 * 3.1415926) * Exp(-0.5 * x * x) * temp
If x < 0 Then cdf = 1 - cdf
End Function
```

VB implementation

In practice if we calculate the implied volatility for many different strikes and expiries on the same underlying then we find that *the volatility is not constant*. A typical result is that of Figure 8.15 which shows the implied volatilities for the S&P500 on 9th September

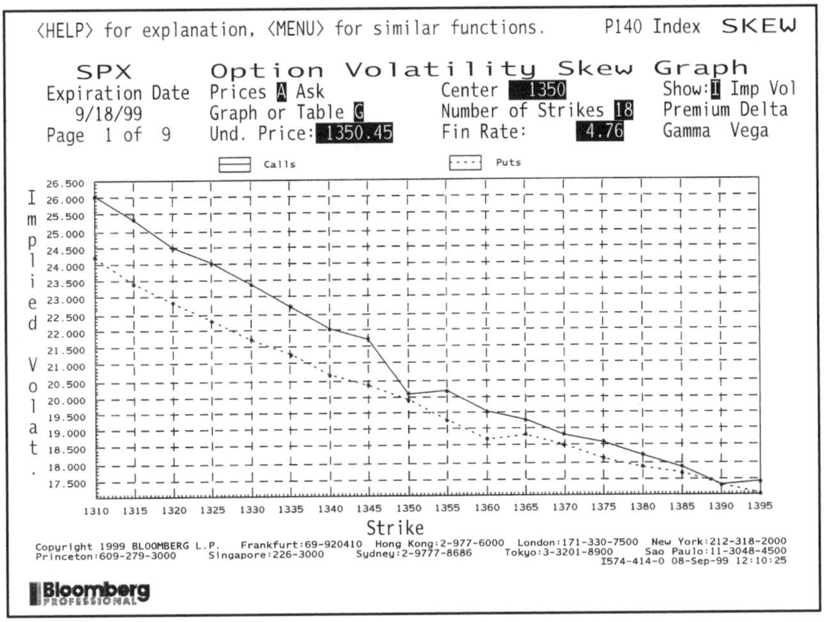

Figure 8.15 Implied volatilities for the S&P500. Source: Bloomberg L.P.

1999 for options expiring later in the month. The implied volatilities for the calls and puts should be identical, because of put-call parity. The differences seen here could be due to bid-offer spread or calculations performed at slightly different times.

This shape is commonly referred to as the **smile**, but it could also be in the shape of a **frown**. In this example it's a rather lopsided wry grin. Whatever the shape, it tends to persist with time, with certain shapes being characteristic of certain markets.

The dependence of the implied volatility on strike and expiry can be interpreted in many ways. The easiest interpretation is that it represents the market's view of future volatility in some complex way.

8.10 **A CLASSIFICATION OF HEDGING TYPES**

8.10.1 Why hedge?

'Hedging' in its broadest sense means the reduction of risk by exploiting relationships or correlation between various risky investments (or bets). The concept is used widely in horse racing, other sports betting and, of course, high finance. The reason for hedging is that it can lead to an improved risk/return. In the classical Modern Portfolio Theory framework (Chapter 21), for example, it is usually possible to construct many portfolios having the same expected return but with different variance of returns ('risk'). Clearly, if you have two portfolios with the same expected return the one with the lower risk is the better investment.

8.10.2 The two main classifications

Probably the most important distinction between types of hedging is between model-independent and model-dependent hedging strategies.

Model-independent hedging: An example of such hedging is put-call parity. There is a simple relationship between calls and puts on an asset (when they are both European and with the same strikes and expiries), the underlying stock and a zero-coupon bond with the same maturity. This relationship is completely independent of how the underlying asset changes in value. Another example is spot-forward parity. In neither case do we have to specify the dynamics of the asset, not even its volatility, to find a possible hedge. Such model-independent hedges are few and far between.

Model-dependent hedging: Most sophisticated finance hedging strategies depend on a model for the underlying asset. The obvious example is the hedging used in the Black–Scholes analysis that leads to a whole theory for the value of derivatives. In pricing derivatives we typically need to at least know the volatility of the underlying asset. If the model is wrong then the option value and any hedging strategy will also be wrong.

8.10.3 Delta hedging

One of the building blocks of derivatives theory is **delta hedging**. This is the theoretically perfect elimination of all risk by using a very clever hedge between the option and its underlying. Delta hedging exploits the perfect correlation between the changes in the option value and the changes in the stock price. This is an example of 'dynamic' hedging; the hedge must be continually monitored and frequently adjusted by the sale or purchase of the underlying asset. Because of the frequent rehedging, any dynamic hedging strategy is going to result in losses due to transaction costs. In some markets this can be very important.

8.10.4 Gamma hedging

To reduce the size of each rehedge and/or to increase the time between rehedges, and thus reduce costs, the technique of **gamma hedging** is often employed. A portfolio that is delta hedged is insensitive to movements in the underlying as long as those movements are quite small. There is a small error in this due to the convexity of the portfolio with respect to the underlying. Gamma hedging is a more accurate form of hedging that theoretically eliminates these second-order effects. Typically, one hedges one, exotic, say, contract with a vanilla contract and the underlying. The quantities of the vanilla and the underlying are chosen so as to make both the portfolio delta and the portfolio gamma instantaneously zero.

8.10.5 Vega hedging

As I said above, the prices and hedging strategies are only as good as the model for the underlying. The key parameter that determines the value of a contract is the volatility of the underlying asset. Unfortunately, this is a very difficult parameter to measure or even estimate. Nor is it usually a constant as assumed in the simple theories. Obviously, the value of a contract depends on this parameter, and so to ensure that our portfolio value is insensitive to this parameter we can **vega hedge**. This means that we hedge one option with both the underlying and another option in such a way that both the delta and the vega, the sensitivity of the portfolio value to volatility, are zero. This is often quite satisfactory in practice but is usually theoretically inconsistent; we should not use a constant volatility (basic Black–Scholes) model to calculate sensitivities to parameters that are assumed not to vary. The distinction between variables (underlying asset price and time) and parameters (volatility, dividend yield, interest rate) is extremely important here. It is justifiable to rely on sensitivities of prices to variables, but usually not sensitivity to parameters. To get around this problem it is possible to independently model volatility, etc. as variables themselves. In such a way it is possible to build up a consistent theory.

8.10.6 Static hedging

There are quite a few problems with delta hedging, on both the practical and the theoretical side. In practice, hedging must be done at discrete times and is costly. Sometimes one has to buy or sell a prohibitively large number of the underlying in order to follow the theory. This is a problem with barrier options and options with discontinuous payoff. On the theoretical side, the model for the underlying is not perfect, at the very least we do not know parameter values accurately. Delta hedging alone leaves us very exposed to the model; this is model risk. Many of these problems can be reduced or eliminated if we follow a strategy of **static hedging** as well as delta hedging: buy or sell more liquid traded contracts to reduce the cashflows in the original contract. The static hedge is put into place now, and left until expiry. In the extreme case where an exotic contract has all of its cashflows matched by cashflows from traded options then its value is given by the cost of setting up the static hedge; a model is not needed.

8.10.7 Margin hedging

Often what causes banks, and other institutions, to suffer during volatile markets is not the change in the paper value of their assets but the requirement to suddenly come up with a large amount of cash to cover an unexpected margin call. Recent examples where margin has caused significant damage are Metallgesellschaft and Long Term Capital Management. Writing options is very risky. The downside of buying an option is just the initial premium, the upside may be unlimited. The upside of writing an option is limited, but the downside could be huge. For this reason, to cover the risk of default in the event of an unfavorable outcome, the clearing houses that register and settle options insist on the deposit of a margin by the writers of options. Margin comes in two forms, the initial margin and the maintenance margin. The initial margin is the amount deposited at the initiation of the contract. The total amount held as margin must stay above a prescribed maintenance margin. If it ever falls below this level then more money (or equivalent in bonds, stocks, etc.) must be deposited. The amount of margin that must be deposited depends on the particular contract. A dramatic market move could result in a sudden large margin call that may be difficult to meet. To prevent this situation it is possible to **margin hedge**. That is, set up a portfolio such that margin calls on one part of the portfolio are balanced by refunds from other parts. Usually over-the-counter contracts have no associated margin requirements and so won't appear in the calculation.

8.10.8 Crash (Platinum) hedging

The final variety of hedging that we discuss is specific to extreme markets. Market crashes have at least two obvious effects on our hedging. First of all, the moves are so large and rapid that they cannot be traditionally delta hedged. The convexity effect is not small. Second, normal market correlations become meaningless. Typically all correlations become one (or minus one). **Crash** or **Platinum hedging** exploits the latter effect in such a way as to minimize the worst possible outcome for the portfolio. The method, called CrashMetrics (Chapter 25), does not rely on difficult to measure parameters such as volatilities and so is a very robust hedge. Platinum hedging comes in two types: hedging the paper value of the portfolio and hedging the margin calls.

8.11 **SUMMARY**

In this chapter we went through the derivation of some of the most important formulæ. We also saw the definitions and descriptions of the hedge ratios. Trading in derivatives would be no more than gambling if you took away the ability to hedge. Hedging is all about managing risk and reducing uncertainty.

FURTHER READING

- See Taleb (1997) for a lot of detailed analysis of vega.

- See Press *et al.* (1992) for more routines for finding roots, i.e. for finding implied volatilities.

- There are many 'virtual' option pricers on the internet. See, for example, `www.cboe.com`.

- I'm not going to spend much time on deriving or even presenting formulæ. There are 1001 books that contain option formulæ, there is even one book with 1001 formulæ (Haug, 2007).

- See the series of articles by Thorp (2002) on how he derived the correct option pricing formulæ in the late 1960s.

- Haug (2003) discusses the sophisticated trader use of the simple equations.

- For the definitions of even more greeks see Wilmott (2006).

Time Out...

Another look at Black–Scholes

Let's take another look at the Black–Scholes equation:

$$\frac{\partial V}{\partial t} + \tfrac{1}{2}\sigma^2 S^2 \frac{\partial^2 V}{\partial S^2} + rS\frac{\partial V}{\partial S} - rV = 0.$$

The option value $V(S,t)$ depends on (or 'is a function of') the asset price S and the time t.

The first derivative of the option value with respect to time is called the theta:

$$\Theta = \frac{\partial V}{\partial t}.$$

Notice that this is a partial derivative and so theta is the gradient of the option value in the direction of changing time, asset price fixed. It measures the rate of change of the option value with time if the asset price doesn't move, hence the other name 'time decay.'

The first derivative of the option value with respect to the asset price is called the delta:

$$\Delta = \frac{\partial V}{\partial S}.$$

This is the slope in the S direction with time fixed. Asset prices change very rapidly and so the dominant change in the option value from moment to moment is the delta multiplied by the change in the asset price. This is just a simple application of Taylor series; the difference between the option price at time t when the asset is at S and a later time $t + \delta t$ when the asset price is $S + \delta S$ is given by

$$V(S + \delta S, t + \delta t) - V(S, t) = \Delta \, \delta S + \cdots.$$

The $\cdots$ are terms which are, generally speaking, smaller than the leading term. They are still important, as we'll see in a moment.

Because the change in option value and the change in asset price are so closely linked we can see that holding a quantity Δ of the underlying asset short we can eliminate, to leading order, fluctuations in our net portfolio value. This is the basis of delta hedging.

The second derivative of the option value with respect to the asset price is called the gamma:

$$\Gamma = \frac{\partial^2 V}{\partial S^2}.$$

This is also just the S derivative of the delta. If the asset changes by an amount δS then the delta changes by an amount $\Gamma \, \delta S$. Thus the gamma is a measure of how much one might to have to rehedge, and gives a measure of the amount of transaction costs from delta hedging.

Now we can interpret all the terms in the Black–Scholes equation, but what does the equation itself mean?

Written in terms of the greeks, the Black–Scholes equation is

$$\Theta + \tfrac{1}{2}\sigma^2 S^2 \Gamma + rS\Delta - rV = 0.$$

Reordering this we have

$$\Theta = rV - rS\Delta - \tfrac{1}{2}\sigma^2 S^2 \Gamma = r(V - S\Delta) - \tfrac{1}{2}\sigma^2 S^2 \Gamma.$$

When we have a delta-hedged position we hold the option with value V and are short Δ of the underlying asset. Thus our portfolio value is at any time

$$V - S\Delta.$$

So we can write the Black–Scholes equation in words as

Time decay = interest received on cash equivalent of portfolio value

$$- \tfrac{1}{2}\sigma^2 S^2 \text{gamma}.$$

The option value grows by an equivalent of interest that would have been received by a riskless pure cash position. But the delta-hedged option is not a cash position. That's where the final, gamma, term comes in.

Ignoring the interest on the cash equivalent, the theta and gamma terms add up to zero. Of course, you can't ignore this interest unless the portfolio has zero value or rates are zero.

The delta hedge is only accurate to leading order. If one is hedging with finite time intervals between rehedges then there is inevitably a little bit of randomness that we can't hedge away. We can see this if we go to higher order in the Taylor series expansion of $V(S + \delta S, t + \delta t)$:

$$V(S + \delta S, t + \delta t) - V(S, t) = \Delta \, \delta S + \Theta \, \delta t + \tfrac{1}{2} \Gamma \, \delta S^2 \cdots.$$

The Θ term is predictable if we know the time δt between hedges (and it has already appeared in the Black–Scholes equation). But the Γ term is multiplied by the random δS^2. We can't hedge this away perfectly. It is, in practice, the source of hedging errors. However, if we rehedge sufficiently frequently (i.e. δt is very small) then the combined effect of the gamma terms is via an *average* of the δS^2. And this average is $\sigma^2 S^2 \, \delta t$. Why is it the average that matters? It's like betting on the toss of a biased coin. If you have an advantage then you can exploit it by betting a small amount but very, very often. In the long run you will certainly win. (In terms of standard deviations, as the time between hedges decreases so does the standard deviation of the hedging error accumulated over the life of the option.)

We can now see that the gamma term in the Black–Scholes equation is to balance the higher-order fluctuations in the option value. Naturally, it therefore depends on the magnitude of these fluctuations, the volatility of the underlying asset.

	Call	Put	Binary Call	Binary Put
Value V Black–Scholes value	$Se^{-D(T-t)}N(d_1)$ $-Ee^{-r(T-t)}N(d_2)$	$-Se^{-D(T-t)}N(-d_1)$ $+Ee^{-r(T-t)}N(-d_2)$	$e^{-r(T-t)}N(d_2)$	$e^{-r(T-t)}(1-N(d_2))$
Delta $\dfrac{\partial V}{\partial S}$ Sensitivity to underlying	$e^{-D(T-t)}N(d_1)$	$e^{-D(T-t)}(N(d_1)-1)$	$\dfrac{e^{-r(T-t)}N'(d_2)}{\sigma S\sqrt{T-t}}$	$-\dfrac{e^{-r(T-t)}N'(d_2)}{\sigma S\sqrt{T-t}}$
Gamma $\dfrac{\partial^2 V}{\partial S^2}$ Sensitivity of delta to underlying	$\dfrac{e^{-D(T-t)}N'(d_1)}{\sigma S\sqrt{T-t}}$	$\dfrac{e^{-D(T-t)}N'(d_1)}{\sigma S\sqrt{T-t}}$	$-\dfrac{e^{-r(T-t)}d_1 N'(d_2)}{\sigma^2 S^2(T-t)}$	$\dfrac{e^{-r(T-t)}d_1 N'(d_2)}{\sigma^2 S^2(T-t)}$
Theta $\dfrac{\partial V}{\partial t}$ Sensitivity to time	$-\dfrac{\sigma Se^{-D(T-t)}N'(d_1)}{2\sqrt{T-t}}$ $+DSN(d_1)e^{-D(T-t)}$ $-rEe^{-r(T-t)}N(d_2)$	$-\dfrac{\sigma Se^{-D(T-t)}N'(-d_1)}{2\sqrt{T-t}}$ $-DSN(-d_1)e^{-D(T-t)}$ $+rEe^{-r(T-t)}N(-d_2)$	$re^{-r(T-t)}N(d_2)$ $+e^{-r(T-t)}N'(d_2)$ $\times\left(\dfrac{d_1}{2(T-t)}-\dfrac{r-D}{\sigma\sqrt{T-t}}\right)$	$re^{-r(T-t)}(1-N(d_2))$ $-e^{-r(T-t)}N'(d_2)$ $\times\left(\dfrac{d_1}{2(T-t)}-\dfrac{r-D}{\sigma\sqrt{T-t}}\right)$
Speed $\dfrac{\partial^3 V}{\partial S^3}$ Sensitivity of gamma to underlying	$-\dfrac{e^{-D(T-t)}N'(d_1)}{\sigma^2 S^2(T-t)}$ $\times(d_1+\sigma\sqrt{T-t})$	$-\dfrac{e^{-D(T-t)}N'(d_1)}{\sigma^2 S^2(T-t)}$ $\times(d_1+\sigma\sqrt{T-t})$	$\dfrac{e^{-r(T-t)}N'(d_2)}{\sigma^2 S^3(T-t)}$ $\times\left(-2d_1+\dfrac{1-d_1 d_2}{\sigma\sqrt{T-t}}\right)$	$\dfrac{e^{-r(T-t)}N'(d_2)}{\sigma^2 S^3(T-t)}$ $\times\left(-2d_1+\dfrac{1-d_1 d_2}{\sigma\sqrt{T-t}}\right)$
Vega $\dfrac{\partial V}{\partial \sigma}$ Sensitivity to volatility	$S\sqrt{T-t}\,e^{-D(T-t)}N'(d_1)$	$S\sqrt{T-t}\,e^{-D(T-t)}N'(d_1)$	$-e^{-r(T-t)}N'(d_2)$ $\times\left(\sqrt{T-t}+\dfrac{d_2}{\sigma}\right)$	$-e^{-r(T-t)}N'(d_2)$ $\times\left(\sqrt{T-t}+\dfrac{d_2}{\sigma}\right)$
Rho $(r)\ \dfrac{\partial V}{\partial r}$ Sensitivity to interest rate	$E(T-t)e^{-r(T-t)}N(d_2)$	$-E(T-t)e^{-r(T-t)}N(-d_2)$	$-(T-t)e^{-r(T-t)}N(d_2)$ $+\dfrac{\sqrt{T-t}}{\sigma}e^{-r(T-t)}N'(d_2)$	$-(T-t)e^{-r(T-t)}(1-N(d_2))$ $-\dfrac{\sqrt{T-t}}{\sigma}e^{-r(T-t)}N'(d_2)$
Rho $(D)\ \dfrac{\partial V}{\partial D}$ Sensitivity to dividend yield	$-(T-t)Se^{-D(T-t)}N(d_1)$	$(T-t)Se^{-D(T-t)}N(-d_1)$	$-\dfrac{\sqrt{T-t}}{\sigma}e^{-r(T-t)}N'(d_2)$	$\dfrac{\sqrt{T-t}}{\sigma}e^{-r(T-t)}N'(d_2)$

$$d_1 = \frac{\log\left(\dfrac{S}{E}\right)+(r-D+\tfrac{1}{2}\sigma^2)(T-t)}{\sigma\sqrt{T-t}}, \quad d_2 = \frac{\log\left(\dfrac{S}{E}\right)+(r-D-\tfrac{1}{2}\sigma^2)(T-t)}{\sigma\sqrt{T-t}} = d_1 - \sigma\sqrt{T-t}, \quad N(x) = \frac{1}{\sqrt{2\pi}}\int_{-\infty}^{x}e^{-\frac{1}{2}\xi^2}\,d\xi \quad \text{and} \quad N'(x) = \frac{1}{\sqrt{2\pi}}e^{-\frac{1}{2}x^2}$$

EXERCISES

1. Find the explicit solution for the value of a European option with payoff $\Lambda(S)$ and expiry at time T, where

$$\Lambda(S) = \begin{cases} S & \text{if } S > E \\ 0 & \text{if } S < E. \end{cases}$$

2. Find the explicit solution for the value of a European supershare option, with expiry at time T and payoff

$$\Lambda(S) = \mathcal{H}(S - E_1) - \mathcal{H}(S - E_2),$$

where $E_1 < E_2$.

3. Consider the pay-later call option. This has payoff $\Lambda(S) = \max(S - E, 0)$ at time T. The holder of the option does not pay a premium when the contract is set up, but must pay Q to the writer at expiry, only if $S \geq E$. What is the value of Q?

4. Find the implied volatility of the following European call. The call has four months until expiry and an exercise price of $100. The call is worth $6.51 and the underlying trades at $101.5, discount using a short-term risk-free continuously compounding interest rate of 8% per annum.

5. Consider a European call, currently at the money. Why is delta hedging self-financing in the following situations?

    (a) The share price rises until expiry,
    (b) The share price falls until expiry.

6. Using the explicit solutions for the European call and put options, check that put-call parity holds.

7. Consider an asset with zero volatility. We can explicitly calculate the future value of the asset and hence that of a call option with the asset as the underlying. The value of the call option will then depend on the growth rate of the asset, μ. On the other hand, we can use the explicit formula for the call option, in which μ does not appear. Explain this apparent contradiction.

8. The range forward contract is specified as follows: at expiry, the holder must buy the asset for E_1 if $S < E_1$, for S if $E_1 \leq S \leq E_2$ and for E_2 if $S > E_2$. Find the relationship between E_1 and E_2 when the initial value of the contract is zero and $E_1 < E_2$.

9. A forward start call option is specified as follows: at time T_1, the holder is given a European call option with exercise price $S(T_1)$ and expiry at time $T_1 + T_2$. What is the value of the option for $0 \leq t \leq T_1$?

10. Consider a delta-neutral portfolio of derivatives, Π. For a small change in the price of the underlying asset, δS, over a short time interval, δt, show that the change in the portfolio value, $\delta \Pi$, satisfies

$$\delta \Pi = \Theta \delta t + \tfrac{1}{2} \Gamma \, \delta S^2,$$

where $\Theta = \frac{\partial \Pi}{\partial t}$ and $\Gamma = \frac{\partial^2 \Pi}{\partial S^2}$.

11. Show that for a delta-neutral portfolio of options on a non-dividend paying stock, Π,

$$\Theta + \tfrac{1}{2}\sigma^2 S^2 \Gamma = r\Pi.$$

12. Show that the vega of an option, v, satisfies the differential equation

$$\frac{\partial v}{\partial t} + \tfrac{1}{2}\sigma^2 S^2 \frac{\partial^2 v}{\partial S^2} + rS\frac{\partial v}{\partial S} - rv + \sigma S^2 \Gamma = 0,$$

where $\Gamma = \frac{\partial^2 V}{\partial S^2}$. What is the final condition?

13. Find the partial differential equation satisfied by ρ, the sensitivity of the option value to the interest rate.

14. Use put-call parity to find the relationships between the deltas, gammas, vegas, thetas and rhos of European call and put options.

15. The fundamental solution, u_δ, is the solution of the diffusion equation on $-\infty < x < \infty$ and $\tau > 0$ with $u(x, 0) = \delta(x)$. Use this solution to solve the more general problem:

$$\frac{\partial u}{\partial \tau} = \frac{\partial^2 u}{\partial x^2}, \quad \text{on } -\infty < x < \infty, \ \tau > 0,$$

with $u(x, 0) = u_0(x)$.

CHAPTER 9
overview of volatility modeling

The aim of this Chapter...

...is to give a hint towards the possible ways to model volatility, the most important parameter in derivatives pricing.

In this Chapter...

- a look at the joys of volatility modeling

9.1 **INTRODUCTION**

In the main, the Black–Scholes model is very robust and does a decent job of pricing derivatives, including exotics. One of the most important flaws in the model concerns the behavior of volatility. Quite frankly, we do not know what volatility currently is, never mind what it may be in the future. And the correct pricing of derivatives requires us to know what the volatility is going to be.

For this reason, volatility analysis and modeling takes a prominent role in the working life of a quant.

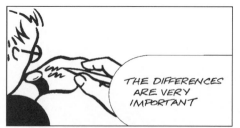

THE DIFFERENCES ARE VERY IMPORTANT

9.2 **THE DIFFERENT TYPES OF VOLATILITY**

We can't *see* volatility in the same way we can see stock prices or interest rates. The best we can hope to do is to measure it statistically. But such a measure is necessarily backwards looking, and we really want to know what volatility is going to be in the future.[1]

For this reason people talk about different volatilities, as proxies for the real thing. Here are a few adjectives you can use with 'volatility.'

- Actual

- Historical/realized

- Implied

- Forward

9.2.1 Actual volatility

This is the measure of the amount of randomness in an asset return at any particular time. It is very difficult to measure, but is supposed to be an input into all option pricing models. In particular, the actual (or 'local') volatility goes into the Black–Scholes *equation*.

- There is no 'timescale' associated with actual volatility, it is a quantity that exists at each instant, possibly varying from moment to moment.

Example: The actual volatility is now 20% . . . now it is 22% . . . now it is 24% . . .

9.2.2 Historical or realized volatility

This is a measure of the amount of randomness over some period in the past. The period is always specified, and so is the mathematical method for its calculation. Sometimes this backward-looking measure is used as an estimate for what volatility will be in the future.

- There are two 'timescales' associated with historical or realized volatility: one short and one long.

---

[1] You can see I am already assuming that volatility is not the nice constant that earlier chapters may have led you to believe.

Example: The 60-day volatility using daily returns. Perhaps of interest if you are pricing a 60-day option, which you are hedging daily.

In pricing an option we are making an estimate of what actual volatility will be over the lifetime of the option. After the option has expired we can go back and calculate what the volatility actually was over the life of the option. This is the realized volatility.

Example: I sold a 30-day option for a 30% volatility, I hedged it every day. Did I make money?

9.2.3 Implied volatility

The implied volatility is the volatility which when input into the Black–Scholes option pricing formulæ gives the market price of the option. It is often described as the market's view of the future actual volatility over the lifetime of the particular option.

However, it is also influenced by other effects such as supply and demand.

- There is one 'timescale' associated with implied volatility: expiration.

Example: A stock is at 100, a call has strike 100, expiration in one year, interest rate 5% and the option market price is $10.45. What volatility are traders using?

9.2.4 Forward volatility

The adjective 'forward' can be applied to many forms of volatility, and refers to the volatility (whether actual or implied) over some period in the future.

- Forward volatility is associated with either a time period, or a future instant.

9.3 **VOLATILITY ESTIMATION BY STATISTICAL MEANS**

9.3.1 The simplest volatility estimate: constant volatility/moving window

If we believe that volatility is constant or slowly varying, and we have N days' data, we can use

$$\sigma^2 = \frac{1}{N} \sum_{i=1}^{N} R_i^2$$

where

$$R_i = \frac{S_i - S_{i-1}}{S_{i-1}}$$

and is the return on the ith day. Note that I haven't annualized quantities yet.

There are obvious major problems associated with this volatility measure, because the returns are equally weighted you will get a plateauing effect associated with a large return. If there is a large one-day return in will increase the volatility instantaneously, but the estimate of volatility will stay raised until N days later when that return drops out of the sample. This is a totally spurious effect. This effect can be seen in Figure 9.1.

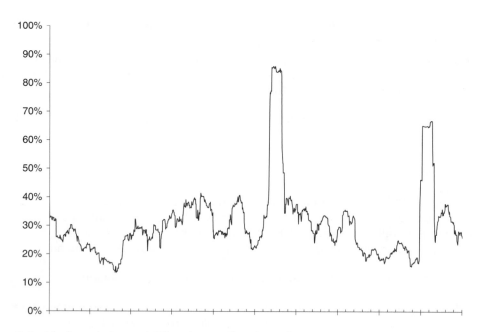

Figure 9.1 Moving-window volatility, observe the plateauing.

9.3.2 Incorporating mean reversion

Now let's consider time-varying volatility. We don't just have one σ but must consider σ_n, our estimate of the volatility on the nth day, using data available up to that point. If we believe that volatility tends to vary about a long-term mean $\bar{\sigma}$, then we could use

$$\sigma_n^2 = \alpha\bar{\sigma}^2 + (1-\alpha)\frac{1}{n}\sum_{i=1}^{n} R_i^2.$$

Here there is a weighting assigned to each long-run volatility estimate and the current estimate based on the last n returns.

  This is called an **ARCH** model, for **Autoregressive Conditional Heteroscedasticity**
  But why should each of the last n returns be equally important?

9.3.3 Exponentially weighted moving average

Consider this estimate for volatility:

$$\sigma_n^2 = (1-\lambda)\sum_{i=1}^{\infty} \lambda^{i-1} R_{n-i+1}^2.$$

The parameter λ must be greater than zero and less than one. This is an example of an **exponentially weighted moving average estimate**. The more recent the return, the more weight is attached. The sum extends back to the beginning of time.

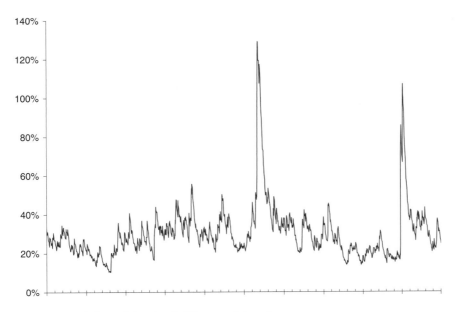

Figure 9.2 Exponentially weighted volatility, no plateauing.

The coefficient of $1 - \lambda$ ensures that the weights all add up to one.
This expression can be simplified to

$$\sigma_n^2 = \lambda\sigma_{n-1}^2 + (1 - \lambda)R_n^2.$$

Note that this uses the most recent return *and* the previous estimate of the volatility. *This is RiskMetrics volatility measure.*

Figure 9.2 uses the same stock price data as in Figure 9.1 but now there is no plateauing.[2]

9.3.4 A simple GARCH model

Put the preceeding models together to get

$$\sigma_n^2 = \alpha\overline{\sigma}^2 + (1 - \alpha)\left(\lambda\sigma_{n-1}^2 + (1 - \lambda)R_n^2\right).$$

This is a **Generalized Autoregressive Conditional Heteroscedasticity** or **GARCH** model.

9.3.5 Expected future volatility

We are currently at day n and we want to estimate the volatility k days into the future, i.e. on day $n + k$.

---

[2] You could say that the obvious exponential decay in the volatility estimate is just as spurious as the discontinuity in the equally weighted case.

Expected future volatility: EWMA

Recall

$$\sigma_{n+k}^2 = \lambda \sigma_{n+k-1}^2 + (1 - \lambda)R_{n+k}^2.$$

Take expectations of this . . .

$$E[\sigma_{n+k}^2] = \lambda E[\sigma_{n+k-1}^2] + (1 - \lambda)E[R_{n+k}^2].$$

But, of course,

$$E[R_{n+k}^2] = \sigma_{n+k}^2.$$

Therefore

$$E[\sigma_{n+k}^2] = \lambda E[\sigma_{n+k-1}^2] + (1 - \lambda)E[\sigma_{n+k}^2]$$

or, on rearranging,

$$E[\sigma_{n+k}^2] = E[\sigma_{n+k-1}^2].$$

In other words, the expected future value of the variance is the same as the previous day's value. Working backwards to the present, the expected future variance is the same as today's.

Expected future volatility: GARCH

Recall

$$\sigma_{n+k}^2 = \alpha \bar{\sigma}^2 + (1 - \alpha)\left(\lambda \sigma_{n+k-1}^2 + (1 - \lambda)R_{n+k}^2\right).$$

Taking expectations of this results in

$$E[\sigma_{n+k}^2] = \alpha \bar{\sigma}^2 + (1 - \alpha)\left(\lambda E[\sigma_{n+k-1}^2] + (1 - \lambda)E[\sigma_{n+k}^2]\right).$$

On rearranging, we get

$$E[\sigma_{n+k}^2] = \frac{\alpha \bar{\sigma}^2}{1 - (1 - \alpha)(1 - \lambda)} + \frac{\lambda(1 - \alpha)}{1 - (1 - \alpha)(1 - \lambda)}E[\sigma_{n+k-1}^2].$$

The next expected value of the variance is a weighting between the most recent value and the long-term mean. Looking further into the future

$$E[\sigma_{n+k}^2] = \bar{\sigma}^2 + \left(E[\sigma_n^2] - \bar{\sigma}^2\right)(1 - v)^k$$

where

$$v = \frac{\alpha}{1 - (1 - \alpha)(1 - \lambda)}.$$

The path of expected future volatility[3] is shown in Figure 9.3.

---

[3] Actually variance, of course, which is anyway more important that volatility.

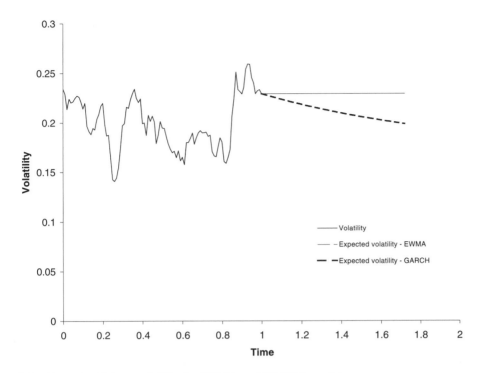

Figure 9.3 Expected future volatility for EWMA and GARCH models.

9.3.6 Beyond close-close estimators: range-based estimation of volatility

The problem with estimating volatility is that you need lots and lots of data to avoid sampling-error problems.

But then if you use too many days' worth of data you will be trying to estimate a parameter during a period when that parameter is almost certainly varying.

A catch-22 situation.

Or is it?

Why not use more information contained within a single day? That is, go down to finer timescales for the data. The problem with that is the behavior of returns over very short timescales, such as minutes, does not appear to be Normally distributed . . . there is even some evidence that the returns do not have a finite standard deviation.

Setting aside such worries(!), let's look at very simple ways of better estimating volatility using readily available price data, and not just closing prices.

Traditional close-to-close measure

When drift is small

$$\sigma_{cc}^2 = \frac{1}{n} \sum_{i=1}^{n} \left(\log \left(\frac{C_i}{C_{i-1}} \right) \right)^2.$$

Here there is a slight change of notation from before; C_i is the closing price on the ith day. Note also that we are looking at logarithms.

To adjust this for the drift take

$$\sigma_{acc}^2 = \frac{1}{n-1} \sum_{i=1}^{n} \left(\left(\log\left(\frac{C_i}{C_{i-1}} \right) \right)^2 - \frac{\left(\log\left(\frac{C_n}{C_0} \right) \right)^2}{n(n-1)} \right).$$

(Don't forget to annualize: multiply by the square root of the number of trading days in a year.)

Parkinson (1980)

This estimator uses extreme value, the highs H and the lows L during the day.

$$\sigma_p^2 = \frac{1}{4n \log(2)} \sum_{i=1}^{n} \left(\log\left(\frac{H_i}{L_i} \right) \right)^2.$$

This is five times more efficient than the close-to-close estimate. (That means, for the same amount of data the variance of the data is one fifth that of the close-to-close measure.)

Garman & Klass (1980)

At 7.4 times more efficient than close to close, we have

$$\sigma_{gk}^2 = \frac{1}{n} \sum_{i=1}^{n} \left(0.511 \left(\log\left(\frac{H_i}{L_i} \right) \right)^2 \right.$$

$$\left. -0.019 \log\left(\frac{C_i}{O_i} \right) \log\left(\frac{H_i L_i}{O_i^2} \right) - 2 \log\left(\frac{H_i}{O_i} \right) \log\left(\frac{L_i}{O_i} \right) \right).$$

Here O_i is the opening price.

Rogers & Satchell (1991)

Parkinson and Garman & Klass are not independent of the drift. Our final simple volatility estimate is

$$\sigma_{rs}^2 = \frac{1}{n} \sum_{i=1}^{n} \left(\log\left(\frac{H_i}{C_i} \right) \log\left(\frac{H_i}{O_i} \right) + \log\left(\frac{L_i}{C_i} \right) \log\left(\frac{L_i}{O_i} \right) \right).$$

9.4 **MAXIMUM LIKELIHOOD ESTIMATION**

A large part of statistical modeling concerns finding model parameters. Two popular ways of doing this are regression and Maximum Likelihood Estimation (MLE). We look at the second method here.

9.4.1 A simple motivating example: taxi numbers

You are attending a math conference. You arrive by train at the city hosting the event. You take a taxi from the train station to the conference venue. The taxi number is 20,922. How many taxis are there in the city?

This is a parameter estimation problem. Getting into a specific taxi is a probabilistic event. Estimating the number of taxis in the city from that event is a question of assumptions and statistical methodology.

The assumptions:

1. Taxi numbers are strictly positive integers.

2. Numbering starts at one.

3. No number is repeated.

4. No number is skipped.

The statistical methodology We will look at the probability of getting into taxi number 20,922 when there are N taxis in the city. This couldn't be simpler, the probability of getting into any specific taxi is

$$\frac{1}{N}.$$

This is shown in Figure 9.4.

Which N maximizes the probability of getting into taxi number 20,922?

$$N = 20,922.$$

This example explains the concept of MLE: *choose parameters that maximize the probability of the outcome actually happening.*

9.4.2 Three hats

You have three hats containing Normally distributed random numbers. One hat's numbers have mean of zero and standard deviation 0.1. This is hat A. Another hat's numbers have

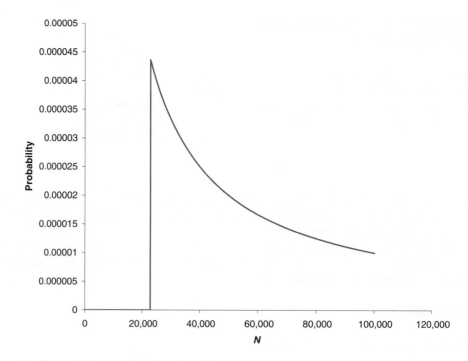

Figure 9.4 Probability of getting into the Nth taxi.

mean of zero and standard deviation 1. This is hat B. The final hat's numbers have mean of zero and standard deviation 10. This is hat C.

You don't know which hat is which.

You pick a number out of one hat, it is −2.6. Which hat do you think it came from?

The 'probability' of picking the number −2.6 from hat A (having a mean of zero and a standard deviation of 0.1) is

$$\frac{1}{\sqrt{2\pi}\ 0.1} \exp\left(-\frac{2.6^2}{2 \times 0.1^2}\right) = 6 \times 10^{-147}.$$

Very, very unlikely!

(N.B. The word 'probability' is in inverted commas to emphasize the fact that this is the value of the probability density function, not the actual probability. The probability of picking exactly −2.6 is, of course, zero.)

The 'probability' of picking the number −2.6 from hat B (having a mean of zero and a standard deviation of 1) is

$$\frac{1}{\sqrt{2\pi}\ 1} \exp\left(-\frac{2.6^2}{2 \times 1^2}\right) = 0.014,$$

and from hat C (having a mean of zero and a standard deviation of 10)

$$\frac{1}{\sqrt{2\pi}\ 10} \exp\left(-\frac{2.6^2}{2 \times 10^2}\right) = 0.039.$$

We would conclude that hat C is the most likely, since it has the highest probability for picking the number −2.6.

We now pick a second number from the same hat, it is 0.37. This looks more likely to have come from hat B. We get the following table of probabilities.

Hat	−2.6	0.37	Joint
A	6×10^{-147}	0.004	2×10^{-149}
B	0.014	0.372	0.005
C	0.039	0.040	0.002

The second column represents the probability of drawing the number −2.6 from each of the hats, the third column represents the probability of drawing 0.37 from each of the hats, and the final column is the joint probability, that is, the probability of drawing both numbers from each of the hats.

Using the information about *both* draws, we can see that the most likely hat is now B.

9.4.3 The math behind this: find the standard deviation

You have one hat containing Normally distributed random numbers, with a mean of zero and a standard deviation of σ which is unknown. You draw N numbers ϕ_i from this hat. Estimate σ.

Q. What is the 'probability' of drawing ϕ_i from a Normal distribution with mean zero and standard deviation σ?

A. It is

$$\frac{1}{\sqrt{2\pi}\sigma} e^{-\frac{\phi_i^2}{2\sigma^2}}.$$

Q. What is the 'probability' of drawing all of the numbers $\phi_1, \phi_2, \ldots, \phi_N$ from independent Normal distributions with mean zero and standard deviation σ?

A. It is

$$\prod_{i=1}^{N} \frac{1}{\sqrt{2\pi}\sigma} e^{-\frac{\phi_i^2}{2\sigma^2}}.$$

. . . choose the σ that maximizes this quantity. This is easy . . .

Differentiate with respect to σ (take logarithms first) and set result equal to zero:

$$\frac{d}{d\sigma}\left(-N\log(\sigma) - \frac{1}{2\sigma^2}\sum_{i=1}^{N}\phi_i^2\right) = 0.$$

(A multiplicative factor has been ignored here.) I.e.

$$-\frac{N}{\sigma} + \frac{1}{\sigma^3}\sum_{i=1}^{N}\phi_i^2 = 0.$$

Therefore our best guess for σ is given by

$$\sigma^2 = \frac{1}{N} \sum_{i=1}^{N} \phi_i^2.$$

This should be a familiar expression!

9.4.4   Quants' salaries

In Figure 9.5 are the results of a 2004 survey on `www.wilmott.com` concerning the salaries of quants using the Forum[4].

This distribution looks vaguely lognormal, with distribution

$$\frac{1}{\sqrt{2\pi}\sigma E} \exp\left(-\frac{(\log E - \log E_0)^2}{2\sigma^2}\right),$$

where E is annual earnings, σ is the standard deviation and E_0 the mean. Using MLE find σ and E_0.

The MLE solution is shown in Figure 9.6.

The mean $E_0 = \$133,284$, with $\sigma = 0.833$.

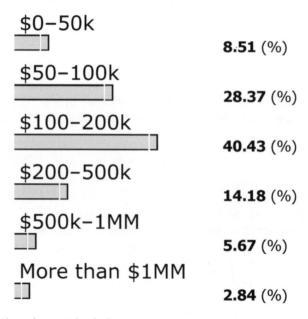

If you are a professional 'quant,' how much do you earn?

Last year I earned:

$0–50k
8.51 (%)

$50–100k
28.37 (%)

$100–200k
40.43 (%)

$200–500k
14.18 (%)

$500k–1MM
5.67 (%)

More than $1MM
2.84 (%)

Figure 9.5   Distribution of quants' salaries.

[4] The respondents were self selecting so the numbers will be biased towards the more forthcoming, that is, less well paid, quant.

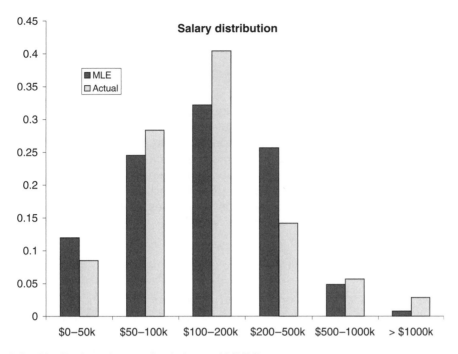

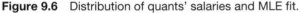

Figure 9.6 Distribution of quants' salaries and MLE fit.

9.5 **SKEWS AND SMILES**

We have briefly already mentioned skews and smiles, but here is a reminder of what they are about.

For a series of options that all expire at the same date, plot the value of implied volatility against strike. *If* actual volatility were constant, and *if* the Black–Scholes model were correct and *if* people priced options correctly then that plot would be flat, all options would have the same implied volatility. Of course, none of those assumptions is correct, and so there is plenty of scope for that plot to be curved, or skewed. If there is an appreciable slant to that curve, for example if it goes from top left to bottom right, then we have what is called a skew. A negative skew is downward sloping and a positive skew upward sloping. If there is curvature so that the curve has a minimum in the middle then we have a smile. Skews and smiles are the market's way of telling us that either they don't believe in the Black–Scholes model or its assumptions or that they don't care.

'They don't care'? If out-of-the-money puts are expensive, does it matter? Perhaps not if they still cost only pennies and they are the easiest or cheapest way of getting downside protection. To not buy needed downside protection because implied volatility seems a bit high would be a foolish economy. 'Penny wise, pound foolish.'

So smiles and skews may give us information about future volatility or they may give us information about people's expectation of future volatility or they may give us an idea of how desperately they need to hedge. All very useful stuff.

You can speculate on what you think implied volatility might be going to do in the future by buying or selling specific portfolios of vanilla options. If you want to speculate on level of implied volatility you may buy or sell a straddle, and if you want to speculate on skew then you would consider a risk reversal. Let's see how this works.

9.5.1 Sensitivity of the straddle to skews and smiles

The straddle is a portfolio made up of a long position in a call and a put, both having the same strike and expiration. Because of put-call parity the market will price these two contracts with the same volatility (bid-offer spread aside) and so there is really only one implied volatility to consider. Figure 9.7 shows the Black–Scholes value of this simple portfolio using three different levels of volatility. The strike is 100, the interest rate is 5% and there is one year to expiration. The Black–Scholes value of this portfolio is monotonic in the volatility; increase the volatility and the value rises. Such a portfolio is therefore ideal when it comes to speculating on implied volatility.

9.5.2 Sensitivity of the risk reversal to skews and smiles

The risk reversal is made up of a long call and a short put, the call having a higher strike than the put. Now that there are two strikes to consider we can see that the implied volatility skew is important. Figure 9.8 shows how the value of the risk reversal varies with the skew. In the case of the negative skew we have used a 25% volatility for the put, having strike 80, and a 15% volatility for the call, having a strike of 120. In the positive skew example these quantities are reversed and with the no-skew example both

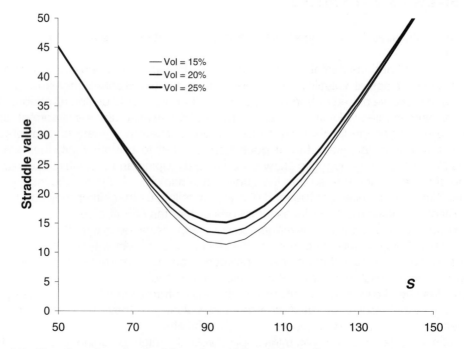

Figure 9.7 How the value of a straddle varies with level of volatility.

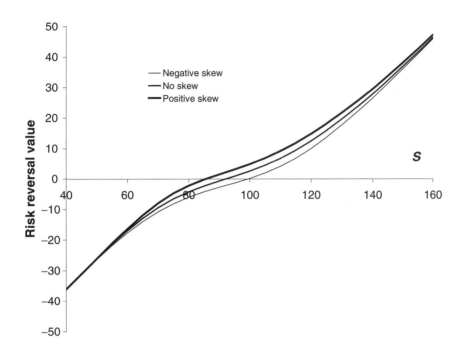

Figure 9.8 How the value of a risk reversal varies with volatility skew.

options have a strike of 20%. The risk reversal's sensitivity to skew makes it perfect for speculation on that skew.[5]

If you want to speculate on the smile what contract would you buy? Simple, you need a payoff with three kinks in it, a butterfly spread.

9.6 DIFFERENT APPROACHES TO MODELING VOLATILITY

For the rest of this chapter I want to provide a brief overview of what is possible in terms of volatility modeling, and to put it all into context. Please see *PWOQF2* for all the details.

9.6.1 To calibrate or not?

Perhaps the biggest question to face is that of how much information should we take from the prices of options in the markets. Given that we can't see what volatility is at any instant, and given that forecasting volatility is not easy (see just a small subset of possibilities above), we might be tempted to use implied volatility as an estimate of future volatility. What we

---

[5] At a meeting of The Committee on 15th September 2005 it was unanimously voted that sensitivity to skew be henceforward called 'Xena.' Present were Dominic Connor, Mike Weber and the author.

might say is that implied volatility is the market's best estimate of what volatility will do in the future. In this sense, the implied volatility of a three-month option can be thought of as containing information about actual volatility over the next three months.

Well, yes and no. In some sense, perhaps. But I personally don't believe that the market is that statistically sophisticated. If people want to spend too much buying an option, or charge too little when selling it that is their business, it doesn't mean that their prices are right. It is no different from the pricing of a liter of milk in your corner shop. Has the shopkeeper done some detailed analysis of the utility of individual customers, pricing in the opportunity cost of going to the corner shop versus the cheaper supermarket, allowing for the future price of gas or bus fares, etc.? No, he knows what it costs to buy the milk and he just tries to sell it for as much above that as he possibly can. Out-of-the-money puts are expensive, due to demand, otherwise known as 'fear.' Out-of-the-money calls are cheap, due to supply, otherwise known as 'greed.'

Yes, there is arbitrage. Every business is based on arbitrage, so it is to be expected that arbitrage (or mispricing as theoreticians call it, or earning a living, as sensible people call it) exists. So I wouldn't be too keen on accepting that there is a great deal of information about volatility within option prices.

Anyway, whether to accept prices as containing information is part of the subject of calibration. If you have an option pricing model, should it output theoretical prices that are exactly the same as quoted market prices?

The subject of calibration will crop up a lot from now on.

9.6.2 Deterministic volatility surfaces

The most straightforward modeling approach that leads to theoretical prices that match market prices is to work in the classical Black–Scholes world, with the one exception that actual volatility is not a constant but a function of stock price and time, $\sigma(S, t)$. This is the simplest model that is consistent with the market prices of options. Stock- and time-dependent actual volatility are still entirely consistent with the Black–Scholes partial differential equation, you just have $\sigma(S, t)$ in the coefficient of the gamma term. The big difference from the constant-volatility world is just that we cannot generally find closed-form solutions for option prices anymore.

The way that this idea works is that you have enough freedom in the function $\sigma(S, t)$ to make the theoretical option values (found numerically, say) consistent with all option values in the market, or, totally equivalently, consistent with all implied vols. Now normally you would specify the actual volatility, work out the option prices and so the implied vols. This is the natural forward problem. Not so with this form of calibration. Here we specify the implied vols and ask what actual volatilities are consistent with them. This is what is known to mathematicians as an inverse problem.

Inverse problems are notoriously tricky to solve. One reason is the sensitivity of the result (actual volatilities) to the input (implied volatilities). If you specify actual volatilities and work out implied, then this is a smoothing operation; implied volatilities are averages of actuals. But going the other way does the opposite of smoothing. Make a very small change to implied volatilities and this can have an enormous effect on $\sigma(S, t)$.

If our problem were a diffusion equation from a nice physical problem, this might not matter. Having faith in the diffusion model, finding the parameters (actual volatilities) is a matter of 'regularization.' Unfortunately, we cannot have faith in our model, it is financial not physical, and so the sensitivity to initial input is something we have to live with.

One reason is that common sense says it cannot be right, the financial world is too complicated to obey the rather simplistic $\sigma(S, t)$ model. A second reason is that it is very, very easy to test scientifically. Do the following. Find $\sigma(S, t)$ using option data one day. Then come back a week later, when stock prices and option prices have all changed. Now recalibrate to find $\sigma(S, t)$ again. If the model is right then the first and second calculations will give exactly the same actual volatilities. Do they? No. Never.[6]

9.6.3 Stochastic volatility

Without a doubt it is impossible to accurately forecast future actual volatility so it makes sense to treat that quantity as being random. After all, modeling stock prices as random was the great breakthrough in pricing derivatives based on stocks, so perhaps modeling volatility as random is also a great breakthrough since options are really all about future volatility.

Although stochastic volatility models are commonly used in practice they do suffer from two major problems. First, what model should we choose? What is the volatility of volatility? Given that we can't even measure volatility at any moment particularly accurately, how on earth can we measure the volatility of that immeasurable volatility?

The second problem concerns hedging. When only the stock price is random we have only one source of randomness. This randomness can be hedged away from an option by using a position in the underlying stock. One source of randomness, one traded quantity for hedging that randomness, end result no randomness at all. Now, when volatility is stochastic we have two sources of randomness, the stock and volatility. But we still only have the one traded quantity to hedge with, the stock. We can't hedge with volatility to remove volatility risk because that isn't traded. We can, sort of, get rid of the volatility risk in one option by hedging with another option, an exchange-traded vanilla. End result is a hedged portfolio, but now we have one equation for two unknowns, the value of the original option and the value of the option used for hedging. Oh dear. To get out of that one requires the introduction of a concept known as the market price of volatility risk.

9.6.4 Uncertain parameters

First deterministic volatility, then random volatility. That just about covers the possibilities, no? No. There is also 'uncertain' volatility. This is subtly, but importantly, different from random. Random is when you have a probabilistic description, perhaps even a probability density function, for the random variable. Uncertainty is when you have no such concept. Models using uncertainty are therefore far more vague than models using randomness. (And I mean 'vague' in a good way.)

---

[6] Phlogiston theory: hypothesis regarding combustion. The theory, advanced by J. J. Becher late in the 17th century, and extended and popularized by G. E. Stahl, postulates that in all flammable materials there is present phlogiston, a substance without color, odor, taste, or weight that is given off in burning. 'Phlogisticated' substances are those that contain phlogiston and, on being burned, are 'dephlogisticated.' The ash of the burned material is held to be the true material. Source: *The Columbia Electronic Encyclopedia,* 6th ed. 2004. Many financial theories seem very phlogiston-like to me. It is time for some debunking!

The simplest such model allows volatility to lie within a range. But there is no mention made of how likely the volatility is to be at any point in that range, it is a genuine model of uncertainty not of randomness. Given a range of possible values for volatility, we find that there is a range of possible values for an option. Furthermore, long and short positions take different values, and the whole business of pricing derivatives becomes non linear.

9.6.5 Static hedging

Hedging is used to reduce or, if possible, to eliminate risk. In options theory and practice we dynamically delta hedge to eliminate the stock-price risk in an option. Such theory we have seen several times in this book. But there are other, perhaps more obscure, risks that we are only just starting to worry about here. One of those risks is caused by volatility. The plain and simple fact is that we don't know what volatility is going to be in the future therefore when we price an option we will be exposed to the input volatility being wrong, we therefore have volatility risk.

In practice, instead of just dynamically hedging with vanilla options, we also statically hedge. To see how this works, imagine that we want to price and hedge some exotic contract. Suppose that the payoff from that exotic contract can somehow be closely matched by the payoff from a portfolio of vanillas. If it can, then you hedge with those vanillas leaving only a small residual payoff which needs delta hedging. The original contract may have been very difficult to delta hedge, and so very exposed to your volatility input. But after statically hedging with the vanillas the delta-hedging task is much easier. And, of course, you know exactly what the portfolio is worth (the contracts are exchange traded) so you know almost exactly what the exotic should be worth. In practice, you won't be able to get a perfect match between the exotic and the vanillas because if you could then the exotic wasn't exotic at all.

9.6.6 Stochastic volatility and mean-variance analysis

As mentioned above, one of the drawbacks with stochastic volatility models is that when you build up the governing equation you assume that you can dynamically hedge with options. And the equation you end up with contains the market price of volatility risk, a wonderful concept in theory but rather too unreliable for practice. There are ways of tidying this all up without these two problems, and that is to accept that not all risk can be dynamically hedged away, and then to assign a value to that risk.

9.6.7 Asymptotic analysis of volatility

When deciding which stochastic volatility model to choose we often face the dilemma of whether to pick an easy-to-compute model that might not be so accurate, or a slower but more scientifically precise model. Practitioners almost always go for fast and inaccurate. However, by exploiting a little known applied math concept known as asymptotic analysis[7] you can actually get the best of both worlds. Asymptotic analysis

---

[7] Little known in finance, at least. To applied mathematicians asymptotic analysis is a very commonly used tool in their toolbox. Prior to succumbing to the lure of finance almost every mathematical model I worked on used asymptotic analysis at some stage, mainly because they would otherwise have been far too complicated to solve or understand.

is all about finding approximate solutions to differential equations, models, whatever, by exploiting the relative largeness or smallness of a parameter in the model. If some terms in a complicated equation are multiplied by a small number then perhaps those terms don't matter so we can ignore them, leaving us with a simpler equation that we may be able to solve. Of course, it is nowhere near as simple as that, but it gives you the flavor of the technique.

9.7 THE CHOICES OF VOLATILITY MODELS

Model	Math	Popularity
Constant vol	$\sigma =$ constant, Black–Scholes formulæ	Very, especially for vanillas
Deterministic vol	$\sigma(S, t)$, Black–Scholes pde	Very, for exotics
Stochastic vol	$d\sigma = \ldots$, higher dimensions, transforms	Very, for exotics
Jump diffusion	Poisson processes, jumps in stock and/or vol.	Increasing
Uncertain vol	$\sigma^- \le \sigma \le \sigma^+$, non-linear pde	Not at all, unfortunately
Stoch vol and mean-variance	$d\sigma = \ldots$, higher dimensions, non-linearity	Not at all, unfortunately

9.8 SUMMARY

Derivatives are all about volatility. You can't price or hedge derivatives without a decent model for volatility. And if your volatility model is better than the market's you could make money by speculating on volatility. We will see this in the next chapter. One point to watch out for is how much information we back out from vanilla option prices into our volatility model. Never forget that volatility is a property of the stock and would still be present even if there weren't any derivatives! Indeed, how on earth can markets possibly have perfect knowledge of the future, and the future volatility of the stock? Of course they can't. Option prices may be governed to some extent by what people expect to happen in the future in some rational sense, but they are also governed by fear and greed as interpreted by option prices through simple supply and demand. Option prices, and hence volatility, will rise when people panic and rush to buy those OTM puts, regardless of whether this panic is rational. And if you do have to pay 10 cents for an option that may only be worth 7 cents, well so what? It's still pennies after all. However, translate those pennies into implied volatility numbers and suddenly it looks like the market is expecting volatility to rise.

FURTHER READING

- Natenberg (1994), of course.
- Shu Zhang (2003) look at data for SP500 index option volatility and compare with realized volatility.

- And for something more (much more) quanty, see Rebonato (2004).

- Javaheri (2005) on volatility arbitrage is a must read.

- A survey of stochastic volatility models, their calibration and how very differently they price the same contracts is given in Schoutens, *et al.* (2004).

- All of the models discussed above are described in great detail in *PWOQF2*.

'A NEAT DERIVATION'

APPENDIX: HOW TO DERIVE BS PDE, MINIMUM FUSS

Here is how to derive the Black–Scholes equation, with the minimum fuss and the minimum (explicit) assumptions. This derivation also shows the special, almost arbitrary role, played by volatility.

Working with any Brownian-motion type model for stock price dynamics will give you a linear diffusion equation for pretty much everything, including option values. If $V(S, t)$ is the option's value then the general linear diffusion equation (and homogeneous, since the value of an empty portfolio should be zero) is

$$\frac{\partial V}{\partial t} + a\frac{\partial^2 V}{\partial S^2} + b\frac{\partial V}{\partial S} + cV = 0$$

where a, b and c are, for the moment, arbitrary.

A solution of this equation must be cash, i.e. $e^{-r(T-t)}$. Plug this function into the partial differential equation to find that

$$c = -r.$$

Another solution is the stock, S. Plug this function in and you will find

$$b = rS.$$

This gives you the risk-neutral pricing equation

$$\frac{\partial V}{\partial t} + a\frac{\partial^2 V}{\partial S^2} + rS\frac{\partial V}{\partial S} - rV = 0.$$

The only remaining 'real' or 'arbitrary' parameter left to determine or fudge/calibrate is a. And we know (from what we've done before) that this is related to volatility. So, this shows us a couple of things:

- Basic considerations pin down the coefficients of most of the terms in the pricing equation, and are clearly risk neutral as well.

- To determine or model the diffusion coefficient you will need to go to greater lengths. Or more simply, just use this function as the only one you can arguably calibrate.

EXERCISES

1. Using real, daily data, for several stocks, plot a time series of volatility using several models.

    (a) Divide the data into yearly intervals and estimate volatility during each year.
    (b) Use a fixed-length, moving window.
    (c) Use an exponentially weighted estimate.

2. Collect real option data from the *Wall Street Journal*, the *Financial Times* or elsewhere, calculate implied volatilities and plot them against expiration, against strike, and, in a three-dimensional plot, against strike and expiration.

CHAPTER 10
how to delta hedge

The aim of this Chapter...

...is to show how classical calculus can be used to model situations in which you believe that there is arbitrage, and want to study risk and return.

In this Chapter...

- how to make money if your volatility forecast is more accurate than the market's

- different ways of delta hedging

- how much profit should you expect to make

10.1 **INTRODUCTION**

In this chapter I am going to boldly assert that there is money to be made from options, because options may be mispriced by the market. In simple terms, *there are arbitrage opportunities*. Shock, horror! I know that the whole of Chicago University has just thrown down this book in disgust. However, I hope the rest of you will enjoy the contents of this chapter for it puts into concrete mathematics some ideas that are most important, and frighteningly under-explained in the literature. This is the subject of how to delta hedge when your estimate of future actual volatility differs from that of the market as measured by the implied volatility.

As I hinted above, to some people, saying that actual volatility and implied volatility can be inconsistent with each other is a heresy, for it implies arbitrage and hence free money. Well, it's only as free as the model is accurate, that is, not at all. But even so, if there is such a difference (and vol arb hedge funds certainly think there is) then we can only get at that money by hedging, and if we have two estimates of volatility, which one goes into the famous Black–Scholes delta formula?

We'll see how you can hedge using a delta based on *either* actual volatility or on implied volatility. Neither is wrong, they just have different risk/return profiles.

If you do doubt that implied volatility and actual volatility can be in disagreement then take a look at Figure 10.1. This is simply a plot of the distributions of the logarithms of the VIX and of the rolling realized SPX volatility. The VIX is an implied volatility measure based on the SPX index and so you would expect it and the realized SPX volatility to bear some

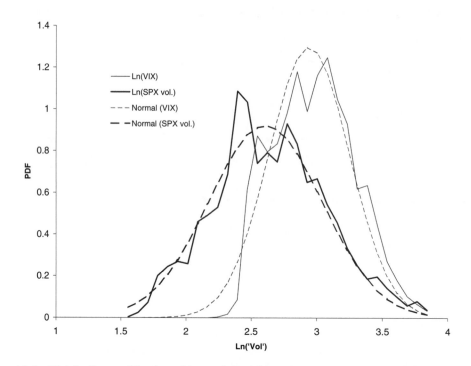

Figure 10.1 Distributions of the logarithms of the VIX and the rolling realized SPX volatility, and the Normal distributions for comparison.

resemblance. Not quite, as can be seen in the figure. The implied volatility VIX seems to be higher than the realized volatility. Both of these volatilities are approximately lognormally distributed (since their logarithms appear to be Normal), especially the realized volatility. The VIX distribution is somewhat truncated on the left. The mean of the realized volatility, about 15%, is significantly less than the mean of the VIX, about 20%, but its standard deviation is greater.

10.2 WHAT IF IMPLIED AND ACTUAL VOLATILITIES ARE DIFFERENT?

Actual volatility is the amount of 'noise' in the stock price, it is the coefficient of the Wiener process in the stock returns model, it is the amount of randomness that 'actually' transpires. Implied volatility is how the market is pricing the option currently. Since the market does not have perfect knowledge about the future these two numbers can and will be different.

Actual volatility being different from implied volatility is the heart of this chapter. Let's look at the simple case of exploiting such a difference by buying or selling options, but not delta hedging them.

Imagine that we have a forecast for volatility over the remaining life of an option, this volatility is forecast to be constant, and, crucially, our forecast turns out to be correct.

If you believe that actual volatility is higher than implied you might want to buy a straddle because there is then a good chance that the stock will move so far before expiry that you will get a payoff of more than the premium you paid, even after allowing for the time value of money. This is a very simple strategy, requiring no maintenance. There is one big problem with this however. It is risky. Sometimes you'll win, sometimes you'll lose. *Unless you can do this strategy many, many times you could end up losing a great deal.* Even if you are right about the actual volatility being large the stock might end up at the money, and you lose out. The relationship between actual volatility and the range over which an asset moves is a probabilistic one, there are no guarantees that a high volatility results in large moves.

If you buy an at-the-money straddle close to expiry the profit you expect to make from this strategy is approximately

$$\sqrt{\frac{2(T-t)}{\pi}} \, (\sigma - \tilde{\sigma}) \, S.$$

The expression uses the close to expiry and ATM approximation we saw in Chapter 8. The notation is obvious; σ is the actual volatility, assumed constant, and $\tilde{\sigma}$ is the implied volatility. Note that this is an *expectation*. It is also a *real* expectation, however the real drift doesn't appear in this expression because it is an approximation valid only when close to expiration.

The standard deviation of the profit (the risk) is approximately

$$\sqrt{1 - \frac{2}{\pi}} \, \sigma S \sqrt{T-t}.$$

Observe how this depends on the actual volatility and not on the implied volatility. This standard deviation is of the same order of magnitude as the expected profit. That is a lot of risk. We can improve the risk-reward profile by delta hedging as we shall see next. The main purpose of writing down the above expressions is to show how they are linear in the two volatilities.

10.3 IMPLIED VERSUS ACTUAL, DELTA HEDGING BUT USING WHICH VOLATILITY?

Let's buy an underpriced option, or portfolio as above, but now, to improve risk and reward, we will delta hedge to expiry. This is a less risky strategy.

But which delta do you choose? Delta based on actual or implied volatility? This is one of those questions that people always ask, and one that no one seems to know the full answer to.

Scenario: Implied volatility for an option is 20%, but we believe that actual volatility is 30%.

Question: How can we make money if our forecast is correct?

Answer: Buy the option and delta hedge. But which delta do we use? We know that

$$\Delta = N(d_1)$$

where

$$N(x) = \frac{1}{\sqrt{2\pi}} \int_{-\infty}^{x} e^{-\frac{s^2}{2}} \, ds$$

and

$$d_1 = \frac{\ln(S/E) + \left(r + \frac{1}{2}\sigma^2\right)(T-t)}{\sigma\sqrt{T-t}}.$$

We can all agree on S, E, $T - t$ and r (almost), but not on σ, should we use $\sigma = 0.2$ or 0.3, implied volatility or actual? In this example,

$$\sigma = \text{actual volatility, 30\%}$$

and

$$\tilde{\sigma} = \text{implied volatility, 20\%}.$$

Which of these goes into the d_1?

10.4 CASE 1: HEDGE WITH ACTUAL VOLATILITY, σ

By hedging with actual volatility we are replicating a short position in a *correctly priced* option. The payoffs for our long option and our short replicated option will exactly cancel. The profit we make will be exactly the difference in the Black–Scholes prices of an option with 30% volatility and one with 20% volatility. (Assuming that the Black–Scholes assumptions hold.) If $V(S, t; \sigma)$ is the Black–Scholes formula then the guaranteed profit is

$$V(S, t; \sigma) - V(S, t; \tilde{\sigma}).$$

But how is this guaranteed profit realized? Let's do the math on a mark-to-market basis.

In the following, superscript 'a' means actual and 'i' means implied, these can be applied to deltas and option values. For example, Δ^a is the delta using the actual volatility in the formula. V^i is the theoretical option value using the implied volatility in the formula. Note also that V, Δ, Γ and Θ are all simple, known, Black–Scholes formulæ.

The model is as usual

$$dS = \mu S \, dt + \sigma S \, dX.$$

Now, set up a portfolio by buying the option for V^i and hedge with Δ^a of the stock. The values of each of the components of our portfolio are shown in Table 10.1.

Leave this hedged portfolio overnight, and come back to it the next day. The new values are shown in Table 10.2. (I have included a continuous dividend yield in this.)

Therefore we have made, mark to market,

$$dV^i - \Delta^a \, dS - r(V^i - \Delta^a \, S)dt - \Delta^a DS \, dt.$$

Because the option would be correctly valued at V^a then we have

$$dV^a - \Delta^a \, dS - r(V^a - \Delta^a \, S)dt - \Delta^a DS \, dt = 0.$$

So we can write the mark-to-market profit over one time step as

$$dV^i - dV^a + r(V^a - \Delta^a \, S)dt - r(V^i - \Delta^a \, S)dt$$

$$= dV^i - dV^a - r(V^i - V^a)dt = e^{rt} \, d\left(e^{-rt}(V^i - V^a)\right).$$

Table 10.1 Portfolio composition and values, today.

Component	Value
Option	V^i
Stock	$-\Delta^a \, S$
Cash	$-V^i + \Delta^a \, S$

Table 10.2 Portfolio composition and values, tomorrow.

Component	Value
Option	$V^i + dV^i$
Stock	$-\Delta^a \, S - \Delta^a \, dS$
Cash	$(-V^i + \Delta^a \, S)(1 + r \, dt) - \Delta^a DS \, dt$

That is the profit from time t to $t + dt$. The present value of this profit at time t_0 is

$$e^{-r(t-t_0)}e^{rt} \, d\left(e^{-rt}(V^i - V^a)\right) = e^{rt_0} \, d\left(e^{-rt}(V^i - V^a)\right).$$

So the total profit from t_0 to expiration is

$$e^{rt_0} \int_{t_0}^{T} d\left(e^{-rt}(V^i - V^a)\right) = V^a - V^i.$$

This confirms what I said earlier about the guaranteed total profit by expiration.

We can also write that one time step mark-to-market profit (using Itô's lemma) as

$$\Theta^i \, dt + \Delta^i \, dS + \tfrac{1}{2}\sigma^2 S^2 \Gamma^i \, dt - \Delta^a \, dS - r(V^i - \Delta^a S) \, dt - \Delta^a DS \, dt$$

$$= \Theta^i \, dt + \mu S(\Delta^i - \Delta^a) \, dt + \tfrac{1}{2}\sigma^2 S^2 \Gamma^i \, dt - r(V^i - \Delta^a S) \, dt + (\Delta^i - \Delta^a)\sigma S \, dX - \Delta^a DS \, dt$$

$$= (\Delta^i - \Delta^a)\sigma S \, dX + (\mu - r + D)S(\Delta^i - \Delta^a) \, dt + \tfrac{1}{2}\left(\sigma^2 - \tilde{\sigma}^2\right)S^2 \Gamma^i \, dt$$

(using Black–Scholes with $\sigma = \tilde{\sigma}$)

$$= \tfrac{1}{2}\left(\sigma^2 - \tilde{\sigma}^2\right)S^2 \Gamma^i \, dt + (\Delta^i - \Delta^a)\left((\mu - r + D)S \, dt + \sigma S \, dX\right).$$

The conclusion is that the final profit is guaranteed (the difference between the theoretical option values with the two volatilities) but how that is achieved is random, because of the dX term in the above. On a mark-to-market basis you could lose before you gain. Moreover, the mark-to-market profit depends on the real drift of the stock, μ. This is illustrated in Figure 10.2. The figure shows several realizations of the same delta-hedged

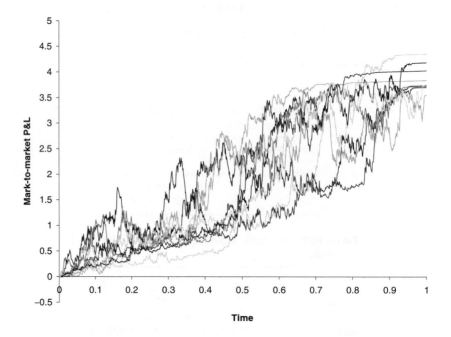

Figure 10.2 P&L for a delta-hedged option on a mark-to-market basis, hedged using actual volatility.

position. Note that the final P&L is not *exactly* the same in each case because of the effect of hedging discretely.

When S changes, so will V. But these changes do not cancel each other out. From a risk management point of view this is not ideal.

There is a simple analogy for this behavior. It is similar to owning a bond. For a bond there is a guaranteed outcome, but we may lose on a mark-to-market basis in the meantime.

10.5 **CASE 2: HEDGE WITH IMPLIED VOLATILITY, $\tilde{\sigma}$**

Compare and contrast now with the case of hedging using a delta based on implied volatility. By hedging with implied volatility we are balancing the random fluctuations in the mark-to-market option value with the fluctuations in the stock price. The evolution of the portfolio value is then 'deterministic' as we shall see.

Buy the option today, hedge using the implied delta, and put any cash in the bank earning r. The mark-to-market profit from today to tomorrow is

$$dV^i - \Delta^i\, dS - r(V^i - \Delta^i S)dt - \Delta^i DS\, dt$$
$$= \Theta^i\, dt + \tfrac{1}{2}\sigma^2 S^2 \Gamma^i\, dt - r(V^i - \Delta^i S)dt - \Delta^i DS\, dt$$
$$= \tfrac{1}{2}\left(\sigma^2 - \tilde{\sigma}^2\right)S^2 \Gamma^i\, dt. \qquad (10.1)$$

THIS IS HOW MUCH YOU SHOULD MAKE EACH DAY

This is a far nicer way to make money. Observe how the daily profit is deterministic, there aren't any dX terms. From a risk management perspective this is much better behaved. There is another, rather wonderful, advantage of hedging using implied volatility . . . we don't even need to know what actual volatility is. And to make a profit all we need to know is that actual is always going to be greater than implied (if we are buying) or always less (if we are selling). This takes some of the pressure off forecasting volatility accurately in the first place.

Add up the present value of all of these profits to get a total profit of

$$\tfrac{1}{2}\left(\sigma^2 - \tilde{\sigma}^2\right)\int_{t_0}^{T} e^{-r(t-t_0)}S^2 \Gamma^i\, dt.$$

This is always positive, but highly path dependent. Being path dependent it will depend on the drift μ. If we start off at the money and the drift is very large (positive or negative) we will find ourselves quickly moving into territory where gamma and hence (10.1) is small, so that there will be not much profit to be made. The best that could happen would be for the stock to end up close to the strike at expiration, this would maximize the total profit. This path dependency is shown in Figure 10.3. The figure shows several realizations of the same delta-hedged position. Note that the lines are not perfectly smooth, again because of the effect of hedging discretely.

The simple analogy is now just putting money in the bank. The P&L is always increasing in value but the end result is random.

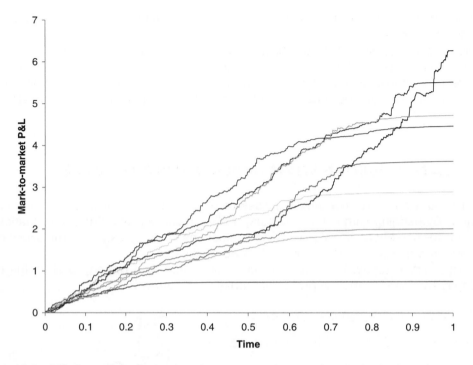

Figure 10.3 P&L for a delta-hedged option on a mark-to-market basis, hedged using implied volatility.

Peter Carr (2005) and Henrard (2001) show that if you hedge using a delta based on a volatility σ_h then the PV of the total profit is given by

$$V(S, t; \sigma_h) - V(S, t; \tilde{\sigma}) + \tfrac{1}{2}\left(\sigma^2 - \sigma_h^2\right) \int_{t_0}^{T} e^{-r(t-t_0)} S^2 \Gamma^h \, dt, \tag{10.2}$$

where the superscript on the gamma means that it uses the Black–Scholes formula with a volatility of σ_h.

10.5.1   The expected profit after hedging using implied volatility

When you hedge using delta based on implied volatility the profit each 'day' is deterministic but the present value of total profit by expiration is path dependent, and given by

$$\tfrac{1}{2}(\sigma^2 - \tilde{\sigma}^2) \int_{t_0}^{T} e^{-r(s-t_0)} S^2 \Gamma^i \, ds.$$

The details of the analysis of this expression are found in *PWOQF2*. Anyway, after some manipulations we end up with the expected profit initially being the single integral

$$\frac{Ee^{-r(T-t_0)}(\sigma^2 - \tilde{\sigma}^2)}{2\sqrt{2\pi}} \int_{t_0}^{T} \frac{1}{\sqrt{\sigma^2(s-t_0) + \tilde{\sigma}^2(T-s)}}$$

$$\exp\left(-\frac{\left(\log(S/E) + \left(\mu - \frac{1}{2}\sigma^2\right)(s-t_0) + \left(r - D - \frac{1}{2}\tilde{\sigma}^2\right)(T-s)\right)^2}{2(\sigma^2(s-t_0) + \tilde{\sigma}^2(T-s))}\right) ds.$$

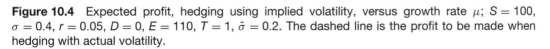

Results are shown in Figures 10.4–10.6.

In Figure 10.4 is shown the expected profit versus the growth rate μ. Parameters are $S = 100$, $\sigma = 0.4$, $r = 0.05$, $D = 0$, $E = 110$, $T = 1$, $\tilde{\sigma} = 0.2$. Observe that the expected profit has a maximum. This will be at the growth rate that ensures, roughly speaking, that the stock ends up close to at the money at expiration, where gamma is largest. In the figure is also shown the profit to be made when hedging with actual volatility. For most realistic parameters regimes the maximum expected profit hedging with implied is similar to the guaranteed profit hedging with actual.

A bit complicated, but implemented on the CD

In Figure 10.5 is shown expected profit versus E and μ. You can see how the higher the growth rate the larger the strike price at the maximum. The contour map is shown in Figure 10.6.

10.5.2 The variance of profit after hedging using implied volatility

Once we have calculated the expected profit from hedging using implied volatility we can calculate the variance in the final profit. Again, all details may be found in *PWOQF2*.

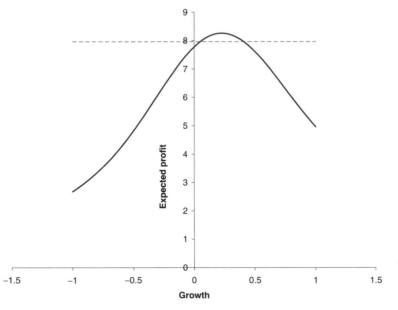

Figure 10.4 Expected profit, hedging using implied volatility, versus growth rate μ; $S = 100$, $\sigma = 0.4$, $r = 0.05$, $D = 0$, $E = 110$, $T = 1$, $\tilde{\sigma} = 0.2$. The dashed line is the profit to be made when hedging with actual volatility.

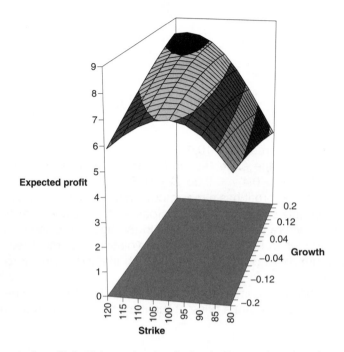

Figure 10.5 Expected profit, hedging using implied volatility, versus growth rate μ and strike E; $S = 100$, $\sigma = 0.4$, $r = 0.05$, $D = 0$, $T = 1$, $\tilde{\sigma} = 0.2$.

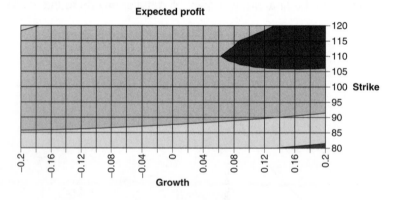

Figure 10.6 Contour map of expected profit, hedging using implied volatility, versus growth rate μ and strike E; $S = 100$, $\sigma = 0.4$, $r = 0.05$, $D = 0$, $T = 1$, $\tilde{\sigma} = 0.2$.

The initial variance is $G(S_0, t_0) - F(S_0, t_0)^2$, where

$$G(S_0, t_0) = \frac{E^2(\sigma^2 - \tilde{\sigma}^2)^2 e^{-2r(T-t_0)}}{4\pi\sigma\tilde{\sigma}} \int_{t_0}^{T} \int_{s}^{T}$$

$$\times \frac{e^{p(u,s;S_0,t_0)}}{\sqrt{s-t_0}\sqrt{T-s}\sqrt{\sigma^2(u-s) + \tilde{\sigma}^2(T-u)}\sqrt{\frac{1}{\sigma^2(s-t_0)} + \frac{1}{\tilde{\sigma}^2(T-s)} + \frac{1}{\sigma^2(u-s)+\tilde{\sigma}^2(T-u)}}} \, du \, ds \quad (10.3)$$

where

$$p(u, s; S_0, t_0) = -\frac{1}{2}\frac{(x - \alpha(T - s))^2}{\tilde{\sigma}^2(T - s)} - \frac{1}{2}\frac{(x - \alpha(T - u))^2}{\sigma^2(u - s) + \tilde{\sigma}^2(T - u)}$$

$$+ \frac{1}{2}\frac{\left(\dfrac{x - \alpha(T - s)}{\tilde{\sigma}^2(T - s)} + \dfrac{x - \alpha(T - u)}{\sigma^2(u - s) + \tilde{\sigma}^2(T - u)}\right)^2}{\dfrac{1}{\sigma^2(s - t_0)} + \dfrac{1}{\tilde{\sigma}^2(T - s)} + \dfrac{1}{\sigma^2(u - s) + \tilde{\sigma}^2(T - u)}}$$

and

$$x = \ln(S_0/E) + \left(\mu - \tfrac{1}{2}\sigma^2\right)(T - t_0), \quad \text{and} \quad \alpha = \mu - \tfrac{1}{2}\sigma^2 - r + D + \tfrac{1}{2}\tilde{\sigma}^2.$$

Even more complicated, but still implemented on the CD

In Figure 10.7 is shown the standard deviation of profit versus growth rate, $S = 100$, $\sigma = 0.4$, $r = 0.05$, $D = 0$, $E = 110$, $T = 1$, $\tilde{\sigma} = 0.2$. Figure 10.8 shows the standard deviation of profit versus strike, $S = 100$, $\sigma = 0.4$, $r = 0.05$, $D = 0$, $\mu = 0.1$, $T = 1$, $\tilde{\sigma} = 0.2$.

Note that in these plots the expectations and standard deviations have not been scaled with the cost of the options.

10.6 **HEDGING WITH DIFFERENT VOLATILITIES**

We will briefly examine hedging using volatilities other than actual or implied, using the general expression for profit given by (10.2).

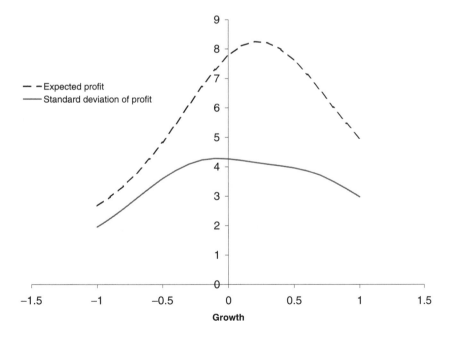

Figure 10.7   Standard deviation of profit, hedging using implied volatility, versus growth rate μ; $S = 100$, $\sigma = 0.4$, $r = 0.05$, $D = 0$, $E = 110$, $T = 1$, $\tilde{\sigma} = 0.2$. (The expected profit is also shown.)

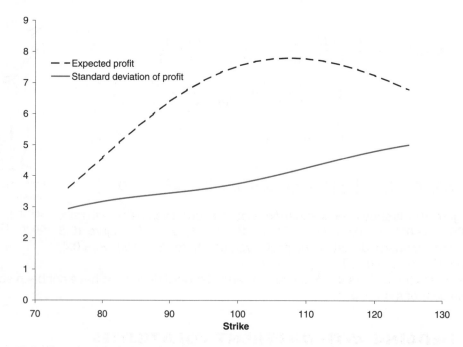

Figure 10.8 Standard deviation of profit, hedging using implied volatility, versus strike E; $S = 100$, $\sigma = 0.4$, $r = 0.05$, $D = 0$, $\mu = 0$, $T = 1$, $\tilde{\sigma} = 0.2$. (The expected profit is also shown.)

The expressions for the expected profit and standard deviations now must allow for the $V(S, t; \sigma_h) - V(S, t; \tilde{\sigma})$, since the integral of gamma term can be treated as before if one replaces $\tilde{\sigma}$ with σ_h in this term. Results are presented in the next sections.

10.6.1 Actual volatility = Implied volatility

For the first example let's look at hedging a long position in a correctly priced option, so that $\sigma = \tilde{\sigma}$. We will hedge using different volatilities, σ^h. Results are shown in Figure 10.9. The figure shows the expected profit and standard deviation of profit when hedging with various volatilities. The chart also shows minimum and maximum profit. Parameters are $E = 100$, $S = 100$, $\mu = 0$, $\sigma = 0.2$, $r = 0.1$, $D = 0$, $T = 1$, and $\tilde{\sigma} = 0.2$.

With these parameters the expected profit is small as a fraction of the market price of the option ($13.3) regardless of the hedging volatility. The standard deviation of profit is zero when the option is hedged at the actual volatility. The upside, the maximum profit is much greater than the downside. Crucially all of the curves have zero value at the actual/implied volatility.

10.6.2 Actual volatility > Implied volatility

In Figure 10.10 is shown the expected profit and standard deviation of profit when hedging with various volatilities when actual volatility is greater than implied. The chart again also shows minimum and maximum profit. Parameters are $E = 100$, $S = 100$, $\mu = 0$, $\sigma = 0.4$, $r = 0.1$, $D = 0$, $T = 1$, and $\tilde{\sigma} = 0.2$. Note that it is possible to lose money if you hedge at

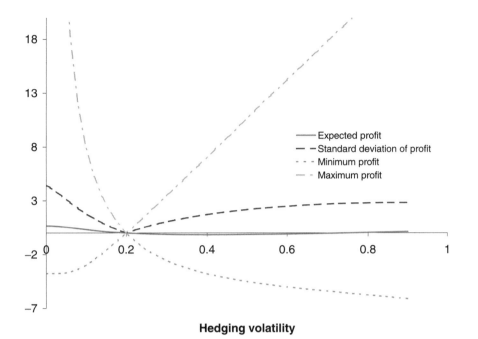

Hedging volatility

Figure 10.9 Expected profit, standard deviation of profit, minimum and maximum, hedging with various volatilities. $E = 100$, $S = 100$, $\mu = 0$, $\sigma = 0.2$, $r = 0.1$, $D = 0$, $T = 1$, $\tilde{\sigma} = 0.2$.

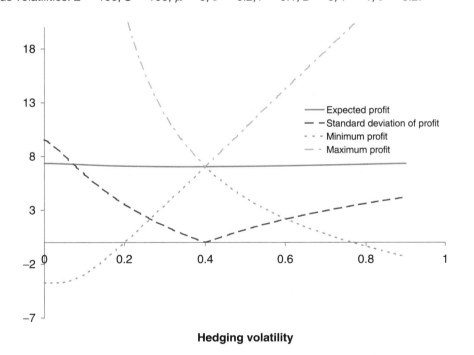

Hedging volatility

Figure 10.10 Expected profit, standard deviation of profit, minimum and maximum, hedging with various volatilities. $E = 100$, $S = 100$, $\mu = 0$, $\sigma = 0.4$, $r = 0.1$, $D = 0$, $T = 1$, $\tilde{\sigma} = 0.2$.

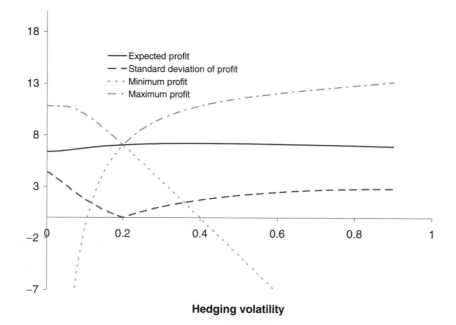

Figure 10.11 Expected profit, standard deviation of profit, minimum and maximum, hedging with various volatilities. $E = 100$, $S = 100$, $\mu = 0$, $\sigma = 0.2$, $r = 0.1$, $D = 0$, $T = 1$, $\tilde{\sigma} = 0.4$.

below implied, but hedging with a higher volatility you will not be able to lose until hedging with a volatility of approximately 75%. The expected profit is again insensitive to hedging volatility.

10.6.3 Actual volatility < Implied volatility

In Figure 10.11 is shown properties of the profit when hedging with various volatilities when actual volatility is less than implied. We are now selling the option and delta hedging it. Parameters are $E = 100$, $S = 100$, $\mu = 0$, $\sigma = 0.4$, $r = 0.1$, $D = 0$, $T = 1$, and $\tilde{\sigma} = 0.2$. Now it is possible to lose money if you hedge at above implied, but hedging with a lower volatility you will not be able to lose until hedging with a volatility of approximately 10%. The expected profit is again insensitive to hedging volatility. The downside is now more dramatic than the upside.

10.7 PROS AND CONS OF HEDGING WITH EACH VOLATILITY

Given that we seem to have a choice in how to delta hedge it is instructive to summarize the advantages and disadvantages of the possibilities.

10.7.1 Hedging with actual volatility

Pros: The main advantage of hedging with actual volatility is that you know exactly what profit you will get at expiration. So in a classical risk/reward sense this seems to be the best choice, given that the expected profit can often be insensitive to which volatility you choose to hedge with whereas the standard deviation is always going to be positive away from hedging with actual volatility.

Cons: The P&L fluctuations during the life of the option can be daunting, and so less appealing from a 'local' as opposed to 'global' risk management perspective. Also, you are unlikely to be totally confident in your volatility forecast, the number you are putting into your delta formula. However, you can interpret the previous two figures in terms of what happens if you intend to hedge with actual but don't quite get it right. You can see from those that you do have quite a lot of leeway before you risk losing money.

10.7.2 Hedging with implied volatility

Pros: There are three main advantages to hedging with implied volatility. The first is that there are no local fluctuations in P&L, you are continually making a profit. The second advantage is that you only need to be on the right side of the trade to profit. Buy when actual is going to be higher than implied and sell if lower. Finally, the number that goes into the delta is implied volatility, and therefore easy to observe.

Cons: You don't know how much money you will make, only that it is positive.

10.7.3 Hedging with another volatility

You can obviously balance the pros and cons of hedging with actual and implied by hedging with another volatility altogether. See Dupire (2005) for work in this area.

In practice which volatility one uses is often determined by whether one is constrained to mark to market or mark to model. If one is able to mark to model then one is not necessarily concerned with the day-to-day fluctuations in the mark-to-market profit and loss and so it is natural to hedge using actual volatility. This is usually not far from optimal in the sense of possible expected total profit, and it has no standard deviation of final profit. However, it is common to have to report profit and loss based on market values. This constraint may be imposed by a risk management department, by prime brokers, or by investors who may monitor the mark-to-market profit on a regular basis. In this case it is more usual to hedge based on implied volatility to avoid the daily fluctuations in the profit and loss.

For the remainder of this chapter we will only consider the case of hedging using a delta based on implied volatility.

10.8 PORTFOLIOS WHEN HEDGING WITH IMPLIED VOLATILITY

A natural extension to the above analysis is to look at portfolios of options, options with different strikes and expirations. Since only an option's gamma matters when we are hedging using implied volatility, calls and puts are effectively the same since they have the same gamma.

The profit from a portfolio is now

$$\frac{1}{2} \sum_k q_k \left(\sigma^2 - \tilde{\sigma}_k^2 \right) \int_{t_0}^{T_k} e^{-r(s-t_0)} S^2 \Gamma_k^i \, ds,$$

where k is the index for an option, and q_k is the quantity of that option.

10.8.1 Expectation

The solution for the present value of the expected profit ($t = t_0$, $S = S_0$, $I = 0$) is simply the sum of individual profits for each option,

$$F(S_0, t_0) = \sum_k q_k \frac{E_k e^{-r(T_k - t_0)} (\sigma^2 - \tilde{\sigma}_k^2)}{2\sqrt{2\pi}} \int_{t_0}^{T_k} \frac{1}{\sqrt{\sigma^2(s - t_0) + \tilde{\sigma}_k^2(T_k - s)}}$$

$$\times \exp\left(-\frac{\left(\ln(S_0/E_k) + \left(\mu - \frac{1}{2}\sigma^2 \right)(s - t_0) + \left(r - D - \frac{1}{2}\tilde{\sigma}_k^2 \right)(T_k - s) \right)^2}{2(\sigma^2(s - t_0) + \tilde{\sigma}_k^2(T_k - s))} \right) ds.$$

10.8.2 Variance

The variance is more complicated, obviously, because of the correlation between all of the options in the portfolio. Nevertheless, we can find an expression for the initial variance as $G(S_0, t_0) - F(S_0, t_0)^2$ where

$$G(S_0, t_0) = \sum_j \sum_k q_j q_k G_{jk}(S_0, t_0)$$

where

$$G_{jk}(S_0, t_0) = \frac{E_j E_k (\sigma^2 - \tilde{\sigma}_j^2)(\sigma^2 - \tilde{\sigma}_k^2) e^{-r(T_j - t_0) - r(T_k - t_0)}}{4\pi \sigma \tilde{\sigma}_k} \int_{t_0}^{\min(T_j, T_k)} \int_s^{T_j}$$

$$\times \frac{e^{p(u, s; S_0, t_0)}}{\sqrt{s - t_0} \sqrt{T_k - s} \sqrt{\sigma^2(u - s) + \tilde{\sigma}_j^2(T_j - u)} \sqrt{\frac{1}{\sigma^2(s - t_0)} + \frac{1}{\tilde{\sigma}_k^2(T_k - s)} + \frac{1}{\sigma^2(u - s) + \tilde{\sigma}_j^2(T_j - u)}}} \, du \, ds$$

(10.4)

where

$$p(u, s; S_0, t_0) = -\frac{1}{2} \frac{(\ln(S_0/E_k) + \bar{\mu}(s - t_0) + \bar{r}_k(T_k - s))^2}{\tilde{\sigma}_k^2(T_k - s)}$$

$$- \frac{1}{2} \frac{(\ln(S_0/E_j) + \bar{\mu}(u - t_0) + \bar{r}_j(T_j - u))^2}{\sigma^2(u - s) + \tilde{\sigma}_j^2(T_j - u)}$$

$$+ \frac{1}{2} \frac{\left(\dfrac{\ln(S_0/E_k) + \bar{\mu}(s - t_0) + \bar{r}_k(T_k - s)}{\tilde{\sigma}_k^2(T_k - s)} + \dfrac{\ln(S_0/E_j) + \bar{\mu}(u - t_0) + \bar{r}_j(T_j - u)}{\sigma^2(u - s) + \tilde{\sigma}_j^2(T_j - u)} \right)^2}{\dfrac{1}{\sigma^2(s - t_0)} + \dfrac{1}{\tilde{\sigma}_k^2(T_k - s)} + \dfrac{1}{\sigma^2(u - s) + \tilde{\sigma}_j^2(T_j - u)}}$$

and

$$\bar{\mu} = \mu - \tfrac{1}{2}\sigma^2, \quad \bar{r}_j = r - D - \tfrac{1}{2}\tilde{\sigma}_j^2 \quad \text{and} \quad \bar{r}_k = r - D - \tfrac{1}{2}\tilde{\sigma}_k^2.$$

10.8.3 Portfolio optimization possibilities

There is clearly plenty of scope for using the above formulae in portfolio optimization problems. Here I give one example.

The stock is currently at 100. The growth rate is zero, actual volatility is 20%, zero dividend yield and the interest rate is 5%. Table 10.3 shows the available options, and associated parameters. Observe the negative skew. The out-of-the-money puts are overvalued and the out-of-the-money calls are undervalued. (The 'Profit total expected' row assumes that we buy a single one of that option.)

Using the above formulae we can find the portfolio that maximizes or minimizes target quantities (expected profit, standard deviation, ratio of profit to standard deviation). Let us consider the simple case of maximizing the expected return, while constraining the standard deviation to be one. This is a very natural strategy when trying to make a profit from volatility arbitrage while meeting constraints imposed by regulators, brokers, investors, etc. The result is given in Table 10.4.

The payoff function (with its initial delta hedge) is shown in Figure 10.12. This optimization has effectively found an ideal risk reversal trade. This portfolio would cost −$0.46 to set up, i.e. it would bring in premium. The expected profit is $6.83.

10.9 HOW DOES IMPLIED VOLATILITY BEHAVE?

Now is the natural time to talk a little bit about how implied volatility behaves in practice.

As the stock price goes up and down randomly we often see that the implied volatility of each option will also vary. This may or may not be consistent with certain models, and

Table 10.3 Available options.

	A	B	C	D	E
Type	Put	Put	Call	Call	Call
Strike	80	90	100	110	120
Expiration	1	1	1	1	1
Volatility, implied	0.250	0.225	0.200	0.175	0.150
Option price, market	1.511	3.012	10.451	5.054	1.660
Option value, theory	0.687	2.310	10.451	6.040	3.247
Profit total expected	−0.933	−0.752	0.000	0.936	1.410

Table 10.4 An optimal portfolio.

	A	B	C	D	E
Type	Put	Put	Call	Call	Call
Strike	80	90	100	110	120
Quantity	−2.10	−2.25	0	1.46	1.28

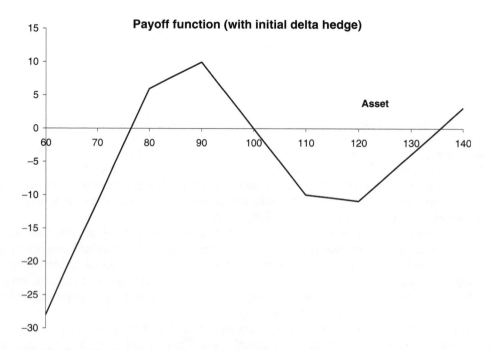

Figure 10.12 Payoff with initial delta hedge for optimal portfolio; $S = 100$, $\mu = 0$, $\sigma = 0.2$, $r = 0.05$, $D = 0$, $T = 1$. See text for additional parameters and information.

may or may not be consistent with no arbitrage. But more importantly, what does it mean for making money if we think that the market is wrong? Below are a couple of 'models' for how implied volatility might change as the market moves.

10.9.1 Sticky strike

In this model implied volatility remains constant for each option (i.e. each strike and expiration). Effectively each option inhabits its own little Black–Scholes world of constant volatility. This behavior seems to be most common in the equity markets. As far as making a profit if the implied volatility is different from actual volatility then the first half of this chapter is clearly very relevant.

10.9.2 Sticky delta

Since the delta of an option is a function of its moneyness, S/E, the sticky delta behavior could also be called the sticky moneyness rule. This behavior is commonly seen in the FX markets, possibly because there it is usual to quote option prices/volatilities for options with specific deltas rather than specific strike. (There is, of course, a one-to-one correspondence for vanillas.)

In this model we have

$$\tilde{\sigma} = g(S/E, t).$$

Therefore

$$d\tilde{\sigma} = \left(\frac{\partial g}{\partial t} + \mu \frac{S}{E} \frac{\partial g}{\partial \xi} + \frac{1}{2} \sigma^2 \frac{S^2}{E^2} \frac{\partial^2 g}{\partial \xi^2} \right) dt + \sigma \frac{S}{E} \frac{\partial g}{\partial \xi} \, dX_1,$$

where $\xi = S/E$. The most important point about this expression is that it is perfectly correlated with dS, $\rho = 1$, so that perfect hedging (in the mark-to-market sense) is possible.

A variation on this theme is to have implied volatility at different strikes being proportional to the ATM volatility and a function of the moneyness, such as

$$\tilde{\sigma} = \sigma_{ATM} \, g \left(\frac{\log(S/E)}{\sqrt{T - t}} \right).$$

See Natenberg (1994) for details of this. Of course, this then requires a model for the behavior of the ATM volatility.

10.9.3 Time-periodic behavior

Just to make matters even more interesting, there appears to be a day-of-the-week effect in implied volatility. The next few figures show how the VIX volatility index (a measure of the implied volatility of the ATM SPX adjusted to always have an expiration of 30 days)

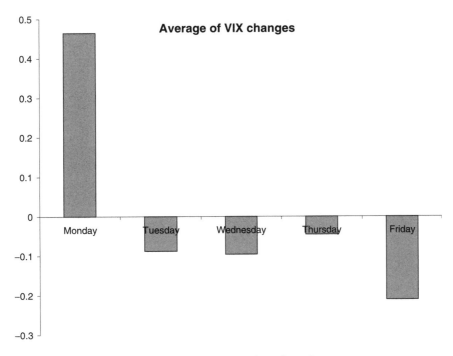

Figure 10.13 Average change in level of VIX versus day of week.

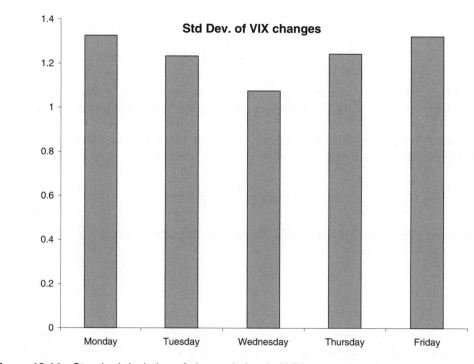

Figure 10.14 Standard deviation of change in level of VIX versus day of week.

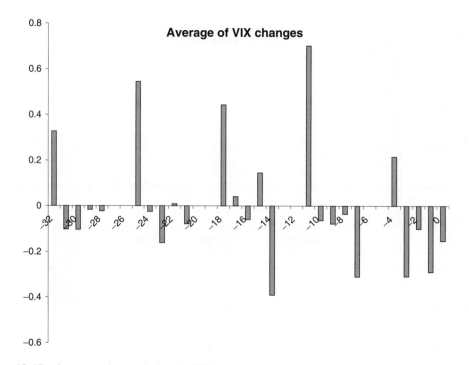

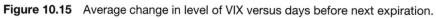

Figure 10.15 Average change in level of VIX versus days before next expiration.

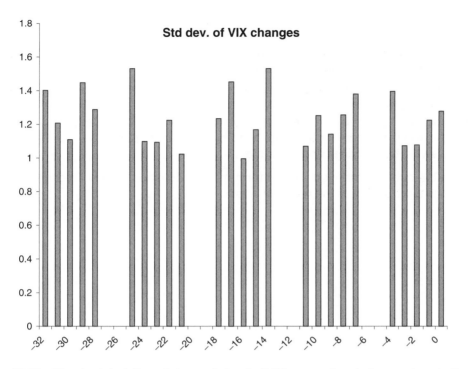

Figure 10.16 Standard deviation of change in level of VIX versus days before next expiration.

changes with day of the week and number of days to next expiration. Both average changes and standard deviation are shown.[1]

10.10 **SUMMARY**

In this chapter we have seen some hints at how we can start to move away from the Black–Scholes world, and perhaps even profit from options.

FURTHER READING

- See Derman (1999) for a description of sticky strike and delta, and other volatility regimes.

- Natenberg's book (Natenberg, 1994) is still the classic reference for volatility trading.

- See Carr's (Carr, 2005) excellent FAQs paper for further insight into which volatility to use for hedging. Also Henrard (2001), who examined the role of the real drift rate.

- Ahmad & Wilmott (2005) delve even deeper into the subject of hedging with different volatilities.

---

[1] Of course, some of this is no doubt related to the role of weekends in the calculation of volatility. There is a lot of 'potential' for volatility over weekends in the sense that there is plenty of news that comes out that will impact on market prices when markets open on the Monday.

EXERCISES

1. Take the How to Hedge spreadsheet on the CD and rewrite using VB, C++, or other code. Now modify the code to do the following.

    (a) Allow for arbitrary fixed period between rehedges. Observe how the hedging error varies with this period.

    (b) Incorporate bid-offer spread on each transaction in the underlying.

    (c) As above but now for the delta hedging of an entire portfolio of vanilla options of varying type, strikes and expiration.

    Write the code so that you can perform many thousands of simulations, and output statistical properties of the hedging error.

CHAPTER 11
an introduction to exotic and path-dependent options

The aim of this Chapter...

...is to give an overview of many of the exciting derivatives above and beyond the basic vanillas. By the end of the chapter you should be able to compare and contrast different sorts of derivative contracts.

In this Chapter...

- how to classify options according to important features

- how to think about derivatives in a way that makes it easy to compare and contrast different contracts

- the names and contract details for many basic types of exotic options

11.1 INTRODUCTION

The contracts we have seen so far are the most basic, and most important, derivative contracts but they only hint at the features that can be found in the more interesting products. Some of these contracts will be explored in following chapters, the more complex ones are covered in *PWOQF2*.

Exotic options are interesting for several reasons. They are harder to price, sometimes being very model dependent. The risks inherent in the contracts are usually more obscure and can lead to unexpected losses. Careful hedging becomes important, whether delta hedging or some form of static hedging to minimize cashflows. Actually, how to hedge exotics is all that really matters. A trader may have a good idea of a reasonable price for an instrument, either from experience or by looking at the prices of similar instruments. But he may not be so sure about the risks in the contract or how to hedge them away successfully.

It is an impossible task to classify all options. The best that we can reasonably achieve is a rough characterization of the most popular of the features to be found in derivative products. I list some of these features in this chapter and give several examples. In the following few chapters I go into more detail in the description of the options and their pricing and hedging. The features that I describe now are time dependence, cashflows, weak path dependence and strong path dependence, dimensionality, the 'order' of an option, and finally options with embedded decisions.

One approach that I will not really be taking is to try to decompose an exotic into a portfolio of vanillas. If such a decomposition is exact then the contract was not exotic in the first place. (Riddle: When can you decompose an exotic into a portfolio of vanillas? Answer: When it isn't exotic.) You may get an idea for an approximate price and how to possibly statically hedge an exotic by such a means but ultimately you will probably have to face a full and proper mathematical analysis of the exotic features in a contract.

11.2 OPTION CLASSIFICATION

In order to figure out how to price and hedge exotic options I have found it incredibly helpful to classify them according to six criteria or features. I can't overemphasize how useful this has been to me. These six features are unashamedly mathematical in nature, having nothing whatsoever to do with what the name of the option is or what is the underlying. Being mathematical in nature they very quickly give you the following information.

- What kind of pricing method should best be used.

- Whether you can reuse some old code.

- How long it will take you to code it up.

- How fast it will eventually run.

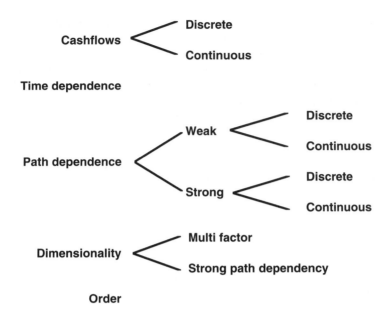

Figure 11.1 Option classification chart.

The six features to look out for are

1. Time dependence

2. Cashflows

3. Path dependence

4. Dimensionality

5. Order

6. Embedded decisions

Some of these classes can be broken down further, as shown in Figure 11.1.

Let's now look at these features one by one, in increasing order of interest.

11.3 TIME DEPENDENCE

Time dependence in the present context means that certain specifications within a term sheet vary with time. For example, early exercise might only be permitted on certain dates or during certain periods.

This intermittent early exercise is a characteristic of **Bermudan options**. Such contracts are referred to as time-inhomogeneous.

Time dependence is first on our list of features, since it is not all that earth shattering. Probably the only reason for the importance of time dependence at all is that it requires us to be a little bit careful with any numerical method we employ. Inevitably when solving for an option price via numerical methods we end up needing to do some discretization of time. If the contract has time dependence then we may have restrictions imposed on our discretization.

- Time dependence in an option contract means that our numerical discretization may have to be lined up to coincide with times at, or periods during, which something happens.

- This means that our code will have to keep track of time, dates, etc. This is not difficult, just annoying.

Time Out...

In terms of the binomial model?

If we have time-dependent interest rate or volatility then this just changes the structure of the tree and the discounting. Time dependence in the term sheet means that some nodes might have to be treated differently from others.

NO ARBITRAGE LEADS TO THIS SIMPLE JUMP CONDITION WHEN MONEY CHANGES HANDS

11.4 **CASHFLOWS**

Imagine a contract that pays the holder an amount q at time t_0. The contract could be a bond and the payment a coupon. If we use $V(t)$ to denote the contract value (ignoring any dependence on any underlying asset) and t_0^- and t_0^+ to denote just before and just after the cashflow date then simple arbitrage considerations lead to

$$V(t_0^-) = V(t_0^+) + q.$$

This is a **jump condition**. The value of the contract jumps by the amount of the cashflow. If this were not the case then there would be an arbitrage opportunity. The behavior of the contract value across the payment date is shown in Figure 11.2.

If the contract is contingent on an underlying variable so that we have $V(S, t)$ then we can accommodate cashflows that depend on the level of the asset, S, i.e. we could have

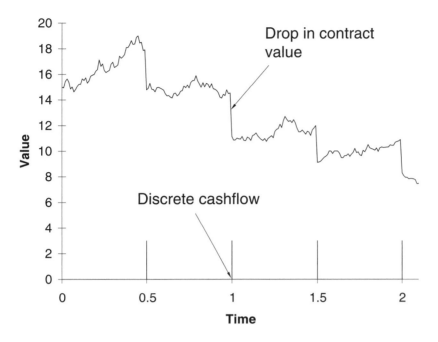

Figure 11.2 A discrete cashflow and its affect on a contract value.

$q(S)$. Furthermore, this also allows us to lump all our options on the same underlying into one large portfolio. Then, across the expiry of each option, there will be a jump in the value of our whole portfolio of the amount of the payoff for that option.

There is one small technical requirement here, the cashflow must be a deterministic function of time and the underlying asset. For example, the contract holder could receive a payment of S^2, for some asset with price S. However, the above argument would not be valid if, for example, the cashflow depended on the toss of a coin; one dollar is received if heads is thrown and nothing otherwise. The jump condition does not necessarily apply, because the cashflow is not deterministic.

If the cashflow is not deterministic the modeling is not so straightforward. There is no 'no-arbitrage' argument to appeal to, and the result could easily depend on an individual's risk preferences. Nevertheless, we could say, for example, that the jump condition would be that the change in value of the contract would be the *expected* value of the cashflow:

$$V(t_0^-) = V(t_0^+) + E[q].$$

Such a condition would not, however, allow for the risk inherent in the uncertain cashflow.

That was an example of a **discrete cashflow**. You may also see **continuous cashflows** in option contracts. The term sheet may specify something, for example, along the lines of 'the holder receives $1 every day that the stock price is below $80.' That would effectively be a continuous cashflow. When the cashflow is paid continuously then we no longer have jump conditions, instead we modify the basic Black–Scholes equation to add a source term. We'll see examples later.

- When a contract has a discretely paid cashflow you should expect to have to apply jump conditions. This also means that the contract has time dependence, see above.

- Continuously paid cashflows mean a modification, although rather simple, to the governing equation.

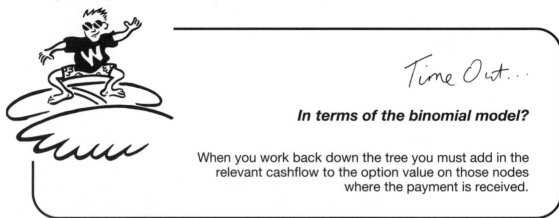

Time Out...

In terms of the binomial model?

When you work back down the tree you must add in the relevant cashflow to the option value on those nodes where the payment is received.

11.5 PATH DEPENDENCE

Many options have payoffs that depend on the path taken by the underlying asset, and not just the asset's value at expiration. These options are called **path dependent**. Path dependency comes in two varieties, strong and weak.

STRONG PATH DEPENDENCE MEANS THAT WE HAVE TO KEEP TRACK OF ANOTHER VARIABLE

11.5.1 Strong path dependence

Of particular interest, mathematical and practical, are the strongly path-dependent contracts. These have payoffs that depend on some property of the asset price path in addition to the value of the underlying at the present moment in time; in the equity option language, we cannot write the value as $V(S, t)$. The contract value is a function of at least one more independent variable. This is best illustrated by an example.

The Asian option has a payoff that depends on the average value of the underlying asset from inception to expiry. We must keep track of more information about the asset price path than simply its present position. The extra information that we need is contained in the 'running average.' This is the average of the asset price from inception until the present, when we are valuing the option. No other information is needed. This running average is then used as a new independent variable, the option value is a function of this as well as the usual underlying and time, and a derivative of the option value with respect to the running average appears in the governing equation. There are many such contracts in existence.

Strong path dependency comes in two forms, **discretely sampled** and **continuously sampled**, depending on whether a discrete subset of asset prices is used or a continuous distribution of them.

- Strong path dependency means that we have to work in higher dimensions. A consequence of this is that our code may take longer to run.

Time Out...

In terms of the binomial model?

This is rather outside the scope of this book. But what you'll have to do is introduce a multi-dimensional tree.
There will be branches orthogonal to the S branches to keep track of the path-dependent quantity.

11.5.2 Weak path dependence

WEAK PATH DEPENDENCE MEANS THAT THE OPTION DEPENDS ONLY ON ASSET AND TIME

A simple example of a contract with weak path dependence is the **barrier**. Barrier (or knock-in, or knock-out) options are triggered by the action of the underlying hitting a prescribed value at some time before expiry. For example, as long as the asset remains below 150, the contract will have a call payoff at expiry. However, should the asset reach this level before expiry then the option becomes worthless; the option has 'knocked out.' This contract is clearly path dependent. Consider the two paths in Figure 11.3; one has a payoff at expiry because the barrier was not triggered, the other is worthless, yet both have the same value of the underlying at expiry.

Time Out...

In terms of the binomial model?

This is usually quite straightforward to implement. But not necessarily very accurate though. For example, with a knock-out barrier option the simplest way to price this is to set all option values to zero beyond the barrier.

We shall see in Chapter 13 that such a contract is only weakly path dependent: we still solve a partial differential equation in the two variables, the underlying and time.

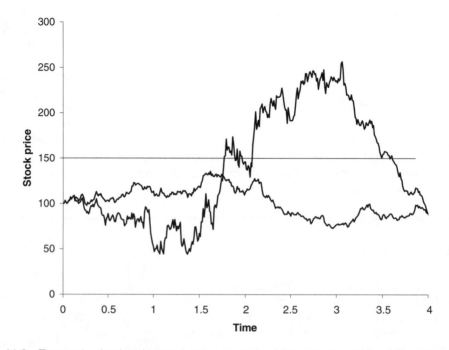

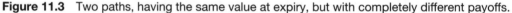

Figure 11.3 Two paths, having the same value at expiry, but with completely different payoffs.

And that is the difference, mathematically speaking, between strong and weak path dependency. A weakly path-dependent contract does not require us to introduce an extra variable to handle the path dependency. Again, we can imagine discrete and continuous versions.

- Weak path dependency means that we *don't* have to work in higher dimensions, so our code should be pretty fast.

11.6 DIMENSIONALITY

Dimensionality refers to the number of underlying independent variables. The vanilla option has two independent variables, S and t, and is thus two dimensional. The weakly path-dependent contracts have the same number of dimensions as their non-path-dependent cousins, i.e. a barrier call option has the same two dimensions as a vanilla call. The roles of the asset dimension and the time dimension are quite different from each other, as discussed in Chapter 7 on the diffusion equation. This is because the governing equation, the Black–Scholes equation, contains a second asset-price derivative but only a first time derivative.

We can have two types of three-dimensional problem. The first type of problem that is three dimensional is the strongly path-dependent contract. Typically, the new independent variable is a measure of the path-dependent quantity on which the option is contingent. The new variable may be the average of the asset price to date, say. In this case, derivatives of the option value with respect to this new variable are only of the first order. Thus the new variable acts more like another time-like variable. This topic is covered in detail in *PWOQF2*.

The second type of three-dimensional problem occurs when we have a second source of randomness, such as a second underlying asset. We might, for example, have an option on the maximum of two equities. Both of these underlyings are stochastic, each with a volatility, and there will be a correlation between them. In the governing equation we will see a second derivative of the option value with respect to each asset. We say that there is diffusion in both S_1 and S_2.

- Higher dimensions means longer computing time.

- The number of dimensions we have also tells us what kind of numerical method to use. High dimensions mean that we probably want to use Monte Carlo, low means finite difference.

Time Out...

In terms of the binomial model?

As with path dependency you will have to have a higher-dimensional tree structure to model the new dependent variables.

11.7 THE ORDER OF AN OPTION

The next classification that we make is the **order** of an option. Not only is this a classification but the idea also introduces fundamental modeling issues.

The basic vanilla options are of first order. Their payoffs depend only on the underlying asset, the quantity that we are *directly* modeling. Other, path-dependent, contracts can still be of first order if the

ORDER WILL AFFECT THE SENSITIVITY OF THE THEORETICAL PRICE TO THE MODEL

payoff depends only on properties of the asset price path. 'Higher order' refers to options whose payoff, and hence value, is contingent on the value of *another* option. The obvious second-order options are compound options, for example a call option giving the holder the right to buy a put option. The compound option expires at some date T_1 and the option on which it is contingent, expires at a later time T_2. Technically speaking, such an option is weakly path dependent. The *theoretical* pricing of such a contract is straightforward as we shall see.

From a practical point of view, the compound option raises some important modeling issues: the payoff for the compound option depends on the *market* value of the underlying option, and not on the theoretical price. If you hold a compound option and want to exercise the first option then you must take possession of the underlying option. If that option is worth less than you think it should (because your model says so) then there is not much you can do about it. High-order option values are very sensitive to the basic pricing model and should be handled with care.

- When an option is second or higher order we have to solve for the first-order option, first. We thus have a layer cake, we must work on the lower levels and the results of those feed into the higher levels.

- This means that computationally we have to solve more than one problem to price our option.

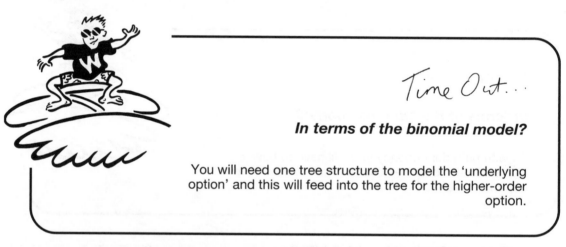

Time Out...

In terms of the binomial model?

You will need one tree structure to model the 'underlying option' and this will feed into the tree for the higher-order option.

11.8 **EMBEDDED DECISIONS**

We have seen early exercise in the American option problem. Early exercise is a common feature of other contracts, perhaps going by other names. For example, the conversion of convertible bonds is mathematically identical to the early exercise of an American option. The key point about early exercise is that the holder of this valuable right should ideally act *optimally*, i.e. they must decide *when* to exercise or convert. In the partial differential equation framework that has been set up, this optimality is achieved by solving a free boundary problem, with a constraint on the option value, together with a smoothness condition. It is this smoothness condition, that the derivative of the option value with respect to the underlying is continuous, that ensures optimality, i.e. maximization of the option value with respect to the exercise or conversion strategy. It is perfectly possible for there to be more than one early-exercise region.[1]

Holding an American option you are faced with the decision whether and when to exercise your rights. The American option is the most common contract that contains within it a decision feature. Other contracts require more subtle and interesting decisions to be made.

When a contract has embedded decisions you need an algorithm for deciding how that decision will be made. That algorithm amounts to assuming that the holder of the contract acts to *make the option value as high as possible for the delta-hedging writer*. The pricing algorithm then amounts to searching across all possible holder decision strategies for the one that maximizes the option value. That sounds hard, but approached correctly is actually remarkably straight-

DOES THE HOLDER OR WRITER HAVE TO MAKE DECISIONS DURING THE LIFE OF THE CONTRACT?

forward, especially if you use the finite-difference method. The justification for seeking the strategy that maximizes the value is that the writer cannot afford to sell the option for anything less, otherwise he would be exposed to 'decision risk.'

When the option writer or issuer is the one with the decision to make then the value is based on seeking the strategy that minimizes the value.

- Decision features mean that we'd really like to price via finite differences.

- The code will contain a line in which we seek the best price, so watch out for $\geq$ or $\leq$ signs.

Time Out...

In terms of the binomial model?

You've seen this already in Chapter 3. Just make sure that the option value stays above the payoff at all times that exercise is allowed.

For other contracts, whether this is easy or not depends on the nature of the contract. But as with the American option, decision making requires a process for ensuring optimality. Mathematically this usually boils down to a $\geq$ sign somewhere.

---

[1] One rarely mentioned aspect of American options, and, generally speaking, contracts with early exercise-type characteristics, is that they are path dependent. Whether the owner of the option still holds the option at expiry depends on whether or not he has exercised the option, and thus on the path taken by the underlying. For American-type options this path dependence is weak, in the sense that the partial differential equation to be solved has no more independent variables than a similar, but European, contract.

I USE THESE CLASSIFICATION TABLES TO HELP ME TURN TERMSHEETS INTO MATH

11.9 CLASSIFICATION TABLES

I find tables like the following very useful for the classification of special contracts.

Classification	Option Name
Time dependence	Do details vary with time? Eg. discrete sampling.
Cashflow	Does money change hands during life of contract?
Path dependence	Weak or Strong?
Dimension	2, 3, 4, ... ?
Order	First, second, ...?
Decisions	Does holder and/or writer have to make decisions?

11.10 EXAMPLES OF EXOTIC OPTIONS

There now follow some basic examples, just to get you into the swing of things.

11.10.1 Compounds and choosers

Compound and **chooser options** are simply options on options. The compound option gives the holder the right to buy (call) or sell (put) another option. Thus we can imagine owning a call on a put, for example. This gives us the right to buy a put option for a specified amount on a specified date. If we exercise the option then we will own a put option which gives us the right to sell the underlying. This compound option is second order because the compound option gives us rights over another derivative. Although the Black–Scholes model can theoretically cope with second-order contracts it is not so clear that the model is completely satisfactory in practice; when we exercise the contract we get an option at the market price, not at our theoretical price.

In the Black–Scholes framework the compound option is priced as follows. There are two steps: first price the underlying option and then price the compound option. Suppose that the underlying option has a payoff of $F(S)$ at time T, and that the compound option can be exercised at time $T_{Co} < T$ to get $G(V(S, T_{Co}))$ where $V(S, t)$ is the value of the underlying option. Step one is to price the underlying option, i.e. to find $V(S, t)$. This satisfies

$$\frac{\partial V}{\partial t} + \tfrac{1}{2}\sigma^2 S^2 \frac{\partial^2 V}{\partial S^2} + rS\frac{\partial V}{\partial S} - rV = 0 \quad \text{with} \quad V(S, T) = F(S).$$

Solve this problem so that you have found $V(S, T_{Co})$. This is the (theoretical) value of the underlying option at time T_{Co}, which is the time at which you can exercise your compound option. Now comes the second step, to value the compound option. The value of this is $Co(S, t)$ which satisfies

$$\frac{\partial\, Co}{\partial t} + \tfrac{1}{2}\sigma^2 S^2 \frac{\partial^2\, Co}{\partial S^2} + rS\frac{\partial\, Co}{\partial S} - r\, Co = 0 \quad \text{with} \quad Co(S, T_{Co}) = G(V(S, T_{Co})).$$

As an example, if we have a call on a call with exercise prices E for the underlying and E_{Co} for the compound option, then we have

$$F(S) = \max(S - E, 0) \quad \text{and} \quad G(V) = \max(V - E_{Co}, 0).$$

In Figure 11.4 is shown the value of a vanilla call option at the time of expiry of a put option on this call. This is obviously some time before the expiry of the underlying call. In the same figure is the payoff for the put on this option. This is the final condition for the Black–Scholes partial differential equation.

It is possible to find analytical formulæ for the price of basic compound options in the Black–Scholes framework when volatility is constant. These formulæ involve the cumulative distribution function for a bivariate Normal variable. However, because of the second-order nature of compound options and thus their sensitivity to the precise nature of the asset price random walk, these formulæ are dangerous to use in practice. Practitioners use either a stochastic volatility model or an implied volatility surface.

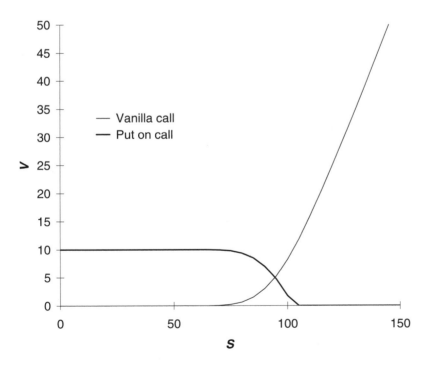

Figure 11.4 The value of a vanilla call option some time before expiry and the payoff for a put on this option.

Chooser options are similar to compounds in that they give the holder the right to buy a further option. With the chooser option the holder can choose whether to receive a call or a put, for example. Generally, we can write the value of the chooser option as $Ch(S, t)$ and the value of the underlying options as $V_1(S, t)$ and $V_2(S, t)$ (or more). Now

$$\frac{\partial Ch}{\partial t} + \frac{1}{2}\sigma^2 S^2 \frac{\partial^2 Ch}{\partial S^2} + rS\frac{\partial Ch}{\partial S} - r\, Ch = 0,$$

$$\frac{\partial V_1}{\partial t} + \frac{1}{2}\sigma^2 S^2 \frac{\partial^2 V_1}{\partial S^2} + rS\frac{\partial V_1}{\partial S} - rV_1 = 0$$

and

$$\frac{\partial V_2}{\partial t} + \frac{1}{2}\sigma^2 S^2 \frac{\partial^2 V_2}{\partial S^2} + rS\frac{\partial V_2}{\partial S} - rV_2 = 0.$$

Final conditions are the usual payoffs for the underlying options at their expiry dates and

$$Ch(S, T_{Ch}) = \max(V_1(S, T_{Ch}) - E_1, V_2(S, T_{Ch}) - E_2, 0),$$

with the obvious notation.

The practical problems with pricing choosers are the same as for compounds.

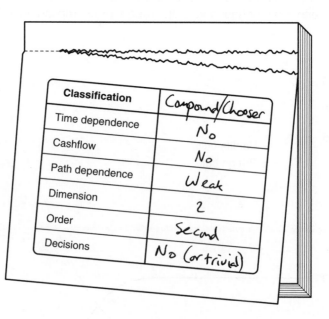

Classification	Compound/Chooser
Time dependence	No
Cashflow	No
Path dependence	Weak
Dimension	2
Order	Second
Decisions	No (or trivial)

In Figure 11.5 is shown the values of a vanilla call and a vanilla put some time before expiry. In the same figure is the payoff for a call on the best of these two options (less an exercise price). This is the final condition for the Black–Scholes partial differential equation.

Figures 11.6 and 11.7 show the Bloomberg screens for valuing chooser options.

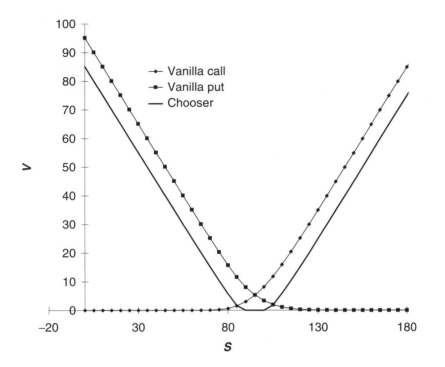

Figure 11.5 The value of a vanilla call option and a vanilla put option some time before expiry and the payoff for the best of these two.

```
<HELP> for explanation.                               DL18 Index  OVX
─────────────────────────────────────────────────────────────────────
               Chooser  Option  Valuation     Page 1 of 2
    DJZ9              DJIA INDEX FUT    Dec99    Currency: USD
                                              Hit 1 GO for save/send screen
                                              Hit 2 GO for notes
  Price of DJZ9 Index    11150                Hit 3 GO to price off fwrd, divds
                                              Hit MENU for exotic option types
                                              Hit PAGE for scenario graph
  Call Strike:         11150.00  (USD)Rate: 4.767%Semiannual
  Put Strike:          11150.00

  Trade Date:          9/11/99   Choice Date:   10/29/99
  Settlement Date:     9/11/99   Exercise Type of chosen option: E European

  Days to Exp. of Call:     96   Days to Exp. of Put:        96
  Expir. Date of Call: 12/16/99  Expir. Date of Put:   12/16/99
  Settle Date of Call: 10/29/99  Settle Date of Put:   10/29/99
  Exercise Delay of Chosen Option:    0

  ┌─ Option Valuation and Risk Parameters ──────┬── Dividends ──┐
        Value    Percent    Time Value:    571.19519
  Price:  571.195   5.123%  7-Day Decay:    29.86389
  Volatility:  14.853%      Premium:         5.12283
  Delta:       0.08757      Parity:          0.00000
  Gamma:       0.00112      Gearing:        19.52047
  Vega:       38.44012
  Copyright 1999 BLOOMBERG L.P.   Frankfurt:69-920410  Hong Kong:2-977-6000  London:171-330-7500  New York:212-318-2000
  Princeton:609-279-3000   Singapore:226-3000   Sydney:2-9777-8686   Tokyo:3-3201-8900   Sao Paulo:11-3048-4500
                                                                      I741-53-0 11-Sep-99 14:23:34
  Bloomberg
  PROFESSIONAL
```

Figure 11.6 Bloomberg chooser option valuation screen. Source: Bloomberg L.P.

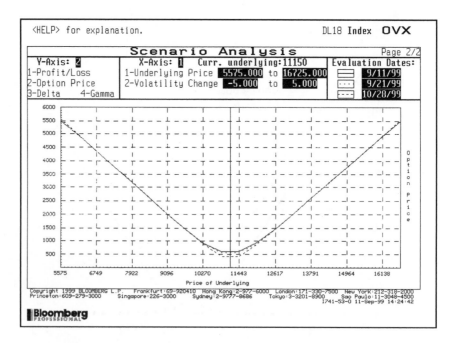

Figure 11.7 Bloomberg scenario analysis for a chooser. Source: Bloomberg L.P.

Extendible options are very, very similar to compounds and choosers. At some specified time the holder can choose to accept the payoff for the original option or to extend the option's life and even change the strike. Sometimes it is the writer who has these powers of extension. The reader has sufficient knowledge to be able to model these contracts in the Black–Scholes framework.

11.10.2 Range notes

Range notes are very popular contracts, existing on the 'lognormal' assets such as equities and currencies, and as fixed-income products. In its basic, equity derivative, form the range note pays at a rate of L all the time that the underlying lies within a given range, $S_l \leq S \leq S_u$. That is, for every dt that the asset is in the range you receive $L\,dt$. Introducing $\mathcal{I}(S)$ as the function taking the value 1 when $S_l \leq S \leq S_u$ and zero otherwise, the range note satisfies

IF WE RECEIVE/PAY MONEY CONTINUOUSLY THEN IT WILL APPEAR AS A SOURCE TERM

$$\frac{\partial V}{\partial t} + \tfrac{1}{2}\sigma^2 S^2 \frac{\partial^2 V}{\partial S^2} + rS\frac{\partial V}{\partial S} - rV + L\mathcal{I}(S) = 0.$$

In Figure 11.8 is shown the term sheet for a range note on the Mexican peso, US dollar exchange rate. This contract pays out the positive part of the difference between number of days the exchange rate is inside the range less the number of days outside the range. This payment is received at expiry. (This contract is subtly different, and more complicated than the basic range note described above. Why?)

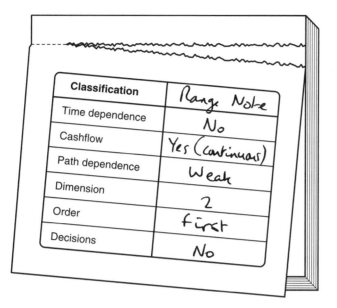

Preliminary and Indicative
For Discussion Purposes Only

6 Month In-Out Range Accrual Option on MXN/USD FX Rate

Settlement Date	One week from Trade Date
Maturity Date	6 months from Trade Date
Option Premium	USD 50,000+
Option Type	In MINUS Out Range Accrual on MXN/USD FX rate
Option Payment Date	2 business days after Maturity Date
Option Payout	USD 125,000 * Index
Where Index	

$$\frac{FX \text{ daily In MINUS } FX \text{ daily Out}}{\text{Total Business Days}} \text{ (subject to a minimum of zero)}$$

FX daily In	The number of business days Spot MXN/USD Exchange Rate is within Range
FX daily Out	The number of business days Spot MXN/USD Exchange Rate is outside Range
Range	MXN/USD 7.7200-8.1300
Spot MXN/USD Exchange Rate	Official spot exchange rate as determined by the Bank of Mexico as appearing on Reuters page "BNMX" at approximately 3:00 p.m. New York time.
Current Spot MXN/USD	7.7800

This indicative termsheet is neither an offer to buy or sell securities or an OTC derivative product which includes options, swaps, forwards and structured notes having similar features to OTC derivative transactions, nor a solicitation to buy or sell securities or an OTC derivative product. The proposal contained in the foregoing is not a complete description of the terms of a particular transaction and is subject to change without limitation.

Figure 11.8 Term sheet for an in-out range accrual note on MXN/USD.

11.10.3 Barrier options

Barrier options have a payoff that is contingent on the underlying asset reaching some specified level before expiry. The critical level is called the barrier, there may be more than one. Barrier options are weakly path dependent. Barrier options are discussed in depth in Chapter 13.

Barrier options come in two main varieties, the 'in' barrier option (or **knock-in**) and the 'out' barrier option (or **knock-out**). The former only have a payoff if the barrier level is reached before expiry and the latter only have a payoff if the barrier is *not* reached before

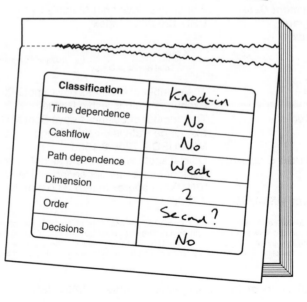

Classification	Knock-Out
Time dependence	No
Cashflow	No
Path dependence	Weak
Dimension	2
Order	first
Decisions	No

Classification	Knock-in
Time dependence	No
Cashflow	No
Path dependence	Weak
Dimension	2
Order	Second?
Decisions	No

expiry. These contracts are weakly path dependent, meaning that the price depends only on the current level of the asset and the time to expiry. They satisfy the Black–Scholes equation, with special boundary conditions as we shall see.

11.10.4 Asian options

Asian options have a payoff that depends on the average value of the underlying asset over some period before expiry. They are the first strongly path-dependent contract we examine. They are strongly path dependent because their value prior to expiry depends on the path taken and not just on where they have reached. Their value depends on the *average to date* of the asset. This average to date will be very important to us, we introduce something like it as a new state variable. (In *PWOQF2* it is shown how to derive a partial differential equation for the value of this Asian contract, but now the differential equation will have *three* independent variables.)

The average used in the calculation of the option's payoff can be defined in many different ways. It can be an arithmetic average or a geometric average, for example. The data could be continuously sampled, so that every realized asset price over the given period is used. More commonly, for practical and legal reasons, the data is usually sampled discretely; the calculated average may only use every Friday's closing price, for example.

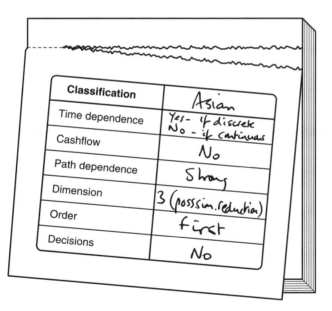

Classification	Asian
Time dependence	Yes– if discrete No – if continuous
Cashflow	No
Path dependence	Strong
Dimension	3 (possim. reduction)
Order	first
Decisions	No

11.10.5 Lookback options

Lookback options have a payoff that depends on the realized maximum or minimum of the underlying asset over some period prior to expiry. An extreme example, which captures the flavor of these contracts, is the option that pays off the difference between that maximum realized value of the asset and the minimum value over the next year. Thus it enables the holder to buy at the lowest price and sell at the highest, every trader's dream. Of course, this payoff comes at a price. And for such a contract that price would be very high.

Again the maximum or minimum can be calculated continuously or discretely, using every realized asset price or just a subset. In practice the maximum or minimum is measured discretely.

Classification	Lookback
Time dependence	Yes - if discrek / No - if continuous
Cashflow	No
Path dependence	Strong
Dimension	3 (possbin. reduction)
Order	first
Decisions	No

11.11 SUMMARY OF MATH/CODING CONSEQUENCES

Classification	Examples	Consequences
Time dependence	Bermudan exercise, discrete sampling, ...	Must keep track of time in code
Cashflow	Swap, instalments, ...	Jump in option value/Source term in pde
Path dependence	Barrier, Asian, lookback, ...	If strong path dependency need extra dimension
Dimension	Strongly path dependent, multi asset, ...	Monte Carlo may be better than finite difference
Order	Compounds, in barriers, ...	Solve lower-level option(s) first and input into higher
Decisions	American, passport, chooser, ...	Finite difference better than Monte Carlo, 'optimize'

11.12 **SUMMARY**

This chapter suggests ways to think about derivative contracts that make their analysis simpler. To be able to make comparisons between different contracts is a big step forward in understanding them.

FURTHER READING

- Geske (1979) discusses the valuation of compound options.

- See Taleb (1997) for more details of classifications of the type I have described. This book is an excellent and entertaining read.

- The book by Zhang (1997) is a discussion of many types of exotic options, with many formulæ.

- See Kyprianou *et al.* (2005) for Lévy processes and exotic option pricing.

- *PWOQF2* has many chapters on exotics and the mathematics used for pricing them.

SOME FORMULÆ FOR ASIAN OPTIONS

There are very few nice formulæ for the values of Asian options. The most well known are for average rate calls and puts when the average is a continuously sampled, geometrical average.

The geometric average rate call   This option has payoff

$$\max(A - E, 0),$$

where A is the continuously sampled geometric average. This option has a Black–Scholes value of

$$e^{-r(T-t)} \left(G \exp\left(\frac{(r - D - \sigma^2/2)(T - t)^2}{2T} + \frac{\sigma^2(T - t)^3}{6T^2} \right) N(d_1) - EN(d_2) \right)$$

where

$$I = \int_0^t \log(S(\tau))d\tau,$$

$$G = e^{I/T} S^{(T-t)/T},$$

$$d_1 = \frac{T \log(G/E) + (r - D - \sigma^2/2)(T - t)^2/2 + \sigma^2(T - t)^3/3T}{\sigma \sqrt{(T - t)^3/3}}$$

and

$$d_2 = \frac{T \log(G/E) + (r - D - \sigma^2/2)(T - t)^2/2}{\sigma \sqrt{(T - t)^3/3}}.$$

The geometric average of a lognormal random walk is itself lognormally distributed, but with a reduced volatility.

The geometric average rate put   This option has payoff

$$\max(E - A, 0),$$

where A is the continuously sampled geometric average. This option has a Black–Scholes value of

$$e^{-r(T-t)} \left(EN(-d_2) - G \exp \left(\frac{(r - D - \sigma^2/2)(T - t)^2}{2T} + \frac{\sigma^2(T - t)^3}{6T^2} \right) N(d_1) \right).$$

SOME FORMULÆ FOR LOOKBACK OPTIONS

Floating strike lookback call   The continuously sampled version of this option has a payoff

$$\max(S - M, 0) = S - M,$$

where M is the realized minimum of the asset price. In the Black–Scholes world the value is

$$Se^{-D(T-t)}N(d_1) - Me^{-r(T-t)}N(d_2)$$

$$+ Se^{-r(T-t)} \frac{\sigma^2}{2(r - D)} \left(\left(\frac{S}{M} \right)^{-\frac{2(r-D)}{\sigma^2}} N\left(-d_1 + \frac{2(r - D)\sqrt{T - t}}{\sigma} \right) - e^{(r-D)(T-t)}N(-d_1) \right),$$

where

$$d_1 = \frac{\log(S/M) + (r - D + \frac{1}{2}\sigma^2)(T - t)}{\sigma\sqrt{T - t}}$$

and

$$d_2 = d_1 - \sigma\sqrt{T - t}.$$

Floating strike lookback put   The continuously sampled version of this option has a payoff

$$\max(M - S, 0) = M - S,$$

where M is the realized maximum of the asset price. The value is

$$Me^{-r(T-t)}N(-d_2) - Se^{-D(T-t)}N(-d_1)$$

$$+ Se^{-r(T-t)} \frac{\sigma^2}{2(r - D)} \left(-\left(\frac{S}{M} \right)^{-\frac{2(r-D)}{\sigma^2}} N\left(d_1 - \frac{2(r - D)\sqrt{T - t}}{\sigma} \right) + e^{(r-D)(T-t)}N(d_1) \right),$$

where

$$d_1 = \frac{\log(S/M) + (r - D + \frac{1}{2}\sigma^2)(T - t)}{\sigma\sqrt{T - t}}$$

and

$$d_2 = d_1 - \sigma\sqrt{T - t}.$$

Fixed strike lookback call   This option has a payoff given by

$$\max(M - E, 0)$$

where M is the realized maximum. For $E > M$ the fair value is

$$Se^{-D(T-t)}N(d_1) - Ee^{-r(T-t)}N(d_2)$$

$$+Se^{-r(T-t)}\frac{\sigma^2}{2(r-D)}\left(-\left(\frac{S}{E}\right)^{-\frac{2(r-D)}{\sigma^2}}N\left(d_1 - \frac{2(r-D)\sqrt{T-t}}{\sigma}\right) + e^{(r-D)(T-t)}N(d_1)\right),$$

where

$$d_1 = \frac{\log(S/E) + (r - D + \frac{1}{2}\sigma^2)(T - t)}{\sigma\sqrt{T-t}}$$

and

$$d_2 = d_1 - \sigma\sqrt{T-t}.$$

When $E < M$ the value is

$$(M - E)e^{-r(T-t)} + Se^{-D(T-t)}N(d_1) - Me^{-r(T-t)}N(d_2)$$

$$+Se^{-r(T-t)}\frac{\sigma^2}{2(r-D)}\left(-\left(\frac{S}{M}\right)^{-\frac{2(r-D)}{\sigma^2}}N\left(d_1 - \frac{2(r-D)\sqrt{T-t}}{\sigma}\right) + e^{(r-D)(T-t)}N(d_1)\right),$$

where

$$d_1 = \frac{\log(S/M) + (r - D + \frac{1}{2}\sigma^2)(T - t)}{\sigma\sqrt{T-t}}$$

and

$$d_2 = d_1 - \sigma\sqrt{T-t}.$$

Fixed strike lookback put   This option has a payoff given by

$$\max(E - M, 0)$$

where M is the realized minimum. For $E < M$ the fair value is

$$Ee^{-r(T-t)}N(-d_2) - Se^{-D(T-t)}N(-d_1)$$

$$+Se^{-r(T-t)}\frac{\sigma^2}{2(r-D)}\left(\left(\frac{S}{E}\right)^{-\frac{2(r-D)}{\sigma^2}}N\left(-d_1 + \frac{2(r-D)\sqrt{T-t}}{\sigma}\right) - e^{(r-D)(T-t)}N(-d_1)\right),$$

where

$$d_1 = \frac{\log(S/E) + (r - D + \frac{1}{2}\sigma^2)(T - t)}{\sigma\sqrt{T-t}}$$

and

$$d_2 = d_1 - \sigma\sqrt{T-t}.$$

When $E > M$ the value is

$$(E - M)e^{-r(T-t)} - Se^{-D(T-t)}N(-d_1) + Me^{-r(T-t)}N(-d_2)$$

$$+Se^{-r(T-t)}\frac{\sigma^2}{2(r-D)}\left(\left(\frac{S}{M}\right)^{-\frac{2(r-D)}{\sigma^2}}N\left(-d_1 + \frac{2(r-D)\sqrt{T-t}}{\sigma}\right) - e^{(r-D)(T-t)}N(-d_1)\right),$$

where

$$d_1 = \frac{\log(S/M) + (r - D + \frac{1}{2}\sigma^2)(T - t)}{\sigma\sqrt{T-t}}$$

and

$$d_2 = d_1 - \sigma\sqrt{T-t}.$$

EXERCISES

1. A chooser option has the following properties:

    At time $T_C < T$, the option gives the holder the right to buy a European call or put option with exercise price E and expiry at time T, for an amount E_C. What is the value of this option when $E_C = 0$?

    Hint: Write down the payoff of the option and then use put-call parity to simplify the result.

2. How would we value the chooser option in the above question if E_C was non-zero?

3. Prove put-call parity for European compound options:

    $$C_C + P_P - C_P - P_C = S - E_2 e^{-r(T_2-t)},$$

    where C_C is a call on a call, C_P is a call on a put, P_C is a put on a call and P_P is a put on a put. The compound options have exercise price E_1 and expiry at time T_1 and the underlying calls and puts have exercise price E_2 and expiry at time T_2.

4. Find the value of the power European call option. This is an option with exercise price E, expiry at time T, when it has a payoff:

    $$\Lambda(S) = \max(S^2 - E, 0).$$

    Hint: Note that if the underlying asset price is assumed to be lognormally distributed then the square of the price is also lognormally distributed.

CHAPTER 12
multi-asset options

The aim of this Chapter...

...is to introduce the idea of correlation between many different assets and so develop a theory for derivatives that depend on several different assets simultaneously.

In this Chapter...

- how to model the behavior of many assets simultaneously

- estimating correlation between asset price movements

- how to value and hedge options on many underlying assets in the Black—Scholes framework

- the pricing formula for European non-path-dependent options on dividend-paying assets

12.1 **INTRODUCTION**

In this chapter I introduce the idea of higher dimensionality by describing the Black–Scholes theory for options on more than one underlying asset. This theory is perfectly straightforward; the only new idea is that of correlated random walks and the corresponding multifactor version of Itô's lemma.

Although the modeling and mathematics is easy, the final step of the pricing and hedging, the 'solution,' can be extremely hard indeed. I explain what makes a problem easy, and what makes it hard, from the numerical analysis point of view.

12.2 **MULTIDIMENSIONAL LOGNORMAL RANDOM WALKS**

The basic building block for option pricing with one underlying is the lognormal random walk

$$dS = \mu S \, dt + \sigma S \, dX.$$

This is readily extended to a world containing many assets via models for each underlying

$$dS_i = \mu_i S_i \, dt + \sigma_i S_i \, dX.$$

Here S_i is the price of the ith asset, $i = 1, \ldots, d$, and μ_i and σ_i are the drift and volatility of that asset respectively and dX_i is the increment of a Wiener process. We can still continue to think of dX_i as a random number drawn from a Normal distribution with mean zero and standard deviation $dt^{1/2}$ so that

$$E[dX_i] = 0 \quad \text{and} \quad E[dX_i^2] = dt$$

but the random numbers dX_i and dX_j are **correlated**:

$$E[dX_i \, dX_j] = \rho_{ij} \, dt.$$

here ρ_{ij} is the correlation coefficient between the ith and jth random walks. The symmetric matrix with ρ_{ij} as the entry in the ith row and jth column is called the **correlation matrix**. For example, if we have seven underlyings $d = 7$ and the correlation matrix will look like this:

$$\Sigma = \begin{pmatrix} 1 & \rho_{12} & \rho_{13} & \rho_{14} & \rho_{15} & \rho_{16} & \rho_{17} \\ \rho_{21} & 1 & \rho_{23} & \rho_{24} & \rho_{25} & \rho_{26} & \rho_{27} \\ \rho_{31} & \rho_{32} & 1 & \rho_{34} & \rho_{35} & \rho_{36} & \rho_{37} \\ \rho_{41} & \rho_{42} & \rho_{43} & 1 & \rho_{45} & \rho_{46} & \rho_{47} \\ \rho_{51} & \rho_{52} & \rho_{53} & \rho_{54} & 1 & \rho_{56} & \rho_{57} \\ \rho_{61} & \rho_{62} & \rho_{63} & \rho_{64} & \rho_{65} & 1 & \rho_{67} \\ \rho_{71} & \rho_{72} & \rho_{73} & \rho_{74} & \rho_{75} & \rho_{76} & 1 \end{pmatrix}$$

Note that $\rho_{ii} = 1$ and $\rho_{ij} = \rho_{ji}$. The correlation matrix is positive definite, so that $\mathbf{y}^T \Sigma \mathbf{y} \geq 0$. The **covariance matrix** is simply

$$\mathbf{M \Sigma M},$$

where $\mathbf{M}$ is the matrix with the σ_i along the diagonal and zeros everywhere else.

To be able to manipulate functions of many random variables we need a multidimensional version of Itô's lemma. If we have a function of the variables $S_1, \ldots, S_d$ and t, $V(S_1, \ldots, S_d, t)$, then

$$dV = \left(\frac{\partial V}{\partial t} + \frac{1}{2} \sum_{i=1}^{d} \sum_{j=1}^{d} \sigma_i \sigma_j \rho_{ij} S_i S_j \frac{\partial^2 V}{\partial S_i\, \partial S_j} \right) dt + \sum_{i=1}^{d} \frac{\partial V}{\partial S_i} dS_i.$$

We can get to this same result by using Taylor series and the rules of thumb:

$$dX_i^2 = dt \quad \text{and} \quad dX_i dX_j = \rho_{ij}\, dt.$$

Time Out...

Correlation

Correlation is a measure of the relationship or dependence between two or more random quantities.

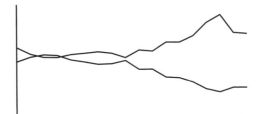

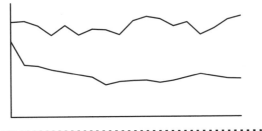

This is most easily explained by reference to the above series of figures. In the first figure we see two random walks that are perfectly correlated, $\rho = 1$. They may be moving apart overall, but that is a long-term phenomenon. In the short term, and correlation is a characteristic of random walks over small periods of time, you can see that each up move in one random walk is matched by an up move in the other.

In the second figure we see a correlation ρ of -1. Now each up move in one walk is matched by a down in the other. The third figure shows two uncorrelated random walks, there is no relationship between the up and down moves in the two walks.

Excel simulation

The correlation can be anywhere between -1 and $+1$. What would two random walks with a correlation of 0.5 look like?

P.S. I don't believe in correlations among financial assets.

12.3 **MEASURING CORRELATIONS**

If you have time series data at intervals of δt for all d assets you can calculate the correlation between the returns as follows. First, take the price series for each asset and calculate the return over each period. The return on the ith asset at the kth data point in the time series is simply

$$R_i(t_k) = \frac{S_i(t_k + \delta t) - S_i(t_k)}{S_i(t_k)}.$$

The historical volatility of the ith asset is

$$\sigma_i = \sqrt{\frac{1}{\delta t(M-1)} \sum_{k=1}^{M} (R_i(t_k) - \overline{R}_i)^2}$$

where M is the number of data points in the return series and $\overline{R}_i$ is the mean of all the returns in the series.

The covariance between the returns on assets i and j is given by

$$\frac{1}{\delta t(M-1)} \sum_{k=1}^{M} (R_i(t_k) - \overline{R}_i)(R_j(t_k) - \overline{R}_j).$$

The correlation is then

$$\frac{1}{\delta t(M-1)\sigma_i\sigma_j} \sum_{k=1}^{M} (R_i(t_k) - \overline{R}_i)(R_j(t_k) - \overline{R}_j).$$

In Excel correlation between two time series can be found using the CORREL worksheet function, or Tools | Data Analysis | Correlation.

Figure 12.1 shows the correlation matrix for Marks & Spencer, Tesco, Sainsbury and IBM.

Correlations measured from financial time series data are notoriously unstable. If you split your data into two equal groups, up to one date and beyond that date, and calculate the correlations for each group you may find that they differ quite markedly. You could calculate a 60-day correlation, say, from several years' data and the result would look something like Figure 12.2. You might want to use a historical 60-day correlation if you have a contract of that maturity. But, as can be seen from the figure, such a historical correlation should be used with care; correlations are even more unstable than volatilities.

The other possibility is to back out an **implied correlation** from the quoted price of an instrument. The idea behind that approach is the same as with implied volatility, it gives an estimate of the market's perception of correlation.

Time Out...

On a spreadsheet

The following spreadsheet shows how to simulate two correlated random walks on a spreadsheet. Both of these random walks are lognormal, but notice the correlation between them.

Excel simulation

	A	B	C	D	E	F	G	H	I
1	**Asset1**	**Asset2**		**Time**	**Random1**	**Random2**	**Asset1**	**Asset2**	
2	100	80		0	0.046223	−1.59903	100	80	
3				0.01	−0.158143	−0.960557	99.78371	77.97375	
4	**Drift1**	**Drift2**		0.02	−0.540749	0.340648	98.80434	78.18732	
5	0.1	0.2		= D3 + $B$12	0.03	0.859933	−1.754755	100.6024	75.78769
6					0.04	−0.268174	0.896078	100.1635	77.3988
7	**Vol1**	**Vol2**		0.05	−0.810562	−2.361049	98.63986	71.86476
8	0.2	0.3	= RAND() + RAN	6	−0.974247	0.569597	96.81651	72.02177
9			D() + RAND() + R	7	0.576045	1.016849	98.02874	74.69084
10	**Correl.**	0.5	AND() + RAND()	8	−0.989892	−0.409346	96.18601	72.93684
11			+ RAND() + RAN	9	−0.839252	−1.013799	94.66771	70.24342
12	**Timestep**	0.01	D() + RAND() + R	1	0.372974	−0.409777	95.46855	70.02906
13			AND() + RAND()	1	−0.542291	−0.597359	94.52858	68.51264
14	**Sqrt(1-correl^2)**		+ RAND() + RAN	2	0.248432	−0.643216	95.09279	67.76004
15	0.866025		D() −6	3	0.963828	1.237832	97.02094	71.05435
16				4	0.591412	2.049829	98.26555	75.61087
17				0.15	−0.243018	0.321826	97.88621	76.11868
18	= SQRT(1−B10*B10)			0.16	0.558761	1.187003	99.078	79.25634
19				0.17	−0.951554	1.985109	97.29151	82.37122
20				0.18	0.502183	−1.61082	98.36597	79.70918
21	= G19*(1 + A$5*$B$12 + A$8*SQRT($B$12)*E20)			2	−1.502543	95.92222	75.212	
22				0.2	0.348241	−1.424413	96.68622	72.97191
23				0.21	2.09392	−1.355961	100.832	72.8391
24				0.22	1.044282	−1.60787	103.0387	71.08298
25				0.23	0.902542	1.108671	105.0017	74.23496
26				4	1.517420	1.260644	2934	73.64175
27	= H24*(1 + B$5*$B$12 + B$8*SQRT($B$12)*($B$10*E25 + $A$15*F25))				8.629	75.89836		
28				0.26	−0.640458	0.532359	107.3462	76.37077
29				0.27	0.344599	−0.17648	108.1934	76.5681
30				0.28	1.082126	0.483641	110.6431	78.92619
31				0.29	0.041153	−0.865378	110.8448	77.35825
32				0.3	−0.029683	0.034647	110.8899	77.54816

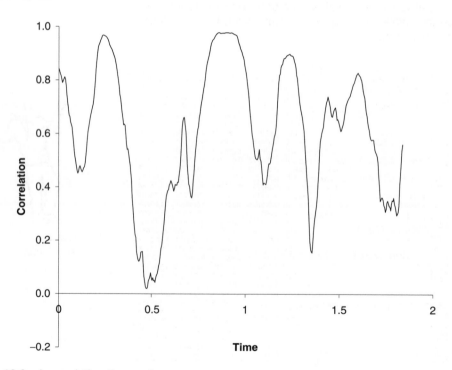

```
<HELP> for explanation.                                P140 Comdty CORR
Start date shifted.  <PAGE> for t-Statistics -or- <MENU> to Update Matrix.
                      CORRELATION  MATRIX
 RANGE  3/ 8/99 TO  9/ 7/99   PERIOD D                           PAGE 1 OF 3
Name:STORES                        -OR-  CHOOSE ONE   0 - Use PDF Default
                                                      1 - Year to Date
 Observations = 132                            0      2 - 3 Month
                                                      3 - 6 Month
                                                      4 - 12 Month
                                                      5 - 5 Year
                      * - observations limited due to this securiy
                   Correlation  Coefficients
         GBp    GBp    GBp    USD
         MKS    TSCO   SBRY * IBM
GBp  MKS  1.000  0.362  0.239 -0.463  n.a.   n.a.  n.a.  n.a.  n.a.  n.a.
GBp  TSCO 0.362  1.000  0.596  0.091  n.a.   n.a.  n.a.  n.a.  n.a.  n.a.
GBp  SBRY 0.239  0.596  1.000  0.457  n.a.   n.a.  n.a.  n.a.  n.a.  n.a.
USD  IBM -0.463  0.091  0.457  1.000  n.a.   n.a.  n.a.  n.a.  n.a.  n.a.
          n.a.   n.a.   n.a.   n.a.   n.a.   n.a.  n.a.  n.a.  n.a.  n.a.
          n.a.   n.a.   n.a.   n.a.   n.a.   n.a.  n.a.  n.a.  n.a.  n.a.
          n.a.   n.a.   n.a.   n.a.   n.a.   n.a.  n.a.  n.a.  n.a.  n.a.
          n.a.   n.a.   n.a.   n.a.   n.a.   n.a.  n.a.  n.a.  n.a.  n.a.
          n.a.   n.a.   n.a.   n.a.   n.a.   n.a.  n.a.  n.a.  n.a.  n.a.

Copyright 1999 BLOOMBERG L.P.   Frankfurt:69-920410  Hong Kong:2-977-6000  London:171-330-7500  New York:212-318-2000
Princeton:609-279-3000   Singapore:226-3000   Sydney:2-9777-8686   Tokyo:3-3201-8900   Sao Paulo:11-3048-4500
                                                              I574-414-0 08-Sep-99 12:17:01
Bloomberg
PROFESSIONAL
```

Figure 12.1   Some correlations. Source: Bloomberg L.P.

Figure 12.2   A correlation time series.

12.4 **OPTIONS ON MANY UNDERLYINGS**

Options with many underlyings are called **basket options**, **options on baskets** or **rainbow options**. The theoretical side of pricing and hedging is straightforward, following the Black–Scholes arguments but now in higher dimensions.

Set up a portfolio consisting of one basket option and short a number Δ_i of each of the assets S_i:

$$\Pi = V(S_1, \dots, S_d, t) - \sum_{i=1}^{d} \Delta_i S_i.$$

The change in this portfolio is given by

$$d\Pi = \left(\frac{\partial V}{\partial t} + \frac{1}{2} \sum_{i=1}^{d} \sum_{j=1}^{d} \sigma_i \sigma_j \rho_{ij} S_i S_j \frac{\partial^2 V}{\partial S_i \, \partial S_j} \right) dt + \sum_{i=1}^{d} \left(\frac{\partial V}{\partial S_i} - \Delta_i \right) dS_i.$$

If we choose

$$\Delta_i = \frac{\partial V}{\partial S_i}$$

for each i, then the portfolio is hedged and is risk-free. Setting the return equal to the risk-free rate we arrive at

$$\frac{\partial V}{\partial t} + \frac{1}{2} \sum_{i=1}^{d} \sum_{j=1}^{d} \sigma_i \sigma_j \rho_{ij} S_i S_j \frac{\partial^2 V}{\partial S_i \, \partial S_j} + r \sum_{i=1}^{d} S_i \frac{\partial V}{\partial S_i} - rV = 0. \qquad (12.1)$$

This is the multidimensional version of the Black–Scholes equation. The modifications that need to be made for dividends are obvious. When there is a dividend yield of D_i on the ith asset we have

$$\frac{\partial V}{\partial t} + \frac{1}{2} \sum_{i=1}^{d} \sum_{j=1}^{d} \sigma_i \sigma_j \rho_{ij} S_i S_j \frac{\partial^2 V}{\partial S_i \, \partial S_j} + \sum_{i=1}^{d} (r - D_i) S_i \frac{\partial V}{\partial S_i} - rV = 0$$

$Time\ Out\dots$

Here we go again

Risk neutrality means that the drift rates of the assets do not appear in the pricing equation.

12.5 THE PRICING FORMULA FOR EUROPEAN NON-PATH-DEPENDENT OPTIONS ON DIVIDEND-PAYING ASSETS

Because there is a Green's function for this problem (see Chapter 7) we can write down the value of a European non-path-dependent option with payoff of Payoff($S_1, \ldots, S_d$) at time T:

$$V = e^{-r(T-t)} (2\pi(T-t))^{-d/2} (\mathrm{Det}\boldsymbol{\Sigma})^{-1/2} (\sigma_1 \ldots \sigma_d)^{-1}$$

$$\int_0^\infty \cdots \int_0^\infty \frac{\mathrm{Payoff}(S_1' \cdots S_d')}{S_1' \ldots S_d'} \exp\left(-\frac{1}{2}\boldsymbol{\alpha}^T \boldsymbol{\Sigma}^{-1} \boldsymbol{\alpha}\right) dS_1' \cdots dS_d'.$$

$$\alpha_i = \frac{1}{\sigma_i(T-t)^{1/2}} \left(\log\left(\frac{S_i}{S_i'}\right) + \left(r - D_i - \frac{\sigma_i^2}{2}\right)(T-t)\right)$$

(12.2)

This has included a constant continuous dividend yield of D_i on each asset.

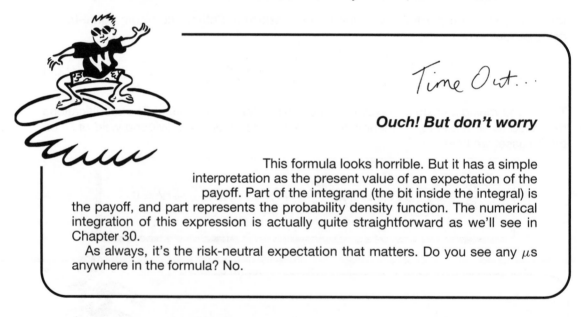

Time Out...

Ouch! But don't worry

This formula looks horrible. But it has a simple interpretation as the present value of an expectation of the payoff. Part of the integrand (the bit inside the integral) is the payoff, and part represents the probability density function. The numerical integration of this expression is actually quite straightforward as we'll see in Chapter 30.

As always, it's the risk-neutral expectation that matters. Do you see any μs anywhere in the formula? No.

12.6 EXCHANGING ONE ASSET FOR ANOTHER: A SIMILARITY SOLUTION

An **exchange option** gives the holder the right to exchange one asset for another, in some ratio. The payoff for this contract at expiry is

$$\max(q_1 S_1 - q_2 S_2, 0),$$

where q_1 and q_2 are constants.

The partial differential equation satisfied by this option in a Black–Scholes world is

$$\frac{\partial V}{\partial t} + \frac{1}{2} \sum_{i=1}^{2} \sum_{j=1}^{2} \sigma_i \sigma_j \rho_{ij} S_i S_j \frac{\partial^2 V}{\partial S_i \, \partial S_j} + \sum_{i=1}^{2} (r - D_i) S_i \frac{\partial V}{\partial S_i} - rV = 0.$$

A dividend yield has been included for both assets. Since there are only two underlyings the summations in these only go up to two.

This contract is special in that there is a similarity reduction. Let's postulate that the solution takes the form

$$V(S_1, S_2, t) = q_1 S_2 H(\xi, t),$$

where the new variable is

$$\xi = \frac{S_1}{S_2}.$$

If this is the case, then instead of finding a function V of three variables, we only need find a function H of two variables, a much easier task.

Time Out...

Similarity reductions

If you skipped much of Chapter 7, as I advised some of you to do, you won't have read about similarity reductions.
This is just a useful trick, not one you can often use, but when you can, you should.

Sometimes it is possible to reduce the number of dimensions in a problem by exploiting the 'nice' form of the problem. The example here is typical.

Changing variables from S_1, S_2 to ξ we must use the following for the derivatives.

$$\frac{\partial}{\partial S_1} = \frac{1}{S_2} \frac{\partial}{\partial \xi}, \quad \frac{\partial}{\partial S_2} = -\frac{\xi}{S_2} \frac{\partial}{\partial \xi},$$

$$\frac{\partial^2}{\partial S_1^2} = \frac{1}{S_2^2} \frac{\partial^2}{\partial \xi^2}, \quad \frac{\partial^2}{\partial S_2^2} = \frac{\xi^2}{S_2^2} \frac{\partial^2}{\partial \xi^2} + \frac{2\xi}{S_2^2} \frac{\partial}{\partial \xi}, \quad \frac{\partial^2}{\partial S_1 \, \partial S_2} = -\frac{\xi}{S_2^2} \frac{\partial^2}{\partial \xi^2} - \frac{1}{S_2^2} \frac{\partial}{\partial \xi}.$$

The time derivative is unchanged. The partial differential equation now becomes

$$\frac{\partial H}{\partial t} + \frac{1}{2} \sigma'^2 \xi^2 \frac{\partial^2 H}{\partial \xi^2} + (D_2 - D_1) \xi \frac{\partial H}{\partial \xi} - D_2 H = 0.$$

where

$$\sigma' = \sqrt{\sigma_1^2 - 2\rho_{12}\sigma_1\sigma_2 + \sigma_2^2}.$$

You will recognize this equation as being the Black–Scholes equation for a single stock with D_2 in place of r, D_1 in place of the dividend yield on the single stock and with a volatility of σ'.

From this it follows, retracing our steps and writing the result in the original variables, that

$$V(S_1, S_2, t) = q_1 S_1 e^{-D_1(T-t)} N(d_1') - q_2 S_2 e^{-D_2(T-t)} N(d_2')$$

where

$$d_1' = \frac{\log(q_1 S_1/q_2 S_2) + (D_2 - D_1 + \frac{1}{2}\sigma'^2)(T-t)}{\sigma'\sqrt{T-t}} \quad \text{and} \quad d_2' = d_1' - \sigma'\sqrt{T-t}.$$

12.7 TWO EXAMPLES

In Figure 12.3 is shown the term sheet for 'La Tricolore' Capital-guaranteed Note. This contract pays off the *second* best performing of three currencies against the French franc, but only if the second-best performing has appreciated against the franc, otherwise

Preliminary and Indicative
For Discussion Purposes Only

'La Tricolore' Capital-guaranteed Note

Issuer	XXXX
Principal Amount	FRF 100,000,000
Issue Price	98.75%
Maturity Date	Twelve months after Issue Date
Coupon	Zero
Redemption Amount	If at least two of the following three appreciation indices, namely: $\frac{\text{USD/FRF} - 6.0750}{6.0750}$; $\frac{\text{GBP/FRF} - 10.2000}{10.2000}$; $\frac{\text{JPY/FRF} - 0.05120}{0.05120}$ are positive at Maturity, the Note will redeem in that currency whose appreciation index is the second highest of the three; in all other circumstances the Note will redeem at Par in FRF. If the Note redeems in a currency other than FRF, the amount of that currency shall be calculated by dividing the FRF Principal Amount by the spot Currency/FRF exchange rate prevailing on the Issue Date.

This indicative termsheet is neither an offer to buy or sell securities or an OTC derivative product which includes options, swaps, forwards and structured notes having similar features to OTC derivative transactions, nor a solicitation to buy or sell securities or an OTC derivative product. The proposal contained in the foregoing is not a complete description of the terms of a particular transaction and is subject to change without limitation.

Figure 12.3 Term sheet for 'La Tricolore' Capital-guaranteed Note.

it pays off at par. This contract does not have any unusual features, and has a value that can be written as a three-dimensional integral, of the form (12.2). But what would the payoff function be? You wouldn't use a partial differential equation to price this contract. Instead you would estimate the multiple integral directly by the methods of Chapter 29.

The next example, whose term sheet is shown in Figure 12.4, is of basket equity swap. This rather complex, high-dimensional contract, is for a swap of interest payment based on three-month LIBOR and the level of an index. The index is made up of the weighted average of 20 pharmaceutical stocks. To make matters even more complex, the index uses a time averaging of the stock prices.

Preliminary and Indicative
For Discussion Purposes Only

International Pharmaceutical Basket Equity Swap

Indicative terms

Trade Date	[ ]
Initial Valuation Date	[ ]
Effective Date	[ ]
Final Valuation Date	26th September 2002
Averaging Dates	The monthly anniversaries of the Initial Valuation Date commencing 26th March 2002 and up to and including the Expiration Date
Notional Amount	US$25,000,000

Counterparty floating amounts (US$ LIBOR)

Floating Rate Payer	[ ]
Floating Rate Index	USD-LIBOR
Designated Maturity	Three months
Spread	Minus 0.25%
Day Count Fraction	Actual/360
Floating Rate Payment Dates	Each quarterly anniversary of the Effective Date
Initial Floating Rate Index	[ ]

The Bank Fixed and Floating Amounts (Fee, Equity Option)

Fixed Amount Payer	XXXX
Fixed Amount	1.30% of Notional Amount
Fixed Amount Payment Date	Effective Date
Basket	A basket comprising 20 stocks and constructed as described in attached Appendix
Initial Basket Level	Will be set at 100 on the Initial Valuation Date
Floating Equity Amount Payer	XXXX

Figure 12.4 Term sheet for a basket equity swap.

Floating Equity Amount

Will be calculated according to the performance of the basket of stocks in the following way:

$$\text{Notional Amount} * \max\left[0,\left(\frac{\text{BASKET}_{average}-100}{100}\right)\right]$$

where

$$\text{BASKET}_{average} = 100 * \sum_{20\ stocks}\left(\text{Weight} * \frac{P_{average}}{P_{initial}}\right)$$

And for each stock the Weight is given in the Appendix
P_initial is the local currency price of each stock on the Initial Valuation Date
P_average is the arithmetic average of the local currency price of each stock on each of the Averaging Dates

Floating Equity Amount Payment Date

Termination Date

Appendix
Each of the following stocks are equally weighted (5%):
Astra (Sweden), Glaxo Wellcome (UK), Smithkline Beecham (UK), Zeneca Group (UK), Novartis (Switzerland), Roche Holding Genus (Switzerland), Sanofi (France), Synthelabo (France), Bayer (Germany), Abbott Labs (US), Bristol Myers Squibb (US), American Home Products (US), Amgen (US), Eli Lilly (US), Medtronic (US), Merck (US), Pfizer (US), Schering-Plough (US), Sankyo (Japan), Takeda Chemical (Japan).

This indicative termsheet is neither an offer to buy or sell securities or an OTC derivative product which includes options, swaps, forwards and structured notes having similar features to OTC derivative transactions, nor a solicitation to buy or sell securities or an OTC derivative product. The proposal contained in the foregoing is not a complete description of the terms of a particular transaction and is subject to change without limitation.

Figure 12.4   (*continued*)

12.8   REALITIES OF PRICING BASKET OPTIONS

The factors that determine the ease or difficulty of pricing and hedging multi-asset options are

- existence of a closed-form solution;
- number of underlying assets, the dimensionality;
- path dependency;
- early exercise.

We have seen all of these except path dependency.
    The solution technique that we use will generally be one of

- finite-difference solution of a partial differential equation;
- numerical integration;
- Monte Carlo simulation.

These methods are the subjects of later parts of the book.

12.8.1 Easy problems

If we have a closed-form solution then our work is done; we can easily find values and hedge ratios. This is provided that the solution is in terms of sufficiently simple functions for which there are spreadsheet functions or other libraries. If the contract is European with no path dependency then the solution may be of the form (12.2). If this is the case, then we often have to do the integration numerically. This is not difficult. Several methods are described in Chapter 30, including Monte Carlo integration and the use of low-discrepancy sequences.

12.8.2 Medium problems

If we have low dimensionality, lower than three or four, say, the finite-difference methods are the obvious choice. They cope well with early exercise and many path-dependent features can be incorporated, though usually at the cost of an extra dimension.

For higher dimensions, Monte Carlo simulations are good. They cope with all path-dependent features. Unfortunately, they are not very efficient for American-style early exercise.

12.8.3 Hard problems

The hardest problems to solve are those with both high dimensionality, for which we would like to use Monte Carlo simulation, and with early exercise, for which we would like to use finite-difference methods. There is currently no numerical method that copes well with such a problem.

12.9 REALITIES OF HEDGING BASKET OPTIONS

Even if we can find option values and the greeks, they are often very sensitive to the level of the correlation. But as I have said, the correlation is a very difficult quantity to measure. So the hedge ratios are very likely to be inaccurate. If we are delta hedging then we need accurate estimates of the deltas. This makes basket options very difficult to delta hedge successfully.

When we have a contract that is difficult to delta hedge we can try to reduce sensitivity to parameters, and the model, by hedging with other derivatives. This was the basis of vega hedging, mentioned in Chapter 8. We could try to use the same idea to reduce sensitivity to the correlation. Unfortunately, that is also difficult because there just aren't enough contracts traded that depend on the right correlations.

12.10 CORRELATION VERSUS COINTEGRATION

The correlations between financial quantities are notoriously unstable. One could easily argue that a theory should not be built up using parameters that are so unpredictable. I would tend to agree with this point of view. One could propose a stochastic correlation model, but that approach has its own problems.

An alternative statistical measure to correlation is **cointegration**. Very loosely speaking, two time series are cointegrated if a linear combination has constant mean and standard deviation. In other words, the two series never stray too far from one another. This is probably a more robust measure of the linkage between two financial quantities but as yet there is little derivatives theory based on the concept.

12.11 **SUMMARY**

The new ideas in this chapter were the multifactor, correlated random walks for assets, and Itô's lemma in higher dimensions. These are both simple concepts, and we will use them often, especially in interest rate-related topics.

FURTHER READING

- See Hamilton (1994) for further details of the measurement of correlation and cointegration.

- The first solution of the exchange option problem was by Margrabe (1978).

- For analytical results, formulæ or numerical algorithms for the pricing of some other multifactor options see Stulz (1982), Johnson (1987), Boyle *et al.* (1989), Boyle & Tse (1990), Rubinstein (1991) and Rich & Chance (1993).

- See Emanuel Derman's autobiography for discussion of quantos (Derman, 2004).

- For details of cointegration, what it means and how it works see the papers by Alexander & Johnson (1992, 1994).

- Krekel *et al.* (2004) compare different pricing methods for basket options.

EXERCISES

1. N shares follow geometric Brownian motions, i.e.

$$dS_i = \mu_i S_i\, dt + \sigma_i S_i\, dX_i,$$

   for $1 \leq i \leq N$. The share price changes are correlated with correlation coefficients ρ_{ij}. Find the stochastic differential equation satisfied by a function $f(S_1, S_2, \ldots, S_N)$.

2. Using tick data for at least two assets, measure the correlations between the assets using the entirety of the data. Split the data in two halves and perform the same calculations on each of the halves in turn. Are the correlation coefficients for the first half equal to those for the second? If so, do these figures match those for the whole data set?

3. Check that if we use the pricing formula for European non-path-dependent options on dividend-paying assets, but for a single asset (i.e. in one dimension), we recover the solution found in Chapter 8:

$$V(S, t) = \frac{e^{-r(T-t)}}{\sigma\sqrt{2\pi(T-t)}} \int_0^\infty e^{-\left(\log(S/S') + \left(r - \frac{1}{2}\sigma^2\right)(T-t)\right)^2 \Big/ 2\sigma^2(T-t)} \text{Payoff}(S') \frac{dS'}{S0'}.$$

4. Set up the following problems mathematically (i.e. what equations do they satisfy and with what boundary and final conditions?) The assets are correlated.

   (a) An option that pays the positive difference between two share prices S_1 and S_2 and which expires at time T.

(b) An option that has a call payoff with underlying S_1 and strike price E at time T only if $S_1 > S_2$ at time T.

(c) An option that has a call payoff with underlying S_1 and strike price E_1 at time T if $S_1 > S_2$ at time T and a put payoff with underlying S_2 and strike price E_2 at time T if $S_2 > S_1$ at time T.

5. What is the explicit formula for the price of a quanto which has a put payoff on the Nikkei Dow index with strike at E and which is paid in yen. $S_\$$ is the yen-dollar exchange rate and S_N is the level of the Nikkei Dow index. We assume

$$dS_\$ = \mu_\$ S_\$ \, dt + \sigma_\$ S_\$ \, dX_\$$$

and

$$dS_N = \mu_N S_N \, dt + \sigma_N S_N \, dX_N,$$

with a correlation of ρ.

CHAPTER 13
barrier options

The aim of this Chapter...

...is to describe and classify barrier options, to show how they can easily be put into a partial differential equation framework for later solution by numerical methods. Such a framework is ideal for pricing barrier options with complex modern volatility models.

In this Chapter...

- the different types of barrier options

- how to price many barrier contracts in the partial differential equation framework

- some of the practical problems with the pricing and hedging of barriers

13.1 INTRODUCTION

I mentioned barrier options briefly in an earlier chapter. In this chapter we study them in detail, from both a theoretical and a practical perspective. **Barrier options** are path-dependent options. They have a payoff that is dependent on the realized asset path via its level; certain aspects of the contract are triggered if the asset price becomes too high or too low. For example, an up-and-out call option pays off the usual $\max(S - E, 0)$ at expiry unless at any time previously the underlying asset has traded at a value S_u or higher. In this example, if the asset reaches this level (from below, obviously) then it is said to 'knock out,' becoming worthless. Apart from 'out' options like this, there are also 'in' options which only receive a payoff if a level is reached, otherwise they expire worthless.

Barrier options are popular for a number of reasons. Perhaps the purchaser uses them to hedge very specific cashflows with similar properties. Usually, the purchaser has very precise views about the direction of the market. If he wants the payoff from a call option but does not want to pay for all the upside potential, believing that the upward movement of the underlying will be limited prior to expiry, then he may choose to buy an up-and-out call. It will be cheaper than a similar vanilla call, since the upside is severely limited. If he is right and the barrier is not triggered he gets the payoff he wanted. The closer that the barrier is to the current asset price then the greater the likelihood of the option being knocked out, and thus the cheaper the contract.

Conversely, an 'in' option will be bought by someone who believes that the barrier level will be realized. Again, the option is cheaper than the equivalent vanilla option.

13.2 DIFFERENT TYPES OF BARRIER OPTIONS

There are two main types of barrier option:

- The **out option**, which only pays off if a level is *not* reached. If the barrier is reached then the option is said to have **knocked out**.

- The **in option**, which pays off as long as a level is reached before expiry. If the barrier is reached then the option is said to have **knocked in**.

Then we further characterize the barrier option by the position of the barrier relative to the initial value of the underlying:

- If the barrier is above the initial asset value, we have an **up** option.

- If the barrier is below the initial asset value, we have a **down** option.

Finally, we describe the payoff received at expiry:

- The payoffs are all the usual suspects, call, put, binary, etc.

The above classifies the commonest barrier options. In all of these contracts the position of the barrier could be time dependent. The level may begin at one level and then rise, say. Usually the level is a piecewise-constant function of time.

USD/MXN Double Knock-Out Note

Principal Amount	USD 10,000,000
Issuer	XXXX
Maturity	6 months from Trade Date
Issue Price	100%
Coupon	If the USD/MXN spot exchange rate trades above the Upper Barrier orbelow the Lower Barrier at any time during the term of the Note:

$$\text{Zero}$$

Otherwise:

$$400\% \times \max\left(0, \frac{8.2500\text{-FX}}{\text{FX}}\right)$$

where FX isthe USD/MXN spot exchage rate at Maturity

Redemption Amount	100%
Upper Barrier Level	8.2500
Lower Barrier Level	7.4500

Figure 13.1   Term sheet for a USD/MXN double knock-out note.

Another style of barrier option is the **double barrier**. Here there is both an upper and a lower barrier, the first above and the second below the current asset price. In a double 'out' option the contract becomes worthless if *either* of the barriers is reached. In a double 'in' option one of the barriers must be reached before expiry, otherwise the option expires worthless. Other possibilities can be imagined, one barrier is an 'in' and the other an 'out,' at expiry the contract could have either an 'in' or an 'out' payoff.

Sometimes a **rebate** is paid if the barrier level is reached. This is often the case for 'out' barriers in which case the rebate can be thought of as cushioning the blow of losing the rest of the payoff. The rebate may be paid as soon as the barrier is triggered or not until expiry.

In Figure 13.1 is shown the term sheet for a double knock-out option on the Mexican peso, US dollar exchange rate. The upper barrier is set at 8.25 and the lower barrier at 7.45. If the exchange rate trades inside this range until expiry then there is a payment. This is a very vanilla example of a barrier contract.

13.3   **PRICING METHODOLOGIES**

13.3.1   Monte Carlo simulation

Pricing via Monte Carlo simulation is simple in principle:

- The value of an option is the present value of the expected payoff under a risk-neutral random walk.

The pricing algorithm:

1. Simulate the risk-neutral random walk starting at today's value of the asset over the required time horizon. This gives one realization of the underlying price path.
2. For this realization calculate the option payoff.
3. Perform many more such realizations over the time horizon.
4. Calculate the average payoff over all realizations.
5. Take the present value of this average, this is the option value.

Advantages of Monte Carlo pricing

- It is easy to code.
- It is hard to make mistakes in the coding.

Disadvantages of Monte Carlo pricing

- More work is needed to get the greeks.
- It can be slow since tens of thousands of simulations are needed to get an accurate answer.

13.3.2 Partial differential equations

Barrier options are path dependent. Their payoff, and therefore value, depends on the path taken by the asset up to expiry.

- Yet that dependence is weak. We only have to know whether or not the barrier has been triggered, we do not need any other information about the path.

13.4 PRICING BARRIERS IN THE PARTIAL DIFFERENTIAL EQUATION FRAMEWORK

I use $V(S, t)$ to denote the value of the barrier contract *before the barrier has been triggered*. This value still satisfies the Black–Scholes equation

$$\frac{\partial V}{\partial t} + \tfrac{1}{2}\sigma^2 S^2 \frac{\partial^2 V}{\partial S^2} + rS\frac{\partial V}{\partial S} - rV = 0.$$

The details of the barrier feature come in through the specification of the boundary conditions.

Time Out...

The framework

Partial differential equations are the natural framework for pricing barrier options. When combined with the kind of numerical method described in Chapter 28 the solution is relatively straightforward. Indeed, in many cases it is easier to solve a barrier option numerically than a vanilla option.

    Once you are working in this framework it is very easy to incorporate modern volatility models. As hinted at later in this chapter, barrier options can be very sensitive to the assumptions made about volatility and very rarely are such options priced using the assumption of constant volatility. In such a situation it's nice to have a framework that can be easily adapted to sophisticated volatility models. This is that framework.

    However, in the following I will also give a few pointers to valuing via trees.

13.4.1 'Out' barriers

If the underlying asset reaches the barrier in an 'out' barrier option then the contract becomes worthless. This leads to the boundary condition

$$V(S_u, t) = 0 \quad \text{for } t < T,$$

for an up-barrier option with the barrier level at $S = S_u$. We must solve the Black–Scholes equation for $0 \le S \le S_u$ with this condition on $S = S_u$ and a final condition corresponding to the payoff received if the barrier is not triggered. For a call option we would have

$$V(S, T) = \max(S - E, 0).$$

If we have a down-and-out option with a barrier at S_d then we solve for $S_d \le S < \infty$ with

$$V(S_d, t) = 0,$$

and the relevant final condition at expiry.

    The boundary conditions are easily changed to accommodate rebates. If a rebate of R is paid when the barrier is hit then

$$V(S_d, t) = R.$$

Time Out...

In terms of the binomial model?

To price out barrier options in the binomial framework you have to specify on which nodes the option becomes valueless. The option value is then set to zero on these nodes, and the usual algorithm is used for all other nodes. (Of course, there is no need to find option values beyond the barrier, so the tree is usually smaller than for a vanilla option.)

13.4.2 'In' barriers

An 'in' option only has a payoff if the barrier is triggered. If the barrier is not triggered then the option expires worthless

$$V(S, T) = 0.$$

The value in the option is in the potential to hit the barrier. If the option is an up-and-in contract then on the upper barrier the contract must have the same value as a vanilla contract:

$$V(S_u, t) = \text{value of vanilla contract, a function of } t.$$

Using the notation $V_v(S, t)$ for value of the equivalent vanilla contract (a vanilla call, if we have an up-and-in call option) then we must have

$$V(S_u, t) = V_v(S_u, t) \quad \text{for } t < T.$$

A similar boundary condition holds for a down-and-in option.

The contract we receive when the barrier is triggered is a derivative itself, and therefore the 'in' option is a second-order contract.

In solving for the value of an 'in' option completely numerically we must solve for the value of the vanilla option first, before solving for the value of the barrier option. The solution therefore takes roughly twice as long as the solution of the 'out' option.[1]

When volatility is constant we can solve for the theoretical price of many types of barrier contract. Some examples are given at the end of the chapter.

---

[1] And, of course, the vanilla option must be solved for $0 \leq S < \infty$.

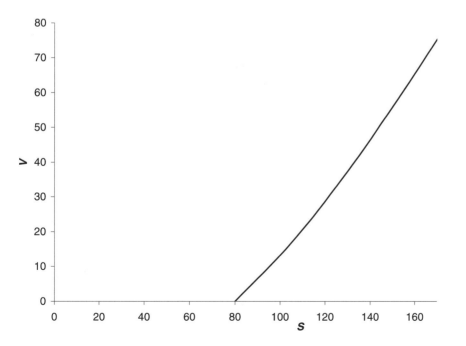

Time Out...

In terms of the binomial model?

The 'in'-barrier option can be thought of as a
second-order contract. So you would need one tree for
pricing the underlying option and the results of this will be
passed to the 'in'-barrier tree. To make things simple, make sure that the two
trees have the same structure.

13.5 EXAMPLES

Down-and-out call option   As the first example, consider the down-and-out call option
with barrier level S_d below the strike price E. The value of this option is shown as a
function of S in Figure 13.2.

Down-and-in call option   In the absence of any rebates the relationship between an
'in'-barrier option and an 'out'-barrier option (with same payoff and same barrier level) is

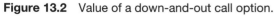

Figure 13.2   Value of a down-and-out call option.

very simple:

$$\text{in} + \text{out} = \text{vanilla}.$$

If the 'in' barrier is triggered then so is the 'out' barrier, so whether or not the barrier is triggered we still get the vanilla payoff at expiry.

The value of this option is shown as a function of S in Figure 13.3. Also shown is the value of the vanilla call. Note that the two values coincide at the barrier.

Up-and-out call option   The barrier S_u for an up-and-out call option must be above the strike price E (otherwise the option would be valueless).

The value of this option is shown as a function of S in Figure 13.4. In Figure 13.5 is shown the delta.

Figure 13.6 shows the Bloomberg barrier option calculator and Figure 13.7 shows the option *profit/loss* against asset price.

13.5.1   Some more examples

The following figures are all taken from Bloomberg, who use the formulæ below, for the pricing.

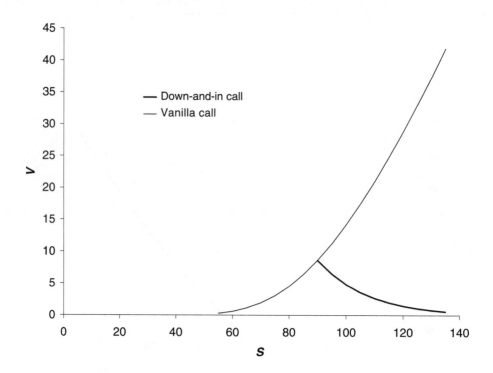

Figure 13.3   Value of a down-and-in call option.

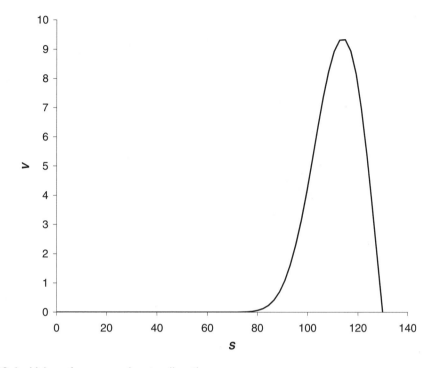

Figure 13.4   Value of an up-and-out call option.

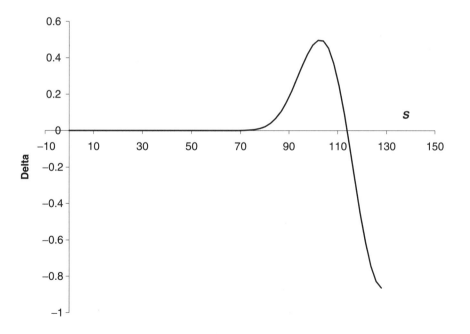

Figure 13.5   Delta of an up-and-out call option.

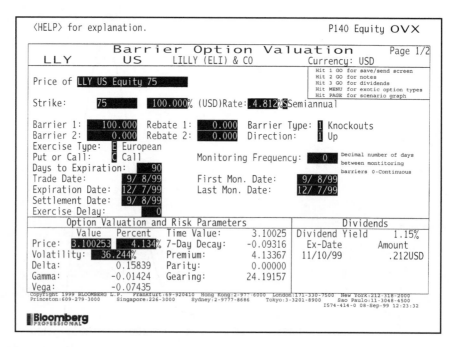

Figure 13.6   An up-and-out call again. Source: Bloomberg L.P.

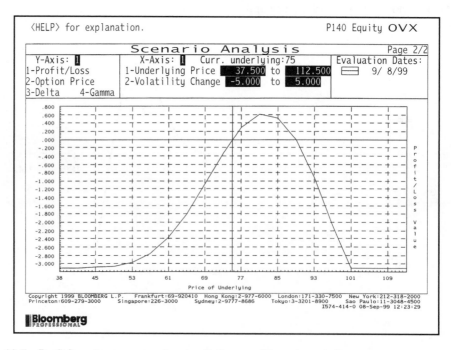

Figure 13.7   Profit/loss for an up-and-out call. Source: Bloomberg L.P.

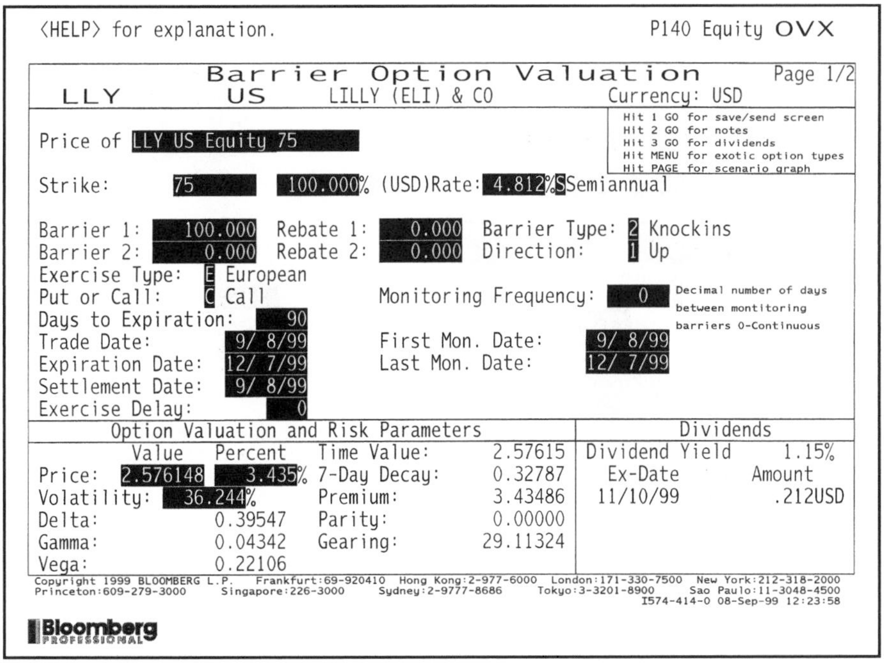

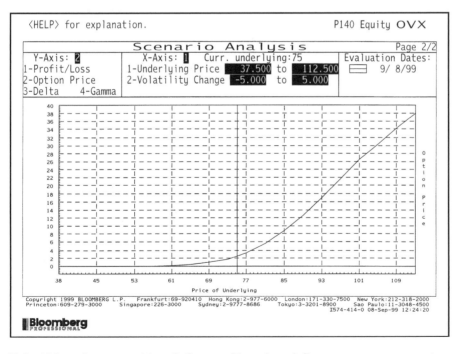

Figure 13.8 Calculator for an up-and-in call. Source: Bloomberg L.P.

Figure 13.9 Value of an up-and-in call. Source: Bloomberg L.P.

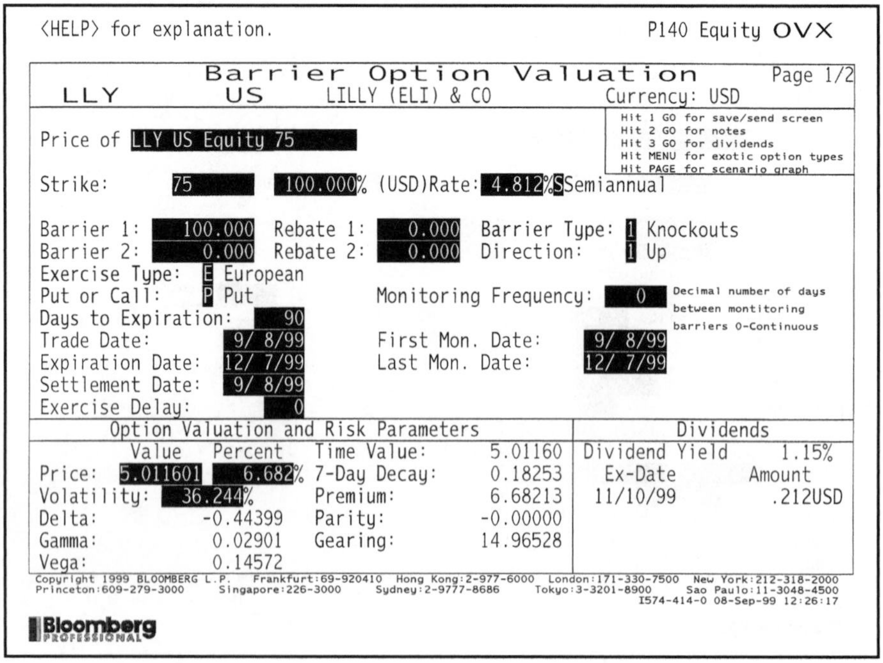

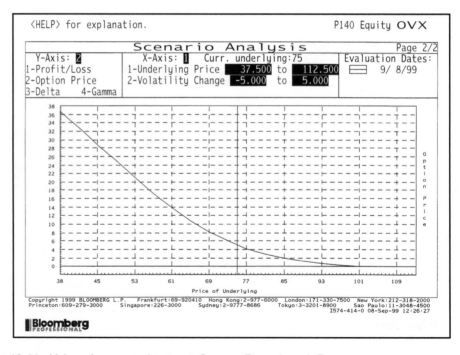

Figure 13.10 Calculator for an up-and-out put. Source: Bloomberg L.P.

Figure 13.11 Value of an up-and-out put. Source: Bloomberg L.P.

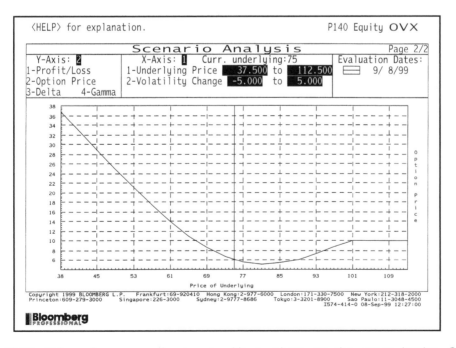

```
⟨HELP⟩ for explanation.                          P140 Equity OVX
                 Barrier  Option  Valuation           Page 1/2
     LLY         US      LILLY (ELI) & CO       Currency: USD
                                              ┌──────────────────────────┐
                                              │ Hit 1 GO for save/send screen│
  Price of  LLY US Equity 75                  │ Hit 2 GO for notes         │
                                              │ Hit 3 GO for dividends     │
  Strike:       75      100.000% (USD)Rate: 4.812%SSemiannual │
                                              │ Hit MENU for exotic option types│
                                              │ Hit PAGE for scenario graph│
                                              └──────────────────────────┘
  Barrier 1:    100.000  Rebate 1:   10.000  Barrier Type: 1 Knockouts
  Barrier 2:      0.000  Rebate 2:    0.000  Direction:    1 Up
  Exercise Type: E European
  Put or Call:   P Put             Monitoring Frequency:   0   Decimal number of days
  Days to Expiration:    90                                    between montitoring
  Trade Date:      9/ 8/99   First Mon. Date:   9/ 8/99        barriers 0-Continuous
  Expiration Date: 12/ 7/99  Last Mon. Date:   12/ 7/99
  Settlement Date:  9/ 8/99
  Exercise Delay:       0
  ────── Option Valuation and Risk Parameters ──────┬──────── Dividends ────────
           Value   Percent  Time Value:    6.03326 │ Dividend Yield    1.15%
  Price:  6.033261    8.044% 7-Day Decay:   0.31150 │ Ex-Date     Amount
  Volatility: 36.244%       Premium:       8.04435 │ 11/10/99      .212USD
  Delta:    -0.28762  Parity:       -0.00000 │
  Gamma:     0.04606  Gearing:      12.43109 │
  Vega:      0.23285
  Copyright 1999 BLOOMBERG L.P.  Frankfurt:69-920410  Hong Kong:2-977-6000  London:171-330-7500  New York:212-318-2000
  Princeton:609-279-3000  Singapore:226-3000  Sydney:2-9777-8686  Tokyo:3-3201-8900  Sao Paulo:11-3048-4500
                                                    I574-414-0 08-Sep-99 12:26:52
  Bloomberg
  PROFESSIONAL
```

Figure 13.12 Calculator for an up-and-out put with a rebate on the upper barrier. Source: Bloomberg L.P.

```
⟨HELP⟩ for explanation.                          P140 Equity OVX
                      Scenario  Analysis             Page 2/2
   Y-Axis: 2      X-Axis: 1  Curr. underlying:75   Evaluation Dates:
  1-Profit/Loss   1-Underlying Price  37.500  to  112.500   ▭  9/ 8/99
  2-Option Price  2-Volatility Change -5.000  to   5.000
  3-Delta   4-Gamma
```

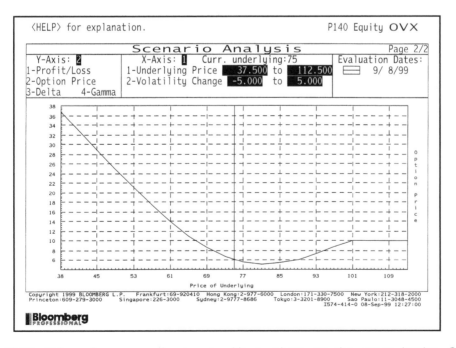

Figure 13.13 Value of an up-and-out put with a rebate on the upper barrier. Source: Bloomberg L.P.

13.6 **OTHER FEATURES IN BARRIER-STYLE OPTIONS**

Not so long ago barrier options were exotic, the market for them was small and few people were comfortable pricing them. Nowadays they are heavily traded and it is only the contracts with more unusual features that can rightly be called exotic. Some of these features are described below.

13.6.1 Early exercise

It is possible to have American-style early exercise. The contract must specify what the payoff is if the contract is exercised before expiry. As always, early exercise is a simple constraint on the value of the option.

In Figure 13.14 is the term sheet for a knock-out installment premium option on the US dollar, Japanese yen exchange rate. This knocks out if the exchange rate ever goes above 140. If the option expires without ever hitting this level there is a vanilla call payoff. I mention this contract in the section on early exercise because it has a similar feature. To keep the contract alive the holder must pay in instalments, every month another payment is due. The question is when to stop paying the instalments. This can be done optimally.

Preliminary and Indicative
For Discussion Purposes Only

USD/JPY KO Installment-Premium Option

Notional Amount	USD 50,000,000
Option Type	133.25 (ATMS) USD Put/JPY Call with KO and Installment Premium
Maturity	6 months from Trade Date
Knockout Mechanism	If, at any time from Trade Date to Maturity, the USD/JPY spot rate trades in the interbank market at or above JPY 140.00per USD, the option will automatically be cancelled, with no further rights or obligations arising for the parties thereto.
Upfront Premium	JPY 1.50 per USD
Installments	JPY 1.50 per USD,payable monthly from Trade Date (5 installments)
Installment Mechanism	As long as the installments continue to be paid, the option will be kept alive, but the Counterparty has the right to cease paying the installments and to thereby let the option becancelled at anytime.
Spot Reference	JPY 133.25 per USD

This indicative termsheet is neither an offer to buy or sell securities or an OTC derivative product which includes options, swaps, forwards and structured notes having similar features to OTC derivative transactions, nor a solicitation to buy or sell securities or an OTC derivative product. The proposal contained in the foregoing is not a complete description of the terms of a particular transaction and is subject to change without limitation.

Figure 13.14 Term sheet for a USD/JPY knock-out installment premium option.

13.6.2 Repeated hitting of the barrier

The double barrier that we have seen above can be made more complicated. Instead of only requiring one hit of either barrier we could insist that *both* barriers are hit before the barrier is triggered.

This contract is easy to value. Observe that the first time that one of the barriers is hit the contract becomes a vanilla barrier option. Thus on the two barriers we solve the Black–Scholes equation with boundary conditions that our double barrier value is equal to an up-barrier option on the lower barrier and a down-barrier option on the upper barrier.

13.6.3 Resetting of barrier

Another type of barrier contract that can be priced by the same two- (or more) step procedure as 'in' barriers is the reset barrier. When the barrier is hit the contract turns into another barrier option with a different barrier level. The contract may be time dependent in the sense that if the barrier is hit before a certain time we get a new barrier option, if it is hit after a certain time we get the vanilla payoff.

Related to these contracts are the **roll-up** and **roll-down options**. These begin life as vanilla options, but if the asset reaches some predefined level they become a barrier option. For example, with a roll-up put if the roll-up strike level is reached the contract becomes an up-and-out put with the roll-up strike being the strike of the barrier put. The barrier level will then be at a prespecified level.

13.6.4 Outside barrier options

Outside or **rainbow barrier options** have payoffs or a trigger feature that depends on a second underlying. Thus the barrier might be triggered by one asset, with the payoff depending on the other. These products are clearly multi-factor contracts.

13.6.5 Soft barriers

The **soft barrier option** allows the contract to be gradually knocked in or out. The contract specifies two levels, an upper and a lower. In the knock-out option a proportion of the contract is knocked out depending on the distance that the asset has reached between the two barriers. For example, suppose that the option is an up and out with a soft barrier range of 100 to 120. If the maximum asset value reached before expiry is 105 then 5/20 or 25% of the payoff is lost.

13.6.6 Parisian options

Parisian options have barriers that are triggered only if the underlying has been beyond the barrier level for more than a specified time. This additional feature reduces the possibility of manipulation of the trigger event and makes the dynamic hedging easier. However, this new feature also increases the dimensionality of the problem.

13.7 MARKET PRACTICE: WHAT VOLATILITY SHOULD I USE?

Practitioners do not price contracts using a single, constant volatility. Let us see some of the pitfalls with this, and then see what practitioners do.

In Figure 13.15 we see a plot of the value of an up-and-out call option using three different volatilities, 15%, 20% and 25%. I have chosen three very different values to make a point. If we are unsure about the value of the volatility (as we surely are) then which value do we use to price the contract? Observe that at approximately $S = 100$ the option value seems to be insensitive to the volatility, the vega is zero. If S is greater than this value perhaps we should only sell the contract for a volatility of 15% to be on the safe side. If S is less than this, perhaps we should sell the contract for 25%, again to play it safe. Now ask the question: Do I believe that volatility will be one of 15%, 20% or 25%, and will be fixed at that level? Or do I believe that volatility could move around between 15% and 25%? Clearly the latter is closer to the truth. But the measurement of vega and the plots in Figure 13.15 assume that volatility is fixed until expiry. If we are concerned with playing it safe we should assume that the behavior of volatility will be that which gives us the lowest value if we are buying the contract. The worst outcome for volatility is for it to be low below the strike price and high around the barrier. Financially, this means that if we are near the strike we get a small payoff, but if we are near the barrier we are likely to hit it. Mathematically, the 'worst' choice of volatility path depends on the sign of the gamma at each point. If gamma is positive then low volatility is bad,

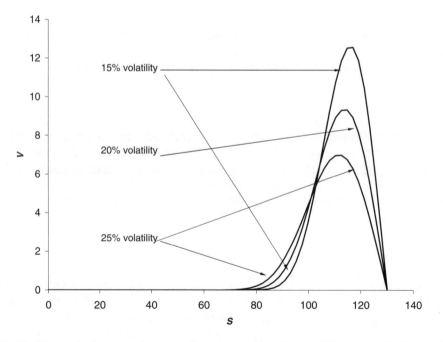

Figure 13.15 Theoretical up-and-out call price with three different volatilities. Source: Bloomberg L.P.

if gamma is negative then high volatility is bad. When the gamma is not single signed, the measurement of vega can be meaningless. Barrier options with non-single-signed gamma include the up-and-out call, down-and-out put and many double-barrier options.

Figures 13.16 through 13.19 show the details of a double knockout put contract, its price versus the underlying, its gamma versus the underlying and its price versus volatility. This is a contract with a gamma that changes sign as can be seen from Figure 13.18. You must be very careful when pricing such a contract as to what volatility to use. Suppose you wanted to know the implied volatility for this contract when the price was 3.2, what value would you get? Refer to Figure 13.19.

To accommodate problems like this, practitioners have invented a number of 'patches.' One is to use two different volatilities in the option price. For example, one can calculate implied volatilities from vanilla options with the same strike, expiry and payoff as the barrier option and also from American-style one-touch options with the strike at the barrier level. The implied volatility from the vanilla option contains the market's estimate of the value of the payoff, but includes all the upside potential that the call has but which is irrelevant for the up-and-out option. The one-touch volatility, however, contains the market's view of the likelihood of the barrier level being reached. These two volatilities can be used to price an up-and-out call by observing that an 'out' option is the same as a vanilla minus an 'in' option. Use the vanilla volatility to price the vanilla call and the one-touch volatility to price the 'in' call.

```
<HELP> for explanation.                              P140 Equity OVX
            B a r r i e r   O p t i o n   V a l u a t i o n        Page 1/2
    LLY        US       LILLY (ELI) & CO      Currency: USD
                                              Hit 1 GO for save/send screen
  Price of  LLY US Equity 75                  Hit 2 GO for notes
                                              Hit 3 GO for dividends
                                              Hit MENU for exotic option types
  Strike:        75       100.000% (USD)Rate: 4.812%S Hit PAGE for scenario graph
                                        Semiannual
  Barrier 1:    100.000  Rebate 1:    0.000  Barrier Type: 3 Double Knock-out
  Barrier 2:     55.000  Rebate 2:    0.000  Direction:     1 Up
  Exercise Type: E European
  Put or Call:   P Put           Monitoring Frequency:    0   Decimal number of days
  Days to Expiration:      90                                 between montitoring
  Trade Date:      9/ 8/99       First Mon. Date:  9/ 8/99    barriers 0-Continuous
  Expiration Date: 12/ 7/99      Last Mon. Date:   12/ 7/99
  Settlement Date: 9/ 8/99
  Exercise Delay:         0
  ─── Option Valuation and Risk Parameters ───┬─────── Dividends ───────
       Value    Percent   Time Value:   3.23694 │ Dividend Yield    1.15%
  Price: 3.236936  4.316% 7-Day Decay: -0.06711 │ Ex-Date      Amount
  Volatility: 36.000%     Premium:      4.31591  │ 11/10/99      .212USD
  Delta:     -0.17192     Parity:      -0.00000
  Gamma:     -0.00856     Gearing:     23.17006
  Vega:      -0.04460
  Copyright 1999 BLOOMBERG L.P.  Frankfurt:69-920410  Hong Kong:2-977-6000  London:171-330-7500  New York:212-318-2000
  Princeton:609-279-3000   Singapore:226-3000   Sydney:2-9777-8686   Tokyo:3-3201-8900   Sao Paulo:11-3048-4500
                                                                    I574-414-0 08-Sep-99 12:28:30
  ‖Bloomberg
   PROFESSIONAL
```

Figure 13.16 Details of a double knockout put. Source: Bloomberg L.P.

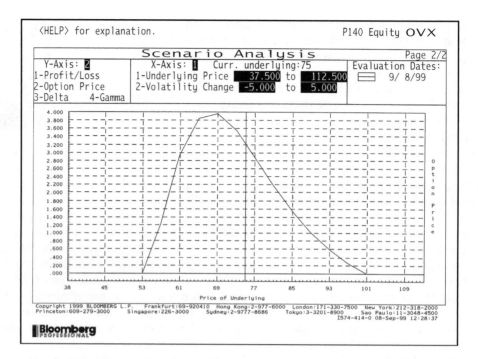

Figure 13.17   Price of the double knockout put. Source: Bloomberg L.P.

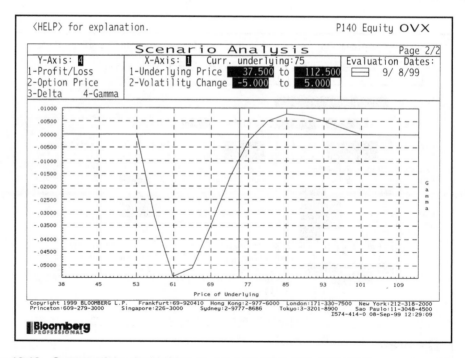

Figure 13.18   Gamma of the double knockout put. Source: Bloomberg L.P.

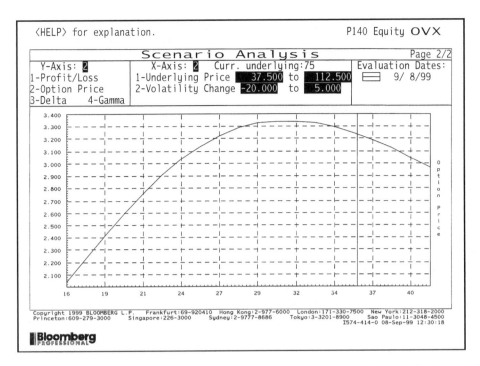

Figure 13.19 Option price versus volatility for the double knockout put. Source: Bloomberg L.P.

13.8 HEDGING BARRIER OPTIONS

Barrier options have discontinuous delta at the barrier. For a knock-out, the option value is continuous, decreasing approximately linearly towards the barrier then being zero beyond the barrier. This discontinuity in the delta means that the gamma is instantaneously infinite at the barrier. Delta hedging through the barrier is virtually impossible, and certainly very costly. This raises the issue of whether there are improvements on delta hedging for barrier options.

There have been a number of suggestions made for ways to *statically* hedge barrier options. These methods try to mimic as closely as possible the value of a barrier option with vanilla calls and puts, or with binary options. A very common practice for hedging a short up-and-out call is to buy a long call with the same strike and expiry. If the option does knock out then you are fortunate in being left with a long call position.

I now describe another simple but useful technique, based on the **reflection principle** and **put-call symmetry**. This technique only really works if the barrier and strike lie in the correct order, as we shall see. The method gives an approximate hedge only.

The simplest example of put-call symmetry is actually put-call parity. At all asset levels we have

$$V_C - V_P = S - Ee^{-r(T-t)},$$

where E is the strike of the two options, and C and P refer to call and put. Suppose we have a down-and-in call, how can we use this result? To make things simple for the moment, let's have the barrier and the strike at the same level. Now hedge our down-and-in call with a short position in a vanilla put with the same strike. If the barrier is reached we have a position worth

$$V_C - V_P.$$

The first term is from the down-and-in call and the second from the vanilla put. This is exactly the same as

$$S - Ee^{-r(T-t)} = E(1 - e^{-r(T-t)}),$$

because of put-call parity and since the barrier and the strike are the same. If the barrier is not touched then both options expire worthless. If the interest rate were zero then we would have a perfect hedge. If rates are non-zero what we are left with is a one-touch option with small and time-dependent value on the barrier. Although this leftover cashflow is non-zero, it is small, bounded and more manageable than the original cashflows.

Now suppose that the strike and the barrier are distinct. Let us continue with the down-and-in call, now with barrier below the strike. The static hedge is not much more complicated than the previous example. All we need to know is the relationship between the value of a call option with strike E when $S = S_d$ and a put option with strike S_d^2/E. It is easy to show from the formulæ for calls and puts that if interest rates are zero, the value of this call at $S = S_d$ is equal to a number E/S_d of the puts, valued at S_d. We would therefore hedge our down-and-in call with E/S_d puts struck at S_d^2/E. Note that the geometric average of the strike of the call and the strike of the put is the same as the barrier level, this is where the idea of 'reflection' comes in. The strike of the hedging put is at the reflection in the barrier of the call's strike. When rates are non-zero there is some error in this hedge, but again it is small and manageable, decreasing as we get closer to expiry. If the barrier is not touched then both options expire worthless (the strike of the put is below the barrier remember).

If the barrier level is above the strike, matters are more complicated since if the barrier is touched we get an in-the-money call. The reflection principle does not work because the put would also be in the money at expiry if the barrier is not touched.

13.8.1 Slippage costs

The delta of a barrier option is discontinuous at the barrier, whether it is an in or an out option. This presents a particular problem to do with **slippage** or **gapping**. Should the underlying move significantly as the barrier is triggered it is likely that it will not be possible to continuously hedge through the barrier. For example, if the contract is knocked out then one finds oneself with a $-\Delta$ holding of the underlying that should have been offloaded sooner. This can have a significant effect on the hedging costs.

It is not too difficult to allow for the *expected* slippage costs, and all that is required is a slight modification to the apparent barrier level.

At the barrier we hold $-\Delta$ of the underlying. The value of this position is $-\Delta X$, since $S = X$ is the barrier level. Suppose that the asset moves by a small fraction k before

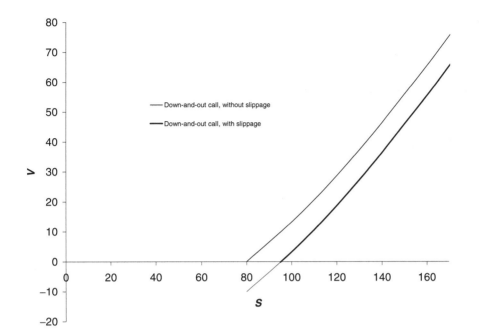

Figure 13.20 Incorporating slippage.

we can close out our asset position, or equivalently, that there is a transaction charge involved in closing. We thus lose

$$-k\Delta X$$

on the trigger event.

Now refer to Figure 13.20 where we'll look at the specific example of a down-and-out option. Because we lose $-k\Delta X$ we should use the boundary condition

$$V(X, t) = -k\Delta X.$$

After a little bit of Taylor series we find that this is approximately the same as

$$V((1 + k)X, t) = 0.$$

In other words, we should apply the boundary condition at a slightly higher value of S and so slightly reduce the option's value.

13.9 SUMMARY

In this chapter we have seen a description of many types of barrier option. We have seen how to put these contracts into the partial differential equation framework. Many of these contracts have simple pricing formulæ. Unfortunately, the extreme nature of these contracts make them very difficult to hedge in practice and in particular, they can be very sensitive to the volatility of the underlying. Worse still, if the gamma of the contract changes sign we cannot play safe by adding a spread to the volatility. Practitioners seem to be most comfortable statically hedging as much of the barrier contract as possible using traded vanillas.

SOME FORMULÆ

In the following I use $N(\cdot)$ to denote the cumulative distribution function for a standardized Normal variable. The dividend yield on stocks or the foreign interest rate for FX are denoted by q. Also

$$a = \left(\frac{S_b}{S}\right)^{-1+\frac{2(r-q)}{\sigma^2}},$$

$$b = \left(\frac{S_b}{S}\right)^{1+\frac{2(r-q)}{\sigma^2}},$$

All implmented on the CD

where S_b is the barrier position (whether S_u or S_d should be obvious from the example),

$$d_1 = \frac{\log(S/E) + \left(r - q + \frac{1}{2}\sigma^2\right)(T-t)}{\sigma\sqrt{T-t}},$$

$$d_2 = \frac{\log(S/E) + \left(r - q - \frac{1}{2}\sigma^2\right)(T-t)}{\sigma\sqrt{T-t}},$$

$$d_3 = \frac{\log(S/S_b) + \left(r - q + \frac{1}{2}\sigma^2\right)(T-t)}{\sigma\sqrt{T-t}},$$

$$d_4 = \frac{\log(S/S_b) + \left(r - q - \frac{1}{2}\sigma^2\right)(T-t)}{\sigma\sqrt{T-t}},$$

$$d_5 = \frac{\log(S/S_b) - \left(r - q - \frac{1}{2}\sigma^2\right)(T-t)}{\sigma\sqrt{T-t}},$$

$$d_6 = \frac{\log(S/S_b) - \left(r - q + \frac{1}{2}\sigma^2\right)(T-t)}{\sigma\sqrt{T-t}},$$

$$d_7 = \frac{\log(SE/S_b^2) - \left(r - q - \frac{1}{2}\sigma^2\right)(T-t)}{\sigma\sqrt{T-t}},$$

$$d_8 = \frac{\log(SE/S_b^2) - \left(r - q + \frac{1}{2}\sigma^2\right)(T-t)}{\sigma\sqrt{T-t}}.$$

Up-and-out call

$$Se^{-q(T-t)}(N(d_1) - N(d_3) - b(N(d_6) - N(d_8))) - Ee^{-r(T-t)}(N(d_2) - N(d_4) - a(N(d_5) - N(d_7))).$$

Up-and-in call

$$Se^{-q(T-t)}(N(d_3) + b(N(d_6) - N(d_8))) - Ee^{-r(T-t)}(N(d_4) + a(N(d_5) - N(d_7))).$$

Down-and-out call

1. $E > S_b$:

$$Se^{-q(T-t)}(N(d_1) - b(1 - N(d_8))) - Ee^{-r(T-t)}(N(d_2) - a(1 - N(d_7))).$$

2. $E < S_b$:

$$Se^{-q(T-t)}(N(d_3) - b(1 - N(d_6))) - Ee^{-r(T-t)}(N(d_4) - a(1 - N(d_5))).$$

Down-and-in call

1. $E > S_b$:

$$Se^{-q(T-t)}b(1 - N(d_8)) - Ee^{-r(T-t)}a(1 - N(d_7)).$$

2. $E < S_b$:

$$Se^{-q(T-t)}(N(d_1) - N(d_3) + b(1 - N(d_6))) - Ee^{-r(T-t)}(N(d_2) - N(d_4) + a(1 - N(d_5))).$$

Down-and-out put

$$-Se^{-q(T-t)}(N(d_3) - N(d_1) - b(N(d_8) - N(d_6))) + Ee^{-r(T-t)}(N(d_4) - N(d_2) - a(N(d_7) - N(d_5))).$$

Down-and-in put

$$-Se^{-q(T-t)}(1 - N(d_3) + b(N(d_8) - N(d_6))) + Ee^{-r(T-t)}(1 - N(d_4) + a(N(d_7) - N(d_5))).$$

Up-and-out put

1. $E > S_b$:

$$-Se^{-q(T-t)}(1 - N(d_3) - bN(d_6)) + Ee^{-r(T-t)}(1 - N(d_4) - aN(d_5)).$$

2. $E < S_b$:

$$-Se^{-q(T-t)}(1 - N(d_1) - bN(d_8)) + Ee^{-r(T-t)}(1 - N(d_2) - aN(d_7)).$$

Up-and-in put

1. $E > S_b$:

$$-Se^{-q(T-t)}(N(d_3) - N(d_1) + bN(d_6)) + Ee^{-r(T-t)}(N(d_4) - N(d_2) + aN(d_5)).$$

2. $E < S_b$:

$$-Se^{-q(T-t)}bN(d_8) + Ee^{-r(T-t)}aN(d_7).$$

The following charts show each of the above types of barrier option, as well as the underlying vanilla option.

Note that with out options the value of the barrier option 'hugs' the vanilla, except that it must be zero at the barrier. With in options, the barrier value hugs zero except that it becomes the vanilla value at the barrier.

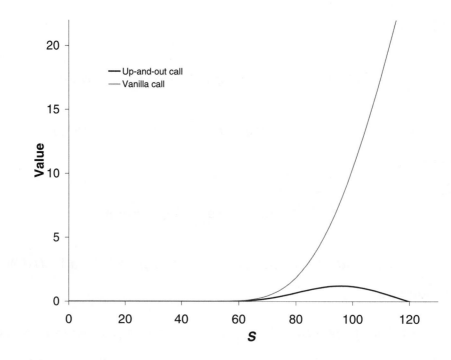

Figure 13.21   Up-and-out call. $\sigma = 0.2, r = 0.05, q = 0, E = 100, T = 1$ and $S_b = 120$.

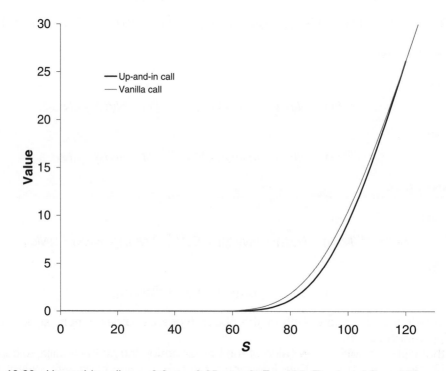

Figure 13.22   Up-and-in call. $\sigma = 0.2, r = 0.05, q = 0, E = 100, T = 1$ and $S_b = 120$.

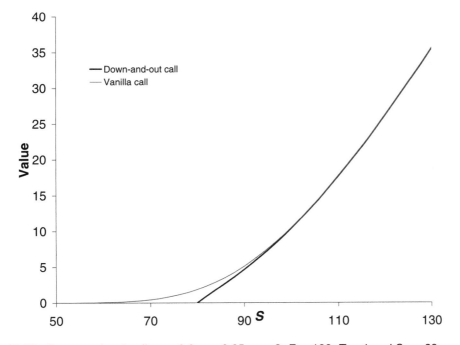

Figure 13.23 Down-and-out call. $\sigma = 0.2$, $r = 0.05$, $q = 0$, $E = 100$, $T = 1$ and $S_b = 80$.

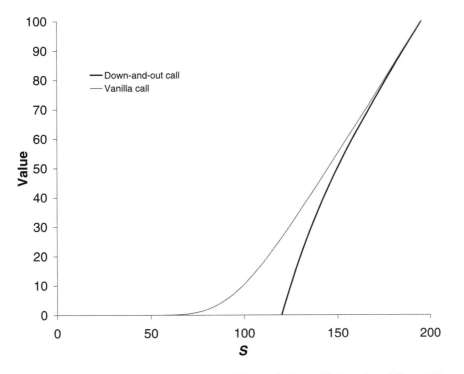

Figure 13.24 Down-and-out call. $\sigma = 0.2$, $r = 0.05$, $q = 0$, $E = 100$, $T = 1$ and $S_b = 120$.

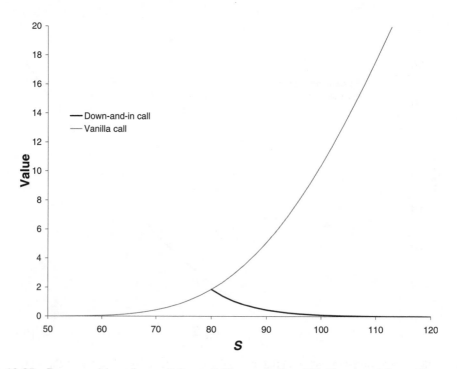

Figure 13.25   Down-and-in call. $\sigma = 0.2$, $r = 0.05$, $q = 0$, $E = 100$, $T = 1$ and $S_b = 80$.

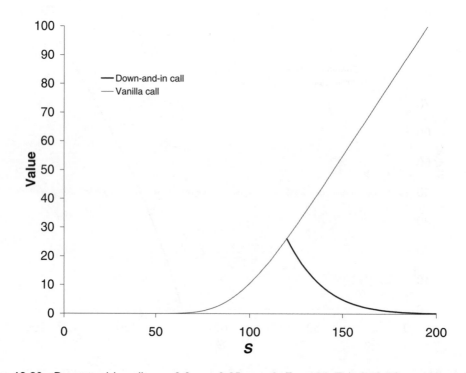

Figure 13.26   Down-and-in call. $\sigma = 0.2$, $r = 0.05$, $q = 0$, $E = 100$, $T = 1$ and $S_b = 120$.

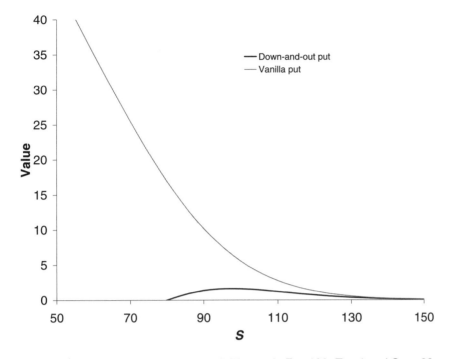

Figure 13.27 Down-and-out put. $\sigma = 0.2$, $r = 0.05$, $q = 0$, $E = 100$, $T = 1$ and $S_b = 80$.

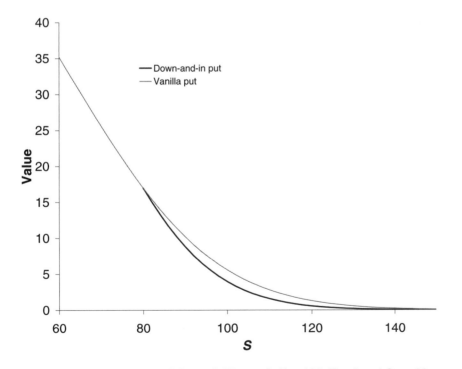

Figure 13.28 Down-and-in put. $\sigma = 0.2$, $r = 0.05$, $q = 0$, $E = 100$, $T = 1$ and $S_b = 80$.

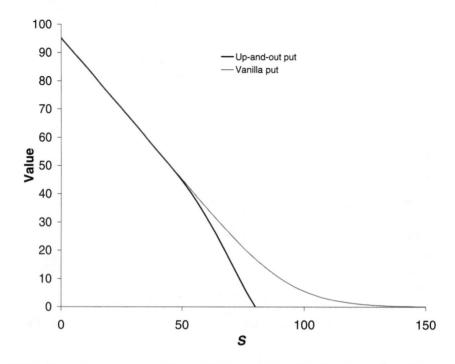

Figure 13.29 Up-and-out put. $\sigma = 0.2$, $r = 0.05$, $q = 0$, $E = 100$, $T = 1$ and $S_b = 80$.

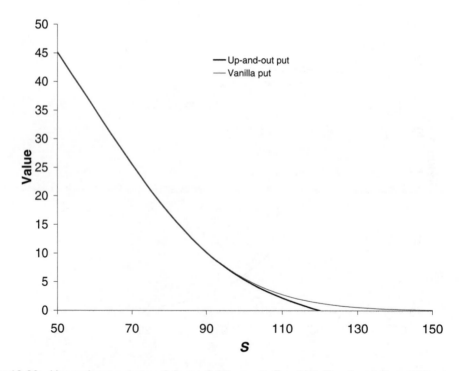

Figure 13.30 Up-and-out put. $\sigma = 0.2$, $r = 0.05$, $q = 0$, $E = 100$, $T = 1$ and $S_b = 120$.

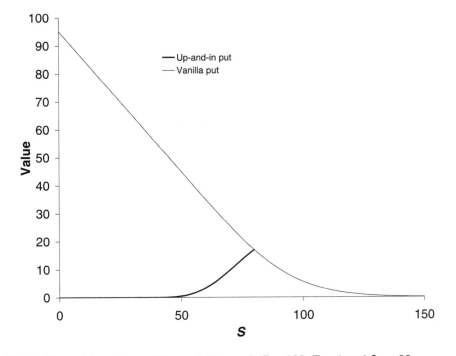

Figure 13.31 Up-and-in put. $\sigma = 0.2$, $r = 0.05$, $q = 0$, $E = 100$, $T = 1$ and $S_b = 80$.

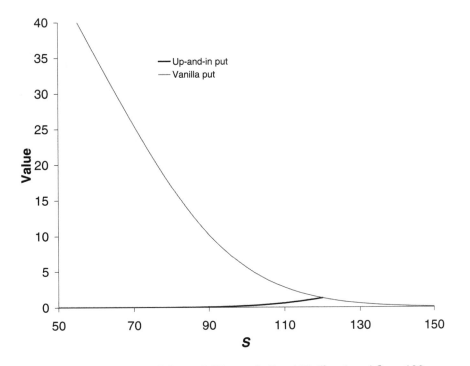

Figure 13.32 Up-and-in put. $\sigma = 0.2$, $r = 0.05$, $q = 0$, $E = 100$, $T = 1$ and $S_b = 120$.

FURTHER READING

- Many of the original barrier formulæ are due to Reiner & Rubinstein (1991).

- The formulæ above are explained in Taleb (1997) and Haug (2007). Taleb discusses barrier options in great detail, including the reality of hedging that I have only touched upon.

- The article by Carr (1995) contains an extensive literature review as well as a detailed discussion of protected barrier options and rainbow barrier options.

- See Derman *et al.* (1997) for a full description of the static replication of barrier options with vanilla options.

- See Carr (1994) for more details of put-call symmetry.

- See Haug & Haug (2002) for the pricing of barrier options that depend on two underlying assets.

- More closed-form solutions can be found in Banerjee (2003).

Time Out...

Binomial model revisited

Using trees to price barrier options can be a bit of a chore. This is because it is tedious to line up nodes with the barrier level. You can be faced with the question of on which node to set the option value to zero. Interpolation methods make the most sense. Those fond of trees will go to extraordinary lengths to justify various *ad hoc* tree modifications. In the finite-difference method the barrier is trivial — the mathematician's favorite word — to incorporate.

EXERCISES

1. Check that the solution for the down-and-out call option, $V_{D/O}$, satisfies Black–Scholes, where

$$V_{D/O}(S, t) = C(S, t) - \left(\frac{S}{S_d}\right)^{1 - \frac{2r}{\sigma^2}} C(S_d^2/S, t),$$

and $C(S, t)$ is the value of a vanilla call option with the same maturity and payoff as the barrier option.

Hint: Show that $S^{1-\frac{2r}{\sigma^2}}V(X^2/S,t)$ satisfies Black–Scholes for any X, when $V(S,t)$ satisfies Black–Scholes.

2. Why do we need the condition $S_d < E$ to be able to value a down-and-out call by adding together known solutions of the Black–Scholes equation (as in question 1)? How would we value the option in the case that $S_d > E$?

3. Check the value for the down-and-in call option using the explicit solutions for the down-and-out call and the vanilla call option.

4. Formulate the following problem for the accrual barrier option as a Black–Scholes partial differential equation with appropriate final and boundary conditions:

   The option has barriers at levels S_u and S_d, above and below the initial asset price, respectively. If the asset touches either barrier before expiry then the option knocks out with an immediate payoff of $\Phi(T-t)$. Otherwise, at expiry the option has a payoff of $\max(S-E,0)$.

5. Formulate the following barrier option pricing problems as partial differential equations with suitable boundary and final conditions:

   (a) The option has barriers at levels S_u and S_d, above and below the initial asset price, respectively. If the asset touches both barriers before expiry, then the option has payoff $\max(S-E,0)$. Otherwise the option does not pay out.

   (b) The option has barriers at levels S_u and S_d, above and below the initial asset price, respectively. If the asset price first rises to S_u and then falls to S_d before expiry, then the option pays out \$1 at expiry.

6. Price the following double knockout option: the option has barriers at levels S_u and S_d, above and below the initial asset price, respectively. The option has payoff \$1, unless the asset touches either barrier before expiry, in which case the option knocks out and has no payoff.

7. Prove put-call parity for simple barrier options:

$$C_{D/O} + C_{D/I} - P_{D/O} - P_{D/I} = S - Ee^{-r(T-t)},$$

   where $C_{D/O}$ is a European down-and-out call, $C_{D/I}$ is a European down-and-in call, $P_{D/O}$ is a European down-and-out put and $P_{D/I}$ is a European down-and-in put, all with expiry at time T and exercise price E.

8. Why might we prefer to treat a European up-and-out call option as a portfolio of a vanilla European call option and a European up-and-in call option?

CHAPTER 14
fixed-income products and analysis: yield, duration and convexity

The aim of this Chapter...

...is to introduce the most common contracts of the fixed-income world and to show simple ways for their analysis. The big assumption of this chapter is that interest rates are deterministic. Greater levels of sophistication are needed for pricing more complex fixed-income contracts such as derivatives, but these will be reached in later chapters.

In this Chapter...

- the names and properties of the basic and most important fixed-income products

- the definitions of features commonly found in fixed-income products

- simple ways to analyze the market value of the instruments: yield, duration and convexity

- how to construct yield curves and forward rates

14.1   **INTRODUCTION**

This chapter is an introduction to some basic instruments and concepts in the world of fixed income, that is, the world of cashflows that are in the simplest cases independent of any stocks, commodities, etc. I will describe the most elementary of fixed-income instruments, the coupon-bearing bond, and show how to determine various properties of such bonds to help in their analysis.

This chapter is self contained, and does not require any knowledge from earlier chapters. A lot of it is also not really necessary reading for anything that follows. The reason for this is that, although the concepts and techniques I describe here are used in practice and are *useful* in practice, it is difficult to present a completely coherent theory for more sophisticated products in this framework.

14.2   **SIMPLE FIXED-INCOME CONTRACTS AND FEATURES**

14.2.1   The zero-coupon bond

The **zero-coupon bond** is a contract paying a known fixed amount, the **principal**, at some given date in the future, the **maturity** date T. For example, the bond pays $100 in 10 years' time, see Figure 14.1. We're going to scale this payoff so that in future all principals will be $1.

This promise of future wealth is worth something now. It cannot have zero or negative value. Furthermore, except in extreme circumstances, the amount you pay initially will be smaller than the amount you receive at maturity.

We discussed the idea of time value of money in Chapter 1. This is clearly relevant here and we will return to this in a moment.

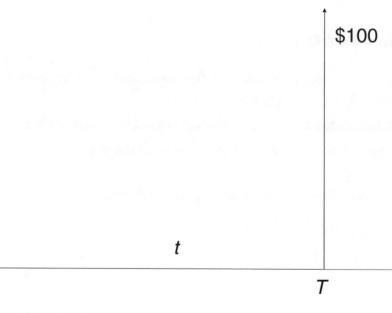

Figure 14.1   The zero-coupon bond.

14.2.2 The coupon-bearing bond

A **coupon-bearing bond** is similar to the above except that as well as paying the principal at maturity, it pays smaller quantities, the coupons, at intervals up to and including the maturity date. See Figure 14.2.

These coupons are usually prespecified fractions of the principal. For example, the bond pays $1 in 10 years and 2%, i.e. 2 cents, every six months. This would be called a 4% coupon. This bond is clearly more valuable than the bond in the previous example because of the coupon payments. We can think of the coupon-bearing bond as a portfolio of zero-coupon bearing bonds; one zero-coupon bearing bond for each coupon date with a principal being the same as the original bond's coupon, and then a final zero-coupon bond with the same maturity as the original.

Figure 14.3 is an excerpt from *The Wall Street Journal Europe* of 14th April 2005 showing US Treasury bonds, notes and bills. Observe that there are many different 'rates' or coupons, and different maturities. The values of the different bonds will depend on the size of the coupon, the maturity and the market's view of the future behavior of interest rates.

14.2.3 The money market account

Everyone who has a bank account has a **money market account**. This is an account that accumulates interest compounded at a rate that varies from time to time. The rate at which interest accumulates is usually a short-term and unpredictable rate. In the sense that money held in a money market account will grow at an unpredictable rate, such an account is risky when compared with a one-year zero-coupon bond. On the other hand, the money market account can be closed at any time but if the bond is sold before maturity there is no guarantee how much it will be worth at the time of the sale.

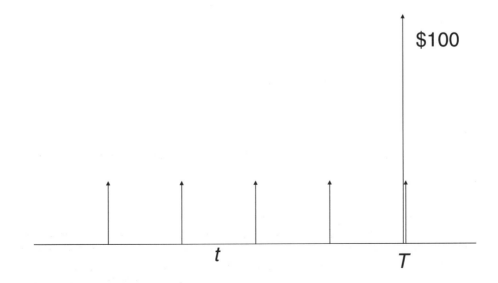

Figure 14.2 The coupon-bearing bond.

Source: Reuters Ltd.

TREASURY BONDS, NOTES AND BILLS

Wednesday, April 13, 2005

Explanatory Notes

Representative Over-the-Counter quotation based on transactions of $1 million or more. Treasury bond, note and bill quotes are as of mid-afternoon. Colons in bid-and-asked quotes represent 32nds; 101:01 means 101 1/32. Net changes in 32nds. n-Treasury note. i-Inflation-Indexed issue. Treasury bill quotes in hundredths, quoted on terms of a rate of discount. Days to maturity calculated from settlement date. All yields are to maturity and based on the asked quote. Latest 13-week and 26-week bills are boldfaced. For bonds callable prior to maturity, yields are computed to the earliest call date for issues quoted above par and to the maturity date for issues below par. *When issued.

Source: eSpeed/Cantor Fitzgerald

Government Bonds & Notes

RATE	MATURITY MO/YR	BID	ASKED	CHG	ASK YLD
1.625	Apr 05n	99:29	99:30	...	2.67
6.500	May 05n	100:10	100:11	...	2.41
6.750	May 05n	100:10	100:11	-1	2.48
12.000	May 05	100:25	100:26	-1	2.20
1.250	May 05n	99:26	99:27	1	2.45
1.125	Jun 05n	99:21	99:22	...	2.59
1.500	Jul 05n	99:18	99:19	...	2.81
6.500	Aug 05n	101:05	101:06	-1	2.89
10.750	Aug 05	102:20	102:21	-1	2.81
2.000	Aug 05n	99:19	99:20	...	2.95
1.625	Sep 05n	99:10	99:11	...	3.06
1.625	Oct 05n	99:05	99:06	...	3.14
5.750	Nov 05	101:13	101:14	-1	3.22
5.875	Nov 05n	101:16	101:17	...	3.21
1.875	Nov 05n	99:05	99:06	...	3.19
1.875	Dec 05n	99:00	99:01	...	3.24
1.875	Jan 06n	98:27	98:28	...	3.29
5.625	Feb 06n	101:29	101:30	1	3.26
9.375	Feb 06	105:01	105:02	...	3.19
1.625	Feb 06n	98:15	98:16	...	3.35
1.500	Mar 06n	98:06	98:07	...	3.38
2.250	Apr 06n	98:25	98:26	1	3.40
2.000	May 06n	98:15	98:16	1	3.40
4.625	May 06n	101:08	101:09	1	3.41
6.875	May 06n	103:20	103:21	1	3.40
2.500	May 06n	98:30	98:31	1	3.42
2.750	Jun 06n	99:04	99:05	1	3.45
7.000	Jul 06n	104:08	104:09	1	3.48
2.750	Jul 06n	99:01	99:02	1	3.48
2.375	Aug 06n	98:16	98:17	1	3.51
2.375	Aug 06n	98:14	98:15	2	3.52
2.500	Sep 06n	98:15	98:16	1	3.55
6.500	Oct 06n	104:08	104:09	1	3.55
2.500	Oct 06n	98:12	98:13	1	3.57
2.625	Nov 06n	98:16	98:17	2	3.57
3.500	Nov 06n	99:27	99:28	1	3.57
2.875	Nov 06n	99:27	99:28	2	3.58
3.000	Dec 06n	98:30	98:31	1	3.61
3.375	Jan 07i	105:00	105:00	-1	0.51
3.125	Jan 07n	99:03	99:04	2	3.62
2.250	Feb 07n	97:17	97:18	2	3.62
6.250	Feb 07	104:22	104:23	2	3.57
3.375	Feb 07n	99:16	99:17	2	3.63
3.750	Mar 07n	100:05	100:06	2	3.65
6.625	May 07n	105:27	105:28	1	3.66
4.375	May 07n	101:12	101:13	2	3.66
3.125	May 07n	98:28	98:29	2	3.67
2.750	Aug 07n	97:27	97:28	2	3.71
3.250	Aug 07n	98:30	98:31	2	3.71
6.125	Aug 07n	105:11	105:12	1	3.70
3.000	Nov 07n	98:05	98:06	2	3.74
3.625	Jan 08i	107:16	107:17	-3	0.85
3.000	Feb 08n	97:26	97:27	2	3.80
5.500	Feb 08	104:18	104:19	2	3.77
3.375	Feb 08n	98:27	98:28	3	3.80
2.625	May 08n	96:15	96:16	2	3.83
5.625	May 08n	105:04	105:05	2	3.83
3.250	Aug 08n	98:01	98:02	2	3.87
3.125	Sep 08n	97:18	97:19	3	3.88
3.125	Oct 08n	97:15	97:16	2	3.89
3.375	Nov 08n	98:08	98:09	2	3.89
4.750	Nov 08n	102:27	102:28	2	3.88
3.375	Dec 08n	98:06	98:07	3	3.90
3.250	Jan 09n	97:22	97:23	2	3.91
3.875	Jan 09i	110:06	110:07	-5	1.09
3.000	Feb 09n	96:22	96:23	2	3.93
2.625	Mar 09n	95:09	95:10	2	3.92
3.125	Apr 09n	97:00	97:00	2	3.94
3.875	May 09n	99:23	99:24	3	3.94
5.500	May 09n	105:28	105:29	2	3.92
4.000	Jun 09n	100:04	100:05	1	3.95
3.625	Jul 09n	98:20	98:21	2	3.97
3.500	Aug 09n	98:05	98:06	2	3.95
6.000	Aug 09n	108:00	108:01	2	3.96
3.500	Sep 09n	97:17	97:18	2	3.98
3.500	Oct 09n	97:14	97:15	3	3.99
3.500	Nov 09n	97:29	97:30	2	3.99
3.500	Dec 09n	97:25	97:26	2	4.01
3.625	Jan 10n	98:08	98:09	2	4.02
4.250	Jan 10i	113:28	113:29	-2	1.23
3.500	Feb 10n	97:23	97:24	2	4.01
6.500	Feb 10n	110:24	110:25	2	4.02
4.000	Mar 10n	99:27	99:28	2	4.02
0.875	Apr 10i	97:30	97:31	-2	1.30
10.000	May 10	100:19	100:20	-2	2.40
5.750	Aug 10n	108:00	108:00	1	4.06
12.750	Nov 10	105:14	105:15	-2	3.21
3.500	Jan 11i	111:28	111:29	-2	1.34
5.000	Feb 11n	104:19	104:20	2	4.10
13.875	May 11	111:00	111:01	-6	3.43
5.000	Aug 11n	104:22	104:23	1	4.14
14.000	Nov 11	115:30	115:31	1	3.55
3.375	Jan 12i	112:15	112:16	-2	1.42
4.875	Feb 12n	104:02	104:03	1	4.18
3.000	Jul 12i	110:14	110:15	-2	1.47
4.375	Aug 12n	101:02	101:03	...	4.23
4.000	Nov 12n	98:16	98:17	...	4.23
11.250	Nov 12	116:04	116:05	...	3.76
4.000	Feb 13n	97:12	97:13	-1	4.26
4.250	May 13n	95:28	95:29	-1	4.23
1.875	Jul 13i	102:05	102:06	-1	1.59
4.250	Aug 13n	99:17	99:17	-1	4.31
12.000	Aug 13	125:06	125:07	-2	3.87
4.250	Nov 13n	99:13	99:14	...	4.33
2.000	Jan 14i	102:25	102:26	-2	1.65
4.000	Feb 14n	97:14	97:15	-1	4.35
4.750	May 14n	102:26	102:27	-2	4.36
2.000	May 14	134:23	134:24	1	3.95
2.000	Jul 14i	102:22	102:23	...	1.68
4.250	Aug 14n	99:00	99:01	-2	4.37
12.500	Aug 14	133:18	133:19	...	3.99
11.750	Nov 14	132:07	132:08	1	3.98
4.250	Nov 14n	98:29	98:30	-1	4.39
1.625	Jan 15i	99:01	99:02	-6	1.73

RATE	MATURITY MO/YR	BID	ASKED	CHG	ASK YLD
4.000	Feb 15n	97:00	97:01	-2	4.37
11.250	Feb 15	154:10	154:11	-2	4.39
10.625	Aug 15	151:01	151:02	-3	4.42
9.875	Nov 15	145:13	145:14	-3	4.44
9.250	Feb 16	140:24	140:25	-2	4.46
7.250	May 16	123:23	123:24	-4	4.50
7.500	Nov 16	126:17	126:18	-4	4.53
8.750	May 17	138:21	138:22	-3	4.55
8.875	Aug 17	140:10	140:11	-3	4.56
9.125	May 18	144:06	144:07	-5	4.59
9.000	Nov 18	143:24	143:25	-4	4.62
8.875	Feb 19	142:27	142:28	-4	4.64
8.125	Aug 19	135:26	135:27	-6	4.67
8.500	Feb 20	140:14	140:15	-6	4.68
8.750	May 20	143:17	143:18	-8	4.69
8.750	Aug 20	144:00	144:00	-8	4.69
7.875	Feb 21	134:28	134:29	-6	4.72
8.125	May 21	137:30	137:31	-7	4.73
8.125	Aug 21	138:09	138:10	-6	4.73
8.000	Nov 21	137:06	137:06	-4	4.74
7.250	Aug 22	129:05	129:06	-5	4.76
7.625	Nov 22	133:26	133:27	-5	4.76
7.125	Feb 23	128:00	128:01	-7	4.77
6.250	Aug 23	117:23	117:24	-5	4.78
7.500	Nov 24	134:09	134:10	-7	4.78
2.375	Jan 25i	107:25	107:26	-8	1.90
7.625	Feb 25	136:03	136:04	-8	4.78
6.875	Aug 25	126:26	126:27	-8	4.79
6.000	Feb 26	115:20	115:21	-8	4.80
6.750	Aug 26	125:27	125:28	-8	4.80
6.500	Nov 26	122:21	122:22	-9	4.80
6.625	Feb 27	124:16	124:17	-9	4.80
6.375	Aug 27	121:13	121:14	-10	4.80
6.125	Nov 27	118:04	118:05	-10	4.80
3.625	Apr 28i	131:25	131:26	-10	1.91
5.500	Aug 28	109:26	109:27	-9	4.79
5.250	Nov 28	106:11	106:12	-9	4.80
5.250	Feb 29	106:14	106:15	-10	4.79
3.875	Apr 29i	137:27	137:28	-12	1.90
6.125	Aug 29	119:02	119:03	-10	4.79
6.250	May 30	121:14	121:15	-12	4.77
5.375	Feb 31	110:08	110:09	-11	4.68
3.375	Apr 32i	133:02	133:03	-8	1.82

Treasury Bills

MATURITY	DAYS TO MAT	BID	ASKED	CHG	ASK YLD
Apr 21 05	7	2.59	2.58	-0.02	2.62
Apr 28 05	14	2.55	2.54	0.01	2.58
May 05 05	21	2.57	2.56	0.01	2.60
May 12 05	28	2.58	2.57	0.02	2.61
May 19 05	35	2.55	2.54	-0.03	2.58
May 26 05	42	2.59	2.58	0.01	2.62
Jun 02 05	49	2.61	2.60	0.01	2.65
Jun 09 05	56	2.64	2.63	0.01	2.68
Jun 16 05	63	2.65	2.64	0.01	2.69
Jun 23 05	70	2.68	2.67	0.02	2.72
Jun 30 05	77	2.69	2.68	0.02	2.73
Jul 07 05	84	2.71	2.70	...	2.75
Jul 14 05	91	2.71	2.70	...	2.76
Jul 21 05	98	2.75	2.74	0.01	2.80
Jul 28 05	105	2.75	2.74	-0.02	2.80
Aug 04 05	112	2.82	2.81	...	2.87
Aug 11 05	119	2.87	2.86	0.01	2.93
Aug 18 05	126	2.89	2.88	0.01	2.95
Aug 25 05	133	2.93	2.92	-0.01	2.99
Sep 01 05	140	2.96	2.95	...	3.03
Sep 08 05	147	2.98	2.97	-0.01	3.05
Sep 15 05	154	2.99	2.98	-0.01	3.06
Sep 22 05	161	3.01	3.00	-0.01	3.08
Sep 29 05	168	2.99	2.98	-0.02	3.06
Oct 06 05	175	3.04	3.03	...	3.12
Oct 13 05	182	3.06	3.05	-0.01	3.14

CURRENCIES

Figure 14.3 *The Wall Street Journal Europe* of 14th April 2005 Treasury bonds, notes and bills.

14.2.4 Floating rate bonds

In its simplest form a **floating interest rate** is the amount that you get on your bank account. This amount varies from time to time, reflecting the state of the economy and in response to pressure from other banks for your business. This uncertainty about the interest rate you receive is compensated by the flexibility of your deposit, it can be withdrawn at any time. We often represent floating payments by wiggly lines as in Figure 14.4.

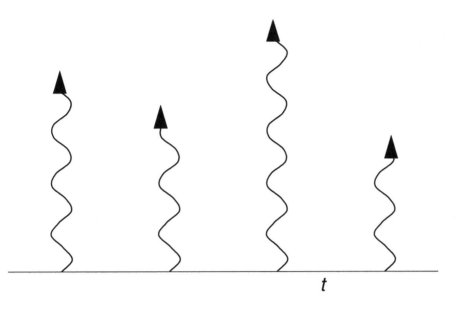

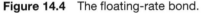

Figure 14.4 The floating-rate bond.

The most common measure of interest is **London Interbank Offer Rate** or **LIBOR**. LIBOR comes in various maturities, one month, three month, six month, etc., and is the rate of interest offered between Eurocurrency banks for fixed-term deposits.

Sometimes the coupon payment on a bond is not a prescribed dollar amount but depends on the level of some 'index,' measured at the time of the payment or before. Typically, we cannot know at the start of the contract what level this index will be at when the payment is made. We will see examples of such contracts in later chapters.

14.2.5 Forward rate agreements

A **forward rate agreement (FRA)** is an agreement between two parties that a prescribed interest rate will apply to a prescribed principal over some specified period in the future. The cashflows in this agreement are as follows: party A pays party B the principal at time T_1 and B pays A the principal plus agreed interest at time $T_2 > T_1$. The value of this exchange at the time the contract is entered into is generally not zero and so there will be a transfer of cash from one party to the other at the start date.

14.2.6 Repos

A **repo** is a repurchase agreement. It is an agreement to sell some security to another party and buy it back at a fixed date and for a fixed amount. The price at which the security is bought back is greater than the selling price and the difference implies an interest rate called the **repo rate**. The commonest repo is the overnight repo in which the agreement is renegotiated daily. If the repo agreement extends for 30 days it is called a **term repo**.

A **reverse repo** is the borrowing of a security for a short period at an agreed interest rate.

Repos can be used to lock in future interest rates. For example, buy a six-month Treasury bill today and repo it out for three months. There is no cash flow today since the bond has been paid for (money out) and then repoed (same amount in). In three months' time you will have to repurchase the bill at the agreed price, this is an outflow of cash. In six months you receive the principal. Money out in three months, money in in six months, for there to be no arbitrage the equivalent interest rate should be that currently prevailing between three and six months' time.

14.2.7 STRIPS

STRIPS stands for Separate Trading of Registered Interest and Principal of Securities. The coupons and principal of normal bonds are split up, creating artificial zero-coupon bonds of longer maturity than would otherwise be available.

14.2.8 Amortization

In all of the above products I have assumed that the principal remains fixed at its initial level. Sometimes this is not the case, the principal can **amortize** or decrease during the life of the contract. The principal is thus paid back gradually and interest is paid on the amount of the principal outstanding. Such amortization is arranged at the initiation of the contract and may be fixed, so that the rate of decrease of the principal is known beforehand, or can depend on the level of some index, if the index is high the principal amortizes faster, for example. We see an example of a complex amortizing structure in Chapter 18.

14.2.9 Call provision

Some bonds have a **call provision**. The issuer can call back the bond on certain dates or at certain periods for a prescribed, possibly time-dependent, amount. This lowers the value of the bond. The mathematical consequences of this are discussed in Chapter 16.

14.3 INTERNATIONAL BOND MARKETS

14.3.1 United States of America

In the US, bonds of maturity less than one year are called **bills** and are usually zero coupon. Bonds with maturity 2–10 years are called **notes**. They are coupon bearing with coupons every six months. Bonds with maturity greater than 10 years are called **bonds**. Again they are coupon bearing. In this book I tend to call all of these 'bonds,' merely specifying whether or not they have coupons.

Bonds traded in the United States foreign bond market but which are issued by non-US institutions are called **Yankee** bonds.

Since the beginning of 1997 the US government has also issued bonds linked to the rate of inflation.

14.3.2 United Kingdom

Bonds issued by the UK government are called **gilts**. Some of these bonds are callable, some are irredeemable, meaning that they are perpetual bonds having a coupon but no repayment of principal. The government also issues convertible bonds which may be converted into another bond issue, typically of longer maturity. Finally, there are index-linked bonds having the amount of the coupon and principal payments linked to a measure of inflation, the Retail Price Index (RPI).

14.3.3 Japan

Japanese government bonds (**JGB**s) come as short-term treasury bills, medium-term, long-term (10-year maturity) and super long-term (20-year maturity). The long- and super long-term bonds have coupons every six months. The short-term bonds have no coupons and the medium-term bonds can be either coupon-bearing or zero-coupon bonds.

Yen denominated bonds issued by non-Japanese institutions are called **Samurai** bonds.

14.4 **ACCRUED INTEREST**

The market price of bonds quoted in the newspapers are **clean prices**. That is, they are quoted without any **accrued interest**. The accrued interest is the amount of interest that has built up since the last coupon payment:

accrued interest = interest due in full period

$$\times \frac{\text{number of days since last coupon date}}{\text{number of days in period between coupon payments}}.$$

The actual payment is called the **dirty price** and is the sum of the quoted clean price and the accrued interest.

14.5 **DAY-COUNT CONVENTIONS**

Because of such matters as the accrual of interest between coupon dates there naturally arises the question of how to accrue interest over shorter periods. Interest is accrued between two dates according to the formula

$$\frac{\text{number of days between the two dates}}{\text{number of days in period}} \times \text{interest earned in reference period}.$$

There are three main ways of calculating the 'number of days' in the above expression.

- **Actual/Actual** Simply count the number of calendar days.

- **30/360** Assume there are 30 days in a month and 360 days in a year.

- **Actual/360** Each month has the right number of days but there are only 360 days in a year.

14.6 CONTINUOUSLY AND DISCRETELY COMPOUNDED INTEREST

To be able to compare fixed-income products we must decide on a convention for the measurement of interest rates. So far, we have used a continuously compounded rate, meaning that the present value of $1 paid at time T in the future is

$$e^{-rT} \times \$1$$

for some r. We have seen how this follows from the cash-in-the-bank or money market account equation

$$dM = rM\,dt.$$

This is the convention used in the options world.

Another common convention is to use the formula

$$\frac{1}{(1+r')^T} \times \$1,$$

for present value, where r' is some interest rate. This represents discretely compounded interest and assumes that interest is accumulated *annually* for T years. The formula is derived from calculating the present value from a single-period payment, and then compounding this for each year. This formula is commonly used for the simpler type of instruments such as coupon-bearing bonds. The two formulæ are identical, of course, when

$$r = \log(1 + r').$$

This gives the relationship between the continuously compounded interest rate r and the discrete version r'. What would the formula be if interest was discretely compounded twice per year?

In this book we tend to use the continuous definition of interest rates.

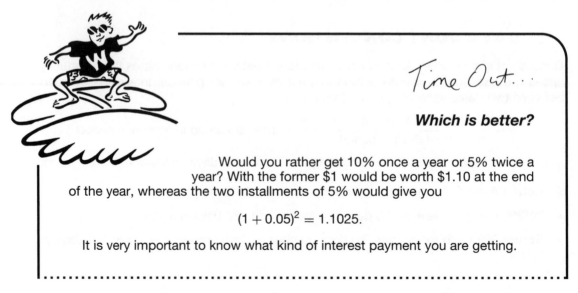

Time Out...

Which is better?

Would you rather get 10% once a year or 5% twice a year? With the former $1 would be worth $1.10 at the end of the year, whereas the two installments of 5% would give you

$$(1 + 0.05)^2 = 1.1025.$$

It is very important to know what kind of interest payment you are getting.

What interest rate paid continuously is equivalent to a one-off 10%? The answer is the r which satisfies

$$e^r = 1.1$$

i.e.

$$r = \log(1.1) = 0.09531018\ldots.$$

So, about 9.53% on an annualized basis. Remember this logarithm is the natural logarithm, also denoted (as in Excel) by $\ln(\cdot)$.

14.7 MEASURES OF YIELD

There is such a variety of fixed-income products, with different coupon structures, amortization, fixed and/or floating rates, that it is necessary to be able to consistently compare different products. Suppose you have to choose between a 10-year zero-coupon bond and a 20-year coupon-bearing bond. One has no income for 10 years but then gets a big lump sum, the other has a trickle of income but you have to wait much longer for the big amount.

One way to do this is through measures of how much each contract earns, there are several measures of this all coming under the name **yield**.

14.7.1 Current yield

The simplest measurement of how much a contract earns is the **current yield**. This measure is defined by

$$\text{current yield} = \frac{\text{annual \$ coupon income}}{\text{bond price}}.$$

For example, consider the 10-year bond that pays 2 cents every six months and $1 at maturity. This bond has a total income per annum of 4 cents. Suppose that the quoted market price of this bond is 88 cents. The current yield is simply

$$\frac{0.04}{0.88} = 4.5\%.$$

This measurement of the yield of the bond makes no allowance for the payment of the principal at maturity, nor for the time value of money if the coupon payment is reinvested, nor for any capital gain or loss that may be made if the bond is sold before maturity. It is a relatively unsophisticated measure, concentrating very much on short-term properties of the bond.

14.7.2 The yield to maturity (YTM) or internal rate of return (IRR)

Suppose that we have a zero-coupon bond maturing at time T when it pays one dollar. At time t it has a value $Z(t; T)$. Applying a constant rate of return of y between t and T, then one dollar received at time T has a present value of $Z(t; T)$ at time t, where

$$Z(t; T) = e^{-y(T-t)}.$$

It follows that

$$y = -\frac{\log Z}{T - t}.$$

A VERY BASIC
AND USEFUL
DEFINITION

Let us generalize this. Suppose that we have a coupon-bearing bond. Discount all coupons and the principal to the present by using some interest rate y. The present value of the bond, at time t, is then

$$V = Pe^{-y(T-t)} + \sum_{i=1}^{N} C_i e^{-y(t_i-t)}, \qquad (14.1)$$

where P is the principal, N the number of coupons, C_i the coupon paid on date t_i.

If the bond is a traded security then we know the price at which the bond can be bought. If this is the case then we can calculate the **yield to maturity** or **internal rate of return** as the value y that we must put into Equation (14.1) to make V equal to the traded price of the bond. This calculation must be performed by some trial and error/iterative procedure. For example, in the bond in Table 14.1 we have a principal of $1 paid in five years and coupons of three cents (three percent) paid every six months.

Suppose that the market value of this bond is 96 cents. We ask 'What is the internal rate of return we must use to give these cash flows a total present value of 96 cents?' This value is the yield to maturity. In the fourth column in this table is the present value (PV) of each of the cashflows using a rate of 6.8406%: since the sum of these present values is 96 cents the YTM or IRR is 6.8406%.

This yield to maturity is a valid measure of the return on a bond if we intend to hold it to maturity.

Table 14.1 An example of a coupon-bearing bond.

Time	Coupon	Principal repayment	PV (discounting at 6.8406%)
0			0
0.5	.03		0.0290
1.0	.03		0.0280
1.5	.03		0.0270
2.0	.03		0.0262
2.5	.03		0.0253
3.0	.03		0.0244
3.5	.03		0.0236
4.0	.03		0.0228
4.5	.03		0.0220
5.0	.03	1.00	0.7316
		Total	0.9600

To calculate the yield to maturity of a portfolio of bonds simply treat all the cashflows as if they were from the one bond and calculate the value of the whole portfolio by adding up the market values of the component bonds.

14.8 THE YIELD CURVE

The plot of yield to maturity against time to maturity is called the **yield curve**. For the moment assume that this has been calculated from zero-coupon bonds and that these bonds have been issued by a perfectly creditworthy source.

If the bonds have coupons then the calculation of the yield curve is more complicated and the 'forward curve,' described below, is a better measure of the interest rate pertaining at some time in the future. Figure 14.5 shows the yield curve for US Treasuries as it was on 9th September 1999.

Time Out...

Discount factors

Once you've calculated the yield curve you can use the results to work out the present value of any fixed-rate cashflows. All you have to do is work out the discount factor for each cashflow and multiply the cashflow by that amount. Typically, you'll find yourself in the situation of having a cashflow on a certain date but no yield associated with that maturity. Then you'll have to interpolate between the two yields either side to get an estimate for the required maturity.

14.9 PRICE/YIELD RELATIONSHIP

From Equation (14.1) we can easily see that the relationship between the price of a bond and its yield is of the form shown in Figure 14.6 (assuming that all cash flows are positive). On this figure is marked the current market price and the current yield to maturity.

Since we are often interested in the sensitivity of instruments to the movement of certain underlying factors it is natural to ask how does the price of a bond vary with the yield, or vice versa. To a first approximation this variation can be quantified by a measure called the duration.

Figure 14.7 shows the price/yield relationship for a specific five-year US Treasury.

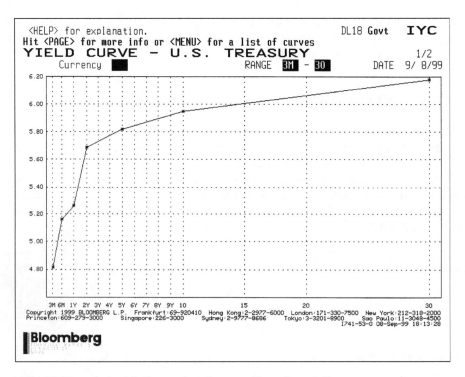

Figure 14.5 Yield curve for US Treasuries. Source: Bloomberg L.P.

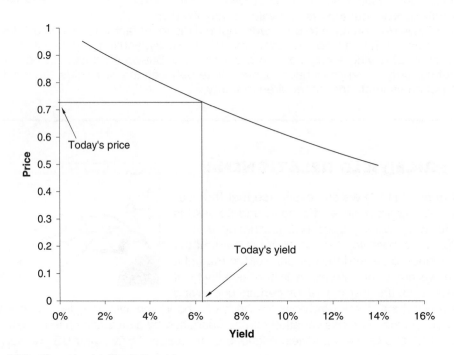

Figure 14.6 The price/yield relationship.

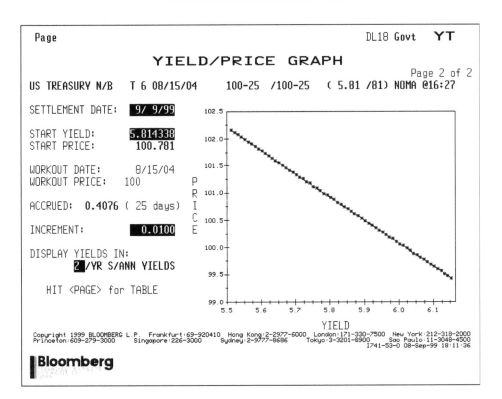

Page | DL18 Govt **YT**

YIELD/PRICE GRAPH

Page 2 of 2

US TREASURY N/B   T 6 08/15/04   100-25 /100-25   (5.81 /81) NOMA @16:27

SETTLEMENT DATE: 9/ 9/99

START YIELD: 5.814338
START PRICE: 100.781

WORKOUT DATE: 8/15/04
WORKOUT PRICE: 100

ACCRUED: 0.4076 (25 days)

INCREMENT: 0.0100

DISPLAY YIELDS IN:
     2 /YR S/ANN YIELDS

   HIT <PAGE> for TABLE

Copyright 1999 BLOOMBERG L.P. Frankfurt:69-920410 Hong Kong:2-2977-6000 London:171-330-7500 New York:212-318-2000
Princeton:609-279-3000   Singapore:226-3000   Sydney:2-9777-8686   Tokyo:3-3201-8900   Sao Paulo:11-3048-4500
                                                                        I741-53-0 08-Sep-99 18:11:36

Bloomberg

Figure 14.7 Bloomberg's price/yield graph. Source: Bloomberg L.P.

14.10 **DURATION**

From Equation (14.1) we find that

$$\frac{dV}{dy} = -(T-t)Pe^{-y(T-t)} - \sum_{i=1}^{N} C_i(t_i - t)e^{-y(t_i - t)}.$$

DURATION IS A SENSITIVITY TO A YIELD, A BIT LIKE DELTA

This is the slope of the price/yield curve. The quantity

$$-\frac{1}{V}\frac{dV}{dy}$$

is called the **Macaulay duration**. (The **modified duration** is similar but uses the discretely compounded rate.) In the expression for the duration the time of each coupon payment is weighted by its present value. The higher the value of the present value of the coupon the more it contributes to the duration. Also, since y is measured in units of inverse time, the units of the duration are time. The duration is a measure of the average life of the bond. It is easily shown that the Macaulay duration for a zero-coupon bond is the same as its maturity.

Let's take a look at the idea of average time. Suppose we asked what zero-coupon bond is our (coupon-bearing) bond equivalent to? That is, what maturity would an 'equivalent' bond have? Take the actual bond's value and equate it to a zero-coupon bond, having

All of this is implemented on the CD

the same yield but an unknown maturity (and unknown quantity!):

$$V = Pe^{-y(T-t)} + \sum_{i=1}^{N} C_i e^{-y(t_i-t)} = X\,e^{-y(\overline{T}-t)}.$$

Differentiate both sides with respect to y:

$$\frac{dV}{dy} = -(T-t)Pe^{-y(T-t)} - \sum_{i=1}^{N} C_i(t_i-t)e^{-y(t_i-t)} = -X\,(\overline{T}-t)\,e^{-y(\overline{T}-t)}.$$

Finally, divide both sides by $-V$:

$$-\frac{1}{V}\frac{dV}{dy} = \cdots = \overline{T} - t.$$

Hence the statement about the bond's *average* life, or effective maturity.

For small movements in the yield, the duration gives a good measure of the change in value with a change in the yield. For larger movements we need to look at higher order terms in the Taylor series expansion of $V(y)$.

One of the most common uses of the duration is in plots of yield versus duration for a variety of instruments. An example is shown in Figure 14.8. Look at the bond marked 'CPU.' This bond has a coupon of 4.75% paid twice per year, callable from June 1998 and maturing in June 2000. We can use this plot to group together instruments with the same or similar durations and make comparisons between their yields. Two bonds having the same duration but with one bond having a higher yield might be suggestive of value for money in the higher-yielding bond, or of credit risk issues. However, such indicators of relative value must be used with care. It is possible for two bonds to have vastly different cashflow profiles yet have the same duration; one may have a maturity of 30 years but an

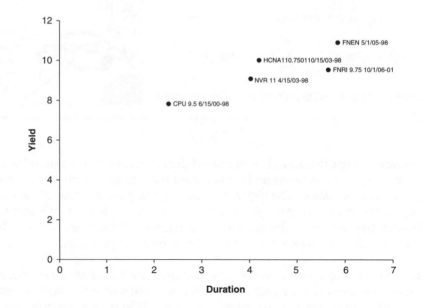

Figure 14.8 Yield versus duration: measuring the relative value of bonds.

average life and hence a duration of seven years, whereas another may be a seven-year zero-coupon bond. Clearly, the former has 23 years more risk than the latter.

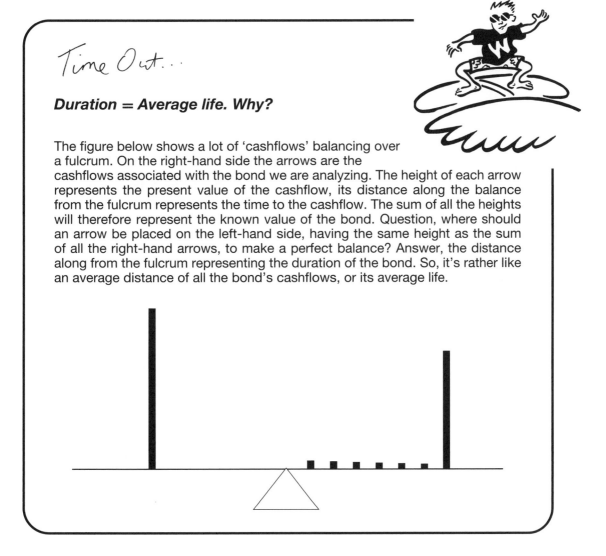

Time Out...

Duration = Average life. Why?

The figure below shows a lot of 'cashflows' balancing over a fulcrum. On the right-hand side the arrows are the cashflows associated with the bond we are analyzing. The height of each arrow represents the present value of the cashflow, its distance along the balance from the fulcrum represents the time to the cashflow. The sum of all the heights will therefore represent the known value of the bond. Question, where should an arrow be placed on the left-hand side, having the same height as the sum of all the right-hand arrows, to make a perfect balance? Answer, the distance along from the fulcrum representing the duration of the bond. So, it's rather like an average distance of all the bond's cashflows, or its average life.

14.11 CONVEXITY

The Taylor series expansion of V gives

$$\frac{dV}{V} = \frac{1}{V}\frac{dV}{dy}\delta y + \frac{1}{2V}\frac{d^2V}{dy^2}(\delta y)^2 + \ldots,$$

where δy is a change in yield. For very small movements in the yield, the change in the price of a bond

CONVEXITY IS LIKE GAMMA, A SECOND-ORDER EFFECT

can be measured by the duration. For larger movements we must take account of the curvature in the price/yield relationship.

The **dollar convexity** is defined as

$$\frac{d^2V}{dy^2} = (T-t)^2Pe^{-y(T-t)} + \sum_{i=1}^{N} C_i(t_i - t)^2 e^{-y(t_i-t)}.$$

and the **convexity** is

$$\frac{1}{V}\frac{d^2V}{dy^2}.$$

To see how these can be used, examine Figure 14.9.

In this figure we see the price/yield relationship for two bonds having the same value and duration when the yield is around 8%, but then they have different convexities. Bond A has a greater convexity than bond B. This figure suggests that bond A is better value than B because a small change in the yields results in a higher value for A. When we develop a consistent theory for pricing bonds when interest rates are stochastic we will see how the absence of arbitrage will lead to relationships between such quantities as yield, duration and convexity, not unlike the Black–Scholes equation.

The calculation of yield to maturity, duration and convexity are shown in the simple spreadsheet in Figure 14.10. Inputs are in the gray boxes.

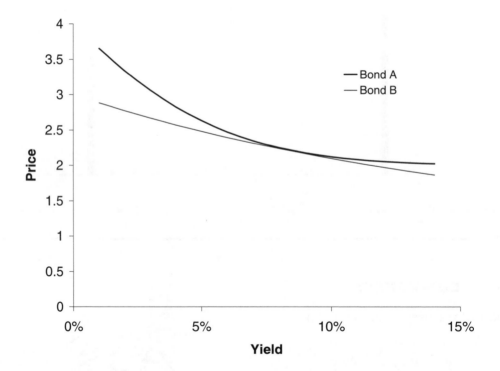

Figure 14.9 Two bonds with the same price and duration but different convexities.

	A	B	C	D	E	F	G	H	I	J	K
1					Date	Coupon	Principal	PVs	Time wtd	Time^2 wtd	
2					0						
3		YTM	4.95%		0.5	2%		0.0195	0.0098	0.0049	
4		Mkt price	0.921		1	2%		0.0190	0.0190	0.0190	
5		Th. Price	0.921		1.5	2%		0.0186	0.0279	0.0418	
6		Error	1.4E-08		2	2%		0.0181	0.0362	0.0725	
7		Duration	8.2544		2.5	2%		0.0177	0.0442	0.1104	
8		Convexity	76.8728		3	2%		0.0172	0.0517	0.1551	
9					3.5	2%		0.0168	0.0589	0.2060	
10		= SUM(H3:H22)			4	2%		0.0164	0.0656	0.2625	
11					4.5	2%		0.0160	0.0720	0.3241	
12					5	2%		0.0156	0.0781	0.3903	
13					5.5	2%		0.0152	0.0838	0.4607	
14					6	2%		0.0149	0.0892	0.5349	
15					6.5	2%		0.0145	0.0942	0.6124	
16		= SUM(I3:I22)/C5			7	2%		0.0141	0.0990	0.6929	
17					7.5	2%		0.0138	0.1035	0.7760	
18					8	2%		0.0135	0.1077	0.8613	
19					8.5	2%		0.0131	0.1116	0.9485	
20		= SUM(J3:J22)/C5			9	2%		0.0128	0.1153	1.0374	
21					9.5	2%		0.0125	0.1187	1.1276	
22					10	2%	1	0.6216	6.2161	62.1614	
23											
24		= F20*EXP(-E20*$C$3)									
25											
26		= (G22+F22)*EXP(-E22*$C$3)					= E20*H20				
27											
28									= E20*I20		

= C4-C5

Goal Seek

Set cell: $C$6
To value: 0
By changing cell: $C$3

OK   Cancel

Figure 14.10 A spreadsheet showing the calculation of yield, duration and convexity.

14.12 **AN EXAMPLE**

Figure 14.11 shows the yield analysis screen from Bloomberg. The yield, duration and convexity have been calculated for a specific US Treasury. Figures 14.12 and 14.13 show time series of the price and yield respectively.

FOR SIMPLE INSTRUMENTS IT'S EASY TO CALCULATE YIELD, DURATION AND CONVEXITY

14.13 **HEDGING**

In measuring and using yields to maturity, it must be remembered that the yield is the rate of discounting that makes the present value of a bond the same as its market value. A yield is thus identified with each individual instrument. It is perfectly possible for the yield on one instrument to rise while another falls, especially if they have significantly different

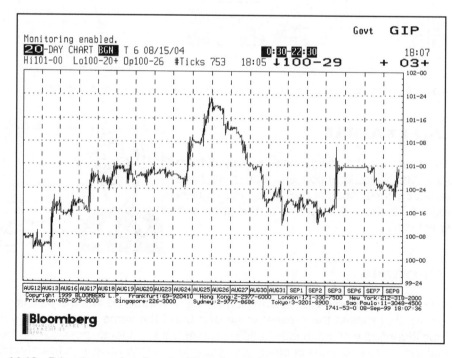

```
YA                                                    DL18 Govt  YA
Bond Matures on a SUNDAY
                      YIELD ANALYSIS          CUSIP    CT05    3
US TREASURY N/B   T 6 08/15/04   100-25 /100-25 ( 5.81 /81) NOMA @16:27
PRICE 100-25              SETTLEMENT DATE  9/ 9/1999
  YIELD              MATURITY     CASHFLOW ANALYSIS
  CALCULATIONS       8/15/2004    To 8/15/2004WORKOUT  1000M FACE
STREET CONVENTION          5.814     PAYMENT INVOICE
TREASURY CONVENTION        5.813   PRINCIPAL[RND(Y/N)N]  1007812.50
TRUE YIELD                 5.811    25 DAYS ACCRUED INT     4076.09
EQUIVALENT 1/YEAR COMPOUND 5.899   TOTAL                 1011888.59
JAPANESE YIELD (SIMPLE)    5.796           INCOME
PROCEEDS/MMKT EQUIVALENT           REDEMPTION VALUE      1000000.00
                                   COUPON PAYMENT         300000.00
REPO EQUIVALENT            5.801   INTEREST @ 5.814%       42449.69
EFFECTIVE @ 5.814 RATE(%)  5.814   TOTAL                 1342449.69
TAXED: INC 39.60% CG 28.00% 3.512*        RETURN
*ISSUE PRICE = 99.940.  BOND PURCHASED WITH PREMIUM.*
 SENSITIVITY ANALYSIS              GROSS PROFIT           330561.10
DURATION(YEARS)            4.328   RETURN                     5.814
ADJ/MOD DURATION           4.206
RISK                       4.256    FURTHER ANALYSIS
CONVEXITY                  0.212   HIT 1 <GO> COST OF CARRY
DOLLAR VALUE OF A  0.01    0.04256 HIT 2 <GO> PRICE/YIELD TABLE
YIELD VALUE OF A   0 1/32  0.00734 HIT 3 <GO> TOTAL RETURN
Copyright 1999 BLOOMBERG L.P. Frankfurt:69-920410  Hong Kong:2-2977-6000  London:171-330-7500  New York:212-318-2000
Princeton:609-279-3000  Singapore:226-3000  Sydney:2-9777-8686  Tokyo:3-3201-8900  Sao Paulo:11-3048-4500
                                                                I741-53-0 08-Sep-99 18:05:35
Bloomberg
```

Figure 14.11   Yield analysis. Source: Bloomberg L.P.

```
                                               Govt  GIP
Monitoring enabled.
20-DAY CHART BGN  T 6 08/15/04      0:30-22:30           18:07
Hi101-00  Lo100-20+ Op100-26  #Ticks 753   18:05 ↓100-29   + 03+
                                                          102-00
                                                          101-24
                                                          101-16
                                                          101-08
                                                          101-00
                                                          100-24
                                                          100-16
                                                          100-08
                                                          100-00
                                                          99-24
AUG12 AUG13 AUG16 AUG17 AUG18 AUG19 AUG20 AUG23 AUG24 AUG25 AUG26 AUG27 AUG30 AUG31 SEP1 SEP2 SEP3 SEP6 SEP7 SEP8
Copyright 1999 BLOOMBERG L.P. Frankfurt:69-920410  Hong Kong:2-2977-6000  London:171-330-7500  New York:212-318-2000
Princeton:609-279-3000  Singapore:226-3000  Sydney:2-9777-8686  Tokyo:3-3201-8900  Sao Paulo:11-3048-4500
                                                                I741-53-0 08-Sep-99 18:07:36
Bloomberg
```

Figure 14.12   Price time series. Source: Bloomberg L.P.

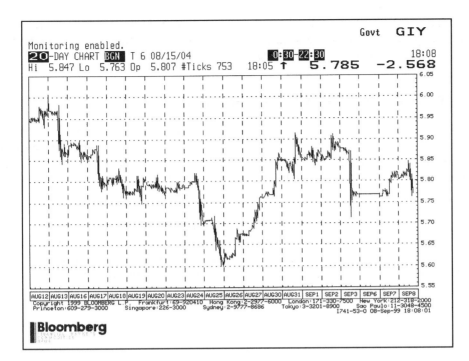

Figure 14.13 Yield time series. Source: Bloomberg L.P.

maturities or durations. Nevertheless, one often wants to hedge movements in one bond with movements in another. This is commonly achieved by making one big assumption about the relative movements of yields on the two bonds. Bond A has a yield of y_A, bond B has a yield of y_B, they have different maturities and durations but we will assume that a move of x% in A's yield is accompanied by a move of x% in B's yield. This is the assumption of **parallel shifts** in the yield curve. If this is the case, then if we hold A bonds and B bonds in the inverse ratio of their durations (with one long position and one short) we will be leading-order hedged:

$$\Pi = V_A(y_A) - \Delta V_B(y_B),$$

with the obvious notation for the value and yield of the two bonds. The change in the value of this portfolio is

$$\delta\Pi = \frac{\partial V_A}{\partial y_A}x - \Delta\frac{\partial V_B}{\partial y_B}x + \text{higher-order terms.}$$

Choose

$$\Delta = \frac{\partial V_A}{\partial y_A} \Big/ \frac{\partial V_B}{\partial y_B}$$

to eliminate the leading-order risk. The higher-order terms depend on the convexity of the two instruments.

Of course, this is a simplification of the real situation; there may be little relationship between the yields on the two instruments, especially if the cash flows are significantly different. In this case there may be twisting or arching of the yield curve.

14.14　**TIME-DEPENDENT INTEREST RATE**

In this section we examine bond pricing when we have an interest rate that is a known function of time. The interest rate we consider will be what is known as a **short-term interest rate** or **spot interest rate** $r(t)$. This means that the rate $r(t)$ is to apply at time t: interest is compounded at this rate at each moment in time but *this rate may change*; generally we assume it to be time dependent.

If the spot interest rate $r(t)$ is a known function of time, then the bond price is also a function of time only: $V = V(t)$. (The bond price is, of course, also a function of maturity date T, but I suppress that dependence except when it is important.) We begin with a zero-coupon bond example. Because we receive 1 at time $t = T$ we know that $V(T) = 1$. I now derive an equation for the value of the bond at a time before maturity, $t < T$.

Suppose we hold one bond. The change in the value of that bond in a time-step dt (from t to $t + dt$) is

$$\frac{dV}{dt}\, dt.$$

Arbitrage considerations again lead us to equate this with the return from a bank deposit receiving interest at a rate $r(t)$:

$$\frac{dV}{dt} = r(t)V.$$

The solution of this equation is

$$V(t; T) = e^{-\int_t^T r(\tau)d\tau}. \tag{14.2}$$

Now let's introduce coupon payments. If during the period t to $t + dt$ we have received a coupon payment of $K(t)\, dt$, which may be either in the form of continuous or discrete payments or a combination, our holdings including cash change by an amount

$$\left(\frac{dV}{dt} + K(t)\right) dt.$$

Again setting this equal to the risk-free rate $r(T)$ we conclude that

$$\frac{dV}{dt} + K(t) = r(t)V. \tag{14.3}$$

The solution of this ordinary differential equation is easily found to be, dropping the parameter T,

$$V(t) = e^{-\int_t^T r(\tau)d\tau} \left(1 + \int_t^T K(t')e^{\int_{t'}^T r(\tau)d\tau}\, dt'\right); \tag{14.4}$$

the arbitrary constant of integration has been chosen to ensure that $V(T) = 1$.

14.15 **DISCRETELY PAID COUPONS**

Equation (14.4) allows for the payment of a coupon. But what if the coupon is paid discretely, as it is in practice, for example, every six months, say? We can arrive at this result by a financial argument that will be useful later. Since the holder of the bond receives a coupon, call it K_c, at time t_c there must be a jump in the value of the bond across the coupon date. That is, the values before and after this date differ by K_c:

$$V(t_c^-) = V(t_c^+) + K_c.$$

This will be recognized as a jump condition. This time the realized bond price is *not* continuous. After all, there is a discrete payment at the coupon date. This jump condition will still apply when we come to consider stochastic interest rates.

Having built up a simple framework in which interest rates are time dependent I now show how to derive information about these rates from the market prices of bonds.

14.16 **FORWARD RATES AND BOOTSTRAPPING**

FORWARD RATES ARE SUPPOSED TO TELL US SOMETHING ABOUT THE FUTURE

The main problem with the use of yield to maturity as a measure of interest rates is that it is not consistent across instruments. One five-year bond may have a different yield from another five-year bond if they have different coupon structures. It is therefore difficult to say that there is a single interest rate associated with a maturity.

One way of overcoming this problem is to use **forward rates**.

Forward rates are interest rates that are assumed to apply over given periods *in the future* for *all* instruments. This contrasts with yields which are assumed to apply up to maturity, with a different yield for each bond.

Let us suppose that we are in a perfect world in which we have a continuous distribution of zero-coupon bonds with all maturities T. Call the prices of these at time t $Z(t; T)$. Note the use of Z for zero coupon.

The **implied forward rate** is the curve of a time-dependent spot interest rate that is consistent with the market price of instruments. If this rate is $r(\tau)$ at time τ then it satisfies

$$Z(t; T) = e^{-\int_t^T r(\tau)d\tau}.$$

On rearranging and differentiating this gives

$$r(T) = -\frac{\partial}{\partial T}(\log Z(t; T)).$$

This is the forward rate for time T as it stands today, time t. Tomorrow the whole curve (the dependence of r on the future) may change. For that reason we usually denote the forward rate at time t applying at time T in the future as $F(t; T)$ where

$$F(t; T) = -\frac{\partial}{\partial T}(\log Z(t; T)).$$

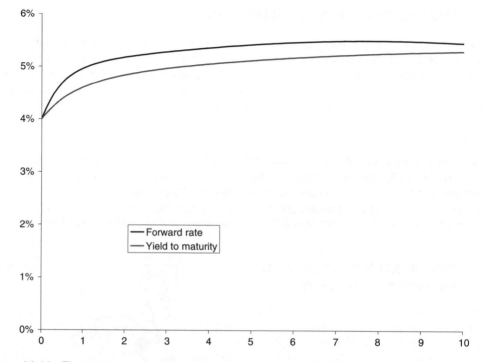

Figure 14.14 The yields and the forward rates.

Writing this in terms of yields $y(t; T)$ we have

$$Z(t; T) = e^{-y(t;T)(T-t)}$$

and so

$$F(t; T) = y(t; T) + \frac{\partial y}{\partial T}.$$

This is the relationship between yields and forward rates when everything is nicely differentiable. See Figure 14.14.

14.16.1 Discrete data

In the less-than-perfect real world we must do with only a discrete set of data points. We continue to assume that we have zero-coupon bonds but now we will only have a discrete set of them. We can still find an implied forward rate curve as follows.

Rank the bonds according to maturity, with the shortest maturity first. The market prices of the bonds will be denoted by Z_i^M where i is the position of the bond in the ranking.

Using only the first bond, ask the question: 'What interest rate is implied by the market price of the bond?' The answer is given by y_1, the solution of

$$Z_1^M = e^{-y_1(T_1-t)},$$

i.e.

$$y_1 = -\frac{\log(Z_1^M)}{T_1 - t}.$$

This rate will be the rate that we use for discounting between the present and the maturity date T_1 of the first bond. And it will be applied to *all* instruments whenever we want to discount over this period.

Now move on to the second bond having maturity date T_2. We know the rate to apply between now and time T_1, but at what interest rate must we discount between dates T_1 and T_2 to match the theoretical and market prices of the second bond? The answer is y_2 which solves the equation

$$Z_2^M = e^{-y_1(T_1-t)}e^{-y_2(T_2-T_1)},$$

i.e.

$$y_2 = -\frac{\log\left(Z_2^M/Z_1^M\right)}{T_2 - T_1}.$$

By this method of **bootstrapping** we can build up the forward rate curve. Note how the forward rates are applied between two dates, for which period we have assumed they are constant. Figure 14.21 gives an example.

This method can easily be extended to accommodate coupon-bearing bonds. Again rank the bonds by their maturities, but now we have the added complexity that we may only have one market value to represent the sum of several cashflows. Thus one often has to make some assumptions to get the right number of equations for the number of unknowns. See Figures 14.15–14.20.

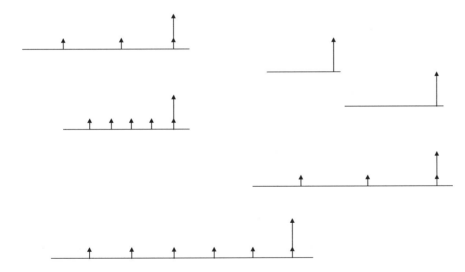

Figure 14.15 The universe of bonds.

14.16.2 On a spreadsheet

Given the market price of zero-coupon bonds it is very easy to calculate yields and forward rates, as shown in the spreadsheet (Figure 14.21). Inputs are in the gray boxes.

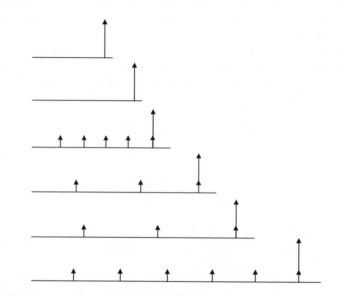

Figure 14.16 The universe of bonds, ranked in order of maturity.

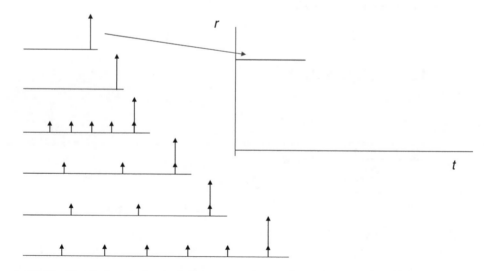

Figure 14.17 The first-maturing bond gives us a forward rate from now until its maturity.

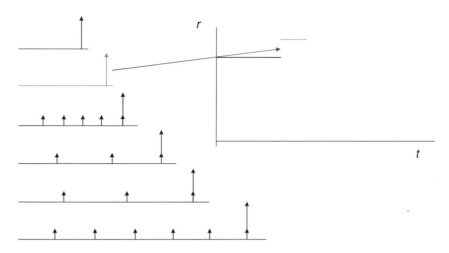

Figure 14.18 The second-maturing bond gives us a forward rate from maturity of the previous bond until its own maturity.

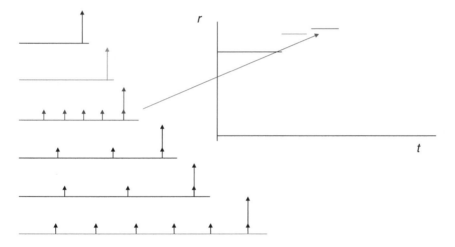

Figure 14.19 The third-maturing bond gives us a forward rate from maturity of the previous bond until its own maturity.

The yields and forward rates for this data are shown in Figures 14.22 and 14.23. Note that in each case the yield begins at zero maturity and extends up to the maturity of each bond. The forward rates pick up where the last forward rates left off.

There are far more swaps of different maturities than there are bonds, so that in practice swaps are used to build up the forward rates by bootstrapping. Fortunately, there is a simple decomposition of swaps prices into the prices of zero-coupon bonds so that bootstrapping is still relatively straightforward. Swaps are discussed in more detail in Chapter 15.

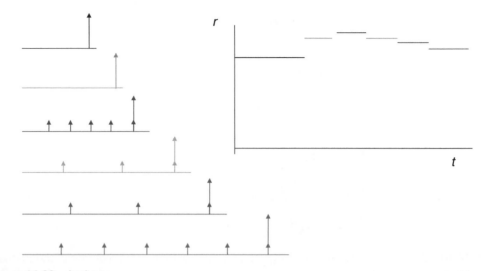

Figure 14.20 And so on.

	A	B	C	D	E
1	**Time to**	**Market**	**Yield to**	**Forward**	
2	**maturity**	**price z-c b**	**maturity**	**rate**	
3	0.25	0.9809	7.71%	7.71%	
4	0.5	0.9612	7.91%	8.12%	
5	1	0.9194	8.40%	8.89%	
6	2	0.8436	8.50%	8.60%	
7	3	0.7772	8.40%	8.20%	
8	5	0.644	8.80%	9.40%	
9	7	0.5288	9.10%	9.85%	
10	10	0.3985	9.20%	9.43%	
11					
12	= -LN(B10)/ A10				
13					
14					
15			= (C10*A10-C9*A9)/ (A10-A9)		
16					

Figure 14.21 A spreadsheet showing the calculation of yields and forward rates from zero-coupon bonds.

14.17 **INTERPOLATION**

We have explicitly assumed in the previous section that the forward rates are piecewise constant, jumping from one value to the next across the maturity of each bond. Other methods of 'interpolation' are also possible. For example, the forward rate curve could be made continuous, with piecewise constant gradient. Some people like to use cubic splines. The correct way of 'joining the dots' (for there are only a finite number of market prices) has been the subject of much debate. If you want to know what rate to apply to a two-and-a-half-year cashflow and the nearest bonds are at two and three years then you

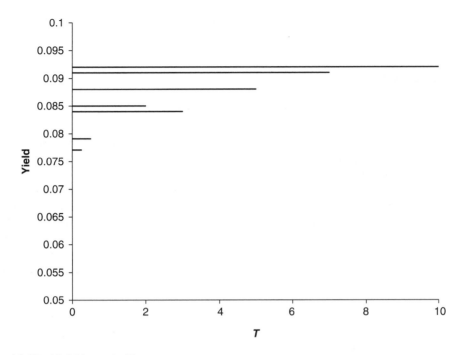

Figure 14.22 Yield to maturities.

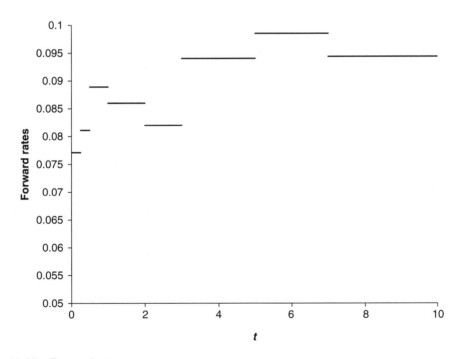

Figure 14.23 Forward rates.

will have to make some assumptions; there is no 'correct' value. Perhaps the best that can be done is to bound the rate.

14.18 SUMMARY

There are good and bad points about the interest rate model of this chapter. First, I mention the advantages.

Compare the simplicity of the mathematics in this chapter with that in previous chapters on option pricing. Clearly there is benefit in having models for which the analysis is so simple. Computation of many values and hedging can be performed virtually instantaneously on even slow computers. Moreover, it may be completely unnecessary to have a more complex model. For example, if we want to compare simple cashflows it may be possible to directly value one bond by summing other bonds, if their cashflows can be made to match. Such a situation, although uncommon, is market-independent modeling. Even if exact cashflow matches are not possible, there may be sufficiently close agreement for the differences to be estimated or at least bounded; large errors are easily avoided.

On the other hand, it is common experience that interest rates are unpredictable, random, and for complex products the movement of rates is the most important factor in their pricing. To assume that interest rates follow forward rates would be financial suicide in such cases. Think back to Jensen's inequality. There is therefore a need for models more closely related to the stochastic models we have seen in earlier chapters.

In this chapter we saw simple yet powerful ways to analyze simple fixed-income contracts. These methods are used very frequently in practice, far more frequently than the complex methods we later discuss for the pricing of interest rate derivatives. The assumptions underlying the techniques, such as deterministic forward rates, are only relevant to simple contracts. As we have seen in the options world, more complex products with non-linear payoffs require a model that incorporates the stochastic nature of variables. Stochastic interest rates will be the subject of later chapters.

FURTHER READING

- The work of Macaulay (1938) on duration wasn't used much prior to the 1960s, but now it is considered fundamental to fixed-income analysis.

- See Fabozzi (1996) for a discussion of yield, duration and convexity in greater detail. He explains how the ideas are extended to more complicated instruments.

- The argument about how to join the yield curve dots is as meaningless as the argument between the Little-Endians and Big-Endians of Swift (1726).

- See Walsh (2003) for issues concerning curve building.

EXERCISES

1. A coupon bond pays out 3% every year, with a principal of $1 and a maturity of five years. Decompose the coupon bond into a set of zero-coupon bonds.

2. Construct a spreadsheet to examine how $1 grows when it is invested at a continuously compounded rate of 7%. Redo the calculation for a discretely compounded rate of 7%, paid once per annum. Which rate is more profitable?

3. A zero-coupon bond has a principal of $100 and matures in four years. The market price for the bond is $72. Calculate the yield to maturity, duration and convexity for the bond.

4. A coupon bond pays out 2% every year on a principal of $100. The bond matures in six years and has a market value of $92. Calculate the yield to maturity, duration and convexity for the bond.

5. Zero-coupon bonds are available with a principal of $1 and the following maturities:

   (a) 1 year (market price $0.93),
   (b) 2 years (market price $0.82),
   (c) 3 years (market price $0.74).

   Calculate the yield to maturities for the three bonds. Use a bootstrapping method to work out the forward rates that apply between 1–2 years and 2–3 years.

6. What assumption do we make when we duration hedge? Is this a reasonable assumption to make?

7. Solve the equation

$$\frac{dV}{dt} + K(t) = r(t)V,$$

PTE 6 Year Non-Call 2 Year Fixed Rate Step-up Note

Aggregate Principal Amount	PTE 10,000,000,000
Trade Date	4 November 1997
Issue Date	25 November 1997
Settlement Date	25 November 1997
Maturity Date	25 November 2003
Issue Price	100%
Coupon	Years 1–2: 5.75%
	Years 3–6: 6.25%
Issuer Optional Redemption	The issuer has the right, but not the obligation, to redeem the Notes at 100% of Nominal, in whole but not in part, on 25 November 1999 with 10 Business Days Prior notice.
Payment Frequency	Annual
Daycount Convention	30/360
Governing Law	English

This indicative termsheet is neither an offer to buy or sell securities or an OTC derivative product which includes options, swaps, forwards and structured notes having similar features to OTC derivative transactions, nor a solicitation to buy or sell securities or an OTC derivative product. The proposal contained in the foregoing is not a complete description of the terms of a particular transaction and is subject to change without limitation.

Figure 14.24   A PTE six-year non-call two-year fixed rate step-up note.

with final data $V(T) = 1$. This is the value of a coupon bond when there is a *known* interest rate, $r(t)$. What must we do if interest rates are not known in advance?

8. Figure 14.24 is a term sheet for a step-up note paying a fixed rate that changes during the life of the contract. Plot the price/yield curve for this product today, ignoring the call feature. What effect will the call feature have on the price of this contract?

CHAPTER 15
swaps

The aim of this Chapter...

...is to introduce the reader to the important world of swaps, one of the most important and fundamental financial contracts. We will also be seeing the simple relationship between swaps and bonds.

In this Chapter...

- the specifications of basic interest rate swap contracts
- the relationship between swaps and zero-coupon bonds
- exotic swaps

15.1 **INTRODUCTION**

A **swap** is an agreement between two parties to exchange, or swap, future cashflows. The size of these cashflows is determined by some formulæ, decided upon at the initiation of the contract. The swaps may be in a single currency or involve the exchange of cashflows in different currencies.

The swaps market is big. The total notional principal amount is, in US dollars, currently comfortably in *14* figures. This market really began in 1981 although there were a small number of swap-like structures arranged in the 1970s. Initially the most popular contracts were currency swaps, discussed below, but very quickly they were overtaken by the interest rate swap.

15.2 **THE VANILLA INTEREST RATE SWAP**

In the **interest rate swap** the two parties exchange cashflows that are represented by the interest on a notional principal. Typically, one side agrees to pay the other a fixed interest rate and the cashflow in the opposite direction is a **floating rate**. The parties to a swap are shown schematically in Figure 15.1. One of the commonest floating rates used in a swap agreement is LIBOR, London Interbank Offer Rate.

Commonly in a swap, the exchange of the fixed and floating interest payments occur every six months. In this case the relevant LIBOR rate would be the six-month rate. At the maturity of the contract the principal is *not* exchanged.

Let me give an example of how such a contract works.

Example Suppose that we enter into a five-year swap on 7th July 2007, with semi-annual interest payments. We will pay to the other party a rate of interest fixed at 6% on a notional principal of $100 million, the counterparty will pay us six-month LIBOR. The cashflows in this contract are shown in Figure 15.2. The straight lines denote a fixed rate of interest and thus a known amount, the curly lines are floating rate payments.

The first exchange of payments is made on 7th January 2008, six months after the deal is signed. How much money changes hands on that first date? We must pay 0.03 × $100,000,000 = $3,000,000. The cashflow in the opposite direction will be at six-month LIBOR, *as quoted six months previously*, i.e. at the initiation of the contract. This is a very important point. The LIBOR rate is set six months before it is paid, so that in the first exchange of payments the floating side is known. This makes the first exchange special.

The second exchange takes place on 7th July 2008. Again we must pay $3,000,000, but now we receive LIBOR, as quoted on 7th January 2008. Every six months there is an

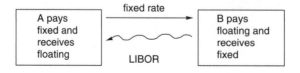

Figure 15.1 The parties to an interest rate swap.

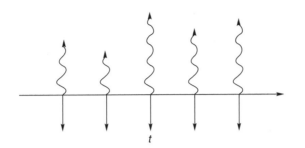

Figure 15.2 A schematic diagram of the cashflows in an interest rate swap.

exchange of such payments, with the fixed leg always being known and the floating leg being known six months before it is paid. This continues until the last date, 7th July 2012.

Why is the floating leg set six months before it is paid? This 'minor' detail makes a large difference to the pricing of swaps, believe it or not. It is no coincidence that the time between payments is the same as the maturity of LIBOR that is used, six months in this example. This convention has grown up because of the meaning of LIBOR, it is the rate of interest on a fixed-term maturity, set now and paid at the end of the term. Each floating leg of the swap is like a single investment of the notional principal six months prior to the payment of the interest. Hold that thought, we return to this point in a couple of sections to show the simple relationship between a swap and bonds.

There is also the **LIBOR in arrears swap** in which the LIBOR rate paid on the swap date is the six-month rate set that day, not the rate set six months before.

15.3 COMPARATIVE ADVANTAGE

Swaps were first created to exploit **comparative advantage**. This is when two companies who want to borrow money are quoted fixed and floating rates such that by exchanging payments between themselves they benefit, at the same time benefiting the intermediary who puts the deal together. Here's an example.

Two companies A and B want to borrow $50MM, to be paid back in two years. They are quoted the interest rates for borrowing at fixed and floating rates shown in Table 15.1.

Note that both must pay a premium over LIBOR to cover risk of default, which is perceived to be greater for company B.

Ideally, company A wants to borrow at floating and B at fixed. If they each borrow directly then they pay the following:

The total interest they are paying is

$$\text{six-month LIBOR} + 30 \text{ bps} + 8.2\% = \text{six-month LIBOR} + 8.5\%.$$

Table 15.1 Borrowing rates for companies A and B.

	Fixed	Floating
A	7%	six-month LIBOR + 30 bps
B	8.2%	six-month LIBOR + 100 bps

Table 15.2 Borrowing rates with no swap involved.

A	six-month LIBOR + 30 bps (floating)
B	8.2% (fixed)

If only they could get together they'd only be paying

six-month LIBOR + 100 bps + 7% = six-month LIBOR + 8%.

That's a saving of 0.5%.

Let's suppose that A borrows fixed and B floating, even though that's not what they want. Their total interest payments are six-month LIBOR plus 8%. Now let's see what happens if we throw a swap into the pot.

* A is currently paying 7% and B six-month LIBOR plus 1%. They enter into a swap in which A pays LIBOR to B and B pays 6.95% to A. They have swapped interest payments.

Looked at from A's perspective they are paying 7% and LIBOR while receiving 6.95%, a net floating payment of LIBOR plus 5 bps. Not only is this floating, as A originally wanted, but it is 25 bps better than if they had borrowed directly at the floating rate. There's still another 25 bps missing, and, of course, B gets this. B pays LIBOR plus 100 bps and also 6.95% to A while receiving LIBOR from A. This nets out at 7.95%, which is fixed, as required, and 25 bps less than the original deal.

Where did I get the 6.95% from? Let's do the same calculation with 'x' instead of 6.95.

Go back to *. A is currently paying 7% and B six-month LIBOR plus 1%. They enter into a swap in which A pays LIBOR to B and B pays x% to A. They have swapped interest payments.

Looked at from A's perspective they are paying 7% and LIBOR while receiving 'x'%, a net floating payment of LIBOR plus $7 - x$%. Now we want A to benefit by 25 bps over the original deal, this is half the 50 bps advantage. (I've just unilaterally decided to divide the advantage equally, 25 bps each.) So . . .

$$\text{LIBOR} + 7 - x + 0.25 = \text{LIBOR} + 0.3,$$

i.e.

$$x = 6.95\%.$$

Not only does A now get floating, as originally wanted, but it is 25 bps better than if they had borrowed directly at the floating rate. There's still another 25 bps missing, and, of course, B gets this. B pays LIBOR plus 100 bps and also 6.95% to A while receiving LIBOR from A. This nets out at 7.95%, which is fixed, as required, and 25 bps less than the original deal.

In practice the two counterparties would deal through an intermediary who would take a piece of the action.

Although comparative advantage was the original reason for the growth of the swaps market, it is no longer the reason for the popularity of swaps. Swaps are now very vanilla products existing in many maturities and more liquid than simple bonds.

Given the ubiquity of swaps you would expect the comparative advantage argument to have been arbed away. This is true. However, the arbitrage still exists in special circumstances. For example, floating loans usually come with provision for reviewing the spread over LIBOR every few months. If the company has become less creditworthy between reviews the spread will be increased. This is difficult to model or anticipate and so is outside the no-arbitrage concept.

15.4 THE SWAP CURVE

When the swap is first entered into it is usual for the deal to have no value to either party. This is done by a careful choice of the fixed rate of interest. In other words, the 'present value,' let us say, of the fixed side and the floating side both have the same value, netting out to zero. Consider the two extreme scenarios, very high fixed leg and very low fixed leg. If the fixed leg is very high the receiver of fixed has a contract with a high value. If the fixed leg is low the receiver has a contract that is worth a negative amount. Somewhere in between is a value that makes the deal valueless. The fixed leg of the swap is chosen for this to be the case.

Such a statement throws up many questions: How is the fixed leg decided upon? Why should both parties agree that the deal is valueless?

There are two ways to look at this. One way is to observe that a swap can be decomposed into a portfolio of bonds (as we see shortly) and so its value is not open to question if we are given the yield curve. However, in practice the calculation goes the other way. The swaps market is so liquid, at so many maturities, that it is the prices of swaps that drive the prices of bonds. The fixed leg of a **par swap** (having no value) is determined by the market.

The rates of interest in the fixed leg of a swap are quoted at various maturities. These rates make up the **swap curve**, see Figure 15.3.

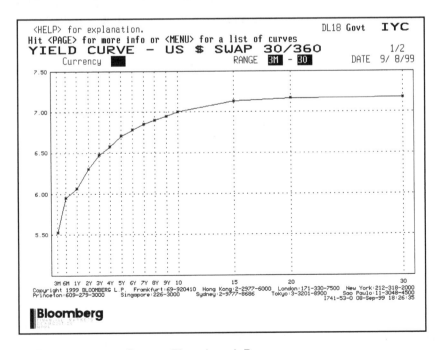

Figure 15.3 The swap curve. Source: Bloomberg L.P.

15.5 **RELATIONSHIP BETWEEN SWAPS AND BONDS**

There are two sides to a swap, the fixed-rate side and the floating-rate side. The fixed interest payments, since they are all known in terms of actual dollar amount, can be

seen as the sum of zero-coupon bonds. If the fixed rate of interest is r_s then the fixed payments add up to

$$r_s \sum_{i=1}^{N} Z(t; T_i).$$

This is the value today, time t, of all the fixed-rate payments. Here there are N payments, one at each T_i. Of course, this is multiplied by the notional principal, but assume that we have scaled this to one.

To see the simple relationship between the floating leg and zero-coupon bonds I draw some schematic diagrams and compare the cashflows. A single floating leg payment is shown in Figure 15.4. At time T_i there is payment of r_τ of the notional principal, where r_τ is the period τ rate of LIBOR, set at time $T_i - \tau$. I add and subtract $1 at time T_i to get the second diagram. The first and the second diagrams obviously have the same present value. Now recall the precise definition of LIBOR. It is the interest rate paid on a fixed-term deposit. Thus the $1 + r_\tau$ at time T_i is the same as $1 at time $T_i - \tau$. This gives the third diagram. It follows that the single floating rate payment is equivalent to two zero-coupon bonds. A single floating leg of a swap at time T_i is *exactly* equal to a deposit of $1 at time $T_i - \tau$ and a withdrawal of $1 at time τ.

Now add up all the floating legs as shown in Figure 15.5, note the cancelation of all $1 (dashed) cashflows except for the first and last. This shows that the floating side of the swap has value

$$1 - Z(t; T_N).$$

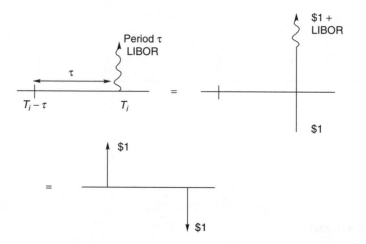

Figure 15.4 A schematic diagram of a single floating leg in an interest rate swap and equivalent portfolios.

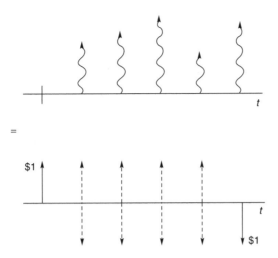

Figure 15.5 A schematic diagram of all the floating legs in a swap.

Bring the fixed and floating sides together to find that the value of the swap, to the receiver of the fixed side, is

$$r_s \tau \sum_{i=1}^{N} Z(t; T_i) - 1 + Z(t; T_N).$$

This result is *model independent*. This relationship is independent of any mathematical model for bonds or swaps.

At the start of the swap contract the rate r_s is usually chosen to give the contract par value, i.e. zero value initially. Thus

$$r_s = \frac{1 - Z(t; T_N)}{\tau \sum_{i=1}^{N} Z(t; T_i)}.$$

(15.1)

This is the quoted swap rate.

15.6 **BOOTSTRAPPING**

Swaps are now so liquid and exist for an enormous range of maturities that their prices determine the yield curve and not *vice versa*. In practice one is given $r_s(T_i)$ for many maturities T_i and one uses (15.1) to calculate the prices of zero-coupon bonds and thus the yield curve. For the first point on the discount-factor curve we must solve

USED IN PRACTICE
ALL THE TIME

$$r_s(T_1) = \frac{1 - Z(t; T_1)}{\tau Z(t; T_1)},$$

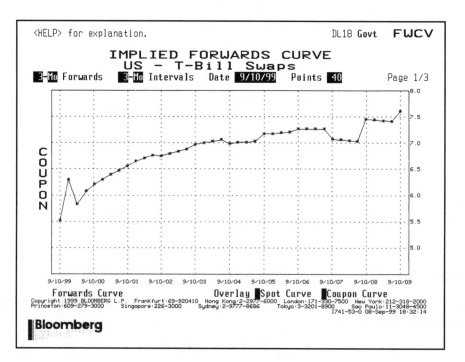

Figure 15.6 Forward rates derived from the swap curve by bootstrapping. Source: Bloomberg L.P.

i.e.

$$Z(t; T_1) = \frac{1}{1 + r_s(T_1)\tau}.$$

After finding the first j discount factors the $j + 1$th is found from

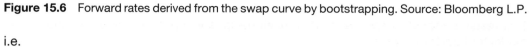

$$Z(t; T_{j+1}) = \frac{1 - r_s(T_{j+1})\tau \sum_{i=1}^{j} Z(t; T_i)}{1 + r_s(T_{j+1})\tau}$$

Figure 15.6 shows the forward curve derived from the data in Figure 15.3 by bootstrapping.

15.7 OTHER FEATURES OF SWAPS CONTRACTS

The above is a description of the vanilla interest rate swap. There any many features that can be added to the contract that make it more complicated, and most importantly, model dependent. A few of these features are mentioned here.

Callable and puttable swaps   A **callable** or **puttable swap** allows one side or the other to close out the swap at some time before its natural maturity. If you are receiving fixed and the floating rate rises more than you had expected you would want to close the position. Mathematically we are in the early exercise world of American-style options. The problem is model dependent and is discussed in Chapter 18.

Extendible swaps   The holder of an **extendible swap** can extend the maturity of a vanilla swap at the original swap rate.

Index amortizing rate swaps   The principal in the vanilla swap is constant. In some swaps the principal declines with time according to a prescribed schedule. The index amortizing rate swap is more complicated still with the amortization depending on the level of some index, say LIBOR, at the time of the exchange of payments. We will see this contract in Chapter 18.

15.8   **OTHER TYPES OF SWAP**

15.8.1   Basis rate swap

In the **basis rate swap** the floating legs of the swap are defined in terms of two distinct interest rates. For example, the prime rate versus LIBOR. A bank may have outstanding loans based on this prime rate but itself may have to borrow at LIBOR. It is thus exposed to **basis risk** and can be reduced with a suitable basis rate swap.

15.8.2   Equity swaps

The basic **equity swap** is an agreement to exchange two payments, one being an agreed interest rate (either fixed or floating) and the other depending on an equity index. This equity component is usually measured by the total return on an index, both capital gains and dividend are included. The principal is not exchanged.

The **equity basis swap** is an exchange of payments based on *two* different indices.

15.8.3   Currency swaps

A **currency swap** is an exchange of interest payments in one currency for payments in another currency. The interest rates can be both fixed, both floating or one of each. As well as the exchange of interest payments there is also an exchange of the principals (in two different currencies) at the beginning of the contract and at the end.

To value the fixed-to-fixed currency swap we need to calculate the present values of the cashflows in each currency. This is easily done, requiring the discount factors for the two currencies. Once this is done we can convert one present value to the other currency using the current *spot* exchange rate. If floating interest payments are involved we first decompose them into a portfolio of bonds (if possible) and value similarly.

15.9 **SUMMARY**

The need and ability to be able to exchange one type of interest payment for another is fundamental to the running of many businesses. This has put swaps among the most liquid of financial contracts. This enormous liquidity makes swaps such an important product that one has to be very careful in their pricing. In fact, swaps are so liquid that you do not price them in any theoretical way, to do so would be highly dangerous. Instead they are almost treated like an 'underlying' asset. From the market's view of the value we can back out, for example, the yield curve. We are helped in this by the fine detail of the swaps structure, the cashflows are precisely defined in a way that makes them exactly decomposable into zero-coupon bonds. And this can be done in a completely model-independent way. To finish this chapter I want to stress the importance of not using a model when a set of cashflows can be perfectly, statically and model-independently hedged by other cashflows. Any mispricing, via a model, no matter how small could expose you to large and risk-free losses.

FURTHER READING

- Two good technical books on swaps are by Das (1994) and Miron & Swannell (1991).

- The pocketbook by Ungar (1996) describes the purpose of the swaps market, how it works and the different types of swaps, with no mathematics.

EXERCISES

1. Consider a swap with the following specification:

   The floating payment is at the six-month rate, and is set six months before the payment (swaplet) date. The swap expires in five years, and payments occur every six months on a principal of $1. Zero-coupon bond prices are known for all maturities up to 10 years. What is the 'fair' level for the fixed rate side of the swap, so that initially the swap has no value?

2. An index amortizing rate swap has a principal which decreases at a rate dependent on the interest rate at settlement dates. Over a payment date, the principal changes from P to $g(r)P$, where $g(r)$ is a function specified in the swap contract, and $0 \leq g(r) \leq 1$. How will this affect the level of the fixed rate if the swap initially has no value?

3. A swap allows the side receiving floating to close out the position before maturity. How does the 'fair' value for the fixed rate side of the swap compare to that for a swap with no call/put features?

CHAPTER 16
one-factor interest rate modeling

The aim of this Chapter...

...is to model interest rates as random walks and bring together the instruments of the fixed-income world and the modeling ideas of Black and Scholes. You will see many familiar ideas and a few new ones that are not seen in the context of equity derivatives.

In this Chapter...

- stochastic models for interest rates
- how to derive the bond pricing equation for many fixed-income products
- the structure of many popular interest rate models

LATER YOU'LL SEE THAT
THE MODELS DON'T MATCH
THE DATA

16.1 **INTRODUCTION**

Until now I have assumed that interest rates are either constant or a known function of time. This may be a reasonable assumption for short-dated equity contracts. But for longer-dated contracts the interest rate must be more accurately modeled. This is not an easy task. In this chapter I introduce the ideas behind modeling interest rates using a single source of randomness. This is **one-factor interest rate modeling**. The model will allow the short-term interest rate, the spot rate, to follow a random walk. This model leads to a parabolic partial differential equation for the prices of bonds and other interest rate derivative products.

The 'spot rate' that we will be modeling is a very loosely defined quantity, meant to represent the yield on a bond of infinitesimal maturity. In practice one should take this rate to be the yield on a liquid finite-maturity bond, say one of one month. Bonds with one *day* to expiry do exist but their price is not necessarily a guide to other short-term rates. I will continue to be vague about the precise definition of the spot interest rate. We could argue that if we are pricing a complex product that is highly model dependent then the *exact* definition of the independent variable will be relatively unimportant compared with the choice of model.

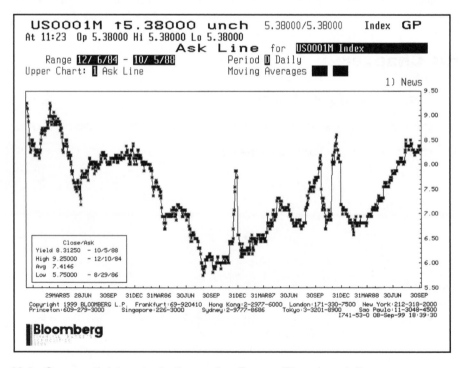

Figure 16.1 One-month interest rate time series. Source: Bloomberg L.P.

16.2 **STOCHASTIC INTEREST RATES**

Since we cannot realistically forecast the future course of an interest rate, it is natural to model it as a random variable. We are going to model the behavior of r, the interest rate received by the shortest possible deposit. From this we will see the development of a model for all other rates. The interest rate for the shortest possible deposit is commonly called the **spot interest rate**.

Figure 16.1 shows the time series of a one-month US interest rate. We will often use the one-month rate as a proxy for the spot rate.

Earlier I proposed a model for the asset price as a stochastic differential equation, the lognormal random walk. Now let us suppose that the interest rate r is governed by another stochastic differential equation of the form

$$dr = u(r, t)\, dt + w(r, t)\, dX. \tag{16.1}$$

The functional forms of $u(r, t)$ and $w(r, t)$ determine the behavior of the spot rate r. For the present I will not specify any particular choices for these functions. We use this random walk to derive a partial differential equation for the price of a bond using similar arguments to those in the derivation of the Black–Scholes equation. Later I describe functional forms for u and w that have become popular with practitioners.

Time Out...

Intuition behind stochastic interest rates

Equation (16.1) is just another recipe for generating random numbers. Until now we've concentrated on the lognormal random walk as the model for asset prices. But there's no reason why interest rates should behave like stock prices, there's no reason why we should use the same model for interest rates as for equities. In fact, such a model would be a very poor one; interest rates certainly do not exhibit the long-term exponential growth seen in the equity markets.

So, we need another model. But we're going to use the same mathematical, stochastic framework, with subtly and suitably different forms. Modeling interest rates in this framework amounts to choosing functional forms for the dt and dX coefficients in our random walk recipe.

From a model for the short-term interest rate r will follow a model for bonds of all maturities and hence interest rates for all maturities. In other words, the spot interest rate model leads to a model for the whole forward curve.

I'll be taking the stochastic calculus and differential equation approach to the pricing of interest rate products. But it can all be done in a binomial or trinomial setting. Actually, trinomial is the more popular for interest rate products. The principle is the same as in the equity tree model. I'll give some details shortly.

SUBTLY DIFFERENT FROM THE DERIVATION OF BS.... ONE EQN TWO UNKNOWNS

16.3 THE BOND PRICING EQUATION FOR THE GENERAL MODEL

When interest rates are stochastic a bond has a price of the form $V(r, t; T)$. The reader should think for the moment in terms of simple bonds, but the governing equation will be far more general and may be used to price many other contracts. That's why I'm using the notation V rather than our earlier Z for zero-coupon bonds.

Pricing a bond presents new technical problems, and is in a sense harder than pricing an option since *there is no underlying asset with which to hedge*. We are therefore not modeling a *traded* asset; the traded asset (the bond, say) is a derivative of our independent variable r. The only way to construct a hedged portfolio is by hedging one bond with a bond of a different maturity. We set up a portfolio containing two bonds with different maturities T_1 and T_2. The bond with maturity T_1 has price $V_1(r, t; T_1)$ and the bond with maturity T_2 has price $V_2(r, t; T_2)$. We hold one of the former and a number $-\Delta$ of the latter. We have

$$\Pi = V_1 - \Delta V_2. \tag{16.2}$$

The change in this portfolio in a time dt is given by

$$d\Pi = \frac{\partial V_1}{\partial t}dt + \frac{\partial V_1}{\partial r}dr + \frac{1}{2}w^2\frac{\partial^2 V_1}{\partial r^2}dt - \Delta\left(\frac{\partial V_2}{\partial t}dt + \frac{\partial V_2}{\partial r}dr + \frac{1}{2}w^2\frac{\partial^2 V_2}{\partial r^2}dt\right), \tag{16.3}$$

where we have applied Itô's lemma to functions of r and t. Which of these terms are random? Once you've identified them you'll see that the choice

$$\Delta = \frac{\partial V_1}{\partial r} \bigg/ \frac{\partial V_2}{\partial r}$$

eliminates all randomness in $d\Pi$. This is because it makes the coefficient of dr zero. We then have

$$d\Pi = \left(\frac{\partial V_1}{\partial t} + \frac{1}{2}w^2\frac{\partial^2 V_1}{\partial r^2} - \left(\frac{\partial V_1}{\partial r}\bigg/\frac{\partial V_2}{\partial r}\right)\left(\frac{\partial V_2}{\partial t} + \frac{1}{2}w^2\frac{\partial^2 V_2}{\partial r^2}\right)\right)dt$$

$$= r\Pi\, dt = r\left(V_1 - \left(\frac{\partial V_1}{\partial r}\bigg/\frac{\partial V_2}{\partial r}\right)V_2\right)dt,$$

where we have used arbitrage arguments to set the return on the portfolio equal to the risk-free rate. This risk-free rate is just the spot rate.

Collecting all V_1 terms on the left-hand side and all V_2 terms on the right-hand side we find that

$$\frac{\frac{\partial V_1}{\partial t} + \frac{1}{2}w^2\frac{\partial^2 V_1}{\partial r^2} - rV_1}{\frac{\partial V_1}{\partial r}} = \frac{\frac{\partial V_2}{\partial t} + \frac{1}{2}w^2\frac{\partial^2 V_2}{\partial r^2} - rV_2}{\frac{\partial V_2}{\partial r}}.$$

At this point the distinction between the equity and interest rate worlds starts to become apparent. This is *one* equation in *two* unknowns. Fortunately, the left-hand side is a function of T_1 but not T_2 and the right-hand side is a function of T_2 but not T_1. The only way for this to be possible is for both sides to be independent of the maturity date. Dropping the subscript from V, we have

$$\frac{\frac{\partial V}{\partial t} + \frac{1}{2}w^2\frac{\partial^2 V}{\partial r^2} - rV}{\frac{\partial V}{\partial r}} = a(r,t)$$

for some function $a(r,t)$. I shall find it convenient to write

$$a(r,t) = w(r,t)\lambda(r,t) - u(r,t);$$

for a given $u(r,t)$ and non-zero $w(r,t)$ this is always possible. The function $\lambda(r,t)$ is as yet unspecified. λ is 'universal' in that through this function all interest rate products are linked.

The bond pricing equation is therefore

$$\frac{\partial V}{\partial t} + \frac{1}{2}w^2\frac{\partial^2 V}{\partial r^2} + (u - \lambda w)\frac{\partial V}{\partial r} - rV = 0. \qquad (16.4)$$

Time Out...

Is this like Black–Scholes?

Pretty much, yes. Mathematically, it's of the same form as the Black–Scholes equation, but with different coefficients in front of two of the partial derivative terms. That's why I like to teach people about BS before interest rates...the math is almost identical but there are no problems with one equation for two unknowns.

The downside of this kind of modeling for interest rates is rather severe. Finding the best (correct?) form for w and $u - \lambda w$ is not easy. And it's not even possible to determine $u - \lambda w$ from observing time series for r, since that time series depends on u and w not on λ.

To find a unique solution of (16.4) we must impose one final and two boundary conditions. The final condition corresponds to the payoff on maturity and so for a zero-coupon bond

$$V(r,T;T) = 1.$$

Boundary conditions depend on the form of $u(r,t)$ and $w(r,t)$ and are discussed later for a special model.

It is easy to incorporate coupon payments into the model. If an amount $K(r, t)\, dt$ is received in a period dt then

$$\frac{\partial V}{\partial t} + \tfrac{1}{2}w^2 \frac{\partial^2 V}{\partial r^2} + (u - \lambda w)\frac{\partial V}{\partial r} - rV + K(r, t) = 0.$$

When this coupon is paid discretely, arbitrage considerations lead to jump condition

$$V(r, t_c^-; T) = V(r, t_c^+; T) + K(r, t_c),$$

where a coupon of $K(r, t_c)$ is received at time t_c.

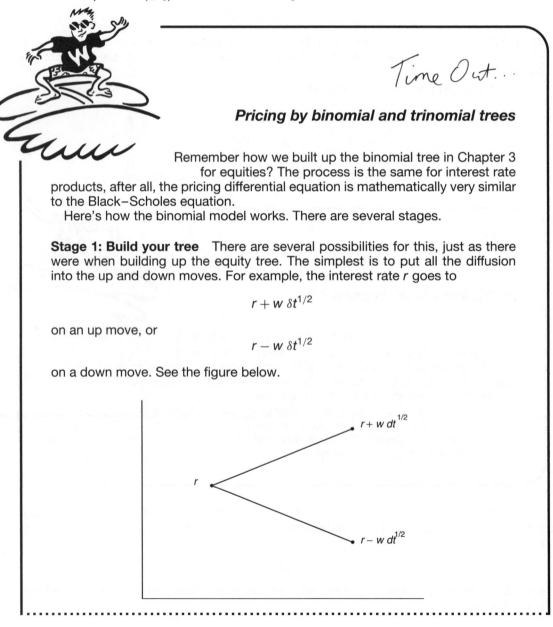

Time Out...

Pricing by binomial and trinomial trees

Remember how we built up the binomial tree in Chapter 3 for equities? The process is the same for interest rate products, after all, the pricing differential equation is mathematically very similar to the Black–Scholes equation.

Here's how the binomial model works. There are several stages.

Stage 1: Build your tree   There are several possibilities for this, just as there were when building up the equity tree. The simplest is to put all the diffusion into the up and down moves. For example, the interest rate r goes to

$$r + w\, \delta t^{1/2}$$

on an up move, or

$$r - w\, \delta t^{1/2}$$

on a down move. See the figure below.

Stage 2: Define the risk-neutral probabilities   Simple. The probability of an up move is

$$\frac{1}{2} + \frac{u\,\delta t^{1/2}}{2w}.$$

But the *risk-neutral* probability is

$$\frac{1}{2} + \frac{(u - \lambda w)\delta t^{1/2}}{2w}.$$

It's the risk-neutral probability you will use when working out expected values.

Stage 3: Discounting   Discount at the rate *r* at the base of the two branches.
   Now you just follow the same procedure as in Chapter 3 to work out contract values. You could even modify the VB code in that chapter for interest rate products.
   Often trinomial models are used because of the extra degree of freedom they allow in choosing parameters — you are still only going to fit the volatility and risk-neutral drift.

16.4   **WHAT IS THE MARKET PRICE OF RISK?**

MARKET PRICE
OF RISK..... YEUGHH

I now give an interpretation of the function $\lambda(r, t)$. Imagine that you hold an unhedged position in one bond with maturity date *T*. In a time-step *dt* this bond changes in value by

$$dV = w\frac{\partial V}{\partial r}dX + \left(\frac{\partial V}{\partial t} + \tfrac{1}{2}w^2\frac{\partial^2 V}{\partial r^2} + u\frac{\partial V}{\partial r}\right)dt.$$

From (16.4) this may be written as

$$dV = w\frac{\partial V}{\partial r}dX + \left(w\lambda\frac{\partial V}{\partial r} + rV\right)dt,$$

or

$$dV - rV\,dt = w\frac{\partial V}{\partial r}(dX + \lambda\,dt). \qquad (16.5)$$

The right-hand side of this expression contains two terms: a deterministic term in *dt* and a random term in *dX*. The presence of *dX* in (16.5) shows that this is not a riskless portfolio. The deterministic term may be interpreted as the excess return above the risk-free rate for accepting a certain level of risk. In return for taking the extra risk the portfolio profits by an extra $\lambda\,dt$ per unit of extra risk, *dX*. The function λ is therefore called the **market price of risk**.

16.5 INTERPRETING THE MARKET PRICE OF RISK, AND RISK NEUTRALITY

The bond pricing equation (16.4) contains references to the functions $u - \lambda w$ and w. The former is the coefficient of the first-order derivative with respect to the spot rate, and the latter appears in the coefficient of the diffusive, second-order derivative. The four terms in the equation represent, in order as written, time decay, diffusion, drift and discounting. We can interpret the solution of this bond pricing equation as the expected present value of all cashflows, just like we could with equity derivatives.

Suppose that we get a 'Payoff' at time T then the value of that contract today would be

$$E\left[e^{-\int_t^T r(\tau)\, d\tau}\text{Payoff}\right].$$

Notice that the present value (exponential) term goes inside the expectation since it is also random when interest rates are random.

We exploit this relationship in Chapter 29, and see exactly how to price via simulations.

As with equity options, this expectation is not with respect to the *real* random variable, but instead with respect to the *risk-neutral* variable. There is this difference because the drift term in the equation is not the drift of the real spot rate u, but the drift of another rate, called the **risk-neutral spot rate**. This rate has a drift of $u - \lambda w$. When pricing interest rate derivatives (including bonds of finite maturity) it is important to model, and price, using the risk-neutral rate. This rate satisfies

$$dr = (u - \lambda w)\, dt + w\, dX.$$

We need the new market-price-of-risk term because our modeled variable, r, is not traded.

Because we can't observe the function λ, except possibly via the whole yield curve (see Chapter 17), I tend to think of it as a great big carpet under which we can brush all kinds of nasty, inconvenient things.

16.6 NAMED MODELS

There are many interest rate models associated with the names of their inventors. The stochastic differential equation (16.1) for the risk-neutral interest rate process incorporates the models of Vasicek, Cox, Ingersoll & Ross, Ho & Lee, and Hull & White.

16.6.1 Vasicek

The Vasicek model takes the form

$$dr = (\eta - \gamma r)dt + \beta^{1/2}dX.$$

This model is so 'tractable' that there are explicit formulæ for many interest rate derivatives. The value of a zero-coupon bond is given by

$$e^{A(t;T) - rB(t;T)}$$

where

$$B = \frac{1}{\gamma}(1 - e^{-\gamma(T-t)})$$

and

$$A = \frac{1}{\gamma^2}(B(t; T) - T + t)(\eta\gamma - \tfrac{1}{2}\beta) - \frac{\beta B(t; T)^2}{4\gamma}.$$

The model is mean reverting to a constant level, which is a good property, but interest rates can easily go negative, which is a very bad property.

In Figure 16.2 are shown three types of yield curves predicted by the Vasicek model, each uses different parameters. (It is quite difficult to get the humped yield curve with reasonable numbers.)

16.6.2 Cox, Ingersoll & Ross

The CIR model takes the form

$$dr = (\eta - \gamma r)\,dt + \sqrt{\alpha r}\,dX.$$

Vasicek simulations and yield curves

The spot rate is mean reverting and if $\eta > \alpha/2$ the spot rate stays positive. There are some explicit solutions for interest rate derivatives, although typically involving integrals of the non-central chi-squared distribution. The

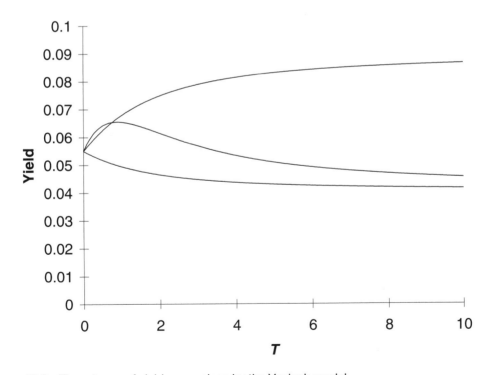

Figure 16.2 Three types of yield curve given by the Vasicek model.

value of a zero-coupon bond is

$$e^{A(t;T)-rB(t;T)}$$

where A and B are given by

$$\frac{\alpha}{2}A = a\psi_2 \log(a-B) + \psi_2 b \log((B+b)/b) - a\psi_2 \log a,$$

and

$$B(t;T) = \frac{2(e^{\psi_1(T-t)} - 1)}{(\gamma + \psi_1)(e^{\psi_1(T-t)} - 1) + 2\psi_1}$$

where

$$\psi_1 = \sqrt{\gamma^2 + 2\alpha} \quad \text{and} \quad \psi_2 = \frac{\eta}{a+b}$$

and

$$b, a = \frac{\pm\gamma + \sqrt{\gamma^2 + 2\alpha}}{\alpha}.$$

In Figure 16.3 are simulations of the Vasicek and CIR models using the same random numbers. The parameters have been chosen to give similar mean and standard deviations for the two processes.

16.6.3 Ho & Lee

Ho & Lee takes the form

$$dr = \eta(t)\,dt + \beta^{1/2}\,dX.$$

CIR simulations and yield curves

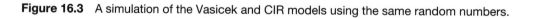

Figure 16.3 A simulation of the Vasicek and CIR models using the same random numbers.

Note the function of time in this. The value of zero-coupon bonds is given by

$$e^{A(t;T)-rB(t;T)}$$

where

$$B = T - t$$

and

$$A = -\int_t^T \eta(s)(T - s)\,ds + \tfrac{1}{6}\beta(T - t)^3.$$

This model was the first 'no-arbitrage model' of the term structure of interest rates. By this is meant that the careful choice of the function $\eta(t)$ will result in theoretical zero-coupon bonds prices, output by the model, which are the same as market prices. This technique is also called **yield curve fitting**. This careful choice is

$$\eta(t) = -\frac{\partial^2}{\partial t^2}\log Z_M(t^*;t) + \beta(t - t^*)$$

where today is time $t = t^*$. In this $Z_M(t^*;T)$ is the market price today of zero-coupon bonds with maturity T. Clearly this assumes that there are bonds of all maturities and that the prices are twice differentiable with respect to the maturity. We'll see the mathematics of this in the next chapter.

16.6.4   Hull & White

Hull & White have extended both the Vasicek and the CIR models to incorporate time-dependent parameters. This time dependence again allows the yield curve (and even a volatility structure) to be fitted.

16.7   **EQUITY AND FX FORWARDS AND FUTURES WHEN RATES ARE STOCHASTIC**

Recall from Chapter 6 that forward prices and futures prices are the same if rates are constant. How does this change, if at all, when rates are stochastic? We must repeat the analysis of that chapter but now with

$$dS = \mu S\,dt + \sigma S\,dX_1$$

and

$$dr = u(r, t)\,dt + w(r, t)\,dX_2.$$

We are in the world of correlated random walks, as described in Chapter 12. The correlation coefficient is ρ.

16.7.1   Forward contracts

$V(S, r, t)$ will be the value of the forward contract at any time during its life on the underlying asset S, and maturing at time T. As in Chapter 6, I'll assume that the delivery price is known and then find the forward contract's value.

Set up the portfolio of one long forward contract and short Δ of the underlying asset, and Δ_1 of a risk-free bond:

$$\Pi = V(S, t) - \Delta S - \Delta_1 Z.$$

I won't go through all the details, because the conclusion is the obvious one:

$$\frac{\partial V}{\partial t} + \tfrac{1}{2}\sigma^2 S^2 \frac{\partial^2 V}{\partial S^2} + \rho\sigma Sw\frac{\partial^2 V}{\partial S\,\partial r} + \tfrac{1}{2}w^2\frac{\partial^2 V}{\partial r^2} + rS\frac{\partial V}{\partial S} + (u - \lambda w)\frac{\partial V}{\partial r} - rV = 0.$$

The final condition for the equation is simply the difference between the asset price S and the fixed delivery price $\overline{S}$. So

$$V(S, r, T) = S - \overline{S}.$$

The solution of the equation with this final condition is

$$V(S, r, t) = S - \overline{S}Z.$$

At this point Z is not just any old risk-free bond, it is a zero-coupon bond having the same maturity as the forward contract. This is the forward contract's value during its life.

Remember that the delivery price is set initially $t = t_0$ as the price that gives the forward contract zero value. If the underlying asset is S_0 at t_0 then

$$0 = S_0 - \overline{S}Z$$

or

$$\overline{S} = \frac{S_0}{Z}.$$

The quoted forward price is therefore

$$\text{Forward price} = \frac{S}{Z}.$$

Remember that Z satisfies

$$\frac{\partial Z}{\partial t} + \tfrac{1}{2}w^2\frac{\partial^2 Z}{\partial r^2} + (u - \lambda w)\frac{\partial Z}{\partial r} - rZ = 0$$

with

$$Z(r, T) = 1.$$

16.8 FUTURES CONTRACTS

Use $F(S, r, t)$ to denote the futures price.

Set up a portfolio of one long futures contract and short Δ of the underlying, and Δ_1 of a risk-free bond:

$$\Pi = -\Delta S - \Delta_1 Z.$$

(Remember that the futures contract has no value.)

$$d\Pi = dF - \Delta\,dS - \Delta_1\,dZ.$$

Following the usual routine we get

$$\frac{\partial F}{\partial t} + \frac{1}{2}\sigma^2 S^2 \frac{\partial^2 F}{\partial S^2} + \rho\sigma Sw \frac{\partial^2 F}{\partial S \partial r} + \frac{1}{2}w^2 \frac{\partial^2 F}{\partial r^2} + rS \frac{\partial F}{\partial S} + (u - \lambda w) \frac{\partial F}{\partial r} = 0.$$

The final condition is

$$F(S, r, T) = S.$$

Let's write the solution of this as

$$F(S, r, t) = \frac{S}{p(r, t)}.$$

Why? Two reasons. First, a similarity solution is to be expected, the price should be proportional to the asset price. Second, I want to make a comparison between the futures price and the forward price. The latter is

$$\frac{S}{Z}.$$

So it's natural to ask, how similar are Z and p?

It turns out that p satisfies

$$\frac{\partial p}{\partial t} + \frac{1}{2}w^2 \frac{\partial^2 p}{\partial r^2} + (u - \lambda w) \frac{\partial p}{\partial r} - rp - w^2 \frac{\left(\frac{\partial p}{\partial r}\right)^2}{q} + \rho\sigma\beta \frac{\partial p}{\partial r} = 0. \qquad (16.6)$$

(Just plug the similarity form into the equation to see this.)

The final condition is

$$p(r, T) = 1.$$

The differences between the p and Z equations are in the underlined terms in Equation (16.6).

16.8.1   The convexity adjustment

There is clearly a difference between the prices of forwards and futures when interest rates are stochastic. From Equation (16.6) you can see that the difference depends on the volatility of the spot interest rate, the volatility of the underlying and the correlation between them. Provided that $\rho \geq 0$ the futures price is always greater than the equivalent forward price. Should the correlation be zero then the volatility of the stock is irrelevant. If the interest rate volatility is zero then rates are deterministic and forward and futures prices are the same.

Since the difference in price between forwards and futures depends on the spot rate volatility, market practitioners tend to think in terms of **convexity adjustments** to get from one to the other. Clearly, the convexity adjustment will depend on the precise nature of the model. For the popular models, described above, the p equation (16.6) still has simple solutions.

16.9 **SUMMARY**

In this chapter I introduced the idea of a random interest rate. The interest rate that we modeled was the 'spot rate,' a short-term interest rate. Several popular spot rate models were described. These models were chosen because simple forms of the coefficients make the solution of the basic bond pricing equation straightforward analytically.

FURTHER READING

- See the original interest rate models by Vasicek (1977), Dothan (1978), Cox *et al.* (1985), Ho & Lee (1986) and Black *et al.* (1990).

- For details of the general affine model see the papers by Pearson & Sun (1989), Duffie (1992), Klugman (1992) and Klugman & Wilmott (1994).

- The comprehensive book by Rebonato (1996) describes all of the popular interest rate models in detail.

- Multi-factor models and some very new ideas are discussed in *PWOQF2*.

EXERCISES

1. Substitute

$$Z(r, t; T) = e^{A(t;T) - rB(t;T)},$$

into the bond pricing equation

$$\frac{\partial V}{\partial t} + \frac{1}{2}w^2\frac{\partial^2 V}{\partial r^2} + (u - \lambda w)\frac{\partial V}{\partial r} - rV = 0.$$

What are the explicit dependencies of the functions in the resulting equation?

2. Simulate random walks for the interest rate to compare the different named models suggested in this chapter.

3. What final condition (payoff) should be applied to the bond pricing equation for a swap, cap, floor, zero-coupon bond, coupon bond and a bond option?

4. What form does the bond pricing equation take when the interest rate satisfies the Vasicek model

$$dr = (\eta - \gamma r)dt + \beta^{1/2}dX?$$

Solve the resulting equations for A and B in this case, to find

$$A = \frac{1}{\gamma^2}(B - T + t)\left(\eta\gamma - \tfrac{1}{2}\beta\right) - \frac{\beta B^2}{4\gamma},$$

and

$$B = \frac{1}{\gamma}(1 - e^{-\gamma(T-t)}).$$

CHAPTER 17
yield curve fitting

The aim of this Chapter...

...is to show how the simple models can be forced to give a theoretical yield curve which is exactly the same as the market's yield curve. But we also see why this is misleading and dangerous.

In this Chapter...

- how to choose time-dependent parameters in one-factor models so that today's yield curve is an output of the model
- the advantages and disadvantages of yield curve fitting

17.1   **INTRODUCTION**

One-factor models for the spot rate build up an entire yield curve from a knowledge of the spot rate and the parameters in the model. In using a one-factor model we have to decide how to choose the parameters and whether to believe the output of the model. If we choose parameters using historical time series data then one of the outputs of the model will be a theoretical yield curve. Unless we are very, very lucky this theoretical curve will not be the same as the market yield curve. Which do we believe? Do we believe the theoretical yield curve or do we believe the prices trading in the market? You have to be very brave to ignore the market prices for such liquid instruments as bonds and swaps. Even if you are pricing very complex products you must still hedge with simpler, more liquid, traded contracts for which you would like to get the price right.

Because of this need to correctly price liquid instruments, the idea of **yield curve fitting** or **calibration** has become popular. When one-factor models are used in practice they are almost always fitted. This means that one or more of the parameters in the model is allowed to depend on time. This functional dependence on time is then carefully chosen to make an output of the model, the price of zero-coupon bonds, exactly match the market prices for these instruments. Yield curve fitting is the subject of this chapter.

17.2   **HO & LEE**

The Ho & Lee spot interest rate model is the simplest that can be used to fit the yield curve. It will be useful to examine this model in detail to see one way in which fitting is done in practice.

In the Ho & Lee model the process for the risk-neutral spot rate is

$$dr = \eta(t)dt + c\,dX.$$

The standard deviation of the spot rate process, c, is constant, the drift rate η is time dependent.

In this model the solution of the bond pricing equation for a zero-coupon bond is simply

$$Z(r, t; T) = e^{A(t;T) - r(T-t)},$$

where

$$A(t; T) = -\int_t^T \eta(s)(T - s)ds + \tfrac{1}{6}c^2(T - t)^3.$$

If we know $\eta(t)$ then the above gives us the theoretical value of zero-coupon bonds of all maturities. Now turn this relationship around and ask the question: 'What functional form must we choose for $\eta(t)$ to make the theoretical value of the discount rates for all maturities equal to the market values?' Call this special choice for η, $\eta^*(t)$. The yield curve is to be fitted today, $t = t^*$, when the spot interest rate is r^* and the discount factors in the market are $Z_M(t^*; T)$. To match the market and theoretical bond prices, we must solve

$$Z_M(t^*; T) = e^{A(t^*;T) - r^*(T-t^*)}.$$

Taking logarithms of this and rearranging slightly we get

$$\int_{t^*}^{T} \eta^*(s)(T-s)ds = -\log(Z_M(t^*;T)) - r^*(T-t^*) + \tfrac{1}{6}c^2(T-t^*)^3. \qquad (17.1)$$

Observe that I am carrying around in the notation today's date t^*. This is a constant but I want to emphasize that we are doing the calibration to *today's* yield curve. If we calibrate again tomorrow, the market yield curve will have changed.

Differentiate (17.1) twice with respect to T to get

$$\eta^*(t) = c^2(t-t^*) - \frac{\partial^2}{\partial t^2}\log(Z_M(t^*;t)).$$

With this choice for the time-dependent parameter $\eta(t)$ the theoretical and actual market prices of zero-coupon bonds are the same. It also follows that

$$A(t;T) = \log\left(\frac{Z_M(t^*;T)}{Z_M(t^*;t)}\right) - (T-t)\frac{\partial}{\partial t}\log(Z_M(t^*;t)) - \tfrac{1}{2}c^2(t-t^*)(T-t)^2.$$

17.3 **THE EXTENDED VASICEK MODEL OF HULL & WHITE**

The Ho & Lee model isn't the only one that can be calibrated, it's just the easiest. Most one-factor models have the potential for fitting, but the more tractable the model the easier the fitting. If the model is not at all tractable, having no nice explicit zero-coupon bond price formula, then we can always resort to numerical methods.

The next easiest model to fit is the Vasicek model. The Vasicek model has the following stochastic differential equation for the risk-neutral spot rate

$$dr = (\eta - \gamma r)dt + c\, dX.$$

Hull & White extend this to include a time-dependent parameter

$$dr = (\eta(t) - \gamma r)dt + c\, dX.$$

Assuming that γ and c have been estimated statistically, say, we choose $\eta = \eta^*(t)$ at time t^* so that our theoretical and the market prices of bonds coincide.

Under this risk-neutral process the value of a zero-coupon bonds

$$Z(r,t;T) = e^{A(t;T)-rB(t;T)},$$

where

$$A(t;T) = -\int_t^T \eta^*(s)B(s;T)ds + \frac{c^2}{2\gamma^2}\left(T-t+\frac{2}{\gamma}e^{-\gamma(T-t)} - \frac{1}{2\gamma}e^{-2\gamma(T-t)} - \frac{3}{2\gamma}\right).$$

and

$$B(t;T) = \frac{1}{\gamma}\left(1 - e^{-\gamma(T-t)}\right).$$

To fit the yield curve at time t^* we must make $\eta^*(t)$ satisfy

$$A(t^*; T) = -\int_{t^*}^{T} \eta^*(s)B(s; T)ds + \frac{c^2}{2\gamma^2}\left(T - t^* + \frac{2}{\gamma}e^{-\gamma(T-t^*)} - \frac{1}{2\gamma}e^{-2\gamma(T-t^*)} - \frac{3}{2\gamma}\right)$$

$$= \log(Z_M(t^*; T)) + r^*B(t^*, T). \tag{17.2}$$

This is an integral equation for $\eta^*(t)$ if we are given all of the other parameters and functions, such as the market prices of bonds, $Z_M(t^*; T)$.

Although (17.2) may be solved by Laplace transform methods, it is particularly easy to solve by differentiating the equation twice with respect to T. This gives

$$\eta^*(t) = -\frac{\partial^2}{\partial t^2}\log(Z_M(t^*; t)) - \gamma\frac{\partial}{\partial t}\log(Z_M(t^*; t)) + \frac{c^2}{2\gamma}\left(1 - e^{-2\gamma(t-t^*)}\right). \tag{17.3}$$

From this expression we can now find the function $A(t; T)$,

$$A(t; T) = \log\left(\frac{Z_M(t^*; T)}{Z_M(t^*; t)}\right) - B(t; T)\frac{\partial}{\partial t}\log(Z_M(t^*; t))$$

$$- \frac{c^2}{4\gamma^3}\left(e^{-\gamma(T-t^*)} - e^{-\gamma(t-t^*)}\right)^2\left(e^{2\gamma(t-t^*)} - 1\right).$$

17.4 YIELD-CURVE FITTING: FOR AND AGAINST

17.4.1 For

The building blocks of the bond pricing equation are delta hedging and no arbitrage. If we are to use a one-factor model correctly then we must abide by the delta-hedging assumptions. We must buy and sell instruments to remain delta neutral. The buying and selling of instruments must be done at the market prices. We *cannot* buy and sell at a theoretical price. But we are not modeling the bond prices directly; we model the spot rate and bond prices are then derivatives of the spot rate. This means that there is a real likelihood that our output bond prices will differ markedly from the market prices. This is useless if we are to hedge with these bonds. The model thus collapses and cannot be used for pricing other instruments, unless we can find a way to generate the correct prices for our hedging instruments from the model; this is yield curve fitting.

Once we have fitted the prices of traded products we then dynamically or statically hedge with these products. The idea being that even if the model is wrong so that we lose money on the contract we are pricing then we should make that money back on the hedging instruments.

17.4.2 Against

If the market prices of simple bonds were correctly given by a model, such as Ho & Lee or Hull & White, fitted at time t^* then, when we come back a week later, $t^* +$ one week, say, to refit the function $\eta^*(t)$, we would find that this function *had not changed* in the meantime. This *never* happens in practice. We find that the function η^* has changed out of all recognition. What does this mean? Clearly the model is wrong.[1]

By simply looking for a Taylor series solution of the bond pricing equation for short times to expiry, we can relate the value of the risk-adjusted drift rate at the short end to the slope and curvature of the market yield curve. This is done as follows. Look for a solution of (16.4) of the form

$$Z(r, t; T) \sim 1 + a(r)(T - t) + b(r)(T - t)^2 + c(r)(T - t)^3 + \ldots$$

Substitute this into the bond pricing equation:

$$- a - 2b(T - t) - 3c(T - t)^2 + \tfrac{1}{2}\left(w^2 - 2(T - t)w\frac{\partial w}{\partial t}\right)\left((T - t)\frac{d^2a}{dr^2} + (T - t)^2\frac{d^2b}{dr^2}\right)$$

$$+ \left((u - \lambda w) - (T - t)\frac{\partial(u - \lambda w)}{\partial t}\right)(T - t)\left(\frac{da}{dr} + (T - t)^2\frac{db}{dr}\right)$$

$$- r\left(1 + a(T - t) + c(T - t)^2\right) + \ldots = 0.$$

Note how I have expanded the drift and volatility terms about $t = T$, in the above these are evaluated at r and T. By equating powers of $(T - t)$ we find that

$$a(r) = -r, \quad b(r) = \tfrac{1}{2}r^2 - \tfrac{1}{2}(u - \lambda w)$$

and

$$c(r) = \tfrac{1}{12}w^2\frac{\partial^2}{\partial r^2}(r^2 - r(u - \lambda w)) - \tfrac{1}{6}(u - \lambda w)\frac{\partial}{\partial r}(r^2 - r(u - \lambda w))$$

$$- \tfrac{1}{3}\frac{\partial}{\partial t}(u - \lambda w) + \tfrac{1}{6}r^2(r - (u - \lambda w)).$$

In all of these $u - \lambda w$ and w are evaluated at r and T.

From the Taylor series expression for Z we find that the yield to maturity is given by

$$-\frac{\log(Z(r, t; T))}{T - t} \sim -a + \left(\tfrac{1}{2}a^2 - b\right)(T - t) + \left(ab - c - \tfrac{1}{3}a^3\right)(T - t)^2 + \ldots$$

for short times to maturity.

The yield curve takes the value $-a(r) = r$ at maturity, obviously. The slope of the yield curve is

$$\tfrac{1}{2}a^2 - b = \tfrac{1}{2}(u - \lambda w),$$

i.e. one half of the risk-neutral drift. The curvature of the yield curve at the short end is proportional to

$$ab - c - \tfrac{1}{3}a^3,$$

---

[1] This doesn't mean that it isn't useful, or profitable. This is a much more subtle point.

which contains a term that is the derivative of the risk-neutral drift with respect to time via c. Let me stress the key points of this analysis. The slope of the yield curve at the short end depends on the risk-neutral drift, and vice versa. The curvature of the yield curve at the short end depends on the time derivative of the risk-neutral drift, and vice versa.

If we choose time-dependent parameters within the risk-adjusted drift rate such that the market prices are fitted at time t^* then we have

$$Z(r^*, t^*; T) = Z_M(t^*; T)$$

which is one equation for the time-dependent parameters.

Thus, for Ho & Lee, for example, the value of the function $\eta^*(t)$ at the short end, $t = t^*$, depends on the slope of the market yield curve. Moreover, the slope of $\eta^*(t)$ depends on the *curvature* of the yield curve at the short end. Results such as these are typical for all fitted models. These, seemingly harmless, results are actually quite profound.

It is common for the slope of the yield curve to be quite large and positive, the difference between very short and not quite so short rates is large. But then for longer maturities typically the yield curve flattens out. This means that the yield curve has a large negative curvature. If one performs the fitting procedure as outlined here for the Ho & Lee or extended Vasicek models, one typically finds the following:

- The value of $\eta^*(t)$ at $t = t^*$ is very large. This is because the yield curve slope at the short end is often large.

- The slope of $\eta^*(t)$ at $t = t^*$ is large and negative. This is because the curvature of the yield curve is often large and negative.

A typical plot of $\eta^*(t)$ versus t is shown in Figure 17.1. This shows the high value for the fitted function and the large negative slope.[2] So far, so good. Maybe this is correct, maybe this is really what the fitted parameter should look like. But what happens when we come back in a few months to look at how our fitted parameter is doing? If the model is correct then we would find that the fitted curve looked like the bold part of the curve in the figure. The previous data should have just dropped off the end, the rest of the curve should remain unchanged. We would then see a corresponding dramatic flattening of the yield curve. Does this in fact happen? No. The situation looks more like that in Figure 17.2, which is really just a translation of the curve in time. Again we see the high value at the short end, the large negative slope and the oscillations. The recalibrated function in Figure 17.2 looks nothing like the bold line in Figure 17.1. This is because the yield curve has not changed that much in the meantime. It still has the high slope and curvature. In fact, we don't even have to wait for a few months for the deviation to be significant, it becomes apparent in weeks or even days.

We can conclude from this that yield curve fitting is an inconsistent and dangerous business. The results presented here are by no means restricted to the models I have named; *no* one-factor model will capture the high slope and curvature that is usual for yield curves; they 'may' give reasonable results when the yield curve is fairly flat.

---

[2] The strange oscillation of the function η^* beyond the short end is usually little more than numerical errors.

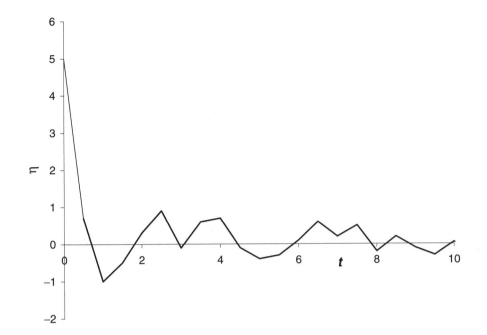

Figure 17.1 Typical fitted function $\eta^*(t)$.

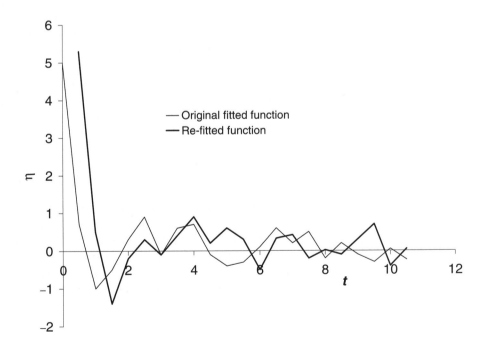

Figure 17.2 Typical *re*-fitted function $\eta^*(t)$, a short time later.

17.5 OTHER MODELS

Other models for the short-term interest rate have been proposed. One of the most popular (but for which there are no explicit solutions) is the **Black, Derman & Toy (BDT)** model where the risk-neutral spot interest rate satisfies

$$d(\log r) = \left(\theta(t) - \frac{\sigma'(t)}{\sigma(t)} \log r \right) dt + \sigma(t)dX.$$

The two functions of time σ and θ allow both zero-coupon bonds and their volatilities to be matched. An even more general model is the **Black & Karasinski** model

$$d(\log r) = (\theta(t) - a(t) \log r) \, dt + \sigma(t)dX.$$

These models are popular because fitting can be done quite simply by a numerical scheme.

Any criticisms of yield curve fitting in general, of course, apply to these models.

17.6 SUMMARY

I have outlined why the yield curve is fitted, and how it is fitted in some simple models. From a practical perspective it is hard to argue against calibration, you cannot hedge with something if your theoretical price is very different from its traded price. But from a modeling and empirical perspective it is hard to argue in its favor, the data shows how inconsistent the concept is. This is always going to be a problem with one-factor Brownian motion models, unless yield curves suddenly decide not to be so steep. There is not a great deal that can be done theoretically.

On the other hand, people seem to make money using these models and I guess that is the correct test of a model. Unless you are speculating with an interest rate derivative, you will have to delta hedge and therefore have to calibrate. Practitioners go much further than I have shown here, they fit as many market prices and properties as they can. Put in another time-dependent parameter and you can fit interest rate volatilities of different maturities, yet another parameter and you can fit the market prices of caps. By fitting more and more data, are you digging a deeper and deeper grave or are you improving and refining the accuracy of your model?

As an aside, suppose we are not interested in hedging but want to speculate with some fixed-income instruments. It is common knowledge that the yield curve is a poor predictor of real future interest rates. In this case it could be unnecessary or even dangerous to fit the yield curve. In this situation one could 'value' the instrument using the *real* spot rate process. This would give a 'value' for the instrument that was the expected present value of all cashflows under the *real* random walk. To do this one needs a model for the real drift u.

FURTHER READING

- A more sophisticated choice of time-dependent parameters is described by Hull & White (1990a).

- Klugman & Wilmott (1994) consider the fitting of the general affine model.

- Baker (1977) gives details of the numerical solution of integral equations.

- See Black *et al.* (1990) for details of their popular model.

- Rebonato (1996) discusses calibration in depth for many popular models.

- See Derman (2004) for the story behind the BDT model.

- In *PWOQF2* is shown a non-linear interest rate model that completely sidesteps the issue of calibration.

EXERCISES

1. Substitute the fitted function for $A(t; T)$, using the Ho & Lee model, back into the solution of the bond pricing equation for a zero-coupon bond,

$$Z(r, t; T) = e^{A(t;T) - r(T-t)}.$$

What do you notice?

2. Differentiate Equation (17.2) twice to solve for the value of $\eta^*(t)$. What is the value of a zero-coupon bond with a fitted Vasicek model for the interest rate?

3. Use market data for the price of zero-coupon bonds to fit a Ho & Lee model. Refit the model with data for a week later in time. Compare the two curves for $\eta^*(t)$.

    Note: The second curve for η^* starts a week after the first curve. They should not be plotted starting at the same point in time.

4. Use market data for zero-coupon bond prices to fit a Vasicek model for the interest rate.

CHAPTER 18
interest rate derivatives

The aim of this Chapter...

...is to examine some of the more important fixed-income products and to explain various ways in which to approach their pricing. You will see how it is common market practice to use simple Black–Scholes pricing formulæ in novel ways.

In this Chapter...

- common fixed-income contracts such as bond options, caps and floors
- how to price interest rate products in the consistent partial differential equation framework
- how to price contracts the market way
- path dependency in interest rate products, such as the index amortizing rate swap

18.1 **INTRODUCTION**

So far in this book I derived a theory for pricing and hedging many different types of options on equities, currencies and commodities. In Chapter 16 I presented the theory for zero-coupon bonds, boldly saying that the model may be applied to other contracts.

In the equity options world we have seen different degrees of complexity. The simple contracts have no path dependency. These include the vanilla calls and puts and contracts having different final conditions such as binaries or straddles. At the next stage of complexity we find the path-dependent contracts such as American options or barriers for which, technically speaking, the path taken by the underlying is important. Many of these ideas are mirrored in the theory of interest rate derivatives.

In this chapter we delve deeper into the subject of fixed-income contracts by considering interest rate derivatives such as bond options, caps and floors, swaptions, captions and floortions, and more complicated and path-dependent contracts such as the index amortizing rate swap.

Time Out...

Pricing methodologies

I'm going to give you some insight into the two main methods for pricing interest rate derivatives. One way is consistent across all instruments but not necessarily accurate, the other is the exact opposite.

The former method is to price contracts using the same stochastic differential equation model for the spot rate and the resulting partial differential equation. Different contracts have different final and boundary conditions. The problem with this approach is that the basic model may not be that accurate. It can therefore be highly dangerous to use this method for pricing popular, highly liquid contracts.

The other approach is to bend and squeeze the instrument so as to make the 'underlying' (suitably defined) look like a lognormal asset. From then on, just apply the basic Black–Scholes formulæ. The main positive point about this rather artificial method is that it is common practice in the market.

18.2 **CALLABLE BONDS**

As a gentle introduction to more complex fixed-income products, consider the **callable bond**. This is a simple coupon-bearing bond, but one that the issuer may call back on specified dates for a specified amount. The amount for which it may be called back may be time dependent. This feature reduces the value of the bond; if rates are low, so that the bond value is high, the issuer will call the bond back.

The callable bond satisfies

$$\frac{\partial V}{\partial t} + \frac{1}{2}w^2\frac{\partial^2 V}{\partial r^2} + (u - \lambda w)\frac{\partial V}{\partial r} - rV = 0,$$

with

$$V(r, T) = 1,$$

and

$$V(r, t_c^-) = V(r, t_c^+) + K_c,$$

across coupon dates. If the bond can be called back for an amount $C(t)$ then we have the constraint on the bond's value

$$V(r, t) \leq C(t),$$

together with continuity of $\partial V/\partial r$.

18.3 **BOND OPTIONS**

The stochastic model for the spot rate presented in Chapter 16 allows us to value contingent claims such as bond options. A **bond option** is identical to an equity option except that the underlying asset is a bond. Both European and American versions exist.

As a simple example, we derive the differential equation satisfied by a call option, with exercise price E and expiry date T, on a zero-coupon bond with maturity date $T_B \geq T$. Before finding the value of the option to buy a bond we must find the value of the bond itself.

Let us write $Z(r, t; T_B)$ for the value of the bond. Thus, Z satisfies

$$\frac{\partial Z}{\partial t} + \frac{1}{2}w^2\frac{\partial^2 Z}{\partial r^2} + (u - \lambda w)\frac{\partial Z}{\partial r} - rZ = 0 \tag{18.1}$$

with

$$Z(r, T_B; T_B) = 1$$

and suitable boundary conditions. Now write $V(r, t)$ for the value of the call option on this bond. Since V also depends on the random variable r, it too must satisfy Equation (18.1). The only difference is that the final value for the option is

$$V(r, T) = \max(Z(r, t; T_B) - E, 0).$$

This payoff is shown in Figure 18.1.

Figure 18.2 shows the Bloomberg option calculator for bond options. In this case the model used is Black, Derman & Toy.

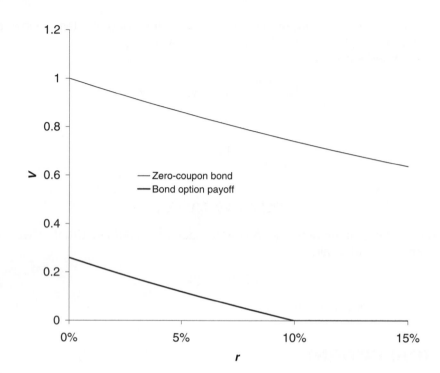

Figure 18.1 Zero-coupon bond price as a function of spot, and the payoff for a call option on the bond.

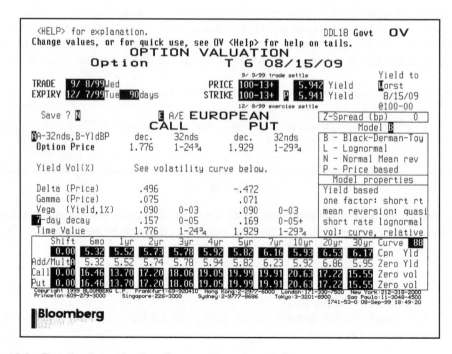

Figure 18.2 Bond option valuation. Source: Bloomberg L.P.

Time Out...

Must we really solve the partial differential equation?

No. There are lots of other things you can do. Here's a brief summary of your choices.

- If there's no 'optionality' in the contract, and all cashflows are fixed or floating as in swaps, you should price by discounting using the yield curve. But first convert floating cashflows to fixed as described in Chapter 15.

- Use the above pde approach if you feel comfortable with such concepts, and are happy to solve numerically by finite-difference methods. I hope you will feel happy with this by the end of the book.

- You can use trees, as hinted at in the previous chapter. Easy to understand, but not very sophisticated from a numerical point of view.

- Risk-neutral expectations are always there for you to fall back on. All the details are covered in Chapter 29.

- Finally, perhaps most popular and robust, fudge. This means pretend that you've got an equity derivative and not a fixed-income derivative and use a Black–Scholes-type formula. Some examples are given below.

18.3.1 Market practice

The above is all well and good, but suffers from the problem that any inaccuracy in the model is magnified by the process of solving once for the bond and then again for the bond option. This makes the contract second order, see Chapter 11. When the time comes to exercise the option the amount you receive will, for a call, be the difference between the *actual* bond price and the exercise price, not the difference between the *theoretical* bond price and the exercise price. So the model had better be correct for the bond price. Of course, this model can never be correct, and so we must treat the pricing of bond options with care. Practitioners tend to use an approach that is internally inconsistent but which is less likely to be very wrong. They use the Black–Scholes equity option pricing equation and formulæ assuming that the underlying is the bond. That is, they assume that the bond behaves like a lognormal asset. This requires them to estimate a volatility for the bond, either measured statistically or implied from another contract, and an interest rate for the lifetime of the bond option. This will be a good model provided that the expiry of the bond option is much shorter than the maturity of the underlying bond. Over short time periods, well away from maturity, the bond does behave stochastically, with a measurable volatility.

This method is called 'Black 76' after the famous paper by that author.

The price of a European bond call option in this model is

$$e^{-r(T-t)}\left(FN(d_1') - EN(d_2')\right),$$

and the put has value

$$e^{-r(T-t)}\left(EN(-d_2') - FN(-d_1')\right),$$

where F is the forward price of the bond at expiry of the option and

$$d_1' = \frac{\log(F/E) + \frac{1}{2}\sigma^2(T-t)}{\sigma\sqrt{T-t}} \quad \text{and} \quad d_2' = d_1' - \sigma\sqrt{T-t}.$$

This model should not be used when the life of the option is comparable to the maturity of the bond, because then there is an appreciable **pull to par**, that is, the value of the bond at maturity is the principal plus last coupon; the bond cannot behave lognormally close to maturity because we know where it must end up, this contrasts greatly with the behavior of an equity for which there is no date in the future on which we know its value for certain. This pull to par is shown in Figure 18.3.

Another approach used in practice is to model the yield to maturity of the underlying bond. The usual assumption is that this yield follows a lognormal random walk. By modeling the yield and then calculating the bond price based on this yield, we get a bond that behaves well close to its maturity; the pull to par is incorporated.

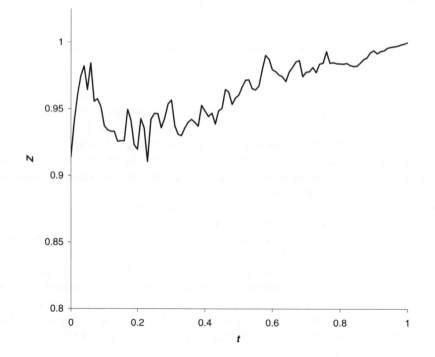

Figure 18.3 The pull to par for a zero-coupon bond.

There is one technical point about the definition of the bond option concerning the meaning of 'price.' One must be careful to use whichever of the clean or dirty price is correct for the option in question. This amounts to knowing whether or not accrued interest should be included in the payoff, see Chapter 14.

18.4 **CAPS AND FLOORS**

A **cap** is a contract that guarantees to its holder that otherwise floating rates will not exceed a specified amount; the variable rate is thus capped.

A typical cap contract involves the payment at times t_i, each quarter, say, of a variable interest on a principal with the cashflow taking the form

$$\max(r_L - r_c, 0),$$

multiplied by the principal. Here r_L is the basic floating rate, for example three-month LIBOR if the payments are made quarterly, and r_c is the fixed cap rate. These payments continue for the lifetime of the cap. The rate r_L to be paid at time t_i is set at time t_{i-1}. Each of the individual cashflows is called a **caplet**; a cap is thus the sum of many caplets.

The cashflow of a caplet is shown in Figure 18.4.

If we assume that the actual floating rate is the spot rate, i.e. $r_L \approx r$ (and this approximation may not be important), then a single caplet may be priced by solving

$$\frac{\partial V}{\partial t} + \tfrac{1}{2}w^2\frac{\partial^2 V}{\partial r^2} + (u - \lambda w)\frac{\partial V}{\partial r} - rV = 0, \tag{18.2}$$

with

$$V(r, T) = \max(r - r_c, 0).$$

Mathematically, this is similar to a call option on the floating rate r.

Figure 18.5 shows the Bloomberg calculator for caps.

A **floor** is similar to a cap except that the floor ensures that the interest rate is bounded below by r_f. A floor is made up of a sum of floorlets, each of which has a cashflow of

$$\max(r_f - r_L, 0).$$

We can approximate r_L by r again, in which case the floorlet satisfies the bond pricing equation but with

$$V(r, T) = \max(r_f - r, 0).$$

A floorlet is thus a put on the spot rate.

18.4.1 Cap/floor parity

A portfolio of a long caplet and a short floorlet (with $r_c = r_f$) has the cashflow

$$\max(r_L - r_c, 0) - \max(r_c - r_L, 0) = r_L - r_c.$$

This is the same cashflow as one payment of a swap. Thus there is the model-independent no-arbitrage relationship

$$\text{cap} = \text{floor} + \text{swap}.$$

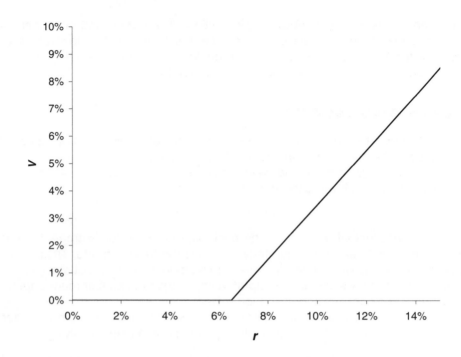

Figure 18.4 The dependence of the payment of a caplet on LIBOR.

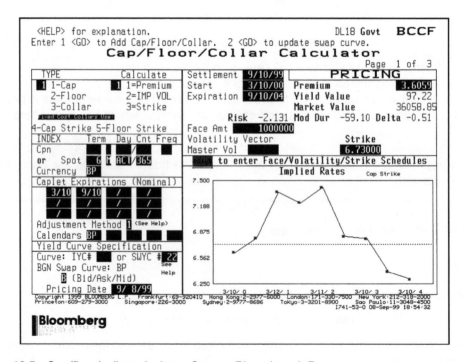

Figure 18.5 Cap/floor/collar calculator. Source: Bloomberg L.P.

18.4.2 The relationship between a caplet and a bond option

A caplet has the following cashflow

$$\max(r_L - r_c, 0).$$

This is received at time t_i but the rate r_L is set at t_{i-1}. This cashflow is *exactly* the same as the cashflow

$$\frac{1}{1 + r_L} \max(r_L - r_c, 0)$$

received at time t_{i-1}, after all, that is the definition of r_L. We can rewrite this cashflow as

$$\max\left(1 - \frac{1 + r_c}{1 + r_L}, 0\right).$$

But

$$\frac{1 + r_c}{1 + r_L}$$

is the price at time t_{i-1} of a bond paying $1 + r_c$ at time t_i. We can conclude that a caplet is equivalent to a put option expiring at time t_{i-1} on a bond maturing at time t_i.

18.4.3 Market practice

Again, because the Black–Scholes formulæ are so simple to use, it is common to use them to price caps and floors. This is done as follows. Each individual caplet (or floorlet) is priced as a call (or put) on a lognormally distributed interest rate. The inputs for this model are the volatility of the interest rate, the strike price r_c (or r_f), the time to the cashflow $t_i - t$, and *two* interest rates. One interest rate takes the place of the stock price and will be the current forward rate applying between times t_{i-1} and t_i. The other interest rate, used for discounting to the present is the yield on a bond maturing at time t_i. For a caplet the relevant formula is

$$e^{-r^*(t_i-t)} \left(F(t, t_{i-1}, t_i)N(d_1') - r_c N(d_2')\right).$$

Here $F(t, t_{i-1}, t_i)$ is the forward rate today between t_{i-1} and t_i, r^* is the yield to maturity for a maturity of $t_i - t$,

$$d_1' = \frac{\log(F/r_c) + \frac{1}{2}\sigma^2 t_{i-1}}{\sigma\sqrt{t_{i-1}}} \quad \text{and} \quad d_2' = d_1' - \sigma\sqrt{t_{i-1}}.$$

σ is the volatility of the $(t_i - t_{i-1})$ interest rate. The floorlet value is

$$e^{-r^*(t_i-t)} \left(-F(t, t_{i-1}, t_i)N(-d_1') + r_c N(-d_2')\right).$$

18.4.4 Collars

A **collar** places both an upper and a lower bound on the interest payments. It can be valued as a long cap and a short floor.

18.4.5 Step-up swaps, caps and floors

Step-up swaps, etc. have swap (cap, etc.) rates that vary with time in a prescribed manner.

18.5 **RANGE NOTES**

The **range note** pays interest on a notional principal for every day that an interest rate lies between prescribed lower and upper bounds. Let us assume that the relevant interest rate is our spot rate r. In this case we must solve

$$\frac{\partial V}{\partial t} + \frac{1}{2}w^2\frac{\partial^2 V}{\partial r^2} + (u - \lambda w)\frac{\partial V}{\partial r} - rV + \mathcal{I}(r) = 0,$$

with

$$V(r, T) = 0,$$

where

$$\mathcal{I}(r) = r \quad \text{if} \quad r_l < r < r_u \quad \text{and is zero otherwise.}$$

This is only an approximation to the correct value since in practice the relevant interest rate will have a finite (not infinitesimal) maturity.

18.6 **SWAPTIONS, CAPTIONS AND FLOORTIONS**

A swaption has a strike rate, r_E, that is the fixed rate that will be swapped against floating if the option is exercised. In a call swaption or **payer swaption** the buyer has the right to become the fixed rate payer; in a put swaption or receiver swaption the buyer has the right to become the payer of the floating leg.

Captions and **floortions** are options on caps and floors respectively. These contracts can be put into the partial differential equation framework with little difficulty. However, these contracts are second order, meaning that their value depends on another, more basic, contract, see Chapter 11. Although the partial differential equation approach is possible, and certainly consistent across instruments, it is likely to be time consuming computationally and prone to serious mispricings because of the high order of the contracts.

18.6.1 Market practice

With some squeezing the Black–Scholes formulæ can be used to value European swaptions. Perhaps this is not entirely consistent, but it is certainly easier than solving a partial differential equation.

The underlying is assumed to be the fixed leg of a par swap with maturity T_S; call this r_f. It is assumed to follow a lognormal random walk with a measurable volatility. If at time

T the par swap rate is greater than the strike rate r_E then the option is in the money. At this time the value of the swaption is

$$\max(r_f - r_E, 0) \times \text{present value of all future cashflows.}$$

It is important that we are 'modeling' the par rate because the par rate measures the rate at which the present value of the floating legs is equal to the present value of the fixed legs. Thus in this expression we only need worry about the excess of the par rate over the strike rate. This expression looks like a typical call option payoff, all we need to price the swaption in the Black–Scholes framework are the volatility of the par rate, the times to exercise and maturity and the correct discount factors. The payer swaption formula in this framework is

$$\frac{1}{F}e^{-r(T-t)}\left(1 - \left(1 + \tfrac{1}{2}F\right)^{-2(T_S-T)}\right)\left(FN(d_1') - EN(d_2')\right)$$

and the receiver swaption formula is

$$\frac{1}{F}e^{-r(T-t)}\left(1 - \left(1 + \tfrac{1}{2}F\right)^{-2(T_S-T)}\right)\left(EN(-d_2') - FN(-d_1')\right)$$

where F is the forward rate of the swap, T_S is the maturity of the swap and

$$d_1' = \frac{\log(F/E) + \frac{1}{2}\sigma^2(T-t)}{\sigma\sqrt{T-t}} \quad \text{and} \quad d_2' = d_1' - \sigma\sqrt{T-t}.$$

These formulæ assume that interest payments in the swap are exchanged every six months.

Figure 18.6 shows the Bloomberg swaption valuation page. They use the Black model for pricing.

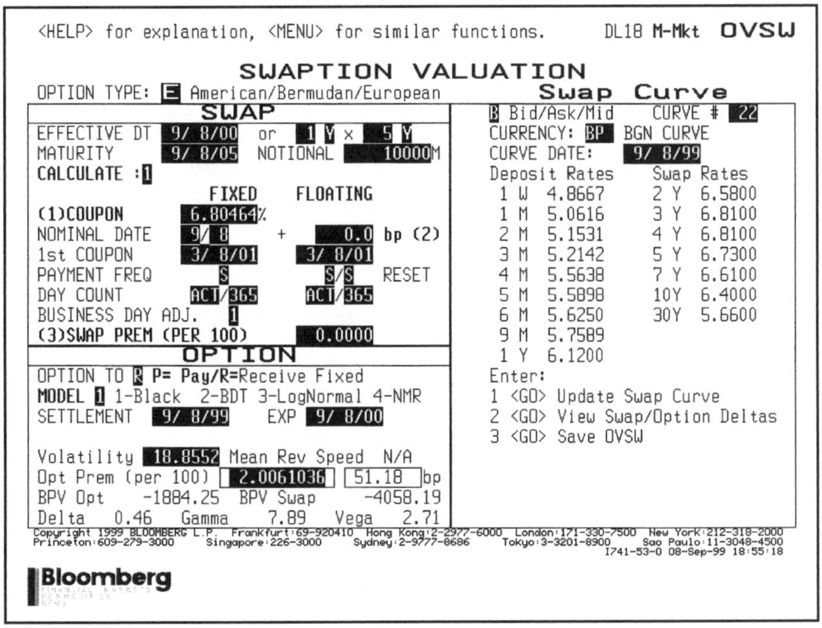
<HELP> for explanation, <MENU> for similar functions. DL18 M-Mkt OVSW

SWAPTION VALUATION

OPTION TYPE: E American/Bermudan/European

SWAP
EFFECTIVE DT 9/ 8/00 or 1 Y x 5 Y
MATURITY 9/ 8/05 NOTIONAL 10000M
CALCULATE : 1
FIXED FLOATING
(1)COUPON 6.80464%
NOMINAL DATE 9/ 8 + 0.0 bp (2)
1st COUPON 3/ 8/01 3/ 8/01
PAYMENT FREQ S S/S RESET
DAY COUNT ACT/365 ACT/365
BUSINESS DAY ADJ. 1
(3)SWAP PREM (PER 100) 0.0000

OPTION
OPTION TO R P= Pay/R=Receive Fixed
MODEL 1 1-Black 2-BDT 3-LogNormal 4-NMR
SETTLEMENT 9/ 8/99 EXP 9/ 8/00
Volatility 18.8552 Mean Rev Speed N/A
Opt Prem (per 100) 2.0061036 51.18 bp
BPV Opt -1884.25 BPV Swap -4058.19
Delta 0.46 Gamma 7.89 Vega 2.71

Swap Curve
B Bid/Ask/Mid CURVE # 22
CURRENCY: BP BGN CURVE
CURVE DATE: 9/ 8/99

Deposit Rates		Swap Rates	
1 W	4.8667	2 Y	6.5800
1 M	5.0616	3 Y	6.8100
2 M	5.1531	4 Y	6.8100
3 M	5.2142	5 Y	6.7300
4 M	5.5638	7 Y	6.6100
5 M	5.5898	10Y	6.4000
6 M	5.6250	30Y	5.6600
9 M	5.7589		
1 Y	6.1200		

Enter:
1 <GO> Update Swap Curve
2 <GO> View Swap/Option Deltas
3 <GO> Save OVSW

Copyright 1999 BLOOMBERG L.P. Frankfurt:69-920410 Hong Kong:2-2977-6000 London:171-330-7500 New York:212-318-2000
Princeton:609-279-3000 Singapore:226-3000 Sydney:2-9777-8686 Tokyo:3-3201-8900 Sao Paulo:11-3048-4500
I741-53-0 08-Sep-99 18:55:18

Bloomberg

Figure 18.6 Swaption valuation. Source: Bloomberg L.P.

18.7 **SPREAD OPTIONS**

Spread options have a payoff that depends on the difference between two interest rates. In the simplest case the two rates both come from the same yield curve, more generally the spread could be between rates on different but related curves (yield curve versus swap curve, LIBOR versus Treasury bills), risky and riskless curves or rates in different currencies.

Can we price this contract in the framework we have built up? No. The contract crucially depends on the tilting of the yield curve. In our one-factor world all rates are correlated and there is little room for random behavior in the spread. One way to price such a contract is to use a two-factor interest rate model that captures both the overall rising and falling of the yield curve and also any titling.

Another method for pricing this contract is to squeeze it into the Black–Scholes-type framework. This amounts to modeling the spread directly as a lognormal (or Normal) variable and choosing suitable rates for discounting. This latter method is the market practice and although intellectually less satisfying it is also less prone to major errors.

18.8 **INDEX AMORTIZING RATE SWAPS**

A swap is an agreement between two parties to exchange interest payments on some principal, usually one payment is at a fixed rate and the other at a floating rate. In an index amortizing rate (IAR) swap the amount of this principal decreases, or **amortizes**, according to the behavior of an 'index' over the life of the swap; typically, that index is a short-term interest rate. The easiest way to understand such a swap is by example, which I keep simple.

Example Suppose that the principal begins at $10,000,000 with interest payments being at 5% from one party to the other, and r%, the spot interest rate, in the other direction. These payments are to be made quarterly.[1] At each quarter, there is an exchange of $(r - 5)$% of the principal. However, at each quarter the principal may also amortize according to the level of the spot rate at that time. In Table 18.1 we see a typical amortizing schedule.

Table 18.1 Typical amortizing schedule.

Spot rate	Principal reduction
less than 3%	100%
4%	60%
5%	40%
6%	20%
8%	10%
over 12%	0%

---

[1] In which case r would, in practice, be a three-month rate and not the spot rate. The IAR swap is so path dependent that this difference will not be of major importance.

We read this table as follows. First, on a reset date, each quarter, there is an exchange of interest payments on the principal as it then stands. What happens next depends on the level of the spot rate. If the spot interest rate (or whatever index the amortization schedule depends on) is below 3% on the date of the exchange of payments then the principal on which future interest is paid is then amortized 100%; in other words, this new level of the principal is zero and thus no further payments are made. If the spot rate is 4% then the amortization is 60%, i.e. the principal falls to just 40% of its level before this reset date. If the spot rate is 8% then the principal amortizes by just 10%. If the rate is over 12% there is no amortization at all and the principal remains at the same level. For levels of the rate between the values in the first column of the table the amount of amortization is a linear interpolation. This interpolation is shown in Figure 18.7 and the function of r that it represents I call $g(r)$.

So, although the principal begins at $10,000,000, it can change after each quarter. This feature makes the index amortizing rate swap path dependent.

The party receiving the fixed rate payments will suffer if rates rise because he will pay out a rising floating rate while the principal does not decrease. If rates fall the principal amortizes and so his lower floating rate payments are unfortunately on a lower principal. Again, he suffers. Thus the receiver of the fixed rate wants rates to remain steady and is said to be selling volatility.

In Figure 18.8 is shown the term sheet for a USD IAR swap. In this contract there is an exchange every six months of a fixed rate and six-month LIBOR. This is a vanilla IAR

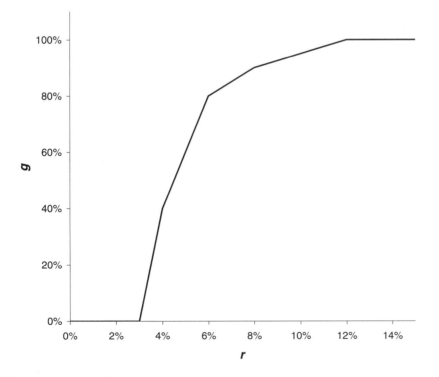

Figure 18.7 A typical amortizing schedule.

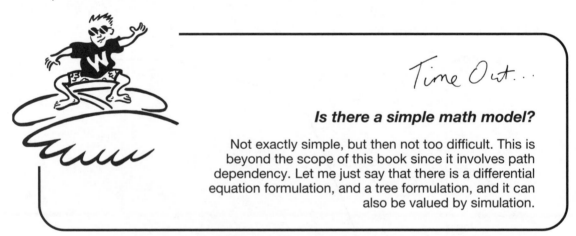

Classification	I. A. R. S.
Time dependence	Yes
Cashflow	Yes
Decisions	No
Path dependence	Strong / discrete
Dimension	3
Order	First

swap with no extra features and can be priced in the way described above. Terms in square brackets would be set at the time that the deal was made.

Time Out...

Is there a simple math model?

Not exactly simple, but then not too difficult. This is beyond the scope of this book since it involves path dependency. Let me just say that there is a differential equation formulation, and a tree formulation, and it can also be valued by simulation.

18.8.1   Other features in the index amortizing rate swap

Lockout period   There is often a 'lockout' period, usually at the start of the contract's life, during which there are no reductions in the principal. During this period the interest payments are like those of a vanilla swap. Mathematically, we can model this feature by allowing the amortizing schedule, previously $g(r)$, to be time dependent: $g(r, i)$. In this case the amount of amortizing depends on the reset date, t_i, as well as the spot interest rate. Such a model can be used for far more sophisticated structures than the simple lockout period.

USD Index Amortizing Swap

Counterparties	XXXX
	The Customer
Notional Amount	USD 50 millions, subject Amortization Schedule
Settlement Date	Two days after Trade Date
Maximum Maturity Date	Five years after Trade Date
Early Maturity Date	On any Fixing Date leading to a Notional Amount equal to 0
Payments made by Customer	**USD 6m LIBOR** paid semiannually, A/360
Payments made by XXXX	**In USD X% p.a.** paid semiannually, 30/360
Index Rate	USD 6m LIBOR
Base Rate	[ ]%

Amortization Schedule (after 1st coupon period)

USD 6m LIBOR – Base Rate	Amortization
–3%	–[ ]%
–2%	–[ ]%
–1%	–[ ]%
0	–[ ]%
1%	0%
2%	0%

NB If the observed difference falls between two entries of this schedule, the amortization amount is interpolated

Fixing Dates	2 business days before each coupon period
USD 6m LIBOR	The USD 6m LIBOR rate as seen on Telerate page 3750 at noon, London time, on each Fixing Date
Documentation	ISDA
Governing Law	English

Figure 18.8 Term sheet for a USD index amortizing swap.

Clean up Some contracts have that if the principal ever falls to a specified percentage of the original principal then it is reduced all the way to zero.

18.9 CONTRACTS WITH EMBEDDED DECISIONS

The following contract is interesting because it requires the holder to make a complex series of decisions on whether to accept or reject cashflows. The contract is path dependent.

This contract, called a **flexiswap**, is a swap with M cashflows of floating minus fixed during its life. The catch is that the holder must choose to accept exactly $m \leq M$ of these cashflows. At each cashflow date the holder must say whether they want the cashflow or not, they cannot later change their mind. When they have taken m of them they can take no more.

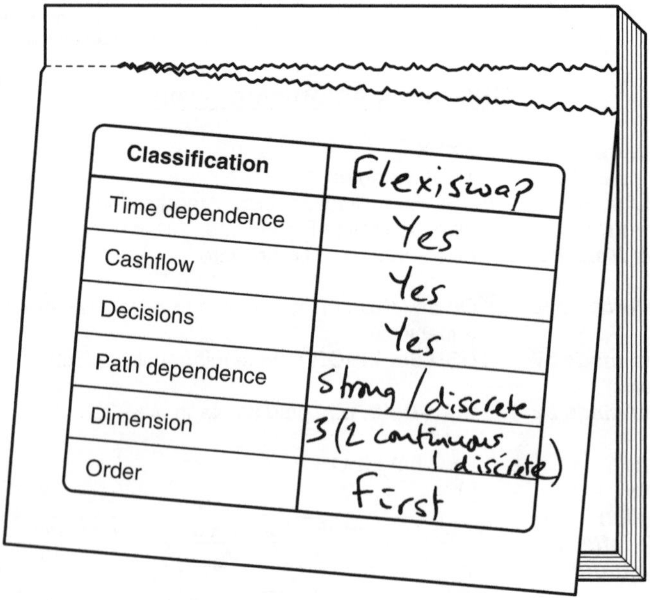

Classification	*Flexiswap*
Time dependence	*Yes*
Cashflow	*Yes*
Decisions	*Yes*
Path dependence	*Strong / discrete*
Dimension	*3 (2 continuous / 1 discrete)*
Order	*First*

18.10   SOME EXAMPLES

The term sheet in Figure 18.9 shows details of a Sterling/Deutschemark deconvergence swap. This contract allows the counterparty to express the view that rates between Germany and the UK will widen. Pricing this contract requires models for both UK and German interest rates and the correlation between them.

Preliminary and Indicative
For Discussion Purposes Only

Sterling/Deutschemark Deconvergence Swap

Start Date	10th March 1999
Maturity Date	10th March 2003
Counterparty 1 payments	
Floating rate	3m DEM LIBOR plus SPREAD
SPREAD	2.35%
Counterparty 2 payments	
Floating rate	3m GBP LIBOR

This indicative termsheet is neither an offer to buy or sell securities or an OTC derivative product which includes options,swaps, forwards and structured notes having similar features to OTC derivative transactions, nor a solicitation to buy or sell securities or an OTC derivative product.The proposal contained in the foregoing is not a complete description of the terms of a particular transaction and is subject to change without limitation.

Figure 18.9   Term sheet for a Sterling/Deutschemark deconvergence swap.

USD 1YR Fixed Rate Note with Redemption linked to World Bank Zero-Coupon Bonds

The note either redeems at par or the investor is delivered World Bank zero-coupon bonds maturing on either 1st March 2009, 15th April 2009 or 15th July 2009. The choice of redemption is at the Issuer's option. If World Bank bonds ar delivered, this will be at effective prices of 57.24% for the March bond, 56.85% for the April bond and 56.05% for the July bond.

Issue Date	15 April 2002
Maturity Date	15 April 2003
Issue price	100%
Coupon	7.00%

Figure 18.10 Term sheet for a USD fixed rate note.

Figure 18.10 shows a one-year USD fixed rate note with redemption linked to World Bank bonds. The interesting point about this contract is that the issuer of the bond gets to choose whether to redeem at par or to redeem using a choice of three World bank bonds. Obviously the issuer chooses whichever will be cheapest to deliver at the time of redemption. Hence this is an example of a **cheapest-to-deliver** bond.

The term sheet in Figure 18.11 is of a GBP two-year chooser range accrual note linked to GBP LIBOR. The contract pays a daily coupon equivalent to an annual six-month

GBP 2YR Chooser Range Accrual Note Linked to 6 month GBP LIBOR

The note pays a coupon based on the number of days that 6-month LIBOR sets within an 80 bps range. The range is chosen by the buyer at the beginning of each coupon period.

Issue Date	24th March 2000
Maturity Date	24th March 2002
Issue Price	100%
Coupon	[6 month LIBOR + 1.00%] x N/D
N	Number of business days that 6-month LIBOR is within the RANGE
D	Number of business days in the OBSERVATION PERIOD
RANGE	Determined by the buyer two days prior to the beginning of each OBSERVATION PERIOD
OBSERVATION PERIOD	Period 1: 24th March 2000–24th September 2000 Period 2: 24th September 2000–24th March 2001 Period 3: 24th March 2001–24th September 2001 Period 4: 24th September 2001–24th March 2002

Figure 18.11 Term sheet for a chooser range accrual note.

LIBOR + 100 bps. But this is only paid while LIBOR is within an 80 bps range. The novel feature about this range note is that the holder chooses the 80 bps range at the start of each coupon period.

18.11   MORE INTEREST RATE DERIVATIVES...

The following require a stochastic interest rate model for their pricing, they are model dependent.

Accordion swap: A swap (fixed-income instrument, see Chapter 15) whose maturity can be lengthened or shortened at the wish of the holder.

Barrier cap/floor: An interest rate cap or floor with a barrier feature.

Basis swap: A swap in which both legs are floating, of different maturities or currencies, say.

Bermudan swaptions: Bermudan swaptions are like vanilla swaptions in that they give the holder the right to pay (payer swaption) or receive (receiver swaption) the fixed leg of a swap. The Bermudan characteristic allows the holder to exercise into this at specified dates.

Bounded cap or floor: An interest rate cap or floor whose total payout is bounded.

Callable swap: A swap which may be called back by the fixed rate payer.

Constant maturity swap: A swap in which one leg is itself a swap rate of constant tenor (rather than the more standard LIBOR rate).

LIBOR-in-arrears swap: LIBOR-in-arrears swap is an interest rate swap in which the floating payment is made at the same time that it is set. In the plain vanilla swap the rate is fixed prior to the payment, so that a swap with six-monthly payments of six-month LIBOR has the floating rate set six months before it is paid. This subtle difference means that the LIBOR-in-arrears swap cannot be decomposed into bonds and the pricing is not model independent. There will be a slight difference between the vanilla swap and the LIBOR-in-arrears swap. Because the difference depends on the slope of the forward curve, the LIBOR-in-arrears swap is often thought of as a play on the steepening or flattening of the yield curve.

Moving average cap/floor: An interest rate cap/floor with payout determined by an average interest rate over a period.

Puttable swap: A swap which may be called back by the floating rate payer.

Ratchets and one-way floaters: Ratchets and one-way floaters are floating rate notes where the amount of the periodic payments is reset, usually in a monotonically increasing (or decreasing) manner. The amount of the reset will depend on a specified floating interest rate.

Reflex cap/floor: As a cap or floor but with payments depending on a trigger being reached.

Reverse floater: A floating rate note with coupon that rises as the underlying rate falls and vice versa.

Rolling cap/floor: A cap or floor in which the out-of-the-money portion of each payment is carried forward into the next period.

Triggers: Triggers are just like barrier options in that payments are received until (or after) a specified financial asset trades above or below a specified level. For example, the trigger swap is like a plain vanilla swap of fixed and floating until the reference LIBOR rate fixes above/below a specified rate. You can imagine that they come in and out and up and down varieties.

18.12 SUMMARY

There are a vast number of contracts in the fixed-income world. It is an impossible task to describe and model any but a small quantity of these. In this chapter I have tried to show two of the possible approaches to the modeling in a few special cases. These two approaches to the modeling are the consistent way via a partial differential equation or the practitioner way via the Black–Scholes equity model and formulæ. The former is nice because it can be made consistent across all instruments, but is dangerous to use for liquid and high-order contracts. Save this technique for the more complex, illiquid and path-dependent contracts. The alternative approach is, as everyone admits, a fudge, requiring a contract to be squeezed and bent until it looks like a call or a put on something vaguely lognormal. Although completely inconsistent across instruments it is far less likely to lead to serious mispricings.

The reader is encouraged to find out more about the pricing of products in these two distinct ways. Better still, the reader should model new contracts for himself as well.

FURTHER READING

- Black (1976) models the value of bond options assuming the bond is a lognormal asset.

- See Hull & White (1996) for more examples of pricing index amortizing rate swaps.

- Everything by Jamshidian on the pricing of interest rate derivatives is popular with practitioners. See the bibliography for some references.

- The best technical book on interest rate derivatives, their pricing and hedging, is by Rebonato (1998).

- See http://my.dreamwiz.com/stoneq/products for a comprehensive list of interest rate derivatives.

- Hagan (2002) explains how to express the volatility risk of exotics in terms of their natural vanilla hedging instruments.

- For an explanation of convexity corrections for several instruments see Hagan (2003).
- See Jäckel (2003) for cap pricing.
- See Berrahoui (2004) for CMS pricing.
- Jäckel & Kawai (2005) present formulæ for the prices of interest rate futures contracts allowing for volatility skew.

EXERCISES

1. Write down the problem we must solve in order to value a puttable bond.

2. Derive a relationship between a floorlet and a call option on a zero-coupon bond.

3. How would a collar be valued practically? What is the explicit solution for a single payment?

4. When an index amortizing rate swap has a lockout period for the first year, we must solve

$$\frac{\partial V}{\partial t} + \tfrac{1}{2}w^2\frac{\partial^2 V}{\partial r^2} + (u - \lambda w)\frac{\partial V}{\partial r} - rV = 0,$$

with jump condition

$$V(r, P, t_i^-) = V(r, g(r, i)P, t_i^+) + (r - r_f)P,$$

where

$$g(r, i) = 1 \quad \text{if} \quad t_i < 1,$$

and with final condition

$$V(r, P, T) = (r - r_f)P.$$

In this case, reduce the order of the problem using a similarity reduction of the form

$$V(r, P, t) = PH(r, t).$$

5. Find the approximate value of a cashflow for a floorlet on the one-month LIBOR, when we use the Vasicek model.

the Heath, Jarrow & Morton and Brace, Gatarek & Musiela models

The aim of this Chapter...

...is to explain in as simple a way as possible the breakthroughs in interest rate modeling known as the Heath, Jarrow & Morton model and the Brace, Gatarek & Musiela model. Unfortunately, even the simplest explanation is tough going and I would understand if you skipped all the math in this chapter.

In this Chapter...

- the Heath, Jarrow & Morton forward rate model
- the relationship between HJM and spot rate models
- the advantages and disadvantages of the HJM approach
- how to decompose the random movements of the forward rate curve into its principal components
- the Brace, Gatarek & Musiela model

19.1 **INTRODUCTION**

The **Heath, Jarrow & Morton** approach to the modeling of the whole forward rate curve was a major breakthrough in the pricing of fixed-income products. They built up a framework that encompassed all of the models we have seen so far (and many that we haven't). Instead of modeling a short-term interest rate and deriving the forward rates (or, equivalently, the yield curve) from that model, they boldly start with a model for the whole forward rate curve. Since the forward rates are known today, the matter of yield curve fitting is contained naturally within their model, it does not appear as an afterthought. Moreover, it is possible to take *real data* for the random movement of the forward rates and incorporate them into the derivative pricing methodology.

19.2 **THE FORWARD RATE EQUATION**

The key concept in the HJM model is that we model the evolution of the whole forward rate curve, not just the short end. Write $F(t; T)$ for the forward rate curve at time t. Thus the price of a zero-coupon bond at time t and maturing at time T, when it pays $1, is

$$Z(t; T) = e^{-\int_t^T F(t;s)\,ds}. \tag{19.1}$$

Let us assume that all zero-coupon bonds evolve according to

$$dZ(t; T) = \mu(t, T)Z(t; T)dt + \sigma(t, T)Z(t; T)dX. \tag{19.2}$$

This is not much of an assumption, other than to say that it is a one-factor model, and I will generalize that later. In this $d\cdot$ means that time t evolves but the maturity date T is fixed. Note that since $Z(t; t) = 1$ we must have $\sigma(t, t) = 0$. From (19.1) we have

$$F(t; T) = -\frac{\partial}{\partial T} \log Z(t; T).$$

Differentiating this with respect to t and substituting from (19.2) results in an equation for the evolution of the forward curve:

$$dF(t; T) = \frac{\partial}{\partial T}\left(\tfrac{1}{2}\sigma^2(t, T) - \mu(t, T)\right)dt - \frac{\partial}{\partial T}\sigma(t, T)dX. \tag{19.3}$$

In Figure 19.1 is shown the forward rate curve today, time t^*, and a few days later. The whole curve has moved according to (19.3).

Where has this got us? We have an expression for the drift of the forward rates in terms of the volatility of the forward rates. There is also a μ term, the drift of the bond. We have seen many times before how such drift terms disappear when we come to pricing derivatives, to be replaced by the risk-free interest rate r. Exactly the same will happen here.

19.3 **THE SPOT RATE PROCESS**

The spot interest rate is simply given by the forward rate for a maturity equal to the current date, i.e.

$$r(t) = F(t; t).$$

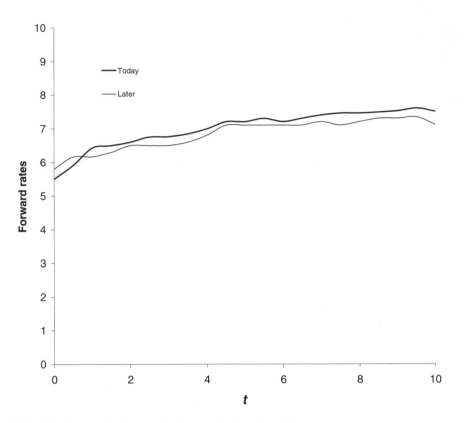

Figure 19.1 The forward rate curve today and a few days later.

In this section I am going to manipulate this expression to derive the stochastic differential equation for the spot rate. In so doing we will begin to see why the HJM approach can be slow to price derivatives.

Suppose today is t^* and that we know the whole forward rate curve today, $F(t^*; T)$. We can write the spot rate for *any* time t in the future as

$$r(t) = F(t; t) = F(t^*; t) + \int_{t^*}^{t} dF(s; t).$$

From our earlier expression (19.3) for the forward rate process for F we have

$$r(t) = F(t^*; t) + \int_{t^*}^{t} \left(\sigma(s, t)\frac{\partial \sigma(s, t)}{\partial t} - \frac{\partial \mu(s, t)}{\partial t} \right) ds - \int_{t^*}^{t} \frac{\partial \sigma(s, t)}{\partial t} dX(s).$$

Differentiating this with respect to time t we arrive at the stochastic differential equation for r

$$dr = \left(\frac{\partial F(t^*; t)}{\partial t} - \frac{\partial \mu(t, s)}{\partial s} \Big|_{s=t} + \int_{t^*}^{t} \left(\sigma(s, t)\frac{\partial^2 \sigma(s, t)}{\partial t^2} + \left(\frac{\partial \sigma(s, t)}{\partial t} \right)^2 - \frac{\partial^2 \mu(s, t)}{\partial t^2} \right) ds \right.$$

$$\left. - \underline{\int_{t^*}^{t} \frac{\partial^2 \sigma(s, t)}{\partial t^2} dX(s)} \right) dt - \frac{\partial \sigma(t, s)}{\partial s} \Big|_{s=t} dX.$$

Eeeek!

This is not a pretty sight. The idea is simple but the math is not. Hold the thought that in the HJM model we move/model *the whole of the forward rate curve*, and not just one end of it. Since we start with today's forward rate curve we don't have to worry about getting discount factors correct initially, they are automatically correct.

If you find the math daunting, just read the words for the rest of this chapter.

19.3.1 The non-Markov nature of HJM

The details of this expression are not important. I just want you to observe one point. Compare this stochastic differential equation for the spot rate with any of the models in Chapter 16. Clearly, it is more complicated, there are many more terms. All but the last one are deterministic, the last is random. The important point concerns the nature of these terms. In particular, the term underlined depends on the history of σ from the date t^* to the future date t, and *it depends on the history of the stochastic increments dX*. This term is thus highly path dependent. Moreover, for a general HJM model it makes the motion of the spot rate **non-Markov**. In a **Markov process** it is only the present state of a variable that determines the possible future (albeit random) state. Having a non-Markov model may not matter to us if we can find a small number of extra state variables that contain all the information that we need for predicting the future. Unfortunately, the general HJM model requires an infinite number of such variables to define the present state; if we were to write the HJM model as a partial differential equation we would need an infinite number of independent variables.

At the moment we are in the real world. To price derivatives we need to move over to the risk-neutral world. The first step in this direction is to see what happens when we hold a hedged portfolio.

19.4 THE MARKET PRICE OF RISK

In the one-factor HJM model all stochastic movements of the forward rate curve are perfectly correlated. We can therefore hedge one bond with another of a different maturity. Such a hedged portfolio is

$$\Pi = Z(t; T_1) - \Delta Z(t; T_2).$$

The change in this portfolio is given by

$$d\Pi = dZ(t; T_1) - \Delta\, dZ(t; T_2)$$

$$= Z(t; T_1)\left(\mu(t, T_1)dt + \sigma(t, T_1)dX\right) - \Delta Z(t; T_2)\left(\mu(t, T_2)dt + \sigma(t, T_2)dX\right).$$

If we choose

$$\Delta = \frac{\sigma(t, T_1)Z(t; T_1)}{\sigma(t, T_2)Z(t; T_2)}$$

then our portfolio is hedged, is risk free. Setting its return equal to the risk-free rate $r(t)$ and rearranging we find that

$$\frac{\mu(t, T_1) - r(t)}{\sigma(t, T_1)} = \frac{\mu(t, T_2) - r(t)}{\sigma(t, T_2)}.$$

The left-hand side is a function of T_1 and the right-hand side is a function of T_2. This is only possible if both sides are independent of the maturity date T:

$$\mu(t, T) = r(t) + \lambda(t)\sigma(t, T).$$

As before, $\lambda(t)$ is the market price of risk (associated with the one factor).

19.5 **REAL AND RISK NEUTRAL**

We are almost ready to price derivatives using the HJM model. But first we must discuss the real and risk-neutral worlds, relating them to the ideas in previous chapters.

All of the variables I have introduced above have been *real* variables. But when we come to pricing derivatives we must do so in the risk-neutral world. In the present HJM context, risk-neutral 'means' $\mu(t, T) = r(t)$. This means that in the risk-neutral world the return on any traded investment is simply $r(t)$. We can see this in (19.2). The risk-neutral zero-coupon bond price satisfies

$$dZ(t; T) = r(t)Z(t; T)dt + \sigma(t, T)Z(t; T)dX.$$

The deterministic part of this equation represents exponential growth of the bond at the risk-free rate. The form of the equation is very similar to that for a risk-neutral equity, except that here the volatility will be much more complicated.

NO ARBITRAGE RESULTS IN A RELATIONSHIP BETWEEN RISK-NEUTRAL DRIFT AND VOL

19.5.1 The relationship between the risk-neutral forward rate drift and volatility

Let me write the stochastic differential equation for the *risk-neutral* forward rate curve as

$$dF(t; T) = m(t, T)dt + v(t, T)dX.$$

From (19.3)

$$v(t, T) = -\frac{\partial}{\partial T}\sigma(t, T)$$

is the forward rate volatility and, from (19.3), the drift of the forward rate is given by

$$\frac{\partial}{\partial T}\left(\tfrac{1}{2}\sigma^2(t, T) - \mu(t, T)\right) = v(t, T)\int_t^T v(t, s)ds - \frac{\partial}{\partial T}\mu(t, T),$$

where we have used $\sigma(t, t) = 0$. In the risk-neutral world we have $\mu(t, T) = r(t)$, and so the drift of the risk-neutral forward rate curve is related to its volatility by

$$m(t, T) = v(t, T) \int_t^T v(t, s)ds. \tag{19.4}$$

And so

$$dF(t; T) = v(t, T) \left(\int_t^T v(t, s)ds \right) dt + v(t, T)dX. \tag{19.5}$$

19.6 **PRICING DERIVATIVES**

Pricing derivatives is all about finding the expected present value of all cashflows in a risk-neutral framework. This was discussed in Chapter 6, in terms of equity, currency and commodity derivatives. If we are lucky then this calculation can be done via a low-dimensional partial differential equation. The HJM model, however, is a very general interest rate model and in its full generality one cannot write down a finite-dimensional partial differential equation for the price of a derivative.

Because of the non-Markov nature of HJM in general a partial differential equation approach is infeasible. This leaves us with two alternatives. One is to estimate directly the necessary expectations by simulating the random evolution of, in this case, the risk-neutral forward rates. The other is to build up a tree structure.

19.7 **SIMULATIONS**

If we want to use a Monte Carlo method, then we must simulate the evolution of the whole forward rate curve, calculate the value of all cashflows under each evolution and then calculate the present value of these cashflows by *discounting at the realized spot rate, $r(t)$.*

To price a derivative using a Monte Carlo simulation, perform the following steps. I will assume that we have chosen a model for the forward rate volatility, $v(t, T)$. Today is t^* when we know the forward rate curve $F(t^*; T)$.

1. Simulate a realized evolution of the whole risk-neutral forward rate curve for the necessary length of time, until T^*, say. This requires a simulation of

$$dF(t; T) = m(t, T)dt + v(t, T)dX,$$

where

$$m(t, T) = v(t, T) \int_t^T v(t, s)ds.$$

After this simulation we will have a realization of $F(t; T)$ for $t^* \leq t \leq T^*$ and $T \geq t$. We will have a realization of the whole forward rate path.

2. At the end of the simulation we will have the realized prices of all maturity zero-coupon bonds at every time up to T^*.

3. Using this forward rate path calculate the value of all the cashflows that would have occurred.

4. Using the realized path for the spot interest rate $r(t)$ calculate the present value of these cashflows. Note that we discount at the continuously compounded risk-free rate, not at any other rate. In the risk-neutral world all assets have an expected return of $r(t)$.

5. Return to Step 1 to perform another realization, and continue until you have a sufficiently large number of realizations to calculate the expected present value as accurately as required.

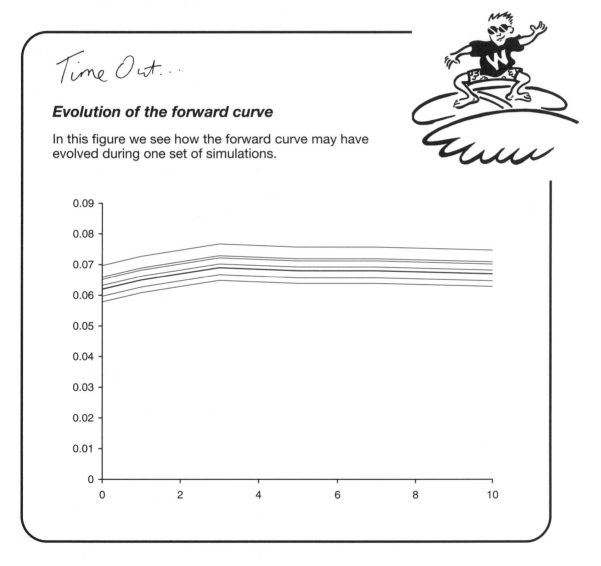

Time Out...

Evolution of the forward curve

In this figure we see how the forward curve may have evolved during one set of simulations.

The disadvantage of the HJM model is that a Monte Carlo simulation such as this can be slow. On the plus side, because the whole forward rate curve is calculated the bond prices at all maturities are trivial to find during this simulation.

19.8 **TREES**

If we are to build up a tree for a non-Markov model then we find ourselves with the unfortunate result that the forward curve after an up move followed by a down is *not* the same as the curve after a down followed by an up. The equivalence of these two paths in the Markov world is what makes the binomial method so powerful and efficient. In the non-Markov world our tree structure becomes 'bushy,' and grows *exponentially* in size with the addition of new time steps.

If the contract we are valuing is European with no early exercise then we don't need to use a tree, a Monte Carlo simulation can be immediately implemented. However, if the contract has some American feature then to correctly price in the early exercise we don't have much choice but to use a tree structure. The exponentially large tree structure will make the pricing problem very slow.

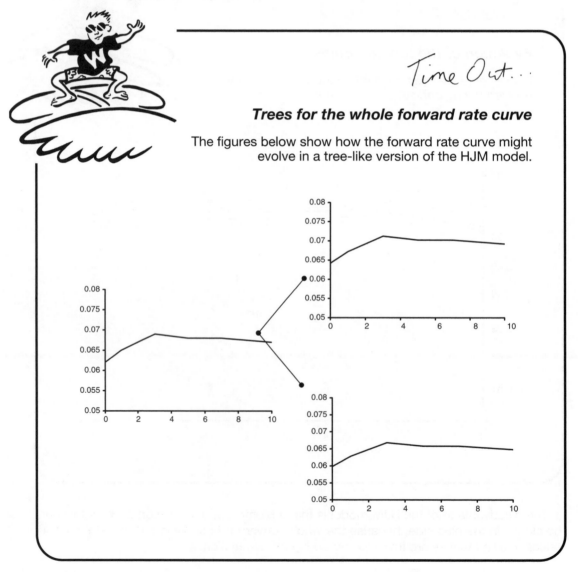

Time Out...

Trees for the whole forward rate curve

The figures below show how the forward rate curve might evolve in a tree-like version of the HJM model.

19.9 **THE MUSIELA PARAMETERIZATION**

Often in practice the model for the volatility structure of the forward rate curve will be of the form

$$v(t, T) = \bar{v}(t, T - t),$$

meaning that we will model the volatility of the forward rate at each maturity, one, two, three years, and not at each maturity date, 2006, 2007, ... If we write τ for the maturity period $T - t$ then it is a simple matter to find that $\bar{F}(t; \tau) = F(t, t + \tau)$ satisfies

$$d\bar{F}(t; \tau) = \bar{m}(t, \tau)dt + \bar{v}(t, \tau)dX,$$

where

$$\bar{m}(t, \tau) = \bar{v}(t, \tau) \int_0^\tau \bar{v}(t, s)ds + \frac{\partial}{\partial \tau}\bar{F}(t, \tau).$$

It is much easier in practice to use this representation for the evolution of the risk-neutral forward rate curve.

19.10 **MULTI-FACTOR HJM**

Often a single-factor model does not capture the subtleties of the yield curve that are important for particular contracts. The obvious example is the spread option that pays off the difference between rates at two different maturities. We then require a multi-factor model. The multi-factor theory is identical to the one-factor case, so we can simply write down the extension to many factors.

If the risk-neutral forward rate curve satisfies the N-dimensional stochastic differential equation

$$dF(t; T) = m(t; T)dt + \sum_{i=1}^{N} v_i(t; T)dX_i,$$

where the dX_i are uncorrelated, then

$$m(t, T) = \sum_{i=1}^{N} v_i(t, T) \int_t^T v_i(t, s)ds.$$

And so

$$dF(t, T) = \left(\sum_{i=1}^{N} v_i(t, T) \int_t^T v_i(t, s)ds \right) dt + \sum_{i=1}^{N} v_i(t, T)dX_i. \tag{19.6}$$

19.11 **SPREADSHEET IMPLEMENTATION**

The HJM model is very easy to implement on a spreadsheet. Figure 19.2 shows the results of such a simulation for a two-factor model. In this example the Musiela parameterization has been used and $\bar{v}$ is a function of $\tau = T - t$ only. This means that the function $\bar{m}$ contains the first volatility term which is just a function of time to maturity (this is row 3 in the figure) and the slope of the forward curve term (this latter is calculated in each of the cells from row 11 down). In this example there are two volatility factors, the first is constant and the second is linear in τ.

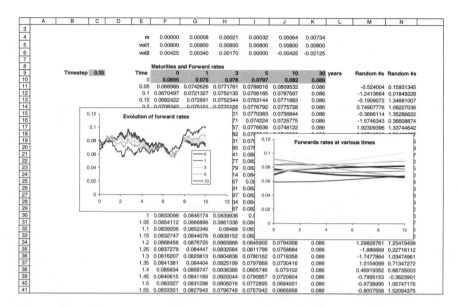

Figure 19.2 Spreadsheet showing results of a two-factor HJM simulation.

19.12 **A SIMPLE ONE-FACTOR EXAMPLE: HO & LEE**

In this section we make a comparison between the spot rate modeling of Chapter 16 and HJM. One of the key points about the HJM approach is that the yield curve is fitted by default. The simplest yield curve fitting spot rate model is Ho & Lee, so we draw a comparison between this and HJM.

In Ho & Lee the risk-neutral spot rate satisfies

$$dr = \eta(t)dt + c\,dX,$$

for a constant c. The prices of zero-coupon bonds, $Z(r, t; T)$, in this model satisfy

$$\frac{\partial Z}{\partial t} + \frac{1}{2}c^2 \frac{\partial^2 Z}{\partial r^2} + \eta(t)\frac{\partial Z}{\partial r} - rZ = 0$$

with

$$Z(r, T; T) = 1.$$

The solution is easily found to be

$$Z(r, t; T) = \exp\left(\frac{1}{6}c^2(T-t)^3 - \int_t^T \eta(s)(T-s)ds - (T-t)r\right).$$

In the Ho & Lee model $\eta(t)$ is chosen to fit the yield curve at time t^*. In forward rate terms this means that

$$F(t^*; T) = r(t^*) - \frac{1}{2}c^2(T-t^*)^2 + \int_{t^*}^T \eta(s)ds,$$

and so

$$\eta(t) = \frac{\partial F(t^*; t)}{\partial t} + c^2(t - t^*).$$

At any time later than t^*

$$F(t; T) = r(t) - \tfrac{1}{2}c^2(T - t)^2 + \int_t^T \eta(s)ds.$$

From this we find that

$$dF(t; T) = c^2(T - t)dt + c \, dX.$$

In our earlier notation, $\sigma(t, T) = -c(T - t)$ and $v(t, T) = c$. This is the evolution equation for the risk-neutral forward rates. It is easily confirmed for this model that Equation (19.4) holds. This is the HJM representation of the Ho & Lee model. Most of the popular models have HJM representations.

19.13 PRINCIPAL COMPONENT ANALYSIS

There are two main ways to use HJM. One is to choose the volatility structure $v_i(t, T)$ to be sufficiently 'nice' to make a tractable model, one that is Markov. This usually leads us back to the 'classical' popular spot-rate models. The other way is to choose the volatility structure to match data. This is where principal component analysis (PCA) comes in.

In analyzing the volatility of the forward rate curve one usually assumes that the volatility structure depends only on the time to maturity, i.e.

$$v = \bar{v}(T - t).$$

I will assume this but examine a more general multi-factor model:

$$dF(t; T) = m(t, T)dt + \sum_{i=1}^N \bar{v}_i(T - t)dX_i.$$

From time series data we can determine the functions $\bar{v}_i$ empirically, this is **principal components analysis**. I will give a loose description of how this is done, with more details in the spreadsheets.

If we have forward rate time series data going back a few years we can calculate the covariances between the *changes* in the rates of different maturities. We may have, for example, the one-, three-, six-month, one-, two-, three-, five-, seven-, 10- and 30-year rates. The covariance matrix would then be a 10×10 symmetric matrix with the variances of the rates along the diagonal and the covariances between rates off the diagonal.

In Figure 19.3 is shown a spreadsheet of daily one-, three- and six-month rates, and the day-to-day changes. The covariance matrix for these changes is also shown.

PCA is a technique for finding common movements in the rates, for essentially finding eigenvalues and eigenvectors of the matrix. We expect to find, for example, that a large part of the movement of the forward rate curve is common between rates, that a parallel

	A	B	C	D	E	F	G
1	Forward rates:				Changes in rates:		
2		1 month	3 month	6 month	1 month	3 month	6 month
3	22-Sep-88	8.25000	8.31250	8.56250			
4	23-Sep-88	8.25000	8.31250	8.56250	0.00000	0.00000	0.00000
5	26-Sep-88	8.31250	8.37500	8.62500	0.06250	0.06250	0.06250
6	27-Sep-88	8.31250	8.43750	8.6[=B4-B3]0000		0.06250	0.06250
7	28-Sep-88	8.42188	8.50000	8.81250	0.10938	0.06250	0.12500
8	29-Sep-88	8.37500	8.68750	8.81250	-0.04688	0.18750	0.00000
9	30-Sep-88	8.31250	8.62500	8.75000	-0.06250	-0.06250	-0.06250
10	3-Oct-88	8.31250	8.62500	8.68750	0.00000	0.00000	-0.06250
11	4-Oct-88	8.31250	8.56250	8.68750	0.00000	-0.06250	0.00000
12	5-Oct-88	8.31250	8.56250	8.68750	0.00000	0.00000	0.00000
13	6-Oct-88	8.31250	8.56250	8.68750	0.00000	0.00000	0.00000
14	7-Oct-88	8.31250	8.62500	8.75000	0.00000	0.06250	0.06250
15	10-Oct-88	8.25000	8.56250	8.56250	-0.06250	-0.06250	-0.18750
16	11-Oct-88	8.25000	8.56250	8.62500	0.00000	0.00000	0.06250
17	12-Oct-88	8.31250	8.62500	8.68750	0.06250	0.06250	0.06250
18	13-Oct-88	8.31250	8.64063	8.68750	0.00000	0.01563	0.00000
19	14-Oct-88	8.31250	8.62500	8.62500	0.00000	-0.01563	-0.06250
20	17-Oct-88	8.31250	8.62500	8.62500	0.00000	0.00000	0.00000
21	18-Oct-88	8.31250	8.62500	8.62500	0.00000	0.00000	0.00000
22	19-Oct-88	8.31250	8.62500	8.62500	0.00000	0.00000	0.00000
23	20-Oct-88	8.37500	8.68750	8.68750	0.06250	0.06250	0.06250
24	21-Oct-88	8.37500	8.68750	8.68750	0.00000	0.00000	0.00000
25	24-Oct-88	8.37500	8.68750	8.75000	0.00000	0.00000	0.06250
26	25-Oct-88	8.37500	8.68750	8.75000	0.00000	0.00000	0.00000
27	26-Oct-88	8.37500	8.68750	8.75000	0.00000	0.00000	0.00000
28	27-Oct-88	8.37500	8.68750	8.68750	0.00000	0.00000	-0.06250

Annotation (columns H–K):

=COVAR(E4:E1721,F4:F1721)

	1 month	3 month	6 month
1 month	0.007501		
3 month	0.003831	0.004225	
6 month	0.003628	0.004020	0.004997

Scaled covariance matrix:

	1 month	3 month	6 month
1 month	0.000189		
3 month	0.000097	0.000106	
6 month	0.000091	0.000101	0.000126

=I8*252/10000

Figure 19.3 One-, three- and six-month rates and the changes.

shift in the rates is the largest component of the movement of the curve in general. The next most important movement would be a twisting of the curve, followed by a bending.

Suppose that we have found the covariance matrix, **M**, for the changes in the rates mentioned above. This 10 by 10 matrix will have 10 eigenvalues, λ_i, and eigenvectors, $\mathbf{v}_i$, satisfying

$$\mathbf{M}\mathbf{v}_i = \lambda_i \mathbf{v}_i;$$

$\mathbf{v}_i$ is a column vector.

The eigenvector associated with the largest eigenvalue is the first principal component. It gives the dominant part in the movement of the forward rate curve. Its first entry represents the movement of the one-month rate, the second entry is the three-month rate, etc. Its eigenvalue is the variance of these movements. In Figure 19.4 we see the entries in this first principal component plotted against the relevant maturity. This curve is relatively flat when compared with the other components. This indicates that, indeed, a parallel shift of the yield curve is the dominant movement. Note that the eigenvectors are orthogonal, there is no correlation between the principal components.

In this figure are also plotted the next two principal components. Observe that one gives a twisting of the curve and the other a bending.

The result of this analysis is that the volatility factors are given by

$$\bar{v}_i(\tau_j) = \sqrt{\lambda_i}(\mathbf{v}_i)_j.$$

Here τ_j is the maturity, i.e. 1/12, 1/4, etc. and $(\mathbf{v}_i)_j$ is the jth entry in the vector $\mathbf{v}_i$. To get the volatility of other maturities will require some interpolation.

The calculation of the covariance matrix is simple, discussed in Chapter 12. The calculation of the eigenvalues and vectors is also simple if you use the following algorithm.

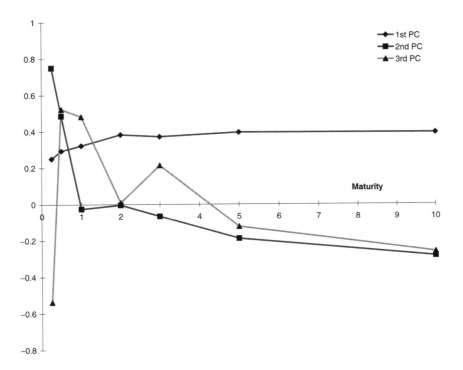

Figure 19.4 The first three principal components for the US forward rate curve. The data run from 1988 until 1996.

19.13.1 The power method

I will assume that all the eigenvalues are distinct, a reasonable assumption given the empirical nature of the matrix. Since the matrix is symmetric positive definite (it is a covariance matrix) we have all the nice properties we need. The eigenvector associated with the *largest* eigenvalue is easily found by the following iterative procedure. First, make an initial guess for the eigenvector, call it $\mathbf{x}^0$. Now iterate using

$$\mathbf{y}^{k+1} = \mathbf{M}\mathbf{x}^k,$$

for $k = 0, \ldots,$ and

$$\beta^{k+1} = \text{element of } \mathbf{y}^{k+1} \text{ having largest modulus}$$

followed by

$$\mathbf{x}^{i+1} = \frac{1}{\beta^{k+1}}\mathbf{y}^{k+1}.$$

As $k \to \infty$, $\mathbf{x}^k$ tends to the eigenvector and β^k to the eigenvalue λ. In practice you would stop iterating once you have reached some set tolerance. Thus we have found the first principal component. It is standard to normalize the vector, and this is our $\mathbf{v}_1$.

To find the next principal component we must define a new matrix by

$$\mathbf{N} = \mathbf{M} - \lambda_1 \mathbf{v}_1 \mathbf{v}_1^T.$$

Now use the power method on this new matrix $\mathbf{N}$ to find the second principal component. This process can be repeated until all (10) components have been found.

19.14   OPTIONS ON EQUITIES, ETC.

The pricing of options contingent on equities, currencies, commodities, indices, etc. is straightforward in the HJM framework. All that we need to know are the volatility of the asset and its correlations with the forward rate factors. The Monte Carlo simulation then uses the risk-neutral random walks for both the forward rates and the asset, i.e. zero-coupon bonds and the asset have a drift of $r(t)$. Of course, there are the usual adjustments, to be made for dividends, foreign interest rate or cost of carry, amounting to a change to the drift rate for the asset.

The only fly in the ointment is that American-style exercise is difficult to accommodate.

19.15   NON-INFINITESIMAL SHORT RATE

One of the problems with HJM is that there is no guarantee that interest rates will stay positive, nor that the money market account will stay finite. These problems are associated with the use of a continuously compounded interest rate; all rates can be deduced from the evolution of this rate, but the rate itself is not actually observable. Modeling rates with a finite accruals period, such as three-month LIBOR, for example, have two advantages: the rate is directly observable, and positivity and finiteness can be guaranteed. Let's see how this works. I use the Musiela parameterization of the forward rates.

I have said that $\overline{F}(t, \tau)$ satisfies

$$d\overline{F}(t, \tau) = \ldots + \overline{v}(t, \tau)dX.$$

A reasonable choice for the volatility structure might be

$$\overline{v}(t, \tau) = \gamma(t, \tau)\overline{F}(t, \tau)$$

for finite, non-zero $\gamma(t, \tau)$. At first sight, this is a good choice for the volatility, after all, lognormality is a popular choice for random walks in finance. Unfortunately, this model leads to exploding interest rates. Yet we would like to retain some form of lognormality of rates, recall that market practice is to assume lognormality of just about everything.

We can get around the explosive rates by defining an interest rate $j(t, \tau)$ that is accrued m times *per annum*. The relationship between the new $j(t, \tau)$ and the old $\overline{F}(t, \tau)$ is then

$$\left(1 + \frac{j(t, \tau)}{m}\right)^m = e^{\overline{F}(t, \tau)}.$$

Now what happens if we choose a lognormal model for the rates? If we choose

$$dj(t, \tau) = \ldots + \gamma(t, \tau)j(t, \tau)dX,$$

it can be shown that this leads to a stochastic differential equation for $\overline{F}(t, \tau)$ of the form

$$d\overline{F}(t, \tau) = \ldots - m\gamma(t, \tau)\left(1 - e^{\overline{F}(t,\tau)/m}\right) dX.$$

The volatility structure in this expression is such that all rates stay positive and no explosion occurs.

If we specify the quantity m, we can of course still do PCA to find out the best form for the function $\gamma(t, \tau) = \gamma(\tau)$.

19.16 THE BRACE, GATAREK & MUSIELA MODEL

The Brace, Gatarek & Musiela[1] model crucially models the actual traded, observable quantities in the fixed-income world. Think of it as a discrete version of the HJM model. This is relatively straightforward, but slightly unnerving if you are used to differential rather than difference equations. The model is popular with practitioners because it can price any contract whose cashflows can be decomposed into functions of the observed forward rates.

We will work in terms of observable, discrete forward rates, i.e. rates that really are quoted in the market, rather than the unrealistic continuous forward curve. With $Z(t; T)$ being the price of a zero-coupon bond at time t that matures at time T we have the forward rates at time t, for the period from T_i to the time T_{i+1}, separated by the time step τ, given by

$$1 + \tau F(t; T_i, T_{i+1}) = 1 + \tau F(t; T_i, T_i + \tau) = 1 + \tau F_i(t) = \frac{Z(t; T_i)}{Z(t; T_{i+1})}.$$

This is the definition of forward rates in terms of zero-coupon bond prices, or vice versa. For simplicity of notation in what follows we shall use F_i to mean $F(t; T_i, T_{i+1})$, and Z_i to mean $Z(t; T_i)$. These are, of course, stochastic quantities, varying with time.

The discount factor in terms of the forward rate is just

$$\frac{1}{1 + \tau F_i(t)}.$$

This is the discount factor for present valuing from T_{i+1} back to T_i.

Note that here we are using the discrete compounding definition of an interest rate, consistent with that introduced in Chapter 14, rather than our usual continuous definition that is more often used in the equity world.

Let's suppose that we can write the dynamics of each forward rate, F_i, as

$$dF_i = \mu_i F_i \, dt + \sigma_i F_i \, dX_i.$$

This looks like a lognormal model, but, of course, the μs and σs could be hiding more Fs. So really it's a lot more general than that. Similarly suppose that the zero-coupon bond dynamics are given by

$$dZ_i = rZ_i \, dt + Z_i \sum_{j=1}^{i-1} a_{ij} \, dX_j \tag{19.7}$$

---

[1] The BGM or BGM/J model, the J standing for Jamshidian.

where

$$Z_i(t) = Z(t; T_i).$$

There are several points to note about this expression. First of all, we are clearly in a risk-neutral world with the drift of the *traded* asset Z being the risk-free rate. If the bond wasn't traded then we couldn't say that its drift was r.[2] That's why we couldn't say that the drift of F_i was r, since the forward rate is *not* a traded instrument.

Actually, we'll see shortly that we don't need a model for r, it will drop out of the analysis. Also, it looks like a lognormal model but again the *a*s could be hiding more Zs.

Finally, the zero-coupon bond volatility is only given in terms of the volatilities of forward rates of shorter maturities. This is because volatility after its maturity will not affect the value of a bond, and that's why there is no a_{ii} term in Equation (19.7).

We can write

$$Z_i = (1 + \tau F_i)Z_{i+1}.$$

Applying Itô's lemma to this we get

$$dZ_i = (1 + \tau F_i)dZ_{i+1} + \tau Z_{i+1}\, dF_i + \tau \sigma_i F_i Z_{i+1} \left(\sum_{j=1}^{i} a_{i+1,j}\rho_{ij} \right) dt, \qquad (19.8)$$

where ρ_{ij} is the correlation between dX_i and dX_j.

Think of Equation (19.8) as containing three types of terms: dX_i; dX_j for $j = 1, \ldots, i - 1$; dt. Equating coefficients of dX_i in Equation (19.8) we get

$$0 = (1 + \tau F_i)a_{i+1,i}Z_{i+1} + \tau Z_{i+1}\sigma_i F_i,$$

($a_{ii} = 0$ remember), that is

$$a_{i+1,i} = -\frac{\sigma_i F_i \tau}{1 + \tau F_i}.$$

Equating the other random terms, dX_j for $j = 1, \ldots, i - 1$, gives

$$a_{ij}Z_i = (1 + \tau F_i)Z_{i+1}a_{i+1,j},$$

that is

$$a_{i+1,j} = a_{ij} \quad \text{for } j < i.$$

It follows that

$$a_{i+1,j} = -\frac{\sigma_j F_j \tau}{1 + \tau F_j} \quad \text{for } j < i.$$

Finally, equating the dt terms we get

$$rZ_i = (1 + \tau F_i)rZ_{i+1} + \tau Z_{i+1}\mu_i F_i + \tau \sigma_i F_i Z_{i+1} \sum_{j=1}^{i} a_{i+1,j}\, \rho_{ij}.$$

---

[2] The drift isn't r, of course, in the real world. But we are in the risk-neutral world for pricing, and in that world all traded instruments have growth r.

From the definition of F_i the terms including r cancel, leaving

$$\mu_i = -\sigma_i \sum_{j=1}^{i} a_{i+1,j} \rho_{ij} = \sigma_i \sum_{j=1}^{i} \frac{\sigma_j F_j \tau \rho_{ij}}{1 + \tau F_j}.$$

And we are done.

The stochastic differential equation for F_i can be written as

$$dF_i = \left(\sum_{j=1}^{i} \frac{\sigma_j F_j \tau \rho_{ij}}{1 + \tau F_j} \right) \sigma_i F_i \, dt + \sigma_i F_i \, dX_i. \tag{19.9}$$

Equation (19.9) is the discrete BGM version of Equation (19.6) for HJM.[3]

Assuming that we can measure or model the volatilities of the forward rates σ_i and the correlations between them ρ_{ij} then we have found the correct risk-neutral drift. We are on familiar territory, Monte Carlo simulations using these volatilities, correlations and drifts can be used to price interest rate derivatives. In practice, one estimates the volatility functions from the market prices of caplets. Invariably, this is how one calibrates the time-dependent functions, rather than estimating them from historical data, say.

19.17 **SIMULATIONS**

We can write (19.9) as

$$d(\log(F_i)) = \left(\sigma_i \sum_{j=1}^{i} \frac{\sigma_j F_j \tau \rho_{ij}}{1 + \tau F_j} - \tfrac{1}{2}\sigma_i^2 \right) dt + \sigma_i \, dX_i.$$

In simulating this random walk we would typically divide time up into equal intervals, we would assume, in order to integrate this expression from one interval to the next, that the Fs (and the σs and ρs) were all piecewise constant during each time interval. Simulation then becomes relatively straightforward.

What is not so obvious, however, is how to present value the cashflows. We know from the risk-neutral concepts that there are two aspects to calculating the expectation that is the contracts value, and they are

- simulating the risk-neutral random walk;

- present valuing the cashflows.

Well, I've explained the first of these, what about the second?

19.18 **PVING THE CASHFLOWS**

Before present valuing the cashflows (in anticipation of later averaging, and hence pricing) we must be able to write them in terms of the quantities we have simulated, that is the forward rates. That may be simple or hard. For the simpler instruments they are already defined in terms of these quantities. The more complicated contracts might have cashflows that are, in the sense of our exotic option classification, higher order. In the

---

[3] Although the notation is slightly different. In the HJM analysis we wrote the random component in terms of uncorrelated dX_i, here we have a different dX_i for each forward rate, but they are all potentially correlated.

HJM framework we present valued these cashflows using the average spot rate r up until each cashflow. In the BGM model we don't have such an r, of course.

In the BGM model we must present value using the discount factors applicable (for each realization) from one accrual period to the next. That is, we present value each cashflow back to the present through all of the dates T_i using the one-period discount factor at each period:[4]

$$\frac{1}{1 + \tau F_i(T_i)}.$$

This is the discrete version of the present valuing we do with the average spot rate in the HJM model. Indeed, if you take the limit as $\tau \to 0$ in all of the above equations you will get back to the HJM model, all the sums become integrals, for example.

19.19 SUMMARY

The HJM and BGM approaches to modeling the whole forward rate curve in one go are very powerful. For certain types of contract it is easy to program the Monte Carlo simulations. For example, bond options can be priced in a straightforward manner. On the other hand, the market has its own way of pricing most basic contracts, such as the bond option, as we discussed in Chapter 18. It is the more complex derivatives for which a model is needed. Some of these are suitable for HJM/BGM.

FURTHER READING

- See the original paper by Heath *et al.* (1992) for all the technical details for making their model rigorous.

- For further details of the finite maturity interest rate process model see Sandmann & Sondermann (1994), Brace *et al.* (1997) and Jamshidian (1997).

EXERCISES

1. Derive the equation for the evolution of the forward rate:

    $$dF(t; T) = \frac{\partial}{\partial T} \left(\tfrac{1}{2}\sigma^2(t, T) - \mu(t, T) \right) dt - \frac{\partial}{\partial T}\sigma(t, T)\,dX,$$

    from

    $$dZ(t; T) = \mu(t, T)Z(t; T)dt + \sigma(t, T)Z(t; T)dX,$$

    and

    $$F(t; T) = -\frac{\partial}{\partial T}\log Z(t; T).$$

---

[4] Notice that I didn't use the word 'step' instead of 'period' here. 'Step' would refer to the small time step in the Monte Carlo simulation. Period refers to the time between T_{i-1} and T_i.

2. Perform a simulation, using the method of section 19.7, to value an option on a zero-coupon bond. You will need to decide upon a suitable form for $v(t, T)$, the forward rate volatility. Does your choice have a standard representation as a model for the spot rate?

3. Using forward rate data, perform a principal component analysis. What are the three main components in the forward price movements and what are their weights?

investment lessons from blackjack and gambling

The aim of this Chapter...

...is to gain as much insight as possible from the world of gambling before embarking on the more 'sophisticated' mathematics of portfolio management.

In this Chapter...

- the rules of blackjack
- blackjack strategy and card counting
- the Kelly criterion and money management
- no arbitrage in horse racing

20.1 **INTRODUCTION**

When I lecture on portfolio management and the mathematics of investment decisions I often start off with a description of the card game blackjack. It is a very simple game, one that most people are familiar with, perhaps by the name of pontoon, 21 or *vingt et un*. The rules are easy to remember, each hand lasts a very short time, the game is easily learned by children and could well give them their first taste of gambling. For without this gambling element there is little point in playing blackjack.

Since the rules are simple and the probabilities can be analyzed, blackjack is also the perfect game to learn about risk and return, and money management and, perhaps most importantly, to help you learn what type of gambler you are. Are you risk averse or a risk seeker? An important question for anyone who later will work in banking and may be gambling with OPM, other people's money.

Despite blackjack being perfect for learning the basics of financial risk and return, and despite bank training managers liking the idea of people being trained in risk management via this game, I am always asked by those training managers to change the title of my lecture. 'You can't call your lecture "Investment Lessons from Blackjack and Gambling," we'll get into trouble with [regulator goes here].' This is a bit silly. Anyone who doesn't think that investment and gambling share the same roots is silly. I can even go so far as to say that most professional gamblers that I know have a better understanding of risk, return and money management than most of the risk managers I know.

In this chapter we will see some of the ideas that these professional gamblers use.

20.2 **THE RULES OF BLACKJACK**

Players at blackjack sit around a kidney-shaped table, with the dealer standing opposite. A bird's eye view is shown in Figure 20.1.

Players

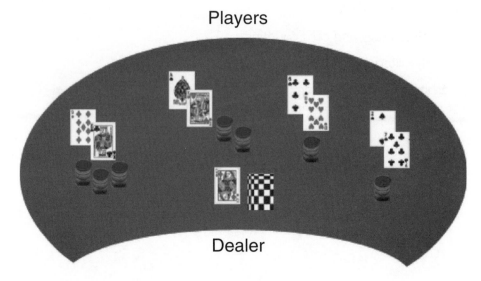

Dealer

Figure 20.1 Blackjack table layout.

Before any cards are dealt, the player must place his bet in front of his table position. The dealer deals two cards to each of the players, and two to himself (one of the dealer's cards is dealt face up and the other face down). This is the state of play shown in the figure. Court cards (kings, queens and jacks) count as 10, ace counts as either one or 11 and all other cards are counted at their face value. The value of the ace is chosen by the player.

The aim of the game for the player is to hold a card count greater than that of the dealer without exceeding 21 (going 'bust').

If the player's first two cards are an ace and a 10-count card he has what is known as 'blackjack' or a natural. If he gets a natural with his first two cards the player wins, unless the dealer also has a natural, in which case it is a standoff or tie (a 'push') and no money changes hands. A winning natural pays the player 3 to 2.

Working clockwise around the table from his immediate left the dealer asks each player in turn whether they want to hit or stand. 'Hit' means to draw another card. 'Stand' means no more cards are taken. If the player hits and busts, his wager is lost. The player can keep taking cards until he is satisfied with his count or busts.

The player also has other decisions to make.

The player is also allowed to double the bet on his first two cards and draw one additional card only. This is called 'doubling down.'

If the first two cards a player is dealt are a pair, he may split them into two separate hands, bet the same amount on each and then play them as two distinct hands. This is called 'splitting pairs.' Aces can receive only one additional card. After splitting, ace + 10 counts as 21 and not as blackjack. If the dealer's up card is an ace, the player may take insurance, a bet not exceeding one half of his original bet. If the dealer's down card is a 10-count card, the player wins 2 to 1. Any other card means a win for the dealer.

It is sometimes permitted to 'surrender' your bet. When permitted, a player may give up his first two cards and lose only one half of his original bet.

The dealer has no decisions to make. He must always follow very simple rules when it comes to hitting or standing. He must draw on 16 and stand on 17. In some casinos, the dealer is required to draw on soft 17 (a hand in which an ace counts as 11, not one). Regardless of the total the player has, the dealer must play this way.

In a tie no money is won or lost, but the bet stays on the table for the next round.

Rules differ subtly from casino to casino, as do the number of decks used.

The casino has an advantage over the player and so, generally speaking, the casino will win in the long run. The advantage to the dealer is that the player can go bust, losing his bet immediately, even if the dealer later busts. This asymmetry is the key to the house's edge. The key to the player's edge, which we will be exploiting shortly, is that he can vary both his bets and his strategy. The first published strategy for winning at blackjack was published by Ed Thorp in 1962 in his book *Beat the Dealer*. In this book Professor Thorp explained that the key ingredients to winning at blackjack were

- the strategy: knowing when to hit or stand, doubledown, etc. — this will depend on what cards you are holding and the dealer's upcard

- information: knowing the approximate makeup of the remaining cards in the deck, some cards favor the player and others the dealer

- money management: how to bet, when to bet small and when to bet large.

20.3 **BEATING THE DEALER**

The first key is in having the optimal strategy. That means knowing whether to hit or stand. You're dealt an 8 and a 4 and the dealer's showing a 6, what do you do? The optimal strategy involves knowing when to split pairs, double down (double your bet in return for only taking one extra card), or draw a new card. Thorp used a computer simulation to calculate the best strategies by playing thousands of blackjack hands. In his best-selling book *Beat the Dealer* Thorp presented tables like the one in Figure 20.2 showing the best strategies.

But the optimal strategy is still not enough without the second key.

You've probably heard of the phrase 'card counter' and conjured up images of Doc Holliday in a 10-gallon hat. The truth is more mundane. Card counting is not about memorizing entire decks of cards but keeping track of the type and percentage of cards remaining in the deck during your time at the blackjack table. Unlike roulette, blackjack has 'memory.' What happens during one hand depends on the previous hands and the cards that have already been dealt out.

A deck that is rich in low cards, 2s to 6s, is good for the house. Recall that the dealer must take a card when he holds 16 or less, the high frequency of low-count cards

	DEALER'S UPCARD									
YOUR HAND	**2**	**3**	**4**	**5**	**6**	**7**	**8**	**9**	**10**	**A**
17+	S	S	S	S	S	S	S	S	S	S
16	S	S	S	S	S	H	H	H	H	H
15	S	S	S	S	S	H	H	H	H	H
14	S	S	S	S	S	H	H	H	H	H
13	S	S	S	S	S	H	H	H	H	H
12	H	H	S	S	S	H	H	H	H	H
11	D	D	D	D	D	D	D	D	D	H
10	D	D	D	D	D	D	D	D	H	H
9	H	D	D	D	D	H	H	H	H	H
5–8	H	H	H	H	H	H	H	H	H	H
A, 8–10	S	S	S	S	S	S	S	S	S	S
A, 7	S	D	D	D	D	S	S	H	H	H
A, 6	H	D	D	D	D	H	H	H	H	H
A, 5	H	H	D	D	D	H	H	H	H	H
A, 4	H	H	D	D	D	H	H	H	H	H
A, 3	H	H	H	D	D	H	H	H	H	H
A, 2	H	H	H	D	D	H	H	H	H	H
A, A; 8, 8	SP	SP	SP	SP	SP	SP	SP	SP	SP	SP
10, 10	S	S	S	S	S	S	S	S	S	S
9, 9	SP	SP	SP	SP	SP	S	SP	SP	S	S
7, 7	SP	SP	SP	SP	SP	SP	H	H	H	H
6, 6	SP	SP	SP	SP	SP	H	H	H	H	H
5, 5	D	D	D	D	D	D	D	D	H	H
4, 4	H	H	H	SP	SP	H	H	H	H	H
3, 3	SP	SP	SP	SP	SP	SP	H	H	H	H
2, 2	SP	SP	SP	SP	SP	SP	H	H	H	H

Figure 20.2 The basic blackjack strategy.

increases his chance of getting close to 21 without busting. For example, take out all the 5s from a single deck and the player has an advantage of 3.3%! On the other hand, a deck rich in 10-count cards (10s and court cards) and aces is good for the player, increasing the chances of either the dealer busting or the player getting a natural (21 with two cards) for which he gets paid at odds of 3 to 2. In the simplest case, card counting means keeping a rough mental count of the percentage of aces and 10s, although more complex systems are possible for the really committed. When the deck favors the player he should increase his bet, when the deck is against him he should lower his bet. (And this bet variation must be done sufficiently subtly so as not to alert the dealers or pit bosses.)

One of the simplest card-counting techniques is to perform the following simple calculation in your head as the cards are being dealt. With a fresh deck(s) start from zero, and then for every ace and 10 that is dealt subtract one, for every 2–6 add one. The larger the count, divided by an estimate of the number of cards left in the deck, the better are your chances of winning. You perform this mental arithmetic as the cards are being dealt around the table.

In *Beat the Dealer*, Ed Thorp published his ideas and the results of his 'experiments.' He combined the card-counting idea, money management techniques (such as the Kelly criterion, below) and the optimal play strategy to devise a system that can be used by anyone to win at this casino game. 'The book that made Las Vegas change the rules,' as it says on the cover, and probably the most important gambling book ever, was deservedly in the *New York Times* and *Time* bestseller lists, selling more than 700,000 copies.

Passionate about probability and gambling, playing blackjack to relax, however, even Ed himself could not face the requirements of being a professional gambler. 'The activities weren't intellectually challenging along that life path. I elected not to do that.'

Once on a film set, Paul Newman asked him how much he could make at blackjack. Ed told him $300,000 a year. 'Why aren't you out there doing it?' Ed's response was that he could make a lot more doing something else, with the same effort, and with much nicer working conditions and a much higher class of people. Truer words were never spoken. Ed Thorp took his knowledge of probability, his scientific rigor and his money management skills to the biggest casino of them all, the stock market.

20.3.1 Summary of winning at blackjack

- If you play blackjack with no strategy you will lose your money quickly. If your strategy is to copy the dealer's rules then there is a house edge of between 5 and 6%.

- The best strategy involves knowing when to hit or stand, when to split, double down, take insurance, etc. This decision will be based on the two cards you hold and the dealer's face up card. If you play the best strategy you can cut the odds down to about evens.

- To win at blackjack takes patience and the ability to count cards.

- If you follow the optimal strategy and simultaneously bet high when the deck is favorable, and low otherwise, then you will win in the long run.

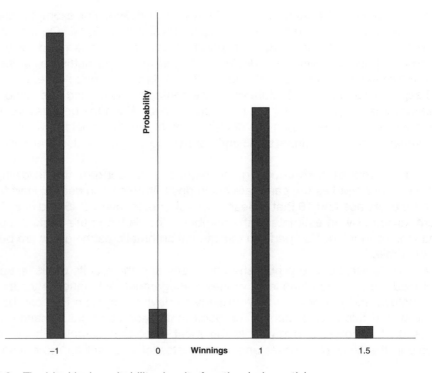

Figure 20.3   The blackjack probability density function (schematic).

What does this have to do with investing?

Over the next two sections we will see how to use estimates of the odds (from card counting in blackjack, say, or statistical analysis of stock price returns) to optimally manage our money.

20.4   **THE DISTRIBUTION OF PROFIT IN BLACKJACK**

Introduce some notation for the distribution of winnings at blackjack. ϕ is a random variable denoting the outcome of a bet. There will be probabilities associated with each ϕ. Suppose that μ is the mean and σ the standard deviation of ϕ.

In blackjack ϕ will take discrete values:

$$\phi = -1, \quad \text{player loses,}$$

$$\phi = 0, \quad \text{a 'push,'}$$

$$\phi = 1, \quad \text{player wins,}$$

$$\phi = 3/2, \quad \text{player gets a 'natural.'}$$

The distribution is shown (schematically) in Figure 20.3.

20.5 **THE KELLY CRITERION**

AN IDEA THAT'S USEFUL IN ASSET MANAGEMENT AND CASINO GAMBLING

To get us into the spirit of asset choice and money management, consider the following real-life example. You have $1000 to invest and the only investment available to you is in a casino playing blackjack.

If you play blackjack with no strategy you will lose your money quickly. The odds, as ever, are in favor of the house. If your strategy is to copy the dealer's rules then there is a house edge of between 5 and 6%. This is because when you bust you lose, even if the dealer busts later. There is, however, an optimal strategy. The best strategy involves knowing when to hit or stand, when to split, double down, take insurance (pretty much never), etc. This decision will be based on the two cards you hold and the dealer's face up card. If you play the best strategy you can cut the odds down to about evens, the exact figure depending on the rules of the particular casino.

To consistently win at blackjack takes two things: patience and the ability to count cards. The latter only means keeping track of, for example, the number of aces and 10-count cards left in the deck. Aces and 10 left in the deck improve your odds of winning. If you follow the optimal strategy and simultaneously bet high when there are a lot of aces and 10 left, and low otherwise, then you will do well in the long run . If there are any casino managers reading this, I'd like to reassure them that I have never mastered the technique of card counting, so it's not worth them banning me. On the other hand, I always seem to win, but that may just be selective memory.

The following is a description of the **Kelly criterion**. It is a very simple way to optimize your bets or investments so as to maximize your long-term average growth rate. This is the subject of *money management*. This technique is not specific to blackjack, although I will continue to use this as a concrete example, but it can be used with any gambling game or investment where you have a positive edge and have some idea of the real probabilities of outcomes. The idea has a long and fascinating history, all told in the book by Poundstone (2005). In that book you will also be able to read how the idea has divided the economics community from the gambling community.

We are going to use the ϕ notation for the outcome of a hand of blackjack, but since each hand is different we will add a subscript. So ϕ_i means the outcome of the ith hand.

Suppose I bet a fraction f of my $1000 on the first hand of blackjack, how much will I have after the hand? The amount will be

$$1000 \left(1 + f\phi_1\right),$$

where the subscript '1' denotes the first hand.

On to the second and subsequent hands. I will consistently bet a constant fraction f of my holdings each hand, so that after two hands I have an amount[1]

Easy to simulate

$$1000 \left(1 + f\phi_1\right)\left(1 + f\phi_2\right).$$

[1] This is not quite what one does when counting cards, since one will change the amount f.

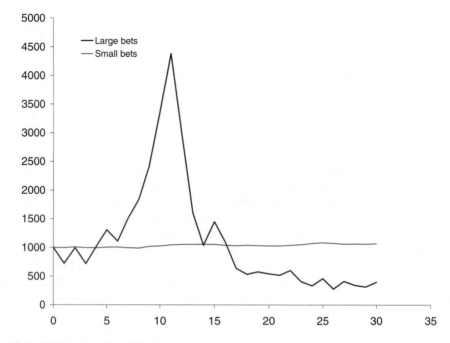

Figure 20.4 Big bets and small bets.

After M hands I have

$$1000 \, \Pi_{i=1}^{M}(1 + f\phi_i).$$

How should I choose the amount f?

If f is large, one say, then I will certainly eventually lose all of my money, even if the expected return is positive. If f is very small then it will take me a very long time to make any sizeable profit. These two extremes are demonstrated in Figure 20.4.

Perhaps there is some middle ground where I will make a reasonable profit without risking it all. This is indeed the case, let's do the math.

I am going to choose the fraction f to *maximize my expected long-term growth rate*. There are other strategies that you can adopt, such as expected wealth maximization. Each goal has its pros and cons.

Expected growth maximization is an obvious goal for a hedge fund since average growth is a number that all potential investors will look at.

This growth rate is given by

$$\frac{1}{M} \log \left(1000 \, \Pi_{i=1}^{M}(1 + f\phi_i) \right) = \frac{1}{M} \sum_{i=1}^{M} \log (1 + f\phi_i) + \frac{1}{M} \log(1000).$$

Assuming that the outcome of each hand is independent,[2] then the expected value of this is

$$E \left[\log (1 + f\phi_i) \right],$$

ignoring the scaling factor $\log(1000)$.

[2] An assumption not strictly true for blackjack, of course.

Expanding the argument of the logarithm in Taylor series, we get

$$E\left[f\phi_i - \tfrac{1}{2}f^2\phi_i^2 + \ldots\right].$$

Now assuming that the mean is small but that the standard deviation is not, we find that the expected long-term growth rate is approximately

$$f\mu - \tfrac{1}{2}f^2\sigma^2. \tag{20.1}$$

This is maximized by the choice

$$f^* = \frac{\mu}{\sigma^2},$$

giving an expected growth rate of

$$\frac{\mu^2}{2\sigma^2}$$

per hand.

If $\mu > 0$ then $f > 0$ and we stand to make a profit, in the long term. If $\mu < 0$, as it is for roulette or if you follow a naive blackjack strategy, then you should invest a negative amount, i.e. own the casino. (If you must play roulette, put all your money you would gamble in your lifetime on a color, and play once. Not only do you stand an almost 50% chance of doubling your money, you will gain an invaluable reputation as a serious player.)

The long-run growth rate maximization and the optimal amount to invest is called the Kelly criterion.

In Figure 20.5 is shown the function given in Equation (20.1) for the expected long-term growth rate. This example uses $\mu = 0.01$ and $\sigma = 1$. In this figure you will see the optimal

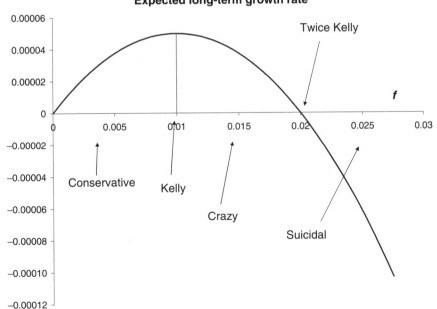

Figure 20.5 The expected long-term growth rate as a function of investment fraction.

betting fraction is the value for *f* which maximizes the function, this is the Kelly criterion. To the left of this is conservative betting, to the right is crazy. I say crazy because going beyond the optimal fraction increases your volatility of winnings, and decreases their expectation. At 'twice Kelly' your expected winnings are zero, and beyond that they become negative.

Given that in practice you rarely know the odds accurately it makes sense to bet conservatively, in case you accidentally stray into the crazy zone. For that reason many people use 'half Kelly,' that is a fraction that is half of the Kelly fraction. This halves your volatility, keeps you nicely away from the crazy zone, yet only decreases your expected growth rate by 25%.

If you can play *M* times in an evening you would expect a total growth of

$$\frac{\mu^2 M}{2\sigma^2} \tag{20.2}$$

using full Kelly.

EVEN WITH A POSITIVE EDGE YOU SHOULDN'T BET TOO MUCH

This illustrates one possible way of choosing a portfolio, which asset to invest in (blackjack) and how much to invest (*f**). Faced with other possible investments, then you could argue in favor of choosing the one with the highest (20.2), depending on the mean of the return, its standard deviation and how often the investment opportunity comes your way. These ideas are particularly important to the technical analyst or chartist who trades on the basis of signal such as golden crosses, saucer bottoms, and head and shoulder patterns. Not only do the risk and return of these signals matter, but so does their frequency of occurence.

The Kelly criterion is about maximizing expected long-term growth. Many people believe this to be a quite aggressive strategy leading to possible large downturns. There are many other quantities to optimize, of course, so the Kelly criterion might not be the right choice for you. You could, for example, choose to minimize downturn, or maximize some risk-adjusted return, as discussed in the next chapter.

20.6 **CAN YOU WIN AT ROULETTE?**

Let's go back to Ed Thorp, but a few years before his work on blackjack.

In spring 1955 Ed Thorp was in his second year of graduate physics at UCLA. At tea time one Sunday he got to chatting with colleagues about how to make 'easy money.' The conversation turned to gambling, and roulette in particular. Was it possible to predict, at least with some exploitable degree of accuracy, the outcome of a spin of the wheel? Some of his colleagues, the ones in the know, were certain that the roulette wheels were manufactured so precisely that there were no imperfections that could be discerned, never mind exploited. But Ed's counter to that was simple, if the wheels are so perfect you should be able to predict, using simple Newtonian principles, the path of the ball and its final resting place.

Ed got to work on this problem in the late 1950s, playing around with a cheap miniature roulette wheel, filming and timing the revolutions. He met up with Claude Shannon, the father of information theory in 1959, originally to discuss his blackjack results, but the conversation soon turned to other games and roulette in particular. Shannon was fascinated. Shortly afterwards they met up at Shannon's house, the basement of which was packed with mechanical and engineering gadgets, the perfect playground for further roulette experiments.

Ed and Shannon together took the roulette analysis to greater heights, investing $1500 in a full-size professional wheel. They calibrated a simple mathematical model to the experiments, to try to predict the moment when the spinning ball would fall into the waiting pockets. From their model they were able to predict any single number with a standard deviation of 10 pockets. This converts to a 44% edge on a bet on a single number. Betting on a specific octant gave them a 43% advantage.

From November 1960 until June 1961 Ed and Shannon designed and built the world's first wearable computer. The 12 transistor, cigarette-pack sized computer was fed data by switches operated by their big toes. One switch initialized the computer and the other was for timing the rotation of the ball and rotor. The computer predictions were heard by the computer wearer as one of eight tones via an earpiece. (Ed and Shannon decided that the best bet was on octants rather than single numbers since the father of information theory knew that faced with n options individuals take a time $a + b \log(n)$ to make a decision.)

This computer was tested out in Las Vegas in the summer of 1961. But for problems with broken wires and earpieces falling out, the trip was a success. Similar systems were later built for the Wheel of Fortune which had an even greater edge, an outstanding 200%. On 30th May 1985 Nevada outlawed the use of any device for predicting outcomes or analyzing probabilities or strategies.

20.7 HORSE RACE BETTING AND NO ARBITRAGE

Several times we have seen how the absence of arbitrage opportunities leads to the idea of risk-neutral pricing. The value of an option can be interpreted as the present value of the expected payoff, with the expectation being with respect to the risk-neutral asset price path. In this context risk neutral just means that the asset price increases with a growth rate that is the same as the risk-free interest rate. In other words, what we really believe that the asset price is going to do in the future (in terms of its growth rate) is irrelevant. We don't even need to know the growth rate of an asset to price its options, only its volatility.

Something related happens in the world of sports betting.

20.7.1 Setting the odds in a sporting game

In a horse race, football or baseball game the odds are set not to reflect the real probabilities of a horse or a team winning but to reflect the betting that has occurred. Depending on how the betting goes, the odds will be set so that the house/bookie cannot lose. For example, in a soccer match between England and Germany the Germans are more likely to win, but the patriotic English will bet more heavily on England (presumably). The odds given by the bookies will reflect this betting and make it look like England is more likely to win.

Of course, in Germany the situation is reversed. The best bet would be on Germany, but placed in England, and one on England placed in Germany.

In practice bookies in one country would lay off their bets on bookies in other countries so all bookies have roughly the same odds. Otherwise there would be straightforward arbitrage opportunities.

In practice it's unlikely for there to be a sure-fire bet (unless the bookie has made a mistake, the race is fixed, or you can find two or more bookies that aren't directly or indirectly laying off their bets on each other).

But you can win, on average, by exploiting the difference between the real probability of a horse winning and the odds you can get. (There are differences between real odds and what you get paid in all casino games, but it's only in blackjack that this can be exploited.)

20.7.2 The mathematics

Suppose that there are N horses in a race, with an amount W_i bet on the ith horse. The odds set by the bookie are $q_i : 1$. This means that if you bet 1 on horse i you will lose the 1 if the horse loses, but will take home $q_i + 1$ if the horse wins, your original 1 plus a further q_i. How does the bookie set the odds to ensure he never loses?

The total takings before the race are

$$\sum_{i=1}^{N} W_i.$$

If horse j wins the bookie has to pay out

$$(q_j + 1)W_j.$$

All that the bookie has to do is to ensure that

$$\sum_{i=1}^{N} W_i \geq (q_j + 1)W_j,$$

or equivalently

$$q_j \leq \frac{\sum_{i=1}^{N} W_i}{W_j} - 1 \quad \text{for all } j.$$

Nothing too complicated.

But see how the odds have been chosen to reflect the betting. Nowhere was there any mention of the likelihood of horse j winning.

20.8 ARBITRAGE

Suppose the bookie made an error when setting the odds. How could you determine whether there was an arbitrage opportunity? (Don't forget that only positive bets are allowed, there's no going short here.)

Let's introduce some more notation. The w_i are the bets that you place. (We can forget about the wagers made by everyone else, the Ws.) Let's assume that your total wager is 1, so that

$$\sum_{i=1}^{N} w_i = 1. \tag{20.3}$$

The amount you win is

$$(q_j + 1)w_j \qquad (20.4)$$

if horse j is the winner.

Can you find a w_i for all i such that they add up to one, are all positive and that expression (20.4) is positive for all j? If you can there is an arbitrage opportunity.

The requirement that (20.4) is positive can be written as

$$w_j \geq \frac{1}{q_j + 1}. \qquad (20.5)$$

Can we find positive ws such that (20.3) and (20.5) hold? This is very easy to visualize, at least when there are two or three horses. Let's look at the two-horse race.

In Figure 20.6 the axes represent the amount of the wager on each of the two horses. The line shows the constraint (20.3). The wagers must lie on this line. The two dots mark the point

$$\left(\frac{1}{q_1 + 1}, \frac{1}{q_2 + 1} \right) \qquad (20.6)$$

in each of two situations. One dot is the typical situation where there is no arbitrage opportunity and the other dot does have an associated arbitrage opportunity. Let's see the details.

To find an arbitrage opportunity we must find a pair (w_1, w_2) lying on the line such that each coordinate is greater than a certain quantity, depending on the qs. Plot the point

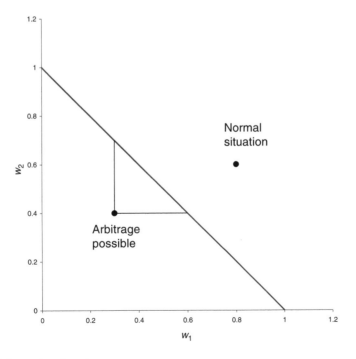

Figure 20.6 Arbitrage in a two-horse race.

(20.6) and draw a line vertically up, and another line horizontally to the right, as shown in the figure, emanating from the dot.

Does the quadrant defined by these two lines include any of the line? If not, as would be the case with the higher dot, then there is no arbitrage possible. If some of the line is included then arbitrage is possible.

20.8.1 How best to profit from the opportunity?

There's a simple test to see whether we are in an arbitrage situation. In general, if

$$\sum_{i=1}^{N} \frac{1}{q_i + 1} \geq 1$$

then there is no arbitrage. If the sum is less than one, there is an arbitrage.

You can benefit from the arbitrage by placing wagers w_i such that they lie on the part of the line encompassed by the quadrant. Which part of the line, though, is up to you. By that I mean that you must make some statement about what you are trying to achieve or optimize in the arbitrage. One possibility is to look at the worst-case scenario and maximize the payback in that case. Alternatively, specify real probabilities for each of the horses winning.

20.9 HOW TO BET

We saw how odds are established by bookies. We even saw how to spot arbitrage opportunities. In practice, of course, you could spend a lifetime looking for arbitrage opportunities that rarely occur in real life. Now we are going to see if we can exploit the difference between the odds as set by the bookie and the odds that you estimate. Remember, the odds set by the bookie are really determined by the wagers placed, which are more to do with irrational sentiment ('I'm going to bet on this horse 'cos it's got the same name as the pet rat I had when I was a child') than with a cold-hearted estimation of the probabilities.

We need some more notation. Let's use p_i as the probability of the ith horse winning the race. This is supposed to be the real probability, not the bookie's probability. Obviously, the odds must sum to one:

$$\sum_{i=1}^{N} p_i = 1.$$

If we wager w_i on the ith horse then we expect to make

$$m = \left(\sum_{i=1}^{N} p_i w_i(q_i + 1)\right) - 1 \tag{20.7}$$

This is under the assumption that the total wager, the sum of all the ws, is one. An obvious goal is to make this quantity positive, we want to get a positive return on average. But there may be many ways to make this positive. How do we decide which way is best?

Table 20.1   Odds and probabilities in a horse race.

Horse	Bookie's odds	Your estimate of probability	Wager
Nijinsky	5	0.2	
Red Rum	6	0.2	
Oxo	1	0.1	
Red Marauder	1	0.1	
Gay Lad	2	0.1	
Roquefort	2	0.1	
Red Alligator	2	0.1	
Shergar	2	0.1	

Another quantity we might want to look at is the standard deviation of winnings. This is given by

$$\sqrt{\sum_{i=1}^{N} p_i \left(w_i(q_i+1)-1-m\right)^2} \tag{20.8}$$

This measures the dispersion of winnings about the average, and is often interpreted as a measure of risk. If this were zero our profit or loss would be a sure thing.

Here's an example, see Table 20.1.

How should you bet? The following calculations are easily done on a spreadsheet.

Scenario 1: Maximize expected return   Since you place no premium on reducing risk you should bet everything on the horse that maximizes

$$p_i(q_i+1).$$

In this case, that is Red Rum. The expected return is 40% with a standard deviation of 280%. A very risky bet. See Table 20.2.

Scenario 2: Minimize standard deviation   An interesting strategy.

I say 'interesting' because this strategy results in zero standard deviation, and a return of −62%. In other words, a guaranteed loss! See Table 20.3.

Table 20.2   Maximizing expectation.

Horse	Bookie's odds	Your estimate of probability	Wager
Nijinsky	5	0.2	0
Red Rum	6	0.2	1
Oxo	1	0.1	0
Red Marauder	1	0.1	0
Gay Lad	2	0.1	0
Roquefort	2	0.1	0
Red Alligator	2	0.1	0
Shergar	2	0.1	0

Table 20.3 Minimizing standard deviation.

Horse	Bookie's odds	Your estimate of probability	Wager
Nijinsky	5	0.2	0.063062
Red Rum	6	0.2	0.054068
Oxo	1	0.1	0.189203
Red Marauder	1	0.1	0.189246
Gay Lad	2	0.1	0.126108
Roquefort	2	0.1	0.126108
Red Alligator	2	0.1	0.126108
Shergar	2	0.1	0.126108

Table 20.4 Maximize return divided by standard deviation.

Horse	Bookie's odds	Your estimate of probability	Wager
Nijinsky	5	0.2	0.459016
Red Rum	6	0.2	0.540984
Oxo	1	0.1	0
Red Marauder	1	0.1	0
Gay Lad	2	0.1	0
Roquefort	2	0.1	0
Red Alligator	2	0.1	0
Shergar	2	0.1	0

Scenario 3: Maximize return divided by standard deviation A strategy that seeks to benefit from a positive expectation but with a smaller risk. For mathematical reasons (the Central Limit Theorem) this is a natural strategy. The solution is given in Table 20.4.

The expected return is now 31% with a standard deviation of 164%.

20.10 SUMMARY

The mathematics of gambling is almost identical to the mathematics of 'investing.' The main difference between gambling and investing is that the parameters are usually easier to measure with gambling games. If you can't cope with the mathematics (and the emotional roller coaster ride) of gambling then you shouldn't be working in a bank;-

FURTHER READING

- See Kelly's original 1956 paper.

- The classic reference texts on blackjack are by Thorp (1962) and Wong (1981).

- The gripping story of John Kelly, Claude Shannon, Ed Thorp and a cast of many intriguing characters can be found in Poundstone (2005).

EXERCISES

1. A die is weighted so that the probability of getting a 6 is 0.3, of getting a 1 is 0.1, and of getting 2, 3, 4 or 5 is 0.15 each. You bet on 6, receiving odds of 5 to 1 (fair odds for an unbiased die). What is your expected profit? What is your standard deviation of profit? What is the formula for the expected return as a function of the fraction of your wealth that you bet? What fraction maximizes this expected return?

2. Build a spreadsheet that simulates the above, in which you keep betting the same fraction of your accumulated wealth.

CHAPTER 21
portfolio management

The aim of this Chapter...

...is to move beyond the world of risk-free hedging and enter the exciting and dangerous world of gambling, also known as investing, in risky assets. You will see some simple ideas for deciding how to allocate your money between all the possible investments on offer.

In this Chapter...

- Modern Portfolio Theory and the Capital Asset Pricing Model

- optimizing your portfolio

- alternative methodologies such as cointegration

- how to analyze portfolio performance

21.1   **INTRODUCTION**

The theory of derivative pricing is a theory of deterministic returns: we hedge our derivative with the underlying to eliminate risk, and our resulting risk-free portfolio then earns the risk-free rate of interest. Banks make money from this hedging process; they sell something for a bit more than it's worth and hedge away the risk to make a guaranteed profit.

But not everyone is hedging. Fund managers buy and sell assets (including derivatives) with the aim of beating the bank's rate of return. In so doing they take risk. In this chapter I explain some of the theories behind the risk and reward of investment. Along the way I show the benefits of diversification, how the return and risk on a portfolio of assets is related to the return and risk on the individual assets, and how to optimize a portfolio to get the best value for money.

For the most part, the assumptions are as follows:

- We hold a portfolio for 'a single period,' examining the behavior after this time.

- During this period returns on assets are Normally distributed.

- The return on assets can be measured by an expected return (the drift) for each asset, a standard deviation of return (the volatility) for each asset and correlations between the asset returns.

21.2   **DIVERSIFICATION**

In this section I introduce some more notation, and show the effects of diversification on the return of the portfolio.

We hold a portfolio of N assets. The value today of the ith asset is S_i and its random return is R_i over our time horizon T. The Rs are Normally distributed with mean $\mu_i T$ and standard deviation $\sigma_i \sqrt{T}$. The correlation between the returns on the ith and jth assets is ρ_{ij} (with $\rho_{ii} = 1$). The parameters μ, σ and ρ correspond to the drift, volatility and correlation that we are used to. Note the scaling with the time horizon.

AN IMPORTANT CONCEPT IN FUND MANAGEMENT.... DON'T PUT ALL YOUR EGGS IN ONE BASKET

If we hold w_i of the ith asset, then our portfolio has value

$$\Pi = \sum_{i=1}^{N} w_i S_i.$$

At the end of our time horizon the value is

$$\Pi + \delta\Pi = \sum_{i=1}^{N} w_i S_i (1 + R_i).$$

We can write the relative change in portfolio value as

$$\frac{\delta\Pi}{\Pi} = \sum_{i=1}^{N} W_i R_i, \tag{21.1}$$

where

$$W_i = \frac{w_i S_i}{\sum_{i=1}^{N} w_i S_i}.$$

The weights W_i sum to one.

From (21.1) it is simple to calculate the expected return on the portfolio

$$\mu_\Pi = \frac{1}{T} E\left[\frac{\delta \Pi}{\Pi}\right] = \sum_{i=1}^{N} W_i \mu_i \tag{21.2}$$

and the standard deviation of the return

$$\sigma_\Pi = \frac{1}{\sqrt{T}} \sqrt{\text{var}\left[\frac{\delta \Pi}{\Pi}\right]} = \sqrt{\sum_{i=1}^{N} \sum_{j=1}^{N} W_i W_j \rho_{ij} \sigma_i \sigma_j}. \tag{21.3}$$

In these, we have related the parameters for the individual assets to the expected return and the standard deviation of the entire portfolio.

21.2.1   Uncorrelated assets

Suppose that we have assets in our portfolio that are uncorrelated, $\rho_{ij} = 0$, $i \neq j$. To make things simple assume that they are equally weighted so that $W_i = 1/N$. The expected return on the portfolio is represented by

$$\mu_\Pi = \frac{1}{N} \sum_{i=1}^{N} \mu_i,$$

the average of the expected returns on all the assets and the volatility becomes

$$\sigma_\Pi = \sqrt{\frac{1}{N^2} \sum_{i=1}^{N} \sigma_i^2}.$$

This volatility is $O(N^{-1/2})$ since there are N terms in the sum. As we increase the number of assets in the portfolio, the standard deviation of the returns tends to zero. It is rather extreme to assume that all assets are uncorrelated but we will see something similar when I describe the Capital Asset Pricing Model below, diversification reduces volatility without hurting expected return.

I am now going to refer to volatility or standard deviation as **risk**, a bad thing to be avoided (within reason), and the expected return as **reward**, a good thing that we want as much of as possible.

Time Out...

Spreadsheet test

In the following spreadsheet you can see the effect of investing all your cash in one risky asset, or of spreading it across four equally risky but uncorrelated assets. A convincing case for diversification... but watch out for those market crashes when all correlations become one.

Simple example of diversification

	A	B	C	D	E	F	G	H	I
1	Drift	0.1		Time	Asset 1	Asset 2	Asset 3	Asset 4	Basket
2	Volatility	0.25		0	100	100	100	100	100
3	Timestep	0.01		0.01	101.4946	102.0604	99.80029	102.4483	101.4509
4			=D2+$B$3	0.02	103.563	100.4693	97.82029	104.2275	101.52
5				0.03	105.7847	102.3088	93.20119	106.3945	101.9223
6				0.04	99.71384	107.1702	91.29877	106.0402	101.0557
7	=E6*(1+$B$1*$B$3+$B$2*SQRT($B$3			0.05	92.86761	106.9663	91.14639	113.5807	101.1402
8	)*(RAND()+RAND()+RAND()+RAND()+			0.06	90.58581	102.5303	91.3095	111.6031	98.00717
9	RAND()+RAND()+RAND()+RAND()+R			0.07	93.42845	100.7858	91.47827	108.5943	98.57169
10	AND()+RAND()+RAND()+RAND()-6))			0.08	=AVERAGE(E8:H8)		91.14564	107.5179	98.5553
11				0.09	90.62362	105.6249	86.09578	106.91	97.31358
12							3	107.3784	98.98025
13							2	108.2679	99.85746
14							7	110.9582	99.38457
15							6	108.1393	99.22791
16							8	108.0873	100.0265
17							9	105.3345	98.15725
18							7	107.7298	98.97677
19							4	107.3138	99.37793
20							9	107.0215	100.223
21							9	107.0683	100.8625
22							8	101.59	100.637
23							4	100.8669	98.90859
24							9	99.30773	97.84018
25							9	101.2298	99.08378
26							8	103.2705	98.91596
27							9	104.8602	98.64734
28							2	111.2662	101.0386
29							5	112.5718	101.8489
30				0.28	105.3536	95.48459	96.4614	114.2369	102.8841
31				0.29	105.6262	93.65618	100.6464	112.8307	103.1899
32				0.3	110.304	92.95482	100.7716	114.2496	104.57
33				0.31	113.8359	92.39261	101.0787	114.2613	105.3921

(Chart in rows 12–29, columns A–G: vertical axis 0 to 160, horizontal axis 0 to 2)

21.3 **MODERN PORTFOLIO THEORY**

We can use the above framework to discuss the 'best' portfolio. The definition of 'best' was addressed very successfully by Nobel Laureate Harry Markowitz. His model provides a way of defining portfolios that are **efficient**. An efficient portfolio is one that has the highest reward for a given level of risk, or the lowest risk for a given reward. To see how this works imagine that there are four assets in the world, A, B, C and D, with reward and risk as shown in Figure 21.1 (ignore E for the moment). If you could buy any one of these (but as yet you are not allowed more than one), which would you buy? Would you choose D? No, because it has the same risk as B but less reward. It has the same reward as C but for a higher risk. We can rule out D. What about B or C? They are both appealing when set against D, but against each other it is not so clear. B has a higher risk, but gets a higher reward. However, comparing them both with A we see that there is no contest. A is the preferred choice. If we introduce asset E with the same risk as B and a higher reward than A, then we cannot objectively say which out of A and E is the better, this is a subjective choice and depends on an investor's **risk preferences**.

Now suppose that I have the two assets A and E of Figure 21.2, and I am now allowed to combine them in my portfolio, what effect does this have on my risk/reward?

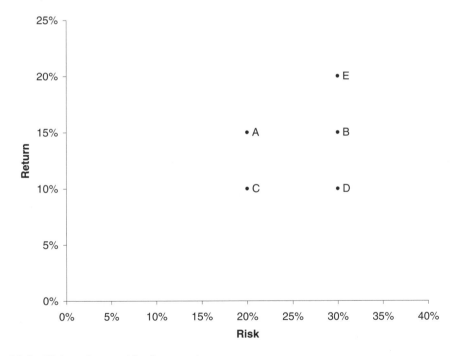

Figure 21.1   Risk and reward for five assets.

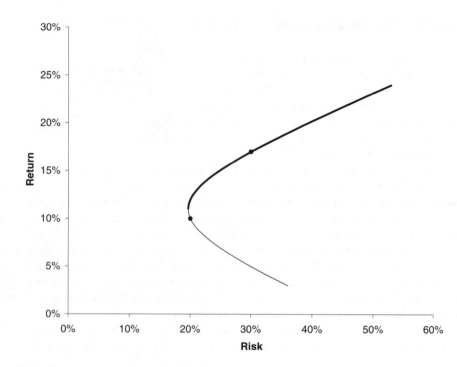

Figure 21.2 Two assets and any combination.

From (21.2) and (21.3) we have

$$\mu_\Pi = W\mu_A + (1 - W)\mu_E$$

and

$$\sigma_\Pi^2 = W^2\sigma_A^2 + 2W(1 - W)\rho\sigma_A\sigma_E + (1 - W)^2\sigma_E^2.$$

Here W is the weight of asset A, and, remembering that the weights must add up to one, the weight of asset E is $1 - W$.

As we vary W, so the risk and the reward change. The line in risk/reward space that is parameterized by W is a hyperbola, as shown in Figure 21.2. The part of this curve in bold is efficient, and is preferable to the rest of the curve. Again, an individual's risk preferences will say where he wants to be on the bold curve. When one of the volatilities is zero the line becomes straight. Anywhere on the curve between the two dots requires a long position in each asset. Outside this region, one of the assets is sold short to finance the purchase of the other. Everything that follows assumes that we can sell short as much of an asset as we want. The results change slightly when there are restrictions.

Demonstration of optimal asset allocation

If we have many assets in our portfolio we no longer have a simple hyperbola for our possible risk/reward profiles, instead we get something like that shown in Figure 21.3. This figure now uses *all* of A, B, C, D and E, not just the A and E. Even though B, C and D are not individually appealing

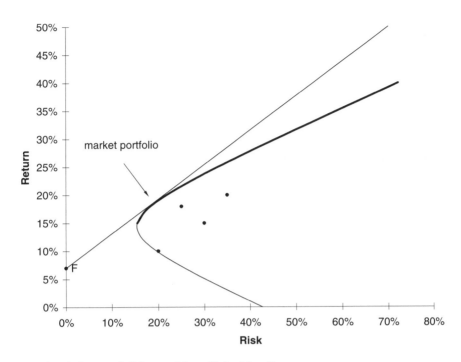

Figure 21.3 Portfolio possibilities and the efficient frontier.

they may well be useful in a portfolio, depending how they correlate, or not, with other investments. In this figure we can see the **efficient frontier** marked in bold. Given any choice of portfolio we would choose to hold one that lies on this efficient frontier.

The calculation of the risk for a given return is demonstrated in the spreadsheet in Figure 21.4. This spreadsheet can be used to find the efficient frontier if it is used many times for different target returns.

21.3.1 Including a risk-free investment

A risk-free investment earning a guaranteed rate of return r would be the point F in Figure 21.3. If we are allowed to hold this asset in our portfolio, then since the volatility of this asset is zero, we get the new efficient frontier which is the straight line in the figure. The portfolio for which the straight line touches the original efficient frontier is called the **market portfolio**. The straight line itself is called the **capital market line**.[1]

21.4 WHERE DO I WANT TO BE ON THE EFFICIENT FRONTIER?

Having found the efficient frontier we want to know whereabouts on it we should be. This is a personal choice; the efficient frontier is objective, given the data, but the 'best' position on it is subjective.

---

[1] In the risk-neutral world they think that all investments lie on the horizontal line going through the point $(0, r)$.

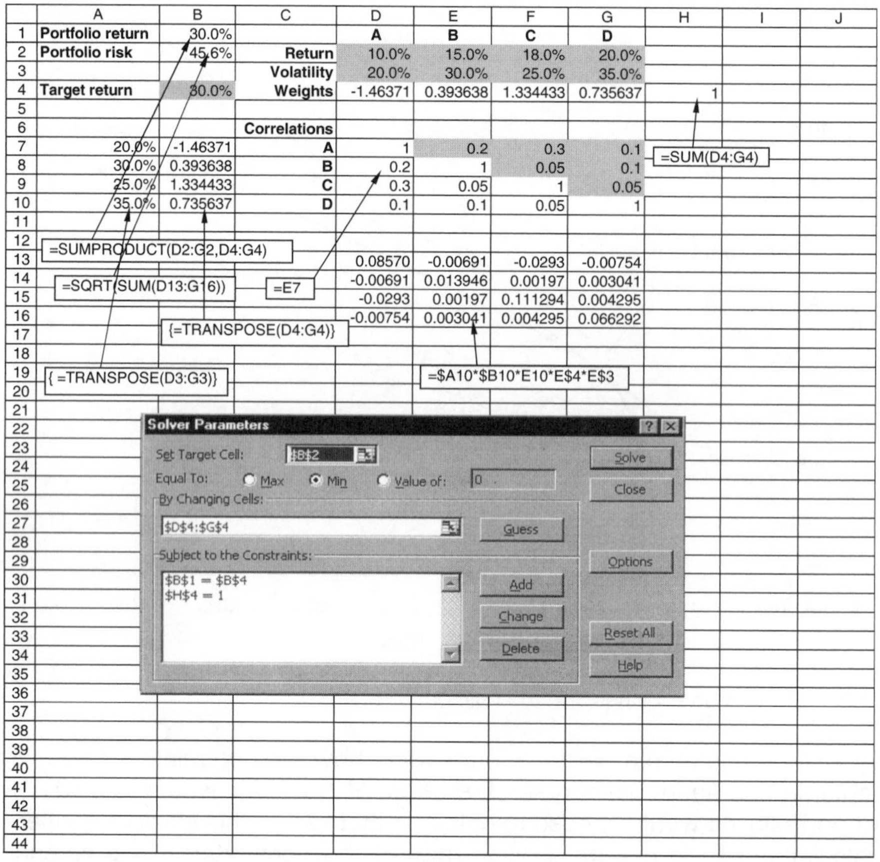

	A	B	C	D	E	F	G	H	I	J
1	Portfolio return	30.0%		A	B	C	D			
2	Portfolio risk	45.6%	Return	10.0%	15.0%	18.0%	20.0%			
3			Volatility	20.0%	30.0%	25.0%	35.0%			
4	Target return	30.0%	Weights	-1.46371	0.393638	1.334433	0.735637	1		
5										
6			Correlations							
7	20.0%	-1.46371	A	1	0.2	0.3	0.1	=SUM(D4:G4)		
8	30.0%	0.393638	B	0.2	1	0.05	0.1			
9	25.0%	1.334433	C	0.3	0.05	1	0.05			
10	35.0%	0.735637	D	0.1	0.1	0.05	1			
11										
12	=SUMPRODUCT(D2:G2,D4:G4)									
13				0.08570	-0.00691	-0.0293	-0.00754			
14	=SQRT(SUM(D13:G16))		=E7	-0.00691	0.013946	0.00197	0.003041			
15				-0.0293	0.00197	0.111294	0.004295			
16			{=TRANSPOSE(D4:G4)}	-0.00754	0.003041	0.004295	0.066292			
17										
18										
19	{=TRANSPOSE(D3:G3)}				=$A10*$B10*E10*E$4*E$3					

Solver Parameters

Set Target Cell: $B$2

Equal To:　○ Max　● Min　○ Value of: 0

By Changing Cells:
$D$4:$G$4

Subject to the Constraints:
$B$1 = $B$4
$H$4 = 1

Solve　Close　Guess　Options　Add　Change　Delete　Reset All　Help

Figure 21.4　Spreadsheet for calculating one point on the efficient frontier.

The following is a way of interpreting the risk/reward diagram that may be useful in choosing the best portfolio.

The return on portfolio Π is Normally distributed because it is comprised of assets which are themselves Normally distributed. It has mean μ_Π and standard deviation σ_Π (I have ignored the dependence on the horizon T).

The slope of the line joining the portfolio Π to the risk-free asset is

$$s = \frac{\mu_\Pi - r}{\sigma_\Pi}.$$

This is an important quantity, it is a measure of the likelihood of Π having a return that exceeds r. If $C(\cdot)$ is the cumulative distribution function for the standardized Normal distribution then $C(s)$ is the probability that the return on Π is at least r. More generally

$$C\left(\frac{\mu_\Pi - r^*}{\sigma_\Pi}\right)$$

is the probability that the return exceeds r^*. This suggests that if we want to minimize the chance of a return of less than r^* we should choose the portfolio from the efficient frontier set Π_{eff} with the largest value of the slope

$$\frac{\mu_{\Pi_{\text{eff}}} - r^*}{\sigma_{\Pi_{\text{eff}}}}.$$

Conversely, if we keep the slope of this line fixed at s then we can say that with a confidence of $C(s)$ we will lose no more than

$$\mu_{\Pi_{\text{eff}}} - s\sigma_{\Pi_{\text{eff}}}.$$

THE EFFICIENT FRONTIER IS SIMPLE TO CALCULATE

Our portfolio choice could be determined by maximizing this quantity. These two strategies are shown schematically in Figure 21.5.

Neither of these methods give satisfactory results when there is a risk-free investment among the assets and there are unrestricted short sales, since they result in infinite borrowing.

Another way of choosing the optimal portfolio is with the aid of a **utility function**. This approach is popular with economists. In Figure 21.6 I show **indifference curves** and the

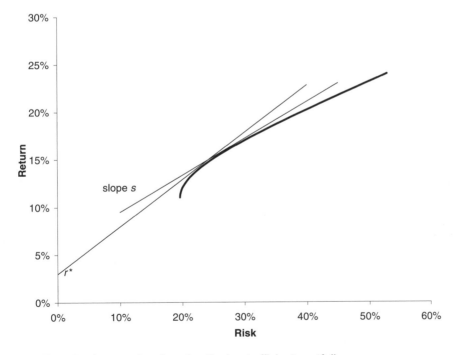

Figure 21.5 Two simple ways for choosing the best efficient portfolio.

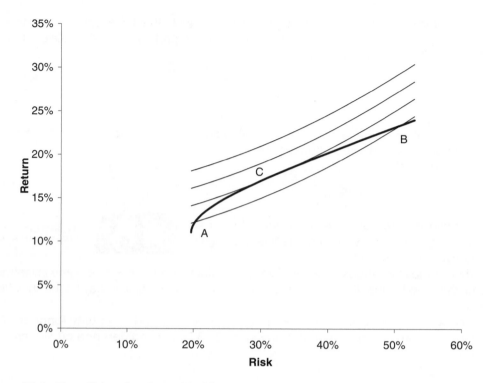

Figure 21.6   The efficient frontier and indifference curves.

efficient frontier. The curves are called by this name because they are meant to represent lines along which the investor is indifferent to the risk/reward tradeoff. An investor wants high return and low risk. Faced with portfolios A and B in the figure, he sees A with low return and low risk, but B has a better reward at the cost of greater risk. The investor is indifferent between these two. However, C is better than both of them, being on a preferred curve.

THE ELEGANT IDEA LOSES
SOMETHING IN PRACTICE

21.5   **MARKOWITZ IN PRACTICE**

The inputs to the Markowitz model are expected returns, volatilities and correlations. With N assets this means $N + N + N(N - 1)/2$ parameters. Most of these cannot be known accurately (do they even exist?), only the volatilities are at all reliable. Having input these parameters, we must optimize over all weights of assets in the portfolio: choose a portfolio risk and find the weights that make the return on the portfolio a maximum subject to this volatility. This is a very time-consuming process computationally unless one only has a small number of assets.

The problem with the practical implementation of this model was one of the reasons for development of the simpler model of the next section.

21.6 **CAPITAL ASSET PRICING MODEL**

Before discussing the **Capital Asset Pricing Model** or **CAPM** we must introduce the idea of a security's beta. The beta, β_i, of an asset relative to a portfolio M is the ratio of the covariance between the return on the security and the return on the portfolio to the variance of the portfolio. Thus

MUCH SIMPLER THAN MPT...FEWER INPUTS, MORE ROBUST

$$\beta_i = \frac{\text{Cov}[R_i R_M]}{\text{Var}[R_M]}.$$

21.6.1 The single-index model

I will now build up a **single-index model** and describe extensions later. I will relate the return on all assets to the return on a representative index, M. This index is usually taken to be a wide-ranging stock market index in the single-index model. We write the return on the ith asset as

$$R_i = \alpha_i + \beta_i R_M + \epsilon_i.$$

Using this representation we can see that the return on an asset can be decomposed into three parts: a constant drift, a random part common with the index M and a random part uncorrelated with the index, ϵ_i. The random part ϵ_i is unique to the ith asset, and has mean zero. Notice how all the assets are related to the index M but are otherwise completely uncorrelated. In Figure 21.7 is shown a plot of returns on Walt Disney stock against returns on the S&P500; α and β can be determined from a linear regression analysis. The data used in this plot ran from January 1985 until almost the end of 1997.

The expected return on the index will be denoted by μ_M and its standard deviation by σ_M. The expected return on the ith asset is then

$$\mu_i = \alpha_i + \beta_i \mu_M$$

and the standard deviation

$$\sigma_i = \sqrt{\beta_i^2 \sigma_M^2 + e_i^2}$$

where e_i is the standard deviation of ϵ_i.

If we have a portfolio of such assets then the return is given by

$$\frac{\delta \Pi}{\Pi} = \sum_{i=1}^{N} W_i R_i = \left(\sum_{i=1}^{N} W_i \alpha_i \right) + R_M \left(\sum_{i=1}^{N} W_i \beta_i \right) + \sum_{i=1}^{N} W_i \epsilon_i.$$

From this it follows that

$$\mu_\Pi = \left(\sum_{i=1}^{N} W_i \alpha_i \right) + E[R_M] \left(\sum_{i=1}^{N} W_i \beta_i \right).$$

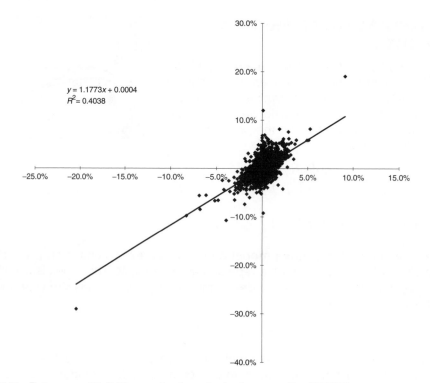

Figure 21.7   Returns on Walt Disney stock against returns on the S&P500.

Let us write

$$\alpha_\Pi = \sum_{i=1}^{N} W_i \alpha_i \quad \text{and} \quad \beta_\Pi = \sum_{i=1}^{N} W_i \beta_i,$$

so that

$$\mu_\Pi = \alpha_\Pi + \beta_\Pi E[R_M] = \alpha_\Pi + \beta_\Pi \mu_M.$$

Similarly the risk in Π is measured by

$$\sigma_\Pi = \sqrt{\sum_{i=1}^{N} \sum_{j=1}^{N} W_i W_j \beta_i \beta_j \sigma_M^2 + \sum_{i=1}^{N} W_i^2 e_i^2}.$$

If the weights are all about the same, N^{-1}, then the final terms inside the square root are also $O(N^{-1})$. Thus this expression is, to leading order as $N \to \infty$,

$$\sigma_\Pi = \left| \sum_{i=1}^{N} W_i \beta_i \right| \sigma_M = |\beta_\Pi| \sigma_M.$$

Observe that the contribution from the uncorrelated ϵs to the portfolio vanishes as we increase the number of assets in the portfolio: the risk associated with the ϵs is called **diversifiable risk**. The remaining risk, which is correlated with the index, is called **systematic risk**.

Time Out...

Finding beta

It's really easy to find beta from asset returns and index returns data using Excel. See the spreadsheet below. I've used the Add Trendline option when drawing the plot. This finds the best-fit straight line through the data, the slope of which is the beta.

	A	B	C	D	E	F	G	H	I
1	Date	SP500	IKON	SP500 Rtn	IKON Rtn				
2	01-Jan-85	167.24	6.11			Beta	0.736802		
3	02-Jan-85	165.37	6.16	-0.011182	0.008183				
4	03-Jan-85	164.57	6.21	-0.004838	0.008117				
5	04-Jan-85	1=(B4-B3)/B3	.19	-0.005408	-0.0032	=LINEST(E3:E3363,D3:D3363,TRUE,FALSE)			
6	07-Jan-85	164.24	6.21	0.003421	0.003231				
7	08-Jan-85	163.99	6.24	-0.001522	0.004831				
8	09-Jan-85	165.18	6.29	0.007257	0.008013				
9	10-Jan-85	168.31	6.26	0.01	=(C6-C5)/C5	39			
10	11-Jan-85	167.91	6.24	-0.002377	-0.003195				
11	14-Jan-85	170.51	6.26	0.015484	0.003205				
12	15-Jan-85	170.81	6.29	0.001759	0.004792				
13	16-Jan-85	171.19	6.29	0.002225	0				
14	17-Jan-85	170.73							
15	18-Jan-85	171.32							
16	21-Jan-85	175.23							
17	22-Jan-85	175.48							
18	23-Jan-85	177.3							
19	24-Jan-85	176.71							
20	25-Jan-85	177.35							
21	28-Jan-85	177.4							
22	29-Jan-85	179.18							
23	30-Jan-85	179.39							
24	31-Jan-85	179.63							
25	01-Feb-85	178.63							
26	04-Feb-85	180.35							
27	05-Feb-85	180.61							
28	06-Feb-85	180.43							
29	07-Feb-85	181.82							
30	08-Feb-85	182.19							
31	11-Feb-85	180.51	7.07	-0.009221	-0.002821				
32	12-Feb-85	180.56	7.04	0.000277	-0.004243				
33	13-Feb-85	183.35	7.09	0.015452	0.007102				

y = 0.7368x + 0.0002
R^2 = 0.1609

IKON Rtn

SP500 Rtn

21.6.2 Choosing the optimal portfolio

The principle is the same as the Markowitz model for optimal portfolio choice. The only difference is that there are a lot fewer parameters to be input, and the computation is a lot faster.

The procedure is as follows. Choose a value for the portfolio return μ_Π. Subject to this constraint, minimize σ_Π. Repeat this minimization for different portfolio returns to obtain efficient frontier. The position on this curve is then a subjective choice.

21.7 **THE MULTI-INDEX MODEL**

The model presented above is a single-index model. The idea can be extended to include further representative indices. For example, as well as an index representing the stock market one might include an index representing bond markets, an index representing currency markets or even an economic index if it is believed to be relevant in linking assets. In the multi-index model we write each asset's return as

$$R_i = \alpha_i + \sum_{j=1}^{n} \beta_{ji} R_j + \epsilon_i,$$

where there are n indices with return R_j. The indices can be correlated to each other. Similar results to the single-index model follow.

It is usually not worth having more than three or four indices. The fewer the parameters, the more robust will be the model. At the other extreme is the Markowitz model with one index per asset.

21.8 **COINTEGRATION**

Whether you use MPT or CAPM you will always worry about the accuracy of your parameters. Both of these methods are only as accurate as the input data, CAPM being more reliable than MPT generally speaking, because it has fewer parameters. There is another method which is gaining popularity, and which I will describe here briefly. It is unfortunately a complex technique requiring sophisticated statistical analysis (to do it properly) but which at its core makes a lot of sense. Instead of asking whether two series are correlated we ask whether they are **cointegrated**.

Two stocks may be perfectly correlated over short timescales yet diverge in the long run, with one growing and the other decaying. Conversely, two stocks may follow each other, never being more than a certain distance apart, but with any correlation, positive, negative or varying. If we are delta hedging then maybe the short timescale correlation matters, but not if we are holding stocks for a long time in an unhedged portfolio. To see whether two stocks stay close together we need a definition of **stationarity**. A time series is stationary if it has finite and constant mean, standard deviation and autocorrelation function. Stocks, which tend to grow, are not stationary. In a sense, stationary series do not wander too far from their mean.

We can see the difference between stationary and non-stationary with our first coin-tossing experiment. The time series given by 1 every time we throw a head and -1 every time we throw a tail is stationary. It has a mean of zero, a standard deviation of 1 and an autocorrelation function that is zero for any non-zero lag. But what if we add up the results, as we might do if we are betting on each toss? This time series is non-stationary. This is because the standard deviation of the sum grows like the square root of the number of throws. The mean may be zero but the sum is wandering further and further away from that mean.

Testing for the stationarity of a time series X_t involves a linear regression to find the coefficients a, b and c in

$$X_t = aX_{t-1} + b + ct.$$

If it is found that $|a| > 1$ then the series is unstable. If $-1 \leq a < 1$ then the series is stationary. If $a = 1$ then the series is non-stationary. As with all things statistical, we can only say that our value for a is accurate with a certain degree of confidence. To decide whether we have got a stationary or non-stationary series requires us to look at the Dickey–Fuller statistic to estimate the degree of confidence in our result. From this point on the subject of cointegration gets complicated.

How is this useful in finance? Even though individual stock prices might be non-stationary it is possible for a linear combination (i.e. a portfolio) to be stationary. Can we find λ_i, with $\sum_{i=1}^{N} \lambda_i = 1$, such that

$$\sum_{i=1}^{N} \lambda_i S_i$$

is stationary? If we can, then we say that the stocks are cointegrated.

For example, suppose we find that the S&P500 is cointegrated with a portfolio of 15 stocks. We can then use these 15 stocks to **track the index**. The error in this tracking portfolio will have constant mean and standard deviation, so should not wander too far from its average. This is clearly easier than using all 500 stocks for the tracking (when, of course, the tracking error would be zero).

We don't have to track the index, we could track anything we want, such as $e^{0.2t}$ to choose a portfolio that gets a 20% return. We could analyze the cointegration properties of two related stocks, Nike and Reebok, for example, to look for relationships. This would be pairs trading. Clearly there are similarities with MPT and CAPM in concepts such as means and standard deviations. The important difference is that cointegration assumes far fewer properties for the individual time series. Most importantly, volatility and correlation do not appear explicitly.

21.9 **PERFORMANCE MEASUREMENT**

If one has followed one of the asset allocation strategies outlined above, or just traded on gut instinct, can one tell how well one has done? Were the outstanding results because of an uncanny natural instinct, or were the awful results simply bad luck?

The ideal performance would be one for which returns outperformed the risk-free rate, but *in a consistent* fashion. Not only is it important to get a high return from portfolio management, but one must achieve this with as little randomness as possible.

The two commonest measures of 'return per unit risk' are the **Sharpe ratio** of 'reward to variability' and the **Treynor ratio** of 'reward to volatility'. These are defined as follows:

$$\text{Sharpe ratio} = \frac{\mu_\Pi - r}{\sigma_\Pi}$$

and

$$\text{Treynor ratio} = \frac{\mu_\Pi - r}{\beta_\Pi}.$$

In these μ_Π and σ_Π are the *realized* return and standard deviation for the portfolio over the period. The β_Π is a measure of the portfolio's volatility. The Sharpe ratio is usually used when the portfolio is the whole of one's investment and the Treynor ratio when one

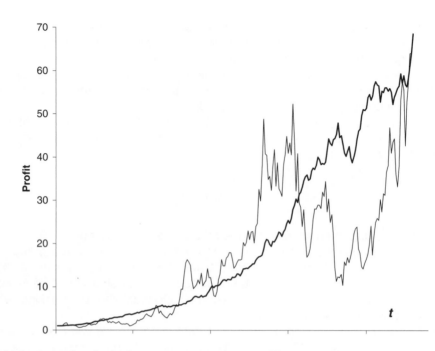

Figure 21.8   A good and a bad manager; same returns, different variablity.

is examining the performance of one component of the whole firm's portfolio, say. When the portfolio under examination is highly diversified the two measures are the same (up to a factor of the market standard deviation).

In Figure 21.8 we see the portfolio value against time for a good manager and a bad manager.

21.10 **SUMMARY**

Portfolio management and asset allocation are about taking risks in return for a reward. The questions are how to decide how much risk to take, and how to get the best return. But derivatives theory is based on not taking any risk at all, and so I have spent little time on portfolio management in the book. On the other hand, as I have stressed, there is so much uncertainty in the subject of finance that elimination of risk is well-nigh impossible and the ideas behind portfolio management should be appreciated by anyone involved in derivatives theory or practice. I have tried to give the flavor of the subject with only the easiest-to-explain mathematics, the following sources will prove useful to anyone wanting to pursue the subject further.

FURTHER READING

- See Markowitz's original book for all the details of MPT, Markowitz (1959).

- One of the best texts on investments, including chapters on portfolio management, is Sharpe (1985).

- For a description of cointegration and other techniques in econometrics see Hamilton (1994) and Hendry (1995).

- See Farrell (1997) for further discussion of portfolio performance.

- I have not discussed the subject of continuous-time asset allocation (yet), but the elegant subject is explained nicely in the collection of Robert Merton's papers, Merton (1992).

- Transaction costs can have a big effect on portfolios that are supposed to be continuously rebalanced. See Morton & Pliska (1995) for a model with costs, and Atkinson & Wilmott (1995), Atkinson *et al.* (1997) and Atkinson & Al-Ali (1997) for asymptotic results.

- For a description of chaos-based methods in finance, and how they won the First International Nonlinear Financial Forecasting Competition, see Alexander & Giblin (1997).

- For a review of current thinking in risk management see Alexander (1998).

EXERCISES

1. Work out the efficient frontier for the following set of assets:

Asset	μ	σ
A	0.08	0.12
B	0.10	0.12
C	0.10	0.15
D	0.14	0.20

The correlation coefficients between the four assets are given by

$$\rho = \begin{pmatrix} 1 & 0.2 & 0.5 & 0.3 \\ 0.2 & 1 & 0.7 & 0.4 \\ 0.5 & 0.7 & 1 & 0.9 \\ 0.3 & 0.4 & 0.9 & 1 \end{pmatrix}.$$

2. Find the efficient frontier for the assets in the table above, when asset D is replaced by a risk-free asset, E, which has a mean of 0.10 over our time horizon of two years. Asset E is uncorrelated with the other assets.

3. Where should we be on the efficient frontier in question 1 if we wish to minimize the chance of a return less than 0.05?

4. What are the economic significances of α and β in the Capital Asset Pricing Model and how are they measured or estimated in practice?

CHAPTER 22
value at risk

The aim of this Chapter...

...is to explain one common way of analyzing risk, to describe the basic methodology and also to hint at some of the difficulties associated with the methodology in practice. Many of the problems arise from the assumptions of stable parameters such as volatilities and correlations, and the absence of large jumps in the asset prices.

In this Chapter...

- the meaning of VaR
- how VaR is calculated in practice
- some of the difficulties associated with VaR for portfolios containing derivatives

I'VE GOT A BAD FEELING ABOUT THIS.....

22.1 **INTRODUCTION**

It is the mark of a prudent investor, be they a major bank with billions of dollars' worth of assets or a pensioner with just a few hundred, that they have some idea of the possible losses that may result from the typical movements of the financial markets. Having said that, there have been well-publicized examples where the institution had no idea what might result from some of their more exotic transactions, often involving derivatives.

As part of the search for more transparency in investments, there has grown up the concept of Value at Risk as a measure of the possible downside from an investment or portfolio.

22.2 **DEFINITION OF VALUE AT RISK**

One of the definitions of **Value at Risk** (VaR), and the definition now commonly intended, is the following.

> Value at Risk is an estimate,
> with a given degree of confidence,
> of how much one can lose from one's
> portfolio over a given time horizon.

The portfolio can be that of a single trader, with VaR measuring the risk that he is taking with the firm's money, or it can be the portfolio of the entire firm. The former measure will be of interest in calculating the trader's efficiency and the latter will be of interest to the owners of the firm who will want to know the likely effect of stock market movements on the bottom line.

The degree of confidence is typically set at 95%, 97.5%, 99%, etc. The time horizon of interest may be one day, say, for trading activities or months for portfolio management. It is supposed to be the timescale associated with the orderly liquidation of the portfolio, meaning the sale of assets at a sufficiently low rate for the sale to have little effect on the market. Thus the VaR is an estimate of a loss that can be realized, not just a 'paper' loss.

As an example of VaR, we may calculate (by the methods to be described here) that over the next week there is a 95% probability that we will lose no more than $10m. We can write this as

$$\text{Prob}\{\delta V \leq -\$10\text{m}\} = 0.05,$$

where δV is the change in the portfolio's value. (I use $\delta \cdot$ for 'the change in' to emphasize that we are considering changes over a finite time.) In symbols,

$$\text{Prob}\{\delta V \leq -\text{VaR}\} = 1 - c,$$

where the degree of confidence is c, 95% in the above example.

VaR is calculated assuming normal market circumstances, meaning that extreme market conditions such as crashes are not considered, or are examined separately. Thus, effectively, VaR measures what can be expected to happen during the day-to-day operation of an institution.

The calculation of VaR requires at least having the following data: the current prices of all assets in the portfolio and their volatilities and the correlations between them. If the assets are traded we can take the prices from the market (**marking to market**). For OTC contracts we must use some 'approved' model for the prices, such as a Black–Scholes-type model; this is then **marking to model**. Usually, one assumes than the movement of the components of the portfolio are random and drawn from Normal distributions. I make that assumption here, but make a few general comments later on.

For more information about VaR and data sets for volatilities and correlations see www.jpmorgan.com and links therein.

22.3 **VaR FOR A SINGLE ASSET**

Let us begin by estimating the VaR for a portfolio consisting of a single asset.

We hold a quantity Δ of a stock with price S and volatility σ. We want to know with 99% certainty what is the maximum we can lose over the next week. I am deliberately using notation similar to that from the derivatives world, but there Δ would be the number held *short* in a hedged portfolio. Here Δ is the number held long.

In Figure 22.1 is the distribution of possible returns over the time horizon of one week. How do we calculate the VaR? First of all we are assuming that the distribution is Normal. Since the time horizon is so small, we can reasonably assume that the mean is zero. The standard deviation of the stock price over this time horizon is

$$\sigma S \left(\frac{1}{52} \right)^{1/2},$$

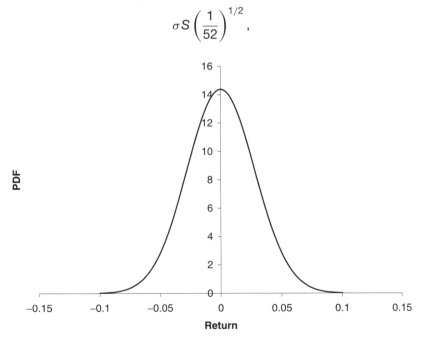

Figure 22.1 The distribution of future stock returns.

Table 22.1 Degree of confidence and the relationship with deviation from the mean.

Degree of confidence	Number of standard deviations from the mean
99%	2.326342
98%	2.053748
97%	1.88079
96%	1.750686
95%	1.644853
90%	1.281551

since the time step is 1/52 of a year. Finally, we must calculate the position of the extreme left-hand tail of this distribution corresponding to $1\% = (100 - 99)\%$ of the events. We only need do this for the standardized Normal distribution because we can get to any other Normal distribution by scaling. Referring to Table 22.1, we see that the 99% confidence interval corresponds to 2.33 standard deviations from the mean. Since we hold a number Δ of the stock, the VaR is given by $2.33\sigma \Delta S(1/52)^{1/2}$.

Time Out...

Degree of confidence in Excel

How to get the number of standard deviations from the mean for a specified degree of confidence on a spreadsheet is shown below.

	A	B	C	D	E	F
1	Mean	0.4				
2	Std dev	1.7				
3						
4	Conf.	No. SDs	Left-hand tail			
5	99%	2.326342	-3.554781			
6	98%	2.053748	-3.091372			
7	97%	1.88079	-2.797342			
8	96%	1.750686	-2.576167			
9	95%	1.644853	-2.39625			
10	90%	1.281551	-1.778636	=$B$1-B8*$B$2		
11						
12		=NORMSINV(A10)				
13						
14						
15						

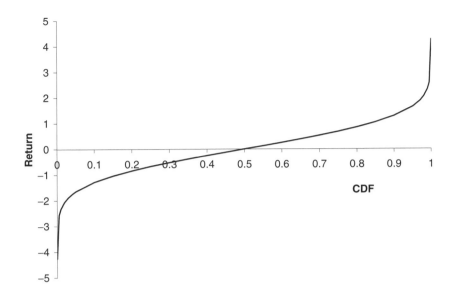

Figure 22.2 The inverse cumulative distribution function for the standardized Normal distribution.

More generally, if the time horizon is δt and the required degree of confidence is c, we have

$$\text{VaR} = -\sigma \, \Delta S(\delta t)^{1/2}\alpha(1-c), \tag{22.1}$$

where $\alpha(\cdot)$ is the inverse cumulative distribution function for the standardized Normal distribution, shown in Figure 22.2.

In (22.1) we have assumed that the return on the asset is Normally distributed *with a mean of zero*. The assumption of zero mean is valid for short time horizons: the standard deviation of the return scales with the square root of time but the mean scales with time itself. For longer time horizons, the return is shifted to the right (one hopes) by an amount proportional to the time horizon. Thus for longer timescales, expression (22.1) should be modified to account for the drift of the asset value. If the rate of this drift is μ then (22.1) becomes

$$\text{VaR} = \Delta S \left(\mu \, \delta t - \sigma \, \delta t^{1/2}\alpha(1-c)\right).$$

Note that I use the *real* drift rate and not the *risk-neutral*. I shall not worry about this adjustment for the rest of this chapter.

22.4 **VaR FOR A PORTFOLIO**

If we know the volatilities of all the assets in our portfolio and the correlations between them then we can calculate the VaR for the whole portfolio.

If the volatility of the ith asset is σ_i and the correlation between the ith and jth assets is ρ_{ij} (with $\rho_{ii} = 1$), then the VaR for the portfolio consisting

VaR for a portfolio
on a spreadsheet

of M assets with a holding of Δ_i of the ith asset is

$$-\alpha(1-c)\delta t^{1/2}\sqrt{\sum_{j=1}^{M}\sum_{i=1}^{M}\Delta_i\Delta_j\sigma_i\sigma_j\rho_{ij}S_iS_j}.$$

Several obvious criticisms can be made of this definition of VaR: returns are not Normal, volatilities and correlations are notoriously difficult to measure, and it does not allow for derivatives in the portfolio. We discuss the first criticism later; I now describe in some detail ways of incorporating derivatives into the calculation.

22.5 VaR FOR DERIVATIVES

The key point about estimating VaR for a portfolio containing derivatives is that, even if the change in the underlying *is* Normal, the essential non-linearity in derivatives means that the change in the derivative can be far from Normal. Nevertheless, if we are concerned with very small movements in the underlying, for example over a very short time horizon, we may be able to approximate for the sensitivity of the portfolio to changes in the underlying by the option's delta. For larger movements we may need to take a higher-order approximation. We see these approaches and pitfalls next.

22.5.1 The delta approximation

Consider for a moment a portfolio of derivatives with a single underlying, S. The sensitivity of an option, or a portfolio of options, to the underlying is the delta, Δ. If the standard deviation of the distribution of the underlying is $\sigma S\,\delta t^{1/2}$ then the standard deviation of the distribution of the option position is

$$\sigma S\,\delta t^{1/2}\Delta.$$

Δ must here be the delta of the whole position, the sensitivity of all of the relevant options to the particular underlying, i.e. the sum of the deltas of all the option positions on the same underlying.

It is but a small, and obvious, step to the following estimate for the VaR of a portfolio containing options:

$$-\alpha(1-c)\delta t^{1/2}\sqrt{\sum_{j=1}^{M}\sum_{i=1}^{M}\Delta_i\Delta_j\sigma_i\sigma_j\rho_{ij}S_iS_j}.$$

Here Δ_i is the rate of change of the *portfolio* with respect to the ith asset.

22.5.2 The delta/gamma approximation

The delta approximation is satisfactory for small movements in the underlying. A better approximation may be achieved by going to higher order and incorporating the gamma or convexity effect.

I demonstrate this by example. Suppose that our portfolio consists of an option on a stock. The relationship between the change in the underlying, δS, and the change in the value of the option, δV, is

$$\delta V = \frac{\partial V}{\partial S}\delta S + \tfrac{1}{2}\frac{\partial^2 V}{\partial S^2}(\delta S)^2 + \frac{\partial V}{\partial t}\delta t + \ldots.$$

Since we are assuming that

$$\delta S = \mu S\,\delta t + \sigma S\,\delta t^{1/2}\phi,$$

where ϕ is drawn from a standardized Normal distribution, we can write

$$\delta V = \frac{\partial V}{\partial S}\sigma S\,\delta t^{1/2}\phi + \delta t\left(\frac{\partial V}{\partial S}\mu S + \tfrac{1}{2}\frac{\partial^2 V}{\partial S^2}\sigma^2 S^2\phi^2 + \frac{\partial V}{\partial t}\right) + \ldots.$$

This can be rewritten as

$$\delta V = \Delta\sigma S\,\delta t^{1/2}\phi + \delta t\left(\Delta\mu S + \tfrac{1}{2}\Gamma\sigma^2 S^2\phi^2 + \Theta\right) + \ldots. \tag{22.2}$$

To leading order, the randomness in the option value is simply proportional to that in the underlying. To the next order there is a deterministic shift in δV due to the deterministic drift of S and the theta of the option. More importantly, however, the effect of the gamma is to introduce a term that is non-linear in the random component of δS.

In Figure 22.3 are shown three pictures. First, there is the assumed distribution for the change in the underlying. This is a Normal distribution with standard deviation $\sigma S\,\delta t^{1/2}$,

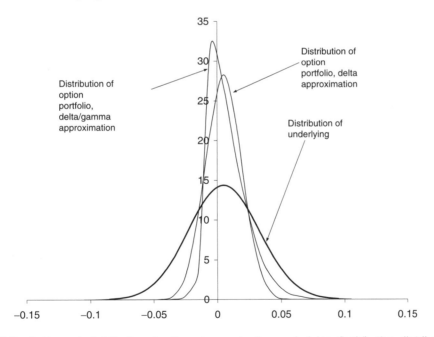

Figure 22.3 A Normal distribution for the change in the underlying (bold), the distribution for the change in the option assuming the delta approximation (another Normal distribution) and the distribution for the change in the option assuming the delta/gamma approximation (definitely not a Normal distribution).

drawn in bold in the figure. Second is shown the distribution for the change in the option assuming the delta approximation only. This is a Normal distribution with standard deviation $\Delta\sigma S\,\delta t^{1/2}$. Finally, there is the distribution for the change in the underlying assuming the delta/gamma approximation.

From this figure we can see that the distribution for the delta/gamma approximation is far from Normal. In fact, because expression (22.2) is quadratic in ϕ, δV must satisfy the following constraint

$$\delta V \geq -\frac{\Delta^2}{2\Gamma} \quad \text{if} \quad \Gamma > 0$$

or

$$\delta V \leq -\frac{\Delta^2}{2\Gamma} \quad \text{if} \quad \Gamma < 0.$$

The extreme value is attained when

$$\phi = -\frac{\Delta}{\sigma S\Gamma\,\delta t^{1/2}}.$$

The question to ask is then 'Is this critical value for ϕ in the part of the tail in which we are interested?' If it is not then the delta approximation may be satisfactory, otherwise it will not be. If we cannot use an approximation we may have to run simulations using valuation formulæ.

One obvious conclusion to be drawn is that positive gamma is good for a portfolio and negative gamma is bad. With a positive gamma the downside is limited, but with a negative gamma it is the upside that is limited.

22.5.3 Use of valuation models

The obvious way around the problems associated with non-linear instruments is to use a simulation for the random behavior of the underlyings and then use valuation formulæ or algorithms to deduce the distribution of the changes in the whole portfolio. This is the ultimate solution to the problem but has the disadvantage that it can be very slow. After all, we may want to run tens of thousands of simulations but if we must solve a multifactor partial differential equation each time then we find that it will take far too long to calculate the VaR.

22.5.4 Fixed-income portfolios

When the asset or portfolio has interest rate dependence then it is usual to treat the yield to maturity on each instrument as the Normally distributed variable. Yields on different instruments are then suitably correlated. The relationship of price to change in yield is via duration (and convexity at higher order). So our fixed-income asset can be thought of as a derivative of the yield. The VaR is then estimated using duration in place of delta (and convexity in place of gamma) in the obvious way.

22.6 SIMULATIONS

Two simulation methods used in VaR estimation are **Monte Carlo**, based on the generation of Normally distributed random numbers, and **bootstrapping** using actual asset price movements taken from historical data.

Within these two simulation methods, there are two ways to generate future scenarios, depending on the timescale of interest and the timescale for one's model or data. If one is interested in a horizon of one year and one has a model or data for returns with this same horizon, then this is easily used to generate a distribution of future scenarios. On the other hand, if the model or data are for a shorter timescale, a stochastic differential equation or daily data, say, and the horizon is one year, then the model must be used to build up a one-year distribution by generating whole year-long paths of the asset. This is more time consuming but is important for path-dependent contracts when the whole path taken must obviously be modeled.

Remember, the simulation must use *real* returns and not *risk-neutral*.

22.6.1 Monte Carlo

Monte Carlo simulation is the generation of a distribution of returns and/or asset price paths by the use of random numbers. This subject is discussed in great depth in Chapter 29. The technique can be applied to VaR: using numbers, ϕ, drawn from a Normal distribution, to build up a distribution of future scenarios. For each of these scenarios use some pricing methodology to calculate the value of a portfolio (of the underlying asset and its options) and thus directly estimate its VaR.

22.6.2 Bootstrapping

Another method for generating a series of random movements in assets is to use historical data. Again, there are two possible ways of generating future scenarios: a one-step procedure if you have a model for the distribution of returns over the required time horizon, or a multi-step procedure if you only have data/model for short periods and want to model a longer time horizon.

The data that we use will consist of daily returns, say, for all underlying assets going back several years. The data for each day is recorded as a vector, with one entry per asset.

Suppose we have real time-series data for N assets and that our data is daily data stretching back four years, resulting in approximately 1000 daily *returns* for each asset. We are going to use these returns for simulation purposes. This is done as follows.

Assign an 'index' to each daily change. That is, we assign 1000 numbers, one for each vector of returns. To visualize this, imagine writing the returns for all of the N assets on the blank pages of a notebook. On page 1 we write the returns in asset values that occurred from 4th August 2000 to 5th August 2000. On page 2 we do the same, but for the returns from 5th August to 6th August 2000. On page 3... from 6th to 7th August, etc. We will fill 1000 pages if we have 1000 data sets. Now, draw a number from 1 to 1000, uniformly distributed; it is 534. Go to page 534 in the notebook. Change all assets from today's value by the vector of returns given on the page. Now draw another number between 1 and 1000 at random and repeat the process. Increment this new value again using one of the vectors.

THE RETURNS DATA GET SHUFFLED FOR SIMULATIONS

	A	B	C	D	E	F	G	H	I	J	K	L	M	N
1	Index	Prob.	TELEBRAS	ELETROBRAS	PETROBRAS	CVDR	USIMINAS	YPF	TAR	TEO	TGS	PEREZ	TELMEX	TELEVISA
2	1	0.001	-0.0152210	0.0180185	0.0118345	-0.0240975	-0.0111733	0.0355909	0.0185764	0.0071943	0.0121214	-0.0182190	-0.0235305	-0.0153849
3	2	0.001	0.0091604	0.0072214	-0.0046130	0.0001039	-0.0226244	0.0207620	0.0121953	0.0106953	0.0000000	-0.0026393	0.0327898	0.0746615
4	3	0.001	-0.0498546	-0.0397883	-0.0324353	-0.0246926	-0.0115608	0.0068260	-0.0121953	-0.0106953	0.0119762	-0.0067506	-0.0139213	-0.0144930
5	4	0.001	-0.0357762	-0.0494712	-0.0358569	-0.1001323	-0.0602100	-0.0068260	-0.0123458	-0.0254097	0.0000000	-0.0144520	-0.0284379	-0.0371790
6	5	0.001	0.0033058	-0.0204013	0.0112413	0.0264184	0.0114388	-0.0068729	0.0061920	0.0036697	-0.0240976	0.0096238	0.0000000	0.0000000
7	6	0.001	0.0424306	0.0260111	-0.0255043	-0.0022909	0.0004155	0.0067340	0.0452054	0.0438519	0.0115608	0.0140863	0.0421608	0.0932575
8	7	0.001	0.0279317	0.0006216	0.0006216	0.0006216	-0.0234759	0.0040080	-0.0208341	0.0000000	-0.0114287	0.0000000	0.0123205	-0.0065147
9	8	0.001	-0.0139801	-0.0383626	-0.0346393	0.0161040	0.0122250	0.0000000	0.0259755	0.0176996	0.0114287	-0.0020299	0.0439192	0.0384663
10	9	0.001	-0.0052219	-0.0036563	0.0403377	0.0142520	0.0229896	0.0063898	0.0101524	0.0085349	0.0114287	-0.0019638	0.0000000	0.0171924
11	10	0.001	-0.0130693	0.0000000	-0.0116961	-0.0047282	0.0112996	0.0000000	0.0100503	0.0112677	0.0112996	0.0081304	-0.0267702	-0.0229895
12	11	0.001	-0.0106656	-0.0148639	0.0069306	-0.0048541	-0.0114030	0.0000000	-0.0100503	-0.0169496	-0.0112996	-0.0166294	-0.0116960	0.0057971
13	12	0.001	0.0079035	0.0184167	-0.0023392	-0.0240975	0.0112996	0.0000000	0.0050633	-0.0085837	0.0335227	-0.0170073	0.0039139	0.0228581
14	13	0.001	0.0000000	-0.0072225	-0.0284021	0.0001035	-0.0226248	0.0000000	-0.0257084	-0.0380719	-0.0110498	-0.0063762	0.0000000	0.0112361
15	14	0.001	0.0000000	-0.0042230	0.0242792	-0.0004134	-0.0126835	-0.0061920	0.0100001	0.0057471	0.0109291	0.0144183	0.0411581	0.0745331
16	15	0.001	-0.0475377	-0.0138620	-0.0251059	-0.0444106	-0.0254146	-0.0062305	-0.0150379	-0.0057471	0.0000000	0.0300138	-0.0080972	0.0000000
17	16	0.001	0.0297428	0.0102652	0.0114445	0.0714950	-0.0008256	0.0415490	0.0277796	0.0309303	0.0408220	-0.0035537	0.0419109	0.0475023
18	17	0.001	-0.0037045	-0.0192060	-0.0248187	0.0078541	-0.0129914	-0.0116280	-0.0045977	0.0052771	0.0000000	0.0007187	-0.0075758	-0.0105264
19	18	0.001	-0.0208341	-0.0205823	-0.0264421	-0.0021947	-0.0267507	0.0231224	0.0091744	-0.0052771	-0.0304592	0.0152095	-0.0269766	-0.0268113
20	19	0.001	0.0568874	0.0828276	0.1052577	0.0477150	0.0612661	0.0271019	0.0753494	0.0746435	0.0388398	0.0599762	0.0498324	0.0438026
21	20	0.001	0.0655911	0.0209154	0.0209922	0.0420456	0.0224756	-0.0173917	0.0165293	0.0223058	0.0000000	0.0232360	0.0036036	0.0194181
22	21	0.001	-0.0091109	0.0309987	0.0615672	-0.0428678	0.0221646	0.0058309	0.0122201	0.0145988	0.0392207	0.0139353	-0.0592766	-0.0342332
23	22	0.001	0.0231470	-0.0036810	-0.0003084	0.0158210	0.0099482	0.0342891	0.0160646	0.0264121	0.0204089	0.0208262	0.0679507	0.0386522
24	23	0.001	0.0157998	-0.0014713	-0.0122804	-0.0094697	-0.0014375	0.0277026	0.0504962	0.0440396	0.0492710	0.0285456	-0.0073260	0.0280392
25	24	0.001	-0.0045147	-0.0054003	-0.0008614	-0.0020500	0.0379553	-0.0054795	-0.0191210	-0.0136988	0.0000000	0.0101176	-0.0073801	-0.0233111
26	25	0.001	0.0270287	0.0275012	0.0583711	0.0001022	0.0361421	0.0280130	-0.0038536	0.0069849	0.0000000	0.0034104	-0.0109690	-0.0432968
27	26	0.001	-0.0089286	0.0068362	0.0038686	0.0248968	-0.0087868	0.0000000	-0.0116506	-0.0093241	0.0000000	0.0110554	-0.0036832	-0.0044346
28	27	0.001	0.0133632	0.0232183	0.0512903	0.0202027	0.0436750	-0.0167135	-0.0117880	-0.0285055	-0.0099503	-0.0080555	0.0000000	0.0088496
29	28	0.001	-0.0110341	0.0417395	0.0176995	0.0506932	0.0085108	0.0000000	-0.0240012	-0.0268636	0.0000000	0.0005324	0.0000000	0.0043956
30	29	0.001	-0.0044544	-0.0289144	0.0069770	-0.0002423	-0.0002043	-0.0056023	0.0000000	0.0024907	0.0000000	-0.0037901	0.0000000	-0.0277796
31	30	0.001	0.0044544	0.0001022	-0.0344781	-0.0075315	0.0086859	0.0056023	0.0202027	0.0049628	0.0204089	0.0147792	0.0038241	0.0277796
32	31	0.001	-0.0044544	-0.0065956	-0.0225751	0.0151071	-0.0173439	0.0111112	-0.0040080	0.0024722	0.0396091	0.0090663	-0.0115164	-0.0184337
33	32	0.001	0.0088685	-0.0067409	0.0284793	0.0204063	0.0261791	0.0096270	0.0043197	-0.0052632	0.0000000	0.0184492	0.0000000	0.1048796
34	33	0.001	-0.0178163	-0.0084174	0.0036982	0.0183391	-0.0186661	-0.0242436	-0.0350913	-0.0240332	-0.0202027	-0.0280518	-0.0234386	-0.1242977
35	34	0.001	-0.0205219	-0.0174839	-0.0199091	-0.0849882	-0.0120831	-0.0061539	-0.0134834	-0.0108697	0.0000000	0.0075047	0.0039448	0.0097562
36	35	0.001	-0.0092167	0.0172806	0.0323986	0.0769500	-0.0145534	-0.0313505	-0.0368705	-0.0221003	0.0202027	-0.0096608	-0.0320027	-0.0600180
37	36	0.001	-0.0256977	-0.0470936	-0.0464976	-0.0325785	-0.0460766	-0.0128207	-0.0189579	-0.0340942	-0.0100503	-0.0547012	-0.0081633	0.0102565
38	37	0.001	0.0303167	0.0398480	0.0188954	0.0204067	0.0278547	0.0625204	0.0421608	0.0396653	0.0000000	0.0471675	0.0322609	0.0497615
39	38	0.001	0.0000000	0.0178185	0.0003050	0.0122735	0.0093548	0.0000000	0.0091325	0.0082988	0.0298530	0.0320480	0.0000000	-0.0097562
40	39	0.001	-0.0113079	-0.0069686	0.0628009	-0.0039604	0.0266682	0.0180185	-0.0091325	-0.0109690	0.0194181	0.0310527	-0.0039604	-0.0148151
41	40	0.001	-0.0479236	-0.0464835	-0.0264332	0.0000000	-0.0266682	-0.0180185	-0.0279088	-0.0198027	-0.0096619	-0.0065198	-0.0119762	-0.0150379
42	41	0.001	-0.0374621	-0.0690578	-0.0427517	-0.0537785	-0.0563828	0.0000000	-0.0094787	-0.0229895	-0.0196085	-0.0109291	-0.0161947	0.0050378

Figure 22.4 Spreadsheet showing bootstrap data.

Continue this process until the required time horizon has been reached. This is one realization of the path of the assets. Repeat this simulation to generate many, many possible realizations to get an accurate distribution of all future prices.

By this method we generate a distribution of possible future scenarios based on historical data.

Note how we keep together all asset changes that happen on a certain date. By doing this we ensure that we capture any correlation that there may be between assets.

This method of bootstrapping is very simple to implement. The advantages of this method are that it naturally incorporates any correlation between assets, and any non-Normality in asset price changes. It does not capture any autocorrelation in the data, but then neither does a Monte Carlo simulation in its basic form. The main disadvantage is that it requires a lot of historical data that may correspond to completely different economic circumstances than those that currently apply.

In Figure 22.4 is shown the daily historical returns for several stocks and the 'index' used in the random choice.

22.7 USE OF VaR AS A PERFORMANCE MEASURE

One of the uses of VaR is in the measurement of performance of banks, desks or individual traders. In the past, 'trading talent' has been measured purely in terms of profit; a trader's bonus is related to that profit. This encourages traders to take risks; think of tossing a coin with you receiving a percentage of the profit but without the downside (which is taken by the bank), how much would you bet? A better measure of trading talent might take into account the risk in such a bet, and reward a good return-to-risk ratio. The ratio

$$\frac{\text{return in excess of risk-free}}{\text{volatility}} = \frac{\mu - r}{\sigma},$$

the **Sharpe ratio**, is such a measure. Alternatively, use VaR as the measure of risk and profit/loss as the measure of return:

$$\frac{\text{daily P\&L}}{\text{daily VaR}}.$$

22.8 **INTRODUCTORY EXTREME VALUE THEORY**

More modern techniques for estimating tail risk use **Extreme Value Theory**. The idea is to more accurately represent the outer limits of returns distributions since this is where the most important risk is. Throw Normal distributions away, their tails are far too thin to capture the frequent market crashes (and rallies). I won't go into the details here, a whole book could be written on this subject (and has been, Embrechts *et al.*, 1997, a very good book).

22.8.1 Some EVT results

Distribution of maxima/minima: If X_i are independent, identically distributed random variables and

$$x = \max(X_1, X_2, \ldots, X_n)$$

then the distribution of x converges to

$$\exp\left(-\left(1 + \frac{\xi(x - \mu)}{\sigma}\right)^{-1/\xi}\right).$$

When $\xi = 0$ this is a Gumbel distribution, $\xi < 0$ a Weibull and $\xi > 0$ Frechet. Frechet is the one of interest in finance because it is associated with fat tails.

Peaks Over Threshold: Consider the probability that loss exceeds u by an amount y (given that the threshold u *has* been exceeded):

$$F_u(y) = P(X - u \le y | X > u).$$

This can be approximated by a Generalized Pareto Distribution:

$$1 - \left(1 + \frac{\xi X}{\beta}\right)^{-1/\xi}.$$

For heavy tails we have $\xi > 0$ in which case not all moments exist:

$$E[X^k] = \infty \quad \text{for} \ k \ge 1/\xi.$$

The parameters in the models are fitted by Maximum Likelihood Estimation using historical data, for example, and from that we can extrapolate to the future.

Example: (From Alexander McNeil, 1998) Fit a Frechet distribution to the 28 annual maxima from 1960 to 16th October 1987, the business day before the big one. Now calculate probability of various returns. E.g. 50-year return level being the level which on average should only be exceeded in one year every 50 years. Result: 24%. And then the next day, 19th October : 20.4%. Note that in the data set the largest fall had been 'just' 6.7%.

22.9   COHERENCE

Some measures of risk make more sense than others. Artzner *et al.* (1997) have stated some properties that sensible risk measures ought to have, they call such sensible measures 'coherent.' If we use $\rho(X)$ to denote this risk measure for a set of outcomes X then the necessary properties are as follows:

1.   Sub-additivity: $\rho(X + Y) \leq \rho(X) + \rho(Y)$. This just says that if you add two portfolios together the total risk can't get any worse than adding the two risks separately. Indeed, there may be cancelation effects or economies of scale that will make the risk better.

2.   Monotonicity: If $X \leq Y$ for each scenario then $\rho(X) \leq \rho(Y)$. Pretty obviously, if one portfolio has better values than another under all scenarios then its risk will be better.

3.   Positive homogeneity: For all $\lambda > 0$, $\rho(\lambda X) = \lambda \rho(X)$. Double your portfolio then you double your risk.

4.   Translation invariance: For all constant c, $\rho(X + c) = \rho(X) - c$. Think of just adding cash to a portfolio.

Do the common measures of risk satisfy these reasonable criteria? Generally speaking, surprisingly and rather unfortunately not! For example, the classical VaR violates sub-additivity.

22.10   SUMMARY

The estimation of downside potential in any portfolio is clearly very important. Not having an idea of this could lead to the disappearance of a bank, and has. In practice, it is more important to the managers in banks, and not the traders. What do they care if their bank collapses as long as they can walk into a new job?

I have shown the simplest ways of estimating Value at Risk, but the subject gets much more complicated. 'Complicated' is not the right word; 'messy' and 'time-consuming' are better. And currently there are many software vendors, banks and academics touting their own versions in the hope of becoming the market standard. In Chapters 24 and 25 we'll see a few of these in more detail.

FURTHER READING

*   See Lawrence (1996) for the application of the Value at Risk methodology to derivatives.

*   See Chew (1996) for a wide ranging discussion of risk management issues and details of important real-life VaR 'crises.'

- See Jorion (1997) for further information about the mathematics of Value at Risk.

- The allocation of bank capital is addressed in Matten (1996).

- Alexander & Leigh (1997) and Alexander (1997a) discuss the estimation of covariance matrices for VaR.

- Artzner *et al*. (1997) discuss the properties that a sensible VaR model must possess.

- Lillo *et al*. (2002) introduce the concept of 'variety' as a measure of the dispersion of stocks.

EXERCISES

1. Assuming a Normal distribution, what percentage of returns are outside the negative two standard deviations from the mean? What is the mean of returns falling in this tail? (This is called the **censored mean**.)

2. What criticisms of Value at Risk as described here can you think of? Consider distributions other than Normal, discontinuous paths and non-linear instruments.

CHAPTER 23
credit risk

The aim of this Chapter...

...is to introduce the concept of creditworthiness and default into our financial modeling. We will also be seeing a new random process, the Poisson process, which is useful for modeling sudden, unexpected changes of state.

In this Chapter...

- the Merton model
- models for instantaneous and exogenous risk of default
- stochastic risk of default and implied risk of default
- credit ratings
- how to model change of rating

23.1 **INTRODUCTION**

In this chapter I describe some ways of looking at default. A recent approach to this subject is to model default as a completely exogenous event, i.e. a bit like the tossing of a coin or the appearance of zero on a roulette wheel, and having nothing to do with how well the company or country is doing. Typically, one then infers from risky bond prices the probability of default as perceived by the market. I'm not wild about this idea but it is very popular.[1]

Later in this chapter I describe the rating service provided by Standard & Poor's and Moody's, for example. These ratings provide a published estimate of the relative creditworthiness of firms.

But first we look at a classic option approach applied to debt valuation, the Merton model.

23.2 **THE MERTON MODEL: EQUITY AS AN OPTION ON A COMPANY'S ASSETS**

The Merton model shows very elegantly how the equity of a company can be thought of as a simple call option on the assets of the company. He starts off by assuming that the assets of the company A follow a random walk

$$dA = \mu A \, dt + \sigma A \, dX.$$

Clearly, the value of the equity equals assets less liabilities:

$$S = A - V.$$

Here S is the value of the equity (just the share price, I've assumed that there is only one share for simplicity) and V the value of the debt.

At maturity of this debt

$$S(A, T) = \max(A - D, 0) \quad \text{and} \quad V(A, T) = \min(D, A),$$

where D is the amount of the debt, to be paid back at time T.

We can now apply ideas from the Black–Scholes model for options, namely the ideas of delta hedging and no arbitrage. Set up a portfolio consisting of the debt and short a quantity Δ of the equity:

$$\Pi = V - \Delta S.$$

We are going to hedge the debt with the stock. (Don't worry about buying and selling a fraction of the one share, in reality there would be millions of shares issued.)

This portfolio changes by

$$d\Pi = dV - \Delta \, dS.$$

---

[1] Bankers are paid such obscene amounts of money, you'd hope they'd feel obliged to think originally once in a while, wouldn't you? Apparently, this is not the case.

So applying Itô's lemma

$$d\Pi = \left(\frac{\partial V}{\partial t} + \tfrac{1}{2}\sigma^2 A^2 \frac{\partial^2 V}{\partial A^2} - \Delta \frac{\partial S}{\partial t} - \tfrac{1}{2}\Delta \sigma^2 A^2 \frac{\partial^2 S}{\partial A^2} \right) dt$$
$$+ \left(\frac{\partial V}{\partial A} - \Delta \frac{\partial S}{\partial A} \right) dA.$$

Now choose

$$\Delta = \frac{\dfrac{\partial V}{\partial A}}{\dfrac{\partial S}{\partial A}}$$

to eliminate risk, and set the return $d\Pi$ equal to the risk-free return $r\Pi \, dt \ldots$
   The end result is, for the current value of the debt V

$$\frac{\partial V}{\partial t} + \tfrac{1}{2}\sigma^2 A^2 \frac{\partial^2 V}{\partial A^2} + rA \frac{\partial V}{\partial A} - rA = 0$$

subject to

$$V(A, T) = \min(D, A)$$

and exactly the same partial differential equation for the equity of the firm S but with

$$S(A, T) = \max(A - D, 0).$$

   Recognize this? The problem for S is exactly that for a call option, but now we have S instead of the option value, the underlying variable are the assets A and the strike is D, the debt. The solution for the equity value is precisely that for a call option.
   And why is this relevant for credit risk? If this 'call option on the assets' ends up out of the money then it is equivalent to a default. So from this model we can find the (risk-neutral) probability of this happening, and if it does happen, what is the recovery rate.

23.3 **RISKY BONDS**

If you are a company wanting to expand, but without the necessary capital, you could borrow the capital, intending to pay it back with interest at some time in the future. There is a chance, however, that before you pay off the debt the company may have got into financial difficulties or even gone bankrupt. If this happens, the debt may never be paid off. Because of this risk of default, the lender will require a significantly higher interest rate than if he were lending to a very reliable borrower such as the US government.
   The real situation is, of course, more complicated than this. In practice it is not just a case of all or nothing. This brings us to the ideas of the seniority of debt and the partial payment of debt.
   Firms typically issue bonds with a legal ranking, determining which of the bonds take priority in the event of bankruptcy or inability to repay. The higher the priority, the more

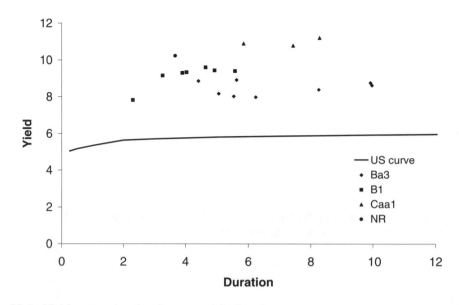

Figure 23.1 Yield versus duration for some risky bonds.

likely the debt is to be repaid, the higher the bond value and the lower its yield. In the event of bankruptcy there is typically a long, drawn out battle over which creditors get paid. It is usual, even after many years, for creditors to get *some* of their money back. Then the question is how much and how soon? It is also possible for the repayment to be another risky bond, this would correspond to a refinancing of the debt. For example, the debt could not be paid off at the planned time so instead a new bond gets issued entitling the holder to an amount further in the future.

In Figure 23.1 is shown the yield versus duration, calculated by the methods of Chapter 14, for some risky bonds. In this figure the bonds have been ranked according to their estimated riskiness. We will discuss this later, for the moment you just need to know that Ba3 is considered to be less risky than Caa1 and this is reflected in its smaller yield spread over the risk-free curve.

The problem that we examine in this chapter is the modeling of the risk of default and thus the fair value of risky bonds. Conversely, if we know the value of a bond, does this tell us anything about the likelihood of default?

23.4 MODELING THE RISK OF DEFAULT

The models that I now describe assume that the likelihood of default is exogenous. These instantaneous risk of default models are simple to use and are therefore the most popular type of credit risk models. In its simplest form the time at which default occurs is completely exogenous. For example, we could roll a die once a month, and when a 1 is thrown the company defaults. This illustrates the exogeneity of the default and also its randomness, a Poisson process is a typical choice for the time of default. We will see that when the intensity of the Poisson process is constant (as in the die example), the pricing of risky bonds amounts to the addition of a time-independent spread to the bond yield. We will also see models for which the intensity is itself a random variable.

A refinement of the modeling that we also consider is the regrading of bonds. There are agents, such as Standard & Poor's and Moody's, who classify bonds according to their estimate of their risk of default. A bond may start life with a high rating, for example, but may find itself regraded due to the performance of the issuing firm. Such a regrading will have a major effect on the perceived risk of default and on the price of the bond. I will describe a simple model for the rerating of risky bonds.

At the end of the chapter we take a quick look at modeling the interrelationships between many risky instruments via copulas.

23.5 THE POISSON PROCESS AND THE INSTANTANEOUS RISK OF DEFAULT

THIS IS PROBABLY THE MOST POPULAR DEFAULT RISK APPROACH

One approach to the modeling of credit risk is via the **instantaneous risk of default**, p. If at time t the company has not defaulted and the instantaneous risk of default is p then the probability of default between times t and $t + dt$ is $p\,dt$. This is an example of a Poisson process; nothing happens for a while, then there is a *sudden* change of state. This is a continuous-time version of our earlier model of throwing a die.

Time Out...

Poisson processes

The basic building block for the random walks we have considered so far is continuous Brownian motion based on the Normally distributed increment. Another stochastic process that is useful in finance is the Poisson process.

A Poisson process dq is defined by

$$dq = \begin{cases} 0 & \text{with probability } 1 - \lambda\,dt \\ 1 & \text{with probability } \lambda\,dt. \end{cases}$$

There is therefore a probability $\lambda\,dt$ of a jump in q in the time step dt. The parameter λ is called the **intensity** of the Poisson process. The scaling of the probability of a jump with the size of the time step is important in making the resulting process 'sensible,' i.e. there being a finite chance of a jump occurring in a finite time, with q not becoming infinite.

Spreadsheet simulation

The simplest example to start with is to take p constant. In this case we can easily determine the risk of default before time T. We do this as follows.

Let $P(t; T)$ be the probability that the company does not default before time T given that it has not defaulted at time t. The probability of default between later times t' and $t' + dt'$ is the product of $p\, dt$ and the probability that the company has not defaulted up until time t'. Thus,

$$P(t' + dt', T) - P(t', T) = p\, dt\, P(t', T).$$

Expanding this for a small time step results in the ordinary differential equation representing the rate of change of the required probability:

$$\frac{\partial P}{\partial t'} = pP(t'; T).$$

If the company starts out not in default then $P(T; T) = 1$. The solution of this problem is

$$e^{-p(T-t)}.$$

The value of a zero-coupon bond paying \$1 at time T could therefore be modeled by taking the present value of the *expected* cashflow. This results in a value of

$$e^{-p(T-t)}Z, \tag{23.1}$$

where Z is the value of a riskless zero-coupon bond of the same maturity as the risky bond. Note that this does not put any value on the risk taken. The yield to maturity on this bond is now given by

$$-\frac{\log(e^{-p(T-t)}Z)}{T-t} = -\frac{\log Z}{T-t} + p.$$

Thus the effect of the risk of default on the yield is to add a spread of p. In this simple model, the spread will be constant across all maturities.

Now we apply this to derivatives, including risky bonds. We will assume that the spot interest rate is stochastic. For simplicity we will assume that there is no correlation between the diffusive change in the spot interest rate and the Poisson process.

Construct a 'hedged' portfolio:

$$\Pi = V(r, p, t) - \Delta Z(r, t).$$

Consider how this changes in a time step. See Figure 23.2 for a diagram illustrating the analysis below.

There is a probability of $(1 - p\, dt)$ that the bond does not default. In this case the change in the value of the portfolio during a time step is

$$d\Pi = \left(\frac{\partial V}{\partial t} + \tfrac{1}{2}w^2\frac{\partial^2 V}{\partial r^2}\right)dt + \frac{\partial V}{\partial r}dr + -\Delta\left(\left(\frac{\partial Z}{\partial t} + \tfrac{1}{2}w^2\frac{\partial^2 Z}{\partial r^2}\right)dt + \frac{\partial Z}{\partial r}dr\right). \tag{23.2}$$

Choose Δ to eliminate the risky dr term.

On the other hand, if the bond defaults, with a probability of $p\, dt$, then the change in the value of the portfolio is

$$d\Pi = -V + O(dt^{1/2}). \tag{23.3}$$

This is due to the sudden loss of the risky bond, the other terms are small in comparison.

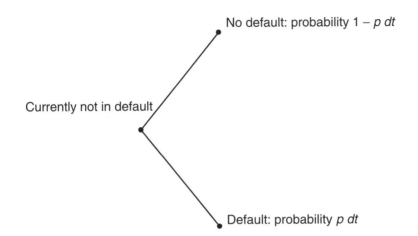

No default: probability $1 - p\,dt$

Currently not in default

Default: probability $p\,dt$

Figure 23.2 A schematic diagram showing the two possible situations: default and no default.

Taking expectations and using the bond pricing equation for the riskless bond, we find that the value of the risky bond satisfies

$$\frac{\partial V}{\partial t} + \tfrac{1}{2}w^2\frac{\partial^2 V}{\partial r^2} + (u - \lambda w)\frac{\partial V}{\partial r} - (r + p)V = 0. \quad (23.4)$$

SEE HOW THE RISK OF DEFAULT AFFECTS THE RATE OF DISCOUNTING

Observe that the spread has been added to the discounting term.

$Time\ Out\dots$

$r \to r + p$

The risk of default has been added to the discounting term. Thus all cashflows are going to be discounted at a rate of $r + p$ instead of r. We can interpret p as a 'spread.' With p being positive this means that all positive cashflows have less present value than if there were no credit risk. The simplicity of this model is the reason for its popularity. (It is not popular because it is a good model.)

Example A four-year US government risk-free zero-coupon bond has a principal of $100 and a current value of $81.11. A similar bond issued by a less reliable source has a value of $77.72. What do these numbers tell you? The yield to maturity of the US government bond is 5.2%. The yield to maturity of the risky bond is 6.3%. The spread of 1.1% between these two means that the market expects (ish) that there is a $1 - e^{-0.011} \approx 1.11\%$ chance per year of the company defaulting.

How would you change this model so that negative cashflows are not affected? After all, why would a company refuse a payment in its favor?

The portfolio is only hedged against moves in the interest rate (assuming that the market price of risk is known, big assumption) and not the event of default. I'll come back to this point below.

This model is the most basic for the instantaneous risk of default. It gives a very simple relationship between a risk-free and a risky bond. There is only one new parameter to estimate, p.

To see whether this is a realistic model for the expectations of the market we take a quick look at the valuation of Brady bonds. In particular we examine the market price of Latin American par bonds, described in full later in this chapter. For the moment, we just need to know that these bonds have interest payments and final return of principal denominated in US dollars. If the above is a good model of market expectations with constant p then we would find a very simple relationship between interest rates in the US and the value of Brady bonds. To find the Brady bond value perform the following:

1. Find the risk-free yield for the maturity of each cashflow in the risky bond.

2. Add a constant spread, p, to each of these yields.

3. Use this new yield to calculate the present value of each cashflow.

4. Sum all the present values.

Conversely, the same procedure can be used to determine the value of p from the market price of the Brady bond: this would be the **implied risk of default**. In Figure 23.3 are shown the implied risks of default for the par bonds of Argentina, Brazil, Mexico and Venezuela using the above procedure and assuming a constant p.

In this simple model we have assumed that the instantaneous risk of default is constant (different for each country) through time. However, from Figure 23.3 we can see that, if we believe the market prices of the Brady bonds, this assumption is incorrect: the market prices are inconsistent with a constant p. This will be our motivation for the stochastic risk of default model which we will see in a moment. Nevertheless, supposing that the figure represents, in some sense, the views of the market (and this constant p model *is* used in practice) we draw a few conclusions from this figure before moving on.

The first point to notice in the graph is the perceived risk of Venezuela, which is consistently greater than the three other countries. Venezuela's risk peaked in July 1994, nine months before the rest of South America, but this had absolutely no effect on the other countries.

The next, and most important, thing to notice is the 'tequila effect' in all the Latin markets. The tequila crisis began with a 50% devaluation of the Mexican peso in December 1994.

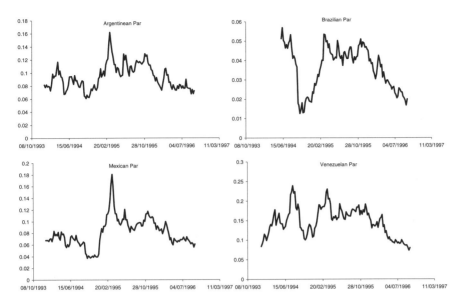

Figure 23.3 The implied risk of default for the par bonds of Argentina, Brazil, Mexico and Venezuela assuming constant p.

Markets followed suit by plunging. Before December 1994 we can see a constant spread between Mexico and Argentina and a contracting spread between Brazil and Argentina. The consequences of tequila were felt through all the first quarter of 1995 and had a knock-on effect throughout South America. In April 1995 the default risks peaked in all the countries apart from Venezuela, but by late 1996 the default risk had almost returned to pre-tequila levels in all four countries. By this time, Venezuela's risk had fallen to the same order as the other countries.

23.5.1 A note on hedging

In the above we have not hedged the event of default. This can sometimes be done (kinda), provided we can hedge with other bonds that will default at exactly the same time, and later we'll see how this introduces a market price of default risk term, as might be expected. Usually, though, there are so few risky bonds that hedging default is not possible. For the

moment I'm going to work in terms of real expectations on the understanding that in the world of default risk, perfect hedging is rarely possible.

23.6 TIME-DEPENDENT INTENSITY AND THE TERM STRUCTURE OF DEFAULT

Suppose that a company issues risky bonds of different maturities. We can deduce from the market's prices of these bonds how the risk of default is perceived to depend on time.

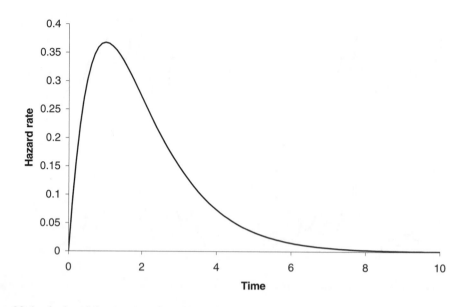

Figure 23.4 A plausible structure for a time-dependent hazard rate.

To make things as simple as possible let's assume that the company issues zero-coupon bonds and that in the event of default in one bond, all other outstanding bonds also default with no recovery rate.

If the risk of default is time dependent, $p(t)$, and uncorrelated with the spot interest rate, then the real expected value of a risky bond paying \$1 at time T is just

$$Ze^{-\int_t^T p(\tau)\,d\tau}.$$

If the market value of the risky bond is Z^* then we can write

$$\int_t^T p(\tau)\,d\tau = \log\left(\frac{Z}{Z^*}\right).$$

Differentiating this with respect to T gives the market's view at the current time t of the **hazard rate** or risk of default at time T. A plausible structure for such a hazard rate is given in Figure 23.4. This figure shows a very small chance of default initially, rising to a maximum before falling off. The company is clearly expected to be around for at least a little while longer, and in the long term it will either have already expired or become very successful. If the area under the curve is finite then there is a finite probability of the company never going bankrupt.

23.7 STOCHASTIC RISK OF DEFAULT

To 'improve' the model, and make it consistent with market prices, we now consider a model in which the instantaneous probability of default is itself random. We assume that it follows a random walk given by

$$dp = \gamma(r,p,t)\,dt + \delta(r,p,t)\,dX_1,$$

with interest rates still given by

$$dr = u(r, t)\,dt + w(r, t)\,dX_2.$$

It is reasonable to expect some interest rate dependence in the risk of default, but not the other way around.

To value our risky zero-coupon bond we construct a portfolio with one of the risky bonds, with value $V(r, p, t)$ (to be determined), and short Δ of a riskless bond, with value $Z(r, t)$ (satisfying our earlier bond pricing equation):

$$\Pi = V(r, p, t) - \Delta Z(r, t).$$

In the next time step either the bond is defaulted or it is not. There is a probability of default of $p\,dt$. We must consider the two cases: default and no default in the next time step. As in the two models above, we take expectations to arrive at an equation for the value of the risky bond.

First, suppose that the bond does not default; this has a probability of $1 - p\,dt$. In this case the change in the value of the portfolio during a time step is

$$d\Pi = \left(\frac{\partial V}{\partial t} + \tfrac{1}{2}w^2 \frac{\partial^2 V}{\partial r^2} + \rho w \delta \frac{\partial^2 V}{\partial r\,\partial p} + \tfrac{1}{2}\delta^2 \frac{\partial^2 V}{\partial p^2} \right) dt + \frac{\partial V}{\partial r}dr + \frac{\partial V}{\partial p}dp$$
$$- \Delta \left(\left(\frac{\partial Z}{\partial t} + \tfrac{1}{2}w^2 \frac{\partial^2 Z}{\partial r^2} \right) dt + \frac{\partial Z}{\partial r}dr \right),$$

where ρ is the correlation between dX_1 and dX_2. Choose Δ to eliminate the risky dr term.

On the other hand, if the bond defaults, with a probability of $p\,dt$, then the change in the value of the portfolio is

$$d\Pi = -V + O(dt^{1/2}).$$

This is due to the sudden loss of the risky bond, the other terms are small in comparison. It is at this point that we could put in a recovery rate, discussed in the next section; as it stands here default means no return whatsoever.

Taking expectations and using the bond pricing equation for the riskless bond, we find that the value of the risky bond satisfies

$$\frac{\partial V}{\partial t} + \tfrac{1}{2}w^2 \frac{\partial^2 V}{\partial r^2} + \rho w \delta \frac{\partial^2 V}{\partial r \partial p} + \tfrac{1}{2}\delta^2 \frac{\partial^2 V}{\partial p^2} + (u - \lambda w)\frac{\partial V}{\partial r} + \gamma \frac{\partial V}{\partial p} - (r + p)V = 0. \quad (23.5)$$

This equation has final condition

$$V(r, p, T) = 1,$$

if the bond is zero coupon with a principal repayment of $1.

Equation (23.5) again shows the similarity between the spot interest rate, r, and the hazard rate, p. The equation is remarkably symmetrical in these two variables, the only difference is in the choice of the model for each. In particular, the final term includes a discounting at rate r and also at rate p. These two variables play similar roles in credit risk equations.

Time Out...

Two-factor models

There are three independent variables in this partial differential equation, t, r and p. And one dependent variable V. If we wanted to think of the meaning of such an equation in terms of our usual mountainside, with slopes in the northerly and westerly directions, then we'd have our job cut out. But the principle is the same. Recall our discussion of the explicit finite-difference method on page 145. The idea works even in this higher-dimensional problem.

As a check on this result, return to the simple case of constant p. In the new framework this case is equivalent to $\gamma = \delta = 0$. The solution of (23.5) is easily seen to be

$$e^{-p(T-t)}Z(r,t),$$

as derived earlier.

If γ and δ are independent of r and the correlation coefficient ρ is zero then we can write

$$V(r,p,t) = Z(r,t)H(p,t),$$

where H satisfies

$$\frac{\partial H}{\partial t} + \frac{1}{2}\delta^2 \frac{\partial^2 H}{\partial p^2} + \gamma \frac{\partial H}{\partial p} - pH = 0,$$

with

$$H(p,T) = 1.$$

In this special, but important case, the default risk decouples from the bond pricing.

23.8 POSITIVE RECOVERY

In default there is usually *some* payment, not all of the money is lost. In Table 23.1, produced by Moody's from historical data, is shown the mean and standard deviations for recovery according to the seniority of the debt. These numbers emphasize the fact that the rate of recovery is itself very uncertain. How can we model a positive recovery?

Table 23.1 Rate of recovery. Source: Moody's.

Class	Mean (%)	Std dev. (%)
Senior secured	53.80	26.86
Senior unsecured	51.13	25.45
Senior subordinated	38.52	23.81
Subordinated	32.74	20.18
Junior subordinated	17.09	10.90

Suppose that on default we know that we will get an amount Q. This will change the partial differential equation. To see this we return to the derivation of Equation (23.4). If there is no default we still have Equation (23.2). However, on default Equation (23.3) becomes instead

$$d\Pi = -V + Q + O(dt^{1/2});$$

we lose the bond but get Q. Taking expectations results in

$$\frac{\partial V}{\partial t} + \tfrac{1}{2}w^2\frac{\partial^2 V}{\partial r^2} + \rho w\delta\frac{\partial^2 V}{\partial r\,\partial p} + \tfrac{1}{2}\delta^2\frac{\partial^2 V}{\partial p^2} + (u - \lambda w)\frac{\partial V}{\partial r} + \gamma\frac{\partial V}{\partial p} - (r + p)V + pQ = 0.$$

Now you are faced with the difficult task of estimating Q, or modeling it as another random variable. It could even be a fraction of V. The last is probably the most sensible approach.

23.9 HEDGING THE DEFAULT

In the above we used riskless bonds to hedge the random movements in the spot interest rate. Can we introduce another risky bond or bonds into the portfolio to help with hedging the default risk? To do this we must assume that default in one bond automatically means default in the other.

Assuming that the risk of default p is constant for simplicity, consider the portfolio

$$\Pi = V - \Delta Z - \Delta_1 V_1,$$

where both V and V_1 are risky.

The choices

$$\Delta_1 = \frac{V}{V_1} \quad \text{and} \quad \Delta = \frac{V_1\dfrac{\partial V}{\partial r} - V\dfrac{\partial V_1}{\partial r}}{V_1\dfrac{\partial Z}{\partial r}}$$

eliminate both default risk and spot rate risk. The analysis results in

$$\frac{\partial V}{\partial t} + \tfrac{1}{2}w^2\frac{\partial^2 V}{\partial r^2} + (u - \lambda w)\frac{\partial V}{\partial r} - (r + \lambda_1(r, t)p)V = 0.$$

Observe that the 'market price of default risk' λ_1 is now where the probability of default appeared before, thus we have a risk-neutral probability of default. This equation is the risk-neutral version of Equation (23.4).

Can you imagine what happens if the risk of default is stochastic? There are actually three sources of randomness:

- the spot rate (the random movement in r)

- the probability of default (the random movement in p)

- the event of default (the Poisson process kicking in)

This means that we must hedge with *three* bonds, two other risky bonds and a risk-free bond, say. Where will you find market prices of risk? Can you derive a risk-neutral version of Equation (23.5)?

23.10 **CREDIT RATING**

There are many **credit rating agencies** who compile data on individual companies or countries and estimate the likelihood of default. The most famous of these are **Standard & Poor's** and **Moody's**. These agencies assign a **credit rating** or **grade** to firms as an estimate of their creditworthiness. Standard & Poor's rate businesses as one of AAA, AA, A, BBB, BB, B, CCC or Default. Moody's use Aaa, Aa, A, Baa, Ba, B, Caa, Ca, C. Both of these companies also have finer grades within each of these main categories. The Moody grades are described in the Table 23.2.

In Figure 23.5 is shown the percentage of defaults over the past 80 years, sorted according to their Moody's credit rating.

The credit rating agencies continually gather data on individual firms and will, depending on the information, grade/regrade a company according to well-specified criteria. A change of rating is called a **migration** and has an important effect on the price of bonds issued by the company. Migration to a higher rating will increase the value of a bond and decrease its yield, since it is seen as being less likely to default.

Clearly there are two stages to modeling risky bonds under the credit-rating scenario. First, we must model the migration of the company from one grade to another and second we must price bonds taking this migration into account.

Figure 23.6 shows the credit rating for Eastern European countries by rating agency.

Table 23.2 The meaning of Moody's ratings.

Aaa	Bonds of best quality. Smallest degree of risk.
	Interest payments protected by a large or stable margin.
Aa	High quality. Margin of protection lower than Aaa.
A	Many favorable investment attributes. Adequate security of principal and interest.
	May be susceptible to impairment in the future.
Baa	Neither highly protected nor poorly secured. Adequate security for the present.
	Lacking outstanding investment characteristics. Speculative features.
Ba	Speculative elements. Future not well assured.
B	Lack characteristics of a desirable investment.
Caa	Poor standing. May be in default or danger with respect to principal or interest.
Ca	High degree of speculation. Often in default.
C	Lowest-rated class. Extremely poor chance of ever attaining any real investment standing.

One-Year Default Rates by Rating and Year

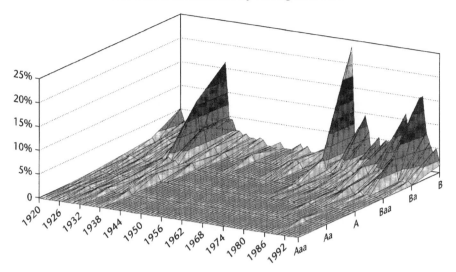

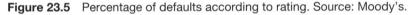

Figure 23.5 Percentage of defaults according to rating. Source: Moody's.

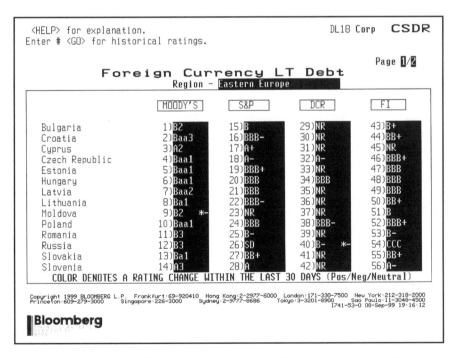

Figure 23.6 Ratings for Eastern European countries by rating agency. Source: Bloomberg L.P.

Table 23.3 An example of a transition matrix.

	AAA	AA	A	BBB	BB	B	CCC	Default
AAA	0.90829	0.08272	0.00736	0.00065	0.00066	0.00014	0.00006	0.00012
AA	0.00665	0.90890	0.07692	0.00583	0.00064	0.00066	0.00029	0.00011
A	0.00092	0.02420	0.91305	0.05228	0.00678	0.00227	0.00009	0.00041
BBB	0.00042	0.00320	0.05878	0.87459	0.04964	0.01078	0.00110	0.00149
BB	0.00039	0.00126	0.00644	0.07710	0.81159	0.08397	0.00970	0.00955
B	0.00044	0.00211	0.00361	0.00718	0.07961	0.80767	0.04992	0.04946
CCC	0.00127	0.00122	0.00423	0.01195	0.02690	0.11711	0.64479	0.19253
Default	0	0	0	0	0	0	0	1

IT'S OFTEN IMPORTANT TO MODEL THE CREDIT RATING NOT JUST THE RISK OF DEFAULT

23.11 A MODEL FOR CHANGE OF CREDIT RATING

Company XYZ is currently rated A by Standard & Poor's. What is the probability that in one year's time it will still be rated A? Suppose that it is 91.305%. Now what is the probability that it will be rated AA or even AAA, or in default? We can represent these probabilities over the one year time horizon by a **transition matrix**. An example is shown in Table 23.3.

This table is read as follows. Today the company is rated A. The probability that in one year's time it will be at another rating can be seen by reading across the A row in the table. Thus the probability of being rated AAA is 0.092%, AA 2.42%, A 91.305%, etc. The highest probability is of no migration. By reading down the rows, this table can be interpreted as either a representation of the probabilities of migration of *all* companies from one grade to another, or of company XYZ had it started out at other than A. Whatever the grade today, the company must have some rating at the end of the year even if that rating is default. Therefore the probabilities reading across each row must sum to one. And once a company is in default, it cannot leave that state, therefore the bottom row must be all zeros except for the last number which represents the probability of going from default to default, i.e. 1.

This table or matrix represents probabilities over a finite horizon. But during that time a bond may have gone from A to BBB to BB, how can we model this sequence of migrations? This is done by introducing a transition matrix over an infinitesimal time period. We can model continuous-time transitions between states via **Markov chains**. This is quite an advanced topic, and I won't be going into this subject any more here.

23.12 COPULAS: PRICING CREDIT DERIVATIVES WITH MANY UNDERLYINGS

Although mentioned briefly above, credit derivatives with many underlyings have become very popular of late. As a natural skeptic when it comes to modeling in finance generally, I have to say that some of the instruments and models being used for the instruments fill me with some nervousness and concern for the future of the global financial markets. Not to mention mankind. Never mind, it's probably just me. We'll see the most important of these ideas and instruments now.

23.12.1 The copula function

The technique now most often used for pricing credit derivatives when there are many underlyings is that of the **copula**. The copula[2] function is a way of simplifying the default dependence structure between many underlyings in a relatively transparent manner. The clever trick is to separate the distribution for default for each individual name from the dependence structure between those names. So you can rather easily analyze names one at a time, for calibration purposes, for example, and then bring them all together in a multivariate distribution. Mathematically the copula way of representing the dependence (one marginal distribution per underlying, and a dependence structure) is no different from specifying a multivariate density function. But it can simplify the analysis.

The copula approach in effect allows us to readily go from a single-default world to a multiple-default world almost seamlessly. And by choosing the nature of the dependence, the copula function, we can explore models with richer 'correlations' than we have seen so far in the multivariate Gaussian world. For example, having a higher degree of dependence during big market moves is quite straightforward.

23.12.2 The mathematical definition

Take N uniformly distributed random variables $U_1, U_2, \ldots, U_N$, each defined on $[0, 1]$. The copula function (see Li, 2000) is defined as

$$C(u_1, u_2, \ldots, u_N) = \text{Prob}(U_1 \leq u_1, U_2 \leq u_2, \ldots, U_N \leq u_N).$$

Clearly we have

$$C(u_1, u_2, \ldots, 0, \ldots, u_N) = 0,$$

and

$$C(1, 1, \ldots, u_i, \ldots, 1) = u_i.$$

So that's the copula function. The way it links many univariate distributions with a single multivariate distribution is as follows.

Let $x_1, x_2, \ldots, x_N$ be random variables with cumulative distribution functions (so-called **marginal** distributions) of $F_1(x_1), F_2(x_2), \ldots, F_N(x_N)$. Combine the Fs with the copula function,

$$C(F_1(x_1), F_2(x_2), \ldots, F_N(x_N)) = F(x_1, x_2, \ldots, x_N)$$

and it's easy to show that this function $F(x_1, x_2, \ldots, x_N)$ is the same as

$$\text{Prob}(X_1 \leq x_1, X_2 \leq x_2, \ldots, X_N \leq x_N).$$

A key reference in this subject is Sklar (1959) who showed that any multivariate distribution can be written in terms of a copula function, i.e. the converse of the above.

In pricing basket credit derivatives we would use the copula approach by simulating default times of each of the constituent names in the basket. And then perform many such simulations in order to be able to analyze the statistics, the mean, standard deviation, distribution, etc., of the present value of resulting cashflows.

---

[2] From the Latin for 'join.'

23.12.3 Examples of copulas

Here are some examples of bivariate copula functions. They are readily extended to the multivariate case.

Bivariate Normal

$$C(u, v) = N_2\left(N_1^{-1}(u), N_1^{-1}(v), \rho\right), \quad -1 \le \rho \le 1,$$

where N_2 is the bivariate Normal cumulative distribution function, and N_1^{-1} is the inverse of the univariate Normal cumulative distribution function.

Frank

$$C(u, v) = \frac{1}{\alpha} \log\left(1 + \frac{(e^{\alpha u} - 1)(e^{\alpha v} - 1)}{e^{\alpha} - 1}\right), \quad -\infty < \alpha < \infty.$$

Fréchet–Hoeffding upper bound

$$C(u, v) = \min(u, v).$$

Gumbel–Hougaard

$$C(u, v) = \exp\left(-\left((-\log u)^\theta + (-\log v)^\theta\right)^{1/\theta}\right), \quad 1 \le \theta < \infty.$$

This copula is good for representing extreme value distributions.

Product

$$C(u, v) = uv$$

Also: Archimedean, Clayton, Student. See Cherubini *et al.* (2004) for a comprehensive list.

One of the simple properties to examine with each of these copulas, and which may help you decide which is best for your purposes, is the **tail index**. Examine

$$\lambda(u) = \frac{C(u, u)}{u}.$$

This is the probability that an event with probability less than u occurs in the first variable given that at the same time an event with probability less than u occurs in the second variable. Now look at the limit of this as $u \to 0$,

$$\lambda_L = \lim_{u \to 0} \frac{C(u, u)}{u}.$$

This tail index tells us about the probability of both extreme events happening together.

23.13 COLLATERALIZED DEBT OBLIGATIONS

Whereas most of the credit instruments described above have a single underlying name, the **collateralized debt obligation** or **CDO** is an instrument designed to give protection against losses in a portfolio, and usually a portfolio containing hundreds of individual companies. As with other credit derivatives there is the protection buyer and the seller.

The CDO gives protection, not against an entire portfolio, but against bits of it, so-called **tranches**. First, define the aggregate loss in the portfolio as the sum of all losses due to default. As more and more companies default so the aggregate loss will increase. Now specify hurdles, as percentages of notional, and these define the tranches. For example, there may be the 0–3% tranche and the 3–7% tranche, etc. As the aggregate loss increases past each of the 3%, 7%, etc. hurdles so the owner of that tranche will begin to receive compensation, at the same rate as the losses are piling up. You will only be compensated once your **attachment point** has been reached and until the **detachment point**.

So there are two types of cashflows in this instrument:

- Premiums: The protection buyer will pay periodic premiums to the seller, quoted in basis points. There may also be an upfront premium.

- 'Compensation:' The holder of the instrument, the protection buyer, receives the loss suffered by his tranche.

To clarify, losses are assigned initially to the first tranche until the threshold is attained, and then to the second tranche until its detachment point is reached, and so on. An example is given in Table 23.4.

To price these instruments you obviously have to consider the probability of each name defaulting and the correlation structure between them. A model often used in practice is the Gaussian copula approach. So far so good. To make the problem tractable, given the large number of underlyings and parameters, it is also often assumed that the structure of the correlation is described by a single random factor. Each has its own stock-specific source of randomness but there is a factor common to all names. Then, to simplify matters further, it is also often assumed that there is a single number to represent all of these correlations, that is, there is just one single correlation parameter. Probably (at least) one simplification too far. One of the reasons for such assumptions is that it leads to simple pricing formulæ.

Working within the framework of a single parameter, how is this parameter used? Suppose we want to price a new CDO, and we have the price of a traded CDO that is not dissimilar. We can back out the **implied** or **compound correlation** from the CDO with the known price and plug it into the model for the other CDO. This is, of course, what is often done in the derivatives world, equity, FX or fixed income, with volatility. It's just another form of calibration.

Table 23.4 A typical CDO and its tranches. Source: St Pierre (2004).

Tranche	Upfront premium	Ongoing premium	(bps)
0–3%	42%	500	
3–7%	0%	331	
7–10%	0%	126	
10-15%	0%	54	
15–30%	0%	16	

There is a major problem with this. As happens in the derivatives world, non-credit, we find that we need a different implied correlation for each tranche. Typically, you might find that the implied correlation falls from first tranche to second, and then rises for third and subsequent tranches (Finger, 2004). This is akin to the implied volatility smile and skews that we have seen before. This suggests that the market is somehow allowing for things not within the one-size-fits-all correlation assumption. Slightly concerning, but not too much. No, the real worry is that you may find that there are *two* possible implied correlations, or no implied correlation at all. This means that a market price is either consistent with two possible constant correlations, or there is no constant correlation which matches theoretical and market prices. Generally speaking, if we were to plot value of a tranche versus implied correlation then we might find a non-monotonic curve. Why is this a worry? Think back to examples we've seen with implied volatility. In particular, the up-and-out call option that we analyzed in some detail (see Chapters 8 and 13). We had the same problem there. Before I expand on this in one paragraph's time, let's see one final way of pricing CDOs.

Using the example in the table, you can think of the 3–7% tranche as long a 0–7% tranche and short the 0–3% tranche. So you can value a non-existent 0–7% tranche very easily. Back out from market data for the 0–3% tranche the implied correlation for that first tranche. Now back out an implied correlation for the 0–7% tranche that you have created. This is called the **base correlation**. Now use these base correlations to price other CDOs with tranches 0–x%, and then construct the y%–x% tranches accordingly.

Now back to the problem with all of this. Do you remember what the non-uniqueness in the implied volatility for the up-and-out call meant? It was because the price versus (constant) volatility graph was non-monotonic. It rose to a peak and then fell. If we have that behavior with a CDO then alarms bells should start ringing. In the knockout example the non-monotonicity was because there were two competing effects going on. If we were out of the money we wanted high volatility so we moved into the money and hence got a nice payoff. But once in the money we wanted low volatility so that we didn't knock out and lose the option. So sometimes volatility was good for us and sometimes bad. Now think bigger than barrier options: two competing effects, one good, one bad. There must be something similar going on with the CDO. Sometimes correlation is good, sometimes bad. What if the good thing didn't kick in and we were only left with the bad? That's what we looked at when we examined the barrier option, we said what if the good volatility, out of the money, didn't appear, but volatility only rose in the money where it hurt us. Net result, much, much lower barrier option prices than if volatility were to rise uniformly everywhere. Exactly the same thing is happening with CDOs. What if the good correlation didn't appear, what if only the bad correlation rose? Ouch. Prices could be much, much lower than you would expect.

With so many potential variables and parameters because of the hundreds of underlyings it is going to be much harder to examine more interesting scenarios. But a step in the right direction would be to at least have two sources of randomness leading to correlations between the underlying names. Or to vary correlation with burn-through (aggregate loss).

23.14 **SUMMARY**

As can be seen from this chapter, credit risk modeling is a very big subject. I have shown some of the popular approaches, but they are by no means the only possibilities. To aid with the assessment of credit risk, the bank JP Morgan has created CreditMetrics, a methodology for assessing the impact of default events on a portfolio. This is described in Chapter 24.

As a final thought for this chapter, suppose that a company issues just the one risky bond so that there is no way of hedging the default. If you believe that the market is underpricing the bond because it overestimates the risk of default then you might decide to buy it. If you intend holding it until expiry, then the market price in the future is only relevant in so far as you may change your mind. But you really do care about the likelihood of default and will pay very close attention to news about the company. On the other hand, if you buy the bond with the intention of only holding it for a short time your main concern should be for how the market is behaving and the real risk of default is irrelevant. You may still watch out for news about the company, but now your concern will be for how the market reacts to the news, not the news itself.

FURTHER READING

- See Black & Scholes (1973), Merton (1974), Black & Cox (1976), Geske (1977) and Chance (1990) for a treatment of the debt of a firm as an option on the assets of that firm. See Longstaff & Schwartz (1994) for more recent work in this area.

- The articles by Cooper & Martin (1996) and Schönbucher (1998) are general reviews of the state of credit risk modeling.

- See Apabhai *et al.* (1998) for more details of the company and debt valuation model, especially for final and boundary conditions for various business strategies. Epstein *et al.* (1997 a, b) describe the firm valuation models in detail, including the effects of advertising and market research.

- The classic reference, and a very good read, for firm-valuation modeling is Dixit & Pindyck (1994). For a non-technical POV see Copeland *et al.* (1990).

- See Kim (1995) for the application of the company valuation model to the question of company mergers and some suggestions for how it can be applied to problems in company relocation and tax status.

- Important work on the instantaneous risk of default model is by Jarrow & Turnbull (1990, 1995), Litterman & Iben (1991), Madan & Unal (1994), Lando (1994a), Duffie & Singleton (1994 a, b) and Schönbucher (1996).

- See Blauer & Wilmott (1998) for the instantaneous risk of default model and an application to Latin American Brady bonds.

- See Duffee (1995) for other work on the estimation of the instantaneous risk of default in practice.

- The original work on change of credit rating was due to Lando (1994b), Jarrow *et al.* (1997) and Das & Tufano (1994). Cox & Miller (1965) describe Markov chains in a very accessible manner.

- See Ahn *et al.* (1998) for the rather sensible use of utility theory in credit risk modeling.

- Current market conditions and prices for Brady bonds can be found at www.bradynet.com.

- See www.emgmkts.com for financial news from emerging markets.

- Clark (2002) uses the implied volatility as a measure of country risk.

EXERCISES

1. A risk-free government, zero-coupon bond, with a principal of $100, maturing in two years has a value of $91.75. A risky corporate zero-coupon bond with the same principal and maturity is worth $88.25. What is the market's estimate of the risk of default assuming zero recovery?

2. The same government and company as in the above question now issue five-year bonds with $100 principal and prices for government bond and corporate bond of $82.15 and $78.89 respectively. What does this now say about the market's view on the probability of the company defaulting?

3. Repeat the analyses of the above two problems but with the extra assumption that on default their is a recovery rate of 10%, i.e. you will receive $10 at maturity if there has been default.

4. Construct the intermediate steps in the derivation of the equation for the value of a risky bond (when default is governed by a Poisson process):

$$\frac{\partial V}{\partial t} + \tfrac{1}{2}w^2\frac{\partial^2 V}{\partial r^2} + (u - \lambda w)\frac{\partial V}{\partial r} - (r + p)V = 0.$$

CHAPTER 24
RiskMetrics and CreditMetrics

The aim of this Chapter...

... is to describe JP Morgan's two popular methodologies for estimating risk associated with general movements of the financial markets, and with credit issues. We will be seeing how parameters are estimated and how the methodologies are implemented.

In this Chapter...

- the methodology of RiskMetrics for measuring value at risk
- the methodology of CreditMetrics for measuring a portfolio's exposure to default events

THIS HAS TOO MANY
UNREALISTIC ASSUMPTIONS...
BUT I GUESS IT'S A START

24.1 INTRODUCTION

In Chapter 22 I described the concept of the 'Value at Risk' (VaR) of a portfolio. I repeat the definition of VaR here: VaR is 'an estimate, with a given degree of confidence, of how much one can lose from one's portfolio over a given time horizon.' In that chapter I showed ways of calculating VaR (and some of the pitfalls of such calculations). Typically the data required for the calculations are parameters for the 'underlyings' and measures of a portfolio's current exposure to these underlyings. The parameters include volatilities and correlations of the assets, and, for longer time horizons, drift rates. The exposure of the portfolio is measured by the deltas, and, if necessary, the gammas (including cross derivatives) and the theta of the portfolio. The sensitivities of the portfolio are obviously best calculated by the owner of the portfolio, the bank. However, the asset parameters can be estimated by anyone with the right data. In October 1994 the American bank JP Morgan introduced the system **RiskMetrics** as a service for the estimation of VaR parameters. Some of this service is free, the datasets are available at www.riskmetrics.com, but the accompanying risk management software is not.

JP Morgan has also proposed a similar approach, together with a data service, for the estimation of risks associated with risk of default: **CreditMetrics**. CreditMetrics has several aims, two of these are the creation of a benchmark for measuring credit risk and the increase in market liquidity. If the former aim is successful then it will become possible to measure risks systematically across instruments and, at the very least, to make relative value judgments. From this follows the second aim. Once instruments, and in particular the risks associated with them, are better understood they will become less frightening to investors, promoting liquidity.

24.2 THE RISKMETRICS DATASETS

The RiskMetrics datasets are extremely broad and comprehensive. They are distributed over the internet. They consist of three types of data: one used for estimating risk over the time horizon of one day, the second having a one-month time horizon and the third has been designed to satisfy the requirements in the latest proposals from the Bank for International Settlements on the use of internal models to estimate market risk. The datasets contain estimates of volatilities and correlations for almost 400 instruments, covering foreign exchange, bonds, swaps, commodities and equity indices. Term-structure information is available for many currencies.

24.3 CALCULATING THE PARAMETERS THE RISKMETRICS WAY

A detailed technical description of the method for estimating financial parameters can be found at the JP Morgan web site. Here I only give a brief outline of major points.

24.3.1   Estimating volatility

The volatility of an asset is measured as the annualized standard deviation of returns. There are many ways of taking this measurement. The simplest is to take data going back a set period, three months, say, calculate the return for each day (or over the typical timescale at which you will be rehedging) and calculate the sample standard deviation of this data. This will result in a time series of three-month volatility.[1] This approach gives equal weight to all of the observations over the previous three months. This estimate of volatility on day i is calculated as

$$\sigma_i = \sqrt{\frac{1}{\delta t(M-1)} \sum_{j=i-M+1}^{i} (R_j - \overline{R})^2},$$

where δt is the time step (typically one day), M is the number of days in the estimate (approximately 63 in three months), R_j is the return on day j and $\overline{R}$ is the average return over the previous M days. If δt is small then we can in practice neglect $\overline{R}$.

   This measurement of volatility has two major drawbacks. First, it is not clear how many days' data we should use; what happened three months ago may not be relevant to today. But the more data we have the smaller will be the sampling error if the volatility really has not changed in that period. Second, a large positive or negative return on one day will be felt in this historical volatility for the next three months. At the end of this period the volatility will apparently drop suddenly, yet there will have been no underlying change in market conditions; the drop will be completely spurious. Thus, the volatility measured in this way will show 'plateauing.' A typical 30-day volatility plot, with plateauing, is shown in Figure 24.1.

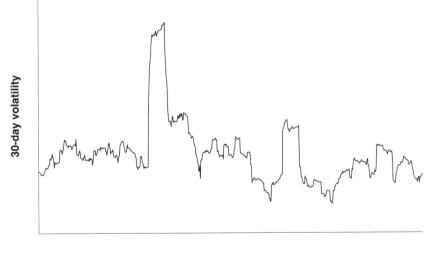

Figure 24.1   Thirty-day volatility.

[1] Which may or may not bear any resemblance to three-month implied volatility.

In RiskMetrics the volatility is measured as the square root of a variance that is an exponential moving average of the square of price returns. This ensures that any individual return has a gradually decreasing effect on the estimated volatility, and plateauing does not occur. This volatility is estimated according to

$$\sigma_i = \sqrt{\frac{1-\lambda}{\delta t} \sum_{j=-\infty}^{i} \lambda^{i-j} R_j^2},$$

where λ represents the weighting attached to the past volatility versus the present return (and we have neglected the mean of R, assuming that the time horizon is sufficiently small). This difference in weighting is more easily seen if we write the above as

$$\sigma_i^2 = \lambda \sigma_{i-1}^2 + (1-\lambda)\frac{R_i^2}{\delta t}.$$

The parameter λ has been chosen by JP Morgan as either 0.94 for an horizon of one day and 0.97 for an horizon of one month. Another possibility is to choose λ to minimize the difference between the squares of the historical volatility and an implied volatility.

The spreadsheet in Figure 24.2 shows how to calculate such an exponentially weighted volatility. As can be seen from the plot, it is much 'better behaved' than the uniformly weighted version.

24.3.2 Correlation

The estimation of correlation is similar to that of volatility. To calculate the covariance σ_{12} between assets 1 and 2 we can take an equal weighting of returns from the two assets over the last M days:

Exponentially weighted moving averages

$$\sigma_{12_i} = \sqrt{\frac{1}{\delta t(M-1)} \sum_{j=i-M+1}^{i} (R_{1_j} - \overline{R}_1)(R_{2_j} - \overline{R}_2)}.$$

Again, this measure shows spurious sudden rises and falls because of the equal weighting of all the returns.

Alternatively, we can use an exponentially weighted estimate:

$$\sigma_{12_i}^2 = \lambda \sigma_{12_{i-1}}^2 + (1-\lambda)\frac{R_{1_i} R_{2_i}}{\delta t}.$$

There are problems with the estimation of covariance due to the synchronicity of asset movements and measurement. Two assets may be perfectly correlated but because of their measurement at different times they may appear to be completely uncorrelated. This is a problem when using data from markets in different time zones. Moreover, there is no guarantee that the exponentially weighted covariances give a positive-definite matrix.

24.4 THE CREDITMETRICS DATASET

The CreditMetrics dataset is available free of charge from www.jpmorgan.com. The CreditMetrics methodology is also described in great detail at that site. The dataset consists of four data types: yield curves, spreads, transition matrices and correlations. Before reading the following sections the reader should be comfortable with the concept of credit rating, see Chapter 23.

	A	B	C	D	E	F	G	H
1	**Start volatility**	0.3		**Date**	**Stock**	**Returns**	**Vol^2**	**Volatility**
2	**Lambda**	0.97		1-Jan-85	218.32		0.09	0.3
3				2-Jan-85	217.16	−0.005313	0.087513	0.295827
4		= (E3−E2)/E2		3-Jan-85	215.24	−0.008841	0.085479	0.292368
5				4-Jan-85	215.24	0.000000	0.082915	0.287949
6		= B1*B1		7-Jan-85	217.16	0.008920	0.081029	0.284655
7				8-Jan-85	220.25	0.014229	0.080129	0.28307
8	= $B$2*G7 + (1-$B$2)*F8*F8*252			Jan-85	224.87	0.020976	0.081051	0.284695
9				10-Jan-85	224.87	0.000000	0.07862	0.280392
10				11-Jan-85	224.1	−0.003424	0.07635	0.276314
11		= SQRT(G11)		14-Jan-85	219.09	−0.022356	0.077838	0.278994
12				15-Jan-86	219.09	0.000000	0.075502	0.274777
13				16-Jan-85	222.17	0.014058	0.074731	0.273371
14				17-Jan-85	226.02	0.017329	0.07476	0.273422
15				18-Jan-85	226.02	0.000000	0.072517	0.26929
16				21-Jan-85	226.79	0.003407	0.070429	0.265385
17				22-Jan-85	234.49	0.033952	0.077031	0.277545
18					57	−0.008188	0.075227	0.274275
19					55	0.013243	0.074296	0.272573
20					27	0.019605	0.074973	0.273812
21					.5	−0.003205	0.072802	0.269818
22					72	−0.024134	0.075021	0.273899
23					35	0.041203	0.085605	0.292583
24					12	0.003164	0.083112	0.288292
25					04	0.007865	0.081086	0.284757
26					04	0.000000	0.078654	0.280453
27					89	0.015648	0.078145	0.279545
28					97	−0.007683	0.076247	0.276129
29				7-Feb-85	247.97	0.000000	0.07396	0.271956
30				8-Feb-85	249.12	0.004638	0.071904	0.268149
31				11-Feb-85	243.35	−0.023162	0.073802	0.271666
32				12-Feb-85	238.34	−0.020588	0.074792	0.273482
33				13-Feb-85	239.5	0.004867	0.072728	0.269681
34				14-Feb-85	238.34	−0.004843	0.070723	0.265938
35				15-Feb-85	235.65	−0.011286	0.069565	0.263751
36				18-Feb-85	232.57	−0.013070	0.068769	0.262239
37				19-Feb-85	234.49	0.008256	0.067221	0.259271
38				20-Feb-85	235.65	0.004947	0.06539	0.255714
39				21-Feb-85	236.42	0.003268	0.063509	0.252009
40				22-Feb-85	235.65	−0.003257	0.061684	0.248362
41				25-Feb-85	234.49	−0.004923	0.060016	0.244982
42				26-Feb-85	235.65	0.004947	0.058401	0.241663
43				27/02/85	232.57	−0.013070	0.05794	0.240708

Figure 24.2   Spreadsheet to calculate an exponentially weighted volatility.

24.4.1   Yield curves

The CreditMetrics yield curve dataset consists of the *risk-free* yield to maturity for major currencies. In Figure 24.3 is shown an example of these risk-free yields. The dataset contains yields for maturities of one, two, three, five, seven, 10 and 30 years. For example, from the yield curve dataset we have information such as the yield to maturity for a three-year US dollar bond is 6.12%.

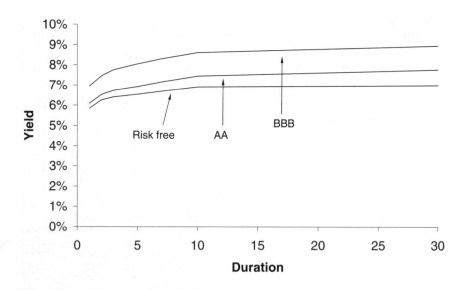

Figure 24.3 Risk-free and two risky yield curves.

24.4.2 Spreads

For each credit rating, the dataset gives the spread above the riskless yield for each maturity. In Figure 24.3 is shown a typical riskless US yield curve, and the yield on AA and BBB bonds. For example, we may be given that the spread for an AA bond is 0.54% above the riskless yield for a three-year bond. Observe that the riskier the bond the higher the yield; the yield on the BBB bond is everywhere higher than that on the AA bond which is in turn higher than the risk-free yield. This higher yield for risky bonds is compensation for the possibility of not receiving future coupons or the principal.

24.4.3 Transition matrices

The concept of the transition matrix has been discussed in Chapter 23. In the CreditMetrics framework, the transition matrix has as its entries the probability of a change of credit rating at the end of a given time horizon, for example the probability of a upgrade from AA to AAA might be 5.5%. The time horizon for the CreditMetrics dataset is one year. Unless the time horizon is very long, the largest probability is typically for the bond to remain at its initial rating, let's say that the probability of staying at AA is 87% in this example. We discussed transition matrices in depth in Chapter 23.

24.4.4 Correlations

In the risk-free yield, the spreads and the transition matrix, there is sufficient information for the CreditMetrics method to derive distributions for the possible future values of a single bond. I show how this is done in the next section. However, when we come to examine the behavior of a portfolio of risky bonds, we must consider whether there is any relationship between the rerating or default of one bond and the rerating or default of another. In other words, are bonds issued by different companies or governments in some sense correlated? This is where the CreditMetrics correlation dataset comes in. This dataset gives the correlations between major indices in many countries.

Each company issuing bonds has the return on its stock decomposed into parts correlated with these indices and a part which is specific to the company. By relating all bond issuers to these indices we can determine correlations between the companies in our portfolio. We will see how this is used in practice later in this chapter.

24.5 THE CREDITMETRICS METHODOLOGY

The CreditMetrics methodology is about calculating the possible values of a risky portfolio at some time in the future (the time horizon) and estimating the probability of such values occurring. Let us consider just a single risky bond currently rated AA. Suppose that the bond is zero coupon, with a maturity of three years and we want to know the possible state of this investment in one year's time. The yield to maturity on this instrument might be 6.12%, for a three-year riskless bond, plus 0.54% for the spread for a three-year AA-rated bond. The total yield is therefore 6.66%, giving a price of 0.819.

The value of the bond will fluctuate between now and one year's time for each of three reasons: the passage of time, the evolution of interest rates and the possible regrading of the bond. Let us take these three points in turn.

First, because of the passage of time our three-year bond will be a two-year bond in one year. But what will be the yield on a two-year bond in one year's time? This is the second point. The assumption that is made in CreditMetrics is that the forward rates do not change between today and the time horizon ('rolling down the curve'). From the yields that we have today we can calculate the forward rates that apply between now and one year, between one and two years, between two and three years, etc. This calculation is described in Chapter 14. We can calculate the value of the bond after one year, suppose it is 0.882. But why should the bond still be rated AA at that time? This is the third point. From our transition matrix we see that the probability of the bond's rating staying AA is 87%. So, there is an 87% chance that the bond's value will be 0.882. We can similarly work out the value of the bond in one year if it is rated AAA, A, BBB, etc. using the relevant forward rates and spreads that we assume will apply in one year's time. And each of these has a probability of occurring that is given in the transition matrix. A probability distribution of the possible bond values is shown in Figure 24.4.

This, highly skewed, distribution tells us all we need to know to determine the risk in this particular bond. We can, for example, calculate the expected value of the bond.

24.6 A PORTFOLIO OF RISKY BONDS

We have seen how to apply the CreditMetrics methodology to a single risky bond, to apply the ideas to a portfolio of risky bonds is significantly harder since it requires the knowledge of any relationship between the different bonds. This is most easily measured by some sort of correlation.

Suppose that we have a portfolio of two bonds. One, issued by ABC, is currently rated AA and the other, issued by XYZ, is BBB. We can calculate, using the method above, the value of each of these bonds at our time horizon for each of the possible states of

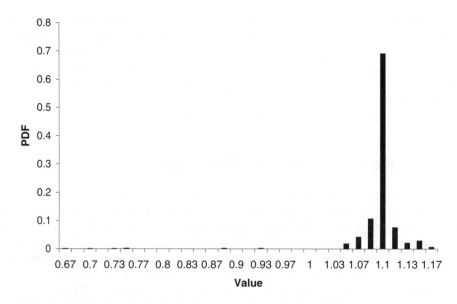

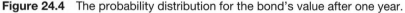

Figure 24.4 The probability distribution for the bond's value after one year.

the two bonds. If we assume that each bond can be in one of eight states (AAA, AA, . . . , CCC, Default) there are $8^2 = 64$ possible joint states at the time horizon. To calculate the expected value of our portfolio and standard deviation we need to know the probability of each of these joint states occurring. This is where the correlation comes in.

There are two stages to determining the probability of any particular future joint state:

1. Calculate the correlations between bonds.

2. Calculate the probability of any joint state.

Stage 1 is accomplished by decomposing the return on the stock of each issuing company into parts correlated with the major indices.

24.7 CREDITMETRICS MODEL OUTPUTS

CreditMetrics is, above all, a way of measuring risk associated with default issues. From the CreditMetrics methodology one can calculate the risk, measured by standard deviation, of the risky portfolio over the required time horizon. Because of the risk of default the distribution of returns from a portfolio exposed to credit risk is highly skewed, as in Figure 24.4. The distribution is far from being Normal. Thus ideas from simple portfolio theory must be used with care. Although it may not be a good absolute measure of risk in the classical sense, the standard deviation is a good indicator of relative risk between instruments or portfolios.

24.8 SUMMARY

This chapter has outlined some of the methodologies for competing and complementary Value at Risk measures. With something as important as Value at Risk there is an obvious case to be made for exploring all of the possible VaR measures to build up as accurate a profile as possible of the dangers lurking in your portfolio. In the next chapter we look at measuring and reducing the risk in stock market crashes.

FURTHER READING

- Download the datasets and very detailed descriptions of the RiskMetrics and Credit-Metrics methodologies from `www.riskmetrics.com`.

- Alexander (1996a) is a critique of RiskMetrics as a risk measurement tool.

- Shore (1997) describes and implements the CreditMetrics methodology.

CHAPTER 25
CrashMetrics

The aim of this Chapter...

...is to explain the analysis of risk associated with market crashes. The methodology is orthogonal to that explained in the previous chapter and is used in conjunction with these other VaR methods and not instead of.

In this Chapter...

- the methodology of CrashMetrics for measuring a portfolio's exposure to sudden, unhedgeable market movements
- Platinum hedging
- crash coefficients
- margin hedging
- counterparty risk
- the CrashMetrics Index for measuring the magnitude of crashes

THIS IS VERY
POPULAR WITH MY
READERS.....
EXCELLENT TASTE

25.1 INTRODUCTION

The final piece of the jigsaw for estimating risk in a portfolio is **CrashMetrics**. If Value at Risk is about normal market conditions then CrashMetrics is the opposite side of the coin, it is about 'fire sale' conditions and the far-from-orderly liquidation of assets in far-from-normal conditions. CrashMetrics is a dataset and methodology for estimating the exposure of a portfolio to extreme market movements or crashes. It assumes that the crash is unhedgeable and then finds the worst outcome for the value of the portfolio. The method then shows how to mitigate the effects of the crash by the purchase or sales of derivatives in an optimal fashion, so-called Platinum hedging. Derivatives have sometimes been thought of as being a dangerous component in a portfolio, in the CrashMetrics methodology they are put to a benign use.

25.2 WHY DO BANKS GO BROKE?

There are two main reasons why banks get into serious trouble. The first reason is the lack of suitable or sufficient control over the traders. Through misfortune, negligence or dishonesty, large and unmanageable positions can be entered into. The consequences are either that the trader concerned becomes a hero and the bank makes a fortune, or the bank loses a fortune, the trader makes a run for it and the bank goes under. The odds are fifty-fifty. The second causes of disaster are the extreme, unexpected and unhedgeable moves in the stock market, the crashes.

25.3 MARKET CRASHES

In typical market conditions one's portfolio will fluctuate rapidly, but not dramatically. That is, it will rise and fall, minute by minute, day by day, but will not collapse. There are times, say once a year on average, when that fluctuation is dramatic... and usually in the downward direction. These are extreme market movements or market crashes. VaR can tell us nothing about these and they must be analyzed separately.

What's special about a crash? Two things spring to mind. Obviously a crash is a sudden fall in market prices, too rapid for the liquidation of a portfolio. But a crash isn't just a rise in volatility. It is also characterized by a special relationship between individual assets. During a crash, all assets fall together. There is no such thing as a crash where half the stocks fall and the rest stay put. Technically this means that all assets become perfectly correlated. In normal market conditions there may be some relationship between stocks, especially those in the same sector, but this connection may not be that strong. Indeed, it is the weakness of these relationships that allows diversification. A small insurance company will happily insure your car, because they can diversify across individuals. Insuring against an earthquake is a different matter. A high degree of correlation makes diversification impossible. This is where traditional VaR falls down, at exactly the time when it is needed most. Figure 25.1 shows the behavior of the correlation of several constituents of the S&P500 around the time of the 1987 stock market crash.

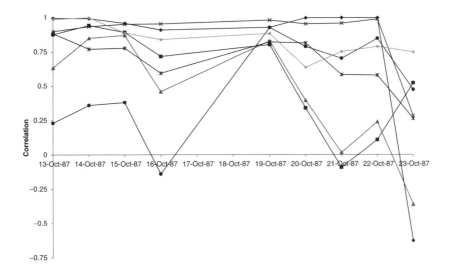

Figure 25.1 The correlation between several assets for a few days before and after the 1987 crash. When the correlation is close to one all assets move in the same direction.

All is not lost. VaR is a very recent concept, created during the 1990s and fast becoming a market standard, with known drawbacks. Many researchers in universities and in banks are turning their thoughts to analyzing and protecting against crashes. Some of these researchers are physicists who concern themselves with examining the tails of returns distributions; are crashes more likely than traditional theory predicts? The answer is a definite yes.

My personal preference though is for models that don't make any assumptions about the likelihood of a crash. One line of work is that of 'worst-case scenarios.' Given that a crash could wipe out your portfolio, wouldn't you like to know what is the worst that could realistically happen, or would you be happy knowing what you would lose on average? CrashMetrics is used to analyze worst cases, and provide advice about how to hedge or insure against a crash.

25.4 **CRASHMETRICS**

CrashMetrics is a methodology for evaluating portfolio performance in the event of extreme movements in financial markets. It is not part of the JP Morgan family of performance measures. We will see how in CrashMetrics the portfolio of financial instruments is valued under a worst-case scenario with few assumptions about the size of the market move or its timing. The only assumptions made are that the market move, the 'crash' is limited in size and that the number of such crashes is limited in some way. There are no assumptions about the probability distribution of the size of the crash or its timing.

This method, used for day-to-day portfolio protection, is concerned with the extreme market movements that may occur when we are not watching, or that cannot be hedged away. These are the fire sale conditions. This is the method I will explain for the rest of this chapter. There are many nice things about the method such as its simplicity and ease of generalization, and no explicit dependence on the annoying parameters volatility and correlation.

25.5 **CRASHMETRICS FOR ONE STOCK**

To introduce the ideas, let's consider a portfolio of options on a single underlying asset. For the moment think in terms of a stock, although we could equally well talk about currencies, commodities or interest rate products.

If the stock changes dramatically by an amount δS how much does the portfolio of options on that stock behave? There will be a relationship between the change in the portfolio value $\delta \Pi$ and δS:

$$\delta \Pi = F(\delta S).$$

The function $F(\cdot)$ will simply be the sum of all the formulæ, expressions, numerical solutions... for each of the individual contracts in the portfolio. Think of it as the sum of lots of Black–Scholes formulæ with lots of different strikes, expiries, payoffs. If there is no change in the asset price there will be no change in the portfolio, so $F(0) = 0$. (There will be a small time decay, which we'll come back to later.) Figure 25.2 shows a possible portfolio change against underlying change.

If we are lucky, and we are not too near to the expiries and strikes of the options, then we could approximate the portfolio by the Taylor series in the change in the underlying asset:

$$\delta \Pi = \Delta \; \delta S + \tfrac{1}{2}\Gamma \; \delta S^2 + \dots . \tag{25.1}$$

In practice this won't be a good enough approximation. Imagine having some knock-out options in the portfolio, we really will have to use the relevant formula or numerical method to capture the sudden drop in value of this contract at the barrier. A simple delta-gamma approximation is not going to work.

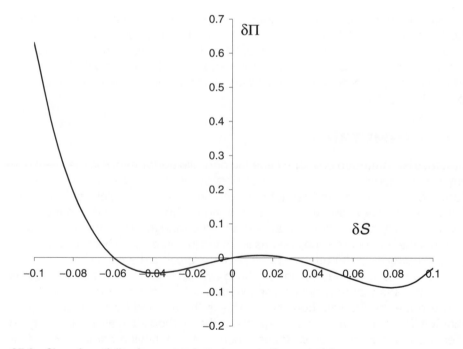

Figure 25.2   Size of portfolio change against change in the underlying.

However, as far as the math is concerned I'm going to show you both the general CrashMetrics methodology and the simple Taylor series version.

Now let's ask what is the worst that could happen to the portfolio overnight say? We want to find the minimum of $F(\delta S)$.

In practice we would only want to look at crashes/rallies of up to a certain magnitude. For this reason we may want to constrain the move in the underlying by

$$-\delta S^- < \delta S < \delta S^+.$$

If we can't use the greek approximation (Taylor series) then we're looking for

$$\min_{-\delta S^- < \delta S < \delta S^+} F(\delta S).$$

Figure 25.2 shows an example where there is one local minimum as well as a global one; it's the global one we want.

In Figure 25.3 we see a plot of the change in the portfolio against δS assuming that a Taylor approximation is valid. Note that it is zero at $\delta S = 0$. If the gamma is positive the portfolio change (25.1) has a minimum at

$$\delta S = -\frac{\Delta}{\Gamma}.$$

The portfolio change in this worst-case scenario is

$$\delta \Pi_{\text{worst}} = -\frac{\Delta^2}{2\Gamma}.$$

This is the worst case given an arbitrary move in the underlying. If the gamma is small or negative the worst case will be a fall to zero or a rise to infinity, both far too unrealistic.

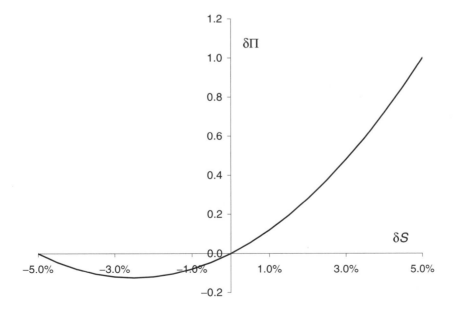

Figure 25.3 Size of portfolio change against change in the underlying, Taylor approximation.

25.6 **PORTFOLIO OPTIMIZATION AND THE PLATINUM HEDGE**

Having found a technique for finding out what could happen in the worst case, it is natural to ask how to make that worst case not so bad. This can be done by optimal static hedging.

To start with, I'll assume the Taylor expansion and then generalize.

Suppose that there is a contract available with which to hedge our portfolio. This contract has a bid-offer spread, a delta and a gamma. I will call the delta of the hedging contract Δ^*, meaning the sensitivity of the hedging contract to the underlying asset. The gamma is similarly Γ^*. Denote the bid-offer spread by $C > 0$, meaning that if we buy (sell) the contract and immediately sell (buy) it back we lose this amount.

Imagine that we add a number λ of the hedging contract to our original position. Our portfolio now has a first-order exposure to the crash of

$$\delta S \left(\Delta + \lambda \Delta^* \right)$$

and a second-order exposure of

$$\tfrac{1}{2} \delta S^2 \left(\Gamma + \lambda \Gamma^* \right).$$

Not only does the portfolio change by these amounts for a crash of size δS but also it loses a *guaranteed* amount

$$|\lambda| \, C$$

just because we cannot close our new position without losing out on the bid-offer spread.

The total change in the portfolio with the static hedge in place is now

$$\delta \Pi = \delta S \left(\Delta + \lambda \Delta^* \right) + \tfrac{1}{2} \delta S^2 \left(\Gamma + \lambda \Gamma^* \right) - |\lambda| \, C.$$

THE MOST IMPORTANT PART OF CRASHMETRICS IS ITS USE IN INSURANCE AGAINST CRASHES

In general, the optimal choice of λ is such that the worst value of this expression for $-\delta S^- \leq \delta S \leq \delta S^+$ is as high as possible. Thus we are exchanging a guaranteed loss (due to bid-offer spread) for a reduced worst-case loss. This is simply insurance and the optimal choice gives the **Platinum hedge**, named for the plastic card that comes after green and gold.[1] For the optimal choice of the λ Figure 25.4 shows the change in the portfolio value as a function of δS. Note that it no longer goes through (0, 0).

In Figure 25.5 is shown a simple spreadsheet for finding the worst-case scenario and the Platinum hedge when there is a single asset.

If we can't use the Taylor approximation, as will generally be the case, we must look for the worst case of

$$F(\delta S) + \lambda F^*(\delta S) - |\lambda| C.$$

Here $F^*(\cdot)$ is the 'formula' for the change in value of the hedging contract.

---

[1] Next, the Centurion hedge?

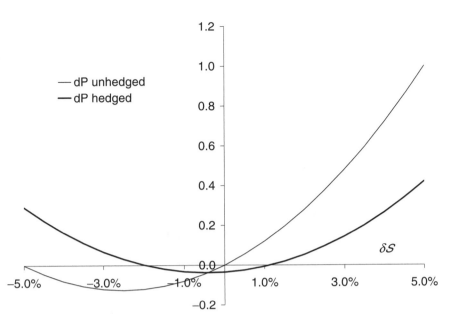

Figure 25.4 Size of portfolio change against δS after optimal hedging, Taylor approximation.

Having found the worst case, we just make this as painless as possible by optimizing over the hedge ratio λ.

Of course, there won't just be the one option with which to statically hedge, there will be many. How does this change the optimization? We'll find out soon.

25.6.1 Other 'cost' functions

In the above we have said that the 'cost' associated with the above is the bid-offer spread on the static hedge part of the portfolio. This is but one of several choices. The reason for this choice is that we may decide tomorrow to get rid of the static hedge, and hence that would genuinely be our cost.

We could also say that the cost function was the value of the bought options, in the sense that we are writing off the 'insurance.' Another choice would be to subtract a cost representing the difference between what we value the static hedge at and the value in the market. This would be suitable for a portfolio that has been constructed for its volatility arbitrage possibilities. An option bought for static hedging that is correctly priced would therefore have no associated cost.

25.7 THE MULTI-ASSET/SINGLE-INDEX MODEL

A bank's portfolio has many underlyings, not just the one. How does CrashMetrics handle them? This is done via an index or benchmark.

We can measure the performance of a portfolio of assets and options on these assets by relating the magnitude of extreme movements in any one asset to one or

	A	B	C	D	E	F	G	H	I	J
1	Max rise	5%								
2	Max fall	-5%		=MIN(IF(AND(G6>B2,G6<B1),-						
3				B6*B6/2/B7,0),B1*B6+0.5*B1*B1*B7,B2*B6+0.5*B2*B2*B7)						
4										
5	Unhedged position					Worst case portfolio fall: unhedged				
6	Δ	10				δS	-0.025		=-B6/B7	
7	Γ	400	=B6+$B$14*B11			Worst fall	-0.125			
8										
9										
10	Hedge contract			Hedged position		Worst case portfolio fall: hedged				
11	Δ	0.5	Δ	1.2771623		δS	-0.004083		=-D11/D12	
12	Γ	5	Γ	312.77162		Worst fall	-0.037499			
13	Cost	0.002								
14	Quantity	-17.4457		=B7+$B$14*B12						
15						=MIN(IF(AND(G11>B2,G11<B1),-				
16						D11*D11/2/D12,0),B1*D11+0.5*B1*B1*D12,B2*D1				
17		δS	δΠ	δΠ		1+0.5*B2*B2*D12)-ABS(B14)*B13				
18			unhedged	hedged						
19	0.005	-5.0%	0.000000	0.292215						
20		-4.5%	-0.045000							
21	=(B1-B2)/20	-4.0%	-0.080000							
22		-3.5%	-0.105000							
23		-3.0%	-0.120000							
24		-2.5%	-0.125000							
25		-2.0%	-0.120000							
26		-1.5%	-0.105000							
27		-1.0%	-0.080000							
28	=$B$6*B25+0.5*$B$7*		0.045000							
29			0.000000							
30		0.5%	0.055000							
31		1.0%	0.120000							
32			195000							
33	=$D$11*B35+0.5*$D$12		280000							
34	*B35*B35-		375000	0.094779						
35			0.480000	0.144171						
36		3.5%	0.595000	0.201382						
37		4.0%	0.720000	0.266412						
38		4.5%	0.855000	0.339262						
39		5.0%	1.000000	0.419931						
40										
41										
42										

Solver Parameters dialog:
Set Target Cell: $G$12
Equal To: ⦿ Max ○ Min ○ Value of: 0
By Changing Cells: $B$14
Subject to the Constraints:
Buttons: Solve, Close, Guess, Options, Add, Change, Delete, Reset All, Help

Figure 25.5   Spreadsheet for implementing basic CrashMetrics in one asset.

more **benchmarks** such as the S&P500. The relative magnitude of these movements is measured by the **crash coefficient** for each asset relative to the benchmark. If the benchmark moves by $x\%$ then the ith asset moves by $\kappa_i x\%$. Estimates of the κ_i for the constituents of the S&P500, with that index as the benchmark, may be downloaded free of charge from www.crashmetrics.com. Note that the benchmark need not be an index containing the assets, but can be any representative quantity. Unlike the RiskMetrics and CreditMetrics datasets, the CrashMetrics dataset does not have to be updated frequently because of the rarity of extreme market movements.

The following tables give the crash coefficients for a few constituents of major indices in several countries. The crash coefficients have been estimated using the tails of the daily return distributions from the beginning of 1985 until the end of 1997, and so include the Black Monday crash of October 1987 and the rice/dragon/sake/Asian 'flu' effect starting in October 1997. For example, in Table 25.1 we see the 10 largest positive and negative daily returns in the S&P500 during that period. In this table are also shown the returns on the same days for several constituents of the index. Tables 25.2 to 25.5 show data for other markets.

Table 25.1 The 10 largest positive and negative moves in several constituents of the S&P500 against the moves in the S&P500 on the same days.

Date	S&P-500	% change	ABBOTT LABS.	ADOBE SYS.	ADVD. MICR.DEVC.	AEROQUIP-VICKERS	AETNA	AHMANSON (H.F.)
19-Oct-87	225	−20.4	−10.5	−22.2	−36.1	−36.6	−15.3	−20.8
26-Oct-87	228	−8.3	−7.3	−20.0	−14.3	−15.2	−4.5	−4.3
27-Oct-97	877	−6.9	−5.3	−6.1	−19.8	−6.7	−8.5	−6.5
08-Jan-88	243	−6.8	−3.8	−14.3	−6.8	−13.5	−7.1	−6.2
13-Oct-89	334	−6.1	−8.2	−12.5	−5.8	−9.3	−5.5	−3.7
16-Oct-87	283	−5.2	−4.6	0.0	−5.3	−6.4	−1.5	−1.3
11-Sep-86	235	−4.8	−5.2	−50.0	−4.7	−5.3	−3.3	−2.9
14-Apr-88	260	−4.4	−4.0	−12.5	−5.6	−2.6	−4.4	−4.8
30-Nov-87	230	−4.2	−6.7	−16.7	−1.4	−9.8	−2.7	−6.1
22-Oct-87	248	−3.9	−4.6	0.0	−5.9	−6.5	−1.9	−1.4
21-Oct-87	258	9.1	4.3	0.0	4.1	11.5	8.0	9.5
20-Oct-87	236	5.3	−0.6	−14.3	6.5	14.3	−3.7	3.3
28-Oct-97	921	5.1	5.2	4.3	19.0	−0.6	4.3	7.4
29-Oct-87	244	4.9	2.4	33.3	10.3	15.5	−1.9	3.2
17-Jan-91	327	3.7	4.3	0.0	4.6	8.0	2.8	3.0
04-Jan-88	255	3.6	0.8	0.0	7.6	−0.4	1.9	−0.7
31-May-88	262	3.4	2.7	0.0	5.3	0.9	3.9	2.5
27-Aug-90	321	3.2	5.4	8.3	4.5	2.2	1.4	3.1
02-Sep-97	927	3.1	3.8	2.6	3.3	0.1	2.5	2.3
21-Aug-91	391	2.9	3.1	4.2	3.5	0.0	−3.3	2.6

Table 25.2 The 10 largest positive and negative moves in several constituents of the FTSE100 against the moves in the FTSE100 on the same days.

Date	FTSE100	% change	ALLIED DOMECQ	ASDA FOODS	ASSD. BRIT	BAA	BANK OF SCOTLAND	BAR-CLAYS
20-Oct-87	1802	−12.2	−7.1	−9.0	−10.1	−7.1	−12.7	−13.2
19-Oct-87	2052	−10.8	−11.5	−9.6	−3.1	−3.7	−3.8	−11.4
26-Oct-87	1684	−6.2	−7.6	−2.4	−3.0	−3.1	−9.0	−7.5
22-Oct-87	1833	−5.7	−4.0	−7.7	−4.7	−2.6	−1.8	−1.0
30-Nov-87	1580	−4.3	−3.0	−4.3	−2.3	−3.8	−2.1	−6.3
05-Oct-92	2446	−4.1	−2.0	−2.9	2.3	−3.4	−6.8	−4.6
03-Nov-87	1653	−4.0	−3.0	−1.7	−2.0	−0.8	−2.0	−7.8
09-Nov-87	1565	−3.4	−3.9	−5.5	−1.0	−4.5	−1.6	−2.2
29-Dec-87	1730	−3.4	−2.3	−1.8	−2.3	−2.1	−0.6	−2.6
16-Oct-89	2163	−3.2	−3.2	−5.0	−3.4	−3.3	0.0	−2.2
21-Oct-87	1943	7.9	7.7	4.9	2.6	2.7	1.5	8.7
10-Apr-92	2572	5.6	8.2	3.3	3.5	7.1	13.1	7.6
17-Sep-92	2483	4.4	3.5	3.6	2.4	2.5	9.6	15.5
11-Nov-87	1639	4.2	2.3	1.8	4.4	2.1	1.0	3.4
30-Oct-87	1749	4.0	1.5	5.0	6.9	3.2	4.6	2.1
12-Nov-87	1702	3.9	1.8	−0.6	−1.0	4.1	0.8	2.2
05-Oct-90	2143	3.6	5.9	0.0	−1.0	3.2	9.3	9.8
18-Sep-92	2567	3.3	6.7	3.4	4.9	3.0	4.2	3.0
26-Sep-97	5226	3.2	1.8	−0.3	1.9	3.2	9.5	8.9
31-Dec-91	2493	3.0	4.0	7.8	1.7	1.3	4.5	2.7

Table 25.3 The 10 largest positive and negative moves in several constituents of the Hang Seng against the moves in the Hang Seng on the same days.

Date	Hang Seng	% change	AMOY PROPS	BANK OF E. ASIA	CHEUNG KONG.	CHINA LT.&POW.	FIRST PACIFIC	GREAT EAGLE
26-Oct-87	2241	−33.3	−37.4	−37.0	−29.2	−32.2	−28.3	−57.3
05-Jun-89	2093	−21.7	−36.4	−22.9	−27.0	−16.6	−28.6	−41.3
28-Oct-97	9059	−13.7	−4.8	−12.7	−9.8	−10.8	−14.7	−19.3
19-Oct-87	3362	−11.1	−18.9	0.0	−9.6	−10.5	−10.7	−20.2
22-May-89	2806	−10.8	−18.6	−8.2	−10.7	−6.2	−14.9	−15.4
23-Oct-97	10426	−10.4	−14.0	−8.9	−13.4	−7.4	−26.9	−6.3
25-May-89	2752	−8.5	−16.6	−7.6	−10.8	−5.0	−9.5	−14.9
19-Aug-91	3722	−8.4	−11.6	−4.7	−6.8	−6.8	−10.2	−9.4
03-Dec-92	4978	−8.0	−2.4	−13.4	−4.8	−9.9	−7.5	−11.3
06-Aug-90	3107	−7.4	−10.3	−6.1	−6.1	−8.2	−6.9	−6.0
29-Oct-97	10765	18.8	9.2	4.9	17.8	20.2	17.3	18.0
23-May-89	3067	9.3	11.4	7.5	9.9	5.2	11.4	14.3
06-Nov-87	2113	7.8	8.5	1.2	12.2	5.4	2.2	9.7
12-Jun-89	2440	7.6	11.7	8.7	10.5	7.0	7.0	16.9
03-Sep-97	14713	7.1	6.0	6.2	5.3	11.9	11.2	5.0
24-Oct-97	11144	6.9	4.1	2.0	9.5	5.9	12.6	7.1
27-Oct-87	2395	6.9	20.1	−2.0	3.8	9.0	−11.4	1.8
03-Nov-97	11255	5.9	5.3	7.8	7.4	−2.9	13.7	6.8
14-Jan-94	10774	5.9	6.1	3.7	6.6	3.6	3.9	4.9
19-Jun-85	1510	5.8	0.0	6.1	6.1	6.2	0.0	13.2

Table 25.4 The 10 largest positive and negative moves in several constituents of the Nikkei against the moves in the Nikkei on the same days.

Date	Nikkei	% change	AJINO-MOTO	ALL NIPPON AIRWAYS	AOKI	ASAHI BREW.	ASAHI CHEM.	ASAHI DENKA KOGYO
20-Oct-87	21910	−14.9	−14.4	−17.9	−18.9	−18.1	−15.7	−10.8
02-Apr-90	28002	−6.6	−3.2	−6.3	−13.7	−5.0	−1.2	−5.8
19-Aug-91	21456	−6.0	−12.1	−7.9	−8.4	−1.6	−5.5	−4.7
23-Aug-90	23737	−5.8	−7.6	−12.0	−9.6	−5.4	−8.4	−7.3
23-Jan-95	17785	−5.6	−8.0	−7.2	−4.9	−1.9	−5.3	−5.2
19-Nov-97	15842	−5.3	−9.0	−3.5	−16.3	−3.4	−3.2	−5.6
24-Jan-94	18353	−4.9	−4.3	−6.0	−6.8	−1.6	−4.1	−7.6
23-Oct-87	23201	−4.9	−4.0	−6.8	−0.9	−4.1	−6.8	−3.4
26-Sep-90	22250	−4.7	−5.2	−2.4	−5.4	−1.6	−2.7	−0.6
03-Apr-95	15381	−4.7	−2.2	−4.1	−2.3	−2.0	−8.4	−6.6
02-Oct-90	22898	13.2	16.0	14.7	9.8	11.4	10.0	15.8
21-Oct-87	23947	9.3	13.5	16.3	11.6	14.7	9.3	5.2
17-Nov-97	16283	8.0	7.3	6.1	0.0	7.4	11.8	9.9
31-Jan-94	20229	7.8	8.5	3.6	13.6	4.2	4.6	9.6
10-Apr-92	17850	7.5	10.5	3.9	13.3	0.0	6.1	3.5
07-Jul-95	16213	6.3	9.8	6.3	9.2	3.0	5.0	1.2
21-Aug-92	16216	6.2	7.9	3.3	21.2	5.6	2.9	2.5
27-Aug-92	17555	6.1	5.6	−1.0	9.4	10.1	5.8	1.8
06-Jan-88	22790	5.6	5.0	6.3	6.4	2.7	6.6	2.4
15-Aug-90	28112	5.4	2.2	6.9	5.4	3.2	3.8	3.8

Table 25.5 The 10 largest positive and negative moves in several constituents of the Dax against the moves in the Dax on the same days.

Date	Dax	% change	ALLIANZ HLDG.	BASF	BAYER	BAYER HYPBK.	BAYERISCHE VBK.	BMW
16-Oct-89	1385	−12.8	−11.3	−10.0	−7.0	−16.1	−13.8	−13.1
19-Aug-91	1497	−9.4	−9.9	−4.8	−5.8	−11.2	−11.2	−10.0
19-Oct-87	1321	−9.4	−10.4	−9.4	−8.5	−7.0	−3.6	−8.2
28-Oct-97	3567	−8.0	−4.7	−8.3	−9.6	−8.6	−7.8	−14.8
26-Oct-87	1193	−7.7	−10.2	−4.0	−5.3	−9.0	−5.5	−6.4
28-Oct-87	1142	−6.8	−7.1	−2.6	−3.2	−8.9	−5.7	−7.5
22-Oct-87	1287	−6.7	−4.2	−4.6	−6.9	−4.6	−5.8	−7.5
10-Nov-87	945	−6.5	−8.9	−4.8	−4.1	−7.4	−6.6	−7.8
04-Jan-88	943	−5.6	−9.9	−6.9	−5.7	−2.1	−5.6	−3.3
06-Aug-90	1740	−5.4	−3.4	−4.3	−6.1	−5.5	−5.2	−6.4
17-Jan-91	1422	7.6	7.8	5.3	6.9	5.8	9.6	9.3
12-Nov-87	1061	7.4	16.6	4.7	7.6	7.6	10.8	6.4
30-Oct-87	1177	6.6	10.2	3.6	8.1	7.8	2.7	7.4
17-Oct-89	1475	6.5	5.8	3.7	2.5	5.9	9.2	5.9
01-Oct-90	1420	6.4	7.8	7.4	9.0	6.0	9.5	7.0
05-Jan-88	1004	6.4	8.6	5.1	4.7	1.7	4.6	4.4
29-Oct-97	3791	6.3	3.5	8.4	8.2	5.9	6.8	12.0
27-Aug-90	1654	6.1	3.9	8.7	5.7	5.0	2.5	6.1
21-Oct-87	1379	5.9	10.9	1.5	8.8	8.7	4.1	4.2
08-Oct-90	1465	5.3	9.1	5.0	5.2	5.1	1.8	3.7

Figure 25.6 uses the same data as used in Chapter 21 for the calculation of the beta for Disney. The fine line in this figure has slope beta. On the figure is shown the line with zero intercept that fits the largest 20 rises and falls in the S&P500, this is the bold line.

In Figure 25.7 are the returns on the Hong Kong and Shanghai Hotel group versus returns on the Hang Seng and in Figure 25.8 are the 40 extreme moves in Daimler–Benz versus returns on the Dax. It is important to note at this stage that the crash coefficient is not the same as the asset's beta with respect to the index. Not only is the number different, but preliminary results suggest that the crash coefficient is more stable than the beta. Moreover, for large moves in the index the stock and the index are far more closely correlated than under normal market conditions. In other words, when there is a crash all stocks move together.

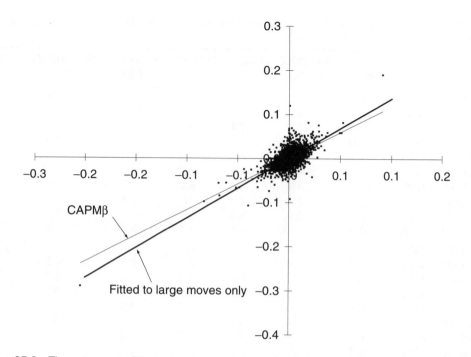

Figure 25.6 The returns on Disney versus returns on the S&P500. Also shown are the line with slope beta, fitted to all points, and the line with slope κ fitted to the 40 extreme moves and having zero intercept.

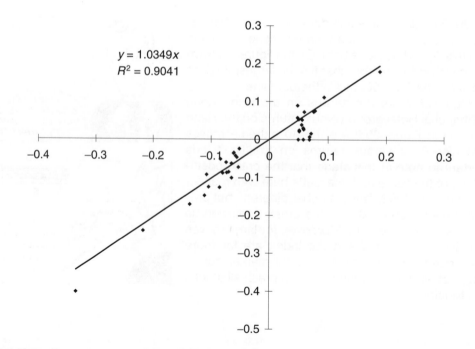

Figure 25.7 The returns on the Hong Kong and Shanghai Hotel group versus returns on the Hang Seng. Also shown is the line with slope κ fitted to the 40 extreme moves and having zero intercept.

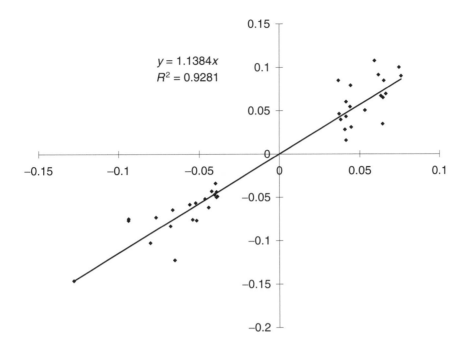

Figure 25.8   The returns on Daimler–Benz versus returns on the Dax. Also shown is the line with slope κ fitted to the 40 extreme moves and having zero intercept.

Figure 25.9 shows the different regimes for the movement of the market as a whole and individual names. There are three scenarios:

1.   Typical day-to-day non-event, small movements in stock and market, perhaps some weak correlation.

2.   Stock-specific event, big rise or fall in individual name, market as a whole is oblivious.

3.   Market crash or dramatic rally, market and stock both move dramatically.

Because of the shape of this figure, I call it the **rings of Saturn** effect.

25.7.1   Assuming Taylor series for the moment

Let's use these ideas, first assuming a Taylor expansion for the portfolio change.
   In the single-index, multi-asset model we can write the change in the value of the portfolio as

$$\delta\Pi = \sum_{i=1}^{N} \Delta_i\, \delta S_i + \tfrac{1}{2}\sum_{i=1}^{N}\sum_{j=1}^{N} \Gamma_{ij}\, \delta S_i\, \delta S_j \qquad (25.2)$$

with the obvious notation. (In particular, observe the cross gammas.) We assume that the percentage change in each asset can be related to the percentage change in the

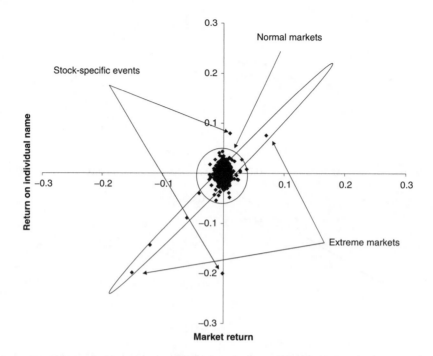

Figure 25.9 Schematic diagram showing the various returns regimes.

benchmark, x, when there is an extreme move:

$$\delta S_i = \kappa_i x S_i.$$

This simplifies (25.2) to

$$\delta \Pi = x \sum_{i=1}^{N} \Delta_i \kappa_i S_i + \tfrac{1}{2} x^2 \sum_{i=1}^{N} \sum_{j=1}^{N} \Gamma_{ij} \kappa_i S_i \kappa_j S_j$$

$$= x D + \tfrac{1}{2} x^2 G.$$

Observe how this contains a first- and a second-order exposure to the crash. The first-order coefficient D is the **crash delta** and the second-order coefficient G is the **crash gamma**.

Now we constrain the change in the benchmark by

$$-x^- \leq x \leq x^+.$$

The worst-case portfolio change occurs at one of the end points of this range or at the internal point

$$x = -\frac{D}{G}.$$

In this last case the extreme portfolio change is

$$\delta \Pi_{\text{worst}} = -\frac{D^2}{2G}.$$

We can also calculate the crash delta and gamma at this worst point.

All of the ideas contained in the single-asset model described above carry over to the multi-asset model, we just use x instead of δS to determine the worst that can happen to our portfolio.

If we can't use the delta-gamma Taylor series expansion then we must look for the worst case of an expression such as

$$\delta\Pi = F(\delta S_1, \ldots, \delta S_N) = F(\kappa_1 x S_1, \ldots, \kappa_N x S_N).$$

This is not hard, or even time consuming as long as we have formulæ for the options in our portfolio.

Suppose you want to look at the exposure of your portfolio of N underlyings in various scenarios then generally you'd want to plot an $N + 1$-dimensional graph, value versus the N underlyings. However, if you want to plot the value of the portfolio in the event of a crash, using the above analysis this $N + 1$-dimensional graph collapses to a more manageable two dimensions, value versus the index.

The single-index, multi-asset model

25.8 **PORTFOLIO OPTIMIZATION AND THE PLATINUM HEDGE IN THE MULTI-ASSET MODEL**

Suppose that there are M contracts available with which to hedge our portfolio. Let us call the deltas of the kth hedging contract Δ_i^k, meaning the sensitivity of the contract to the ith asset, $k = 1, \ldots, M$. The gammas are similarly Γ_{ij}^k. Denote the bid-offer spread by $C_k > 0$, meaning that if we buy (sell) the contract and immediately sell (buy) it back we lose this amount.[2]

Imagine that we add a number λ_k of each of the available hedging contracts to our original position. Our portfolio now has a first-order exposure to the crash of

$$x\left(D + \sum_{k=1}^{M}\lambda_k \sum_{i=1}^{N}\Delta_i^k\kappa_i S_i\right)$$

and a second-order exposure of

$$\frac{1}{2}x^2\left(G + \sum_{k=1}^{M}\lambda_k \sum_{i=1}^{N}\sum_{j=1}^{N}\Gamma_{ij}^k\kappa_i S_i\kappa_j S_j\right).$$

Not only does the portfolio change by these amounts for a crash of size x but also it loses a guaranteed amount:

$$\sum_{k=1}^{M}|\lambda_k|C_k$$

just because we cannot close our new positions without losing out on the bid-offer spread.[3]

---

[2] Of course, as explained above, other cost functions could be used.

[3] We can get an idea of which options are good value for Platinum hedging purposes by looking at the ratio $\kappa/\sigma_{\text{imp}}$. The cost of an at-the-money option is roughly proportional to its implied volatility while its effectiveness in a crash depends on its crash coefficient.

The total change in the portfolio with the static hedge in place is now

$$\delta\Pi = x\left(D + \sum_{k=1}^{M}\lambda_k \sum_{i=1}^{N}\Delta_i^k \kappa_i S_i\right) + \tfrac{1}{2}x^2\left(G + \sum_{k=1}^{M}\lambda_k \sum_{i=1}^{N}\sum_{j=1}^{N}\Gamma_{ij}^k \kappa_i S_i \kappa_j S_j\right) - \sum_{k=1}^{M}|\lambda_k|\,C_k.$$

And if we can't use the Taylor series expansion? We must examine

$$\delta\Pi = F(\kappa_1 x S_1, \ldots, \kappa_N x S_N) + \sum_{k=1}^{M}\lambda_k F_k(\kappa_1 x S_1, \ldots, \kappa_N x S_N) - \sum_{k=1}^{M}|\lambda_k|\,C_k.$$

Here F is the original portfolio and the F_ks are the available hedging contracts.

From now on I'll stick to the delta-gamma approximation and leave it to you to do the more robust and realistic whole-formulæ approach.

25.8.1 The marginal effect of an asset

We can separate the contribution to the portfolio movement in the worst case into components due to each of the underlyings:

$$\delta\Pi_i = x^*\Delta_i\,\delta S_i + \tfrac{1}{2}x^{*2}\sum_{j=1}^{N}\Gamma_{ij}\,\delta S_i\,\delta S_j,$$

Platinum hedging

where x^* is the value of x in the worst case. This has, rather arbitrarily, divided up the parts with exposure to two assets (when the cross gamma is non-zero) equally between those assets. The ratio

$$\frac{\delta\Pi_i}{\delta\Pi_{\text{worst}}}$$

measures the contribution to the crash from the ith asset.

25.9 THE MULTI-INDEX MODEL

In the same way that the CAPM model can accommodate multiple indices, so we can have a multiple index CrashMetrics model. I will skip most of the details, the implementation is simple.

We fit the extreme returns in each asset to the extreme returns in the indices according to

$$\delta S_i = \sum_{j=1}^{n}\kappa_i^j x_j,$$

where the n indices are denoted by the j sub/superscript.

The change in value of our portfolio of stocks and options is now quadratic in all of the x_js. At this point we must decide over what range of index returns do we look for the worst case. Consider just the two index case, because it is easy to draw the pictures.

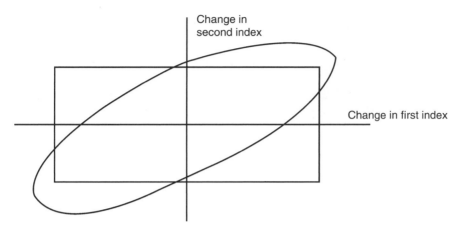

Figure 25.10 Regions of interest in the two-index model.

One possibility is to allow x_1 and x_2 to be independent, to take any values in a given range. This would correspond to looking for the minimum of the quadratic function over the rectangle in Figure 25.10. Note that there is no correlation in this between the two indices, fortunately this difficult-to-measure parameter is irrelevant. Alternatively if you believe that there is some relationship between the size of the crash in one index and the size of the crash in the other you may want to narrow down the area that you explore for the worst case. An example is given in the figure.

25.10 INCORPORATING TIME VALUE

Generally we are interested in the behavior over a longer period than overnight. Can we examine the worst case over a finite time horizon? We can expand the portfolio change in a Taylor series in both δS and δt, the time variable, to get:

$$\delta \Pi - r\Pi \, \delta t = (\Theta - r\Pi) \, \delta t + \Delta \, \delta S + \tfrac{1}{2} \Gamma \, \delta S^2. \tag{25.3}$$

Observe that we examine the portfolio change in excess of the return at the risk-free rate. We must now determine the lowest value taken by this for

$$0 < \delta t < \tau \text{ and } -\delta S^- < \delta S < \delta S^+,$$

where τ is the horizon of interest. Since the time and asset changes decouple, the problem for the worst-case asset move is exactly the same as the above, overnight, problem. The worst-case time decay up to the horizon will be

$$\min \left((\Theta - r\Pi) \, \tau, 0 \right).$$

The idea of Platinum hedging carries over after a simple modification. The modification we need is to the theta. We must incorporate the Θ^* for each of the hedging contracts, suitably multiplied by the number of contracts.

OBVIOUS, BUT NEVER DISCUSSED IN THE LITERATURE

25.11 **MARGIN CALLS AND MARGIN HEDGING**

Stock market crashes are more common than one imagines, if one defines a crash as any unhedgeable move in prices. Although we have focused on the change in value of our portfolio during a crash this is not what usually causes trouble. One of the reasons for this is that in the long run stock markets rise significantly faster than the rate of interest, and banks are usually net long the market. What causes banks, and other institutions, to suffer is not the paper value of their assets but the requirement to suddenly come up with a large amount of cash to cover an unexpected margin call. Banks can weather extreme markets provided they do not have to come up with large amounts of cash for margin calls. For this reason it makes sense to be 'margin hedged.' Margin hedging is the reduction of future margin calls by buying/selling contracts so that the net margin requirement is insensitive to movements in underlyings. In the worst-case crash scenario discussed here, this means optimally choosing hedging contracts so that the worst-case margin requirement is optimized. Typically, over-the-counter (OTC) options will not play a role in the optimal margin hedge since they do not usually have margin call requirements.

Recent examples where margin has caused significant damage are Metallgesellschaft and Long Term Capital Management.[4]

I now show how the basic CrashMetrics methodology can be easily modified to estimate and ameliorate worst-case margin calls.

25.11.1 What is margin?

Writing options is very risky. The downside of buying an option is just the initial premium, the upside may be unlimited. The upside of writing an option is limited, but the downside could be huge. For this reason, to cover the risk of default in the event of an unfavorable outcome, the clearing houses that register and settle options insist on the deposit of a margin by the writers of options. Clearing houses act as counterparty to each transaction.

Margin comes in two forms, the initial margin and the maintenance margin. The initial margin is the amount deposited at the initiation of the contract. The total amount held as margin must stay above a prescribed maintenance margin. If it ever falls below this level then more money (or equivalent in bonds, stocks, etc.) must be deposited. The levels of these margins vary from market to market.

25.11.2 Modeling margin

The amount of margin that must be deposited depends on the particular contract. Obviously, we are not too concerned with the initial margin since this is known in advance of the purchase/sale of the contract. It is the variation margin that will concern us since a dramatic market move could result in a sudden large margin call that may be difficult to meet.

---

[4] The latter suffered after a 'once in a millennium...10 sigma event.' Unfortunately it happened in only their fourth year of trading.

We will model the margin call as a percentage of the change in value of the contract. We denote that percentage by the Greek letter χ. Note that for an over-the-counter (OTC) contract there is usually no margin requirement so $\chi = 0$.

With the same notation as above, the change in the value of a single contract with a single underlying is

$$\delta\Pi = \Delta\ \delta S + \tfrac{1}{2}\Gamma\ \delta S^2.$$

Therefore the margin call would be

$$\delta M = \chi\left(\Delta\ \delta S + \tfrac{1}{2}\Gamma\ \delta S^2\right).$$

The reader can imagine the details of extending this formula to many underlyings and many contracts, and to include time decay.

The final result is simply

$$\delta M - rM\ \delta t = \left(\sum_{i=1}^{N}\overline{\Theta}_i - rM\right)\delta t + \sum_{i=1}^{N}\overline{\Delta}_i\ \delta S_i + \tfrac{1}{2}\sum_{i=1}^{N}\sum_{j=1}^{N}\overline{\Gamma}_{ij}\ \delta S_i\ \delta S_j.$$

This assumes that interest is received by the margin. Here

$\overline{\Theta}_i =$ **margin theta** of all options with S_i as the underlying

$\quad = \sum \chi\Theta$, where the sum is taken over all options

$\overline{\Delta}_i =$ **margin delta** of all options with S_i as the underlying

$\quad = \sum \chi\Delta$, where the sum is taken over all options

$\overline{\Gamma}_{ij} =$ **margin gamma** of all options with S_i and S_j as the underlyings

$\quad = \sum \chi\Gamma$, where the sum is taken over all options

$r =$ risk-free interest rate

$\delta t =$ time horizon

$\delta S_i =$ change in value of ith asset

The notation is self-explanatory.

The conclusion is that the CrashMetrics methodology will carry over directly to the analysis of margin provided that the Greeks are suitably redefined. We have therefore introduced the new Greeks, $\overline{\Theta}$, $\overline{\Delta}$ and $\overline{\Gamma}$, margin theta, margin delta and margin gamma, respectively.

The reader who is aware of the Metallgesellschaft fiasco will recall that they were delta hedged but not margin hedged.

I've assumed a Taylor series/delta-gamma approximation that almost certainly won't be realistic during a crash. We are lucky when modeling margin that virtually every contract on which there is margin has a nice formula for its price. The complex products which require numerical solution are typically OTC contracts with no margin requirements at all. I leave it to the reader to go through the details when using formulæ rather than greek approximations.

25.11.3   The single-index model

As in the original CrashMetrics methodology we relate the change in asset value to the change in a representative index via

$$\delta S_i = \kappa_i x S_i.$$

Thus we have

$$\delta M - rM\,\delta t = \left(\sum_{i=1}^{N} \overline{\Theta}_i - rM\right)\delta t + x\sum_{i=1}^{N}\overline{\Delta}_i\kappa_i S_i + \tfrac{1}{2}x^2\sum_{i=1}^{N}\sum_{j=1}^{N}\overline{\Gamma}_{ij}\kappa_i S_i \kappa_j S_j$$

$$= \overline{Th}\,\delta t + x\overline{D} + \tfrac{1}{2}x^2\overline{G}.$$

Here $\overline{Th}$ is the portfolio margin theta *in excess of the risk-free growth*. Observe how this expression contains a first- and a second-order exposure to the crash. The first-order coefficient $\overline{D}$ is the crash margin delta and the second-order coefficient $\overline{G}$ is the crash margin gamma.

We've seen worst-case scenarios, Platinum hedging and the multi-index model applied to portfolio analysis and hedging. All of these carry over unchanged to the case of margin analysis, provided that the greeks are suitably redefined. In particular Platinum margin hedging is used to optimally reduce the size of margin calls in the event of a market crash.

25.12   COUNTERPARTY RISK

If OTC contracts do not have associated margin calls, they do have another serious kind of risk: counterparty risk. During extreme markets counterparties may go broke, having a knock-on effect on other banks. For this reason, one should divide up one's portfolio by counterparty initially and examine the worst-case scenario counterparty by counterparty. Everything that we have said above about worst-case scenarios and Platinum hedging carries over to the smaller portfolio associated with each counterparty.

25.13   SIMPLE EXTENSIONS TO CRASHMETRICS

In this section I want to briefly outline ways in which CrashMetrics has been extended to other situations and to capture other market effects. Because of the simplicity of the basic form of CrashMetrics, many additional features can be incorporated quite straightforwardly.

First of all, I haven't described how the CrashMetrics methodology can be applied to interest rate products. This is not difficult, simply use a yield (or several) as the benchmark and relate changes in the values of products to changes in the yield via durations and convexities. The reader can imagine the rest.

A particularly interesting topic is what happens to parameter values after a crash. After a crash there is usually a rise in implied volatility and an increase in bid-offer spread. The rise in volatility can be incorporated into the methodology by including vega terms, dependent also on the size of the crash. This is conceptually straightforward,

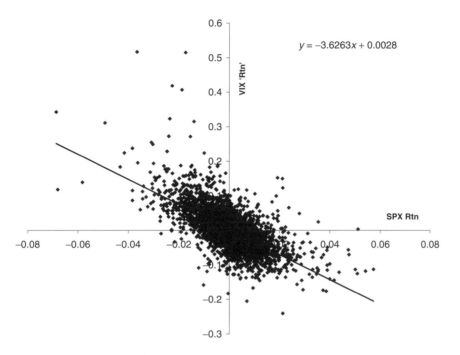

Figure 25.11   VIX return versus SPX return.

but requires analysis of option price data around the times of crashes. If you are long vanilla options during a crash, you will benefit from this rise in volatility. Similarly, a crash-dependent bid-offer spread can be incorporated but again requires historical data analysis to model the relationship between the size of a crash and the increase in the spread. See Figure 25.11.

Finally, it is common experience that shortly after a crash stocks bounce back, so that the real fall in price is not as bad as it seems. Typically 20% of the sudden loss is recovered shortly afterwards, but this is by no means a hard and fast rule. You can see this in the earlier data tables, a date on which there is a very large fall is followed by a date on which there is a large rise. To incorporate such a dynamic effect into the relatively static CrashMetrics is an interesting task.

25.14   **THE CRASHMETRICS INDEX (CMI)**

The results and principles of CrashMetrics have been applied to a **CrashMetrics Index (CMI)**. This is an index that measures the magnitude of market moves and whether or not we are in a crash scenario. It's like a Richter scale for the financial world. Unlike most measures of market movements this one is *not* a volatility index in disguise, it is far more subtle than that. However, being proprietary, I can't tell you how it's defined. Sorry. I can give you some clues: it's based on a logarithmic scale; It has only one timescale (unlike volatility which needs a long timescale such as thirty days, and a short one, a day, say); it exploits the effect shown in Figure 25.1. Figure 25.12 shows a time series of the CMI applied to the S&P500.

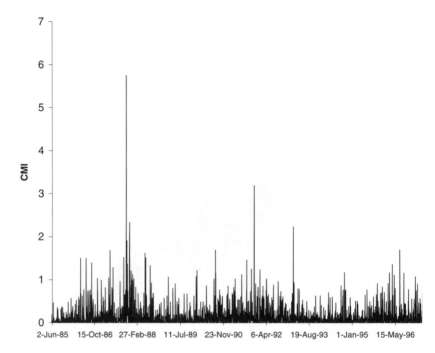

Figure 25.12 The S&P500 CMI.

25.15 **SUMMARY**

This chapter described a VaR methodology that is specifically designed for the analysis of and protection against market crashes. Such analysis is fundamental to the well-being of financial institutions and for that reason I have taken a non-probabilistic approach to the modeling.

FURTHER READING

- Download the CrashMetrics technical documents, datasets and demonstration software for CrashMetrics from www.crashmetrics.com.

EXERCISES

1. Extend the example CrashMetrics spreadsheet to incorporate many underlyings, all related via an index. How would interest rate products be incorporated?

2. Sudden, large movements in a stock are usually accompanied by an increase in implied volatilities. Incorporate a vega term into the one-asset CrashMetrics model. What is the role of actual volatility in CrashMetrics?

CHAPTER 26
derivatives **** ups

The aim of this Chapter...

...is to warn the reader of the dangers associated with the naive use of derivatives, and to encourage the application of common sense at all times. The chapter is also a nice break from the intense mathematics of preceding chapters.

In this Chapter...

- Orange County
- Proctor and Gamble
- Metallgesellschaft
- Gibson Greetings
- Barings
- LTCM

IT'S FRIGHTENING WHAT THESE GUYS GET AWAY WITH..

26.1 INTRODUCTION

Derivatives, in the wrong hands, can be dangerous weapons. They can destroy careers and institutions. In this chapter we take a look of some of the more well-publicized cases of derivatives **** ups. In many cases the details are not in the public domain but where possible I include what *is* known, and offer some analysis.

26.2 ORANGE COUNTY

Orange County is in California. For the first half of the 1990s the County Treasurer was the aptly named Robert Citron. He was in charge of the County investment fund, a pool of money into which went various taxes of the townsfolk. From 1991 until the beginning of 1994 Citron steadily made money, totaling some $750 million, by exploiting low interest rates. This was a very good return on investment, representing approximately 400 basis points above US government rates. How was this possible? He had invested the good people's money in leveraged inverse floating rate notes.

A floating rate note is a bond that pays coupons linked to a floating interest rate such as three- or six-month LIBOR. Normally, the coupon rises when rates rise, not so with inverse floaters. Typically inverse floaters have a coupon of the form

$$\max(\alpha r_f - r_L, 0)$$

where r_f is a fixed rate, r_L some LIBOR rate and $\alpha > 1$ a multiplicative factor. As rates rise, the coupons fall but with a floor at zero; the bond holder never has to return money. Citron bought leveraged inverse floaters[1] having coupons of the form

$$\max(\alpha r_f - \beta r_L, 0)$$

with $\beta > 1$. (If $\beta < 1$ it is a deleveraged note.) While rates are low, coupons are high. This was the situation in the early 1990s, and Citron and Orange County benefited. But what if rates rise? These notes have a high degree of gearing.

Citron gambled that rates would stay low.

In mid-1994 US rates rose dramatically, by a total of 3%. The leveraging in the notes kicked in big time and Orange County lost some $1.6 billion. Figure 26.1 shows US interest rates during the early 1990s. For about 18 months short-term yields had been below 4%, the horizontal line in the figure. But in early 1994 they started a rise that was dramatic in comparison with the previous period of 'stability.' Citron (and others, see below) were 'caught out' by this rise (to the right of the vertical line in the figure).

Orange County didn't have to declare bankruptcy, they were still in the black and money was still pouring into the fund. But as part of the tactics in their damage suit against the brokers of the deal, they declared bankruptcy on 6th December 1994.

It seems that no one had much of a clue how the losses were piling up. There was no frequent marking to market necessary. Had there been, presumably the losses would have been anticipated and someone would have taken action. At the time of the bankruptcy

---

[1] Actually, he bought a lot of other things as well. He was not a lucky boy, our Bob.

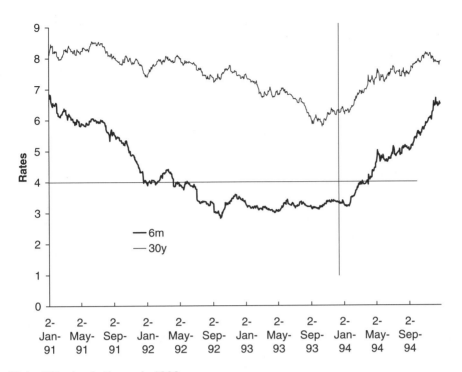

Figure 26.1   US rates in the early 1990s.

filing S&P's rated Orange County as AA and Moody's as Aa1, very high ratings and thought very unlikely to default.

'Leveraged inverse floating rate note' is a very long name for a very simple instrument. The risks should be obvious. After all, how difficult is it to understand $\max(\alpha r_f - \beta r_L, 0)$?

If Orange County lost who gained? The counterparties selling the floaters were various US government housing agencies. Amusingly, the money flowed from the Orange County taxpayers to the US taxpayers everywhere. Hee, hee.

Citron was found guilty of violating state investment laws and was sentenced to one year of community service. During the sentencing phase psychologists found that he had the math skills of a seventh grader and that he was in the lowest 5% of the population in terms of ability to think and reason.

26.3   **PROCTOR AND GAMBLE**

Proctor and Gamble (P&G) is a major multinational company who manufactures beauty and health care products, food and beverages, and laundry and cleaning products. They have a large exposure to interest rates and to exchange rates. To reduce this exposure they use interest rate and currency swaps.

In late 1993 P&G wanted to enter into a swap from fixed to floating, having the view that rates then low would remain low. A vanilla swap would be fine as long as rates didn't rise, but what if they did? Bankers Trust (BT), the counterparty to the deal, suggested some modifications to the swap that satisfied P&G's concerns.

The deal, struck on 2nd November 1993 was a five-year swap on a notional $200 million. It contained something a little out of the ordinary, but not outrageously so. P&G had sold BT something like a put on long-term bond prices.

The deal went like this. BT pays P&G a fixed rate of interest on the $200 million for five years. In return P&G pays BT a fixed rate for the first six months, thereafter a rate defined by

$$r_C - 0.0075 + 0.01 \times \max\left(\frac{98.5}{5.78}Y_5 - P_{30}, 0\right) \tag{26.1}$$

where r_C was the rate on P&G's own corporate bonds, Y_5 the five-year Treasury yield and P_{30} the price of the 30-year Treasury bond. The Treasury yield and price would be known at the time of the first payment, 2nd May 1994, *at which time it would be fixed in the formula*. In other words, the yield and price pertaining on that date would be locked in for the remaining four and a half years.

The best that P&G could achieve would be for rates to stay near the level of November 1993 for just a few more months in which case they would benefit by

$$0.0075 \times \$200 \, \text{million} \times 5 = \$7.5 \, \text{million}.$$

Not a vast amount in the scheme of things. Five- and 30-year rates had been falling fairly steadily for the whole of the 1990s so far, see Figure 26.1, perhaps they would continue to do so, matching the stability of the short-term yields.

However, if rates were to rise between November and May...

Expression (26.1) increases as the five-year yield increases and decreases if the 30-year bond rises in value. But, of course, if the 30-year yield rises the bond price falls and (26.1) increases. Although there is some small exposure to the slope of the yield curve, the dominant effect is due to the level of the yield curve.

In November 1993 the 6.25% coupon bond maturing in August 2023 had a price of about 103.02, corresponding to a yield of approximately 5.97%. The five-year rate was around 4.95%. With those values expression (26.1) was safely the required $r_C - 0.0075$. However, rates rose at the beginning of 1994 and the potential $7.5 million was not realized, instead P&G lost close to $200 million.

Subsequently, P&G sued BT on the grounds that they failed to disclose pertinent information. The case was settled out of court.

The following was taken from P&G Corporate News Releases

P&G Settles Derivatives Lawsuit With Bankers Trust
May 9, 1996

CINCINNATI, May 9, 1996–The Procter & Gamble Company today reached an agreement to settle its lawsuit against Bankers Trust. The suit involves two derivative contracts on which Bankers Trust claimed P&G owed approximately $200 million. Under the terms of the agreement, P&G will absorb $35 million of the amount in dispute, and Bankers Trust will absorb the rest, or about 83% of the total.

'We are pleased with the settlement and are glad to have this issue resolved,' said John E. Pepper, P&G chairman and chief executive.

It's not difficult to work out the potential losses *a priori* from a shift in the yield curve, and I've done just that in Table 26.1 assuming a parallel shift. P&G start to lose out after about

Table 26.1   Effect of parallel shift in yield curve on P&G's losses.

Parallel shift (bps)	0	50	100	150	200
Five-year yield	4.95%	5.45%	5.95%	6.45%	6.95%
Price of 30-year bond	103.02	97.77	93.04	88.74	84.82
30-year yield	5.97%	6.47%	6.97%	7.47%	7.97%
Total loss over 4.5 years $m	0	0	75	190	302

a 70 bps rise in the yield curve. Thereafter they lose about $2.3 million per basis point. On 2nd May 1994 the five-year and 30-year rates were 6.687% and 7.328% respectively, an average rate rise of over 150 bps.

In Figure 26.2 is shown the distribution of changes in US five-year rates over a six-month period during the 10 years prior to November 1993, data readily available at the time that the contract was signed.[2] This historical data suggests that there is a 14% chance of rates rising more than the 70 bps at which P&G start to lose out (the black bars in the figure). There is a 3% chance of a 150 bps or worse rise. Using this data to calculate the expected profit over the five-year period one finds that it is −$8.7 million, rather than the hoped for +$7.5 million.

When you get to the end of this chapter I want you to do a little exercise. Perform the above parallel shift calculation on a spreadsheet. Time yourself to find out how long it would have taken you to save $200 million. (If you use Excel's built-in spreadsheet functions to calculate yields and prices then it should take less than 10 minutes of typing, and that includes switching on your PC and a comfort break.)

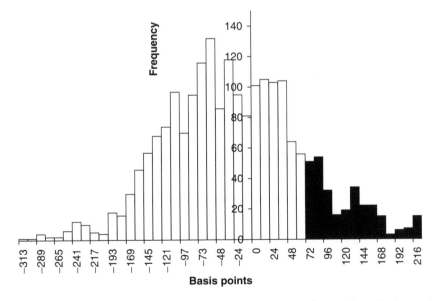

Figure 26.2   Distribution of changes in US five-year rates over a six-month period covering the 10 years prior to November 1993.

---

[2] I've cheated a bit in using overlapping data. Using non-overlapping data gives the same, or slightly worse for P&G, results.

The following, taken from the P&G website (www.pg.com), seems a decent enough principle (I don't know when it was written):

> Integrity: We always try to do the right thing. We are honest and straightforward with each other. We operate within the letter and spirit of the law. We uphold the values and principles of P&G in every action and decision. We are data-based and intellectually honest in advocating proposals, including *recognizing risks*.

The italics are mine.

26.4 METALLGESELLSCHAFT

Metallgesellschaft (*pron.* Met Al gazelle shaft, emphasis on 'Al') is a large German conglomerate with a US subsidiary called MG Refining and Marketing (MGRM). In 1992 MGRM issued forward contracts to its clients, locking in the price of heating oil and gasoline for 10 years. The forward price was fixed at about $3 above the then spot prices. Each month the client received a delivery of oil, paying fixed price. The contract also allowed for both parties to close the position. For example, the client could cancel the contract at any time that the shortest-dated oil futures price exceeded the fixed price. On exercise they would receive 50% of the difference in price between the short future and the fixed price, multiplied by the total volume of oil remaining on the contract. MGRM could also close some of the contracts if the short futures price exceeded some prescribed exit price.

These contracts proved popular with clients because they were the only long-dated contracts available with which to lock in a fixed price. No such contracts existed on an exchange. The total volume of oil in the contracts amounted to some 180 million barrels, the equivalent of 85 days of the output of Kuwait.

Since these contracts were OTC forwards no money changed hands until each delivery. At which time the net cash flow to MGRM was fixed minus spot. The lower the spot price the more that the contracts were of value to MGRM.

MGRM naturally wanted to hedge the oil price risk. But the only exchange traded contracts available were one- to three-month futures. MGRM implemented a strategy of hedging the long-term short OTC forward position with long positions in short-term futures traded on the New York Mercantile Exchange (NYMEX). Because the short-term contracts expired every few months the position had to be rolled over; as one position expired so another was entered into for the next shortest maturity. Theoretically this strategy would have been successful provided that MGRM had a good model for interest rates and the cost of carry. We will return to this point in a moment. Even if MGRM did have a decent model they hit problems because of the important distinction between futures and OTC forwards.

Oil prices fell during the latter half of 1993. Because they held long positions in the futures, a fall in price had to be met on a daily basis by an increase in margin. Futures are marked to market. The extra margin requirements amounted to $900 million during 1993, a large sum of money. MGRM turned to its parent company to help with the funding. Metallgesellschaft responded by taking control of MGRM, installing a new management. In December 1993 the new management closed out half of the short-term contracts. Oil prices then started to rise in early 1994 so that MGRM started to lose out on the long-term contracts. Their response was to cancel the OTC forward contracts and close all positions. By this time losses had amounted to $1.3 billion.

But were they really losses? MGRM were losing out on the short-term futures positions as oil prices fell but remember that these contracts were for hedging purposes. As they lost money on the hedging position they also made money on the OTC forward contracts. The problem was that because these were forward contracts the profit on them was not realized until the positions expired. Marking to model should have resulted in a net flat position regardless of what the oil price did. Think back to margin hedging, discussed in Chapter 25.

Some say that the MGRM management panicked; they say otherwise.

26.4.1 Basis risk

There was a slight complication in this story due to the behavior of futures prices. The relationship between forward prices and spot prices is not as simple in the commodity markets as it is in the FX markets, for example. Arbitrage considerations lead to the theoretical result

$$F = Se^{(r+q)(T-t)}$$

where T is the maturity, r is the relevant risk-free yield and q is the cost of carry. This relationship leads to forward prices that are higher than spot prices, the graph of forward prices as a function of maturity would be upward sloping. In this case the market is said to be in **contango**.

In practice the strategy required to take advantage of the arbitrage opportunity is so impractical, involving the buying, transporting, storing, transporting, ... of the commodity that the theoretical arbitrage is irrelevant. It is therefore possible, and even common, for the forward curve to be downward sloping. The market is said to be in **backwardation**.

In the Metallgesellschaft story the oil markets were in a state of backwardation initially. By rolling over the futures contract it was possible to make a profit, benefiting from the slope of the forward curve at the short end. During 1993 the spot oil price fell sharply and the market moved into contango. Now the rolling over led to losses, amounting to $20 million per month. The question remains, did MGRM price into the OTC forward contracts this possible behavior of effectively the cost of carry? If they did (which seems unlikely, or even impossible *a priori*) then their hedging strategy would have been successful had it not been cut off in its prime.

It is difficult to build an accurate interest rate and/or cost of carry model. MGRM was therefore exposed to the risk of hedging one instrument with an imperfectly correlated one. Such a risk is generally termed **basis risk**.

26.5 **GIBSON GREETINGS**

I think we should use this as an opportunity. We should just call [the Gibson contact], and maybe chip away at the differential a little more. I mean we told him $8.1 million when the real number was 14. So now if the real number is 16, we'll tell him that it is 11. You know, just slowly chip away at the differential between what it really is and what we're telling him.

... when there's a big move, you know, if the market backs up like this, and he is down another 1.3, we can tell him he is down another 2 ... If the market really rallies like crazy, and he's made back a couple of million dollars, you can say you have only made back a half a million.

February 23, 1994, BT Securities tape of a BT Securities manager discussing the BT internal valuation of the Gibson's positions and the valuation given to Gibson.

Gibson Greetings is a US manufacturer of greetings cards. In May 1991 they issued $50 million worth of bonds with a coupon of 9.33% and with maturities of between four and 10 years. In the early 1990s interest rates fell and Gibson were left paying out a now relatively high rate of interest. To reduce the cost of their debt they entered into vanilla interest rate swaps with Bankers Trust in November 1991.

Swap 1: Notional $30 million, two-year maturity, BT pay Gibson six-month LIBOR and Gibson pay BT 5.91%.

Swap 2: Notional $30 million, five-year maturity, BT pay 7.12% and Gibson pay six-month LIBOR.

For the first two years the LIBOR cashflows cancel and Gibson receive $7.12 - 5.91 = 1.21\%$.

In July 1992 both swaps were canceled. Shortly afterwards Gibson entered into a more leveraged swap contract, and so began a sequence of buying and canceling increasingly complex products. Some of these products are described below.

Ratio swap: For five years Gibson were to pay

$$\frac{50}{3} r_L^2$$

to BT every six months and receive 5.5% on a notional of $30 million. Here r_L is six-month LIBOR. Since the first fixing of LIBOR was at approximately 3.08% the first payment by Gibson was just 1.581%. The second payment was 1.893% corresponding to LIBOR of 3.4%.

Interest rates were starting to rise. And judging by the implied forward curve at the time the market was 'expecting' rates to go higher. Should six-month LIBOR reach $5.7\%(= \sqrt{0.06 \times 0.055})$ the net cashflow would be towards BT from Gibson. Fearing that rates would go beyond this level, the swap contract was amended three times and finally canceled in April 1993, six months after its initiation.

LIBOR did not rise as rapidly as the forward curve had suggested (it usually doesn't). With hindsight it probably would have been in Gibson's best interests to have retained the swap in its original form.

Periodic floor: For five years BT were to pay 28 bps above six-month LIBOR on a notional of $30 million. Gibson were to pay

$$r_L$$

where r_L' is six-month LIBOR measured at the previous swap date as long as $r_L > r_L' - 0.15\%$. This is a path-dependent contract. At the end of 1992 BT informed Gibson that the value of the periodic floor was negative and it was canceled nine months after its initiation. The loss was incorporated into a later contract.

Treasury-linked swap: This swap was entered into in exchange for BT decreasing the maturity of the above ratio swap. Gibson were to pay BT LIBOR and BT were to pay Gibson LIBOR plus 2%. The catch was in the amount of the principal repayment at maturity. Gibson were to pay $30 million while BT were to pay

$$\min \left(\$30.6 \text{ million}, \$30 \text{ million} \times \left(1 + \frac{103 \times Y_2}{4.88} - \frac{P_{30}}{100} \right) \right),$$

where Y_2 is the two-year Treasury yield and P_{30} is the 30-year Treasury price. Does this formula look familiar?

Knock-out call option: To reduce its exposure under the terms of the Treasury-linked swap due to an anticipated small principal repayment by BT, Gibson entered into a knock-out call option in June 1993. In return for an up-front premium Gibson were to receive at expiry

$$12.5 \times \$25 \text{ million} \times \max \left(0, 6.876\% - Y_{30} \right)$$

where Y_{30} is the yield on 30-year Treasuries. The downside for Gibson was that the contract expired if the 30-year Treasury yield fell below 6.48%. Long-term rates would have had to stay remarkably stable since the payoff would only be received if $6.48\% < Y_{30} < 6.876\%$ at expiry with Y_{30} *never* having fallen below 6.48%.

The time swap/corridor swap: In August 1993 Gibson entered into a corridor swap with BT. The maturity of the contract was three years and the notional $30 million. BT were to pay Gibson six-month LIBOR plus 1%. Gibson's payments were as follows:

$$r_L + 0.05 \times N\%$$

where r_L is six-month LIBOR and N is the number of days during each six-month calculation period that r_L was outside the range specified in Table 26.2.

After much modification of the multiplier (0.05 initially), the ranges and the termination date, the contract was canceled in January 1994.

In all there were approximately 29 contracts. Gibson's losses amounted to over $20 million, equivalent to almost a year's profits. They sued BT and in an out-of-court settlement agreed in November 1994 they were released from paying BT $14 million outstanding from some swap contracts, only paying BT $6.2 million. Gibson's argument was that they had been misled by BT as to the true value of their contracts. As the tape recording transcribed at the start of this section shows, BT had their own internal models for the value of the contracts but consistently understated the losses to Gibson.

Table 26.2 Ranges for LIBOR in the corridor swap.

6 Aug 1993–6 Feb 1994	3.1875–4.3125%
6 Feb 1994–6 Aug 1994	3.2500–4.5000%
6 Aug 1994–6 Feb 1995	3.3750–5.1250%
6 Feb 1995–6 Aug 1995	3.5000–5.2500%

26.6 **BARINGS**

The Barings story is actually very simple, and the role of derivatives is relatively small. The reasons for all the fuss are the magnitude of the losses ($1.3 billion), that it involved a very staid, 200-year old bank, and that its main protagonist, 28-year old Nick Leeson, did a runner.

Nick Leeson was a trader for Barings Futures, working in Singapore. In 1994 he was reported to have made $20 million for Barings and was expecting to be rewarded with a bonus of $1 million on top of his $150,000 basic. It is likely that he had in fact lost a considerable amount already, with the real position only appearing in the infamous 'Error Account 88888.' Leeson had been given too much freedom. At the time, late 1994 and early 1995, Leeson had control over both a trading desk and back office operations; in effect he was allowed to police his own activities.

The trades that caused the downfall of Barings involved the Japanese stock market, specifically futures and options on the Nikkei 225 index. In November and December 1994 Leeson had been selling straddles on the Nikkei with strikes in the region of 18,500–20,000. The Nikkei index was then trading in a similar range. As long as the index was stable and volatility remained low he would profit from this almost delta-neutral strategy. On 17th January 1995 an earthquake hit Kobe and the Nikkei started to fall, see Figure 26.3. The figure also shows Leeson's trading range. Over the next few days Neeson began buying index futures with March expiry. One of the reasons behind this strategy was the belief that the magnitude of his trades would act to reverse the declining market. If he could bring the Nikkei up to the pre-earthquake levels his option positions would be safe.

Although his trades had a significant impact on the index they could not hold back the fall. Over the next month the index was to fall to 17,400. As the index continued its fall, Leeson increased his trades to shore up the index. Margin was required for the futures mark-to-market and vast sums of money were transferred from Barings in London. Finally,

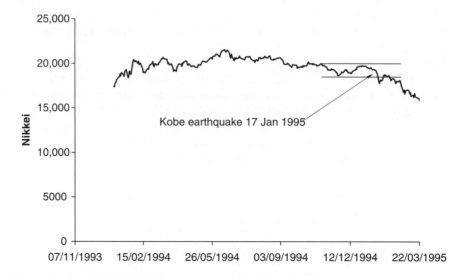

Figure 26.3 The Nikkei 225 index from the beginning of 1994 until March 1995.

the margin calls became too much to cover. On 23rd February 1995 Nick Leeson went on the lam, fleeing Singapore. Finally, he took a flight to Frankfurt, where he was arrested. On 1st December 1995 he pleaded guilty to two offenses of deceiving Barings' auditors in a way likely to cause harm to their reputation as well as cheating SIMEX. The next day he was sentenced to six and a half years in prison.

Leeson was released from the Tanah Merah wing of Changi jail on 3rd July 1999. While in prison he developed cancer of the colon, his wife divorced him and remarried, and they made a movie of the story starring Ewan McGregor and Anna Friel.

Meanwhile Barings went broke. The Sultan of Brunei was approached to bail them out but declined. The Dutch bank ING 'was finally persuaded to take on the corpse of Barings,' as Richard Thomson put it, for the grand sum of £1.

26.7   **LONG-TERM CAPITAL MANAGEMENT**

Long-Term Capital Management (LTCM) is a hedge fund. Hedge funds are supposed to hedge, you'd think. Yet there are few regulations governing their activities. The term 'hedge fund' came about because these funds take short as well as long positions, but this is *not* the same as hedging. LTCM was founded by John Meriwether, ex-Salomon bond arbitrage team, with Nobel Laureates Myron Scholes and Robert Merton as partners in the firm. (The excellent book by Lewis is an account of dodgy dealings at Salomon's during Meriwether's time there.)

Edward Thorp (of blackjack fame, see Chapter 20) started one of the first hedge funds in 1969. It has been a very successful hedge fund and Thorp was invited to invest in LTCM in 1994 when it was founded. Thorp declined, 'I didn't want to have anything to do with it because I knew these guys were just dice rollers. It was just a mutual admiration society at Long-Term and nobody was focusing clearly enough on the model.'

If Thorp didn't want to invest, he was in the minority. It was a glamorous line-up and many who should have known better got sucked in. For the first couple of years they made good returns, of the order of 40%. But look at Figure 26.4, *everyone* was making 40%. And in 1997 they made 27%.

The hype surrounding LTCM, its legendary team and the friends they had in high places meant that they had three benefits that other firms would kill to have:

- They were able to leverage $4.8 billion into $100 billion. Its notional position in swaps was at one time $1.25 trillion, 5% of the entire market.

- They were excused collateral on many deals.

- When they finally went under the Federal Reserve organized a bail-out.

During 1998 LTCM took huge leveraged bets on the relative value of certain instruments. They were expecting a period of financial calm and convergence of first and emerging world interest rates and credit risk. Here are some of the strategies LTCM had in place, what they gambled would happen and what actually did happen. Observe how many of these trades come in pairs; LTCM were making relative value trades.

European government bonds   LTCM sold German Bunds and bought other European bonds in the expectation of interest rate convergence in the run-up to EMU. They did ultimately converge but not before first diverging further.

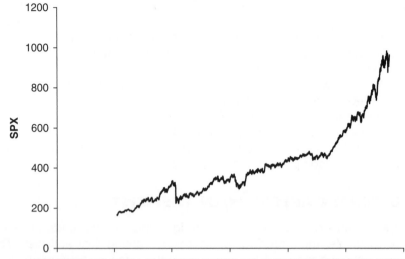

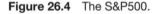

Figure 26.4 The S&P500.

Emerging market bonds and US Treasuries LTCM had long positions in Brazilian and Argentinian bonds and short positions in US Treasuries. They expected credit spreads to decrease, instead they widened to as much as 2000 bps.

Russian GKOs and Japanese bonds They expected Russian yields to fall and Japanese to rise, and so bought Russian GKOs and sold Japanese bonds. They were wrong about the direction of Japanese yields, and Russia defaulted.

Long- and short-term German bonds LTCM bought 30-year German bonds, sold 10-year bonds, expecting the German yield curve to flatten. Instead, demand for the short-term bonds caused the yield curve to steepen.

Long- and short-dated swaption straddles They bought long-dated swaption straddles and sold short-dated swaption straddles. This is an almost delta-neutral strategy and therefore a volatility trade. Short-term volatility rose, resulting in losses.

The main point to note about these trades is that all seem to have the same view of the world market. They were expecting a period of relative stability, with emerging markets in particular benefiting. In fact, the default by Russia on 17th August 1998 sent markets into a panic, investors 'fled to quality' and all the above trades went wrong. LTCM had most definitely made a big bet on one aspect of the market, and were far from being diversified. Along the way the partners lost 90% of their investment and a couple of Nobel prize winners had very red faces. They say on Wall Street that if you lose $5 million you'll never work on the Street again, lose $50 million and you'll walk into a new job the next day. But lose billions? It's good to have friends.

Figure 26.5 shows the price of the $9\frac{1}{4}$% 2001 USD Argentine bond. Prior to the August Russian default the price is quite stable. But then the price plummeted in the overall panic. As things calmed down the price returned. LTCM may have been correct in their views

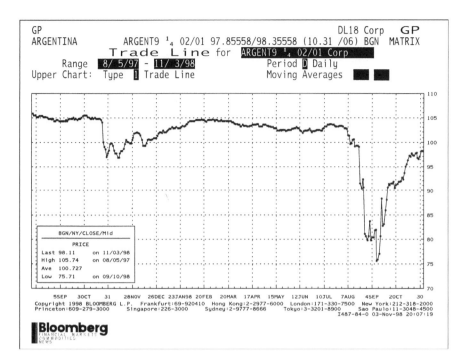

Figure 26.5 Time series of the $9\frac{1}{4}$% 2001 USD Argentine bond. Source: Bloomberg L.P.

long term, but if you can't weather the storm in the *short term* your correct market view is irrelevant. As hedge fund is a misnomer, so, perhaps, is LTCM . . . a more accurate name might be STCMM.

On 21st August 1998 they managed to lose $550 million, and there was more to come.

It was deemed too dangerous for LTCM to be allowed to fail completely, the impact on the US economy could have been disastrous. So the New York Federal Reserve organized, in September 1998, a bail-out in which 14 banks invested a total of $3.6 billion in return for a 90% stake in LTCM.

Much of the LTCM story is still unknown, they were so glamorous that many of their investors didn't even know what they were up to. However, it seems that LTCM were using only rudimentary VaR estimates, with little or no emphasis on stress testing. They estimated that daily swings in the portfolio should be of the order of $45 million. But this didn't allow for extreme market moves and problems with liquidity. In trying to reduce risks LTCM even sold off liquid assets, leaving the (theoretically) more profitable illiquid trades stay on their books. Not a sensible move at times of crisis. Simple VaR as described in Chapter 22 is fine as far as it goes, but cannot deal with global financial meltdowns.

'When we examine banks, we expect them to have systems in place that take account of outsized market moves,' said Alan Greenspan, chairman of the Federal Reserve.

There's another aspect to the LTCM tale that should make anyone using simple quantitative analysis a little bit wary. And that is the matter of liquidity. In August 1998 there was a worldwide drying up of liquidity. Without liquidity it is impossible to offload your positions and the idea of 'value' for any product becomes meaningless. You just have to wait until the market decides to loosen up. Part of the problem was that many of the banks they dealt with knew of LTCM's trades. Many of these were simply copying LTCM's strategies. This wouldn't have mattered if LTCM and all these banks were dealing in small quantities. However, they weren't and in some cases completely cornered the market. It's one thing to corner the market in one of the necessities of life, such as beer, but to corner the market in something obscure makes you a sitting duck when you want to sell.

26.8 **SUMMARY**

Most of these stories have similar themes, overconfidence, lack of understanding of the risks, pure speculation at inappropriate times or for inappropriate reasons, overgearing.

We're only human but what is the point of the math modeling when any profits gets thrown away by a few individuals who don't know what they are doing? If they *do* know what they are doing, I would assume they are crooks.

I'll end with a note of caution sounded by Robert Merton in 1993: 'Any virtue can become a vice if taken to extreme, and just so with the application of mathematical models in finance practice... At times the mathematics of the models become too interesting and we lose sight of the models' ultimate purpose. The mathematics of the models are precise, but the models are not, being only approximations to the complex, real world... The practitioner should therefore apply the models only tentatively, assessing their limitations carefully in each application.' Doh!

FURTHER READING

- Leeson (1997) explains the Barings disaster from his own perspective.

- Chew (1996) is an excellent book covering the risks of derivative transactions. She discusses the technical side of contracts, the legal side and the morality.

- Partnoy (1998) is a cracking good tale of goings-on at Morgan Stanley (coincidentally one of my least favorite banks).

- For background on Meriwether, the LTCM partner, see Lewis (1989).

- Dunbar (1998), Kolman (1999) and Jorion (1999) are nice accounts of LTCM.

- Miller (1997) discusses Metallgesellschaft in detail.

- Thomson (1998) has plenty of inside gen on many of the derivatives stories.

- Read Merton (1995) for his thoughts on the influence of mathematical models on the finance world.

CHAPTER 27
overview of numerical methods

The aim of this Chapter...

...is to introduce the main numerical methods used in quantitative finance, and to propose a program of study.

In this Chapter...

- finite-difference methods
- Monte Carlo simulation
- numerical integration
- programs of study

27.1 **INTRODUCTION**

We are in the home straight now, only numerical methods separate us from the appendices and bibliography. This chapter, before we get to the meat of the numerical methods, is to put these techniques into context, to explain what they are used for, why, and give you some initial thoughts on how they are implemented. I'll also explain how efficient these techniques are in terms of computational time, and suggest a program of self study to help you build up your experience of implementation.

27.2 **FINITE-DIFFERENCE METHODS**

Finite-difference methods are designed for finding numerical solutions of differential equations. Since we work with a mesh, not unlike the binomial method, we will find the contract value at all points is stock price-time space. In quantitative finance that differential equation is almost always of diffusion or parabolic type, as explained. The only real differences between the partial differential equations are the following:

- number of dimensions;
- functional form of coefficients;
- boundary/final conditions;
- decision features;
- linear or non-linear.

Number of dimensions: Is the contract an option on a single underlying or many? Is there any strong path dependence in the payoff? Answers to these questions will determine the number of dimensions in the problem. At the very least we will have two dimensions: S or r, and t. Finite-difference methods cope extremely well with smaller number of dimensions, up to four, say. Above that they get rather time consuming.

Functional form of coefficients: The main difference between an equity option problem and a single-factor interest rate option problem is in the functional form of the drift rate and the volatility. These appear in the governing partial differential equations as coefficients. The standard model for equities is the lognormal model, but there are many more 'standard' models in fixed income. Does this matter? No, not if you are solving the equations numerically, only if you are trying to find a closed-form solution in which case the simpler the coefficients the more likely you are to find a closed-form solution. When we look at the details of the finite-difference methods we won't be assuming any particular functional forms at all.

Boundary/final conditions: In a numerical scheme the difference between a call and a put is in the final condition. You tell the finite-difference scheme how to start. And in finite-difference schemes in finance we start, strangely, at expiration and work towards the present. Boundary conditions are where we tell the scheme about things like knock-out barriers. When we write our code we'd like it to be as general and reusable as possible. That means writing it so that it doesn't have to be changed too much in going from one contract or model to another. So we might put things like final conditions in some external function, to be changed easily.

Decision features: Early exercise, installment premiums, chooser features, are all examples of embedded decisions seen in exotic contracts. Coping with these numerically is quite straightforward using finite-difference methods, making these numerical techniques the natural ones for such contracts. The difference between a European and an American option is about three lines of code in a finite-difference program and less than a minute's work.

Linear or non-linear: Almost all finance models are linear, so that you can solve for a portfolio of options by solving each contract at a time and adding. Some more modern models are non-linear. Linear or non-linear doesn't make that much difference when you are solving by finite-difference methods. So choosing this method gives you a lot of flexibility in the type of model you can use.

27.2.1 Efficiency

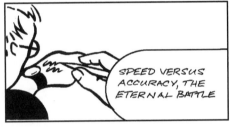

Finite differences are very good at coping with low dimensions, and are the method of choice if you have a contract with embedded decisions. They are excellent for non-linear differential equations.

Here I will just quote an expression for the calculation time of a typical finite-difference scheme used to price a portfolio of options. The time taken to price an option, and calculate the sensitivities to underlying(s) and time, will be

$$O\left(M\epsilon^{-1-d/2}\right),$$

where M is the number of options in the portfolio and we want an accuracy of ϵ, and d is the number of dimensions other than time.[1]

27.2.2 Program of study

If you are new to numerics and you really want to study them to implement the models I describe then you need a program of study. Here I make some suggestions for how you should approach the numerical methods you'll be seeing.

- **Explicit method/European calls, puts and binaries**: To get started you should learn the explicit method as applied to the Black–Scholes equation for a European option. This is very easy to program and you won't make many mistakes.

- **Explicit method/American calls, puts and binaries**: Not much harder is the application of the explicit method to American options.

---

[1] So if we have a non-path-dependent option on a single underlying then $d = 1$.

- **Crank–Nicolson/European calls, puts and binaries**: Once you've got the explicit method under your belt you should learn the Crank–Nicolson implicit method. This is harder to program, but you will get a better accuracy. See *PWOQF2* for details concerning this numerical method and many of those below.

- **Crank–Nicolson/American calls, puts and binaries**: There's not much more effort involved in pricing American-style options than in the pricing of European-style options.

- **Explicit method/path-dependent options**: By now you'll be quite sophisticated and it's time to price a path-dependent contract. Start with an Asian option with discrete sampling, and then try a continuously sampled Asian. Finally, try your hand at lookbacks.

- **Interest rate products**: Repeat the above program for non-path-dependent and then path-dependent interest rate products. First, price caps and floors and then go on to the index amortizing rate swap.

- **Two-factor explicit**: To get started on two-factor problems price a convertible bond using an explicit method, with both the stock and the spot interest rate being stochastic. Again. see *PWOQF2* for details.

- **Two-factor implicit**: The final stage is to implement the implicit two-factor method as applied to the convertible bond.

27.3 MONTE CARLO METHODS

Monte Carlo methods simulate the random behavior underlying the financial models. So, in a sense they get right to the heart of the problem. Always remember, though, that when pricing you must simulate the risk-neutral random walk(s), the value of a contract is then the expected present value of all cashflows. When implementing a Monte Carlo method look out for the following:

- number of dimensions;
- functional form of coefficients;
- boundary/final conditions;
- decision features;
- linear or non-linear;

again!

Number of dimensions: For each random factor you will have to simulate a time series. It will obviously take longer to do this, but the time will only be proportional to number of factors, which isn't so bad. This makes Monte Carlo methods ideal for higher dimensions when the finite-difference methods start to crawl.

Functional form of coefficients: As with the finite-difference methods it doesn't matter too much what the drift and volatility functions are in practice, since you won't be looking for closed-form solutions.

Boundary/final conditions: These play a very similar role to finite differences. The final condition is the payoff function and the boundary conditions are where we implement trigger levels, etc.

Decision features: When you have a contract with embedded decisions the Monte Carlo method becomes cumbersome. This is easily the main drawback of simulation methods. You'll see that when we use the Monte Carlo method we are only finding the option value at today's stock price and time. But to correctly price an American option, say, we need to know what the option value *would be* at every point in stock price-time space. We don't typically find this as part of the Monte Carlo solution.

Linear or non-linear: Simulation methods also cope poorly with non-linear models. Some models just don't have a useful interpretation in terms of probabilities and expectations so you wouldn't expect them to be amenable to solution by methods based on random simulations.

27.3.1 Efficiency

If we want an accuracy of ϵ and we have d underlyings then the calculation time is

$$O\left(d\epsilon^{-3}\right).$$

It will take longer to price the greeks, but, on the positive side, we can price many options at the same time.

27.3.2 Program of study

Here is a program of study for the Monte Carlo path-simulation methods.

- **European calls, puts and binaries on a single equity**: Simulate a single stock path, the payoff for an option, or even a portfolio of options, calculate the expected payoff and present value to price the contract.

- **Path-dependent option on a single equity:** Price a barrier, Asian, lookback, etc.

- **Options on many stocks:** Price a multi-asset contract by simulating correlated random walks. You'll see how time taken varies with number of dimensions.

- **Interest rate derivatives, spot rate model:** This is not that much harder than equities. Just remember to present value along each realized path of rates *before* taking the expectation across all paths.

- **HJM model:** Slightly more ambitious is the HJM interest rate model. Use a single factor, then two factors, etc.

- **BGM model:** A discrete version of HJM.

27.4 **NUMERICAL INTEGRATION**

Occasionally one can write down the solution of an option-pricing problem in the form of a multiple integral. This is because you can interpret the option value as an expectation of a payoff, and an expectation of the payoff is mathematically just the integral of the product of that payoff function and a probability density function. This is only possible in special cases. The option has to be European, the underlying stochastic differential equation must be explicitly integrable (so the lognormal random walk is perfect for this) and the payoff shouldn't usually be path dependent. So if this is possible then pricing is easy … you have a formula. The only difficulty comes in turning this formula into a number. And that's the subject of numerical integration or quadrature. Look out for the following:

- Can you write down the value of an option as an integral?

That's it in a nutshell.

27.4.1 Efficiency

There are several numerical quadrature methods we'll describe in Chapter 30. But the two most common are based on random number generation again. One uses Normally distributed numbers and the other uses what are called low-discrepancy sequences. The low-discrepancy numbers are clever in that they appear superficially to be random but don't have the inevitable clustering that truly random numbers have.

Using the simple Normal numbers, if you want an accuracy of ϵ and you are pricing M options the time taken will be

$$O\left(M\epsilon^{-2}\right).$$

If you use the low-discrepancy numbers the time taken will be

$$O\left(M\epsilon^{-1}\right).$$

You can see that this method is very fast, unfortunately it isn't often applicable.

27.4.2 Program of study

Here is a program of study for the numerical quadrature methods.

- **European calls, puts and binaries on a single equity using Normal numbers**: Very simple. You will be evaluating a single integral.

- **European calls, puts and binaries on several underlying lognormal equities, using Normal numbers**: Very simple again. You will be evaluating a multiple integral.

- **Arbitrary European, non-path-dependent payoff, on several underlying lognormal equities, using Normal numbers**: You'll only have to change a single function.

- **Arbitrary European, non-path-dependent payoff, on several underlying lognormal equities, using low-discrepancy numbers**: Just change the source of the random numbers in the previous code.

27.5 **SUMMARY**

Subject	FD	MC	Quad.
Low dimensions	Good	Inefficient	Good
High dimensions	Slow	Excellent	Good
Path dependent	Depends	Excellent	Not good
Greeks	Excellent	Not good	Excellent
Portfolio	Inefficient	Very good	Very good
Decisions	Excellent	Poor	V. poor
Non-linear	Excellent	Poor	V. poor

If you get to the end of this program successfully then you will have reached a very high level of sophistication.

FURTHER READING

- Finite differences and Monte Carlo aren't the only numerical methods we can use. See Topper (2005) for a description of the finite-element method, a technique commonly used in the hard sciences and now finding its way into finance.

CHAPTER 28
finite-difference methods for one-factor models

The aim of this Chapter...

...is to put in place one of the final pieces of the quantitative finance jigsaw. By the end of this chapter you will know one of the most important methods for solving the equations that we have derived in previous chapters.

In this Chapter...

- finite-difference grids

- how to approximate derivatives of a function

- how to go from the Black—Scholes partial differential equation to a *difference* equation

- the explicit finite-difference method, a generalization of the binomial method

28.1 INTRODUCTION

Rarely can we find closed-form solutions for the values of options. Unless the problem is very simple indeed we are going to have to solve a problem numerically. In an earlier chapter I described the binomial method for pricing options. This used the idea of a finite tree structure branching out from the current asset price and the current time right up to the expiry date. One way of thinking of the binomial method is as a method for solving a partial differential equation. Finite-difference methods are no more than a generalization of this concept, although we tend to talk about **grids** and **meshes** rather than 'trees.' Once we have found an equation to solve numerically then it is much easier to use a finite-difference grid than a binomial tree, simply because the transformation from a differential equation (Black–Scholes) to a difference equation is easier when the grid/mesh/tree is nice and regular. Moreover, there are many, many ways the finite-difference method can be improved upon, making it faster and more accurate. The binomial method is not so flexible. And finally, there is a great deal in the mathematical/numerical analysis literature on these and other methods, it would be such a shame to ignore this. The main difference between the binomial method and the finite-difference methods is that the former contains the diffusion, the volatility, in the tree structure. In the finite-difference methods the 'tree' is fixed but parameters change to reflect a changing diffusion.

To those of you who are new to numerical methods let me start by saying that you will find the parabolic partial differential equation very easy to solve numerically. If you are not new to these ideas, but have been brought up on binomial methods, now is the time to wean yourself off them. On a personal note, for solving problems in practice I would say that I use finite-difference methods about 75% of the time, Monte Carlo simulations 20%, and the rest would be explicit formulæ. Those explicit formulæ are almost always just the regular Black–Scholes formulæ for calls and puts, never for barriers for which it is highly dangerous to use constant volatility. Only once have I ever seriously used a binomial method, and that was more to help with modeling than with the numerical analysis.

In this chapter I'm going to show how to approximate derivatives using a grid and then how to write the Black–Scholes equation as a difference equation using this grid. I'll show how this can be done in many ways, discussing the relative merits of each.

When I describe the numerical methods I often use the Black–Scholes equation as the example. *But the methods are all applicable to other problems, such as stochastic interest rates.* I am therefore assuming a certain level of intelligence from my reader, that once you have learned the methods as applied to the equity, currency, commodity worlds you can use them in the fixed-income world. I am sure you won't let me down.

28.2 GRIDS

Figure 28.1 is the binomial tree figure from Chapter 3. This is the structure commonly used for pricing simple non-path-dependent contracts. The idea was explained in Chapter 3. In the world of finite differences we use the grid or mesh shown in Figure 28.2. In the former figure the **nodes** are spaced at equal time intervals and at equal intervals in $\log S$. The finite-difference grid usually has equal **time steps**, the time between nodes, and either equal S steps or equal $\log S$ steps. If we wanted, we could make the grid any shape we wanted.

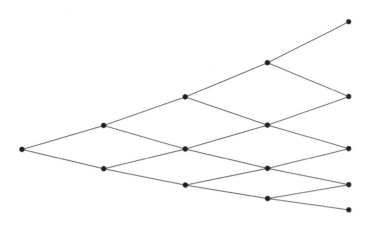

Figure 28.1   The binomial tree.

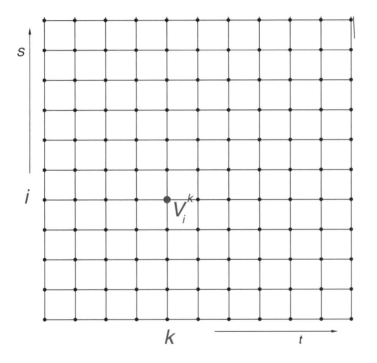

Figure 28.2   The finite-difference grid.

I am only going to describe finite-difference methods with constant time and asset step. There are advantages and disadvantages in this. If we are solving the Black–Scholes equation there is something appealing in having a grid with constant $\log S$ steps, after all, the underlying is following a lognormal random walk. But if you want to use constant $\log S$ steps then it is conceptually simpler to change variables, to write the Black–Scholes equation in terms of the new variable $x = \log S$. Once you have done this then constant $\log S$ step size is equivalent to constant x step size. You could even go so far as to transform to the much neater heat equation as in Chapter 7. One downside to such a transformation is that equal spacing in log S means that a lot of grid points are spread around small values of S where there is usually not very much happening. The main reason that I rarely do any transforming of the equation when I am solving it numerically is that I like to solve in terms of the real financial variables since terms of the contract are specified using these real variables: transforming to the heat equation could cause problems for contracts such as barrier options. For other problems such a transformation to something nicer is not even possible. Examples would be an underlying with asset- and time-dependent volatility, or an interest rate product.

I'm also going to concentrate on backward parabolic equations. Every partial differential equation or numerical analysis book explains methods with reference to the forward equation. But of course, the difference between forward and backward is no more than a change of the sign of the time (but make sure you apply initial conditions to forward equations and final conditions to backward).

Time Out...

Varying volatility

Here's a simple reason why finite differences beat binomial trees. Look at the figures below. They show the effect of increasing vol in a tree and in a grid. As volatility increases the tree spreads out more. The finite-difference mesh stays fixed. This is particularly important when you want to price contracts with important features (such as barriers) at specified asset levels.

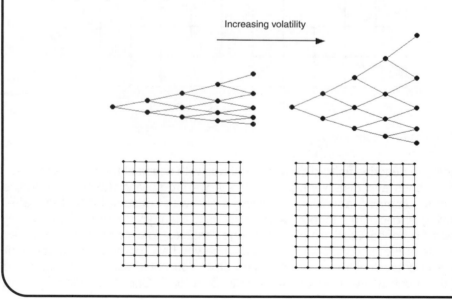

Increasing volatility

28.3 **DIFFERENTIATION USING THE GRID**

Let's introduce some notation. The time step will be δt and the asset step δS, both of which are constant. Thus the grid is made up of the points at asset values

$$S = i\,\delta S$$

and times

$$t = T - k\,\delta t$$

where $0 \leq i \leq I$ and $0 \leq k \leq K$. This means that we will be solving for the asset value going from zero up to the asset value $I\,\delta S$. Remembering that the Black–Scholes equation is to be solved for $0 \leq S < \infty$ then $I\,\delta S$ is our approximation to infinity. In practice, this upper bound does not have to be too large. Typically it should be three or four times the value of the exercise price, or more generally, three or four times the value of the asset at which there is some important behavior. In a sense barrier options are easier to solve numerically because you don't need to solve over all values of S; for an up-and-out option there is no need to make the grid extend beyond the barrier.

I will write the option value at each of these grid points as

$$V_i^k = V(i\,\delta S, T - k\,\delta t),$$

so that the superscript is the time variable and the subscript the asset variable. Notice how I've changed the direction of time, as k increases so real time decreases.

Suppose that we know the option value at each of the grid points, can we use this information to find the derivatives of the option value with respect to S and t? That is, can we find the terms that go into the Black–Scholes equation?

28.4 **APPROXIMATING** θ

The definition of the first time derivative of V is simply

$$\frac{\partial V}{\partial t} = \lim_{h \to 0} \frac{V(S, t+h) - V(S, t)}{h}.$$

It follows naturally that we can approximate the time derivative from our grid of values using

OUR FIRST DISCRETE APPROXIMATION

$$\frac{\partial V}{\partial t}(S, t) \approx \frac{V_i^k - V_i^{k+1}}{\delta t}. \qquad (28.1)$$

This is our approximation to the option's theta. It uses the option value at the two points marked in Figure 28.3.

How accurate is this approximation? We can expand the option value at asset value S and time $t - \delta t$ in a Taylor series about the point S, t as follows.

$$V(S, t - \delta t) = V(S, t) - \delta t \frac{\partial V}{\partial t}(S, t) + O(\delta t^2).$$

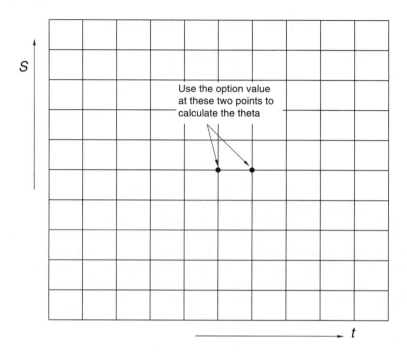

Figure 28.3 An approximation to the theta.

In terms of values at grid points this is just

$$V_i^k = V_i^{k+1} + \delta t \frac{\partial V}{\partial t}(S, t) + O(\delta t^2).$$

Which, upon rearranging, is

$$\frac{\partial V}{\partial t}(S, t) = \frac{V_i^k - V_i^{k+1}}{\delta t} + O(\delta t).$$

Our question is answered, the error is $O(\delta t)$. It is possible to be more precise than this, the error depends on the magnitude of the second t derivative. But I won't pursue the details here.

There are other ways of approximating the time derivative of the option value, but this one will do for now.

THERE ARE (AT LEAST) THREE SIMPLE WAYS TO APPROX DELTA

28.5 **APPROXIMATING** Δ

The same idea can be used for approximating the first S derivative, the delta. But now I *am* going to present some choices.

Let's examine a cross-section of our grid at one of the time steps. In Figure 28.4 is shown this cross-section. The figure shows three things: the function

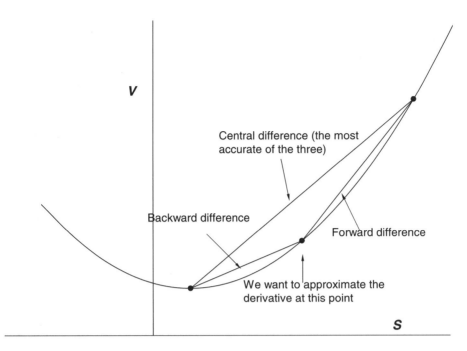

Figure 28.4 Approximations to the delta.

we are approximating (the curve), the values of the function at the grid points (the dots) and three possible approximations to the first derivative (the three straight lines). These three approximations are

$$\frac{V_{i+1}^k - V_i^k}{\delta S}, \quad \frac{V_i^k - V_{i-1}^k}{\delta S} \quad \text{and} \quad \frac{V_{i+1}^k - V_{i-1}^k}{2\,\delta S}.$$

These are called a **forward difference**, a **backward difference** and a **central difference** respectively.

One of these approximations is better than the others, and it is obvious from the diagram which it is. From a Taylor series expansion of the option value about the point $S + \delta S$, t we have

$$V(S + \delta S, t) = V(S, t) + \delta S \frac{\partial V}{\partial S}(S, t) + \tfrac{1}{2}\delta S^2 \frac{\partial^2 V}{\partial S^2}(S, t) + O(\delta S^3).$$

Similarly,

$$V(S - \delta S, t) = V(S, t) - \delta S \frac{\partial V}{\partial S}(S, t) + \tfrac{1}{2}\delta S^2 \frac{\partial^2 V}{\partial S^2}(S, t) + O(\delta S^3).$$

Subtracting one from the other, dividing by $2\,\delta S$ and rearranging gives

$$\frac{\partial V}{\partial S}(S, t) = \frac{V_{i+1}^k - V_{i-1}^k}{2\,\delta S} + O(\delta S^2).$$

Approximations to the delta

The central difference has an error of $O(\delta S^2)$ whereas the error in the forward and backward differences are both much larger, $O(\delta S)$. The central difference is that much more accurate because of the fortunate cancelation of terms, due to the symmetry about S in the definition of the difference.

The central difference calculated at S requires knowledge of the option value at $S + \delta S$ and $S - \delta S$. However, there will be occasions when we do not know one of these values, for example if we are at the extremes of our region, i.e. at $i = 0$ or $i = I$. Then there are times when it may be beneficial to use a one-sided derivative for reasons of stability, an important point which I will come back to. If we do need to use a one-sided derivative, must we use the simple forward or backward difference or is there something better?

The simple forward and backward differences use only two points to calculate the derivative, if we use three points we can get a better order of accuracy. To find the best approximations using three points we need to use Taylor series again.

Suppose I want to use the points S, $S + \delta S$ and $S + 2\,\delta S$ to calculate the option's delta, how can I do this as accurately as possible? First, expand the option value at the points $S + \delta S$ and $S + 2\,\delta S$ in a Taylor series:

$$V(S + \delta S, t) = V(S, t) + \delta S \frac{\partial V}{\partial S}(S, t) + \tfrac{1}{2} \delta S^2 \frac{\partial^2 V}{\partial S^2}(S, t) + O(\delta S^3)$$

and

$$V(S + 2\,\delta S, t) = V(S, t) + 2\,\delta S \frac{\partial V}{\partial S}(S, t) + 2\,\delta S^2 \frac{\partial^2 V}{\partial S^2}(S, t) + O(\delta S^3).$$

If I take the combination

$$-4V(S + \delta S, t) + V(S + 2\,\delta S, t)$$

I get

$$-3V(S, t) - 2\,\delta S \frac{\partial V}{\partial S}(S, t) + O(\delta S^3),$$

since the second derivative, $O(\delta S^2)$, terms both cancel. Thus

$$\frac{\partial V}{\partial S}(S, t) = \frac{-3V(S, t) + 4V(S + \delta S, t) - V(S + 2\,\delta S, t)}{2\,\delta S} + O(\delta S^2).$$

This approximation is of the same order of accuracy as the central difference, but of better accuracy than the simple forward difference. It uses no information about V for values below S.

If we want to calculate the delta using a better *backward* difference then we would choose

$$\frac{\partial V}{\partial S}(S, t) = \frac{3V(S, t) - 4V(S - \delta S, t) + V(S - 2\,\delta S, t)}{2\,\delta S}$$
$$+ O(\delta S^2).$$

28.6 **APPROXIMATING Γ**

The gamma of an option is the second derivative of the option with respect to the underlying. The natural approximation for this is

$$\frac{\partial^2 V}{\partial S^2}(S, t) \approx \frac{V_{i+1}^k - 2V_i^k + V_{i-1}^k}{\delta S^2}.$$

Again, this comes from a Taylor series expansion. The error in this approximation is also $O(\delta S^2)$. I'll leave the demonstration of this as an exercise for the reader.

28.7 **EXAMPLE**

In Figure 28.5 are shown some option values on the grid. The time step is 0.1 and the asset step is 2.

From these numbers we can estimate the theta as

$$\frac{12 - 13}{0.1} = -10.$$

The delta is approximately

$$\frac{15 - 10}{2 \times 2} = 1.25.$$

Approximating gamma

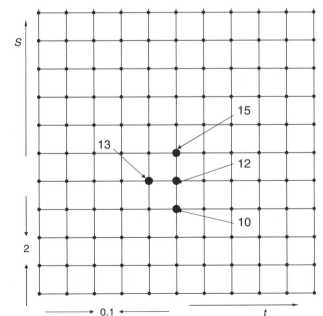

Figure 28.5 Calculation of the greeks.

And the gamma is approximately

$$\frac{15 - 2 \times 12 + 10}{2 \times 2} = 0.25.$$

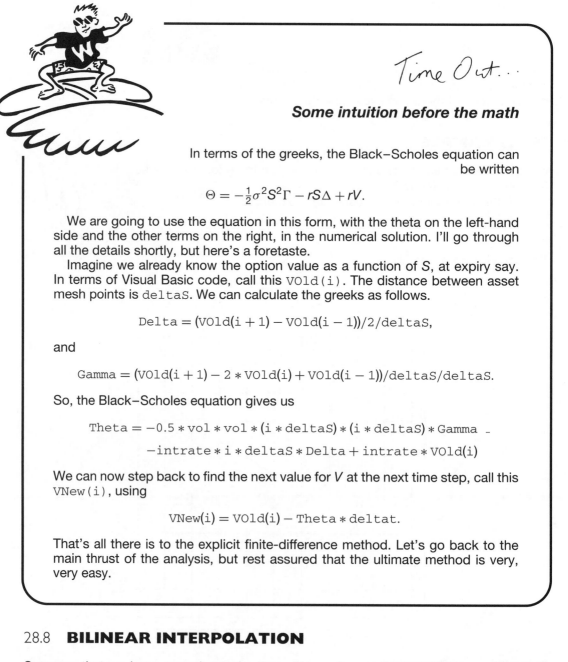

Time Out...

Some intuition before the math

In terms of the greeks, the Black–Scholes equation can be written

$$\Theta = -\tfrac{1}{2}\sigma^2 S^2 \Gamma - rS\Delta + rV.$$

We are going to use the equation in this form, with the theta on the left-hand side and the other terms on the right, in the numerical solution. I'll go through all the details shortly, but here's a foretaste.

Imagine we already know the option value as a function of S, at expiry say. In terms of Visual Basic code, call this `VOld(i)`. The distance between asset mesh points is `deltaS`. We can calculate the greeks as follows.

$$\texttt{Delta} = (\texttt{VOld}(i+1) - \texttt{VOld}(i-1))/2/\texttt{deltaS},$$

and

$$\texttt{Gamma} = (\texttt{VOld}(i+1) - 2 * \texttt{VOld}(i) + \texttt{VOld}(i-1))/\texttt{deltaS}/\texttt{deltaS}.$$

So, the Black–Scholes equation gives us

$$\texttt{Theta} = -0.5 * \texttt{vol} * \texttt{vol} * (i * \texttt{deltaS}) * (i * \texttt{deltaS}) * \texttt{Gamma} \_$$
$$-\texttt{intrate} * i * \texttt{deltaS} * \texttt{Delta} + \texttt{intrate} * \texttt{VOld}(i)$$

We can now step back to find the next value for V at the next time step, call this `VNew(i)`, using

$$\texttt{VNew}(i) = \texttt{VOld}(i) - \texttt{Theta} * \texttt{deltat}.$$

That's all there is to the explicit finite-difference method. Let's go back to the main thrust of the analysis, but rest assured that the ultimate method is very, very easy.

28.8 BILINEAR INTERPOLATION

Suppose that we have an estimate for the option value, or its derivatives, on the mesh points, how can we estimate the value at points in between? The simplest way to do

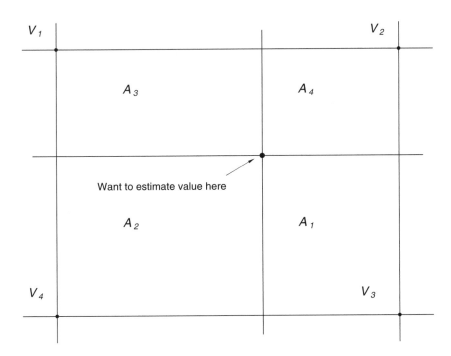

Figure 28.6 Bilinear interpolation.

this is to use a two-dimensional interpolation method called **bilinear interpolation**. This method is most easily explained via the following schematic diagram, Figure 28.6.

We want to estimate the value of the option, say, at the interior point in the figure. The values of the option at the four nearest neighbors are called V_1, V_2, V_3 and V_4, simplifying earlier notation just for this brief section. The areas of the rectangles made by the four corners and the interior point are labeled A_1, A_2, A_3 and A_4. But note that the subscripts for the areas correspond to the subscripts of the option values at the corners *opposite*. The approximation for the option value at the interior point is then

$$\frac{\sum_{i=1}^{4} A_i V_i}{\sum_{i=1}^{4} A_i}.$$

28.9 FINAL CONDITIONS AND PAYOFFS

We know that at expiry the option value is just the payoff function. This means that we don't have to solve anything for time T. At expiry we have

$$V(S, T) = \text{Payoff}(S)$$

or, in our finite-difference notation,

$$V_i^0 = \text{Payoff}(i \, \delta S).$$

The right-hand side is a known function. For example, if we are pricing a call option we put

$$V_i^0 = \max(i\,\delta S - E, 0).$$

This final condition will get our finite-difference scheme started. It will be just like working down the tree in the binomial method.

28.10 BOUNDARY CONDITIONS

When we come to solving the Black–Scholes equation numerically in the next section, we will see that we must specify the option value at the extremes of the region. That is, we must prescribe the option value at $S = 0$ and at $S = I\,\delta S$. What we specify will depend on the type of option we are solving. I will give some examples.

Example 1 Suppose we want to price a call option. At $S = 0$ we know that the value is always zero, therefore we have

$$V_0^k = 0.$$

Example 2 For large S the call value asymptotes to $S - Ee^{-r(T-t)}$ (plus exponentially small terms). Thus our upper boundary condition could be

$$V_I^k = I\,\delta S - Ee^{-rk\,\delta t}.$$

This would be slightly different if we had a dividend.

Example 3 For a put option we have the condition at $S = 0$ that $V = Ee^{-r(T-t)}$. This becomes

$$V_0^k = Ee^{-rk\,\delta t}.$$

Example 4 The put option becomes worthless for large S and so

$$V_I^k = 0.$$

Example 5 A useful boundary condition to apply at $S = 0$ for most contracts (including calls and puts) is that the diffusion and drift terms 'switch off.' This means that on $S = 0$ the payoff is guaranteed, resulting in the condition

$$\frac{\partial V}{\partial t}(0, t) - rV(0, t) = 0.$$

Numerically, this becomes

$$V_0^k = (1 - r\,\delta t)V_0^{k-1}.$$

Example 6 When the option has a payoff that is at most linear in the underlying for large values of S then you can use the upper boundary condition

$$\frac{\partial^2 V}{\partial S^2}(S, t) \to 0 \quad \text{as } S \to \infty.$$

Almost all common contracts have this property. The finite-difference representation is

$$V_I^k = 2V_{I-1}^k - V_{I-2}^k.$$

This is particularly useful because it is independent of the contract being valued meaning that your finite-difference program does not have to be too intelligent.[1]

Often there are natural boundaries at finite, non-zero values of the underlying, which means that the domain in which we are solving either does not extend down to zero or up to infinity. Barrier options are the most common form of such contracts.

By way of example, suppose that we want to price an up-and-out call option. This option will be worthless if the underlying ever reaches the value S_u. Clearly,

$$V(S_u, t) = 0.$$

If we are solving this problem numerically how do we incorporate this boundary condition?

The ideal thing to do first of all is to choose an asset step size such that the barrier $S = S_u$ is a grid point, i.e. $S_u/\delta S$ should be an integer. This is to ensure that the boundary condition

$$V_I^k = 0$$

is an accurate representation of the correct boundary condition. Note that we are no longer solving over an asset price range that extends to large S. The upper boundary at $S = S_u$ may be close to the current asset level. In a sense this makes barrier problems easier to solve, the solution region is always smaller than the region over which you would solve a non-barrier problem.

Sometimes it is not possible to make your grid match up with the barrier. This would be the case if the barrier were moving, for example. If this is the case then you are going to have to find an approximation to the boundary condition. There is something that you must not do, and that is to set V equal to zero at the nearest grid point to the barrier. Such an approximation is very inaccurate, of $O(\delta S)$, and will ruin your numerical solution. The trick that we can use to overcome such problems is to introduce a **fictitious point**. This is illustrated in Figure 28.7.

The point $i = I - 1$ is a real point, within the solution region. The point $i = I$ is just beyond the barrier.

Example 7 Suppose that we have the condition that

$$V(S_u, t) = f(t).$$

If we have an 'out' option then f would be either zero or the value of the rebate. If we have an 'in' option then f is the value of the option into which the barrier option converts.

---

[1] Sometimes I even use this condition for small values of S, not taking the grid down to $S = 0$.

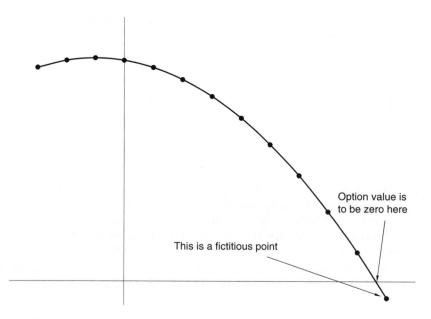

Figure 28.7 A fictitious point, introduced to ensure accuracy in a barrier option boundary condition.

This condition can be approximated by ensuring that the straight line connecting the option values at the two grid points straddling the barrier has the value f at the barrier. Then a good discrete version of this boundary condition is

$$V_I^k = \frac{1}{\alpha}\left(f - (1-\alpha)V_{I-1}^k\right)$$

where

$$\alpha = \frac{S_u - (I-1)\delta S}{\delta S}.$$

This is accurate to $O(\delta S^2)$, the same order of accuracy as in the approximation of the S derivatives.

I have set up all the foundations for us to begin solving some equations. Remember, there has been nothing difficult in what we have done so far, everything is a simple application of Taylor series.

28.11 **THE EXPLICIT FINITE-DIFFERENCE METHOD**

The Black–Scholes equation is

$$\frac{\partial V}{\partial t} + \tfrac{1}{2}\sigma^2 S^2 \frac{\partial^2 V}{\partial S^2} + rS\frac{\partial V}{\partial S} - rV = 0.$$

I'm going to write this as

$$\frac{\partial V}{\partial t} + a(S,t)\frac{\partial^2 V}{\partial S^2} + b(S,t)\frac{\partial V}{\partial S} + c(S,t)V = 0$$

to emphasize the wide applicability of the finite-difference methods. The only constraint we must pose on the coefficients is that if we are solving a backward equation, i.e. imposing final conditions, we must have $a > 0$.

I'm going to take the approximations to the derivatives, explained above, and put them into this equation:

$$\frac{V_i^k - V_i^{k+1}}{\delta t} + a_i^k \left(\frac{V_{i+1}^k - 2V_i^k + V_{i-1}^k}{\delta S^2} \right) + b_i^k \left(\frac{V_{i+1}^k - V_{i-1}^k}{2 \, \delta S} \right) + c_i^k V_i^k = O(\delta t, \delta S^2).$$

I have used a different line for each of the terms in the original equation.

Points to note:

- The time derivative uses the option values at 'times' k and $k + 1$, whereas the other terms all use values at k.

- The gamma term is a central difference, in practice one never uses anything else.

- The delta term uses a central difference. There are often times when a one-sided derivative is better. We'll see examples later.

- The asset- and time-dependent functions a, b and c have been valued at $S_i = i \, \delta S$ and $t = T - k \, \delta t$ with the obvious notation.

- The error in the equation is $O(\delta t, \delta S^2)$.

I am going to rearrange this **difference equation** to put all of the $k + 1$ terms on the left-hand side:

$$V_i^{k+1} = A_i^k V_{i-1}^k + (1 + B_i^k)V_i^k + C_i^k V_{i+1}^k \tag{28.2}$$

where

$$A_i^k = v_1 a_i^k - \tfrac{1}{2} v_2 b_i^k,$$
$$B_i^k = -2v_1 a_i^k + \delta t \, c_i^k$$

and

$$C_i^k = v_1 a_i^k + \tfrac{1}{2} v_2 b_i^k$$

where

$$v_1 = \frac{\delta t}{\delta S^2} \quad \text{and} \quad v_2 = \frac{\delta t}{\delta S}.$$

The error in this is $O(\delta t^2, \delta t \, \delta S^2)$, I will come back to this in a moment. The error in the approximation of the differential equation is called the **local truncation error**.

Equation (28.2) only holds for $i = 1, \ldots, I - 1$, i.e. for interior points, since V_{-1}^k and V_{I+1}^k are not defined. Thus there are $I - 1$ equations for the $I + 1$ unknowns, the V_i^k. The remaining two equations come from the two boundary conditions on $i = 0$ and $i = I$. These two end points are treated separately.

If we know V_i^k for all i then Equation (28.2) tells us V_i^{k+1}. Since we know V_i^0, the payoff function, we can easily calculate V_i^1, which is the option value one time step

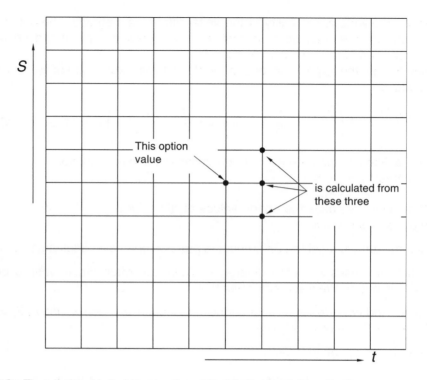

Figure 28.8 The relationship between option values in the explicit method.

before expiry. Using these values we can work step by step back down the grid as far as we want. Because the relationship between the option values at time step $k + 1$ is a simple function of the option values at time step k this method is called the **explicit finite-difference method**. The relationship between the option values in Equation (28.2) is shown in Figure 28.8.

Equation (28.2) is only used to calculate the option value for $1 \leq i \leq I - 1$ since the equation requires knowledge of the option values at $i - 1$ and $i + 1$. This is where the boundary conditions come in. Typically we either have a V_i^k being prescribed at $i = 0$ and $i = I$ or, as suggested above, we might prescribe a relationship between the option value at an end point and interior values. This idea is illustrated in the following Visual Basic code fragment. This code fragment does not have all the declarations, etc. at the top, nor the return of any answers. I will give a full function shortly, for the moment I want you to concentrate on setting up the final condition and the finite-difference time loop.

The array V(i, k) holds the option values. Unless we wanted to store all option values for all time steps this would not be the most efficient way of writing the program, I will describe a better way in a moment.

First, set up the final condition, the payoff.

```
For i = 0 To NoAssetSteps
    S(i) = i * AssetStep
    V(i, 0) = CallPayoff(S(i)) ' Set up final condition
Next i
```

Now we can work backwards in time using the following time loop.

```
' Time loop
For k = 1 To NoTime steps
    RealTime = Expiry - k * Time step
    For i = 1 To NoAssetSteps - 1
        V(i, k + 1) = A(S(i), RealTime) _
                    * V(i - 1, k) + _
                    B(S(i), RealTime) _
                    * V(i, k) + _
                    C(S(i), RealTime) _
                    * V(i + 1, k)
    Next i
' BC at S=0
    V(0, k + 1) = 0
' BC at "infinity"
    V(NoAssetSteps, k + 1) = 2 * V(NoAssetSteps - 1, k + 1) _
                    - V(NoAssetSteps - 2, k + 1)
Next k
```

The explicit finite-difference algorithm is simple, the functions `A(S(i), RealTime)`, `B(S(i), RealTime)` and `C(S(i), RealTime)` are defined elsewhere and are in terms of the asset price `S(i)` and the time `RealTime`. Since I am valuing a call option here the boundary condition at $S = 0$ is simply `V(0, k + 1) = 0` but the boundary condition I have used at the upper boundary `i = NoAssetSteps` is that the gamma is zero.

28.11.1 The Black–Scholes equation

For the Black–Scholes equation with dividends the coefficients above simplify to

$$A_i^k = \frac{1}{2}\left(\sigma^2 i^2 - (r - D)i\right)\,\delta t,$$

$$B_i^k = -\left(\sigma^2 i^2 + r\right)\,\delta t$$

and

$$C_i^k = \frac{1}{2}\left(\sigma^2 i^2 + (r - D)i\right)\,\delta t.$$

This uses $S = i\,\delta S$. If the volatility, interest rate and dividend are constant then there is no time or k dependence in these coefficients.

28.11.2 Convergence of the explicit method

I can write the value of the option at any i point at the final time step K as

$$V_i^K = V_i^0 + \sum_{k=0}^{K-1}(V_i^{k+1} - V_i^k).$$

Each of the terms in this summation is in error by $O(\delta t^2, \delta t\, \delta S^2)$. This means that the error in the final option value is

$$O(K\delta t^2, K\delta t\, \delta S^2)$$

since there are K terms in the summation. If we value the option at a finite value of T then $K = O(\delta t^{-1})$ so that the error in the final option value is $O(\delta t, \delta S^2)$.

Although the explicit method is simple to implement it does not always converge. Convergence of the method depends on the size on the time step, the size of the asset step and the size of the coefficients a, b and c.

The technique often used to demonstrate convergence is quite fun, so I'll show you how it is done. The method, as I describe it, is not rigorous but it can be made so.

Ask the question, 'If a small error is introduced into the solution, is it magnified by the numerical method or does it decay away?' If a small error, introduced by rounding errors for example, becomes a large error then the method is useless. The usual way to analyze such stability is to look for a solution of the equation, Equation (28.2), of the form[2]

$$V_i^k = \alpha^k e^{2\pi i \sqrt{-1}/\lambda}. \tag{28.3}$$

In other words, I'm going to look for an oscillatory solution with a wavelength of λ. If I find that $|\alpha| > 1$ then there is instability. Note that I am not worried about how the oscillation gets started, I could interpret this special solution as part of a Fourier series analysis.

Substituting (28.3) into (28.2) I get

$$\alpha = \left(1 + c_i^k\, \delta t + 2a_i^k \nu_1(\cos(2\pi/\lambda) - 1)\right) + \sqrt{-1}\, b_i^k \nu_2 \sin(2\pi/\lambda).$$

It turns out that to have $|\alpha| < 1$, for stability, we require

$$c_i^k \le 0,$$

$$2\nu_1 a_i^k - \delta t\, c_i^k \le 1$$

and

$$\tfrac{1}{2}\nu_2 |b_i^k| \le \nu_1 a_i^k.$$

To get this result, I have assumed that all the coefficients are slowly varying over the δS length scales.

In financial problems we almost always have a negative c, often it is simply $-r$ where r is the risk-free interest rate. The other two constraints are what really limit the applicability of the explicit method.

Typically we choose ν_1 to be $O(1)$ in which case the second constraint is approximately

$$\nu_1 \le \frac{1}{2a}$$

(ignoring sub- and superscripts on a). This is a serious limitation on the size of the time step,

$$\delta t \le \frac{\delta S^2}{2a}.$$

---

[2] This is the only place in the book that I use $\sqrt{-1}$. Normally I'd write this as i but I need i for other quantities.

If we want to improve accuracy by halving the asset step, say, we must reduce the time step by a factor of four. The computation time then goes up by a factor of *eight*. The improvement in accuracy we would get from such a reduction in step sizes is a factor of four since the explicit finite-difference method is accurate to $O(\delta t, \delta S^2)$.

In the Black–Scholes equation this time step constraint becomes

$$\delta t \le \frac{\delta S^2}{2a} = \frac{\delta S^2}{\sigma^2 S^2} = \frac{1}{\sigma^2}\left(\frac{\delta S}{S}\right)^2.$$

This constraint depends on the asset price. Since δt will be independent of S the constraint is most restrictive for the largest S in the grid. If there are I equally spaced asset grid points then the constraint is simply

$$\delta t \le \frac{1}{\sigma^2 I^2}.$$

If the time step constraint is not satisfied, if it is too large, then the instability is obvious from the results. The instability is so serious, and so oscillatory, that it is easily noticed. It is unlikely that you will get a false but believable result if you use the explicit method.

The final constraint can also be a serious restriction. It can be written as

$$\delta S \le \frac{2a}{|b|}. \tag{28.4}$$

If we are solving the Black–Scholes equation this restriction does not make much difference in practice unless the volatility is very small. It can be important in other problems though and I will show how to get past this restriction after the next Visual Basic programs.

28.12 THE CODE #1: EUROPEAN OPTION

The following VB code will output the value of a call or put option (depending on whether `PType` is C or P). The time step is hard coded and depends on the asset step. It has been chosen to be just about as big as possible while still satisfying the constraint on ν_1, so that the scheme shouldn't be unstable.

A whole array of option value versus stock price and time is output in this example.

Explicit finite-difference code

```
Function Option_Value_3D(Vol, Int_Rate, _
    PType, Strike, Expiration, NAS)
' NAS is number of asset steps

ReDim S(0 To NAS) As Double ' Asset array

dS = 2 * Strike / NAS ' 'Infinity' is _
    twice the strike
dt = 0.9 / Vol ^ 2 / NAS ^ 2 ' For _
    stability
NTS = Int(Expiration / dt) + 1 ' Number _
    of time steps
```

A COMPLETE EXPLICIT SCHEME FOR BS

```
dt = Expiration / NTS ' To ensure that expiration is an integer number _
    of time steps away

ReDim V(0 To NAS, 0 To NTS) As Double ' Option value array

q = 1
If PType = "P" Then q = -1 ' Test for call or put

For i = 0 To NAS
S(i) = i * dS ' Set up S array
V(i, 0) = Application.Max(q * (S(i) - Strike), 0) ' Set up payoff
Next i

For k = 1 To NTS ' Time loop
For i = 1 To NAS - 1 ' Asset loop. End points treated separately
Delta = (V(i + 1, k - 1) - V(i - 1, k - 1)) / 2 / dS ' Central difference
Gamma = (V(i + 1, k - 1) - 2 * V(i, k - 1) + V(i - 1, k - 1)) / dS / dS _
        ' Central difference
Theta = -0.5 * Vol ^ 2 * S(i) ^ 2 * Gamma - _
                    Int_Rate * S(i) * Delta + Int_Rate * _
                    V(i, k - 1) ' Black-Scholes
V(i, k) = V(i, k - 1) - dt * Theta
Next i

V(0, k) = V(0, k - 1) * (1 - Int_Rate * dt) ' Boundary condition at S=0
V(NAS, k) = 2 * V(NAS - 1, k) - V(NAS - 2, k) ' Boundary condition at _
            S=infinity

Next k

Option_Value_3D = V ' Output array

End Function
```

Results from this program for $\sigma = 0.2$, $r = 0.05$, $E = 100$, $T = 1$ and NAS $= 20$ are shown in Table 28.1 and Figure 28.9 for a call option.

Table 28.1   Call option values output by the explicit finite-difference code. Stock price ranges from 60 to 100, time from 0 (expiration) to 1. Only showing results for every other time step.

	0.000	0.111	0.222	0.333	0.444	0.556	0.667	0.778	0.889	1.000
60	0.000	0.000	0.000	0.000	0.001	0.004	0.011	0.023	0.041	0.066
70	0.000	0.000	0.001	0.008	0.028	0.067	0.126	0.207	0.308	0.430
80	0.000	0.000	0.037	0.141	0.310	0.534	0.799	1.096	1.416	1.754
90	0.000	0.128	0.592	1.182	1.812	2.450	3.080	3.700	4.306	4.899
100	0.000	2.253	3.819	5.054	6.109	7.054	7.925	8.741	9.515	10.255
110	10.000	10.671	11.587	12.535	13.455	14.337	15.180	15.990	16.770	17.523
120	20.000	20.555	21.159	21.826	22.529	23.247	23.967	24.683	25.391	26.089
130	30.000	30.555	31.109	31.680	32.272	32.882	33.504	34.134	34.768	35.402
140	40.000	40.555	41.106	41.658	42.213	42.777	43.348	43.926	44.509	45.095

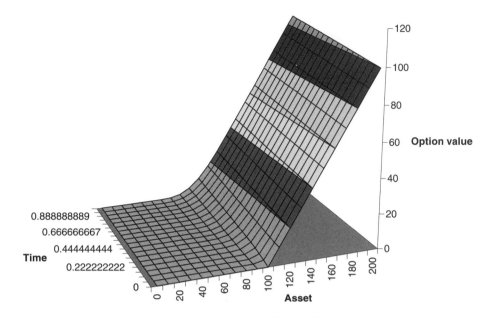

Figure 28.9 Call option values output by the explicit finite-difference code.

Table 28.2 and Figure 28.10 show the results for a put, same parameter values.

The error between the results of this explicit finite-difference program and the exact Black–Scholes formula as a function of the underlying is shown in Figure 28.11 for 50 asset points, a volatility of 20%, and interest rate of 10% an expiry of one year and a strike of 100. The option is a call.

The logarithm of the absolute error as a function of the logarithm of the square of the asset step size is shown in Figure 28.12. The $O(\delta S^2)$ behavior is very obvious. In these calculations I have kept v_1 constant.

In Figure 28.13 is shown the error as a function of calculation time; time units will depend on your machine.

Table 28.2 Put option values output by the explicit finite-difference code. Stock price ranges from 60 to 100, time from 0 (expiration) to 1. Only showing results for every other time step.

	0.000	0.111	0.222	0.333	0.444	0.556	0.667	0.778	0.889	1.000
60	40.000	39.445	38.894	38.345	37.801	37.261	36.728	36.204	35.688	35.182
70	30.000	29.445	28.894	28.353	27.827	27.323	26.843	26.387	25.955	25.546
80	20.000	19.445	18.930	18.486	18.110	17.790	17.516	17.276	17.063	16.871
90	10.000	9.573	9.486	9.527	9.612	9.706	9.798	9.880	9.953	10.015
100	0.000	1.699	2.713	3.399	3.909	4.311	4.642	4.921	5.162	5.372
110	0.000	0.116	0.481	0.880	1.254	1.593	1.898	2.171	2.417	2.639
120	0.000	0.000	0.052	0.171	0.328	0.503	0.684	0.864	1.038	1.205
130	0.000	0.000	0.003	0.025	0.071	0.138	0.221	0.315	0.415	0.518
140	0.000	0.000	0.000	0.002	0.013	0.033	0.065	0.106	0.156	0.211

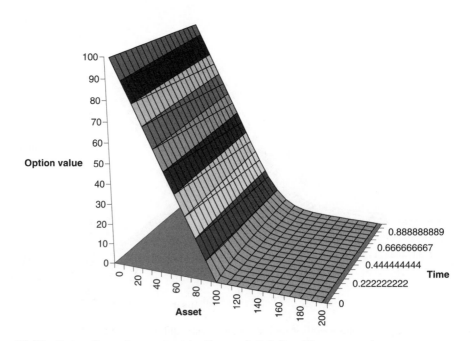

Figure 28.10 Put option values output by the explicit finite-difference code.

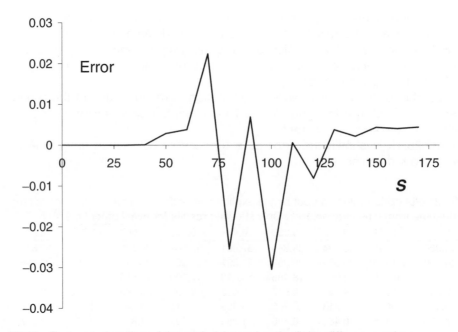

Figure 28.11 Error as a function of the underlying using the finite-difference scheme.

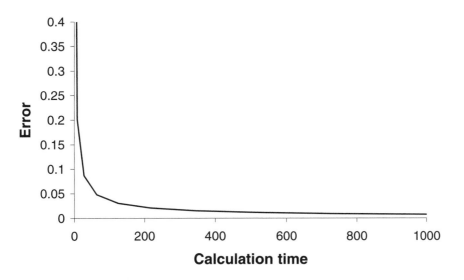

Figure 28.12 Log(Error) as a function of log(δS^2) using the finite-difference scheme.

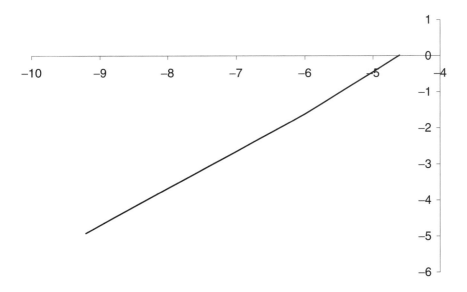

Figure 28.13 Absolute error as a function of the calculation time using the finite-difference scheme.

28.13 **THE CODE #2: AMERICAN EXERCISE**

The code changes trivially when we have early exercise.

```
Function Option_Value_3D_US(Vol, Int_Rate, PType, Strike, Expiration, _
                            EType, NAS)
' NAS is number of asset steps
```

```
ReDim S(0 To NAS) As Double ' Asset array
ReDim Payoff(0 To NAS) As Double ' Payoff array

dS = 2 * Strike / NAS ' 'Infinity' is twice the strike
dt = 0.9 / Vol ^ 2 / NAS ^ 2 ' For stability
NTS = Int(Expiration / dt) + 1 ' Number of time steps
dt = Expiration / NTS ' To ensure that expiration is an integer number _
    of time steps away

ReDim V(0 To NAS, 0 To NTS) As Double ' Option value array

q = 1
If PType = "P" Then q = -1 ' Test for call or put

For i = 0 To NAS
S(i) = i * dS ' Set up S array
V(i, 0) = Application.Max(q * (S(i) - Strike), 0) ' Set up payoff
Payoff(i) = V(i, 0) ' Store payoff
Next i

For k = 1 To NTS ' Time loop
For i = 1 To NAS - 1 ' Asset loop. End points treated separately
Delta = (V(i + 1, k - 1) - V(i - 1, k - 1)) / 2 / dS ' Central difference
Gamma = (V(i + 1, k - 1) - 2 * V(i, k - 1) + V(i - 1, k - 1)) / dS / _
        dS ' Central difference
Theta = -0.5 * Vol ^ 2 * S(i) ^ 2 * Gamma - _
                        Int_Rate * S(i) * Delta + Int_Rate * _
                        V(i, k - 1) ' Black-Scholes
V(i, k) = V(i, k - 1) - dt * Theta
Next i

V(0, k) = V(0, k - 1) * (1 - Int_Rate * dt) ' Boundary condition at S=0
V(NAS, k) = 2 * V(NAS - 1, k) - V(NAS - 2, k) ' Boundary condition _
            at S=infinity

If EType = "Y" Then ' Check for early exercise
For i = 0 To NAS
V(i, k) = Application.Max(V(i, k), Payoff(i))
Next i
End If

Next k

Option_Value_3D_US = V ' Output array

End Function
```

In Table 28.3 and Figure 28.14 are results for the American put, same parameters as above.

Table 28.3 American put option values output by the explicit finite-difference code. Stock price ranges from 60 to 100, time from 0 (expiration) to 1.

	0.000	0.111	0.222	0.333	0.444	0.556	0.667	0.778	0.889	1.000
60	40.000	40.000	40.000	40.000	40.000	40.000	40.000	40.000	40.000	40.000
70	30.000	30.000	30.000	30.000	30.000	30.000	30.000	30.000	30.000	30.000
80	20.000	20.000	20.000	20.000	20.000	20.000	20.000	20.000	20.000	20.000
90	10.000	10.000	10.000	10.060	10.226	10.434	10.653	10.869	11.074	11.267
100	0.000	1.726	2.810	3.549	4.102	4.551	4.935	5.275	5.581	5.859
110	0.000	0.116	0.491	0.909	1.305	1.666	1.994	2.294	2.571	2.827
120	0.000	0.000	0.053	0.174	0.338	0.523	0.714	0.905	1.093	1.276
130	0.000	0.000	0.003	0.025	0.073	0.143	0.230	0.328	0.434	0.544
140	0.000	0.000	0.000	0.002	0.013	0.034	0.067	0.110	0.162	0.221

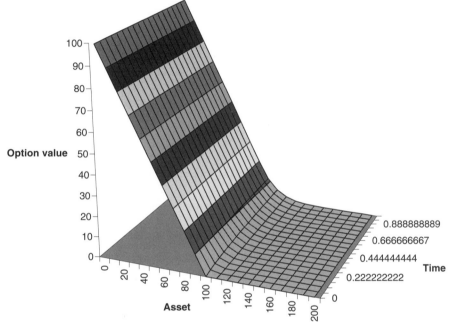

Figure 28.14 American put option values output by the explicit finite-difference code.

28.14 **THE CODE #3: 2-D OUTPUT**

The above code is fine if you want to output the entire function $V(S, t)$. But if you only want to know today's curve or value it is very inefficient since it stores too much information. The following code only uses `VOld` and `VNew` to store enough information to calculate the curve today. The code also outputs the greeks.

```
Function Option_Value_2D_US(Vol, Int_Rate, PType, Strike, Expiration, _
                            EType, NAS)
' NAS is number of asset steps
```

```
ReDim S(0 To NAS) As Double ' Asset array
ReDim VOld(0 To NAS) As Double ' One option array
ReDim VNew(0 To NAS) As Double ' Second option array
ReDim Payoff(0 To NAS) As Double ' Payoff array
ReDim Dummy(0 To NAS, 1 To 6) As Double ' Used for storing data for _
        output

dS = 2 * Strike / NAS ' 'Infinity' is twice the strike
dt = 0.9 / Vol ^ 2 / NAS ^ 2 ' For stability
NTS = Int(Expiration / dt) + 1 ' Number of time steps
dt = Expiration / NTS ' To ensure that expiration is an integer number _
        of time steps away

q = 1
If PType = "P" Then q = -1 ' Test for call or put

For i = 0 To NAS
S(i) = i * dS ' Set up S array
VOld(i) = Application.Max(q * (S(i) - Strike), 0) ' Set up payoff
Payoff(i) = VOld(i) ' Store payoff
Dummy(i, 1) = S(i) ' First column of Dummy is the stock price
Dummy(i, 2) = Payoff(i) ' Second column of Dummy is the payoff
Next i

For k = 1 To NTS ' Time loop
For i = 1 To NAS - 1 ' Asset loop. End points treated separately
Delta = (VOld(i + 1) - VOld(i - 1)) / 2 / dS ' Central difference
Gamma = (VOld(i + 1) - 2 * VOld(i) + VOld(i - 1)) / dS / dS ' Central _
        difference
Theta = -0.5 * Vol ^ 2 * S(i) ^ 2 * Gamma - _
                        Int_Rate * S(i) * Delta + Int_Rate * _
                        VOld(i) ' Black-Scholes
VNew(i) = VOld(i) - dt * Theta ' Update option value
Next i

VNew(0) = VOld(0) * (1 - Int_Rate * dt) ' Boundary condition at S=0
VNew(NAS) = 2 * VNew(NAS - 1) - VNew(NAS - 2) ' Boundary condition at _
            S=infinity

For i = 0 To NAS ' Replace Old with New
VOld(i) = VNew(i)
Next i

If EType = "Y" Then ' Check for early exercise
For i = 0 To NAS
VOld(i) = Application.Max(VOld(i), Payoff(i))
Next i
End If

Next k
```

```
For i = 1 To NAS - 1
Dummy(i, 3) = VOld(i) ' Third column of Dummy is option value
Dummy(i, 4) = (VOld(i + 1) - VOld(i - 1)) / 2 / dS ' Fourth column of _
            Dummy is delta
Dummy(i, 5) = (VOld(i + 1) - 2 * VOld(i) + VOld(i - 1)) / dS / dS
                        ' Fifth column of Dummy is gamma
Dummy(i, 6) = -0.5 * Vol ^ 2 * S(i) ^ 2 * Dummy(i, 5) - _
            Int_Rate * S(i) * Dummy(i, 4) + Int_Rate * VOld(i) ' Sixth _
            column of Dummy is theta
Next i

Dummy(0, 3) = VOld(0)
Dummy(NAS, 3) = VOld(NAS)
Dummy(0, 4) = (VOld(1) - VOld(0)) / dS ' End points need to be treated _
            separately for delta, gamma and theta
Dummy(NAS, 4) = (VOld(NAS) - VOld(NAS - 1)) / dS
Dummy(0, 5) = 0
Dummy(NAS, 5) = 0
Dummy(0, 6) = Int_Rate * VOld(0)
Dummy(NAS, 6) = -0.5 * Vol ^ 2 * S(NAS) ^ 2 * Dummy(NAS, 5) - _
            Int_Rate * S(NAS) * Dummy(NAS, 4) + Int_Rate * VOld(NAS)

Option_Value_2D_US = Dummy ' Output array

End Function
```

Table 28.4 shows the results from this code, same parameters but now 40 asset steps.

28.15 **UPWIND DIFFERENCING**

The constraint (28.4) can be avoided if we use a one-sided difference instead of a central difference for the first derivative of the option value with respect to the asset. As I said in Chapter 7 the first S derivative represents a drift term. This drift has a direction associated with it, as t decreases, moving away from expiry, so the drift is towards smaller S. In a sense, this makes

SOMETIMES YOU SHOULDN'T USE CENTRAL DIFFERENCES FOR DELTA

the forward price of the asset a better variable to use. Anyway, the numerical scheme can make use of this by using a one-sided difference. That is the situation for the Black–Scholes equation. More generally, the approximation that we use for delta in the equation could depend on the sign of b. For example, use the following

$$\text{if } b(S, t) \geq 0 \quad \text{then} \quad \frac{\partial V}{\partial S}(S, t) = \frac{V_{i+1}^k - V_i^k}{\delta S}$$

but if

$$b(S, t) < 0 \quad \text{then} \quad \frac{\partial V}{\partial S}(S, t) = \frac{V_i^k - V_{i-1}^k}{\delta S}.$$

Table 28.4   Call option values and greeks output by the explicit finite-difference code.

Stock	Payoff	Option	Delta	Gamma	Theta
0	0.000	0.000	0.000	0.000	0.000
5	0.000	0.000	0.000	0.000	0.000
10	0.000	0.000	0.000	0.000	0.000
15	0.000	0.000	0.000	0.000	0.000
20	0.000	0.000	0.000	0.000	0.000
25	0.000	0.000	0.000	0.000	0.000
30	0.000	0.000	0.000	0.000	0.000
35	0.000	0.000	0.000	0.000	0.000
40	0.000	0.000	0.000	0.000	−0.001
45	0.000	0.001	0.000	0.000	−0.005
50	0.000	0.003	0.002	0.000	−0.023
55	0.000	0.016	0.005	0.001	−0.086
60	0.000	0.058	0.016	0.003	−0.256
65	0.000	0.173	0.038	0.006	−0.617
70	0.000	0.437	0.078	0.010	−1.235
75	0.000	0.953	0.139	0.015	−2.113
80	0.000	1.832	0.222	0.019	−3.168
85	0.000	3.174	0.321	0.021	−4.255
90	0.000	5.044	0.429	0.022	−5.224
95	0.000	7.461	0.536	0.021	−5.962
100	0.000	10.403	0.636	0.019	−6.425
105	5.000	13.816	0.723	0.016	−6.625
110	10.000	17.628	0.795	0.013	−6.614
115	15.000	21.764	0.852	0.010	−6.459
120	20.000	26.149	0.896	0.007	−6.225
125	25.000	30.722	0.928	0.005	−5.965
130	30.000	35.430	0.951	0.004	−5.712
135	35.000	40.235	0.968	0.003	−5.488
140	40.000	45.107	0.979	0.002	−5.301
145	45.000	50.023	0.986	0.001	−5.153
150	50.000	54.969	0.991	0.001	−5.039
155	55.000	59.935	0.994	0.001	−4.954
160	60.000	64.913	0.997	0.000	−4.892
165	65.000	69.900	0.998	0.000	−4.848
170	70.000	74.892	0.999	0.000	−4.817
175	75.000	79.886	0.999	0.000	−4.796
180	80.000	84.883	0.999	0.000	−4.781
185	85.000	89.881	1.000	0.000	−4.770
190	90.000	94.880	1.000	0.000	−4.761
195	95.000	99.878	1.000	0.000	−4.754
200	100.000	104.877	1.000	0.000	−4.754

This removes the limitation (28.4) on the asset step size, improving stability. However, since these one-sided differences are only accurate to $O(\delta S)$ the numerical method is less accurate.

The use of one-sided differences that depend on the sign of the coefficient b is called **upwind differencing**.[3] There is a small refinement of the technique in the choice of the value chosen for the function b:

$$\text{if } b(S, t) \geq 0 \quad \text{then} \quad b(S, t)\frac{\partial V}{\partial S}(S, t) = b^k_{i+\frac{1}{2}} \frac{V^k_{i+1} - V^k_i}{\delta S}$$

but if

$$b(S, t) < 0 \quad \text{then} \quad b(S, t)\frac{\partial V}{\partial S}(S, t) = b^k_{i-\frac{1}{2}} \frac{V^k_i - V^k_{i-1}}{\delta S}.$$

Notice how I have used the midpoint value for b.[4]

Below is a Visual Basic code fragment that uses a one-sided difference, which one depending on the sign of the drift term. This code fragment can be used for interest rate products, since it is solving

$$\frac{\partial V}{\partial t} + \frac{1}{2}\sigma(r)^2 \frac{\partial^2 V}{\partial r^2} + (\mu(r) - \lambda(r)\sigma(r))\frac{\partial V}{\partial r} - rV = 0.$$

Note the arbitrary $\sigma(r) = \texttt{Volatility(IntRate(i))}$ and $\mu(r) - \lambda(r)\sigma(r) = \texttt{RiskNeutral}$ $\texttt{Drift(IntRate(i))}$.

This fragment of code is just the time stepping, above it would go declarations and setting up the payoff. Below it would go the outputting. It does not implement any boundary conditions at $\texttt{i = 1}$ or at $\texttt{i = NoIntRateSteps}$, these would depend on the contract being valued.

```
For i = 1 To NoIntRateSteps - 1
    If RiskNeutralDrift(IntRate(i)) > 0 Then
        Delta(i) = (VOld(i + 1) - VOld(i)) / dr
        RNDrift = RiskNeutralDrift(IntRate(i) + 0.5 * dr)
    Else
        Delta(i) = (VOld(i) - VOld(i - 1)) / dr
        RNDrift = RiskNeutralDrift(IntRate(i) - 0.5 * dr)
    End If
    Gamma(i) = (VOld(i + 1) - 2 * VOld(i) + VOld(i - 1)) / (dr * dr)
    VNew(i) = VOld(i) + Time step * (0.5 * Volatility(IntRate(i)) _
                * Volatility(IntRate(i)) * Gamma(i) + RNDrift _
                * Delta(i) - IntRate(i) * VOld(i))
Next i
```

---

[3] That's 'wind' as in breeze, not as in to wrap or coil.

[4] This choice won't make much difference to the result but it does help to make the numerical method 'conservative,' meaning that certain properties of the partial differential equation are retained by the solution of the difference equation. Having a conservative scheme is important in computational fluid dynamics applications, otherwise the scheme will exhibit mass 'leakage.'

To get back the $O(\delta S^2)$ accuracy of the central difference with a one-sided difference you can use the approximations described in section 28.5.

We have seen that the explicit finite-difference method suffers from restrictions in the size of the grid steps. The explicit method is similar in principle to the binomial tree method, and the restrictions can be interpreted in terms of risk-neutral probabilities. The terms A, B and C are related to the risk-neutral probabilities of reaching the points $i - 1$, i and $i + 1$. Instability is equivalent to one of these being a negative quantity, and we can't allow negative probabilities. More sophisticated numerical methods exist that do not suffer from such restrictions.

The advantages of the explicit method

- It is very easy to program and hard to make mistakes.
- When it does go unstable it is usually obvious.
- It copes well with coefficients that are asset and/or time dependent.
- It is easy to incorporate accurate one-sided differences.

The disadvantage of the explicit method

- There are restrictions on the time step so the method can be slower than other schemes.

28.16 SUMMARY

The diffusion equation has been around for a *long* time. Numerical schemes for the solution of the diffusion equation have been around quite a while too, not as long as the equation itself but certainly a lot longer than the Black–Scholes equation and the binomial method. This means that there is a great deal of academic literature on the efficient solution of parabolic equations in general.

FURTHER READING

- For general numerical methods see Johnson & Riess (1982) and Gerald & Wheatley (1992).

- The first use of finite-difference methods in finance was due to Brennan & Schwartz (1978). For its application in interest rate modeling see Hull & White (1990b).

- An excellent, well-written, book on numerical methods in finance is Ahmad (2008).

- See *PWOQF2* for more on finite-difference methods including techniques for higher dimensions.

$Time\ Out...$

Over and over again

Once you're happy with writing explicit finite-difference code you'll find yourself using it for many pricing problems. In fact, you may even use the same piece of core code for many types of instruments, it's that robust. But even writing the code from scratch will become second nature. Eventually, expect to take no more than 10 minutes to write basic pricing code *with no mistakes*.

EXERCISES

1. Write a program to value European call and put options by solving the Black–Scholes equation with suitable final and boundary conditions. Include a constant, continuous dividend yield on the underlying share. Output option value, delta, gamma and theta.

2. Adjust your program to value call options with the forward price as underlying.

3. Write a program to value a down-and-out call option, with barrier below the strike price.

4. Write a program to value compound options of the following form:
   (a) call on a call;
   (b) call on a put;
   (c) put on a call;
   (d) put on a put.

5. Alter your compound option program to value a chooser option which allows you to buy a call or a put at expiry.

CHAPTER 29
Monte Carlo simulation

The aim of this Chapter...

...is to explain what is possibly the most useful technique for pricing derivatives and also for examining future scenarios in a probabilistic manner, the Monte Carlo simulation. You will see how the idea is applied to pricing hedged contracts and also to estimating the risks in unhedged positions.

In this Chapter...

- the relationship between option values and expectations for equities, currencies, commodities and indices

- the relationship between derivative products and expectations when interest rates are stochastic

- how to do Monte Carlo simulations to calculate derivative prices and to see the results of speculating with derivatives

- how to do simulations in many dimensions using Cholesky factorization

29.1 **INTRODUCTION**

The foundation of the theory of derivative pricing is the random walk of asset prices, interest rates, etc. We have seen this foundation in Chapter 4 for equities, currencies and commodities, and the resulting option pricing theory from Chapter 6 onwards. This is the Black–Scholes theory leading to the Black–Scholes parabolic partial differential equation. In Chapter 6 I mentioned the relationship between option prices and expectations. In this chapter we exploit this relationship, and see how derivative prices can be found from special simulations of the asset price, or interest rate, random walks. Briefly, the value of an option is the expected present value of the payoff. The catch in this is the precise definition of 'expected.'

I am going to distinguish between the valuation of options having equities, indices, currencies, or commodities as their underlying with interest rates assumed to be deterministic and those products for which it is assumed that interest rates are stochastic. First, I show the relationship between derivative values and expectations with deterministic interest rates.

29.2 **RELATIONSHIP BETWEEN DERIVATIVE VALUES AND SIMULATIONS: EQUITIES, INDICES, CURRENCIES, COMMODITIES**

Recall from Chapter 6 that the fair value of an option in the Black–Scholes world is the present value of the expected payoff at expiry under a *risk-neutral* random walk for the underlying.

The risk-neutral random walk for S is

$$dS = rS\,dt + \sigma S\,dX.$$

We can therefore write

$$\text{option value } = e^{-r(T-t)}E\left[\text{payoff}(S)\right]$$

provided that the expectation is with respect to the risk-neutral random walk, not the *real* one.

This result leads to an estimate for the value of an option by following these simple steps:

1. Simulate the risk-neutral random walk as discussed below, starting at today's value of the asset S_0, over the required time horizon. This time period starts today and continues until the expiry of the option. This gives one realization of the underlying price path.

2. For this realization calculate the option payoff.

3. Perform many more such realizations over the time horizon.

4. Calculate the average payoff over all realizations.

Pricing by
simulations

5. Take the present value of this average, this is the option value.

29.3 **GENERATING PATHS**

The initial part of this algorithm requires first of all the generation of random numbers from a standardized Normal distribution (or some suitable approximation). We discuss this issue below, but for the moment assume that we can generate such a series in sufficient quantities. Then one has to update the asset price at each time step using these random increments. Here we have a choice how to update S.

MONTE CARLO IS EASY TO IMPLEMENT ON A SPREADSHEET, AT LEAST TO GET STARTED

An obvious choice is to use

$$\delta S = rS\,\delta t + \sigma S\,\sqrt{\delta t}\,\phi,$$

where ϕ is drawn from a standardized Normal distribution. This discrete way of simulating the time series for S is called the **Euler method**. Simply put the latest value for S into the right-hand side to calculate δS and hence the next value for S. This method is easy to apply to any stochastic differential equation. This discretization method has an error of $O(\delta t)$.[1]

The above algorithm is illustrated in the spreadsheet of Figure 29.1. The stock begins at time $t = 0$ with a value of 100, it has a volatility of 20%. The spreadsheet simultaneously

	A	B	C	D	E	F	G	H	I
1	**Asset**	100		**Time**	**Sim1**	**Sim2**	**Sim3**	**Sim4**	**Sim5**
2	**Drift**	5%		0	100.00	100.00	100.00	100.00	100.00
3	**Volatility**	20%		0.01	100.15	101.27	100.79	100.16	98.54
4	**Timestep**	0.01		0.02	99.80	100.84	102.72	102.31	101.66
5	**Int.rrate**	5%		0.03	97.35	103.77	105.27	102.00	105.64
6				0.04	96.50	103.08	104.72	97.65	105.35
7			= D3+$B$4	0.05	101.25	101.61	102.37	102.76	103.63
8				0.06	97.53	100.49	104.47	106.86	99.04
9				0.07	97.41	103.00	107.70	105.73	99.20
10			=E3*EXP(($B$5-0.5*$B$3*$B$3)*$B$4+$B$3*SQRT($B$4)*NORMSINV(RAND()))						3.77
11				0.09	85.74	100.79	109.07	106.01	97.95
12				0.1	81.32	100.99	105.13	105.40	100.32
94				0.92	102.25	105.44	88.51	96.74	96.08
95				0.93	100.68	105.48	90.44	97.04	95.36
96				0.94	102.26	104.01	92.40	99.26	94.67
97				0.95	102.10	103.47	88.99	95.27	97.09
98				0.96	100.11	103.36	88.95	92.74	96.30
99				0.97	101.34	104.06	89.26	93.59	97.19
100				0	= MAX($B$104-F102,0)		= MAX(G102-$B$104,0)		9
101		=AVERAGE(E104:IV104)		0.99	103.71	102.73			8
102				1	104.94	104.47	91 86	95.05	98.79
103									
104	**Strike**	105	**CALL**	**Payoff**	0.00	0.00	0.00	0.00	0.00
105	= D105*EXP(-		**Mean**	8.43					
106	$B$5*$D$102)		**PV**	8.02					
107			**PUT**	**Payoff**	0.06	0.53	13.14	9.95	6.21
108			**Mean**	8.31					
109			**PV**	7.9					
110									
111									

Figure 29.1 Spreadsheet showing a Monte Carlo simulation to value a call and a put option.

[1] There are better approximations, for example the **Milstein method** which has an error of $O(\delta t^2)$.

calculates the values of a call and a put option. They both have an expiry of one year and a strike of 105. The interest rate is 5%. In this spreadsheet we see a small selection of a large number of Monte Carlo simulations of the random walk for S, *using a drift rate of 5%*. The time step was chosen to be 0.01. For each realization the final stock price is shown in row 102 (rows 13–93 have been hidden). The option payoffs are shown in rows 104 and 107. The mean of all these payoffs, over all the simulations, is shown in rows 105 and 108. In rows 106 and 109 we see the present values of the means, these are the option values. For serious option valuation you would not do such calculations on a spreadsheet. For the present example I took a relatively small number of sample paths.

The method is particularly suitable for path-dependent options. In the spreadsheet in Figure 29.2 I show how to value an Asian option. This contract pays an amount max($A - 105, 0$) where A is the average of the asset price over the one-year life of the contract. The remaining details of the underlying are as in the previous example. How would the spreadsheet be modified if the average were only taken of the last six months of the contract's life?

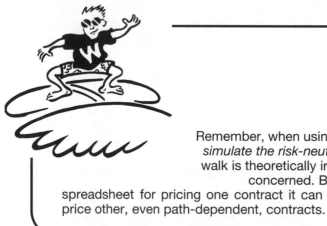

Time Out...

Recap ... risk neutrality

Remember, when using simulations for pricing *you must simulate the risk-neutral random walk*. The real random walk is theoretically irrelevant as far as option pricing is concerned. But once you've set up the code or spreadsheet for pricing one contract it can often be modified quite easily to price other, even path-dependent, contracts.

29.4 LOGNORMAL UNDERLYING, NO PATH DEPENDENCY

For the lognormal random walk we are lucky that we can find a simple, and *exact*, time stepping algorithm. We can write the risk-neutral stochastic differential equation for S in the form

$$d(\log S) = \left(r - \tfrac{1}{2}\sigma^2\right)dt + \sigma\,dX.$$

This can be integrated exactly to give

$$S(t) = S(0)\exp\left(\left(r - \tfrac{1}{2}\sigma^2\right)t + \sigma\int_0^t dX\right).$$

Or, over a time step δt,

$$S(t + \delta t) = S(t) + \delta S = S(t)\exp\left(\left(r - \tfrac{1}{2}\sigma^2\right)\delta t + \sigma\sqrt{\delta t}\,\phi\right). \tag{29.1}$$

	A	B	C	D	E	F	G	H	I
1	Asset	100		Time	Sim1	Sim 2	Sim 3	Sim 4	Sim 5
2	Drift	5%		0	100.00	100.00	100.00	100.00	100.00
3	Volatility	20%		0.01	98.62	97.68	99.73	99.42	102.98
4	Timestep	0.01		0.02	100.69	96.45	101.13	101.28	101.36
5	Int.rate	5%		0.03	99.60	99.67	102.62	99.37	101.95
6				0.04	99.19	101.15	104.14	98.60	99.51
7		= D3+$B$4		0.05	104.10	100.00	105.03	98.97	96.86
8				0.06	104.71	99.11	103.22	96.93	98.89
9	=E3*EXP(($B$5-0.5*$B$3*$B$3)*$B$4+$B$3*SQRT($B$4)*NORMSINV(RAND()))								
10									
11				0.09	110.57	100.93	101.59	99.34	98.75
12				0.1	114.50	100.24	99.36	95.67	99.88
13				0.11	114.43	101.32	100.22	94.92	102.90
93				0.91	101.02	111.09	119.38	77.82	85.23
94				0.92	101.54	109.58	118.06	80.13	83.75
95				0.93	101.38	108.20	118.49	79.96	83.54
96				0.94	103.38	107.87	119.79	82.21	83.12
97				0.95	107.58	108.43	116.24	81.58	84.69
98			=AVERAGE(E2:E102)		109.39	115.79	81.61	88.50	
99				0.97	107.20	112.81	115.56	83.07	90.72
100				0.98	109.18	113.45			
101		= AVERAGE(E106:IV106)			110.49	114.04	=MAX(G104-$B$106,0)		
102					113.23	117.67	120.05	81.49	93.27
103									
104				Average	105.98	106.95	109.21	87.43	97.22
105									
106	Strike	105	ASIAN	Payoff	0.98	1.95	4.21	0.00	0.00
107	=D107*EXP(-		Mean	4.79					
108	$B$5*$D$102)		PV	4.55					
109									
110									

Figure 29.2 Spreadsheet showing a Monte Carlo simulation to value an Asian option.

Note that δt need not be small, since the expression is exact. Because this expression is exact and simple it is the best time stepping algorithm to use. Because it is exact, if we have a payoff that only depends on the final asset value, i.e. is European and path independent, then we can simulate the final asset price in one giant leap, using a time step of T.

If the option is path dependent then we have to go back to smaller time increments generally.

29.5 ADVANTAGES OF MONTE CARLO SIMULATION

Now that we have some idea of how Monte Carlo simulations are related to the pricing of options, I'll give you some of the benefits of using such simulations:

YOU NEED TO KNOW WHEN TO USE MONTE CARLO... AND WHEN NOT TO

- The mathematics that you need to perform a Monte Carlo simulation can be very basic.
- Correlations can be easily modeled.

- There is plenty of software available, at the least there are spreadsheet functions that will suffice for most of the time.

- To get a better accuracy, just run more simulations.

- The effort in getting *some* answer is very low.

- The models can often be changed without much work.

- Complex path dependency can often be easily incorporated.

- People accept the technique and will believe your answers.

29.6 USING RANDOM NUMBERS

The Black–Scholes theory as we have seen it has been built on the assumption of either a simple up-or-down move in the asset price, the binomial model, or a Normally distributed return. When it comes to simulating a random walk for the asset price it doesn't matter very much what distribution we use for the random increments as long as the time step is small and thus that we have a large number of steps from the start to the finish of the asset price path. All we need are that the variance of the distribution must be finite and constant. (The constant must be such that the *annualized* volatility, i.e. the annualized standard deviation of returns, is the correct value. In particular, this means that it must scale with $\delta t^{1/2}$.) In the limit as the size of the time step goes to zero the simulations have the same probabilistic properties over a finite timescale regardless of the nature of the distribution over the infinitesimal timescale. This is a result of the central limit theorem.

Nevertheless, the most accurate model is the lognormal model with Normal returns. Since one has to worry about simulating sufficient paths to get an accurate option price one would ideally like not to have to worry about the size of the time step too much. As I said above, it is best to use the exact expression (29.1) and then the choice of time step does not affect the accuracy of the random walk. In some cases we can take a single time step since the time stepping algorithm is exact. If we do use such a large time step then we must generate Normally distributed random variables. I will discuss this below, where I describe the Box–Muller method.

If the size of the time step is δt then, for more complicated products, such as path-dependent ones, we may still introduce errors of $O(\delta t)$ by virtue of the discrete approximation to continuous events. An example would be of a continuous barrier. If we have a finite time step we miss the possibility of the barrier being triggered between steps. Generally speaking, the error due to the finiteness of the time step is $O(\delta t)$.

Because we are only simulating a finite number of an infinite number of possible paths, the error due to using N, say, realizations of the asset price paths is $O(N^{-1/2})$.

The total number of calculations required in the estimation of a derivative price is then $O(N/\delta t)$. This is then also a measure of the time taken in the calculation of the price. The error in the price is

$$O\left(\max\left(\delta t, \frac{1}{\sqrt{N}}\right)\right),$$

i.e. the worst out of either the error due to the discreteness of the time step or the error in having only a finite number of realizations. To minimize this quantity, while keeping the total computing time fixed such that $O(N/\delta t) = K$, we must choose

$$N = O(K^{2/3}) \quad \text{and} \quad \delta t = O(K^{-1/3}).$$

29.7 GENERATING NORMAL VARIABLES

Some random number generators are good, others are bad, repeating themselves after a finite number of samples, or showing serial autocorrelation. Then they can be fast or slow. A particularly useful distribution that is easy to implement on a spreadsheet, and is fast, is the following approximation to the Normal distribution:

GENERATE YOUR OWN NORMAL VARIABLES

$$\left(\sum_{i=1}^{12} \psi_i \right) - 6,$$

where the ψ_i are independent random variables, drawn from a uniform distribution over zero to one. This distribution is close to Normal, having a mean of zero, a standard deviation of one, and a third moment of zero. It is in the fourth and higher moments that the distribution differs from Normal. I would use this in a spreadsheet when generating asset price paths with smallish time steps.

To get a better approximation you can just add up more uniform random variables. The general formula is

$$\sqrt{\frac{12}{N}} \left(\left(\sum_{i=1}^{N} \psi_i \right) - \frac{N}{2} \right).$$

This has a mean of zero and a standard deviation of one. As N gets larger so the approximation gets better. But if N gets too large we may as well use the following technique to produce genuinely Normal numbers.

29.7.1 Box–Muller

If you need to generate genuinely Normally distributed random numbers then the simplest technique is the **Box–Muller method**. This method takes uniformly distributed variables and turns them into Normal. The basic uniform numbers can be generated by any number of methods, see Press *et al.* (1992) for some algorithms. The Box–Muller method takes two uniform random numbers x_1 and x_2 between zero and one and combines them to give two numbers y_1 and y_2 that are both Normally distributed:

$$y_1 = \sqrt{-2\ln x_1} \, \cos(2\pi x_2) \quad \text{and} \quad y_2 = \sqrt{-2\ln x_1} \, \sin(2\pi x_2).$$

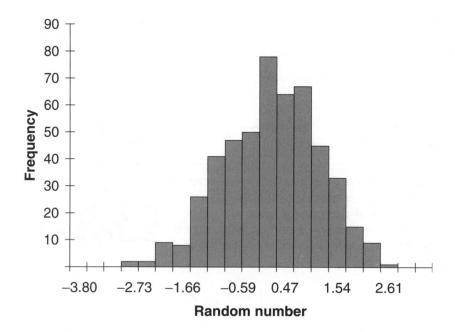

Figure 29.3 The approximation to the Normal distribution using 500 uniformly distributed points and the Box–Muller method.

Here is a Visual Basic function that outputs a Normally distributed variable.

```
Function BoxMuller()
Randomize
Do
        x = 2 * Rnd() - 1
        y = 2 * Rnd() - 1
        dist = x * x + y * y
Loop Until dist < 1
BoxMuller = x * Sqr(-2 * Log(dist) / dist)
End Function
```

In Figure 29.3 is the approximation to the Normal distribution using 500 points from the uniform distribution and the Box–Muller method.

For more efficient, more recent algorithms for generating Normal random variables see Jäckel (2002).

29.8 **REAL VERSUS RISK NEUTRAL, SPECULATION VERSUS HEDGING**

In Figure 29.4 are shown several realizations of a risk-neutral asset price random walk with 5% interest rate and 20% volatility. These are the thin lines. The bold lines in this figure are the corresponding *real* random walks using the same random numbers but here with a drift of 20% instead of the 5% interest rate drift. Although I am here emphasizing the use of Monte Carlo simulations in valuing options we can of course use them to estimate the payoff distribution from holding an *unhedged* option position. In this situation we are

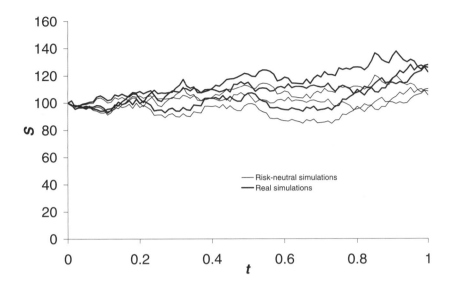

Figure 29.4 Several realizations of an asset price random walk.

interested in the whole distribution of payoffs (and their present values) and not just the average or expected value. This is because in holding an unhedged position we cannot guarantee the return that we (theoretically) get from a hedged position. It is therefore valid and important to have the real drift as one of the parameters; it would be incorrect to estimate the probability density function for the return from an unhedged position using the risk-neutral drift.

In Figure 29.5 I show the estimated probability density function and cumulative distribution function for a call with expiry one year and strike 105 using Monte Carlo simulations with $\mu = 20\%$ and $\sigma = 20\%$. The probability density function curve does not show the zero payoffs. The probability of expiring out of the money and receiving no payoff is approximately 25%.

In Figure 29.6 I show the estimated probability density function and cumulative distribution function for a put with the same expiry and strike, again using Monte Carlo simulations with $\mu = 20\%$ and $\sigma = 20\%$. The probability density function curve does not show the zero payoffs. The probability of expiring out of the money and receiving no payoff is approximately 75%.

Time Out...

Recap ... reality

If you use simulations to get an idea of what may happen in the future to unhedged positions *use the real random walk for the underlying.* You can estimate probability density functions, real expectations and standard deviations. These are all useful in risk management.

29.9 **INTEREST RATE PRODUCTS**

The relationship between expected payoffs and option values when the short-term interest rate is stochastic is slightly more complicated because there is the question of what rate to use for discounting.

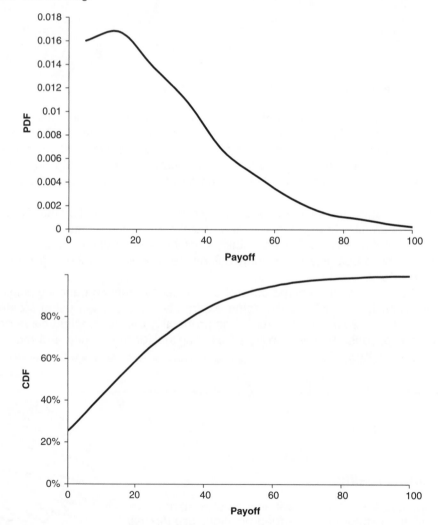

Figure 29.5 Real probability density function (top) and cumulative distribution function (bottom) for the payoff for a call.

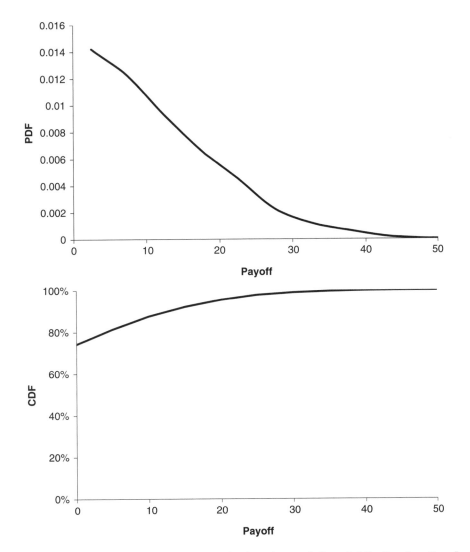

Figure 29.6 Real probability density function (top) and cumulative distribution function (bottom) for the payoff for a put.

The correct way to estimate option value with stochastic interest rates is as follows:

1. Simulate the random walk for the risk-adjusted spot interest rate r, as discussed below, starting at today's value of the spot rate, over the required time horizon. This time period starts today and continues until the expiry of the option. This gives one realization of the spot rate path.

2. For this realization calculate two quantities, the payoff and the *average* interest rate realized up until the payoff is received.

Pricing interest rate products

ITS A LITTLE BIT DIFFERENT WHEN VALUING INTEREST RATE PRODUCTS

3. Perform many more such realizations.

4. For each realization of the r random walk calculate the present value of the payoff for this realization discounting at the average rate for this realization.

5. Calculate the average present value of the payoffs over all realizations, this is the option value.

In other words,

$$\text{option value} = E\left[e^{-\int_t^T r(\tau)d\tau}\text{payoff}(r)\right].$$

Why is this different from the deterministic interest rate case? Why discount at the average interest rate? We discount all cashflows at the average rate because this is the interest rate received by a money market account, and in the risk-neutral world all assets have the same risk-free growth rate. Recall that cash in the bank grows according to

$$\frac{dM}{dt} = r(t)M.$$

The solution of which is

$$M(t) = M(T)e^{-\int_t^T r(\tau)d\tau}.$$

This contains the same discount factor as in the option value.

The choice of discretization of spot rate models is usually limited to the Euler method

$$\delta r = (u(r, t) - \lambda(r, t)w(r, t))dt + w(r, t)\sqrt{\delta t}\,\phi.$$

Rarely can the spot rate equations be exactly integrated.

In the next spreadsheet I demonstrate the Monte Carlo method for a contract with payoff $\max(r - 10\%, 0)$. Maturity is in one year. The model used to perform the simulations is Vasicek with constant parameters. The spot interest rate begins at 10%. The option value is the average present value in the last row.

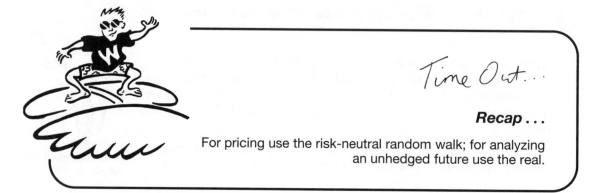

Time Out...

Recap...

For pricing use the risk-neutral random walk; for analyzing an unhedged future use the real.

	AB		C	D	E	F	G	H
1	Spot rate	10%		Time	Sim 1	Sim2	Sim33	Sim44
2	Mean rate	8%		0	10.00%	10.00%	10.00%	10.00%
3	Reversion rate	0.2		0.01	9.99%	10.04%	10.10%	9.88%
4	Volatility	0.007		0.02	9.95%	10.07%	10.14%	9.87%
5	Timestep	0.01		0.03	9.88%	10.08%	10.08%	9.81%
6				0.04	9.78%	10.12%	10.18%	9.84%
7			= D3+$B$5	0.05	9.87%	10.17%	10.15%	9.75%
8				0.06	9.87%	10.18%	10.10%	9.82%
9				0.07	9.73%	10.20%	10.11%	9.81%
10				0.08	9.72%	10.21%	10.27%	9.82%
11				0.09	9.60%	10.22%	10.25%	9.73%
12	= F5+$B$3*($B$2-						9%	9.79%
13	F5)*$B$5+$B$4*SQRT($B$5)*(RAND()+RAND()+RAND()+RAND()+RAND()						4%	9.77%
14	+RAND()+RAND()+RAND()+RAND()+RAND()+RAND()-6)						7%	9.75%
15				0.13	9.57%	10.15%	10.38%	9.73%
95				0.93	8.85%	10.44%	10.21%	9.27%
96			= AVERAGE(E2:E102)	0.94	8.81%	10.47%	10.23%	9.21%
97				0.95	8.83%	10.49%	10.17%	9.10%
98				0.96	8.81%	10.62%	10.19%	9.01%
99				0.97	8.73%	10.63%	10.29%	9.14%
100			= MAX(E102-$B$106,0)	0.98	8.68%	10.71%	10.28%	9.18%
101				0.99	8.56%	10.68%	10.15%	9.09%
102				1	8.42%	10.64%	10.33%	9.22%
103	= E106*EXP(-$D$102*E104)							
104				Mean rate	9.19%	10.32%	10.18%	9.56%
105								
106	Strike	10%		Payoff	0.0000	0.0064	0.0033	0.0000
107	= AVERAGE(E107:IV107)			PV'd	0.0000	0.0058	0.0030	0.0000
108				Mean	0.001352			
109								
110								
111								
112								
113								
114								

Figure 29.7 Spreadsheet showing a Monte Carlo simulation to value a contract with a payoff max$(r - 10\%, 0)$.

29.10 CALCULATING THE GREEKS

The simplest way to calculate the delta of an option using Monte Carlo simulation is to estimate the option's value twice. The delta of the option is the derivative of the option with respect to the underlying

$$\Delta = \lim_{h \to 0} \frac{V(S + h, t) - V(S - h, t)}{2h}.$$

This is a central difference, discussed in Chapter 28. This is an accurate estimate of the first derivative, with an error of $O(h^2)$. However, the error in the measurement of the two option values at $S + h$ and $S - h$ can be much larger than this for the Monte Carlo simulation. These Monte Carlo errors are then magnified when divided by h, resulting in an error of $O(1/hN^{1/2})$. To overcome this problem, estimate the value of the option at $S + h$ and $S - h$ *using the same values for the random numbers*. In this way the errors in the Monte Carlo simulation will cancel each other out. The same principal is used to calculate the gamma and the theta of the option.

If we are dealing with a lognormal random walk then things are much simpler than this in practice. Simulate many lognormal random paths as usual, starting with stock at S. Now imagine that the stock had started at $(1 + \epsilon)S$. Do you have to resample the paths? No, because all you need do is multiple the final stock prices, at expiration, by the factor $1 + \epsilon$. Of course, this only works for a lognormal random walk. Now use these new, scaled, prices to calculate payoffs and hence an option value. Do the same but with a factor of $1 - \epsilon$. And then difference these two new option values and divide by $2\epsilon S$ and you have your delta, for almost no extra computational time.

Finally, we can also find the delta by observing what equation it satisfies.

The solution of the Black–Scholes partial differential equation

$$\frac{\partial V}{\partial t} + \frac{1}{2}\sigma^2 S^2 \frac{\partial^2 V}{\partial S^2} + rS\frac{\partial V}{\partial S} - rV = 0 \qquad (29.2)$$

has the interpretation of being the expected value of the present value of the payoff, under a risk-neutral random walk.

The first 'r' in this equation represents the 'r' in

$$dS = rS\, dt + \sigma S\, dX.$$

The second 'r' represents present valuing.

Differentiate Equation (29.2) with respect to S to get

$$\frac{\partial \Delta}{\partial t} + \frac{1}{2}\sigma^2 S^2 \frac{\partial^2 \Delta}{\partial S^2} + (r + \sigma^2)S\frac{\partial \Delta}{\partial S} = 0,$$

where

$$\Delta = \frac{\partial V}{\partial S}.$$

A comparison with the Black–Scholes equation shows that the solution of this equation represents the expected value of the final Δ (a step function) under the random walk

$$dS = (r + \sigma^2)S\, dt + \sigma S\, dX.$$

We can use the same paths for S as used for calculating the option value but shifted according to

$$Se^{\int_0^t \sigma^2(\tau)d\tau}.$$

Now calculate the expected value of the step function (delta at expiration) using this shifted random walk. Since there is no discounting term in the partial differential equation there is no need to take the present value.

29.11 HIGHER DIMENSIONS: CHOLESKY FACTORIZATION

Monte Carlo simulation is a natural method for the pricing of European-style contracts that depend on many underlying assets. Supposing that we have an option paying off some function of $S_1, S_2, \ldots, S_d$ then we could, in theory, write down a partial differential equation in $d + 1$ variables. Such a problem would be horrendously time consuming to compute. The simulation methods discussed above can easily be extended to cover such a problem. All we need to do is to simulate

$$S_i(t + \delta t) = S_i(t) \exp\left(\left(r - \tfrac{1}{2}\sigma_i^2\right)\delta t + \sigma_i\sqrt{\delta t}\,\phi_i\right).$$

The catch is that the ϕ_i are correlated,

$$E[\phi_i\phi_j] = \rho_{ij}.$$

How can we generate *correlated* random variables? This is where **Cholesky factorization** comes in.

Let us suppose that we can generate d *uncorrelated* Normally distributed variables $\epsilon_1, \epsilon_2, \ldots, \epsilon_d$. We can use these variables to get correlated variables with the transformation

$$\phi = \mathbf{M}\epsilon \tag{29.3}$$

where ϕ and ϵ are the column vectors with ϕ_i and ϵ_i in the ith rows. The matrix $\mathbf{M}$ is special and must satisfy

$$\mathbf{M}\mathbf{M}^T = \Sigma$$

with Σ being the correlation matrix.

It is easy to show that this transformation will work. From (29.3) we have

$$\phi\phi^T = \mathbf{M}\epsilon\epsilon^T\mathbf{M}^T. \tag{29.4}$$

Taking expectations of each entry in this matrix equation gives

$$E\left[\phi\phi^T\right] = \mathbf{M}E\left[\epsilon\epsilon^T\right]\mathbf{M}^T = \mathbf{M}\mathbf{M}^T = \Sigma.$$

We can take expectations through the matrix multiplication in this because the right-hand side of (29.4) is linear in the terms $\epsilon_i\epsilon_j$.

This decomposition of the correlation matrix into the product of two matrices is not unique. The Cholesky factorization gives one way of choosing this decomposition. It results in a matrix $\mathbf{M}$ that is lower triangular. Here is an algorithm for the factorization.

The matrix `Sigma` contains the correlation matrix with dimension n. The output matrix is contained in M.

```
Function cholesky(Sigma As Object)
Dim n As Integer
Dim k As Integer
Dim i As Integer
Dim j As Integer
Dim x As Double
Dim a() As Double
Dim M() As Double
n = Sigma.Columns.Count
ReDim a(1 To n, 1 To n)
ReDim M(1 To n, 1 To n)
```

Cholesky

CODE FOR CHOLESKY
FACTORIZATION

```
For i = 1 To n
    For j = 1 To n
        a(i, j) = Sigma.Cells(i, j).Value
        M(i, j) = 0
    Next j
Next i
For i = 1 To n
    For j = i To n
    x = a(i, j)
    For k = 1 To (i - 1)
        x = x - M(i, k) * M(j, k)
    Next k
    If j = i Then
        M(i, i) = Sqr(x)
    Else
        M(j, i) = x / M(i, i)
    End If
    Next j
Next i
cholesky = M
End Function
```

One health warning, Cholesky decomposition can become unstable if you have any perfect correlation. To get more insight into this and for other decomposition methods see Jäckel (2002).

29.12 CALCULATION TIME

If we want an accuracy of ϵ and we have d underlyings (dimensions), how long will it take for us to get the price of an option?

Since the accuracy is proportional to the time step, δt, and inversely proportional to the square root of the number of paths, N, then we must have

$$\delta t = O(\epsilon) \quad \text{and} \quad N = O\left(\epsilon^{-2}\right).$$

The total calculation time is therefore

$$O\left(\delta t^{-1} \times N \times d\right) = O\left(\epsilon^{-1} \times \epsilon^{-2} \times d\right) = O\left(d\epsilon^{-3}\right).$$

The factor d appears because we will have to simulate d correlated assets.

Note that we don't get the greeks from this calculation. If we want to calculate the greeks then we will have to repeat the calculation as many more times as we need greeks. But, on the other hand, we can price many different options as the same time with little extra time cost, since the time is taken up generating the paths and not in calculating payoffs.

29.13 SPEEDING UP CONVERGENCE

Monte Carlo simulation is inefficient, compared with finite-difference methods, in dimensions fewer than about three. It is natural, therefore, to ask how can one speed up the convergence. There are several methods in common use, two of which I now describe.

29.13.1   Antithetic variables

In this technique one calculates two estimates for an option value using the one set of random numbers. We do this by using our Normal random numbers to generate one realization of the asset price path, an option payoff and its present value. Now take the same set of random numbers but change their signs, thus replace ϕ with $-\phi$. Again simulate a realization, and calculate the option payoff and its present value. Our estimate for the option value is the average of these two values. Perform this operation many times to get an accurate estimate for the option value.

This technique works because of the symmetry in the Normal distribution. This symmetry is guaranteed by the use of the antithetic variable.

29.13.2   Control variate technique

Suppose we have two similar derivatives, the former is the one we want to value by simulations and the second has a similar (but 'nicer') structure such that we have an explicit formula for its value. Use the *one* set of realizations to value *both* options. Call the values estimated by the Monte Carlo simulation V_1' and V_2'. If the accurate value of the second option is V_2 then a better estimate than V_1' for the value of the first option is

$$V_1' - V_2' + V_2.$$

The argument behind this method is that the error in V_1' will be the same as the error in V_2', and the latter is known.

A refinement of this technique is **martingale variance reduction**. In this method, one simulates one or more new dependent variables at the same time as the path of the underlying. This new stochastic variable is chosen so as to have an *expected value of zero* after each time step. This new variable, the 'variate,' is then added on to the value of the option. Since it has an expected value of zero it cannot make the estimate any worse, but if the variate is chosen carefully it can reduce the variance of the error significantly.

Let's see how this is done in practice using a single variate. Suppose we simulate

$$\delta S = \mu S \, \delta t + \sigma S \sqrt{\delta t} \, \phi$$

to price our contract. Now introduce the variate y, satisfying

$$\delta y = f(S, t) \, (\delta S - E[\delta S]) ,$$

with zero initial value. Note that this has zero expectation. The choice of $f(S, t)$ will be discussed in a moment. The new estimate for the option value is simply

$$\overline{V} - \alpha e^{-r(T-t)} \overline{y},$$

where $\overline{V}$ is our usual Monte Carlo estimate and $\overline{y}$ is the average over all the realizations of the new variate at expiry. The choice of α is simple, choose it to minimize the variance of the error, i.e. to minimize

$$E\left[(V - \alpha e^{-r(T-t)} y)^2 \right].$$

I leave the details to the reader.

And the function $f(S, t)$? The natural choice is the delta of an option that is closely related to the option in question, one for which there is a closed-form solution. Such a choice corresponds to an approximate form of delta hedging, and thus reduces the fluctuation in the contract value along each path.

29.14 PROS AND CONS OF MONTE CARLO SIMULATIONS

The Monte Carlo technique is clearly very powerful and general. The concept readily carries over to exotic and path-dependent contracts, just simulate the random walk and the corresponding cash flows, estimate the average payoff and take its present value.

The main disadvantages are twofold. First, the method is slow when compared with the finite-difference solution of a partial differential equation. Generally speaking this is true for problems up to three or four dimensions. When there are four or more stochastic or path-dependent variables the Monte Carlo method becomes relatively more efficient. Second, the application to American options is far from straightforward. The reason for the problem with American options is to do with the optimality of early exercise. To know when it is optimal to exercise the option one must calculate the option price *for all values of S and t up to expiry* in order to check that at no time is there any arbitrage opportunity. However, the Monte Carlo method in its basic form is only used to estimate the option price at one point in S, t-space, now and at today's value.

Because Monte Carlo simulation is based on the generation of a finite number of realizations using series of random numbers, the value of a option derived in this way will vary each time the simulations are run. Roughly speaking, the error between the Monte Carlo estimate and the correct option price is of the order of the inverse square root of the number of simulations. More precisely, if the standard deviation in the option value using a single simulation is ϵ then the standard deviation of the error after N simulations is $\epsilon/\sqrt{N}$. To improve our accuracy by a factor of 10 we must perform 100 times as many simulations.

29.15 AMERICAN OPTIONS

Applying Monte Carlo methods to the valuation of European contracts is simple, but applying them to American options is harder. The problem is to do with the time direction in which we are solving. We have seen how it is natural in the partial differential equation framework to work backwards from expiry to the present. If we do this numerically then we find the value of a contract at every mesh point between now and expiry. This means that along the way we can ensure that there is no arbitrage, and in particular ensure that the early-exercise constraint is satisfied.

When we use the Monte Carlo method in it basic form for valuing a European option we only ever find the option's value at the one point, the current asset level and the current time. We have no information about the option value at any other asset level or time. So if our contract is American we have no way of knowing whether or not we violated the early-exercise constraint somewhere in the future.

In principle, we could find the option value at each point in asset-time space using Monte Carlo. For every asset value and time that we require knowledge of the option value we start a new simulation. But when we have early exercise we have to do this at a large number of points in asset-time space, keeping track of whether the constraint is violated. If we find a value for the option that is below the payoff then we mark this point in asset-time space as one where we must exercise the option. And then for every other path that goes through this point we must exercise at this point, if not before. Such a procedure is possible, but the time taken grows exponentially with the number of points at which we value the option.

In Chapter 12 I said that there were no 'good' algorithms for Monte Carlo and early exercise. Well, that's not strictly true anymore, as we'll see in the next section.

29.16 LONGSTAFF & SCHWARTZ REGRESSION APPROACH FOR AMERICAN OPTIONS

There are several algorithms for pricing American options using Monte Carlo simulations, see Jäckel (2002) and Glasserman (2003) for details. But the one that is currently most popular with practitioners is that by Longstaff & Schwartz (2001). This method combines the forward simulation of stock price paths from startup to expiration, with the present valuing of cashflows along paths, but at each time step one looks at the benefit of exercising versus holding using a simple regression across stock prices. Let's walk through the algorithm in detail with an example.

Consider an American put with strike price $100, expiring in one year's time. The stock is currently $100, it has a volatility of 20% and the risk-free interest rate is 5%.

Step one, simulate many, N, realizations of the asset path from now to expiration using time steps of δt. If the random walk is lognormal then we will simulate

$$S_{j+1} = S_j \exp\left(\left(r - \tfrac{1}{2}\sigma^2\right)\delta t + \sigma\sqrt{\delta t}\,\phi\right)$$

where ϕ is a Normally distributed random variable, and S_j is the stock price after j time steps. We start each path at $j = 0$ with $S_0 = 100$. In Figure 29.8 are shown 10 such paths, using five time steps from now to expiration. The numbers are shown in Figure 29.9.

Next step, calculate the payoffs at expiration for each of these 10 paths. These payoffs are shown in Figure 29.10. Notice that five paths end in the money and five out. Of course, this assumes that we haven't exercised the put option at any time before expiration. We'll get to that point in a moment. If we were to present value the average of all of these payoffs then we'd get the value of a European option.

The above tells us what we would receive if we exercised only at expiration, but we might have exercised earlier than that. Let's go back to the fourth time step, time 0.8, and look at the decision to exercise at that time for each of the paths. In what follows I use the notation of Longstaff & Schwartz.

Figure 29.11 has an X and a Y column. The X column are the stock prices at time 0.8 *for those paths which are in the money at that time*. The Y column are the payoffs for these paths, discounted back from expiration to time 0.8. We want to calculate the cashflow from holding on to the option, conditional on the stock price at time 0.8. To do this we perform a regression of Y against a constant, X and X^2. In this example[2] we find the least-squares fit to be

$$Y = -0.1472\,X^2 + 25.347\,X - 1075.2. \tag{29.5}$$

---

[2] Other regressions are possible and to be preferred. We'll look at the subject of basis functions shortly.

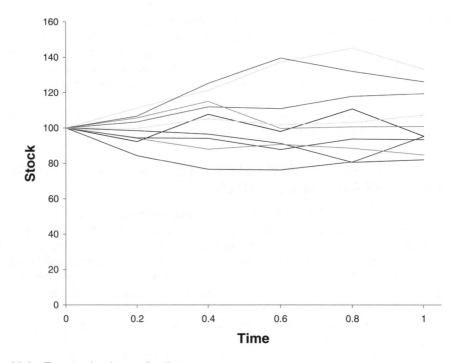

Figure 29.8   Ten stock price realizations.

Realization	0	0.2	0.4	0.6	0.8	1
1	100	92.30759	107.7357	98.04343	110.7416	95.34586
2	100	103.4446	111.9465	110.9322	117.8379	119.4419
3	100	111.2298	121.2417	137.1683	145.1687	133.1789
4	100	105.7152	115.0572	99.73054	100.6804	100.9471
5	100	98.47278	96.5825	91.32007	80.63689	82.1163
6	100	94.40168	94.16078	87.83702	93.84797	93.45847
7	100	106.7042	125.264	139.4822	132.0177	126.2041
8	100	84.37568	76.60055	76.21345	80.85454	95.19434
9	100	94.21698	88.00477	90.81541	88.63676	84.80556
10	100	99.81029	105.2631	101.747	103.1483	107.3703

Figure 29.9   The stock prices.

Realization	0	0.2	0.4	0.6	0.8	1	Payoff
1	100	92.30759	107.7357	98.04343	110.7416	95.34586	4.654138
2	100	103.4446	111.9465	110.9322	117.8379	119.4419	0
3	100	111.2298	121.2417	137.1683	145.1687	133.1789	0
4	100	105.7152	115.0572	99.73054	100.6804	100.9471	0
5	100	98.47278	96.5825	91.32007	80.63689	82.1163	17.8837
6	100	94.40168	94.16078	87.83702	93.84797	93.45847	6.541526
7	100	106.7042	125.264	139.4822	132.0177	126.2041	0
8	100	84.37568	76.60055	76.21345	80.85454	95.19434	4.805663
9	100	94.21698	88.00477	90.81541	88.63676	84.80556	15.19444
10	100	99.81029	105.2631	101.747	103.1483	107.3703	0

Figure 29.10   The stock prices and payoffs.

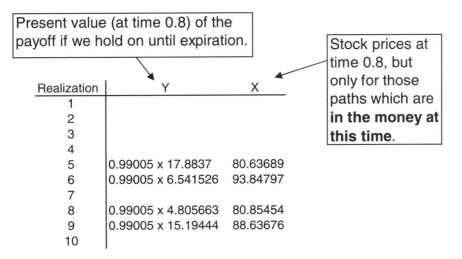

Figure 29.11 Discounted payoffs and stock prices, for in the money at time 0.8 only. The discount factor is 0.99005.

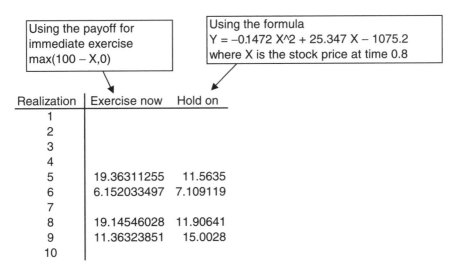

Figure 29.12 What you get from exercising versus holding on.

Now, for these same in-the-money-at-time-0.8 paths we compare the value of exercising immediately, time 0.8, with that from holding on using (29.5), see Figure 29.12. These numbers show that it is optimal to exercise now (time 0.8) for paths five and eight.

The next step is to build up a matrix of cashflows, as in Figure 29.13. This represents what is optimal *assuming that we don't exercise at any time step before 0.8*. Note that if there is a positive entry in the time 0.8 column it means that we should have exercised there (if not earlier) and so the cashflows for later times are set to zero.

Obviously we must continue to work backwards, next asking whether it would have been optimal to have exercised at time 0.6 for any of the paths. In Figure 29.14 are the cashflows, the Y column, present valued to time 0.6, and the stock prices, X, for those

Realization	0.2	0.4	0.6	0.8	1
1				0	4.654138
2				0	0
3				0	0
4				0	0
5				19.36311	0
6				0	6.541526
7				0	0
8				19.14546	0
9				0	15.19444
10				0	0

Figure 29.13 Cashflow matrix so far.

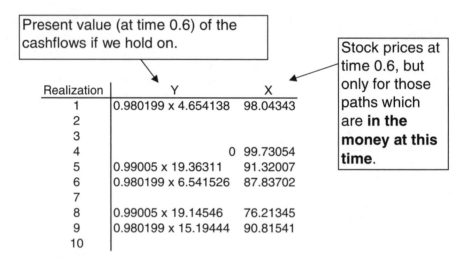

Realization	Y	X
1	0.980199 x 4.654138	98.04343
2		
3		
4	0	99.73054
5	0.99005 x 19.36311	91.32007
6	0.980199 x 6.541526	87.83702
7		
8	0.99005 x 19.14546	76.21345
9	0.980199 x 15.19444	90.81541
10		

Figure 29.14 Regression at time 0.6.

paths which are in the money at time 0.6. Note that there are now two discount factors because some cashflow has to be discounted one time step and others two time steps. The regression now gives

$$Y = -0.0361 \, X^2 + 5.6613 \, X - 203.95.$$

And off we go again, compare what you would get from exercising $\max(100 - X, 0)$ with the value from holding on $-0.0361 \, X^2 + 5.6613 \, X - 203.95$. After which we can draw up a new cashflow matrix.

Continue this process right back to time zero, and you should get the final cashflow matrix as shown in Figure 29.15. The last step in pricing the option is to present value all of these cashflows back to time zero and average. End result, 6.409. A finite-difference scheme gives the answer as 6.092.

Realization	0.2	0.4	0.6	0.8	1
1	0	0	0	0	4.6541375
2	0	0	0	0	0
3	0	0	0	0	0
4	0	0	0	0	0
5	0	0	0	19.363113	0
6	0	0	0	0	6.541526
7	0	0	0	0	0
8	0	0	23.786554	0	0
9	0	11.995234			0
10	0	0	0	0	0

Figure 29.15 Final cashflow matrix.

29.17 **BASIS FUNCTIONS**

I have used the simple quadratic basis function for the regression, since it is easiest to explain, and does a decent job. There are, however, better ones you can use. The original paper by Longstaff & Schwartz discusses this matter. When it comes to using this method in higher dimensions (which is the point after all) the choice of basis functions can become important.

29.18 **SUMMARY**

Simulations are at the very heart of finance. With simulations you can explore the unknown future, and act accordingly. Simulations can also be used to price options, although the future is uncertain, the result of hedging an option is theoretically guaranteed.

In this chapter I have tried to give a flavor of the potential of Monte Carlo and related methods. The reader should now be in a position to begin to use these methods in practice. The subject is a large and growing one, and the reader is referred to the section below for more information.

FURTHER READING

- See Boyle (1977) for the original application of Monte Carlo simulations to pricing derivatives.

- Duffie (1992) describes the important theory behind the validity of Monte Carlo simulations and also gives some clues about how to make the method efficient.

- The subject of Monte Carlo simulations is described straightforwardly and in detail by Vose (1997).

- For a review of Monte Carlo methods applied to American options see Boyle *et al.* (1995).

- For a very technical look at Monte Carlo see Jäckel (2002).

- For an American option algorithm see Longstaff & Schwartz (2001). This is a very good piece of work, nicely presented, understandable and with plenty of convincing examples. If only all papers were written like this.

EXERCISES

1. Simulate the risk-neutral random walk for an asset using a spreadsheet package, or otherwise. Use these data to calculate the value of a European call option.

2. Modify the spreadsheet in the above to ouput the option's delta.

3. Modify the above spreadsheet to value various exotic options such as barriers, Asians and lookbacks.

4. Why is it difficult to use Monte Carlo simulations to value American options?

CHAPTER 30
numerical integration

The aim of this Chapter...

...is to describe how to perform multiple integration numerically in an arbitrary number of dimensions. This is a method that is very useful when valuing certain types of high-dimensional exotic options.

In this Chapter...

- how to do numerical integration in high dimensions to calculate the price of options on baskets

30.1 **INTRODUCTION**

Often the fair value of an option can be written down analytically as an integral. This is certainly the case for non-path-dependent European options contingent upon d lognormal underlyings, for which we have

$$V = e^{-r(T-t)} (2\pi(T-t))^{-d/2} (\mathrm{Det}\Sigma)^{-1/2}(\sigma_1 \ldots \sigma_d)^{-1}$$

$$\int_0^\infty \cdots \int_0^\infty \frac{\mathrm{Payoff}(S'_1 \ldots S'_d)}{S'_1 \ldots S'_d} \exp\left(-\frac{1}{2}\alpha^T \Sigma^{-1}\alpha\right) dS'_1 \ldots dS'_d$$

where

$$\alpha_i = \frac{1}{\sigma_i(T-t)^{1/2}} \left(\log\left(\frac{S_i}{S'_i}\right) + \left(r - D_i - \frac{\sigma_i^2}{2}\right)(T-t)\right)$$

and Σ is the correlation matrix for the d assets and Payoff($\cdots$) is the payoff function. Sometimes the value of path-dependent contracts can also be written as a multiple integral. American options, however, can rarely be expressed so simply.

If we do have such a representation of an option's value then all we need do to value it is to estimate the value of the multiple integral. Let us see how this can be done.

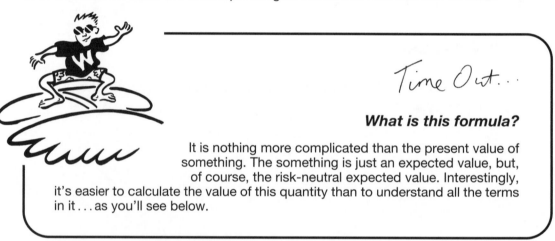

Time Out...

What is this formula?

It is nothing more complicated than the present value of something. The something is just an expected value, but, of course, the risk-neutral expected value. Interestingly, it's easier to calculate the value of this quantity than to understand all the terms in it . . . as you'll see below.

30.2 **REGULAR GRID**

We can do the multiple integration by evaluating the function on a uniform grid in the d-dimensional space of assets. There would thus be $N^{1/d}$ grid points in each direction where N is the total number of points used. Supposing we use the trapezium or mid-point rule, the error in the estimation of the integral will be $O(N^{-2/d})$ and the time taken approximately $O(N)$ since there are N function evaluations. As the dimension d increases this method becomes prohibitively slow. Note that because the integrand is generally not smooth there is little point in using a higher order method than a mid-point rule unless one goes to the trouble of finding out the whereabouts of the discontinuities in the derivatives. To overcome this 'curse of dimensionality' we can use Monte Carlo integration or low-discrepancy sequences.

30.3 **BASIC MONTE CARLO INTEGRATION**

Suppose that we want to evaluate the integral

$$\int \ldots \int f(x_1, \ldots, x_d)dx_1 \ldots dx_d,$$

over some volume. We can very easily estimate the value of this by Monte Carlo simulation. The idea behind this is that the integral can be rewritten as

$$\int \ldots \int f(x_1, \ldots, x_d)dx_1 \ldots dx_d = \text{volume of region of integration} \times \text{average } f,$$

where the average of f is taken over the whole of the region of integration. To make life simple we can rescale the region of integration to make it the unit hypercube. Assuming that we have done this

$$\int_0^1 \ldots \int_0^1 f(x_1, \ldots, x_d)dx_1 \ldots dx_d = \text{average } f$$

because the volume is one. Such a scaling will obviously be necessary in our financial problems because the range of integration is typically from zero to infinity. I will return to this point later.

We can sample the average of f by Monte Carlo sampling using uniformly distributed random numbers in the d-dimensional space. After N samples we have

$$\text{average } f \approx \frac{1}{N} \sum_{i=1}^{N} f(x_i) \tag{30.1}$$

where x_i is the vector of values of $x_1, \ldots, x_d$ at the ith sampling. As N increases, so the approximation improves. Expression (30.1) is only an approximation. The size of the error can be measured by the standard deviation of the correct average about the sampled average, this is

$$\sqrt{\frac{1}{N}\left(\overline{f^2} - \overline{f}^2\right)}$$

(which must be multiplied by the volume of the region), where

$$\overline{f} = \frac{1}{N} \sum_{i=1}^{N} f(x_i)$$

and

$$\overline{f^2} = \frac{1}{N} \sum_{i=1}^{N} f^2(x_i).$$

Thus the error in the estimation of the value of an integral using a Monte Carlo simulation is $O(N^{-1/2})$ where N is the number of points used, and is independent of the number of dimensions. Again there are N function evaluations and so the computational time is $O(N)$. The accuracy is much higher than that for a uniform grid if we have five or more dimensions.

I have explained Monte Carlo integration in terms of integrating over a d-dimensional unit hypercube. In financial problems we often have integrals over the range zero to infinity.

The choice of transformation from zero-one to zero-infinity should be suggested by the problem under consideration. Let us suppose that we have d assets following correlated random walks. The risk-neutral value of these assets at a time t can be written as

$$S_i(T) = S_i(t)e^{\left(r - D_i - \frac{1}{2}\sigma_i^2\right)(T-t) + \sigma_i\phi_i\sqrt{T-t}},$$

in terms of their initial values at time t. The random variables ϕ_i are Normally distributed and correlated. We can now write the value of our European option as

$$e^{-r(T-t)} \int_{-\infty}^{\infty} \cdots \int_{-\infty}^{\infty} \text{Payoff}(S_1(T), \ldots, S_d(T)) p(\phi_1, \ldots, \phi_d) \, d\phi_1 \ldots d\phi_d,$$

where $p(\phi_1, \ldots, \phi_d)$ is the probability density function for d correlated Normal variables with zero mean and unit standard deviation. I'm not going to write down p explicitly since we won't need to know its functional form *as long as we generate numbers from this distribution*. In effect, all that I have done here is to transform from lognormally distributed values of the assets to Normally distributed returns on the assets.

Now to value the option we must generate suitable Normal variables. The first step is to generate uncorrelated variables and then transform them into correlated variables. Both of these steps have been explained above; use Box–Muller and then Cholesky. The option value is then estimated by the average of the payoff over all the randomly generated numbers.

Here is a very simple code fragment for calculating the value of a European option in NDim assets using NoPts points. The interest rate is IntRate, the dividend yields are Div(i), the volatilities are Vol(i), time to expiry Expiry. The initial values of the assets are Asset(i). The Normally distributed variables are the x(i) and the S(i) are the lognormally distributed future asset values.

```
a = Exp(-IntRate * Expiry) / NoPts
suma = 0
For k = 1 To NoPts
For i = 1 To NDim
If test = 0 Then
    Do
        y = 2 * Rnd() - 1
        z = 2 * Rnd() - 1
        dist = y * y + z * z
    Loop Until dist < 1
x(i) = y * Sqr(-2 * Log(dist) / dist)
test = 1
Else
x(i) = z * Sqr(-2 * Log(dist) / dist)
test = 0
End If
Next i
For i = 1 To NDim
    S(i) = Asset(i) * Exp((IntRate - Div(i) - _
              0.5 * Vol(i) * Vol(i)) * Expiry + _
              Vol(i) * x(i) * Sqr(Expiry))
```

```
Next i
term = Payoff(S(1), S(2), S(3), S(4), S(5))
suma = suma + term
Next k
Value = suma * a
```

This code fragment is Monte Carlo in its most elementary form, and does not use any of the tricks described below. Some of these tricks are trivial to implement, especially those that are independent of the particular option being valued.

A more general piece of VB code

30.4 LOW-DISCREPANCY SEQUENCES

An obvious disadvantage of the basic Monte Carlo method for estimating integrals is that we cannot be certain that the generated points in the d-dimensional space are 'nicely' distributed. Indeed, there is inevitably a good deal of clumping. One way around this is to use a non-random series of points with better distributional properties.

SIMPLE AND FAST IF YOU'VE GOT AN EXPLICIT INTEGRAL FORMULATION

Let us motivate the low-discrepancy sequence method by a Monte Carlo example. Suppose that we want to calculate the value of an integral in two dimensions and we use a Monte Carlo simulation to generate a large number of points in two dimensions at which to sample the integrand. The choice of points may look something like Figure 30.1. Notice how the points are not spread out evenly.

Now suppose we want to add a few hundred more points to improve the accuracy. Where should we put the new points? If we put the new points in the gaps between others then we increase the accuracy of the integral. If we put the points close to where there are already many points then we could make matters worse.

The above shows that we want a way of choosing points such that they are not too bunched, but nicely spread out. At the same time we want to be able to add more points later without spoiling our distribution. Clearly Monte Carlo is bad for evenness of distribution, but a uniform grid does not stay uniform if we add an arbitrary number of extra points. **Low discrepancy sequences** or **quasi-random sequences** have the properties we require.[1]

There are two types of low discrepancy sequences, open and closed. The open sequences are constructed on the assumption that we may want to add more points later. The closed sequences are optimized for a given size of sample, to give the best estimate of the integral for the number of points. The regular grid is an example of a closed low-discrepancy sequence. I will describe the open sequences here.

The first application of these techniques in finance was by Barrett *et al.* (1992).[2] There are many such sequences with names such as **Sobol'**, **Faure**, **Haselgrove** and **Halton**. I shall describe the Halton sequence here, it is by far the easiest to describe.

---

[1] There is actually nothing random about quasi-random sequences.

[2] Andy Morton says that this has been my best piece of work, knowing full well that the numerical analysts John Barrett and Gerald Moore should have all the credit.

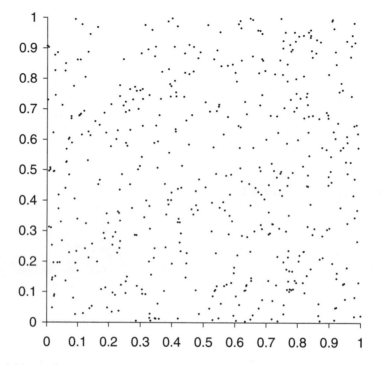

Figure 30.1 A Monte Carlo sample in two dimensions.

The Halton sequence is a sequence of numbers $h(i; b)$ for $i = 1, 2, \ldots$. The integer b is the base. The numbers all lie between zero and one.[3] The numbers are constructed as follows. First, choose your base. Let us choose 2. Now write the positive integers in ascending order in base 2, i.e. 1, 10, 11, 100, 101, 110, 111, etc. The Halton sequence base 2 is the reflection of the positive integers in the decimal point, i.e.

Integers base 10	Integers base 2	Halton sequence base 2	Halton number base 10
1	1	$1 \times \frac{1}{2}$	0.5
2	10	$0 \times \frac{1}{2} + 1 \times \frac{1}{4}$	0.25
3	11	$1 \times \frac{1}{2} + 1 \times \frac{1}{4}$	0.75
4	100	$0 \times \frac{1}{2} + 0 \times \frac{1}{4} + 1 \times \frac{1}{8}$	0.125
. . .	. . .	. . .	. . .

This has been called reflecting the numbers about the decimal point. If you plot the Halton points successively you will see that the next number in the sequence is always as

---

[3] So we must map our integrand onto the unit hypercube.

far as possible from the previous point. Generally, the integer n can be written as

$$i = \sum_{j=1}^{m} a_j b^j$$

in base b, where $0 \le a_j < b$. The Halton numbers are then given by

$$h(i; b) = \sum_{j=1}^{m} a_j b^{-j-1}.$$

Here is an algorithm for calculating Halton numbers of arbitrary base; the nth term in a Halton sequence of base b is given by `Halton(n, b)`.

Generating Halton numbers

```
Function Halton(n, b)
Dim n0, n1, r As Integer
Dim h As Double
Dim f As Double
    n0 = n
    h = 0
    f = 1 / b
While (n0 > 0)
    n1 = Int(n0 / b)
    r = n0 - n1 * b
    h = h + f * r
    f = f / b
    n0 = n1
Wend
Halton = h
End Function
```

The resulting sequence is nice because as we add more and more numbers, more and more 'dots,' we fill in the range zero to one at finer and finer levels.

In Figure 30.2 is the approximation to the Normal distribution using 500 points from a Halton sequence and the Box–Muller method. Compare this distribution with that in Figure 29.3. (You can get erroneous results if you combine the rejection-method Box–Muller with low-discrepancy numbers. See Jäckel, 2002.)

When distributing numbers in two dimensions choose, for example, Halton sequence of bases 2 and 3 so that the integrand is calculated at the points $(h(i, 2), h(i, 3))$ for $i = 1, \ldots, N$. The bases in the two sequences should be prime numbers. The distribution of these points is shown in Figure 30.3, compare the distribution with that in the Figure 30.1.

The estimate of the d-dimensional integral

$$\int_0^1 \cdots \int_0^1 f(x_1, \ldots, x_d) dx_1, \ldots, dx_d$$

is then

$$\frac{1}{N} \sum_{i=1}^{N} f(h(i, b_1), \ldots, h(i, b_n)),$$

where b_j are distinct prime numbers.

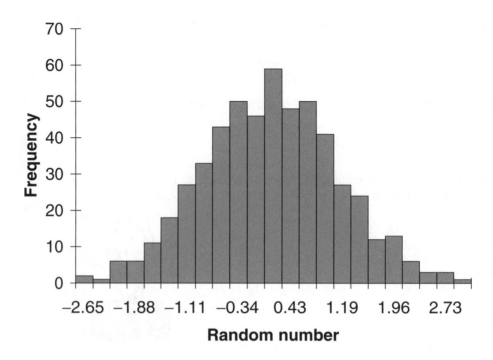

Figure 30.2 The approximation to the Normal distribution using 500 points from a Halton sequence and the Box–Muller method.

The error in these quasi-random methods is

$$O((\log N)^d N^{-1})$$

and is even better than Monte Carlo at all dimensions. The coefficient in the error depends on the particular low-discrepancy series being used. Sobol' is generally considered to be about the best sequence to use... but it's much harder to explain. See Press *et al.* (1992) for code to generate Sobol' points. In three or more dimensions the method beats the uniform grid.

The error is clearly sensitive to the number of dimensions d. To fully appreciate the inverse relationship to N can require an awful lot of points. However, even with fewer points, in practice the method at its worst has the same error as Monte Carlo.

In Figure 30.4 is shown the relative error in the estimate of value of a five-dimensional contract as a function of the number of points used. The inverse relationship with the Halton sequence is obvious.

Another advantage of these low-discrepancy sequences is that if you collapse the points onto a lower dimension (for example, let all of the points in a two-dimensional plot fall down onto the horizontal axis) they will not be repeated, they will not fall on top of one another. This means that if there is any particularly strong dependence on one of the variables over the others then the method will still give an accurate answer because it will distribute points nicely over lower dimensions.

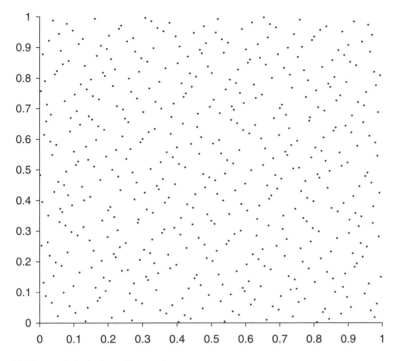

Figure 30.3 Halton points in two dimensions.

30.5 **ADVANCED TECHNIQUES**

There are several sophisticated techniques that can be used to improve convergence of Monte Carlo and related numerical integration methods. They can be generally classified as techniques for the **reduction of variance**, and hence for the increase in accuracy. None of these methods improve the speed of convergence with respect to N (for example, the error remains $O(N^{-\frac{1}{2}})$ for Monte Carlo) but they can significantly reduce the coefficient in the error term.

The method of **antithetic variables** described above is *very* easily applied to numerical integration. It should always be used since it can do no harm and is completely independent of the product being valued.

Control variates can also be used in exactly the same way as described above. As with the pathwise simulation for pricing, the method depends on there being a good approximation to the product having an analytic formula.

The idea behind **importance sampling** is to change variables so that the resulting integrand is as close as possible to being constant. In the extreme case, when the integrand becomes exactly constant, the 'answer' is simply the volume of the region in the new variables. Usually, it is not possible to do so well. But the closer one gets to having a constant integrand, then the better the accuracy of the result. The method is rarely used in finance.

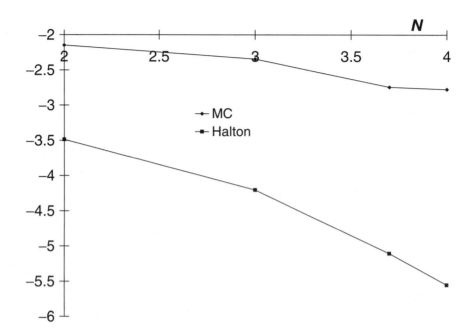

Figure 30.4 Estimate of the error in the value of a five-dimensional contract using basic Monte Carlo and a low-discrepancy sequence.

Stratified sampling involves dividing the region of integration into smaller subregions. The number of sampling points can then be allocated to the subregions in an optimal fashion, depending on the variance of the integral in each subregion. In more than one dimension it is not always obvious how to bisect the region, and can amount to laying down a grid, so defeating the purpose of Monte Carlo methods. The method can be improved upon by **recursive stratified sampling** in which a decision is made whether to bisect a region, based on the variance in the regions. Stratified sampling is rarely used in finance.

30.6 **SUMMARY**

Low-discrepancy sequences, where number theory meets high finance.

FURTHER READING

- See Sloan & Walsh (1990) and Stetson *et al.* (1995) for details of how to optimize a grid.

- See Barrett *et al.* (1992) for details of the Haselgrove method applied to options. And see Haselgrove (1961) for more details of the method in abstract.

- For a practical example of pricing mortgage backed securities see Ninomiya & Tezuka (1996).

- For more financial examples see Paskov & Traub (1995), Paskov (1996) and Traub & Wozniakowski (1994).

- See Niederreiter (1992) for an in-depth discussion of low-discrepancy sequences.

- See the amazing Press *et al.* (1992) for samples of code for random number generation and numerical integration. Make sure you use the latest edition, the random number generators in the first edition are not so good. They also describe more advanced integration techniques.

EXERCISES

1. Value a European call option using a Monte Carlo simulation. Use the simulation to estimate the value of an integral, as opposed to simulating the random walk for the asset.

2. Repeat the above using Halton sequences.

3. Calculate Halton sequences for bases 2, 3 and 4. Compare the results (you may wish to plot one base against another). What do you notice? How should this affect the bases you choose for a multi-factor problem?

all the math you need... and no more (an executive summary)

The aim of this Appendix...

...is to give you an understanding of almost all the mathematics you need in quantitative finance, and to give you the confidence to read through the more technical parts of this and other books.

In this Appendix...

- e
- log
- differentiation and Taylor series
- expectations and variances

QUANTITATIVE
FINANCE REALLY
IS SIMPLE .... IF
APPROACHED CORRECTLY

A.1 **INTRODUCTION**

This book is for *everyone* interested in quantitative finance. This subject is increasingly technical. Some people don't have a high-level math training but may still be interested in the technical side of things. In this chapter we look at the mathematics that you need to cope with the vast majority of derivatives theory and practice. Although often couched in very high level mathematics almost all finance theory can be interpreted using only the basics that I describe here.

The most useful math is the simplest math. This is particularly true in finance where the beauty of the mathematics can and does lead to people not seeing the wood for the trees. All basic finance theory and a great deal of the advanced research really require only elementary mathematics if approached in the right way. In this chapter I explain this elementary mathematics. I am trying to do for mathematical finance what Seuss (1999) did for the English language.

A simple,
ubiquitous function

A.2 **e**

The first bit of math you need to know about is e.

e is

- a number, 2.7183 ...

- a function when written e^x, this function is a.k.a. exp(x)

The function e^x is just the number 2.7183... raised to the power x; e^2 is just $2.7183...^2 = 7.3891...$, e^1 is 2.7183... and $e^0 = 1$. What about non-integer powers?

The function e^x can be written as an infinite series

$$e^x = 1 + x + \tfrac{1}{2}x^2 + \tfrac{1}{6}x^3 + \ldots = \sum_{i=0}^{\infty} \frac{x^i}{i!}.$$

This gets around the non-integer power problem.

A plot of e^x as a function of x is shown in Figure A.1.

The function e^x has the special property that the slope or gradient of the function is also e^x. Plot this slope as a function of x and for e^x you get the same curve again. It follows that the slope of the slope is also e^x, etc.

A.3 **log**

Take the plot of e^x, Figure A.1, and rotate it about a 45° line to get Figure A.2. This new function is $\ln x$, the natural logarithm of x. The relationship between ln and e is

$$e^{\ln x} = x \quad \text{or} \quad \ln(e^x) = x.$$

The inverse of the
exponential

So, in a sense, they are inverses of each other.

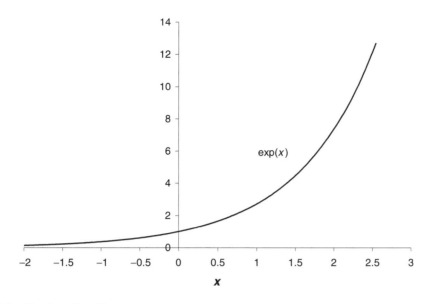

Figure A.1 The function e^x.

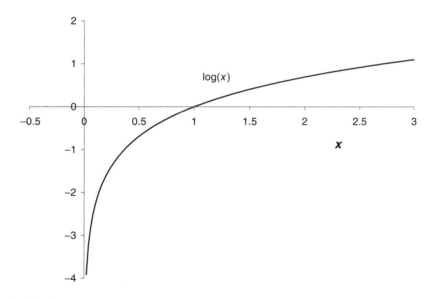

Figure A.2 The function $\log x$.

The function $\ln x$ is also often denoted by $\log x$, as in this book. Sometimes $\log x$ refers to the function with the properties

$$10^{\log x} = x \quad \text{and} \quad \log(10^x) = x.$$

This function would be called 'logarithm base 10.' The most useful logarithm has base $e = 2.7183\ldots$ because of the properties of the gradient of e^x.

The slope of the $\log x$ function is x^{-1}.

From the figure you can see that there don't appear to be any values for $\log x$ for negative x. The function can be defined for these but you'd need to know about complex numbers, something we won't be requiring here.

A.4 DIFFERENTIATION AND TAYLOR SERIES

I've introduced the idea of a gradient or slope in the section above. If we have a function denoted by $f(x)$, then we denote the gradient of this function at the point x by

$$\frac{df}{dx}.$$

Mathematically the slope is defined as

$$\frac{df}{dx} = \lim_{\delta x \to 0} \frac{f(x + \delta x) - f(x)}{\delta x}.$$

The action of finding the gradient is also called 'differentiating' and the slope can also be called the 'derivative' of the function. This use of 'derivative' shouldn't be confused with the use meaning an option contract.

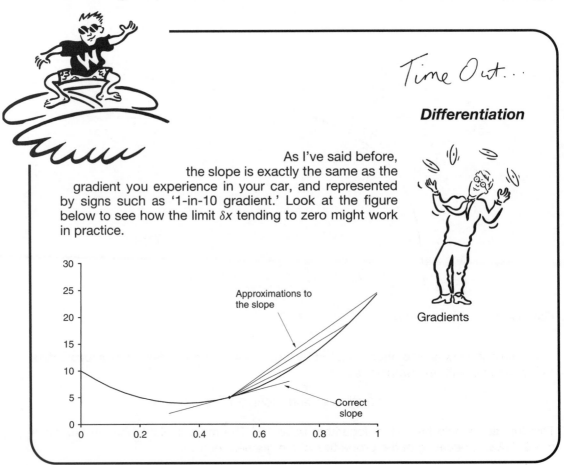

Time Out. . .

Differentiation

As I've said before, the slope is exactly the same as the gradient you experience in your car, and represented by signs such as '1-in-10 gradient.' Look at the figure below to see how the limit δx tending to zero might work in practice.

Approximations to the slope

Correct slope

Gradients

The slope can also be differentiated, resulting in a second derivative of the function $f(x)$. This is denoted by

$$\frac{d^2f}{dx^2}.$$

We can take this differentiation to higher and higher orders.

Take a look at Figure A.3. In particular, note the two dots marked on the bold curve. The bold curve is the function $f(x)$. The dot on the left is at the point x on the horizontal axis and the function value is $f(x)$, the distance up the vertical axis. The dot to the right of this is at $x + \delta x$ with function value $f(x + \delta x)$. What can we say about the vertical distance between the two dots in terms of the horizontal distance?

Start with a trivial example. If the distance δx is zero then the vertical distance is also zero. Now consider a very small but non-zero δx.

The straight line tangential to the bold curve $f(x)$ at the point x is shown in the figure. This line has slope $\frac{df}{dx}$ evaluated at x. Notice that the right-hand hollow dot is almost on this bold line. This suggests that a good approximation to the value $f(x + \delta x)$ is

Gradients of gradients

$$f(x + \delta x) \approx f(x) + \delta x \frac{df}{dx}(x).$$

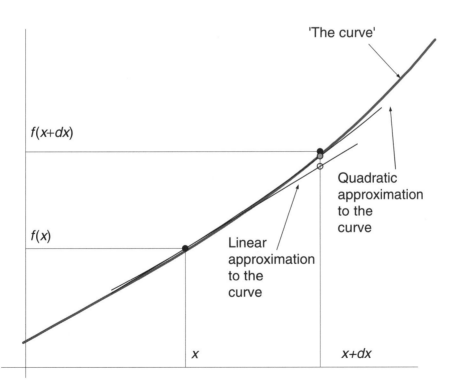

Figure A.3   A schematic diagram of Taylor series.

This is a linear relationship between $f(x + \delta x) - f(x)$ and δx. This makes sense since on rearranging we get

$$\frac{df}{dx} \approx \frac{f(x + \delta x) - f(x)}{\delta x}$$

which as δx goes to zero becomes our earlier definition of the gradient.

But the right-hand hollow dot is not *exactly* on the straight line. It is slightly above it. Perhaps a quadratic relationship between $f(x + \delta x) - f(x)$ and δx would be a more accurate approximation. This is indeed true (provided δx is small enough) and we can write

$$f(x + \delta x) \approx f(x) + \delta x \frac{df}{dx}(x) + \tfrac{1}{2}\delta x^2 \frac{d^2 f}{dx^2}(x).$$

This approximation, shown on the figure as the gray dot, is more accurate. One can take this approximation to cubic, quartic, ... The Taylor series representation of $f(x + \delta x)$ is the infinite sum

See how accurate this can be

$$f(x + \delta x) = f(x) + \sum_{i=1}^{\infty} \frac{1}{i!} \delta x^i \frac{d^i f}{dx^i}(x).$$

Taylor series is incredibly useful in derivatives theory. In derivatives theory the function that we are interested in, instead of being f, is V, the value of an option. The independent variable is no longer x but is S, the price of the underlying asset. From day to day the asset price changes by a small, random amount. This asset price change is just δS (instead of δx). The first derivative of the option value with respect to the asset is known as the delta, and the second derivative is the gamma.

The value of an option is not only a function of the asset price S but also the time t: $V(S, t)$. This brings us into the world of partial differentiation.

Think of the function $V(S, t)$ as a surface with coordinates S and t on a horizontal plane. The function V is the height of a hill above sea level with S and t being distances, or map coordinates, in the northerly and westerly directions. The *partial* derivative of $V(S, t)$ with respect to S is written

$$\frac{\partial V}{\partial S}$$

and is defined as

$$\frac{\partial V}{\partial S} = \lim_{\delta S \to 0} \frac{V(S + \delta S, t) - V(S, t)}{\delta S}.$$

Note that in this V is only ever evaluated at time t. This is like measuring the gradient of the function $V(S, t)$ in the S direction along a constant value of t, i.e. the slope of our hillside in the northerly direction. Note also that we are now using a special curly ∂ instead of the roman d. The partial derivative of $V(S, t)$ with respect to t is similarly defined as

$$\frac{\partial V}{\partial t} = \lim_{\delta t \to 0} \frac{V(S, t + \delta t) - V(S, t)}{\delta t}$$

and is the slope of the hill in the westerly direction.

Higher-order derivatives are defined in the obvious manner.

The Taylor series expansion of the value of an option is then

$$V(S + \delta S, t + \delta t) \approx V(S, t) + \delta t \frac{\partial V}{\partial t} + \delta S \frac{\partial V}{\partial S} + \tfrac{1}{2} \delta S^2 \frac{\partial^2 V}{\partial S^2} + \ldots.$$

This series goes on for ever, but I've only written down the largest and most important terms, those which are required for the Black–Scholes analysis.

A.5   **DIFFERENTIAL EQUATIONS**

Right at the beginning of the book we saw a differential equation. Remember the equation for money in the bank

$$\frac{dM}{dt} = rM?$$

This is an example of an **ordinary differential equation**. 'Ordinary' because it involves only derivatives with respect to a single variable; there are no curly ∂s. This equation can be solved to find M as a function of the other variable t.

Throughout this book there are **partial differential equations**. These involve the curly ∂s because there are derivatives/slopes/gradients with respect to more than one variable. The Black–Scholes equation is an example. In our mountain example, think of a partial differential equation as relating the height of the mountain to its slope in each direction, and maybe even the slope of the slope. Again, such equations must be solved to find the height of the mountain, the option value. How this is done analytically (if possible) or numerically (always possible) will be discussed later.

A.6   **MEAN, STANDARD DEVIATION AND DISTRIBUTIONS**

Much of the modeling in finance uses ideas from probability theory. Again you don't need to know that much to understand most of quantitative finance.

The first idea is that of the mean. The mean is the same as the average or the expectation. What is the average shoe size of US males?

If you roll a die there is an equal, $\frac{1}{6}$, probability of each number coming up. What is the expected number or the average number if you roll the die many times. The answer is

$$1 \times \tfrac{1}{6} + 2 \times \tfrac{1}{6} + 3 \times \tfrac{1}{6} + 4 \times \tfrac{1}{6} + 5 \times \tfrac{1}{6} + 6 \times \tfrac{1}{6} = 3\tfrac{1}{2}.$$

Here we just multiply each of the possible numbers that could turn up by the probability of each, and sum. Although $3\tfrac{1}{2}$ is the expected value, it cannot, of course, be thrown since only integers are possible.

Generally, if we have a random variable X (the number thrown, say) which can take any of the values x_i (1, 2, 3, 4, 5, 6 in our example) for $i = 1, \ldots, N$ each of which has a probability $P(X = x_i)$ (in the example, $\frac{1}{6}$) then the expected value is

$$E[X] = \sum_{i=1}^{N} x_i P(X = x_i).$$

Expectations have the following properties:

$$E[cX] = cE[X]$$

and

$$E[X + Y] = E[X] + E[Y].$$

If the outcome of two random events X and Y have no impact on each other they are said to be independent. If X and Y are independent we have

$$E[XY] = E[X]E[Y].$$

Expectations are important in finance because we often want to know what we can expect to make from an investment on average.

The expectation or mean is also known as the first moment of the distribution of the random variable X. It can be thought of as being a typical value for X. The scatter of values around the mean can be measured by the second moment or the variance:

$$\text{Var}(X) = E\left[(X - E[X])^2\right].$$

Variances have the following property:

$$\text{Var}(cX) = c^2 \text{Var}(X).$$

When X and Y are independent

$$\text{Var}(X + Y) = \text{Var}(X) + \text{Var}(Y).$$

The standard deviation is the square root of the variance and is perhaps more useful as a measure of dispersion since it has the same units as the variable X:

$$\text{Standard deviation}(X) = \sqrt{\text{Var}(X)}.$$

The standard deviation is just a measure of the spread around that mean. The smaller the standard deviation of shoe sizes, the less variation in sizes among the population. If the standard deviation is large, there is a great deal of variation in shoe sizes.

Standard deviations are important in finance because they are often used as a measure of risk in an investment. The higher the standard deviation of investment returns the greater the dispersion of the returns and the greater the risk.

If we were to plot a bar chart (histogram) of number of the population with each shoe size on the vertical axis and shoe size on the horizontal we'd have a frequency distribution of shoe sizes. Now scale the height of each bar with the total number in the population and you've got a probability density function. Why did I ask you to scale the distribution? So that the heights of all the bars add up to one, the probability of having *some* shoe size is one.

That was an example of a discrete distribution. Shoe sizes are a discrete set. Contrast that with foot length. The length of a foot can

Some examples

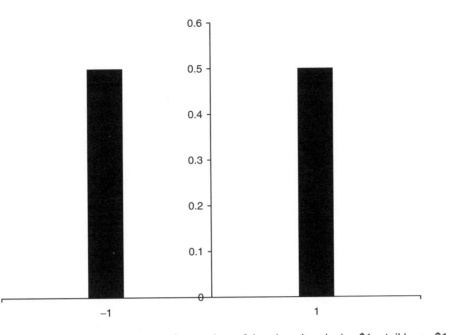

Figure A.4 Probability density functions for tossing a fair coin; a head wins $1 a tail loses $1. The mean is zero.

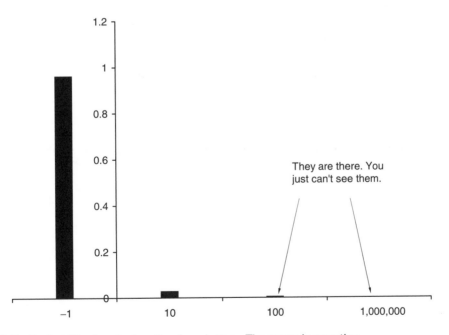

Figure A.5 Probability density function for a lottery. The mean is negative.

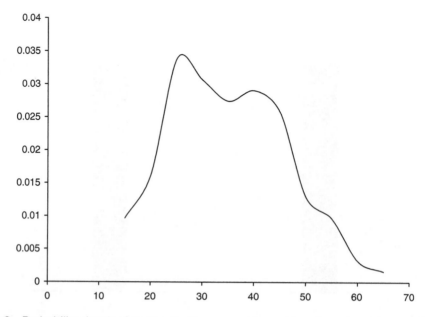

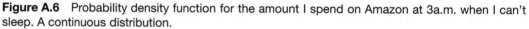

Figure A.6 Probability density function for the amount I spend on Amazon at 3a.m. when I can't sleep. A continuous distribution.

be any number, not confined to a discrete set. Foot lengths form a continuous distribution. In practice, given a continuous distribution such as foot length you will have to assign each length to a finite sized 'bucket.' Think of the bucket as being the corresponding shoe size.

Above are a few examples of probability density functions.

A.7 **SUMMARY**

The math you need in quantitative finance is surprisingly little. And you've just seen all of it.

APPENDIX B
forecasting the markets?
A small digression

The aim of this Appendix...

...is to explain ways in which people supposedly predict future movements in the financial markets. There is little scientific evidence that these methods work in practice but you, a future bond trader perhaps, must know about such matters and eventually decide for yourself.

In this Appendix...

- some of the commonly used technical methods for predicting market direction
- some modern approaches to modeling markets and their microstructure

WE'VE ALL DONE IT, THO' IT'S NOTHING TO BE PROUD OF

B.1 **INTRODUCTION**

People have been making predictions about the future since the dawn of time. And predicting the future of the financial markets has been especially popular. Despite the claims of many 'legendary' investors it is not clear whether there is any validity in any of the methods they use, or whether the claims are examples of survivor bias. The big losers tend to keep quiet.

In this appendix we look at some of the traditional methods for determining trends, technical analysis, and also some of the more recent methods, often emanating from physics. I won't be describing some of the more dubious ideas, such as astrology, but then we Scorpios tend to be skeptical.

In the book generally, I'm taking the view that the markets are best modeled via probabilities. This appendix is very much a digression from the main thrust of the book.

B.2 **TECHNICAL ANALYSIS**

Technical analysis is a way of predicting future price movements based only on observing the past history of prices. This price history may also include other quantities such as volume of trade. These methods contrast with **fundamental analysis** in which prediction is made based on an examination of the factors underlying the stock or other instrument. This may include general economic or political analysis, or analysis of factors specific to the stock, such as the effect of global warming on snowfall in the Alps, if one is concerned with a travel company. In practice, most traders will use a combination of both technical and fundamental analysis.

Technical analysis is also called **charting** because the graphical representation of prices, etc. plays an important part. Technical analysis is thought to be particularly good for timing market moves; fundamental analysis may get the direction right, but not necessarily when the move will happen.

B.2.1 Plotting

The simplest chart types just join together the prices from one day to the next, with time along the horizontal axis. These are the sort of plots we have seen throughout this book. Sometimes a logarithmic scale is used for the vertical price axis to represent return rather than absolute level. Later on we'll see some more complicated types of plotting. Sometimes you will see trading volume on the same graph, this is also used for prediction but I won't go into any details here, see Figure B.1.

B.2.2 Support and resistance

Resistance is a price level which an asset seems to have difficulty rising above. This may be a previously realized highest value, or it may be a psychologically important (round) number. **Support** is a level below which an asset price seems to be reluctant to fall.

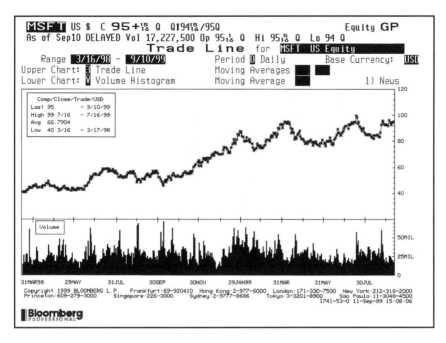

Figure B.1 Price and volume. Source: Bloomberg L.P.

There may be sufficient demand at this low price to stop it falling any further. Examples of support and resistance are shown in Figure B.2.

When a support or resistance level finally breaks it is said to do so quite dramatically.

B.2.3 Trendlines

Similar to support and resistance are **trendlines**. These are formed by joining together successive peaks and/or troughs in the price history to form a rising or falling support or resistance level. An example is shown in Figure B.3.

B.2.4 Moving averages

Moving averages are calculated in many ways. Different time windows can be used, or even exponentially weighted averages can be calculated. Moving averages are supposed to distill out the basic trend in a price by smoothing the random noise.

Sometimes two moving averages are calculated, say a 10-day and a 250-day average. The crossing of these two would signify a change in the underlying trend and a time to buy or sell.

Although I'm not the greatest fan of technical analysis, there is some evidence that there may be predictive power in moving averages.

Figure B.4 shows a Bloomberg screen with Microsoft share price, five- and 15-day moving averages.

Moving averages may actually be useful

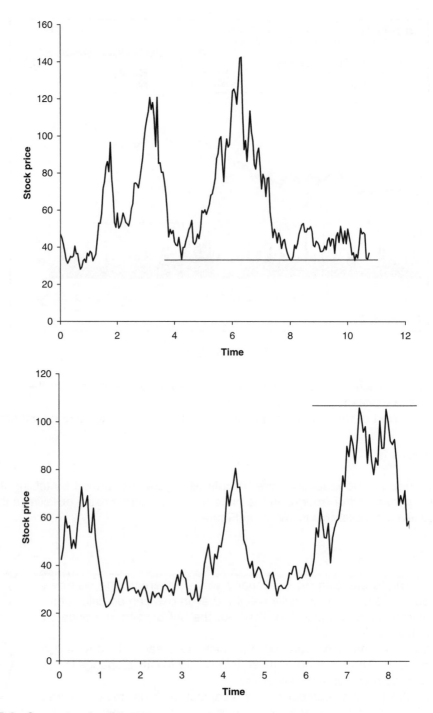

Figure B.2 Support and resistance.

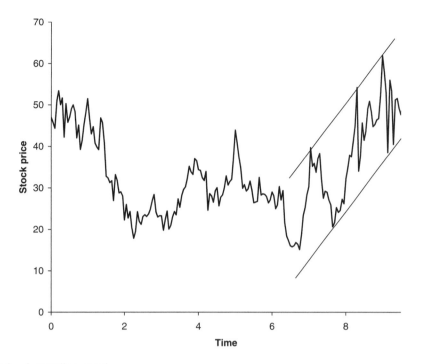

Figure B.3 A trending stock.

Figure B.4 Two moving averages. Source: Bloomberg L.P.

B.2.5 Relative strength

The **relative strength index** is the percentage of up moves in the last N days. A number higher than 70% is said to be overbought and is therefore likely to fall, and below 30% is said to be oversold and should rise.

B.2.6 Oscillators

An **oscillator** is another indicator of over/underbought conditions. One way of calculating it is as follows.
Define k by

RSI

$$100 \times \frac{\text{Current close} - \text{lowest over } n \text{ periods}}{\text{Highest over } n \text{ periods} - \text{lowest over } n \text{ periods}}.$$

Now take a moving average of the last three days, say. This average is plotted against time and any move outside the range 30–70% could be an indication of a move in the asset. See Figure B.5.

B.2.7 Bollinger bands

Bollinger bands are plots of a specified number of standard deviations above and below a specified moving average, see Figure B.6.

Oscillators

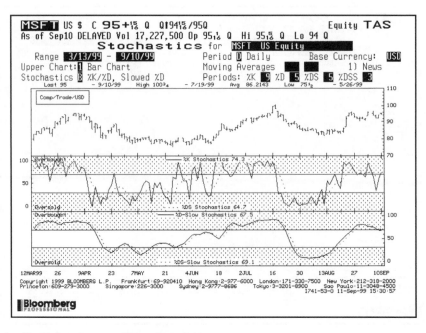

Figure B.5 Oscillator. Source: Bloomberg L.P.

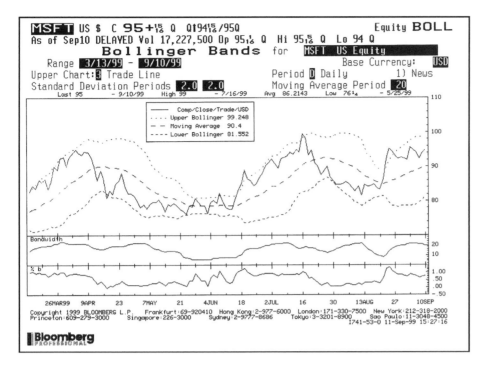

Figure B.6 Bollinger bands. Source: Bloomberg L.P.

B.2.8 Miscellaneous patterns

As well as the 'quantitative' side of charting there is also the 'artistic' side. Practitioners say that certain patterns anticipate certain future moves. It's rather like your grandmother reading tea leaves.

Head and shoulders is a common pattern and is best described with reference to Figure B.7. There are a left and a right shoulder with the head rising above. Following on from the right shoulder should be a dramatic decline in the asset price.

This pattern is supposed to be one of the most reliable predictors. It is also seen in an upside-down formation.

Saucer tops and bottoms are also known as **rounding tops** and **bottoms**. They are the result of a gradual change in supply and demand. The shape is generally fairly symmetrical as the prices rise and fall. These patterns are quite rare. They contain no information about the strength of the new trend. See Figure B.8.

Double and triple tops and bottoms are quite rare patterns, the triple being even rarer than the double. The double top looks like an 'M' and a double bottom like a 'W.' The triple top is similar but with three peaks, as shown in Figure B.9. The key point about the peaks and troughs is that they should all be at approximately the same level.

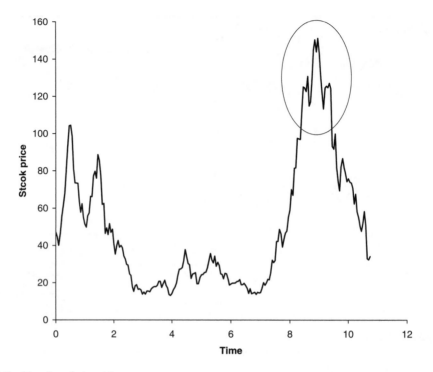

Figure B.7   Head and shoulders.

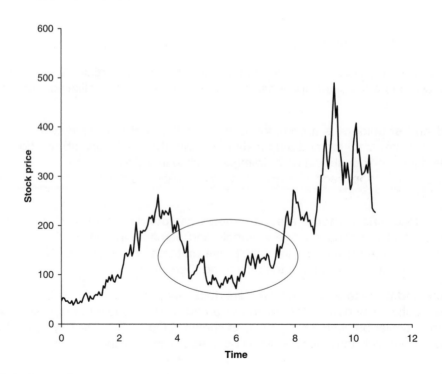

Figure B.8   Saucer bottom.

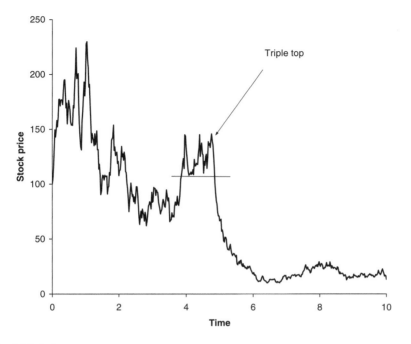

Figure B.9 A triple top.

B.2.9 Japanese candlesticks

Japanese candlesticks contain more information than the simple plots described so far. They record the opening and closing prices as well as the day's high and low. A rectangle is drawn extending from the close to the open, and is colored white if close is above open and black if close is below open. The high-low range is marked by a continuous line.

Certain combinations of candlesticks, appearing consecutively, have special meanings and names like 'Hanging Man' and 'Upside Gap Two Crows.' See Figure B.10 for the two types of candlestick and see Figure B.11 for candlesticks in action. On this chart are shown 'HR' = Bearish Harami, 'D' = Doji (representing indecision), 'BH' Bullish Harami, 'EL' = Bearish Engulfing Line, and 'H' = Hanging Man (representing reversal after a trend).

Figure B.12 shows some of the possible candlestick shapes and their interpretation.

Excel has options for plotting candlesticks

B.2.10 Point and figure charts

Point and figure charts are different from the charts described above in that they do not have any explicit timescale on the horizontal axis. Figure B.13 is an example of a point and figure chart. Each box on the chart represents a prespecified asset price move. The boxes are a way of discretizing asset price moves, instead of discretizing in time. For each consecutive asset price rise of the box size draw an 'X' in the box, in a rising column,

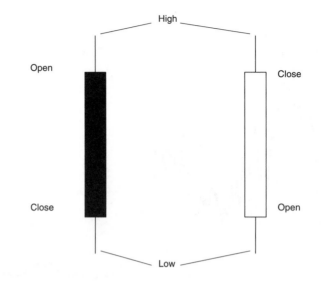

Figure B.10 Japanese candlesticks.

Figure B.11 A candlestick chart. Source: Bloomberg L.P.

one above the other. When this uptrend finishes, and the asset falls, start putting 'O' in a descending column, to the right of the previous rising Xs.

- A long column of Xs denotes demand exceeding supply.

- A long column of Os denotes supply exceeding demand.

- Short up and down columns denote a balance of supply and demand.

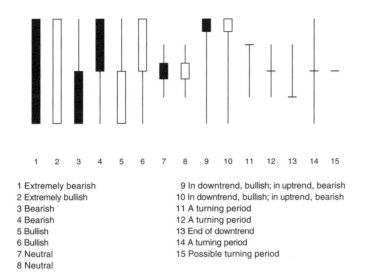

1 Extremely bearish
2 Extremely bullish
3 Bearish
4 Bearish
5 Bullish
6 Bullish
7 Neutral
8 Neutral

9 In downtrend, bullish; in uptrend, bearish
10 In downtrend, bullish; in uptrend, bearish
11 A turning period
12 A turning period
13 End of downtrend
14 A turning period
15 Possible turning period

Figure B.12   The meanings of the various candlesticks.

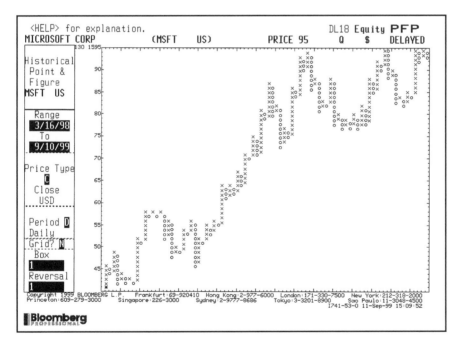

Figure B.13   A point and figure chart of Microsoft. Source: Bloomberg L.P.

B.3   **WAVE THEORY**

As well as plotting and spotting trends in price movements there have been some theories for price prediction based on market cycles or waves. Below, I briefly mention a couple.

B.3.1   Elliott waves and Fibonacci numbers

Ralph N. Elliott observed repetitive patterns, waves or cycles in prices. Roughly speaking, there are supposed to be five points in a bullish wave and then three in a bearish one. See Figure B.14. Within this **Elliott wave theory** there is also supposed to be some predictive ability in terms of the sizes of the peaks in each wave. For some reason, the ratio of peaks in a trend are supposed to be fairly constant; the ratio of second peak to first should be approximately 1.618 and of the third to the second 2.618. Unfortunately, the number 1.618 is approximately the **Golden ratio** of the ancient Greeks; $\frac{1}{2}(\sqrt{5}+1)$. It is also the ratio of successive numbers in the **Fibonacci series** given by $a_n = a_{n-1} + a_{n-2}$ for large n. I say, unfortunately, because people extrapolate wildly from this. And if it's a coincidence then . . . Figure B.15 shows the key levels coming from the Fibonacci series.

B.3.2   Gann charts

Figure B.16 shows a Gann chart. The lines all have slopes which are fractions of the slope of the lowest line. Need I say more?

B.4   **OTHER ANALYTICS**

There's an almost endless number of ways that chartists analyze data. I'll mention just a couple more before moving on.

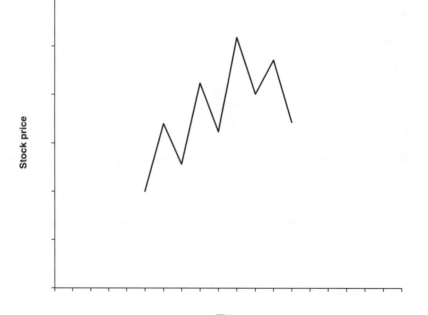

Figure B.14   Elliot waves.

Figure B.15 Fibonacci lines. Source: Bloomberg L.P.

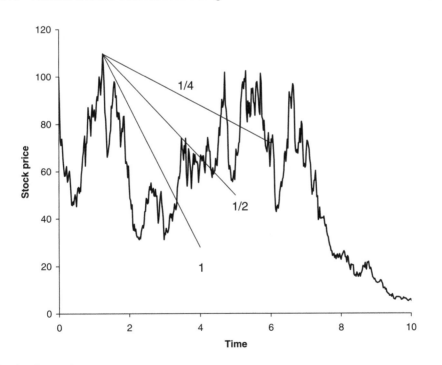

Figure B.16 Gann charts.

Volume is simply the number of contracts traded in a given period. A rising price and high volume means a strong, upwardly trending market. But a rising price with low volume could be a sign that the market is about to turn.

Open interest is the number of still outstanding futures contracts, those which have not been closed out. Because there are equal numbers of buyers and sellers, open interest does not necessarily give any directional info, but an increase in open interest can mean that an existing trend is strong.

B.5 MARKET MICROSTRUCTURE MODELING

The financial markets are made up of many types of players. There are the 'producers' who manufacture or produce or sell various goods to who may be involved in the financial markets for hedging. There are the 'speculators' who try to spot trends in the market, to exploit them and make money. These speculators may be using technical analysis methods, such as those described above, or fundamental analysis, whereby they examine the records and future plans of firms to determine whether stocks are under- or overpriced. Almost all traders use technical analysis at some time. Then there are the market makers who buy and sell financial instruments, holding them for a very short time, often seconds, and profit on bid-offer spreads.

There have been many attempts to model the interaction of these agents, sometimes in a game theoretic way, to try to model the asset price movements that in this book we have taken for granted. For example, can the dynamics induced by the actions of a combination of these three types of agent result in Brownian motion and lognormal random walks?

Below are just a very few examples of work in this area.

B.5.1 Effect of demand on price

Buying and selling assets moves their prices. Market makers respond to demand by increasing price, and reduce prices when the market is selling. If one can model the relationship between demand and price then it should be possible to analyze the effect that various types of technical trading rule have on the evolution of prices. And eventually to model the dynamics of prices.

A common starting point is to assume that there are two types of trader and one market maker. One trader follows a technical trading rule such as watching a moving average and the other is a **noise trader** who randomly buys or sells.

Interesting results follow from such models. For example:

- trend followers can induce patterns in asset price time series;

- these artificially induced patterns can only be exploited for gain by someone following a suitably different trend;

- the more people following the same trend as you, the more money you will lose.

There are good reasons for there being genuine trends in the market: there is a slow diffusion of information from the knowledgeable to the less knowledgeable; the piece-by-piece secret acquisition of a company will gradually move a stock price upwards.

On the other hand, if there is no genuine reason for a trend, if it is simply a case of trend followers begetting a trend, then it may be beneficial to be a contrarian.

B.5.2 Combining market microstructure and option theory

Arbitrage does exist, many people make money from its existence. Yet the action of arbitragers will, via a demand/price relationship, remove the arbitrage. But there will be a timescale associated with this removal. What is the optimal way to exploit the arbitrage opportunity while knowing that your actions will to some extent be self-defeating?

B.5.3 Imitation

Another approach to market microstructure modeling is based on the true observation that people copy each other. In these models there are a number of traders who act partly in response to private information about a stock, partly randomly as noise traders, and partly to imitate their nearest neighbors. These models can result in market bubbles or market crashes.

B.6 CRISIS PREDICTION

There has been some work on analyzing data over various timescales to determine the likelihood of a market crash. Some ideas from earthquake modeling have been used to derive a 'Richter'-like measure of market moves. Of course, an effective predictor of market crashes could either

- increase the chance or size of a crash as everyone panics or

- reduce the chance or size of the crash since everyone gets advance warning and can calmly and logically act accordingly.

B.7 SUMMARY

I started out in finance many years ago plotting all of the technical indicators. I was not very successful at it. I could only get directions right for those assets with obvious seasonality effects, such as some commodities.

There is only one technical indicator that I believe in. There is definitely a strong correlation between hemlines and the state of the economy. The shorter the skirts, the better the economy.

FURTHER READING

- The book on technical analysis written by the news agency Reuters (1999) is excellent, as is Meyers (1994).

- Farmer & Joshi (2000) discusses and models trend following, and the creation of trends. They also demonstrate properties of the relationship between demand and price that prevent arbitrage.

- Bhamra (2000) has worked on imitation in financial markets.

- Olsen & Associates `www.olsen.ch` are currently working in the area of crisis modeling and prediction.

- Johnson *et al*. (1999) models self-organized segregation of traders, and concludes that cautious traders perform poorly.

- The above is only a brief description of a very few examples from an expanding field. See O'Hara (1995) for a wide-ranging discussion of market microstructure models.

- Bernstein (1998) has a whole chapter on the Golden ratio.

- Elton & Gruber (1995) describe the efficient market hypothesis and criticize technical analysis.

- Prast (2000a, b) discusses 'herding' in the financial markets.

APPENDIX C
a trading game

C.1   **INTRODUCTION**

A lot of people reading this book will never have traded options or even stocks. In this appendix I describe a very simple trading game so that a group of people can try out their skill without losing their shirts. The game is based on that by one of my ex-students David Epstein.

C.2   **AIMS**

The aims of this game are to familiarize students with the basic market-traded derivative contracts and to promote an understanding of the concepts involved in trading, such as bid, offer, arbitrage and liquidity.

C.3   **OBJECT OF THE GAME**

To make more money than your opponents. After the final round of trading, each player sums up their profits and losses. The player who has made the most profit is the winner.

C.4   **RULES OF THE GAME**

1. One person (possibly a lecturer) is the game organizer and in charge of choosing the types of contracts available for trading, the number and length of the trading rounds, judging any disputes and jollying the game along during slack periods.

2. The trading game takes place over a number of rounds. At the end of each round, a six-sided die is thrown. After the last round, the 'share price' is deemed to be the sum of all of the die rolls.

3. Traded contracts may include some or all of forwards, calls and puts at the discretion of the organizer. The organizer must also decide what exercise prices are available for call or put options.

4. All contracts expire at the end of the final round. The settlement value of each traded contract can then be determined by substituting the share price into the appropriate formula. A player's profits and losses on each trade can then be calculated and the resultant profit/loss is their final score.

5. During a round, players can offer to buy or sell any of the traded contracts. If another player chooses to take them up on their offer, then the deal is agreed and both parties must record the transaction on their trading sheet.

6. A deal on a contract must include the following information:

    *   Forward: forward price and quantity
    *   Call or put: type of option (call or put), exercise price, cost and quantity

    The organizer chooses the types of contracts available and the strike prices.

    The forward price or option cost and the quantity in a deal are chosen by the players.

For beginners, play three games in succession, with the following structures:

1. Play with just the forward contract.
2. Play with the forward contract and the call option with exercise price 15.
3. Play with the forward and the call and put options with exercise price 15.

All three games take place over five rounds, each five minutes in length.

C.5 **NOTES**

1. Depending on the level of prior knowledge of the players, the organizer may need to explain the characteristics of the various traded contracts. It will be instructive to emphasize that the forward contract has no cost initially.

2. There will probably be times when the organizer has to act as a 'market-maker' and promote trading, for instance, asking the group if anyone wants to buy shares or at what price someone is willing to do so.

3. For more advanced students, consider introducing some of the following ideas:

    *   Increase the number of rounds
    *   Decrease the length of each round
    *   Include extra calls and puts with different exercise prices or which either come into existence or expire at different times. You must fix the details of these extra contracts in advance of the game
    *   Include other contracts, e.g. Asian options or barriers
    *   Include a second die for a second underlying share price

4. Including futures with 'daily' marking to market can be tried, but slows down the game. Nevertheless, it does illustrate the importance of margin, especially if the students have a limit on how much 'in debt' they are allowed to become.

C.6 HOW TO FILL IN YOUR TRADING SHEET

C.6.1 During a trading round

In the 'Contract' column, fill in the specifications of the instrument that you have bought/sold. Specify the forward price or exercise price if applicable (e.g. if there is more than one contract of this type in the game).

In the 'Buy/Sell' column, fill in whether you have bought or sold the contract and the quantity.

In the 'Cost per contract' column, fill in the cost of a single contract.

C.6.2 At the end of the game

In the 'Settlement value' column, fill in the value of a single contract with the final share price.

In the 'Profit/loss per contract' column, fill in the profit/loss for a single contract.

In the 'Total profit/loss' fill in the total profit/loss for the trade (= profit/loss × quantity).

Example During a round, your transactions are:

Buy 10 call options, with exercise price 20, at a cost of 2 each. Sell 1 put option, with exercise price 15, at a cost of $1. Buy 5 forwards, with forward price 19.

Your trading sheet should be filled in as below.

Contract	Buy/sell	Cost per contract	Total cost	Settlement value	Profit/loss
Call 20	Buy 10	2			
Put 15	Sell 1	1			
Forward 19	Buy 5	–			

At the end of the game, the final share price is 21. Consequently, the trading sheet is completed as follows.

Contract	Buy/sell	Cost per contract	Total cost	Settlement value	Profit/loss
Call 20	Buy 10	2	$21 - 20 = 1$	$1 - 2 = -1$	$-1 \times 10 = -10$
Put 15	Sell 1	1	0	$1 - 0 = +1$	$+1 \times 1 = +1$
Forward 19	Buy 5	–	$21 - 19 = 2$	$+2$	$+2 \times 5 = +10$

The total profit and loss for the trader is therefore $-10 + 1 + 10 = +1$.

Remember that:

If you buy a contract, your profit/loss = settlement value − cost per contract

If you sell a contract, your profit/loss = cost per contract − settlement value

Trading sheet

Contract	Buy/sell	Cost per contract	Total cost	Settlement value	Profit/loss

The Trading Game–designed by David Epstein, 1999.

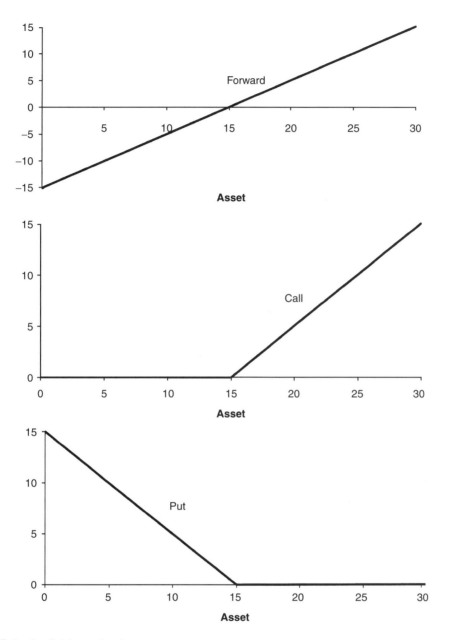

Figure C.1 Available contracts.

contents of CD accompanying *Paul Wilmott Introduces Quantitative Finance, second edition*

There are three folders on the CD, 'Spreadsheets and VBA,' 'Standalone' and 'Wilmott magazine Lyceum.'

In the 'Spreadsheets and VBA' folder there are 25 Excel workbooks. Each corresponds to a chapter of *Paul Wilmott Introduces Quantitative Finance, second edition*. (A few chapters don't have workbooks.) Each workbook typically has several sheets. In order to run some macros you may need to install an add-in to Excel called Solver. When you install Excel, the standard installation does not include this add-in. If Solver is not installed you will need to re-run the Excel setup program and select this component before the macros will work. C++ versions of some of these programs are also available, just email *paul@wilmott.com* if you would like these emailed to you.

In the 'Standalones' folder there are nine simple programs useful for calculating various simple quantities, such as option values, greeks, etc.

In the 'Wilmott magazine Lyceum' folder are 16 Lyceum articles from *Wilmott* magazine in pdf form.

As always, email paul@wilmott.com if you have any problems.

In the following an asterisk denotes VBA code.

1. Products and Markets.xls
A fictitious asset path possibly?
Exponentials

2. Derivatives.xls
A fictitious asset path possibly?
Gearing
Put-call parity

3. Binomial Model.xls
One step in the binomial model
The tree
European Call *
American Call *

4. Random Behavior of Assets.xls
Asset returns

The Normal distribution
Simulations
Approximating the Normal distribution

5. Stochastic Calculus.xls
Brownian motion with drift
The lognormal random walk
Mean-reverting random walk
Another mean-reverting random walk

6. Black–Scholes Model.xls
Simulation of delta hedging *

8. Black–Scholes Formulæ .xls
Spreadsheet and VB functions
Greeks *
Implied volatility *

10. How to Delta Hedge
Simulation of delta hedging
Expected profit

12. Multi-asset Options.xls
Correlated random walks

13. Barrier Options.xls
All the formulæ

14. Fixed-income Products and Analysis.xls
Yield, duration and convexity *
Forward rates

15. Swaps.xls
Bootstrapping

16. One-factor Interest Rate Modeling.xls
Vasicek simulation
Vasicek yield curve
CIR simulation
CIR yield curve
Ho & Lee *

19. Heath, Jarrow and Morton.xls
2-factor HJM *

20. Investment Lessons from Black-jack and Gambling.xls
Kelly
Horses *

21. Portfolio Management.xls
Diversification
Modern Portfolio Theory
Maximize Sharpe ratio *
Alpha and beta

22. Value at Risk.xls
Value at Risk for a portfolio

23. Credit Risk.xls
Poisson process
CB with risk of default

24. RiskMetrics and CreditMetrics.xls
Exponentially weighted moving average volatility

25. CrashMetrics.xls
Single index, multi-asset model *
Platinum hedging *

28. Finite-difference Methods for One-factor Models.xls
3D *
US *
2D *

29. Monte Carlo Simulation.xls
Pricing vanilla by simulation
Pricing exotics by simulation
Box–Muller *
Pricing interest rate products by simulation
Cholesky factorization *
Longstaff Schwartz *

30. Numerical Integration.xls
Numerical integration *
Halton sequence *

A. All the Math You Need.xls
Exponential
The logarithmic function
Calculating gradients
Gradients of gradients
Taylor series
Probability

B. Predicting the Markets.xls
Moving averages *
Relative strength *
Oscillators *
Japanese candlesticks

what you get if (when) you upgrade to *PWOQF2*

INTRODUCTION

The book you've just read is a self-contained account of 'classical' quantitative finance, at a university level. But it's not the whole story. *Paul Wilmott On Quantitative Finance, second edition*, full version, is used by 'serious' quants, in both financial institutions and academia as *the* reference for models, methods and inspiration. But it's still written in the same easy-to-digest style that you are by now familiar with :)

In the 'full' version of *PWOQF2* you'll see four types of extra material:

- More mathematical techniques, useful for valuing almost all exotic derivatives

- Beyond Black–Scholes, errors in the classical models and new models to account for them, in equity, FX, commodity markets and fixed income

- Descriptions and models for more unusual financial markets

- More advanced numerical methods

PWOQF2 is divided up into three volumes and six parts. Volume 1 contains Mathematical and Financial Foundations, Basic Theory of Derivatives, Risk and Return. Volume 2 contains Exotic Contracts and Path Dependency, Fixed-income Modeling and Derivatives, Credit Risk. Volume 3 contains Advanced Topics, Numerical Methods and Programs.

List of chapters in *Paul Wilmott On Quantitative Finance, second edition* (material not contained in the university edition is in bold).

Volume 1: Mathematical and Financial Foundations; Basic Theory of Derivatives; Risk and Return

Volume 2: Exotic Contracts and Path Dependency; Fixed Income Modeling and Derivatives; Credit Risk

Volume 3: Advanced Topics; Numerical Methods and Programs

bibliography

Essential books for your derivatives library

Some of these books are for daily reference, others are insightful, others are simply 'classics.' Some are pure finance, some mathematics and some in between. They are my own favorites.

Abensur, N 1996 *The New Cranks Recipe Book*. Phoenix Illustrated

Ahmad, R 2008 *Numerical and Computational Methods for Derivative Pricing*. John Wiley & Sons

Alexander, CO 2001 *Market Models*. John Wiley & Sons

Cox, DR & Miller, HD 1965 *The Theory of Stochastic Processes*. Chapman & Hall

Cox, J & Rubinstein, M 1985 *Options Markets*. Prentice Hall

Crank, JC 1989 *Mathematics of Diffusion*. Oxford

Derman, E 2004 *My Life as a Quant*. John Wiley & Sons

Dixit, AK & Pindyck, RS 1994 *Investment Under Uncertainty*. Princeton

Elton, EJ & Gruber, MJ 1995 *Modern Portfolio Theory and Investment Analysis*. John Wiley & Sons

Haug, EG 2007 *The Complete Guide to Option Pricing Formulas*. 2nd edition McGraw-Hill

Hull, J 2005 *Options, Futures and Other Derivative Securities*. 6th edition Prentice Hall

Ingersoll, JE Jr 1987 *Theory of Financial Decision Making*. Rowman & Littlefield

Jäckel, P 2002 *Monte Carlo Methods in Finance*. John Wiley & Sons

Jackson, M & Staunton, M 2001 *Advanced Modelling in Finance Using Excel and VBA*. John Wiley & Sons

Lewis, A 2000 *Option Valuation under Stochastic Volatility*. Finance Press

Malkiel, BG 1990 *A Random Walk Down Wall Street*. Norton

Mandelbrot, B & Hudson, R 2004 *The (Mis)Behaviour of Markets: A Fractal View of Risk, Ruin and Reward*. Profile Books

Markowitz, H 1959 *Portfolio Selection: Efficient diversification of investment*. John Wiley & Sons

Merton, RC 1992 *Continuous-time Finance*. Blackwell

Morton, KW & Mayers, DF 1994 *Numerical Solution of Partial Differential Equations*. Cambridge

Neftci, S 1996 *An Introduction to the Mathematics of Financial Derivatives*. Academic Press

Øksendal, B 1992 *Stochastic Differential Equations*. Springer-Verlag

Osband, K 2002 *Iceberg Risk: An Adventure in Portfolio Theory*. Texere

Partnoy, F 1998 *F.I.A.S.C.O.* Profile Books

Poundstone, W 2005 *Fortune's Formula*. Hill & Wang

Press, WH, Teukolsky, SA, Vetterling, WT & Flannery, BP 1992 *Numerical Recipes in C*. Cambridge

Samuelson, P 1948 *Economics*. McGraw-Hill

Schönbucher, PJ 2003 *Credit Derivatives Pricing Models*. John Wiley & Sons

Schuss, Z 1980 *Theory and Applications of Stochastic Differential Equations*. John Wiley & Sons

Schwager, JD 1990 *Market Wizards*. HarperCollins

Schwager, JD 1992 *New Market Wizards*. HarperCollins

Seuss, Dr 1999 *The Cat in the Hat*. HarperCollins

Sharpe, WF 1985 *Investments*. Prentice Hall

Smith, GD 1985 *Numerical Solution of Partial Differential Equations: Finite Difference Methods*. Oxford

Taleb, NN 1997 *Dynamic Hedging*. John Wiley & Sons

Taleb, NN 2001 *Fooled by Randomness*. Texere

Thorp, EO 1962 *Beat the Dealer*. Vintage

Wilmott, P 2006 *Paul Wilmott On Quantitative Finance, second edition*. John Wiley & Sons

Wilmott, P, Dewynne, J & Howison, SD 1993 *Option Pricing: Mathematical models and computation*. Oxford Financial Press www.oxfordfinancial.co.uk

Wong, S 1981 *Professional Blackjack*. Pi Yee Press www.bj21.com

Other books and key research articles

Abboud, T & Zhang, Y 2004 Accurate early exercise free boundaries for American puts. *Wilmott* magazine 98–102 (January)

Ahmad, R, & Wilmott, P 2005 Which free lunch would you like today, Sir? Delta hedging volatility arbitrage and optimal portfolios. *Wilmott* magazine 64–79 (November)

Ahn, H, Arkell, R, Choe, K, Holstad, E & Wilmott, P 1999 Optimal static vega hedge. MFG Working Paper, Oxford University

Ahn, H, Danilova, A & Swindle, G 2002 Storing arb. *Wilmott* magazine (September)

Ahn, H, Dayal, M, Grannan, E & Swindle, G 1998 Option replication with transaction costs: general diffusion limits. To appear in *Annals of Applied Probability* **8** (3) 676–707

Ahn, H, Hua, P, Penaud, A & Wilmott 1999 Compensating traders and bonus maximization. Wilmott Associates Working Paper

Ahn H, Khadem, V & Wilmott, P 1998 On the utility of risky bonds. MFG Working Paper, Oxford University

Ahn, H, Muni, A & Swindle, G 1997 Misspecified asset price models and robust hedging strategies. *Applied Mathematical Finance* **4** (1) 21–36

Ahn, H, Muni, A & Swindle, G 1998 Optimal hedging strategies for misspecified asset price models. *Applied Mathematical Finance* **6** (3) 197–208

Ahn, H, Penaud & Wilmott, P 1998 Various passport options and their valuation. MFG Working Paper, Oxford University

Ahn, H & Wilmott, P 1998 On trading American options. MFG Working Paper, Oxford University

Ahn, H & Wilmott, P 2003a On exercising American options: the risk of making more money than you expected. *Wilmott* magazine 52–63 (March)

Ahn, H & Wilmott, P 2003b Stochastic volatility and mean-variance analysis. *Wilmott* magazine 84–90 (November)

Alexander, CO 1994 History debunked. *Risk* magazine **7** (12) 59–63

Alexander, CO 1995 Volatility and correlation forecasts. *Derivatives Week* (August)

Alexander, CO 1996a Evaluating the use of Riskmetrics as a risk measurement tool for your operation. *Derivatives: Use Trading and Regulation* **2** (3) 277–285

Alexander, CO 1996b Estimating and forecasting volatility and correlation: methods and applications. *Financial Derivatives and Risk Management* **7** 64–72 (September)

Alexander, CO 1996c Volatility and correlation forecasting. In the *Handbook of Risk Management and Analysis* (C. Alexander, ed) John Wiley & Sons 233–260

Alexander, CO 1997a Splicing methods for generating large covariance matrices. *Derivatives Week* (June)

Alexander, CO 1997b Estimating and forecasting volatility and correlation: methods and applications. In *Risk Management and Financial Derivatives: A Guide to the Mathematics* (S. Das, ed) 337–354

Alexander, CO 1998 *The Handbook of Risk Management and Analysis*. John Wiley & Sons

Alexander, CO & Chibuma, A 1997 Orthogonal GARCH: an empirical validation in equities, foreign exchange and interest rates. Working Paper, Sussex University

Alexander, CO & Giblin, I 1997 Multivariate embedding methods: forecasting high-frequency data in the first INFFC. Proceedings of the First International Nonlinear Financial Forecasting Competition, Finance and Technology Publishing

Alexander, CO & Leigh, C 1997 On the covariance matrices used in VAR models. *Journal of Derivatives* **4** (3) 50–62

Alexander, CO & Johnson, A 1992 Are foreign exchange markets really efficient? *Economics Letters* **40** 449–453

Alexander, CO & Johnson, A 1994 Dynamic Links. *Risk* magazine **7** (2) 56–61

Alexander, CO & Riyait, N 1992 The world according to GARCH. *Risk* magazine **5** (8) 120–125

Alexander, CO & Thillainathan, R 1996 The Asian connections. *Emerging Markets Investor* **2** (6) 42–47

Alexander, CO & Williams, P 1997 Modelling the term structure of kurtosis: a comparison of neural network and GARCH methods. Working Paper, Sussex University

Amram, M & Kulatilaka, N 1999 *Real Options*. Harvard Business School Press

Andreasen, J, Jensen, B & Poulson, R 1998 Eight valuation methods in financial mathematics: the Black–Scholes formula as an example. *Mathematical Scientist* **23** 18–40

Angus, J 1999 A note on pricing Asian derivatives with continuous geometric averaging. *J. Fut. Mkts* **19** (7) 845–858

Apabhai, MZ 1995 Term structure modelling and the valuation of yield curve derivative securities. D.Phil. thesis, Oxford University

Apabhai, MZ, Choe, K, Khennach, F & Wilmott, P 1995 Spot-on modelling. *Risk* magazine, **8** (11) 59–63 (December)

Apabhai, MZ, Georgikopoulos, NI, Hasnip, D, Jamie, RKD, Kim, M & Wilmott, P 1998 A model for the value of a business, some optimisation problems in its operating procedures and the valuation of its debt. *IMA Journal of Applied Mathematics* **60** 1–13

Arditti, FD 1996 *Derivatives*. Harvard Business School Press

Artzner, P, Delbaen, F, Eber, J-M & Heath, D 1997 Thinking coherently. *Risk* magazine **10** (11) 68–72 (November)

Atkinson, C & Al-Ali, B 1997 On an investment-consumption model with transaction costs: an asymptotic analysis. *Applied Mathematical Finance* **4** 109–133

Atkinson, C & Wilmott, P 1993 Properties of moving averages of asset prices. *IMA Journal of Mathematics in Business and Industry* **4** 331–341

Atkinson, C & Wilmott, P 1995 Portfolio management with transaction costs: an asymptotic analysis. *Mathematical Finance* **5** 357–367

Atkinson, C, Pliska, S & Wilmott, P 1997 Portfolio management with transaction costs. *Proceedings of the Royal Society A*

Avellaneda, M, Friedman, C, Holmes, R & Samperi D, 1997 Calibrating volatility surfaces via relative-entropy minimization. *Applied Mathematical Finance* **4** 37–64

Avellaneda, M, Levy, A & Parás, A 1995 Pricing and hedging derivative securities in markets with uncertain volatilities. *Applied Mathematical Finance* **2** 73–88

Avellaneda, M & Parás, A 1994 Dynamic hedging portfolios for derivative securities in the presence of large transaction costs. *Applied Mathematical Finance* **1** 165–194

Avellaneda, M & Parás, A 1996 Managing the volatility risk of derivative securities: the Lagrangian volatility model. *Applied Mathematical Finance* **3** 21–53

Avellaneda, M & Buff, R 1997 Combinatorial implications of nonlinear uncertain volatility models: the case of barrier options. Courant Institute, NYU

Ayache, E, Forsyth, PA & Vetzal, KR 2002 Next generation models for convertible bonds with credit risk. *Wilmott* magazine (December)

Ayache, E, Henrotte, P, Nassar, S & Wang, X 2004 Can anyone solve the smile problem? *Wilmott* magazine 78–97 (January)

Babbs, S 1992 Binomial valuation of lookback options. Midland Montagu Working Paper

Baker, CTH 1977 *The Numerical Treatment of Integral Equations*. Oxford University Press

Bakstein, D & Wilmott, P 1999 Equity dividend models. Wilmott Associates Working Paper

Ball, C & Roma, A 1994 Stochastic volatility option pricing. *Journal of Financial and Quantitative Analysis* **29** 589–607

Banerjee, P 2003 Close-form pricing of plain and partial outside double barrier options. *Wilmott* magazine 46–49 (November)

Barles, G, Burdeau, J, Romano, M & Samsen, N 1995 Critical stock price near expiration. *Mathematical Finance* **5** 77–95

Barone-Adesi, G & Whaley, RE 1986 The valuation of American call options and the expected ex-dividend stock price decline. Journal of Financial Economics **17** 91–111

Barone-Adesi, G & Whaley, RE 1987 Efficient analytic approximation of American option values. Journal of Finance **41** 301–320

Barrett, JW, Moore, G & Wilmott, P 1992 Inelegant efficiency. *Risk* magazine **5** (9) 82–84

Beletski, T & Korn, R 2005 Optimal investment with inflation-linked products. Working paper, Universität Kaiserslautern

Bergman, YZ, 1985 Pricing path contingent claims. *Research in Finance* **5** 229–241

Bergman, YZ, 1995 Option pricing with differential interest rates. *Review of Financial Studies* **8** 475–500

Bernstein PL 1998 *Against the Gods*. John Wiley & Sons

Berrahoui, M 2004 Pricing CMS spread options and digital CMS spread options with a smile. *Wilmott* magazine 63–69 (May)

Bhamra, HS 2000 Imitation in financial markets. *Int. J. Theor. Appl. Fin.* **3** 473–478

Black F 1976 The pricing of commodity contracts. *Journal of Financial Economics* **3** 167–179

Black, F & Cox, J 1976 Valuing corporate securities: some effects of bond indenture provisions. *Journal of Finance* **31** 351–367

Black, F, Derman, E & Toy, W 1990 A one-factor model of interest rates and its application to Treasury bond options. *Financial Analysts Journal* **46** 33–39

Black, F & Scholes, M 1973 The pricing of options and corporate liabilities. *Journal of Political Economy* **81** 637–659

Blauer, I & Wilmott, P 1998 Risk of default in Latin American Brady bonds. *Net Exposure* **5** www.netexposure.co.uk

Bloch, D 1995 One-factor inflation rate modelling. M.Phil. dissertation, Oxford University

Bollerslev, T 1986 Generalized Autoregressive Conditional Heteroskedasticity. *Journal of Econometrics* **31** 307–327

Bouchaud, J-P, Potters, M & Cornalba, L 2002 Option pricing and hedging with temporal correlations. *Int. J. Theor. Appl. Fin.* **5** 1–14

Bowie, J & Carr, P 1994 Static simplicity. *Risk* magazine **7** 45–49

Boyle, P 1977 Options: a Monte Carlo approach. *Journal of Financial Economics* **4** 323–338

Boyle, P 1991 Mulit-asset path-dependent options. FORC conference, Warwick

Boyle, P, Broadie, M & Glasserman, P 1995 Monte Carlo methods for security pricing. Working Paper, University of Waterloo

Boyle, P & Emanuel, D 1980 Discretely adjusted option hedges. *Journal of Financial Economics* **8** 259–282

Boyle, P, Evnine, J & Gibbs, S 1989 Numerical evaluation of multivariate contingent claims. *Review of Financial Studies* **2** 241–250

Boyle, P & Tse, Y 1990 An algorithm for computing values of options on the maximum or minimum of several assets. *Journal of Financial and Quantitative Analysis* **25** 215–227

Boyle, P & Vorst, T 1992 Option replication in discrete time with transaction costs. *Journal of Finance* **47** 271

Brace, A, Gatarek, D & Musiela, M 1997 The market model of interest rate dynamics. *Mathematical Finance* **7** 127–154

Brandt, M & Jones, C 2002 Volatility forecasting with range-based EGARCH models. Working Paper, Fuqua

Brennan, M & Schwartz, E 1977 Convertible bonds: valuation and optimal strategies for call and conversion. *Journal of Finance* **32** 1699–1715

Brennan, M & Schwartz, E 1978 Finite-difference methods and jump processes arising in the pricing of contingent claims: a synthesis. *Journal of Financial and Quantitative Analysts* **13** 462–474

Brennan, M & Schwartz, E 1982 An equilibrium model of bond pricing and a test of market efficiency. *Journal of Financial and Quantitative Analysis* **17** 301–329

Brennan, M & Schwartz, E 1983 Alternative methods for valuing debt options. *Finance* **4** 119–138

Brenner, M & Subrahmanyam, MG 1994 A simple approach to option valuation and hedging in the Black–Scholes model. *Financial Analysts Journal* 25–28

Brooks, M 1967 *The Producers*. MGM

Briys, EL, Mai, HM, Bellalah, MB & de Varenne, F 1998 *Options, Futures and Exotic Derivatives*. John Wiley & Sons

Carr, P 1994 European put-call symmetry. Cornell University Working Paper

Carr, P 1995 Two extensions to barrier option pricing. *Applied Mathematical Finance* **2** 173–209

Carr, P 2005 FAQs in option pricing theory. *J. Derivatives* (Forthcoming)

Carr, P & Chou, A 1997 Breaking barriers. *Risk* magazine **10** 139–144

Carr, P, Ellis, K & Gupta, V 1998 Static hedging of exotic options. *Journal of Finance* 1165–1190

Carr, P & Madan, D 1999 Introducing the covariance swap. *Risk* magazine 47–51 (February)

Carr, P & Verma, A 2005 Potential problems in market models of implied volatility. Working Paper

Carslaw, HS & Jaeger, JC 1989 *Conduction of Heat in Solids*. Oxford

Chan, K, Karolyi, A, Longstaff, F & Sanders, A 1992 An empirical comparison of alternative models of the short-term interest rate. *Journal of Finance* **47** 1209–1227

Chance, D 1990 Default risk and the duration of zero-coupon bonds. *Journal of Finance* **45** (1) 265–274

Cherubini, U, Luciano, E & Vecchiato, W 2004 *Copula Methods in Finance*. John Wiley & Sons

Chesney, M, Cornwall, J, Jeanblanc-Picqué, M, Kentwell, G & Yor, M 1997 Parisian pricing. *Risk* magazine **1** (1) 77–80

Chew, L 1996 *Managing Derivative Risk: The use and abuse of leverage*. John Wiley & Sons

Clark, E 2002 Measuring country risk as implied volatility. *Wilmott* magazine (September)

Connolly, KB 1997 *Buying and Selling Volatility*. John Wiley & Sons

Conze, A & Viswanathan 1991 Path-dependent options — the case of lookback options. *Journal of Finance* **46** 1893–1907

Cooper, I & Martin, M 1996 Default risk and derivative products. *Applied Mathematical Finance* **3** 53–74

Copeland, T, Koller, T & Murrin, J 1990 *Valuation: Measuring and managing the value of companies*. John Wiley & Sons

Cox, J, Ingersoll, J & Ross, S 1980 An analysis of variable loan contracts. *Journal of Finance* **35** 389–403

Cox, J, Ingersoll, J & Ross, S 1981 The relationship between forward prices and futures prices. *Journal of Financial Economics* **9** 321–346

Cox, J, Ingersoll, J & Ross, S 1985 A theory of the term structure of interest rates. *Econometrica* **53** 385–467

Cox, JC, Ross, S & Rubinstein M 1979 Option pricing: a simplified approach. *Journal of Financial* Economics **7** 229–263

Crank, J & Nicolson, P 1947 A practical method for numerical evaluation of solutions of partial differential equations of the heat conduction type. *Proceedings of the Cambridge Philosophical Society* **43** 50–67

Curran, M 1992 Beyond average intelligence. *Risk* magazine **60** (October)

Das, S 1994 *Swaps and Financial Derivatives*. IFR

Das, S 1995 Credit risk derivatives. *Journal of Derivatives* **2** 7–23

Das, S & Tufano, P 1994 Pricing credit-sensitive debt when interest rates, credit ratings and credit spreads are stochastic. Working Paper, Harvard Business School Press

Davidson, AS & Herskovitz, MD 1996 *The Mortgage-backed Securities Handbook*. McGraw-Hill

Davis, MHA & Norman, AR 1990 Portfolio selection with transaction costs. *Mathematics of Operations Research* **15** 676–713

Davis, MHA, Panas, VG & Zariphopoulou, T 1993 European option pricing with transaction costs. *SIAM Journal of Control and Optimization* **31** 470–493

Demeterfi, K, Derman, E, Kamal, M & Zou, J 1999 Everything you ever wanted to know about volatility swaps. Goldman Sachs Quantitative Strategies Research Notes

Derman, E, Ergener, D & Kani, I 1997 Static options replication. In *Frontiers in Derivatives*. (Konishi, A & Dattatreya, RE eds) Irwin

Derman, E & Kani, I 1994 Riding on a smile. *Risk* magazine **7** (2) 32–39 (February)

Derman, E & Kani, I 1997 Stochastic implied trees: arbitrage pricing with stochastic term and strike structure of volatility. Goldman Sachs Quantitative Strategies Technical Notes April 1997

Derman, E & Zou, J 1997 Predicting the response of implied volatility to large index moves. Goldman Sachs Quantitative Strategies Technical Notes November 1997

Derman, E 1999 Regimes of volatility. Goldman Sachs Quantitative Strategies Technical Notes January 1999

Dewynne, JN, Erhlichman, S & Wilmott, P 1998 A simple volatility surface parametrization. MFG Working Paper, Oxford University

Dewynne, JN, Whalley, AE & Wilmott, P 1994 Path-dependent options and transaction costs. *Philosophical Transactions of the Royal Society A* **347** 517–529

Dewynne, JN, Whalley, AE & Wilmott, P 1995 Mathematical models and partial differential equations in finance. In *Quantitative Methods, Super Computers and AI in Finance* (S. Zenios ed) 95–124

Dewynne, JN & Wilmott, P 1993 Partial to the exotic. *Risk* magazine **6** (3) 38–46

Dewynne, JN & Wilmott, P 1994a Exotic financial options. *Proceedings of the 7th European Conference on Mathematics in Industry* 389–397

Dewynne, JN & Wilmott, P 1994b Modelling and numerical valuation of lookback options. MFG Working Paper, Oxford University

Dewynne, JN & Wilmott, P 1994c Untitled. MFG Working Paper, Oxford University

Dewynne, JN & Wilmott, P 1995a A note on American options with varying exercise price. *Journal of the Australian Mathematical Society* **37** 45–57

Dewynne, JN & Wilmott, P 1995b A note on average-rate options with discrete sampling. *SIAM Journal of Applied Mathematics* **55** 267–276

Dewynne, JN & Wilmott, P 1995c Asian options as linear complementarity problems: analysis and finite-difference solutions. *Advances in Futures and Options Research* **8** 145–177

Dewynne, JN & Wilmott, P 1996 Exotic options: mathematical models and computation. In *Frontiers in Derivatives* (Konishi and Dattatreya eds) 145–182

Dothan, MU 1978 On the term structure of interest rates. *Journal of Financial Economics* **6** 59–69

Duffee, G 1995 The variation of default risk with treasury yields. Working Paper, Federal Reserve Board, Washington

Duffie, D 1992 *Dynamic Asset Pricing Theory*. Princeton

Duffie, D & Harrison, JM 1992 Arbitrage pricing of Russian options and perpetual lookback options. *Annals of Applied Probability* **3** 641–651

Duffie, D, Ma, J, Yong, J 1994 Black's consol rate conjecture. Working Paper, Stanford

Duffie, D & Singleton, K 1994a Modeling term structures of defaultable bonds. Working Paper, Stanford

Duffie, D & Singleton, K 1994b An econometric model of the term structure of interest rate swap yields. Working Paper, Stanford

Duffy, D 2004 A critique of the Crank–Nicolson scheme. *Wilmott* magazine 68–77 (July)

Dumas, B, Fleming, J & Whaley, RE 1998 Implied volatility functions: empirical tests. *Journal of Finance* **53** (6) 2059–2106

Dunbar, N 1998 Meriwether's meltdown. *Risk* magazine **10** 32–36

Dupire, B 1993 Pricing and hedging with smiles. *Proc AFFI Conf*, La Baule (June)

Dupire, B 1994 Pricing with a smile. *Risk* magazine **7** (1) 18–20 (January)

Dupire, B 2005 *Volatility Derivatives Modeling.* Bloomberg NY

Eberlein, E & Keller, U 1995 Hyperbolic distributions in finance. *Bernoulli* **1** 281–299

El Karoui, Jeanblanc-Picqué & Viswanathan 1991 Bounds for options. *Lecture notes in Control and Information Sciences* **117** 224–237, Springer-Verlag

Embrechts, P, Klüppelberg, C & Mikosch, T 1997 *Modelling Extremal Events*. Springer-Verlag

Engle, R 1982 Autoregressive conditional heteroscedasticity, with estimates of the variance of United Kingdom inflation. *Econometrica* **50** 987–1007

Engle, R & Bollerslev, T 1987 Modelling the persistence of conditional variances. *Econometric Reviews* **5** 1–50

Engle, R & Granger, C 1987 Cointegration and error correction: representation, estimation and testing. *Econometrica* **55** 251–276

Engle, R 1995 (ed) *ARCH: Selected Readings*. Oxford

Engle, R & Mezrich, J 1996 GARCH for groups. *Risk* magazine **9** (8) 36–40

Epstein, D, Mayor, N, Schönbucher, PJ, Whalley, AE & Wilmott, P 1997a The valuation of a firm advertising optimally. MFG Working Paper, Oxford University

Epstein, D, Mayor, N, Schönbucher, PJ, Whalley, AE & Wilmott, P 1997b The value of market research when a firm is learning: option pricing and optimal filtering. MFG Working Paper, Oxford University

Epstein, D & Wilmott, P 1997 Yield envelopes. *Net Exposure* **2** (August) www.netexposure.co.uk

Epstein, D & Wilmott, P 1998 A new model for interest rates. *Int. J. Theor. and Appl. Fin.* **1** 195–226

Epstein, D & Wilmott, P 1999 A nonlinear non-probabilistic spot interest rate model. *Phil. Trans.* A **357** 2109–2117

Fabozzi, FJ 1996 *Bond Markets, Analysis and Strategies*. Prentice Hall

Fabozzi, FJ & Kipnis, GM (eds) 1984 *Stock Index Futures*. Dow Jones-Irwin

Fama, E 1965 The behaviour of stock prices. *Journal of Business* **38** 34–105

Farmer, JD & Joshi, S 2000 The price dynamics of common trading strategies. SFI Working Paper 00-12-069

Farrell, JL Jr 1997 *Portfolio Management*. McGraw-Hill

Finger, C 2004 Issues in pricing of synthetic CDOs. RiskMetrics Working Paper

Fitt, AD, Dewynne, JN & Wilmott, P 1994 An integral equation for the value of a stop-loss option. *Proceedings of the 7th European Conference on Mathematics in Industry* 399–405

Fong, G & Vasicek, O 1991 Interest rate volatility as a stochastic factor. Working Paper

Fouque, JP, Papanicolaou, G & Sircar, KR 1998a Asymptotics of a two-scale stochastic volatility model. In *Equations auk derives particles of applications*, Articles decides a Jacques-Louis Lions. Gauthier-Villers, Paris.

Fouque, JP, Papanicolaou, G & Sircar, KR 1998b Financial modeling in a fast mean-reverting stochastic volatility environment. *Asia-Pacific Finanacial Markets* **6** 37–48

Fouque, JP, Papanicolaou, G & Sircar, KR 2000 Mean-reverting stochastic volatility. *International Journal of Theoretical and Applied Finance,* **3** 101–142

Fouque, JP, Papanicolaou, G, Sircar, KR & Solna, K 2004 Timing the smile. *Wilmott* magazine 59–65 (March)

Frey, R & Stremme, A 1995 Market volatility and feedback effects from dynamic hedging. Working Paper, Bonn

Gabillon, J 1995 Analyzing the forward curve. In *Managing Energy Risk*. Financial Engineering, London

Garman, M 1976 A general theory of asset valuation under diffusion state processes, Technical Report 50, Center for Research in Management Science, Berkeley

Garman, M & Klass, M 1980 On the estimation of security price volatilities from historical data. *Journal of Business* **53** 67–78

Garman, MB & Kohlhagen, SW 1983 Foreign currency option values. *Journal of International Money and Finance* **2** 231–237

Geman, H & Yor, M 1993 Bessel processes, Asian options and perpetuities. *Mathematical Finance* **3** 349–375

Gemmill, G 1992 *Options Pricing*. McGraw-Hill

Gerald, CF & Wheatley, PO 1992 *Applied Numerical Analysis*. Addison Wesley

Geske, R 1977 The valuation of corporate liabilities as compound options. *Journal of Financial and Quantitative Analysis* **12** 541–552

Geske, R 1978 Pricing of options with stochastic dividend yield. *Journal of Finance* **33** 617–625

Geske, R 1979 The valuation of compound options. *Journal of Financial Economics* **7** 63–81

Glasserman, P 2003 *Monte Carlo Methods in Financial Engineering*. Springer Verlag

Goldman, MB, Sosin, H & Gatto, M 1979 Path dependent options: buy at the low, sell at the high. *Journal of Finance* **34** 1111–1128

Gould, SJ 1985 The median is not the message. *Discover* 40–42 (June)

Grindrod, P 1991 *Patterns and Waves: The theory and applications of reaction-diffusion equations*. Oxford

Haber, R, Schönbucher, PJ & Wilmott, P 1997 Parisian options. MFG Working Paper, Oxford University

Hagan, P & Woodward, DE 1999 Equivalent Black volatilities. *Applied Mathematical Finance* **6** (3) 147–157

Hagan, P, Kumar, D, Lesniewski, A & Woodward, D 2002 Managing smile risk. *Wilmott* magazine (September)

Hagan, P 2002 Adjusters: turning good prices into great prices. *Wilmott* magazine (December)

Hagan, P 2003 Convexity conundrums: pricing CMS swaps, caps and floors. *Wilmott* magazine (March)

d'Halluin, Y, Pooley, D & Forsyth, P 2004 No fear of jumps. *Wilmott* magazine 62–70 (January)

Hamermesh, DS & Soss, NM 1974 An economic theory of suicide. *Journal of Political Economy* **82** 83–90

Hamilton, JD 1994 *Time Series Analysis*. Princeton

Harrison, JM & Kreps, D 1979 Martingales and arbitrage in multiperiod securities markets. *Journal of Economic Theory* **20** 381–408

Harrison, JM & Pliska, SR 1981 Martingales and stochastic integrals in the theory of continuous trading. *Stochastic Processes and their Applications* **11** 215–260

Haselgrove, CB 1961 A method for numerical integration. *Mathematics of Computation* **15** 323–337

Haug, E 2003 Know your weapon. *Wilmott* magazine (May and July)

Haug, E & Haug, J 2002 Knock-in/out Margrabe. *Wilmott* magazine (December)

Haug, E, Haug, J & Margrabe, W 2003 Asian pyramid power. *Wilmott* magazine (March)

Heath, D, Jarrow, R & Morton, A 1992 Bond pricing and the term structure of interest rates: a new methodology. *Econometrica* **60** 77–105

Hendry, DF 1995 *Dynamic Econometrics*. Oxford

Henrard, M 2001 Parameter risk in the Black and Scholes model. Working Paper

Henrotte, P 1993 Transaction costs and duplication strategies. Working Paper, Stanford University

Heston, S 1993 A closed-form solution for options with stochastic volatility with application to bond and currency options. *Review of Financial Studies* **6** 327–343

Heynen, RC & Kat, HM 1995 Lookback options with discrete and partial monitoring of the underlying price. *Applied Mathematical Finance* **2** 273–284

Hilliard, JE & Reis, J 1998 Valuation of commodity futures and options under stochastic convenience yields, interest rates, and jump diffusions in the spot. *Journal of Financial and Quantitative Analysis* **33** 61–86

Ho, T & Lee, S 1986 Term structure movements and pricing interest rate contingent claims. *Journal of Finance* **42** 1129–1142

Hodges, SD & Neuberger, A 1989 Optimal replication of contingent claims under transaction costs. *The Review of Futures Markets* **8** 222–239

Hogan, M 1993 Problems in certain two-factor term structure models. *Annals of Applied Probability* **3** (2) 576–581

Hoggard, T, Whalley, AE & Wilmott, P 1994 Hedging option portfolios in the presence of transaction costs. *Advances in Futures and Options Research* **7** 21–35

Hua, P 1997 Modelling stock market crashes. Dissertation, Imperial College, London

Hua, P & Wilmott, P 1997 Crash courses. *Risk* magazine **10** (6) 64–67 (June)

Hughston, LP 1998 Inflation derivatives. Unpublished Merrill Lynch and King's College London Working Paper

Hull, JC & White, A 1987 The pricing of options on assets with stochastic volatilities. *Journal of Finance* **42** 281–300

Hull, JC & White, A 1988 An analysis of the bias in option pricing caused by a stochastic volatility. *Advances in Futures and Options Research* **3** 29–61

Hull, JC & White, A 1990a Pricing interest rate derivative securities. *Review of Financial Studies* **3** 573–592

Hull, JC & White, A 1990b Valuing derivative securities using the finite difference method. *Journal of Financial and Quantitative Analysis* **25** 87–100

Hull, JC & White, A 1996 Finding the keys. In *Over the Rainbow* (R Jarrow ed) *Risk* magazine

Hyer, T, Lipton-Lifschitz, A & Pugachevsky, D 1997 Passport to success. *Risk* magazine **10** (9) 127–132

Jackwerth, JC & Rubinstein, M 1996 Recovering probability distributions from contemporaneous security prices. *Journal of Finance* **51** 1611–1631

Jäckel, P 2003 Mind the cap. *Wilmott* magazine (September)

Jäckel, P & Kawai, A 2005 The future is convex. *Wilmott* magazine 44–55 (January)

Jamshidian, F 1989 An exact bond option formula. *Journal of Finance* **44** 205–209

Jamshidian, F 1990 Bond and option evaluation in the gaussian interest rate model. Working Paper, Merrill Lynch Capital Markets

Jamshidian, F 1991 Forward induction and construction of yield curve diffusion models. *Journal of Fixed Income*, 62–74 (June)

Jamshidian, F 1994 Hedging, quantos, differential swaps and ratios. *Applied Mathematical Finance* **1** 1–20

Jamshidian, F 1995 A simple class of square-root interest-rate models. *Applied Mathematical Finance* **2** 61–72

Jamshidian, F 1996a Sorting out swaptions. *Risk* magazine **9**

Jamshidian, F 1996b Bonds, futures and options evaluation in the quadratic interest rate model. *Applied Mathematical Finance* **3** 93–115

Jamshidian, F 1997 LIBOR and swap market models and measures. *Finance and Stochastics* **1** 293–330

Jarrow, R, Lando, D & Turnbull, S 1997 A Markov model for the term structure of credit spreads. *Review of Financial Studies* **10** 481–523

Jarrow, R & Turnbull, S 1990 Pricing options on financial securities subject to credit risk. Working Paper, Cornell University

Jarrow, R & Turnbull, S 1995 Pricing derivatives on securities subject to credit risk. *Journal of Finance* **50** 53–85

Javaheri, A 2005 *Inside Volatility Aribtrage*. John Wiley & Sons

Jefferies, S 1999 Hedging equity and interest rate derivatives in the presence of transaction costs. M.Sc. dissertation, Oxford

Johnson, HE 1983 An analytical approximation to the American put price. *Journal of Financial and Quantitative Analysis* **18** 141–148

Johnson, HE 1987 Options on the maximum or minimum of several assets. *Journal of Financial and Quantitative Analysis* **22** 277–283

Johnson, LW & Riess, RD 1982 *Numerical Analysis*. Addison-Wesley

Johnson, NF, Hui, PM & Lo, TS 1999 Self-organized segregation of traders within a market. *Phil. Trans. A* **357** 2013–2018

Jordan, DW & Smith, P 1977 *Nonlinear Ordinary Differential Equations*. Oxford

Jorion, P 1997 *Value at Risk*. Irwin

Jorion, P 1999 Risk management lessons from Long-Term Capital Management. Working Paper, University of California at Irvine

Joshi, M 2003 *The Concepts and Practice of Mathematical Finance*. CUP

Kaplanis, C 1986 Options, taxes and ex-dividend day behaviour. *Journal of Finance* **41** 411–424

Kelly, FP, Howison, SD & Wilmott, P (eds) 1995 *Mathematical Models in Finance*. Chapman and Hall

Kelly, JL 1956 A new interpretation of information rate. *Bell Systems Tech. J.* **35** 917–926

Kemna, AGZ & Vorst, ACF 1990 A pricing method for options based upon average asset values. *Journal of Banking and Finance* **14** 113–129 (March)

Khasminskii, RZ & Yin, G 1996 Asymptotic series for singularly perturbed Kolmogorov–Fokker–Planck equations. *SIAM J. Appl. Math.* **56** 1766–1793

Kim, M 1995 Modelling company mergers and takeovers. M.Sc. thesis, Imperial College, London

Klein, A 2002 Determining the future of mortality. *Contingencies* 39–43 (September/October)

Klugman, R 1992 Pricing interest rate derivative securities. M.Phil. thesis, Oxford University

Klugman, R & Wilmott, P 1994 A class of one-factor interest rate models. *Proceedings of the 7th European Conference on Mathematics in Industry* 419–426

Kolman, J 1999 LTCM speaks. *Derivatives Strategy* 12–17 (April)

Korn, R & Wilmott, P 1996 Room for a view. MFG Working Paper, Oxford University

Korn, R & Wilmott, P 1998 A general framework for hedging and speculating with options. *Int. J. Theor. Appl. Fin.* **1** 507–522

Korn, R & Wilmott, P 2002 Optimal portfolios under the threat of a crash. *Int. J. Th. Appl. Fin.* **5** 171-188

Korn, R 1997 *Optimal Portfolios*. World Scientific

Korn, R 2003 Worst-case investment with applications for banks and insurance companies. In: Conference Proceedings, ERC-Conference, METU Ankara

Korn, R & Menkens, O 2004 On worst-case investment with applications for banks and insurance companies. In: *Interacting Stochastic Systems* (Deuschel, JD & Greven, A eds) Springer 397–408

Korn, R & Menkens, O 2005 Worst-case scenario portfolio optimization: a new stochastic control approach. *Mathematical Methods of Operations Research* **62** (1) 123–140

Korn, R 2005 Worst-case scenario investment for insurers. *Insurance Mathematics and Economics* **36** 1–11

Krekel, M 2003 The pricing of Asian options on average spot with average strike. *Wilmott* magazine (July)

Krekel, M, de Kock, J, Korn, R & Man T-K, 2004 An analysis of pricing methods for basket options. *Wilmott* magazine 82–89

Kruske, RA & Keller, JB 1998 Optimal exercise boundary for an American put option. *Applied Mathematical Finance* **5** (2) 107–116

Kyprianou, A, Schoutens, W & Wilmott P (eds) 2005 *Exotic Options and Advanced Levy Models.* John Wiley & Sons

Lacoste, V 1996 Wiener chaos: a new approach to option pricing. *Mathematical Finance* **6** 197–213

Lando, D 1994a Three essays on contingent claims pricing. Ph.D. thesis, Graduate School of Management, Cornell University

Lando, D 1994b On Cox processes and credit risky bonds. Working Paper, Institute of Mathematical Statistics, University of Copenhagen

Lawrence, D 1996 *Measuring and Managing Derivative Market Risk*. International Thompson Business Press

Leeson, N 1997 *Rogue Trader*. Warner

Leland, HE 1985 Option pricing and replication with transaction costs. *Journal of Finance* **40** 1283–1301

Levy, E 1990 Asian arithmetic. *Risk* magazine **3** (5) 7–8 (May)

Levy, E 1992 Pricing European average rate currency options. *Journal of International Money and Finance* **14** 474–491

Lewicki, P & Avellaneda, M 1996 Pricing interest rate contingent claims in markets with uncertain volatilities. CIMS Preprint

Lewis, A 2002a Asian connections. *Wilmott* magazine 57–63 (September)

Lewis, A 2002b Fear of jumps. *Wilmott* magazine 60–67 (December)

Lewis, A 2003a Perpetual American options made easy. *Wilmott* magazine 56–62 (January)

Lewis, A 2003b American options under jump diffusions: an introduction. *Wilmott* magazine 46–51 (March)

Lewis, A 2003c Barrier options under jump diffusions: the analytic theory. *Wilmott* magazine 60–66(May) and 57–60 (July)

Lewis, A 2003d American-style options with one-sided jumps. *Wilmott* magazine 42–45 (November)

Lewis, A, Haug, J & Haug, E 2003 Back to basics: a new approach to the discrete dividend problem. *Wilmott* magazine 46–47 (September)

Lewis, A 2004a Volatility jump diffusions. *Wilmott* magazine 46–53 (January)

Lewis, A 2004b Double barrier options with jump–a simple universal algorithm. *Wilmott* magazine 34–37 (March)

Lewis, A 2004c Diffusions, jumps and the distribution of the maximum. *Wilmott* magazine 48–53 (May)

Lewis, A 2004d Asian option pricing under jump diffusions. *Wilmott* magazine 52–55 (July)

Lewis, M 1989 *Liar's Poker*. Penguin

Li, D 2000 On default correlation: a copula function approach. RiskMetrics Working Paper

Lillo, F, Mantegna, R, Bouchaud, J-P & Potters, M 2002 Introducing variety in risk management. *Wilmott* magazine (December)

Litterman, R & Iben, T 1991 Corporate bond valuation and the term structure of credit spreads. *Financial Analysts Journal* 52–64 (Spring)

Longstaff, FA & Schwartz, ES 1992 A two-factor interest rate model and contingent claims valuation. *Journal of Fixed Income* **3** 16–23

Longstaff, FA & Schwartz, ES 1994 A simple approach to valuing risky fixed and floating rate debt. Working Paper, Anderson Graduate School of Management, University of California

Longstaff, FA & Schwartz, ES 2001 Valuing American options by simulation: a simple least-squares approach. *Rev. Fin. Studies* **14** 113–147

Lucic, V 2003 Forward start options in stochastic volatility model. *Wilmott* magazine (September)

Lyons, TJ 1995 Uncertain volatility and the risk-free synthesis of derivatives. *Applied Mathematical Finance* **2** 117–133

Macaulay, F 1938 Some theoretical problems suggested by movement of interest rates, bond yields and stock prices since 1856. National Bureau of Economic Research, New York

Madan, D & Seneta, E 1990 The variance gamma model for share price returns. *J. Bus.* **63** 511–524

Madan, D, Carr, P & Change, E 1998 The variance gamma process and option pricing. *Euro. Fin. Rev.* **2** 79–105

Madan, DB & Unal, H 1994 Pricing the risks of default. Working Paper, College of Business and Management, University of Maryland

Majd, S & Pindyck, RS 1987 Time to build, option value, and investment decisions. *Journal of Financial Economics* **18** 7–27

Mandelbrot, B 1963 The variation of certain speculative prices. *Journal of Business* **36** 394–419

Margrabe, W 1978 The value of an option to exchange one asset for another. *Journal of Finance* **33** 177–186

Matten, C 1996 *Managing Bank Capital*. John Wiley & Sons

McDonald, R & Siegel, D 1986 The value of waiting to invest. *Quarterly Journal of Economics* **101** 707–728

McKee, S, Wall, D & Wilson, S 1996 An alternating direction implicit scheme for parabolic equations with mixed derivative and convective terms. *J. Comp. Phys.* **126** 64–76

McMillan, LG 1996 *McMillan on Options*. John Wiley & Sons

McNeil, A 1998 On extremes and crashes.*Risk* magazine (January)

Mercurio, F & Vorst, TCF 1996 Option pricing with hedging at fixed trading dates. *Applied Mathematical Finance* **3** 135–158

Mercurio, F 2004 Pricing inflation-indexed derivatives. Working Paper

Merton, RC 1973 Theory of rational option pricing. *Bell Journal of Economics and Management Science* **4** 141–183

Merton, RC 1974 On the pricing of corporate debt: the risk structure of interest rates. *Journal of Finance* **29** 449–470

Merton, RC 1976 Option pricing when underlying stock returns are discontinuous. Journal of Financial Economics **3** 125–144

Merton, RC 1995 Influence of mathematical models in finance on practice: past, present and future. In *Mathematical Models in Finance* (Howison, Kelly & Wilmott ed)

Meyers, TA 1994 *The Technical Analysis Course*. Probus

Mikhailov, S & Nögel, U 2003 Heston's stochastic volatility model: implementation, calibration and some extensions. *Wilmott* magazine (July)

Miller, M 1997 *Merton Miller on Derivatives*. John Wiley & Sons

Miller, M & Modigliani, F 1961 Dividend policy, growth and the valuation of shares. *Journal of Business* **34** 411–433

Miron, P & Swannell, P 1991 *Pricing and Hedging Swaps*. Euromoney Publications

Mitchell, AR & Griffiths, DF 1980 *The Finite Difference Method in Partial Differential Equations*. John Wiley & Sons

Mohamed, B 1994 Simulation of transaction costs and optimal rehedging. *Applied Mathematical Finance* **1** 49–62

Morton, A & Pliska, SR 1995 Optimal portfolio management with fixed transaction costs. *Mathematical Finance* **5** 337–356

Murphy, G 1995 Generalized methods of moments estimation of the short process in the UK. Bank of England Working Paper

Murray, J 1989 *Mathematical Biology*. Springer-Verlag

Naik, V 1993 Option valuation and hedging strategies with jumps in the volatility of asset returns.*Journal of Finance* **48** 1969–1984

Natenberg, S 1994 *Option Volatility and Pricing*. McGraw-Hill

Nelken, I 1999 *Implementing Credit Derivatives*. McGraw-Hill

Nelsen, R 1999 *An Introduction to Copulas*. Springer-Verlag

Nelson, D 1990 Arch models as diffusion approximations. *Journal of Econometrics* **45** 7–38

Neuberger, A 1994 Option replication with transaction costs: an exact solution for the pure jump process. *Advances in Futures and Options Research* **7** 1–20

Neuberger, A 1994 The log contract: a new instrument to hedge volatility. *Journal of Portfolio Management* **20** 74–80

Niederreiter, H 1992 *Random Number Generation and Quasi-Monte Carlo Methods*. SIAM

Nielson, JA & Sandmann, K 1996 The pricing of Asian options under stochastic interest rates. *Applied Mathematical Finance* **3** 209–236

Ninomiya, S & Tezuka, S 1996 Toward real-time pricing of complex financial derivatives. *Applied Mathematical Finance* **3** 1–20

Nyborg, KG 1996 The use and pricing of convertible bonds. *Applied Mathematical Finance* **3** 167–190

O'Hara, M 1995 *Market Microstructure Theory*. Blackwell

Options Institute 1995 *Options: Essential Concepts and Trading Strategies*. Irwin

Osband, K 2004 Support and resistance for support/resistance. *Wilmott* magazine 58–61 (November)

Ouachani, N & Zhang, Y 2004 Pricing cross-currency convertible bonds with pde. *Wilmott* magazine 54–61 (January)

Owen, G 1995 *Game Theory*. Academic Press

Oztukel, A 1996 Uncertain parameter models. M.Sc. dissertation, Oxford University

Oztukel, A & Wilmott, P 1998 Uncertain parameters, an empirical stochastic volatility model and confidence limits. *International Journal of Theoretical and Applied Finance* **1** 175–189

Parkinson, M 1980 The extreme value method for estimating the variance of the rate of return. *Journal of Business* **53** (1) 61–65

Paskov 1996 New methodologies for valuing derivatives. In *Mathematics of Derivative Securities* (Pliska, SR and Dempster, M eds)

Paskov, SH & Traub, JF 1995 Faster valuation of financial derivatives. *Journal of Portfolio Management*.113–120 (Fall)

Pearson, N & Sun, T-S 1989 A test of the Cox, Ingersoll, Ross model of the term structure of interest rates using the method of moments. Sloan School of Management, MIT

Penaud, A 2004 Fast valuation of a portfolio of barrier options under Merton's jump diffusion hypothesis. *Wilmott* magazine 88–91 (September)

Penaud, A, Wilmott, P & Ahn, H 1998 Exotic passport options. MFG Working Paper, Oxford University

Penaud, A & Selfe, J 2003 First to default swaps. *Wilmott* magazine (January)

Peters, EE 1991 *Chaos and Order in the Capital Markets*. John Wiley & Sons

Peters, EE 1994 *Fractal Market Analysis*. John Wiley & Sons

Pilopović, D 1998 *Energy Risk*. McGraw-Hill

Porter, DP & Smith, VL 1994 Stock market bubbles in the laboratory. *Applied Mathematical Finance* **1** 111–128

Prast, H 2000a Herding and financial panics: a role for cognitive psychology? De Nederlandische Bank report

Prast, H 2000b A cognitive dissonance model of financial market behaviour. De Nederlandische Bank report

Ramamurtie, S, Prezas, A & Ulman, S 1993 Consistency and identification problems in models of term structure of interest rates. Working Paper, Georgia State University

Rasmussen, H & Wilmott, P 2002 Asymptotic analysis of stochastic volatility models. In *New Directions in Mathematical Finance*. (Wilmott, P & Rasmussen, H eds) John Wiley & Sons

Ravanelli, C 1999 M.Sc. dissertation, Universita degli Studi di Milano

Rebonato, R 1996 *Interest-rate Option Models*. John Wiley & Sons

Rebonato, R 2004 *Volatility and Correlation*. John Wiley & Sons

Reiner, E & Rubinstein, M 1991 Breaking down the barriers. *Risk* magazine **4** (8) 28–35

Reuters 1999 *Introduction to Technical Analysis* (Reuters Financial Training Series). John Wiley & Sons

Rich, D & Chance, D 1993 An alternative approach to the pricing of options on multiple assets. *Journal of Financial Engineering* **2** 271–285

Richtmyer, RD & Morton, KW 1976 *Difference Methods for Initial-value Problems*. John Wiley & Sons

Roache PJ 1982 *Computational Fluid Dynamics*. Hermosa

Rogers, LCG & Satchell, SE 1991 Estimating variance from high, low and closing prices. *Annals of Applied Probability* **1** 504–512

Roll, R 1977 An analytical formula for unprotected American call options on stocks with known dividends. *Journal of Financial Economics* **5** 251–258

Rubinstein, M 1991 Somewhere over the rainbow. *Risk* magazine **4** (10) 63–66

Rubinstein, M 1994 Implied binomial trees. *Journal of Finance* **69** 771–818

Rupf, I, Dewynne, JN, Howison, SD & Wilmott, P 1993 Some mathematical results in the pricing of American options. *European Journal of Applied Mathematics* **4** 381–398

Sandmann, K & Sondermann, D 1994 On the stability of lognormal interest rate models. Working Paper, University of Bonn, Department of Economics

St Pierre, M 2004 Valuing and hedging synthetic CDO tranches using base correlation. Credit Derivatives, Bear Stearns, May

Schönbucher, PJ 1993 The feedback effect of hedging in illiquid markets. M.Sc. thesis, Oxford University

Schönbucher, PJ 1996 The term structure of defaultable bond prices. Discussion Paper B–384, University of Bonn

Schönbucher, PJ 1997a Modelling defaultable bond prices. Working Paper, London School of Economics, Financial Markets Group

Schönbucher, PJ 1997b Pricing credit risk derivatives. Working Paper, London School of Economics, Financial Markets Group

Schönbucher, PJ 1998 A review of credit risk and credit derivative modelling. To appear in *Applied Mathematical Finance* **5**

Schönbucher, PJ & Wilmott, P 1995a Hedging in illiquid markets: nonlinear effects. *Proceedings of the 8th European Conference on Mathematics in Industry*

Schönbucher, PJ & Wilmott, P 1995b The feedback effect of hedging in illiquid markets. MFG Working Paper, Oxford University

Schönbucher, PJ & Schlögl, E 1996 Credit derivatives and competition in the loan market. Working Paper, University of Bonn, Department of Statistics

Schönbucher, PJ 1999 A market model for stochastic impled volatility. *Phil. Trans.* A **357** 2071–2092

Schoutens, W, Simons, E & Tistaert, J 2004 A perfect calibration! Now what? *Wilmott* magazine 66–78 (March)

Sepp, A & Skachkov, I 2003 Option pricing with jumps. *Wilmott* magazine 50–58 (November)

Shore, S 1997 The modelling of credit risk and its applications to credit derivatives. M.Sc. dissertation, Oxford University

Shu, J & Zhang, J 2003 The relationship between implied and realized volatility of S&P500 index. *Wilmott* magazine (January)

Sircar, KR & Papanicolaou, G 1996 General Black–Scholes models accounting for increased market volatility from hedging strategies. Stanford University, Working Paper

Sircar, KR & Papanicolaou, GC 1999 Stochastic volatility, smile and asymptotics. *Applied Mathematical Finance* **6** (2) 107–145

Sklar, A 1959 Fonctions de repartition á *n* dimensions et leur marges. *Publ. Int. Stat Univ., Paris,* **8** 229–231

Skorokhod, AV 1989 *Asymptotic Methods in the Theory of Stochastic Differential Equations* (Nauka, 1987; AMS, *Translations of Mathematical Monographs*, vol. 78)

Sloan, IH & Walsh, L 1990 A computer search of rank two lattice rules for multidimensional quadrature. *Mathematics of Computation* **54** 281–302

Sneddon, I 1957 *Elements of Partial Differential Equations*. McGraw-Hill

Soros, G 1987 *The Alchemy of Finance*. John Wiley & Sons

Stein, E & Stein, J 1991 Stock price distributions with stochastic volatility: an analytic approach. *Review of Financial Studies* **4**, 727–752

Stetson, C, Marshall, S & Loeball, D 1995 Laudable lattices. *Risk* magazine **8** (12) 60–63 (December)

Strang, G 1986 *Introduction to Applied Mathematics*. Wellesley-Cambridge

Stulz, RM 1982 Options on the minimum or maximum of two risky assets. *Journal of Financial Economics* **10** 161–185

Swift, J 1726 *Travels into Several Remote Nations of the World . . . by Lemuel Gulliver*. B. Motte

Swishchuk, A 2004 Modeling of variance and volatility swaps for financial markets with stochastic volatility. *Wilmott* magazine 64–77 (September)

Taylor, SJ & Xu, X 1994 The magnitude of implied volatility smiles: theory and empirical evidence for exchange rates. *The Review of Futures Markets* **13** 355–380

Thompson, G 2000 Fast narrow bounds on the value of asian options. Technical Report, University of Cambridge

Thomson, R 1998 *Apocalypse Roulette: The lethal world of derivatives*. Pan

Thorp, EO & Kassouf, S 1967 *Beat the Market*. Random House

Thorp, E 2002 What I knew and when I knew it. *Wilmott* magazine (September, December 2002, January 2003)

Topper, J 2005 *Financial Engineering with Finite Elements*. John Wiley & Sons

Traub, JF & Wozniakowski, H 1994 Breaking intractability. *Scientific American* 102–107 (January)

Trigeorgis, L 1998 *Real Options*. MIT Press

Turnbull, SM & Wakeman, LM 1991 A quick algorithm for pricing European average options. *Journal of Financial and Quantitative Finance* **26** 377–389

Ungar, E 1996 *Swap Literacy*. Bloomberg

Vasicek, OA 1977 An equilibrium characterization of the term structure. *Journal of Financial Economics* **5** 177–188

de la Vega, J 1688 *Confusión de Confusiones*. Republished by John Wiley & Sons

Vose, D 1997 *Quantitative Risk Analysis: A guide to Monte Carlo simulation modelling*. John Wiley & Sons

Walsh, O 2003 The art and science of curve building. *Wilmott* magazine (November)

Whaley, RE 1981 On the valuation of American call options on stocks with known dividends. *Journal of Financial Economics* **9** 207–211

Whaley, RE 1993 Derivatives on market volatility: hedging tools long overdue. *Journal of Derivatives* **1** 71–84

Whaley, RE 1997 Building on Black–Scholes. *Risk* magazine **10** 149–156

Whalley, AE & Wilmott, P 1993a Counting the costs. *Risk* magazine **6** (10) 59–66 (October)

Whalley, AE & Wilmott, P 1993b Option pricing with transaction costs. MFG Working Paper, Oxford University

Whalley, AE & Wilmott, P 1994a Hedge with an edge. *Risk* magazine **7** (10) 82–85 (October)

Whalley, AE & Wilmott, P 1994b A comparison of hedging strategies. *Proceedings of the 7th European Conference on Mathematics in Industry* 427–434

Whalley, AE & Wilmott, P 1995 An asymptotic analysis of the Davis, Panas and Zariphopoulou model for option pricing with transaction costs. MFG Working Paper, Oxford University

Whalley, AE & Wilmott, P 1996 Key results in discrete hedging and transaction costs. In *Frontiers in Derivatives* (Konishi, A and Dattatreya, R eds) 183–196

Whalley, AE & Wilmott, P 1997 An asymptotic analysis of an optimal hedging model for option pricing with transaction costs. *Mathematical Finance* **7** 307–324

Wiggins, J 1987 Option values and stochastic volatility. *J. Financial Economics* **19** 351–372

Wilmott, P 1994 Discrete charms. *Risk* magazine **7** (3) 48–51 (March)

Wilmott, P 1995 Volatility smiles revisited. *Derivatives Week* **4** (38) 8

Wilmott, P 1998 *Derivatives*. John Wiley & Sons

Wilmott, P 2002 Cliquet options and volatility models. *Wilmott* magazine (December)

Wilmott, P & Wilmott, S 1990 Dispersion of pollutant along a river, an asymptotic analysis. OCIAM Working Paper

Zhang, PG 1997 *Exotic Options*. World Scientific

Zhu, Y & Avellaneda, M 1998 A risk-neutral stochastic volatility model. *International Journal of Theoretical and Applied Finance* **1** (2) 289–310

index

Note: Page references in *italics* refer to Figures

Index compiled by Annette Musker